INDIANA'S 200

INDIANA'S 200
1816–2016
THE PEOPLE WHO SHAPED THE HOOSIER STATE

EDITED BY LINDA C. GUGIN AND JAMES E. ST. CLAIR

Indiana Historical Society Press | Indianapolis 2015

© 2015 Indiana Historical Society Press. All rights reserved.

This book is a publication of the
Indiana Historical Society Press
Eugene and Marilyn Glick Indiana History Center
450 West Ohio Street
Indianapolis, Indiana 46202-3269 USA
www.indianahistory.org
Telephone orders 1-800-447-1830
Fax orders 1-317-234-0562
Online orders @ http://shop.indianahistory.org

Library of Congress Cataloging-in-Publication Data

Indiana's 200 : the people who shaped the Hoosier State / edited by Linda Gugin and James E. St. Clair.
    pages cm
Includes index.
ISBN 978-0-87195-387-2 (cloth : alk. paper)
1. Indiana–Biography. 2. Indiana–History. I. Gugin, Linda C., editor. II. St. Clair, James E., editor. III. Title: Indiana's two hundred.
F525.I59 2015
977.2—dc23
                                2015012287

The paper in this publication meets the minimum requirements of American National
Standard for Information Sciences—Permanence of Paper for Printed Library Materials,
ANSI Z39. 48–1984

No part of this publication may be reproduced, stored in or introduced into a retrieval system, or transmitted, in any form or by any means (electronic, mechanical, photocopying, recording, or otherwise) without the prior written permission of the copyright owner.

Indiana's 200: The People Who Shaped the Hoosier State
was made possible through the generous support of
Care Institute Group, Inc.

CONTENTS

ix   Acknowledgments
xi   A Word from the Editors
xiii   Subjects by Category
1   Essays
391   Contributor Biographies
405   Index

ACKNOWLEDGMENTS

First, we would like to thank the Indiana Historical Society Press for asking us to undertake what has been an exciting, rewarding, and educational experience. This is our fourth book project with the IHS Press and, as with the previous ones, we have thoroughly enjoyed working with the expert staff there. In particular, we are grateful for the support of Ray E. Boomhower, senior editor, and Kathy Breen, editor, who have patiently guided us through every phase of this four-year project.

We are also indebted to the members of our advisory panel who offered valuable assistance in the selection of subjects and authors and several of whom contributed essays to the book. The panel consisted of Robert G. Barrows, professor of history at Indiana University-Purdue University, Indianapolis; Paula Corpuz, retired senior director of the IHS Press; Ralph Gray, professor emeritus of history, IUPUI; James H. Madison, professor emeritus of history, Indiana University, Bloomington; Wilma Moore, IHS senior archivist, African American history; and Randall Shepard, retired Chief Justice of the Indiana Supreme Court. While each of the members were engaged in their own research, teaching, and writing projects, they were never too busy to answer questions we had or to help guide us through various issues that arose from time to time. We also want to thank the many county historians who made suggestions on potential subjects to profile.

Obviously, this endeavor would not have been possible without access to the vast storehouses of information and knowledge in public, university, and governmental libraries. First and foremost, the Indiana University Southeast library deserves our gratitude for providing us work space, computers, printers, and ready access to its holdings, as well as technical assistance. A special thanks goes to Steven Clark, who helped us overcome many thorny computer problems. We had additional assistance from the staff and resources of the following: the Indiana Room at the New Albany–Floyd County Public Library, the Indiana State Library, and the IHS William H. Smith Memorial Library.

Others deserving special thanks and recognition are Brigette Adams, secretary of the School of Social Sciences at IU Southeast, who provided clerical assistance; Margaret "Peggy" Fukunaga, who helped us navigate various editing issues; and Claudia Crump, professor emeritus of elementary education at IU Southeast and founding director of the IUS Center for Cultural Resources, who provided valuable information about notable women of Indiana.

Finally, we offer our profound thanks to our 136 authors, whose hard work made this book possible.

A WORD FROM THE EDITORS

The main objective of this book commemorating Indiana's bicentennial is to recognize the people who made enduring contributions to the state in its two-hundred-year history. The biographical essays in this book are intended to promote the public's knowledge and appreciation of those who made a difference in the lives of Hoosiers. While the essays contain standard biographical information, they mainly highlight what these people accomplished and the resulting impact for the state. In some cases the effect has been a direct one, such as Richard Lieber's role in creating Indiana's state park system. The impact of others, however, transcended the state. For example, James Dean influenced a generation of teenagers across the country, including those in Indiana, through his films.

Taken as a whole, these essays offer a broad examination of the state's history through the lives and accomplishments of a remarkable collection of people. The achievements of some profiled will be familiar, for example, Hoagy Carmichael, Eli Lilly, Ernie Pyle, and Madam C. J. Walker. Readers, however, may be surprised to learn of contributions of others whose lives and careers have not been widely chronicled such as Paul Emrick, a Purdue band director who invented the forming of letters for marching bands; Zerna Sharp, creator of the Dick and Jane texts that taught generations of first graders to read; Vivian Carter, whose Vee-Jay Records introduced the music of The Beatles to America; and Robert Borkenstein, who invented the Breathalyzer.

The challenge of limiting the number of people selected to profile for this work to two hundred out of the vast number of worthy candidates was obviously a daunting task. We the editors started with some broad parameters to help guide the process, the first being that only individuals who were deceased were considered for inclusion. Additional considerations included having subjects from a wide of range of professions and fields of endeavor, statewide representation, and diversity in gender, race, and ethnicity. Applying these guidelines, we then developed specific criteria to help narrow the choices.

Impact and significance were defined by whether the individual (1) improved the lives of citizens of Indiana in areas such as health, education, economics, culture, governance, entertainment, and transportation; (2) transformed a profession or institution or created a new institution; (3) influenced the lives and behaviors of people in the state by creating new ideas or advancing knowledge; (4) reformed ways of doing things and being an agent of change; or (5) affected how people perceive the state and its people. Also it should be noted that subjects did not have to be born in Indiana to be included but had to have had a significant link to the state.

At the outset, some people such as Abraham Lincoln, Herman B Wells, Cole Porter, Michael Jackson, Red Skelton, Kurt Vonnegut, Ryan White, and Gene Stratton-Porter were obvious choices. To explore other possibilities, the editors researched numerous sources that identified prominent Hoosiers. This research resulted in a list of potential subjects that exceeded the number that could be included. An advisory panel of distinguished scholars helped to refine the list of possible subjects, which was immensely valuable to the editors in making their final selections. We realize that some readers might wonder why this or that person was selected and another was not, but while the process was very rigorous, some subjectivity was inevitable.

A total of 136 dedicated authors, representing a broad range of professional backgrounds, contributed essays for this book and they spent considerable time researching and writing the biographical profiles without any financial compensation. As the editors we were responsible for insuring the essays are engaging and, of course, that the information is accurate. We went to great lengths to verify facts and details, but naturally, given the sheer volume of material produced it is possible that this volume is not error free.

Two features of the essays are included for the benefit of readers. One is the use of small capitals to indicate the names of people who are the subject of one essay who appear in another. Also, at the end of each essay is a For Further Reading section that lists sources for additional information.

SUBJECTS BY CATEGORY

Agriculture
Meredith, Virginia Claypool
Oliver, James
Peden, Rachel
Redenbacher, Orville Clarence

Religion
Cadle, E. Howard
Feuerlicht, Howard
Grutka, Andrew
Guerin, Saint Theodora
Hesburgh, Theodore
McCulloch, Oscar
Sorin, Edward
Sunday, Billy

Reformers
Bacon, Albion Fellows
Bailey, Katherine "Flossie"
Clarke, Grace Julian
Coffin, Levi and Catharine
Coffin, Rhoda
Fletcher, William B.
Gougar, Helen
Harper, Ida Husted
Leach, Antionette
Owen, Robert
Ransom, Willard
Rapp, George
Richardson, Henry
Sewall, May Wright
Thomas, Mary
Wallace, Zerelda G.
White, Esther Griffin
White, Ryan

Education
Ahern, Mary Eileen
Black, Glenn
Blaker, Eliza
Brown, Herbert C.
Butler, Ovid
DePauw, Washington
Hamilton, Edith
Hovey, Edmund
Kinsey, Alfred
Lynd, Robert and Helen
Maclure, William
Maxwell, David
Mills, Caleb
Ostrom, Eleanor and Vincent
Purdue, John
Sharp, Zerna
Wells, Herman B
Wylie, Andrew

Artists
Adams, J. Ottis
Dudley, Frank
Forsyth, William
Goth, (Jesse) Marie
Gruelle Family
Hardrick, John
Hopper, Floyd
Overbeck Sisters
Scott, William Edouard
Shulz, Ada
Stark, Otto
Steele, Theodore Clement
Webster, Marie

Music
Carmichael, "Hoagy" Hoagland
Dresser, Paul
Emrick, Paul "Spotts"
Gennett Family
Gingold, Josef
Monroe, Bill
Montgomery, Wes
Porter, Cole
Sissle, Noble Lee

Inventors
Borkenstein, Robert Frank
Gilbreth, Lillian
Haynes, Elwood
Jenkins, Charles Francis
Muhler, Joseph Charles

Governance
Baker, Conrad
Beveridge, Albert J.
Blackford, Issac
Bowen, Otis R.
Bowers, Claude G.
Brokenburr, Robert L.
Capehart, Homer E.
Carson, Julia
Cornish, Clarence
Debs, Eugene Victor
Harrison, Benjamin
Harrison, William Henry
Hays, William (Will) Harrison, Sr.
Hendricks, Thomas Andrews
Holman, Jesse L.
Jenckes, Virginia
Jennings, Jonathan
Julian, George Washington
Lincoln, Abraham
McNutt, Paul
Marshall, Thomas
Milligan, Lambdin Purdy
Minton, Sherman
Monks, Leander
Morton, Oliver
Orr, Robert
Taggart, Thomas
Welsh, Matthew Empson
Wiley, Harvey
Willkie, Wendell

Conservationists/Naturalists/Preservationists
Caldwell, Lynton Keith
Deam, Charles
Lieber, Richard N.
O'Brien, Cornelius
Owen, Jane Blaffer
Stratton-Porter, Gene

Business
Allison, James
Ball Brothers
Bell, Lawrence D.

Clowes Family
Conn, Charles Gerard
Conner, William
Cook, William Alfred "Bill"
Crosley, Powel Jr.
Cummins, Clessie Lyle
Duesenberg, August and Fredrick
Efromyson Family
Fisher, Carl
Fletcher, Calvin
Glick, Eugene and Marilyn
Hapgood, Powers
Hapgood, William Powers
Lilly Family
Lanier, James F. D.
Miller, J. Irwin
Ransom, Freeman Briley
Richardville, Jean Baptiste
Simon, Melvin
Studebaker, Clement
Van Camp Family
Walker, Madam C. J.
Zimmer, Justin

Media
Chambers, David Laurance
Davis, Elmer
Fox, Lillian Thomas
Hubbard, Frank McKinney "Kin"
Knox, George L.
Martin, John Bartlow
Pulliam, Eugene C. and Eugene S.
Pyle, Ernie
Stewart, George P.
Stout, Elihu
Strauss, Juliet

Sports
Charleston, Oscar
Counsilman, James "Doc"
Crowe, Ray
Hinkle, Tony
Hulman, Tony
Garrett, Bill
Lambert, Ward
Rockne, Knute
Shaw, Wilbur
Wooden, John
Zollner, Fred

Military
Grissom, Virgil "Gus"
Smith, Walter Bedell "Beetle"
Spruance, Raymond

Photographers
Bushemi, John
Cushman, Charles
Hohenberger, Frank

Medicine
Hamilton, Alice
Hurty, John
Link, Geothe
Rumley, Edward
Scheele, Leonard A.
Schweitzer, Ada Estelle

Authors
Dreiser, Theodore
Nicholson, Meredith
Nolan, Jeannette
Tarkington, Booth
Thompson, J. Maurice
Vonnegut, Kurt
Wallace, Lew

Poets
Bolton, Sarah T.
Riley, James Whitcomb

Humorists
Ade, George
Shepherd, Jean
Shriner, Herb

Historians
Carmony, Donald
Dillon, John Brown
Dunn, Jacob P., Jr.
Esarey, Logan
Thornbrough, Emma Lou
Thornbrough, Gayle
Woodburn, James Albert

Entertainment
Carter, Vivian
Dean, James
Jackson, Michael
Koch Family
Skelton, Richard "Red"

Leaders and Builders
Chief Little Turtle (Mihšihkinaahkwa)
Clark, George Rogers
Tecumseh and Tenskwatawa

Notorious
Dillinger, John H., Jr.
Stephenson, D. C.

Adams, J. Ottis

July 8, 1851–January 28, 1927

Landscape painter and instructor who was one of the five members of the Hoosier Group artists.

John Ottis Adams was born on July 8, 1851, in a log cabin five miles south of Franklin, Indiana, built on land settled by his great-grandfather, Elisha Adams. John Ottis's grandfather, John Adams, and his father, Alban Housely Adams, ran a general mercantile store alongside the newly opened Madison and Indianapolis Railroad. After John died in 1856, Alban moved his family to Franklin, Shelbyville, and then Martinsville, where John Ottis attended high school. His teacher remembered him as a good student, a gentleman, and an able artist who was not strong enough to take exercise with the other boys, as a congenital defect had left one leg shorter than the other. His aptitude for art manifested itself in numerous replications of a strikingly realistic painting of a slice of watermelon exhibited at the 1869 state fair by the prodigious William Merritt Chase, only two years Adams senior.

After graduation, Adams attended Wabash College in Crawfordsville until, in September 1872, he chose his career by enrolling in a branch of the South Kensington School of Art in London. In July 1873 Adams was awarded a second-year certificate, and after another year studying privately with English genre painter, John Parker, he returned to his parents' home, now in Seymour, Indiana. Adams opened a portrait studio in Martinsville, which he transferred to Muncie in 1876. He was the only professional portrait painter in the city, but its population of 5,000 could not sustain a painter, so Adams associated with town photographer George Gamble, tinting photographs and painting backgrounds.

In the last months of 1879, a small circle of Indiana artists decided to follow the path of their now celebrated Hoosier confrere, Chase, and perfect their art by studying at the Royal Academy of Painting in Munich. On July 23, 1880, Adams and the Munich-bound Indiana contingent of T. C. STEELE, Samuel Richards, Carrie Wolff, and August Metzner set sail for Europe. WILLIAM FORSYTH followed eighteen months later.

The regimen at the Royal Academy was

J. Ottis Adams in his studio at The Hermitage

rigorous. Adams and Steele were accepted into Gyula Benczur's nature class, where six to eight hours a day were spent drawing from life, usually producing closely observed "study heads" of paid academy models. After two years Adams progressed to the painting class, where he spent two years on similar exercises, but now in oils.

Landscape painting was not taught at the academy, but the Indiana artists spent their holidays in the German countryside sketching and painting. Steele and Forsyth, living outside of Munich in the village of Schleissheim, became ever more inclined in this direction, while Adams, either because of his disability or because of his methodical nature, remained largely a studio painter, creating genre scenes of German peasants in their homes or in their fields.

Adams, Steele, and Forsyth concluded that they would return to Indiana rather than follow Chase's lead and settle in the more conducive art centers of the East. They were induced by family and friendly connections, but also by the notion that they might contribute to the development of an American idiom if they applied their new skills to subjects that they knew best at home, just as they had seen done by the Dutch and Norwegians.

When Adams returned to Muncie on October 28, 1887, he found a changed city, one that was much larger and more prosperous. To supplement his income, Adams began taking students, and in 1888 his colleague, Forsyth, who had recently returned from Europe, joined him. With the support of fourteen Muncie businessmen who guaranteed expenses for two years, Adams and Forsyth organized a formal art school, which opened with thirty-five students in November 1889. Their effort was trumped at the outset by the establishment of a competing school in Indianapolis headed by Steele, which doomed the Muncie Art School and caused temporary bad blood between the three former compatriots.

In November 1894 the Central Art Association of Chicago borrowed a local exhibition of the summer's work of four Indianapolis artists—Steele, Forsyth, RICHARD B. GRUELLE, and OTTO STARK. Its success codified the notion of a Hoosier Group of painters and only a last-minute request from Steele to Adams to contribute to the exhibition secured his inclusion in this coincidental alliance.

Adams's progression from a portrait and genre painter to full-fledged landscape artist had gone unnoticed in Indianapolis until an exhibition in January 1895 of his recent work that was full of the flavor of an Indiana summer and fall. He painted the works at the little crossroads south of Muncie known as Prairie Dell. Reviewing the fourteen oils for the *Indianapolis News*, Steele rhapsodized: "To me, these pictures are pure poetry."

Steele and Adams worked side by side that autumn at Black's Mill on the Mississinewa River creating canvases that shared a lyricism of color, mood, and title. They were companions again the next summer at Metamora along the old Whitewater Canal in southwestern Indiana, the fruits of which they showed at the first exhibition of the Society of Western Artists. The society was a consortium of painters representing six midwestern states who organized themselves in Chicago in March 1896 for the purpose of mounting an annual circulating exhibition of regional paintings. Adams, Steele, and Forsyth formed the Indiana contingent.

At the end of their second season in Metamora, Steele and Adams made an exploratory horseback ride down the east fork of the Whitewater River to Brookville. They found a rambling seventy-year-old house whose three acres and situation made it an ideal retreat for the painters. They bought it in February 1898 and Steele's wife, Libbie, dubbed it the Hermitage. They added a studio on the south end for Steele overlooking two picturesquely abandoned mills, and another on the north for Adams looking up the valley of the Whitewater. Adams brought his new wife, Winifred Brady, to the Hermitage the day after their wedding in Muncie on October 1, 1898. Winifred had been Adams's student in the Muncie Art School and was a first-rate still-life painter. She would add the formal flower gardens, whose flaming poppies and flower-bordered paths provided endless subjects for her husband and the other artists who gathered at the Hermitage, as did the old mills, the rapid river, and the surrounding timbered hills in all seasons. Three sons arrived in rapid succession: John Alban in 1900, Edward Wolfe in 1902, and Robert Brady in 1904.

Family obligations induced Adams to accept the position of chief instructor in the new art school attached to Indianapolis's John Herron Art Institute in 1902. This required his residency in the capital from October through May; consequently, his output shrank from about twenty canvases a year to ten. He kept the six-day-a-week job until commencement in June 1906, then turned the duties over to Forsyth, who was in greater financial need than himself and who, unlike Adams, was stern enough to be a good teacher. The Adamses returned to the Hermitage, which became their formal address with his purchase of Steele's half interest in 1907. In 1905 Adams, or Jack, as everyone called him, Winifred, and the three boys began summering south of the fishing village of Leland, Michigan. They built a cottage next to their close friends the F. C. Balls in the "Indiana Woods." The site provided Adams with vivid sunsets to paint along with a wealth of new material. In later years Stark joined him, pitching a tent next to the Adames' cottage.

Ill health in 1915 sent the sixty-five-year-old Adams to convalesce on Big Bayou by Tampa Bay south of Saint Petersburg on Florida's Gulf coast. He returned for the next four winters, adding flamboyant, subtropical landscapes to his repertoire. In 1920 he shifted his winter headquarters across Florida to New Smyrna on the Atlantic side. He found the biosphere so profuse and paintable that he built a seasonal studio there in 1922. He returned unwell from New Smyrna in the spring of 1926 and failed to improve during the summer at Leland. He had an operation for an intestinal disorder in Indianapolis, but never regained health, dying at his Indianapolis residence on January 28, 1927.

MARTIN KRAUSE

For Further Reading

Griner Ned H. *Side by Side with Coarser Plants: The Muncie Art Movement, 1885–1985*. Muncie, IN: Ball State University, 1985.

Krause, Martin. *The Passage: Return of Indiana Artists from Germany, 1880–1905*. Indianapolis: Indianapolis Museum of Art, 1990.

Newton, Judith Vale. *The Hoosier Group: Five American Painters*. Indianapolis: Eckert Publications, 1985.

Ade, George

February 9, 1866–May 23, 1944

Journalist, playwright, and author.

The 1908 presidential contest pitted two would-be reformers against each other. Republicans nominated William Howard Taft, groomed for the post by former president Theodore Roosevelt, and Democrats responded by selecting William Jennings Bryan, who would be making his third, and last, attempt for the nation's highest office. And while Bryan was shocked by his staggering million-vote loss to Taft at the polls, perhaps the campaign's biggest surprise came at the beginning when Taft decided to open his race for the White House in the small Indiana town of Brook.

Brook may have been a tiny dot on Indiana's map, but it did have something other Hoosier towns did not—the home of George Ade, a leading figure, along with JAMES WHITCOMB RILEY, BOOTH TARKINGTON, and MEREDITH NICHOLSON, of the golden age of Indiana literature in the late nineteenth and early twentieth centuries. Hazelden Farm was the scene of a number of large parties and celebrations in the thirty-nine years Ade resided there. Ade himself noted in an autobiographical piece: "I love to put on big parties or celebrations and see a throng of people having a good time."

Born in Kentland, Indiana, Ade was the second youngest of seven children raised by John and Adaline Bush Ade. "From the time I could read," Ade remembered later in life, "I had my nose in a book, and I lacked enthusiasm for manual labor." His aversion to physical work, especially his dislike for farming, troubled his father, who wondered how his son would make a living. In 1883 Ade started classes at Purdue University, where he enrolled in scientific coursework because he "had no ambition to be an engineer or an agriculturist." His attention, however, soon focused on the Grand Opera House in Lafayette, where he became a regular patron—sometimes to the detriment of his studies. Ade noted that he was a "star student as a Freshman but wobbly later on and a total loss in Mathematics." Still, while at the university he met and began a lifelong friendship with Hoosier cartoonist John T. McCutcheon.

After graduating from Purdue in 1887 with a bachelor of science degree, Ade flirted for a time with the idea of becoming a lawyer, but abandoned that career for journalism, beginning work as a reporter for the *Lafayette Morning News*, later moving to the *Lafayette Call* for the princely sum of six dollars per week. Along with his low salary, Ade had to cope with a frugal editor, who, for example, liked to use old envelopes as copy paper. Ade later moved on to a job writing testimonials for a patent medicine company's tobacco-habit cure. In recalling Ade's work for the firm, McCutcheon noted that the cure was not a fake remedy, "for it was guaranteed to cure the most persistent tobacco habit if the tobacco user followed the directions. The first direction was to discontinue the use of tobacco and then take the tablets."

By 1890 Ade had joined McCutcheon on the staff of the *Chicago Morning News*. The two men were roommates, sharing a hallway bedroom at a rooming house, earning for them the nickname "the hall-bedroom twins." Ade's first regular assignment at the newspaper was a daily weather story. His big break came when the steamer *Tioga* exploded on the Chicago River and Ade, because no other reporters were available, rushed to the scene and produced the best account of the tragedy. His success led to his covering such important events as the heavyweight championship fight between John L. Sullivan and James J. "Gentleman Jim" Corbett in New Orleans and the 1893 Chicago World's Fair.

In November 1893 Ade was put in charge of the column "Stories of the Streets and of the Town," which also featured McCutcheon's illustrations. In his writing Ade captured life on Chicago's bustling streets through the antics of such characters as Artie, a young office boy; Doc' Horne, a "gentlemanly liar"; and Pink Marsh, a shoeshine boy in a barbershop. The key to the popularity of his columns, Ade noted, came in his interest "in all kinds of people and what they were doing and hoping to do." McCutcheon also pointed out that his friend possessed a good memory, a knack for knowing a person's true motives, and keen powers of observation. Ade's column was also the birthplace of the work that made his writing famous across the country—fables.

Fables in Slang, published in 1899, was an immediate hit, selling sixty-nine thousand copies that year alone. These "modern fables," complete with morals drawn at their end based on the shortcomings of their subjects, often written in colloquial speech, and featuring Ade's idiosyncratic capitalization style, were syndicated nationally, produced as movies by the Essanay Film Company, and turned into comic strips by cartoonist Art Helfant. Ade's work won the attention of fellow humorist Mark Twain, literary critic William Dean Howells, and Kansas newspaper editor William Allen White, who was moved to write that he "would rather have written *Fables in Slang* than be President."

Despite such lavish attention, Ade remained levelheaded, wryly noting: "By a queer twist of circumstances I have become known to the general public as a 'humorist' and a writer of 'slang.' I never wanted to be a comic or tried to be one. Always I wrote for the 'family trade' and I used no word or phrase which might give offense to mother and the girls or a professor of English."

Ade next turned his humorist's pen to the theater, writing his first Broadway play, *The Sultan of Sulu*, a comic opera about America's activities in the Philippines, in 1902, in which he collaborated with composer Alfred Wathall. Other hit plays soon followed, including *Peggy from Paris*, a musical comedy; *The County Chairman*, a drama

George Ade

about small-town politics; and his best-known play, *The College Widow*, a comedy about college life and football set on the Wabash College campus in Crawfordsville, Indiana. Although his plays lost favor on Broadway, Ade continued to pursue the form, producing a few one-act plays that became popular with small theater companies across the United States.

While Ade was busy writing and traveling, frequently abroad, including trips to Europe, China, and Japan, back in Indiana his brother, William, acquired on Ade's behalf numerous acres of farmland in Newton County. In 1902 William bought 417 acres near the town of Brook. Impressed by the wooded land, Ade called on his friend Billy Mann, a Chicago architect, to design a small dwelling for him that would cost $2,500. A suggestion here and a suggestion there later, Ade ended up with an impressive English Manor/Tudor-style home that cost approximately $25,000.

Moving into his Hazelden Farm estate in the summer of 1904, Ade described his home as "about the size of a girl's school, with added wings for the managers, otherwise known as employees." Once settled into his new home, Ade wasted little time in making his neighbors feel welcome, hosting numerous parties. Along with Taft's visit, Hazelden was the site of celebrations for the Indiana Society of Chicago, Purdue alumni, and local children. Ade also hosted a rally for Theodore Roosevelt's Bull Moose Party in 1912; a homecoming for soldiers and sailors on July 4, 1919; and a party and speech for vice presidential candidate Charles W. Dawes in 1924. A lifelong bachelor, Ade, in addition to traveling, also enjoyed golf and horse racing, and noted that he disliked "social show-offs, bigots on religion, fanatics on total abstinence, and all persons who take themselves seriously."

Ade retained close ties with his alma mater and fraternity, making donations to Purdue and Sigma Chi. Along with fellow Purdue graduate David E. Ross, Ade, in 1922, bought sixty-five acres on the outskirts of West Lafayette to be used as a site for a new football stadium for the university. Named Ross-Ade Stadium in their honor, the facility was formally dedicated on November 22, 1924. After an illness of several months, Ade died on May 23, 1944, in Brook. His grave is at the Fairlawn Cemetery in Kentland.

RAY E. BOOMHOWER

For Further Reading

Kelly, Fred C. *George Ade: Warmhearted Satirist.* Indianapolis: Bobbs-Merrill, 1947.

Lazarus, A. L. *The Best of George Ade.* Bloomington: Indiana University Press, 1985.

Tobin, Terence. *Letters of George Ade.* West Lafayette: Purdue University Press, 1973.

Ahern, Mary Eileen
October 1, 1860–May 22, 1938

A leader of the modern library movement, crusader for public libraries, and Indiana state librarian.

At the end of World War I, Mary Eileen Ahern, a longtime board member of the American Library Association, traveled to postwar France to take part in the ALA's Library War Service program, a national undertaking that ultimately sent more than four million books to camp libraries serving the American Expeditionary Force in Europe.

When Ahern arrived in Paris, the program director, Burton Stevenson, asked her what she believed she could contribute. According to her own account, she replied, "I will do anything you want me to do, if I can, and I am Irish enough to think that I can do anything." That straightforward confidence and clarity of thought was Ahern's hallmark throughout a distinguished and influential career in librarianship—and one is tempted to claim that it is a reflection of the Hoosier background and values she brought to her career.

By the time she traveled to Europe, Ahern had been a leader in the field of librarianship for some thirty years. The second of three children born to the farming family of William and Mary Ahern, she was raised in southwest Marion County. After graduating from Spencer High School in Owen County, Indiana, in 1878, and Central Normal College in Danville, Indiana, in 1881, Ahern worked as a schoolteacher until 1889, when she was appointed Indiana's assistant state librarian. In that post, she arranged a gathering of librarians from across the state and established the Indiana Library Association, subsequently serving as ILA secretary from 1889 to 1896, and as president in 1895.

In 1893 the Indiana General Assembly appointed Ahern as state librarian, at that time a political position. During her tenure, she pressed the case that the state library should be depoliticized and moved to the Indiana Department of

Education. Always blunt, she said that libraries should not be "used as a shuttlecock in the political game of battledore." She was successful in that pursuit, but the political compromise she forged included an agreement that she would not seek reappointment to her post; she stepped down in 1895.

The 1890s were a critical era in the history of American libraries, an era when new office technologies, organizational structures, cataloging and classification techniques, the role of public libraries as instruments of self-education, and new local, state, and federal funding mechanisms were combining with philanthropic support to shape what would become the twentieth-century library. Ahern played an active role at state, national, and international levels. In 1893 she attended the seminal ALA national conference in Chicago in conjunction with the World's Columbian Exposition. At that meeting, she began taking an active leadership role in matters related to ensuring library access to both U.S. federal documents and official documents published by foreign countries.

Upon leaving her post as state librarian, Ahern formalized her credentials as a librarian by attending the Library School of the Armour Institute of Technology in Chicago, the first library school in the Midwest and the fourth founded in the United States. By the time her studies ended, Ahern had been invited by the leaders of Library Bureau, a firm founded in 1876 by Melvil Dewey to furnish support and equipment to the emerging American library community, to serve as founding editor of a new journal called *Public Libraries*.

For the next thirty-six years, until failing eyesight forced her retirement from the editorship in 1931, Ahern was at the epicenter of American librarianship. By all accounts she was a forceful and influential figure whose vision of public librarianship became foundational for generations of librarians. In her first *Public Libraries* editorial, she argued that rather than merely being a repository for books, the library must be "a workshop, a laboratory, a people's school."

From her base in Chicago, Ahern naturally became a leader in Illinois and midwestern library organizations. Her journal became the formal publication of the Illinois Library Association. She became an authoritative writer and speaker on public policy issues such as the role of board members in public libraries, the educational role of the school librarian, the ways in which public libraries could serve immigrant children, the working environment in libraries, educational standards for library training, and a host of other subjects. She delivered lectures across the country, and was an active member in nonlibrary organizations as well, including the Illinois Women's Press Association, the Fortnightly Club in Indianapolis, and others. After joining the ALA in 1897, she chaired and served on many committees and was on the organization's leadership council for some twenty years.

In addition to setting forth a philosophical vision for librarianship, Ahern brought a pragmatic concern with day-to-day realities to her editorship of *Public Libraries*, and the journal served as a professional-development resource for librarians in the field coping with all sorts of matters, from cataloging materials to dealing with the needs of patrons.

As librarianship grew into a field of great opportunity for American women, Ahern also became both an advocate for women in the profession and—thanks to her connections both with library school directors and public library boards—an influential consultant who helped many library boards find the right librarian for specific placements. Her published correspondence suggests that she had a well-defined notion of the desirable attributes of a librarian. In recommending one candidate, she wrote, "[she] seems to have considerable intelligence, dresses well, and pleased me by expressing disapproval of some of the flighty performances of the unintelligent."

By the end of her career, Ahern's legacy as a librarian was clear. No less a figure than Dewey, the de facto founder of American librarianship, and an advocate of "simplified spelling," wrote in 1931, "Her keen mind & fasil pen wer enlisted promptly in everi good library cauz."

More recently scholars have begun to examine Ahern's role as a library leader in the shifting dynamics of gender relations in the twentieth century. In that realm, Ahern is a fascinating mix of traditional nineteenth century values and progressive ambitions. In a memorable passage, she wrote, "One of the first and most important lessons which a woman who enters the business world needs to learn is the seeming paradox to forget that she is a woman, and at the same time keep ever before her that she is a woman." It is a formula that might seem outdated in our time, but for a woman who was born during the Civil War, whose life spanned seven turbulent decades, and whose career helped shape one of America's most enduring institutions, the public library, it seems to have been an extraordinarily successful strategy.

C. MARTIN ROSEN

For Further Reading

Ahern, M. E. "A. L. A. News from Overseas." *Bulletin of the American Library Association* 13 (1919): 309–12.

American Library Association Papers and Proceedings of the Sixteenth General Meeting, 55 (1894): 127. http://books.google.com/books?id=x1QwAQAAMAAJ&pg=PA127&dq=indiana+state+legislature+1893+ahern&hl=en&sa=X&ei=46WlU-rDMYa2yATaqIDIAg&ved=0CCkQ6AEwAA#v=onepage&q=indiana%20state%20legislature%201893%20ahern&f=false. (Accessed 6/21/2014.)

Maack, M. N. "Gender, Culture, and the Transformation of American Librarianship, 1890–1920." *Libraries & Culture* 33 (1998): 51–61.

Passet, J. "Entering the Profession: Women Library Educators and the Placement of Female Students, 1887–1912." *History of Education Quarterly* 31(1991): 207–28.

Allison, James A.

August 11, 1872–August 4, 1928

Indianapolis industrialist, entrepreneur, inventor, businessman, and one of the founders of the Indianapolis Motor Speedway and 500-mile race.

It was generally considered that CARL FISHER, James A. Allison's longtime friend and partner, was a visionary and Allison was the man who could make the visions happen. Allison's partnership with Fisher, Arthur Newby, and Frank Wheeler made a lasting impact on Indianapolis, the sports community, and the development of the town of Speedway.

Allison, who was born August 11, 1872, in Marcellus, Michigan, was the second of three sons of Noah Samuel and Myra Jane Allison. Noah, who was from Worthington, Indiana, decided to move back to Indiana, first settling in South Bend in 1874 and then relocating to Indianapolis in 1880. The senior Allison was involved in various enterprises before establishing the Allison Coupon Company in 1888. The firm printed coupon books that individuals bought at a small discount and used for purchases instead of cash. He began by printing them for use at coal mine company stores and later expanded into other markets such as grocery stores, restaurants, and streetcars.

James quit school when he was twelve to work in the family business along with his two brothers. After his father's death at age forty-two in 1890, James and his siblings became directors in the company, with eighteen-year-old James being named vice president. Frustrated with the writing instruments he used at the coupon company, James invented a new style of pen, which would be the beginning of his career as a dynamic and creative innovator. He left the coupon company by the late 1890s to run his own firm, the James Allison Manufacturing Company, which produced the Allison Perfection Fountain Pens, his first major business venture during the first decades of the twentieth century.

Allison's next enterprise involved making better automobile headlights. An inventor named Percy Avery had an idea for improving this accessory and held a patent for compressing and storing acetylene in small, steel cylinders for use as headlights. He described this invention to Fisher, who instantly saw the possibility of a business that would serve the whole automobile industry. However, it would require a great sum of money. Fisher and Avery approached Allison with the proposal of a partnership to produce the cylinders, and in 1904 Allison became a partner in the venture. With a capital stock of $10,000 the Concentrated Acetylene Company was formed with offices in Fisher's automobile agency in downtown Indianapolis. A small plant was soon built and then Allison and Fisher purchased Avery's shares and changed the company's name to Prest-O-Lite.

Explosions at the plant, three in one year, prompted a city ordinance prohibiting production of the volatile gas within the city limits. In 1912 Allison and Fisher spent approximately half a million dollars to build a new 300,000-square-foot Prest-O-Lite plant on land adjacent to the newly established Speedway track. Five years later, Allison and Fisher, already millionaires, sold their controlling interest in Prest-O-Lite to Union Carbide and Carbon Corporation for $9 million, though Allison retained large blocks of stock in Prest-O-Lite and Union Carbide.

The Speedway track, another Allison-Fisher joint enterprise with Newby and Wheeler, was built as auto racing was just getting started on horse tracks and public roads. It was dangerous, so Fisher proposed developing a circular track that would give automobile manufacturers a chance to test their cars at sustained speeds and allow drivers a chance to learn their limits. With dozens of carmakers and suppliers in Indiana, Fisher asked, "Indianapolis is going to be the world's greatest center of horseless carriage manufacturing, what could be more logical than building the world's greatest racetrack right here?"

Fisher believed the 328-acre Pressley Farm just five miles outside of Indianapolis was perfect. In December 1908 he persuaded Allison, Newby, and Wheeler to join in purchasing the property for $72,000. The group incorporated the Indianapolis Motor Speedway Company on March 20, 1909, with capital of $250,000. Construction of the track began in March 1909, and two years later became the site of the inaugural Indianapolis 500.

The Allison Speedway Team Company, a machine shop that was also an Allison-Fisher venture, was established primarily to work on improving the design and performance of racecars. Allison, however, entered cars in the 500-mile race only once. In 1919 Howard "Howdy" Wilcox drove one of Allison's two entries to victory with an average speed of 88.050 miles per hour.

Allison became sole owner of the Allison Speedway Team Company in 1916 and four years later moved his company, which had been renamed the Allison Engineering Company, to a new building across from the Indianapolis Motor Speedway. During World War I the company supplied the Nordyke and Marmon Company, an Indianapolis manufacturer, with a variety of parts used in production of the Liberty aircraft engines. Additionally, Allison received government contracts to build crawler-type tractors, tank tracks, and Whippet tanks, which were lighter and faster armored vehicles.

The Allison-Fisher partnership also involved real estate development in South Florida, the Miami area in particular, where Allison built a large home, hospital, and an aquarium, as well as being active in civic and business affairs.

Allison was twice married, first to Sarah Cornelius in 1907. In 1910 they began planning a grand estate on sixty-four acres of land in Indianapolis to be called Riverdale. No expense was spared in the construction of the house, which took three years to complete and was built of reinforced concrete with an exterior of red brick. Circassia walnut was heavily harvested for the extensive paneling in the mansion's Great Hall. During the last winter of construction Allison did not want inclement weather to be an obstacle. With typical creativity he had a huge wooden barn-like structure built over the partially constructed home, thus allowing the workers to continue throughout the winter. Riverdale was completed in 1914 at a cost of $2 million.

While he had great financial success, Allison's personal life was not so smooth. He divorced his wife in 1928. One month later he married his former secretary, Lucile Musset. However, he contracted a fatal case of pneumonia, and died at age fifty-six shortly after marrying his second wife and was buried in Crown Hill Cemetery.

Allison had no children and after his death the two wives and his mother fought bitterly over who should inherit the estate. His mother won and lived there until her death. The house stood vacant for several years until the Sisters of Saint Francis bought it and transformed the estate into Marian College in 1937.

After Allison's death in 1928, the Allison Engineering Company was sold and briefly owned by the Fisher brothers, who in turn sold it to General Motors. As the Allison Division of GM, the former machine shop grew to become the second largest Indianapolis employer and a major supplier of aircraft engines and other aircraft related hardware. In 1995 Rolls-Royce purchased Allison from GM for $525 million.

WANDA LOU WILLIS

For Further Reading

Sonnenburg, Paul, and William A. Schoneberger. *Allison: Power of Excellent, 1915–1990; Allison Gas Turbine Division, General Motors Corporation*. Malibu, CA: Coastline Publishers, 1990.

Whitaker, Sigur E. *James Allison: A Biography of the Engine Manufacturer Indianapolis 500 Co-founder*. Jefferson, NC: McFarland and Company, 2011.

Willis, Wanda Lou. "James A. Allison: The Man and His Legacy." *Engineering Info* (June 1990).

Bacon, Albion Fellows

April 8, 1865–December 10, 1933

Social welfare activist and author.

The social welfare initiatives that Albion Fellows Bacon championed were not unique to her or to the state of Indiana, and there was nothing truly distinctive in the methods she used in an effort to secure the reforms she sought. Bacon was unusual, however, in the range of her reform interests, the zeal she brought to them, the doggedness with which she pursued her goals, and the fact that she combined what she once called her "frenzied philanthropy" with prolific authorship in a variety of genres.

Albion Fellows was born in Evansville, Indiana, the daughter of Reverend Albion and Mary Erskine Fellows. Reared in the nearby hamlet of McCutchanville, she later credited nostalgia for the pastoral environment of her youth with motivating her urban-oriented reform efforts. Following graduation as salutatorian from Evansville High School in 1883, she worked as a legal secretary, toured Europe with her sister, Annie, married local merchant Hilary Bacon in 1888, and settled into a comfortable routine of middle-class domesticity. She gave birth to daughters in 1889 and 1892, followed by fraternal twins, a boy and girl, in 1901. Shortly after the birth of her second daughter, she was afflicted with an illness that lasted for several years. The diagnosis at the time was the catchall term "nervous prostration." In retrospect it seems likely that Bacon suffered from clinical depression that may have resulted from an absence of outlets for her intelligence and creativity.

She eventually found such outlets in voluntary associations and social welfare campaigns. Like many turn-of-the-century Americans, she was troubled by the pernicious effects of late-nineteenth-century industrialization and urbanization and sought to improve conditions that she perceived to be physically unhealthy and morally unwholesome. Her earliest such activities were local and included "friendly visiting" in homes of the city's poor, helping to organize a Visiting Nurse's Circle, and founding a Working Girls' Association to aid rural migrants to the city.

Bacon became best known, however, regionally and even nationally, for her work on behalf of tenement reform. As she later wrote: "I began to notice how the threads of the social problems, the civic problems and even the business problems of a city are all tangled up with the housing problem, and to realise that *housing reform is fundamental*." When the Evansville City Council pigeonholed a proposed building ordinance that included a section concerning tenement house regulation that she had prepared, Bacon concluded that a statewide housing law was essential. She set about drafting such legislation, and during the spring of 1908 she sought information from all over the country.

Two of Bacon's correspondents were Jacob Riis of *How the Other Half Lives* fame, and Lawrence Veiller, the author of the New York tenement law of 1901 and the nation's acknowledged expert on housing reform. Both men provided useful advice, and over the summer Bacon drafted a proposed state law and sought support for it. The Indianapolis Commercial Club, also interested in the issue, met with her and agreed to sponsor the bill *if* she would attend the next session of the Indiana General Assembly and lobby for it. Bacon had never anticipated direct involvement in the legislative process and she acceded to the club's request very reluctantly. She "took the leap," she later recalled, "with the desperate deliberation of a suicide who jumps into the icy water."

Although she was initially loath to take on such a public role and never became entirely comfortable in the spotlight, Bacon rose to the challenge and was remarkably effective as an unpaid lobbyist—an ambassador of the poor—on

Albion Fellows Bacon

behalf of government regulation of housing conditions. Between 1909 and 1917 she attended every biennial session of the state legislature to push that agenda. In three of those sessions (1909, 1913, and 1917) she came away with meaningful legislation.

The 1909 law applied only to multifamily dwellings and was amended to affect only the state's two largest cities—Indianapolis and Evansville. New legislation, drafted by Veiller, was shepherded by Bacon through the 1911 legislative session, only to be defeated on the final day. To this point Bacon had run virtually a one-woman campaign, but in the wake of her failure in 1911 she rallied others to the cause, helped to educate them on the issues, and coordinated their efforts. The Indiana Federation of Clubs, the state affiliate of the General Federation of Women's Clubs, was particularly important in extending the lobbying effort throughout the state. This networking paid off in 1913 when the legislature passed a bill that was almost a clone of the defeated 1911 proposal. Four years later, in her last foray to the general assembly, she successfully advanced a so-called death trap bill that sought to control dwellings deemed "infected and uninhabitable."

Bacon's reputation rests principally on her work as a housing reformer, but to describe her as only that is to ignore several other areas of her activity and accomplishment. As an *Evansville Courier* obituary about Bacon observed, "her interests were amazing in their catholicity." She played a particularly important role with regard to improving the lives of Indiana's children. During World War I she headed a child welfare committee that was part of the State Council of Defense. Among other things, she oversaw a drive to assess the physical development and well-being of preschool children, an effort that detected correctable health problems in hundreds, perhaps thousands, of cases. After the war, when the legislature created an advisory committee to guide Indiana's juvenile probation operation, Bacon was appointed to the committee, elected president of it by her fellow members, and served in the position from 1921 until her death. She was also active in city planning and zoning initiatives (especially in Evansville, where she was either president or vice president of the City Plan Commission throughout the 1920s), as well as a variety of public health efforts. She lectured often, especially in the Midwest, regarding housing reform and other social welfare issues. She found time to write articles, pamphlets, and even a book related to her reform interests, as well as several pieces that proclaimed her strong Methodist faith. In addition, she wrote poetry, authored several pageants, and published a volume of children's stories.

Bacon did not accomplish all that she wished, either personally or in the realm of public policy; she probably overemphasized environmental causes for urban social pathologies; and she was not immune to the racial prejudices of her time and place. Still, few Hoosiers of her era expended so much personal time and energy to ensure that all might have, as the title of her book put it, *Beauty for Ashes*.

ROBERT G. BARROWS

For Further Reading

Albion Fellows Bacon Papers. Willard Library, Evansville, Indiana.

Bacon, Albion Fellows. *Beauty for Ashes*. New York: Dodd, Mead and Company, 1914.

Barrows, Robert G. *Albion Fellows Bacon: Indiana's Municipal Housekeeper*. Bloomington: Indiana University Press, 2000.

Bailey, Katherine "Flossie"
1895–February 6, 1952

Leader of the Indiana National Association for the Advancement of Colored People and anti-lynching and civil rights activist.

She was named Katherine at her birth in Kokomo in 1895, but everyone called her "Flossie." Some also called her a "hot rod" because she sped through life full of determination. Flossie Bailey became an "uppity" woman ready to challenge Indiana's traditions of racial discrimination as she rose to leadership in the National Association for the Advancement of Colored People.

Flossie Harvey married Walter Bailey in 1917. He had grown up in New Castle, Indiana, and after graduation from Meharry Medical College in Nashville, Tennessee, settled in Marion, Indiana. The Baileys had a son whom they named Walter Charles, their only surviving child. Flossie's status as the wife of the leading black doctor in town was an asset, as was Walter's commitment to her causes. She was sometimes addressed as "Mrs. Dr. Bailey."

Flossie's primary cause was equality and justice for all. Her vehicle was the NAACP, the nation's leading civil rights organization. Founded in 1909, the NAACP received most of the media's attention for its national office in New York City, but the organization's real work was done by the local branches, where nearly all members were African Americans. By 1915 black Hoosiers had formed branches in Indianapolis, Terre Haute, Evansville, Gary, and Vincennes. In 1918 Bailey formed a Marion NAACP branch, but not until the late 1920s did the organization take off. Serving as branch president, Bailey enrolled 155 members by the end of 1930, collecting a dollar from each, including a few white citizens.

Leadership of the Marion branch gave Bailey a strong voice when Indiana suffered one of the greatest tragedies in its history. On the night of August 7, 1930, an angry mob responded to rumors of murder and rape by breaking into the Grant County Jail, dragging Abe Smith and Tom Shipp to the Courthouse Square, and lynching the two teenagers from a tree. Local authorities made only halfhearted efforts to stop the mob or to bring its leaders to justice.

Bailey was outraged. Before the lynching she made phone calls and sent telegrams to seek police protection at the jail. Afterward she organized a delegation of NAACP leaders to call on Indiana governor Harry Leslie, who gave them a cold reception and refused to make a public statement. Bailey convinced the national NAACP head, Walter White, to travel to Marion to investigate the lynching. She pushed for indictments, over the objections of Grant County's white leaders and even some African Americans. Largely because of her efforts two of the several dozen members of the lynch mob were eventually indicted and tried.

At the two trials in the Grant County Courthouse, Baily sat quietly and regally. Twelve white Grant County men refused to find either of the accused guilty. One of the great regrets of Bailey's life was that no one was ever punished for two deaths on the Marion lynching tree.

Bailey did not give up. Assuming the state NAACP presidency in 1930, she worked closely with White to plan the state organization's second annual meeting. Soon after, she received the national MADAM C. J. WALKER Medal, given "to the person who has done the best work in the NAACP during the years. Bailey's life was a whirlwind of telephone calls, telegrams, letters, and meetings by which she created and invigorated NAACP branches in the early 1930s. She reported regularly to the New York office about mass meetings, baby contests, fund-raisers, and dues paid in Crawfordsville, French Lick, Greencastle, South Bend, and Gary. It was largely from her efforts that the national NCAAP board in late 1931 singled out Indiana as "developing an able and militant leadership in the Association."

Bailey's spirit burst off the pages of the dozens of letters she wrote to NAACP leaders. One of her primary correspondents in the New York office scribbled on the top of one letter, "What a woman! If only we had one in every town!"

The Baileys' home at 1907 South Adams Street was the Indiana headquarters of the NAACP. Visiting African Americans sometimes stayed overnight because the Spencer Hotel, like many in Indiana, did not take black guests.

Bailey was determined there would never be another lynching in Indiana. The state had enacted antilynching legislation as early as 1899, after which, it seemed that the horror had ceased. (Indiana's infamous Ku Klux Klan of the 1920s was not interested in lynching and lynched no one, ever.) Bailey wrote to every branch in the state and to leaders of black and white lodges, clubs, and churches urging them to badger state legislators. In 1931 the general assembly passed an antilynching bill that provided for immediate dismissal of any sheriff from whose jail a prisoner was taken. Now, the *Indianapolis Recorder* stated, "Indiana has automatically retrieved its high status as a safe place in which to live."

Bailey's fight for justice and equality extended beyond lynching. She took up the cause of racial discrimination at Indiana University's Robert W. Long Hospital in Indianapolis, which did not admit black patients or allow black medical students to train on its floors. She attacked the "increasing tendency to have separate schools." She and her husband brought suit against a Marion movie theater after they were denied admission. A local jury ruled against them. The Baileys then pushed the case to the Indiana Supreme Court, which refused to challenge Hoosier traditions of segregated movie theaters.

Gender and race hampered Flossie's hot rod leadership. Although her colleagues in leadership positions in the NAACP were male, NAACP records show high regard for this Marion woman. It was foolish men who took her frivolously, as did Leslie.

Another obstacle was race. The lines of color always limited choices and skewed outcomes. Bailey knew defeat, yet she "held her head high and set an example for everyone," one old friend remembered. She was a "born leader," "very cultured," and "good looking," another said. People remembered that she dressed with style and wore especially striking hats.

The long years of the Great Depression took their toll. The NAACP struggled. Doctor Bailey suffered a stroke and closed his medical practice around 1940. The couple fell on such hard times that friends had to help them financially. They moved to Indianapolis, where Doctor Bailey died in 1942. Flossie died in the capital city in 1952. Both were buried in the Marion cemetery.

Flossie's last letter in the NAACP Papers at the Library of Congress is an apology to White, written in early 1941, a regret that she could not do more and a hope that other capable leaders would take over. At her death, White wrote, "never did I see greater courage and integrity than was displayed by herself and her late husband as they demonstrated in the Marion riot." She was, he concluded, "a courageous and gallant lady." This uppity woman made a way for others to follow. Her leadership in the 1930s helped build the foundation for the civil rights movement that came in the 1950s.

JAMES H. MADISON

For Further Reading

Hine, Darlene Clark. *Black Women in American History: The Twentieth Century*. Brooklyn, NY: Carlson Publishing, 1990.

Madison, James H. "Flossie Bailey: 'What a Woman!'" *Traces of Indiana and Midwestern History* 12, no. 1 (Winter 2000): 22–27.

———. *A Lynching in the Heartland: Race and Memory in America*. New York: Saint Martin's-Palgrave, 2001.

Thornbrough, Emma Lou. *Indiana Blacks in the Twentieth Century*. Bloomington: Indiana University Press, 2000.

Baker, Conrad

February 12, 1817—April 28, 1885

Lawyer, judge, lieutenant governor and governor.

Conrad Baker spent much of his political career standing just behind the larger-than-life figure of OLIVER P. MORTON, and the record of popular history has treated him as barely visible in Morton's shadow.

Any fair look at Baker's contributions to the Civil War and to the era following it, however, leads inevitably to the conclusion that he not only contributed mightily to Morton's fame but also laid foundations for much of the state's later progress. In fields such as corrections, education, and women's rights, Baker created a new state government readily recognizable more than a century later.

Baker was born on a farm near Chambersburg, Pennsylvania, on February 12, 1817, the son of Presbyterian farmers. He studied at what is now Gettysburg College, but left before graduating to read law under Thaddeus Stevens, later famous as a leader of the "radical Republicans" who so tormented President Andrew Johnson.

While studying with Stevens, Baker married Matilda Escon Sommers. The couple had two children before Matilda died in 1855. Three years later, Baker married Charlotte Francis Chute, with whom he had four children, including a son they named Thaddeus.

A law practice in Gettysburg lasted until 1841, when the Bakers moved westward and settled in Evansville. In addition to building his law business, Baker won election to the Indiana House of Representatives and as judge of the court of common pleas. Baker's local ascendancy paralleled that of his brother, William, still the only person elected mayor of Evansville four times.

Judge Baker was fresh off the bench when the new Republican Party named its first state ticket in 1856: Morton for governor and Baker for lieutenant governor—the same team that would prove so successful just eight years later.

When the Civil War broke out, William was mayor and Conrad was still practicing law in Evansville. William called a rally for April 17, and Conrad proposed a resolution of loyalty to the enormous crowd at the county courthouse. The brothers soon raised a regiment from counties along the Ohio River.

Baker became a cavalry colonel and led a regiment in the southwestern states. Correspondence and cable traffic between Baker and Morton was substantial. It suggested that Baker's special talent was not tactics but organization and a no-nonsense approach. When a soldier in the regiment complained directly to Morton about the food, Baker replied that he had made some changes and that as for the complainant, "I shall issue him double rations for a week . . . and insist on his eating them."

Baker eventually returned to Indianapolis to serve as assistant provost marshal. This assignment consisted chiefly of leading the recruiting drive for Indiana's massive contribution of men to the Union armies, one of the very things for which the Morton administration became so famous. "I tender to you 50,000 men," Morton replied to Abraham Lincoln's first call for troops. It was Baker who rounded them up.

Morton had served nearly four years without a lieutenant governor when the Morton-Baker pair again went to the voters in 1864, winning by a landslide. Their victory celebration had hardly subsided when Morton suffered a paralytic stroke. Morton decided to travel to Paris for treatment and informed the legislature that Baker would administer the executive department during his absence.

The five months of Baker's temporary leadership featured the sort of groundbreaking plans that later characterized his own gubernatorial years. He launched a series of institutions that remain central to Indiana's life. Most dramatically, he laid the groundwork for two of the state's universities. Convinced that an educated populace was crucial to the state's future, acting governor Baker invited communities to compete for hosting a new normal school. The people of Terre Haute proved the most energetic suitors, and the institution now known as Indiana State University opened in 1870. Baker used the opening of the new school to urge that Indiana's schools and universities be open for the advancement of women, a broadminded view for the era.

Baker likewise saw opportunity when Congress offered the states vast acreage for supporting what became known as land-grant colleges. While Baker was acting governor, the general assembly voted to accept this gift. In his 1869 legislative address, Baker declared support for an agricultural and mechanical arts college, although he expressed doubt about whether the funds available were sufficient. This declaration virtually crossed in the mail with the remarkable offer of John Purdue, promising $150,000 if the college was located in Tippecanoe County and bore his name. Baker signed legislation setting this plan in motion in May 1869, and Purdue University opened soon after Baker left office.

Baker was also a leader in corrections reform, joining reformers such as the Quakers and women's groups in pursuing more humane and effective institutions. These alliances produced the Indiana Boys' School, which opened in 1868 with inmates whose prison terms Baker commuted so that they could be transferred. Baker and many of the same reformers prompted creation of a women's prison and a girls reformatory at a joint site in Indianapolis. In the fall after Baker left office, it began receiving inmates previously held at the Jeffersonville prison. Baker was also a force behind building an institution for disabled veterans of the Civil War and the war's many orphans—the Soldiers' and Seamans' Home at Knightstown (later renamed Soldiers' and Sailors' Children's Home).

The most contentious political issue during the Baker administration involved the Civil War amendments to the U.S. Constitution. The Thirteenth Amendment, abolishing slavery, was ratified over Democratic opposition while Baker was acting governor. Democrats also opposed the Fourteenth Amendment, extending civil rights to blacks, ratified in January 1867. These debates were but a warm-up for the struggle over the Fifteenth Amendment, assuring blacks the right to vote.

Baker submitted the proposed amendment to the legislature in March 1869. With no hope of winning a vote on the merits, the Democratic members resigned so that the quorum requirement of two-thirds could not be met. Baker immediately called special elections, but the voters in the affected districts promptly reelected the same members.

Baker sent up the Fifteenth Amendment again in May 1869. Democrats resigned yet again. This time the Republicans met and voted to ratify anyway, saying the quorum requirement meant two-thirds of those holding office. When Democrats later gained control of the legislature, they voted to rescind Indiana's ratification, but the right of blacks to vote had by then become part of the U.S. Constitution.

The Governors Portrait Collection is yet another Baker legacy. In his 1869 legislative address, he urged an appropriation to begin such a collection. The legislature responded favorably, and Baker himself began engaging artists and writing families of former governors asking for photographs or older portraits.

Baker's career after leaving the governor's office took an ironic but positive turn. He joined the law practice launched by his friend and political opponent Thomas Hendricks, whom Baker had defeated during the 1868 election.

Hendricks had opened an office in Indianapolis and associated himself with attorney general Oscar B. Hord. When Hendricks was elected governor in 1872, he went to the statehouse and Baker went to the law firm. All three founders died during the 1880s, and Baker's son and a lawyer named Edward Daniels took over the firm. It has long since become one of the nation's leading law firms. Now called Faegre Baker Daniels, it is still a place characterized by commitment to public affairs and to bipartisanship.

RANDALL T. SHEPARD

For Further Reading

Baker, Conrad. Papers. Indiana State Archives, Indianapolis.
Foulke, William D. *Life of Oliver P. Morton, Including His Important Speeches.* Indianapolis: Bowen-Merrill Company, 1899.
McCutchan, Kenneth P. *At the Bend in the River: The Story of Evansville.* Woodland Hills, CA: Windsor Publications, 1982.
Mueller, Arnold Ernst R. "Conrad Baker, Former Governor of Indiana." MA thesis, Butler University, 1944.

The Ball Brothers

Lucius Lorenzo, March 29, 1850–July 22, 1932; William Charles, August 13, 1852–April 30, 1921; Edmund Burke, October 27, 1855–March 8 1925; Frank Clayton, November 24, 1857–March 19, 1943; and George Alexander, November 5, 1862–October 22, 1955

Industrialists and philanthropists, manufacturers of glass home-canning jars, and benefactors of Ball State University.

While the name Ball immediately brings to mind the iconic glass jars for home canning that became a household name worldwide, the company the Ball brothers built in Muncie, Indiana, became so much more through innovation, expansion, and diversification. The name is renowned not only for the family's business successes but also for philanthropic endeavors enshrined in such institutions as Ball State University, Ball Memorial Hospital, Ball Brothers Foundation, and the forty-acre Minnetrista Cultural Center.

The brothers Edmund and Frank Ball first went into business together in 1878 in Buffalo, New York. After trying various ventures, the duo received in 1880 from their uncle, George, a $200 loan to buy a business that produced tins cans of various sizes from one to ten gallons encased in wood jackets that were used to hold paint, varnishes, and kerosene. Soon brothers Lucius and George joined the business, and then came William, who sold the old family home in Canandaigua, New York, and moved with their mother to Buffalo.

Although fire destroyed the brothers' first factory and then struck again at a rebuilt plant, the brothers recovered and began expanding through increased production, new products, and added manufacturing capabilities, including glassmaking, which led to the introduction of glass home-canning jars with metal lids. The company incorporated as the Ball Brothers Glass Manufacturing Company in 1886, but was soon on the move westward. After Frank realized the advantage that natural gas had over coal for glassmaking, the brothers moved their glass factory to Muncie to take advantage of the natural gas boom there. Frank became president of the company in 1888 and the business continued to grow even during the severe economic panic of 1893, when many businesses faltered. The brothers did well with their glass jars because many families relied on home canning of fruits and vegetables from their gardens.

The company confronted a problem around this time when the supply of natural gas in the area diminished, but it solved that dilemma by installing gas converters that could use Indiana coal, which allowed it to remain in Muncie. In 1898 the brothers invented and patented a glass-blowing machine that completely changed the method of making jars—an innovation that gave them a competitive edge in the market, worldwide name recognition, and expanded production. By 1905 the company had seven plants in addition to the main Muncie facility employing 1,200 workers who produced sixty million jars a year using continuous tank furnaces equipped with Ball's patented blowing machines.

Ball made a practice of branching out into other industries whenever doing so would improve the company's products and profits. In this way, the company continued to expand, improve methods, and diversify. It got into the zinc business to make lids for its glass fruit jars and at one time owned the largest zinc strip rolling mill

The Ball Brothers Glass Manufacturing Company, Muncie, Indiana, circa 1919

in the world. Its entry into the rubber business began with the manufacture of sealing rings for the jars. When the company switched its shipping method from heavy wooden cases packed with straw to corrugated paper boxes, it purchased a paper mill.

Thus, the four components of the fruit jar business—glass, zinc, rubber, and paper—became the basic products from which the Ball Corporation evolved. Later, its zinc products included roofing material, battery shells, and engraving plates. Rubber products were made for the appliance and automotive industries. Ball also bought tin, steel, and plastic companies. Anticipating the commercial opportunities presented by the dawning of the Space Age in the 1950s, the company launched the Ball Brothers Research Corporation with laboratories in Muncie and Boulder, Colorado. Ball began manufacturing aerospace equipment in 1959 and in 1962 its OSO-1 (Orbiting Solar Observatory) satellite, built for the National Aeronautics and Space Administration, was launched from Cape Canaveral in Florida.

Ball has been in more than forty-five businesses since its founding. The company name was changed to Ball Brothers Company in 1922, to Ball Corporation in 1969, and became a publicly traded company in 1973. Having sold its last glass interests in 1996, the famous Ball canning supplies are now made by a spun-off independent company. Ball corporate headquarters moved from Muncie to Broomfield, Colorado, in 1998. Ball Corporation is now a worldwide manufacturer of plastic and metal food and beverage containers as well as providing equipment and services to the aerospace industry.

According to Edmund F. Ball, son of one of the founders and himself an eventual company president, the Ball brothers had personalities and talents that were remarkably well balanced. He said Frank, who served as president for fifty-five years, was a born leader, a strong, dynamic, and shrewd businessman. He described his father, Edmund B., as a great humanitarian who loved people and liked to work with his hands, and excelled at planning and building. His Uncle William, he said, was an exceptional salesman and traveler, elocutionist, and raconteur. The oldest of the brothers, Lucius L., fulfilled his lifelong ambition, after he had seen to it that his younger brothers and sisters were educated and established, to study and become a physician at the age of forty. The youngest brother, George A., lived to age ninety-two, keen, active, and alert up until his death in 1955. During his long and active lifetime, he served the company as bookkeeper, secretary, treasurer, vice president, president, and board chairman. "He participated in all the changes from kerosene cans and fruit jars to the threshold of the space age," his nephew noted.

The Ball brothers' success allowed them to be very generous to their community. In 1912 they provided $150,000 in matching funds for the construction of a Young Men's Christian Association building in downtown Muncie. The family gave an additional $200,000 to furnish the building and to support Camp Crosley, a youth camp that was named in memory of one of Edmund's sons. In 1926 the Balls contributed $100,000 toward a new Young Women's Christian Association building in Muncie.

In 1917 the Ball brothers bought the grounds and buildings of the defunct Eastern Indiana Normal University in Muncie and in 1918 donated them to the state. The institution was named Ball Teachers College in 1922 and became Ball State University in 1965. In 1927 the brothers gave $300,000 for the construction of a women's dormitory named for their sister, Lucina, an educator. The Minnetrista Museum and Cultural Center, which opened in 1988 with the purpose of preserving the cultural heritage of East Central Indiana, is named for a tract of land where the five brothers built homes.

The family established the Ball Brothers Foundation in 1926 for charitable purposes. The initial funds came from the estate of Edmund B., who had died the year before. One of the foundation's first projects was the creation of Ball Memorial Hospital, which opened in Muncie in 1929. It is now affiliated with Indiana University Health.

Outside of Muncie, the Balls contributed generously to a memorial at the site of Abraham Lincoln's boyhood home in southern Indiana; to the James Whitcomb Riley Memorial Hospital for Children in Indianapolis; to Hanover College in Madison, Indiana; Indiana University at Bloomington; Hillsdale College in Michigan; and Keuka College in New York. Ball family members, including their uncle, George, and their sister, Mary Frances Ball Mauck, served as trustees or in some other capacity for several of these institutions. By 1937 the monetary value of the family's philanthropies was estimated at $7 million.

In September 1937 a statue was unveiled on the Ball State campus to honor the Ball brothers for all their contributions to the Muncie community. The bronze statue, titled *Beneficence*, was accompanied by five columns of Indiana limestone, representing the five brothers.

BARBARA QUIGLEY

For Further Reading

Ball, Frank Clayton. *Memoirs of Frank Clayton Ball*. Muncie, IN: Scott Printing Company, 1937.

Birmingham, Frederic A. *Ball Corporation: The First Century*. Indianapolis: Curtis Publishing Company, 1980.

Conn, Earl L. *Beneficence: Stories about the Ball Families of Muncie*. Muncie, IN: Minnetrista Cultural Foundation, 2003.

Bell, Lawrence D.
April 5, 1894–October 20, 1956

Aviation pioneer and founder of Bell Aircraft Corporation and Bell Helicopter.

Lawrence D. Bell, who was born on a farm in Mentone, Indiana, believed that anyone could be successful if they applied themselves—a theory Bell put into practice during a pioneering career of nearly forty-five years in aircraft design, development, and manufacturing that spanned pre–World War I flying to the start of the space age.

Bell's interest in aviation began after his family moved to California in 1907 and he attended an air show in Long Beach with his brother, Grover. This outing inspired them to build their own wood-and-cloth airplane that actually flew and later both went to work in aviation, Grover as a pilot and Larry as his mechanic. However, Bell wanted to quit the field after Grover was killed in a plane crash, but friends persuaded him to remain in aviation.

Bell went to work for the Glenn L. Martin Company, an aircraft manufacturer, becoming shop foreman at age twenty and later promoted to vice president and general manager. Martin then sent him to build a new plant in Cleveland, Ohio, during World War I. Bell left Martin in 1928 to join Consolidated Aircraft Company in Buffalo, New York, a leading military aircraft manufacturer. When Consolidated moved to California, Bell remained in Buffalo and, in the summer of 1935, started his own company, Bell Aircraft Corporation.

Speaking about that decision, Leston Faneuf, who became president of Bell Aircraft prior to Bell's death and a Bell biographer, said, "It is typical of the indomitable spirit and supreme determination of Larry Bell that he chose the very middle of the Depression to fulfill a dream that he nurtured since first he went to work for Glenn Martin in 1912 at $9 a week. Larry always had wanted his own company. He was willing to accept full responsibility by putting his own name on it. He wanted to operate it so it could do some of the things he felt it was high time that aviation should do."

The growth and development of Bell Aircraft depended in large part on military contracts for fighter aircraft, a market that escalated at the dawn of World War II and continued strong through a succession of wars, both cold and hot, that followed. The first contract, awarded less than a year after the company's formation, was for the twin-engine Airacuda, a pusher aircraft, meaning the propellers were located behind the engines. This plane had two .37 mm cannons and four .55-caliber machine guns. Next came the P-39 Airacobra, one of America's main fighter aircraft when the country entered World War II and known for its innovative design, including placement of the engine in the center fuselage behind the pilot, a .37 mm cannon that could be fired through the hollow hub of the propeller, and a tricycle landing gear, the first modern airplane to use this type of landing gear. It was followed by the P-63 Kingcobra, which could fly higher, farther, and faster than the P-39, and then the P-59 Airacomet, developed and built under extreme secrecy, that became America's first jet fighter. For the war effort, Bell's Buffalo plant was building four hundred fighter planes a month, and the company also produced more than six hundred B-29 Superfortress bombers during the war at a plant in Marietta, Georgia, an average of one B-29 a day. In addition, Bell made large quantities of machine-gun mounts and mortar shells at its ordnance division in Vermont and established Camp Bell, where more than seven thousand soldiers were trained as mechanics to service and repair planes.

While fighter planes were still in mass production and war still raged, Bell was thinking ahead, launching development work on helicopters, collaborating with Arthur M. Young, who had devoted years to helicopter research. On March 8, 1946, the Bell helicopter, designated the NC-1H by the Civil Aeronautics Administration, became the world's first commercially licensed helicopter. Bell created a separate division for his latest innovation and built a new production plant in Fort Worth, Texas, for helicopters. Although helicopters were used during the Korean War, they achieved workhorse status in Vietnam, where the UH-1 or Huey was a constant presence in the air, engaging in firefights, transporting troops to battles, and swiftly evacuating wounded soldiers. The combination of jet and helicopter was achieved by Bell in 1954 with the first jet-powered convertiplane, which could take off and land like a helicopter and fly at the faster speed of a fixed-wing plane when propeller assemblies mounted on the wings tilted 90 degrees forward.

Bell's other landmark achievements in aviation paved the way for the country's entry into the space age, including the Bell-X1, which on October 14, 1947, with Chuck Yeager in the cockpit, became the first aircraft to break the sound barrier. A series of rocket-powered research planes followed that developed supersonic flight and heralded manned space travel by breaking into the thermal barrier. These efforts led to the manufacturing of missiles that could deliver nuclear and hydrogen bombs from a remote bomber.

In recognition of his remarkable career, Bell received a host of honors, including induction into the National Aviation Hall of Fame, the Daniel Guggenheim Medal for achievements in design and construction of military aircraft, the Collier Trophy for his work on the X-1 Supersonic plane, a presidential citation, and the U.S. Air Force's highest civilian award.

Bell's name and legacy live on in his hometown and in other parts of the country. Mentone is home to the Lawrence D. Bell Aircraft Museum and the Bell Memorial Public Library. The library was constructed with a donation from Bell, who requested that the money be used to honor his parents. There is a Lawrence D. Bell Hall at the University of Buffalo and a namesake high school in Hurst, Texas, a suburb of Fort Worth. Textron purchased the three divisions of Bell in 1960 and in 1976 combined operations into Bell Helicopter Textron.

Recounting Bell's path from Mentone to acclaim as the dean of the country's aviation executives, Faneuf said that he "had more than proved to be a pioneer with the courage and the ability to penetrate new frontiers and to leave aviation a list of technological feats probably not yet achieved anywhere else by any one man."

LINDA COCHRAN

For Further Reading

Faneuf, Leston. "Lawrence D. Bell, a Man and His Company." *Bell Aircraft* (May 15, 1958).

Museum Contributors (2013). Collections, Lawrence D. Bell Aircraft Museum Inc., Mentone, IN.

Norton, D. J. *Larry, a Biography of Lawrence D. Bell*. Chicago: Nelson-Hall, 1981.

Beveridge, Albert J.

October 6, 1862–April 27, 1927

U.S. senator, historian, and biographer of Chief Justice John Marshall and Abraham Lincoln.

On September 16, 1898, at Tomlinson Hall in Indianapolis, a Hoosier lawyer and would-be politician opened the election season for the Republican Party by addressing an issue the entire country had been pondering: Should the United States become an imperial power by maintaining control of such countries as Cuba, Puerto Rico, and the Philippines captured in the Spanish-American War? Such prominent voices as writer Mark Twain counseled against such foreign adventures, but for staunch imperialist Albert J. Beveridge, it was America's destiny to see its flag fly throughout the world.

In what came to be known as "The March of the Flag" speech, Beveridge, selected by the Republican-controlled Indiana General Assembly for election to the U.S. Senate in 1899, pointed out that if England and Germany could govern "foreign lands," so could America. Also, distance and oceans were no impediment to the march of the flag. "We cannot fly from our world duties; it is ours to execute the purpose of a fate that has driven us to be greater than our small intentions," Beveridge told his audience. "We cannot retreat from any soil where Providence has unfurled our banner; it is ours to save that soil for liberty and civilization."

Although known during his early senatorial career as an advocate on behalf of U.S. economic growth, Beveridge later supported the progressive measures pushed by the liberal wing of his party, including stricter control of big business by the federal government, pure food laws, the direct primary, and leading the fight against child labor in the nation's factories. Losing his seat in the Senate in 1911 when the Democrats took control of the Indiana legislature, Beveridge joined Theodore Roosevelt's insurgent Progressive (Bull Moose) Party, delivering the keynote address at the party's national convention. Beveridge ran as the Progressive candidate for Indiana governor in 1912, but finished second, losing to Democratic candidate Samuel M. Ralston. Beveridge tried to regain his Senate seat in 1914 and 1922, but failed in both contests.

Born on a farm in Highland County, Ohio, Albert was the child of Thomas and Frances Eleanor Beveridge. Thomas was a Union army veteran whose venture as the owner of a general store in Level, Ohio, ended in bankruptcy, forcing the family to move to Illinois. As a young man Albert held a series of jobs, including helping to build a railroad, clerking in a post office, and as a teamster for a lumber company. Encouraged by a teacher, however, Beveridge decided to pursue a career in law. "Lawyers were the biggest men in our own and neighboring counties," he recalled, "and they were regarded as a very superior type of human being."

After graduating from high school in 1881, Beveridge attended Indiana Asbury University (renamed DePauw University in 1884), earning a reputation as a gifted orator and becoming a fixture in the library, where he read such authors as William Shakespeare, Robert Burns, Charles Dickens, and William Makepeace Thackeray. "I would be willing to go to hell," Beveridge told a fellow student, "if I could make a reputation as great as that of Napoleon."

In the fall of 1884 Beveridge took a month off from school to campaign for GOP candidates in the state, winning for him the title "young man eloquent" from the *Indianapolis Journal*. "I was a partisan Republican of that white hot kind that in those days resulted from being the son and brother of Union soldiers," said Beveridge, who spoke in other states as well. After graduating from DePauw in 1885 with a bachelor of philosophy degree, he read law in the Indianapolis firm

Albert J. Beveridge

McDonald, Butler and Mason and also served as a clerk in the Republican-controlled Indiana House. Shortly before being admitted to the bar, Beveridge, on November 24, 1887, married his college sweetheart, Kate Maude Langsdale; she died in 1900 and in 1907 he married Catherine Eddy and the couple had two children.

Beveridge left the McDonald, Butler and Mason firm to start his own practice in 1899. His firm prospered and he became active in a variety of civic organizations, including the Commercial Club, Young Men's Christian Association, the Indianapolis Art Association, and the Indianapolis Literary Club. These associations, and his skill as a speaker, won the attention of GOP leaders, who offered Beveridge the nomination as the Republican candidate in 1894 for the state's attorney general position—an offer he declined. "It is firing off my gun too soon," he noted. "I think there may be something higher ahead for me—but I shall not care even for that unless I can [do] good for my country—good in the better and nobler sense."

In 1899, with Republicans in control of the Indiana legislature, Beveridge had his chance to gain a higher office, that of U.S. senator. Young friends of his who had been active in the Republican Party rallied around his candidacy over that of better-known, and older, candidates, including J. Frank Hanly, Robert S. Taylor, and George W. Steele. When he heard rumblings of discontent about his being too young (thirty-six at the time) for such a high office, Beveridge told a friend to remind his opponents that Thomas Jefferson had been only thirty-three when he wrote the Declaration of Independence, Alexander Hamilton was thirty-two when he became Secretary of the Treasury, and Henry Clay was only thirty when he joined the U.S. Senate. After numerous rounds of balloting by the eighty-nine GOP members of the legislature on January 10, Beveridge captured the nomination, and he was formally elected by the general assembly on January 17, 1899. "Appreciation is a poor word for the honor that you have conferred upon me," he said in remarks at the Statehouse following the balloting, "obligation does not adequately describe the duty which your kindness has placed upon me."

Reelected to the Senate in 1905, Beveridge made his mark as a progressive with his support of two key pieces of legislation. Reacting to the unsanitary practices in the meatpacking industry exposed by Upton Sinclair's 1906 novel *The Jungle*, Beveridge sponsored the Meat Inspection Act. Alarmed by the harm it might do to the country, he also campaigned vigorously in the Senate for a bill that banned the interstate commerce of goods made by child labor. "When these children grow up and understand they are ruined for life," he told a friend, John C. Shaffer, "there is developed the classes which we all fear and have reason to fear."

Thwarted in his political career by the 1912 election that saw Democrats win control of the Indiana legislature and Woodrow Wilson capturing the presidency, Beveridge decided to pursue writing a biography of John Marshall, chief justice of the U.S. Supreme Court from 1801 to 1835. The project resulted in a four-volume work published by the Houghton Mifflin Company to glowing reviews and gaining for Beveridge the Putlizer Prize for Biography or Autobiography in 1920. He turned next to another anticipated four-volume biography, this one on the life of ABRAHAM LINCOLN. Beveridge's death on April 27, 1927, however, saw him only up to the 1858 debates between Lincoln and Stephen A. Douglas. Historian Worthington S. Ford finished the work on Beveridge's behalf, and it was published in two volumes in 1928 by Houghton Mifflin. Thanks to a contribution from Beveridge's widow, Catherine, the American Historical Association in 1939 established the Albert J. Beveridge Award to promote and honor outstanding historical writing.

RAY E. BOOMHOWER

For Further Reading

Bowers, Claude G. *Beveridge and the Progressive Era*. New York: Literary Guild, 1932.

Braeman, John. *Albert J. Beveridge: American Nationalist*. Chicago: University of Chicago Press, 1971.

———. "The Rise of Albert J. Beveridge to the United States Senate." *Indiana Magazine of History* 53 (December 1957): 355–82.

Levine, Daniel. "The Social Philosophy of Albert J. Beveridge." *Indiana Magazine of History* 58 (June 1962): 101–16.

Black, Glenn Albert

August 5, 1900–September 2, 1964

Indiana's first professional archaeologist who established Indiana's first archaeology program.

Glenn Black, who was the first and for many years the only full-time, professional archaeologist in Indiana, spent most of his career investigating archaeological questions about occupations at Angel Mounds, a Mississippian Period (AD 1100–1400) town near Evansville. He was a self-taught scholar who by circumstance, persistence, and ability established Indiana's first archaeology program—initially through the Indiana Historical Society and then Indiana University.

Born in Indianapolis in 1900, Black died in Evansville in 1964 after suffering a heart attack while excavating at Angel Mounds. Although his research was mainly confined to Indiana, his career spanned a time when archaeology was first developing as a profession and archaeologists were just starting to appreciate the value of North American prehistory. Black helped articulate and shape the questions that still drive archaeological research today.

Black's publications reflect a lifelong interest in field techniques and ethnography, the scientific study of cultures and people. Nevertheless, Black, who worked as a drummer in a Dixieland band and an estimating engineer during the 1920s, received little formal postsecondary training and came into archaeology circuitously. His development and successes as an archaeologist coincided with the Great Depression and were intimately related to his relationship with ELI LILLY, president of Eli Lilly and Company, the pharmaceutical giant. In 1927 he volunteered at Albee Mound, the first professional excavation in Indiana, and later on the Whitewater valley survey, both sponsored by the IHS and led by Christopher B. Coleman, director of the Indiana Historical Commission, and J. Arthur MacLean, director of the John Herron Art Institute. These projects introduced Black to the IHS and Lilly, and launched his career as a professional archaeologist.

As an archaeologist, Black was well respected nationwide. A founding member of the Society for American Archaeology, he served in most of its leadership roles: vice president (1939–40), council member (1940–41), president (1941–42), and treasurer (1947–51). His national prominence and the respect accorded him are particularly impressive because Black only held a high school diploma. Although awarded an honorary doctor of science degree from Wabash College in 1951, Black's only formal professional training came at the Ohio State Museum, where he worked with H. C. Shetron from October 1931 to May 1932. Like many prewar archaeologists, Black was largely self-taught, commenting that he "taught at the only university he ever attended," and often quipping that the only degree he ever received was from a college that he never attended (Wabash College). Few nondegreed archeologists, however, rose to his level of national prominence.

Throughout his career, Black was closely tied to Lilly, who was fascinated by and supported archaeology. Their relationship started business-like but soon became very personal, as they often took family vacations together. Black's professional career began in 1931 when, unemployed by the Depression, he was hired as an IHS archaeologist. Partly through Lilly's influence as IHS president (1931–45) but mostly by his performance, Black was appointed as the IHS archaeologist later that year. His duties took him across Indiana and allowed him to broadly investigate the state's archaeology, including many well-known IHS projects. The report on his excavation of Nowlin Mound remains one of the more precise descriptions of mound structure. Black is best known, however, for his 1938 to 1964 investigations of Angel Mounds, which was published posthumously.

The connection between Black and Angel Mounds began serendipitously. In June 1931 the IHS hired Black to be the driver and a guide for a weeklong archaeological tour of sites in Indiana that included Angel Mounds among many others. The tour, whose purpose was to select sites upon which to focus future research, brought together Black, Lilly, and W. K. Moorehead, a nationally prominent archaeologist from Ohio State University and the Peabody Foundation, and by happenstance introduced them to Angel Mounds. Black saw the potential for a detailed, long-term study of village life, and the IHS, mainly with the support of Lilly, ultimately purchased Angel Mounds in 1938. Black devoted the last twenty-seven years of his life to the site. Although the resources spent at a single site subjected him to criticism, Black maintained that constructing site ethnographies, which he believed must be the overarching purpose of archaeological research, could only be accomplished through extensive, long-term excavations. His successful Angel Mounds excavation is his testament to this obligation.

During the 1930s, Lilly, Black, and Paul Weer, a childhood friend of Lilly who was closely

Glenn A. Black (far right) talks with other members of the Indiana University Anthropology Department, March 1947. From left to right: William J. Wallace, Charles F. Voegelin, Georg Karl Neumann, and Black.

associated with his historical research, created a research program for Indiana archaeology that was visionary in its multidisciplinary perspective, technological scope, and scientific purposes. It involved Chautaqua-like meetings with other invited professionals and yearly research goals. One of their more controversial investigations was the scientific evaluation of the *Walam Olum*, which purportedly chronicled the pre/proto-historic migration of the Delaware Tribe but is now considered a hoax. This topic fit into Black's early interests in potential direct prehistoric/historic connections in northern Indiana, but because the *Walam Olum* work was rejected, even ridiculed, by other professionals, Black terminated similar investigations. What Black never abandoned, however, was his conviction that archaeologists should be ethnographers who chronicle how common people lived, which is a central theme of his Angel Mounds monograph.

Black reflected his contemporaries' belief that archaeologists must master many skills. He became a proficient surveyor, cartographer, draftsman, photographer, and geophysicist, each of which was necessary to his research at Angel Mounds. As a first task, Black created an incredibly detailed topographic map by surveying 250,000 points in a five-by-five foot grid across the site using only a plane table. During his twenty-seven years of work at Angel Mound and with support from the IHS and Lilly, Black surrounded himself with innovative technology and creative scientists from many fields. For example, many initial, proof-of-concept radiocarbon dates derived from Angel Mounds and the results are archived at the Glenn A. Black Laboratory of Archaeology. Between 1958 and 1962, with support from two National Science Foundation grants, Black pioneered geophysical applications at archaeological sites in North American. Using a proton magnetometer built in Bloomington by Irwin Scolar, Black and IU field school students traced segments of the palisade walls not visible on the surface.

Except during World War II, Angel Mounds was excavated continuously from 1938 to 1965—first through the Works Progress Administration and later though the IU Archaeology Field School. Black directed an ambitious WPA project at Angel Mounds (1938–42) that employed more than two hundred workers and excavated more than 11,400 square meters. He resumed excavations at Angel Mounds in 1945 through IU—a relationship that became increasingly important to him. In 1944 Black was appointed to the Zoology Department at IU, where archaeology first resided. Black became a founding member of the Anthropology Department in 1947 and remained there until his death.

Although he taught at IU, Black never moved to Bloomington from his home at Angel Mounds, preferring to commute weekly from Evansville. Black ultimately trained more than 120 students through his Angel Mounds Field School and hundreds of others in his IU classes. Students were important to Black and he kept detailed files about his former students to help him guide students throughout their careers. He maintained a "highly personal" relationship and "was easily approached by the rawest undergraduate and more than once saw students through some financial crisis." Black's weekly commute during the 1950s and 1960s is testimony to his commitment to students. Their devotion to him was apparent when many of his former students returned to celebrate the seventieth anniversary of Angel Mounds in 2007. Black would likely agree that no finer testament could be made to him.

G. WILLIAM MONAGHAN
TIMOTHY BAUMANN

For Further Reading

Black, Glenn A. "Excavation of the Nowlin Mound." *Indiana History Bulletin* 14, no.2. (April 1937): 207–305.

———. *The Angel Site: An Historical, Archaeological and Ethological Study.* Indianapolis: Indiana Historical Society, 1967.

Kellar, James H. "Glenn A. Black, 1900–1964." *American Antiquity* 31, no. 3 (July 1966): 402–5

Madison, James H. *Eli Lilly: A Life, 1885–1977.* Indianapolis: Indiana Historical Society, 1989.

Blackford, Isaac

November 6, 1786–December 31, 1859

Speaker of the Indiana House of Representatives, legal scholar, and longest-serving justice of the Indiana Supreme Court.

It does no disservice to the other hundred or so justices of the Indiana Supreme Court to say that Isaac Blackford still has no peer as someone of genuine international reputation.

Much of this reputation rests on Blackford's seminal contribution to nineteenth-century legal scholarship. In our nation's early decades, there was little printed American law, and most lawyers relied on works such as *Blackstone's Commentaries*. Blackford embarked on assembling a series of reports of the court's decisions that marked Indiana as a place of respectable lawyering. He undertook this effort as a personal venture, editing all the decisions himself, paying for the printing, and selling the volumes.

When the first volume appeared in 1830, it was an instant hit in a very large legal community. A young Washington Irving, then secretary to the American legation in London, wrote: "I meet with it frequently and am often asked as to the antecedents of its author, whose name is already quite familiar at Westminster." When Harvard librarian John Gage Marvin, regarded as the founder of American legal bibliography, first examined American law reports in 1847, he declared that Blackford's volumes had "the reputation of being among the best American reports." National figures such as Chancellor Kent praised the reports, and *American Jurist and Law Magazine* acclaimed the opinions themselves as "creditable to the court and bar."

Blackford's demonstrated legal talent and his long tenure—longer even than John Marshall—propelled him to national prominence. When William Draper Lewis, founder of the American Law Institute, undertook to identify and write of the "Great American Lawyers" in 1907, he ranked Blackford as a figure of "permanent national reputation," alongside Joseph Story and Daniel Webster. When twenty-first-century scholars such as Kermit Hall did similar biographies a century later, Blackford was still featured.

Blackford's work was well known beyond legal circles. Indiana governor Albert G. Porter said that there was not a single Indiana community where

Blackford was not "a household word." Citizens commonly quoted Blackford, rather than the statutes. To be sure, Blackford was part of the state's political establishment from the time Indiana was a territory. Governor Thomas Posey named him the first clerk of Washington County in January 1814, and the territorial legislature engaged him as its clerk for successive sessions. In late 1815 Posey named him territorial judge, prompting Blackford's move to Vincennes. He won election to the very first Indiana House of Representatives, and became speaker when it met in Corydon. Governor JONATHAN JENNINGS named him to the Supreme Court in 1817 over Blackford's protestations that at age thirty-one he was not senior enough for the post.

Blackford's diligence, competence, and his connections led to roles in such early institutions as the Bank of Vincennes, designated by the first legislature as the state bank (indeed he became its second officer). This banking service reflected a lifelong interest in business. Usually living as a bachelor or widower under modest circumstances, Blackford accumulated assets and invested regularly in real estate and other ventures in southwest Indiana and in Indianapolis. The land surrounding today's Military Park in Indianapolis was a Blackford real-estate venture, still marked by Blackford Avenue alongside the park and the Indiana University McKinney School of Law. His most monumental project was a five-story office building at Meridian and Washington Streets that was demolished in 1912 to build what is now the headquarters of the law firm Barnes and Thornburg. Of course, even his law reports were a business of sorts—a business of sufficient success that the Constitutional Convention of 1850–51 resolved to create a public office of reporter, presumably expecting that the state could profit from it.

Blackford played leadership roles in the major social movements of his time—opposing slavery and promoting education. He was a founder and president of Indiana's chapter of the American Colonization Society, which sponsored free blacks in returning to Africa. Modern generations view this effort with skepticism, but it once drew support from abolitionists, religious leaders, and people such as James Madison and Bushrod Washington. Blackford was also prominent in the "common school" movement, seeking to establish free and general education as a way of building Indiana's future. He allied himself with reformers such as CALEB MILLS and presided at the common school convention of May 1847, where advocates laid the groundwork for the strong plank on free, public education that became part of Indiana's 1851 constitution. This very public role complemented a lifetime of leadership in education, such as serving as a director of Vincennes's early public library and as a trustee and law professor for Indiana University.

Blackford was not an Indiana native. He was born in Bound Brook, New Jersey, in 1786, and returned there after graduating from Princeton in 1806, part of a remarkable class that produced senators, governors, justices, and a vice president. He studied law in the offices of Colonel George MacDonald and with Judge Gabriel Ford, later a member of New Jersey's supreme court. Blackford moved to Indiana in 1811 and was practicing law in Vincennes when MacDonald and his family arrived there in 1819.

Blackford married young Caroline MacDonald in 1820. She died while giving birth to their son, George, the following year. Blackford considered Vincennes as his home, although he lived in what was called the Governor's Residence on the Circle in downtown Indianapolis for some twenty years. It was there that he closeted himself in grief over George's death in 1846.

When Indiana began electing its judges in 1852, Blackford had been so long out of political circulation that the Democratic Party nominated instead a younger candidate, fellow justice Samuel Perkins. Blackford drifted a bit until President Franklin Pierce appointed him to the new U.S. Court of Claims in March 1855—a choice the nation's newspapers said drew "universal commendation." He became that court's chief judge, and was serving there when he died in Washington, D.C., on the last day of December 1859. His body lay in state in the chambers of the Indiana Senate.

Upon Blackford's death, the editors of the *Indianapolis Journal* declared him "a giant" and the *New York Times* called him "indefatigable" and "much esteemed." The verdict of history, rendered over and over, has been that they were right.

RANDALL T. SHEPARD

For Further Reading

Lupton, Suzanne Weber. "Isaac N. Blackford: First Man of the Court." *Indiana Law Review* 30, no. 1 (1997) 319–28.

Marvin, John Gage. *Legal Bibliography; or, a Thesaurus of American, English, Irish, and Scotch Law Books*. Philadelphia: T. and J. W. Johnson, 1847.

Thornton, W. W. *Isaac Blackford: The Indiana Blackstone*. Edited by Douglas Fivecoat. Indianapolis, IN: Indiana Supreme Court, 2005.

———. "Supreme Court Judges of Indiana." *The Green Bag* 4 (May–June 1882).

Blaker, Eliza

March 5, 1854–December 4, 1926

Teacher, educator, and pioneer of the free kindergarten movement.

When he took over as minister for the Plymouth Church in Indianapolis in 1877, Reverend Oscar Carleton McCulloch noticed that churchgoers in the capital city "had not much hand in relieving the poor." He soon set out to change that, rejuvenating the Indianapolis Benevolent Society and creating the Charity Organization Society to aid those he called the "worthy" distressed. In the summer of 1881, after investigating the condition of children whose families were being helped by the Benevolent Society, McCulloch called on five influential women in the community to attempt to help underprivileged children improve their lives.

Eliza Blaker

That summer a trial free kindergarten program was started to assist underprivileged youngsters in the corridor of School Number 12 at West and McCarty Streets. Pleased with this trial run, the women organized the Indianapolis Free Kindergarten and Children's Aid Society.

Indianapolis's free kindergarten movement, which began in that school corridor, grew by leaps and bounds until, by the mid-1910s, it included as many as sixty schools. The accomplishments of the Indianapolis free kindergartens, which became a model for the rest of the country, were achieved through the untiring efforts of Eliza A. Blaker, the daughter of a Philadelphia seamstress and Quaker Civil War veteran. She watched over the education of thousands of Indianapolis youngsters as superintendent for the free kindergartens and trained numerous teachers by starting the Kindergarten Normal Training School, known to those in the community as "Mrs. Blaker's College."

The woman who inspired such devotion that following her death alumnae and faculty of the Kindergarten Normal Training School formed the Eliza A. Blaker Club was born in Philadelphia on March 5, 1854, the eldest of three children raised by Jacob and Mary Jane Core Cooper. In 1876 at the Philadelphia Centennial Exposition, Blaker became familiar with a system of education that became her life's work. One of the exposition's most popular features was a demonstration kindergarten taught by Ruth Burritt of Boston. "There I found what I had been groping for," Eliza said. The idea for kindergartens originated in Germany in the 1830s through the work of Friedrich Froebel. Using a child's love of play as its base, Froebel's system attempted to "give the children employment in agreement with their whole nature, to strengthen their bodies, to exercise their senses, to engage their wakening mind, and through their senses to make them acquainted with nature and their fellow creatures."

For it to succeed, Froebel believed that his kindergarten idea needed to have the support of what he described as an "intellectually active women:" a definition that fit the young Eliza. Fascinated by what she saw at the exposition, she enrolled in the new Centennial Training School for Kindergartners, operated by Burritt through the auspices of the Friends' Society of Philadelphia. After graduating from the school, she found a job at Philadelphia's Vine Street Kindergarten. Before assuming her new responsibilities, however, she took time out to become the wife of her former childhood playmate, Louis J. Blaker.

In 1882 officials from the Hadley Roberts Academy, a private school in Indianapolis located on Meridian and Vermont Streets, hired Blaker to start a kindergarten class for children of the community's well-to-do families. Shortly after moving to Indianapolis, however, Blaker left the academy and accepted an offer from the Indianapolis Free Kindergarten Society to direct the group's efforts to aid underprivileged children. Blaker helped to open a new kindergarten adjacent to the Friendly Inn, a charitable home established by Reverend McCulloch on West Market Street.

Seeing the "sad and old faces" and "vacant, far away expressions" of the countless underprivileged youths who flocked to the free kindergartens inspired Blaker to provide for them a "miniature world in which the little one is happy, is harmoniously developed and learns to think and act as a reasonable being endowed with a high destiny."

This high purpose, however, had to be achieved with limited financial resources. The benches the children sat on at the first free kindergarten on Market Street consisted of bundles of kindling chopped by indigent men to earn their room and board at the Friendly Inn. When teachers could not find enough paper for students, Blaker sent them out to seek donations of materials from Washington Street merchants. Even before they could start attending the schools, many children had to be given shoes and clothes by the Children's Aid Society. Some kindergartens served breakfast to their charges and all offered free lunches.

Blaker outlined her philosophy of teaching in numerous speeches over the years to local clubs and organizations, and in yearly reports from her superintendent's office. She described the role of the kindergarten as providing a wholesome environment in which students were free to form the proper habits needed for their future schooling and life. Such an institution, said Blaker, also gave poorer students the "opportunity to get a fair start in life; in fact, to feed the soul and, where necessary, to feed and clothe the physical body. To sum the divisions of this aim—"it [the kindergarten] is character-forming." Students spent three hours each morning in the classroom engaged in activities under the guidance of trained teachers.

To further the work of the free kindergarten, Blaker realized from the beginning that it was crucial to have available trained kindergarten teachers. Preschool students, she maintained, had to be under the guidance of a well-trained teacher, one who combined the talents of "a gardener, a mother, a nurse, an elder sister, [and] a wise play-fellow. She must be a psychologist, a woman of good education, [and] of definite training for her work." In 1882 Blaker opened in her own home a training school for kindergarten teachers called the Kindergarten Normal Training School, which became the Teachers College of Indianapolis in 1905.

Despite early hardships, Blaker had faith in the school. "There have been times when I knew not where the money was to come from, but it came, because by the middle of the month I began to 'dig in' and work to get it," she said. Through hard work and "the guidance of a Higher Power than I," Blaker soon had students flocking to her side. From an enrollment of twelve students in 1883, the school's population grew over the next decade to 344 pupils. Graduates of the program had gone on to start kindergarten programs in other Hoosier cities, including Evansville, Lafayette, and Bloomington, as well as establishing programs in such states as Tennessee, Michigan, Ohio, and Pennsylvania.

Shortly before her death on December 4, 1926, Blaker worked out an arrangement between the Teacher's College and Butler University whereby students at each institution who wished training in a particular field—elementary education at the Teacher's College and secondary education at Butler—had the opportunity to do so and receive course credit. "Mrs. Blaker's School" continued to produce teachers until 1930, when control passed to Butler. The free kindergartens had a longer life, continuing to ease the way for Indianapolis youngsters until 1952, when they were incorporated into the Indianapolis school system.

During her forty-four years in the capital city, Blaker oversaw the education of thousands of youngsters and provided training for thousands of preschool teachers. Her devotion to education resulted in her receiving an honorary doctorate from Hanover College in 1917. Even after her death, Blaker continued to be honored for her work, with the Eliza Blaker Club, members of whom were all graduates of her school, establishing a room in her honor at Butler University in 1943 and the Indianapolis school system naming a school for Blaker in 1958. Blaker, however, always refused to let such tributes go to her head. "The cause," she said, "is greater than the individual."

RAY E. BOOMHOWER

For Further Reading

Eliza Blaker Papers. Rare Books and Special Collections. Irwin Library, Butler University, Indianapolis.

Boomhower, Ray E. "'The Thing is Right!' Eliza Blaker and the Free Kindergarten Movement," *Traces of Indiana and Midwestern History* 16, no. 1 (Winter 2004): 28–37.

Thornbrough, Emma Lou. *Eliza Blaker: Her Life and Work.* Indianapolis: Eliza A. Blaker Club, 1956.

A collection of material on the Indianapolis Free Kindergarten and Children's Aid Society can be found at the Indiana Historical Society William Henry Smith Memorial Library, Indianapolis.

Bolton, Sarah T.

December 18, 1814–August 4, 1893

Prominent poet and advocate for women's rights and social justice.

"Nothing great is lightly won, / Nothing won is lost, / Every good deed, nobly done, / Will repay the cost." These stirring sentiments in dated language from Sarah Bolton's most famous poem, "Paddle Your Own Canoe," were once widely known by every schoolchild (as were numerous other of her works) and sung in thousands of parlors when its words were set to music. Most educated Hoosiers knew her poem "Indiana" and could recite it proudly: "The circling sunlight never spanned / The borders of a better land / Than our own Indiana." It, too, became a song.

Her many poems are mostly forgotten today, even in her home state, but it was Bolton who began Indiana's rich literary tradition as a published poet by the time she was fourteen in the early years of Indiana statehood. She was born in Kentucky but her family soon moved to a farm in Jennings County near Vernon, Indiana, an area still largely wilderness. Her father later moved the family to Madison, where the children could be schooled. The precocious Sarah Tittle Barrett (or Barritt) contributed poems regularly to the newspapers in Madison and Cincinnati and caught the eye of Nathaniel Bolton, editor and copublisher of the *Indianapolis Gazette*. They married in 1831 and moved to Indianapolis, purchasing a farm at Mount Jackson on the National Road a few miles west of the capital.

The Boltons lived in town for a few years, then, when their fortunes suffered, moved back to the farm, where they ran a tavern that became something of a salon and destination for legislators and others to discuss the topics of the day. Always interested in current events, Sarah participated in these lively conversations and continued to write and publish poetry in newspapers and magazines on a wide variety of subjects. By this time she was becoming recognized, unofficially, as the poet laureate of Indiana.

After selling the farm in 1845 to the state for what was then called a hospital for the insane, the Boltons, with their two children, moved back into town, where Sarah became actively involved in advocating property rights for women, lobbying first the 1851 Constitutional Convention and later, through Robert Dale Owen, the legislature. Owen is rightly credited for his successful efforts, but in an 1851 letter to Sarah, he congratulated her that "by dint of perseverance through many obstacles, you have so efficiently contributed to the good cause of property rights of your sex." Writing scores of articles and letters advocating reform did not slow her output of poetry; it was in this period that Sarah wrote "Paddle Your Own Canoe."

After a stint as state librarian, Nathaniel was appointed by President Franklin Pierce to be consul to Geneva, Switzerland, in 1855. While Nathaniel attended to his diplomatic duties, Sarah and her daughter explored Switzerland and other parts of Europe, all the while gathering subject matter for her poetry. She wrote lyrically of stunning sights and historical places and created long narrative poems based on both real and fictional characters. Her husband's declining health forced him to resign his post after two years, and after returning home he died in 1858.

Sarah continued to write and remained active in social reform. In 1863 she married Judge Addison Reese of Missouri and lived with him there for two years, but the marriage did not last. Thereafter, Sarah never used the name Reese except for business purposes. Her first collection of poetry, simply titled *Poems*, was published in 1865. She spent the next few years traveling in Europe and lived for a time in Dresden. Upon her return to Indiana, Sarah purchased Beech Bank farm southeast of Indianapolis (at the edge of present-day Beech Grove) in 1871 and lived there until her

Sarah T. Bolton

death. She maintained a wide acquaintance among her literary colleagues. Bolton never stopped writing and published two more collections, *The Life and Poems of Sarah T. Bolton* (1880) and *Songs of a Life-Time* (1892) with an introduction by Lew Wallace and a short ode by James Whitcomb Riley. A posthumous collection, *Paddle Your Own Canoe and Other Poems* (1897), is virtually a reprinting of *Songs* with a few additional poems. It contains the same introductory material as well as a sketch of Bolton's life.

Bolton wrote idealistically and nostalgically of pioneers and farmers, penning paeans to Indiana scenes of her youth as well as the state and its stalwart citizens in general. In her narrative poems that were set in Indiana she created characters and stories, some likely based upon real people that she knew, others entirely invented.

Not surprisingly, she wrote of inequality in regard to women in poems such as "Ne Dormiat Deus," and, in words that ring strangely familiar today, of the yawning gap between the rich and the laboring poor in "Evicted," "Two Scenes," and "Ye Sons of Toil," whose stanzas include:

> Come, swart-browned toilers of the mines,
> Whose labor buys the rich, red wines,
> The silver plate on which he dines,
> Who never toils,
> The silken couch where he reclines,
> Who wins the spoils.

Bolton even wrote against the execution of the anarchists convicted in the 1886 Haymarket riot in Chicago in "The Doomed Anarchists." She took no position on their innocence; rather, she used this event to protest the death penalty.

Her works fit well into the style of many better-known nineteenth-century poets. Several are similar to those of John Greenleaf Whittier, for example, or, indeed, Riley, who called Bolton "this queen / In lilied cadence voiced and raimented." That being said, some of her poems perhaps are better left buried in the sands of time. One such example might be her tribute to Edgar Allan Poe, which she wrote in the meter of and in direct response to the subject of "The Raven." To the modern ear it sounds trite and affected.

Little exists today to commemorate this important literary figure. Beech Grove (a town founded after Bolton's death) purchased the former Beech Bank farm from the Bolton estate in 1930; largely developed by New Deal agencies in the 1930s, the site became Sarah T. Bolton Park. And in the rotunda of the Indiana Statehouse is a bronze portrait relief of Bolton by the sculptor Emma Sangernebo. Dedicated in 1941, it is emblazoned with lines from her poem "Indiana."

GLORY-JUNE GREIFF

For Further Reading

Banta, R. E. *Indiana Authors and Their Books, 1816–1916*. Crawfordsville, IN: Wabash College, 1949.

Bolton, Sarah Tittle. *Paddle Your Own Canoe and Other Poems*. Indianapolis: Bowen-Merrill, 1897.

Dunn, Jacob Piatt, Jr. *Greater Indianapolis*. Chicago: Lewis Publishing Company, 1910.

Borkenstein, Robert Frank

August 31, 1912–August 10, 2002

Forensic scientist, educator, author, and inventor of the Breathalyzer.

Born in Fort Wayne, Indiana, to German immigrant parents, Robert Borkenstein from an early age exhibited tendencies for scientific experimentation. Finishing high school just on the eve of the Great Depression, he was unable to afford a college education and instead began work as a photograph technician. He acquired considerable expertise and the *Indianapolis Star* reported in 1940 that he "developed a simplified color printing process which eliminates the black printing plate, which has a tendency to dull color brilliance" at a time before it was marketed by Kodak. He also built two color cameras with an optical system similar to the Technicolor camera.

As a result of his experience, in 1936 he was hired to establish a photo-processing laboratory at the Indiana State Police headquarters in Indianapolis. While he originally only intended to stay for a short time, he reminisced in a 1996 interview that "at that time photography was a very new science. . . . I had to do a lot of original work. I intended to go back to that kind of work but the more I got into this field, the more I could see the possibilities in the forensic sciences that there were no fixed horizons, and that tempted me."

Those original few months turned into a twenty-two year career, during which he rose through the ranks and ultimately became commander of the laboratory that he helped to found. Drawing upon his photography skills at the ISP, he advanced its use in criminal and accident investigation and designed and built several small labs for photo and fingerprint development in addition to the cameras for those facilities. Furthermore, he made contributions to the evaluation and improvement of the first major electronic speed measurement device in traffic law enforcement, worked to refine polygraph instrumentation, and tested the Drunkometer with Indiana University professor Rolla Harger, inventor of the device. The latter, while considered the first breath sensor for measuring blood-alcohol levels, was cumbersome, prone to user error, and thus susceptible to question in the court of law.

Aware of these challenges, over the course of his February 1954 vacation Borkenstein developed a smaller, more efficient device in the basement workshop of his home in Indianapolis. This Breathalyzer, as it was called, eliminated the need for a physician to collect blood and for the long wait for laboratory results. It also was remarkably simple, consisting of only two photo cells, two filters, a device for collecting the breath sample, and about six wires and thus required little training on the part of the operator. To defray the costs to obtain a patent on the new instrument, Borkenstein sold his English roadster. The first public demonstration of the new device was held at the National Safety Congress in Chicago in October 1954 and six prototypes were initially built and field tested by police agencies in the United States

Robert Borkenstein works on his Breathalyzer invention

and Canada. The device was rapidly adopted in the United States and several other counties. In naming Borkenstein to the Safety and Health Hall of Fame in 1988, the National Safety Council stated that his "technological innovation enabled traffic enforcement authorities to determine and quantify blood alcohol concentrations with sufficient accuracy to be the demands of legal evidence."

In 1962 Borkenstein continued his research as the principal investigator for the large-scale roadside Grand Rapids Study that compared the blood alcohol content levels of drivers involved in accidents to a large control group of drivers who passed the same locations under similar circumstances. The study found an increasing accident risk curve relative to blood alcohol content and today is considered a "classic in the field." The blood alcohol content legal limit of 0.08 percent has become widely accepted internationally as a direct result. Over the following decades, the device underwent several modifications, including an electronic model that produces a digital readout and even a coin-operated version.

Largely self-taught for most of his career, over the years Borkenstein gradually began taking science and foreign language courses offered by the IU extension center in Indianapolis. In 1958 he earned enough credits to receive his bachelor's degree in forensic science. The same year he joined the university as chairman of the Department of Police Administration (now Criminal Justice), which he transformed from a traditional police training program to a four-year degree program of national prominence with a multidisciplinary approach to teaching, research, and service. Both theoretical and practical, the program included courses in psychology, political science, sociology, law, and philosophy.

Over the course of the next several decades, Borkenstein led what has become known as "the golden age of criminal justice education." At IU and across the United States there was an explosion of college-level police administration and criminal justice courses and programs. Eventually the program expanded to include both a master's and doctoral program. In 1970 he formed the Center for Studies of Law in Action, which has a mission to expose practitioners to new academic developments and vice versa. One of the center's most successful programs—the course "Supervision of Chemical Tests for Alcohol"—was established in 1958 and brings people from around the world to learn the latest developments in the field and develop new solutions. Today the course is known as "the Robert F. Borkenstein Course in Alcohol."

Borkenstein officially retired in 1983 from an active role at the university, but continued to conduct research and serve as a guest lecturer. He was recognized nationally and internationally for his contributions to the field and served in professional positions, including chair of the National Safety Council's Committee on Alcohol and Other Drugs; consultant to the Presidential Task Force on Highway Safety; president of the International Committee on Alcohols, Drugs, and Traffic Safety; president of the Academy of Criminal Justice Sciences; a fellow of the American academic of Forensic Sciences; and a charter member of the International Association for Chemical Testing. In 1982 he received the National Safety Council's Distinguished Service to Traffic Award, at that time only the fifteenth person to receive such an honor. He was awarded two honorary degrees, one from Wittenberg University in 1963 and one from IU in 1987, and published numerous articles.

CARRIE LYNN SCHWEIR

For Further Reading

Borkenstein, Robert. Interview by Peter Kramer, August 22, 1996. Indiana University Oral History Archive. Center for the Study of History and Memory, Indiana University, Bloomington.

Borkenstein, Robert, and Allen Dale. *The Role of the Drinking Driver in Traffic Accidents*. Bloomington: Indiana University Press, 1964.

Lucas, D. M. "Professor Robert F. Borkenstein: An Appreciation of His Life and Work." *Forensic Science Review* 12, no. 1 (January 2000): 1–21.

Bowen, Otis R.

February 26, 1918–May 4, 2013

Two-term governor, cabinet secretary in Reagan administration, House Speaker, and physician.

Otis R. "Doc" Bowen came across as an old-fashioned country doctor, yet he became one of the most influential and effective politicians in Indiana history. The first person to serve two consecutive four-year terms as governor after a constitutional change lifted the one-term limit, Bowen stayed well ahead of his time on key policy issues. During his first term he engineered a major overhaul of the state's tax structure, including property tax reform that kept Indiana from suffering the economic woes many other states confronted in the 1970s.

Prior to winning his first race as governor in 1972, Bowen was a longtime member of the Indiana House of Representatives and served two terms in the powerful position of House Speaker. In his postgubernatorial years he joined President Ronald Reagan's cabinet as secretary of the Department of Health and Human Services, the first physician to hold that office.

Bowen, who was born on February 26, 1918, in Fulton County in north central Indiana, said that growing up he was "taught honest, hard work, thrift and persistence." His most influential teacher was his father, Vernie, a schoolteacher, Sunday schoolteacher, township trustee, and Bowen's high school basketball coach. The Bowen home was full of love but also discipline. A paddling at school meant another one at home. Bowen also credited both sets of grandparents for their influence, fondly recalling, in particular, the summers he spent working and playing on his paternal grandparents' sixty-acre farm.

After graduating high school in 1935, Bowen, an honor roll student all twelve years, went to Indiana University for his undergraduate studies in premed while his parents moved to Crown Point. During visits there in the summer, Bowen got to know Elizabeth Anna Agnes "Beth" Steinmann. The daughter of German immigrants, she grew up in the Lutheran Church Missouri Synod, with the same Bible emphasis as Bowen's Brethren church. After they were married in February 1939, Beth stayed in Crown Point to work and in the fall Bowen moved to Indianapolis to finish medical school. He also got a job at the Wheeler Rescue Mission for homeless men. Bowen and his fellow orderlies listened to their medical problems, checked for lice, and referred them to a doctor if necessary. He said that although "we dispensed only aspirin and blue ointment (for lice), the work made us feel like doctors."

Bowen graduated from the IU Medical School in 1942 just after the start of World War II. After a brief internship at Memorial Hospital in South Bend, he joined the U.S. Army Medical Corps, serving in the Pacific and accompanying troops ashore during the invasion of Okinawa in 1945. When the war ended, he returned home in early 1946.

He and Beth settled in Bremen in Marshall County and Bowen began his all-purpose practice as a family doctor. Always on call, Bowen estimated that over the course of his long career, he delivered three thousand babies. "I became accustomed to long hours, lost sleep and missed meals," he recalled. "I learned to remain calm and unflustered and to be patient with and tolerant of others."

The training prepared him well for part-time duty in politics, which began when he was elected Marshall County Coroner in 1952. Four years later he won a seat in the Indiana House of Representatives, losing his race for re-election two years later by four votes. The voters returned him to the state assembly in 1960.

By 1965 Bowen was elected minority leader of the House Republicans. After helping lead the GOP takeover of the House in 1966, he announced his candidacy for Speaker shortly after John Coppes of Nappanee said he was seeking the post. Bowen and Coppes had tangled a few years earlier over increased funding for mental health, causing Coppes to call Bowen a "yellow-bellied bastard" in a caucus meeting. The adage that politics makes strange bedfellows prevailed when Coppes withdrew his candidacy and supported Bowen in his narrow 34 to 32 victory.

From the Speaker's chair Bowen worked on property tax reform, believing that schools and local government needed a broader tax base in an urban economy, while homeowners and businesses could not sustain big rate hikes. His proposals were blocked in the state senate, but they became the key plank in his 1972 campaign for governor, which he won by more than 300,000 votes over former governor MATTHEW WELSH. Once in office, Bowen's long-sought goal of enacting legislation to reduce property taxes was achieved, though narrowly, in 1973.

Easily reelected in 1976, Bowen left an impressive record of achievements during his eight years as the state's chief executive. He led an expansion of state parks, adding several new ones such as Potato Creek and Wyandotte Woods as well as the addition of more than forty nature preserves. He helped enact medical malpractice reforms that made Indiana friendlier for doctors, heading off a problem that hurt medical care in other states. Also under Bowen, a statewide emergency medical system was created. As House

Speaker and governor, he played a key part in the expansion of the IU School of Medicine in Indianapolis.

Bowen postponed the state's addiction to gambling revenues, vetoing legalized gambling several times. Even after he left office, Bowen's opposition played a part in the Indiana General Assembly's reluctance in the 1980s to plunge the state into gambling.

The end of his second term in 1980 might have been cause for celebration. His property tax reforms made him one of the most popular governors in state history. Republicans swept the 1980 elections, with Reagan becoming president and Bowen's Lieutenant Governor ROBERT ORR winning the governor's race. But Beth was losing her fight with cancer, prompting Bowen's decision not to run for the U.S. Senate seat that Dan Quayle won in an upset over Birch Bayh. Beth died on New Year's Day, 1981.

After leaving office Bowen joined the faculty of the IU School of Medicine and later married one of his former patients, a widow, Rose Hochstetler. Bowen returned to government service in 1985 when Reagan appointed him secretary of the Department of Health and Human Services. He was again ahead of the curve, this time it was the AIDS crisis. Bowen and Surgeon General Everett Koop led a public-health campaign that resulted in a mass mailing to households providing advice on avoiding contracting the virus that causes the disease and safe-sex practices. Bowen's major accomplishment as secretary was passage of legislation that covered the costs of catastrophic illnesses for Medicare recipients. However, the victory was short-lived after higher-income seniors objected to paying a higher surtax to fund the program and Congress repealed the act.

At the end of the Reagan administration, Bowen returned to Bremen, but suffered another tragedy when Rose died in 1992. He later married another former patient, Carol Mikesell, and they lived on five acres near his youngest son, Robert, a Marshall County judge.

To honor Bowen's service to the state and country, Ball State University established the Bowen Center for Public Affairs, which sponsors an annual event to encourage citizen participation in politics and public services and also an initiative to assist local communities and local government officials. In addition, the Bowen Center serves counties in northeast Indiana and is so named in recognition of Bowen's support for community mental health centers.

RUSSELL PULLIAM

For Further Reading

Bowen, Otis R. *Doc: Memories from a Life in Public Service.* Bloomington: Indiana University Press, 2000.

Huseland, Stanley. *The Life and Times of L. Keith Bulen.* Carmel, IN: Hawthorne Publishing, 2006.

Watt, William J. *Bowen: The Years as Governor.* Indianapolis: Bierce Associates, 1981.

Bowers, Claude G.

November 20, 1878–January 21, 1958

Journalist, orator, speechwriter, political adviser, historian, and ambassador to Spain and Chile.

Claude Bowers enjoyed a national and international reputation as a spokesman for democracy. As a journalist in Indiana and New York, an aide to U.S. Senator John W. Kern of Indiana, an adviser to U.S. Senator Robert F. Wagner and Governors Alfred E. Smith and Franklin D. Roosevelt, all of New York, and a political orator, Bowers was a partisan Democrat who promoted liberal reforms during the Progressive Era and the New Deal. His historical works praised Presidents Thomas Jefferson and Andrew Jackson and Hoosier Senators ALBERT J. BEVERIDGE and Kern for defending the rights of the majority. While ambassador to Spain during the Spanish Civil War and to Chile during the Cold War, he defended the Spanish Republic and championed the United States' support of Chile's economy and democratic leaders. Bowers's history of Reconstruction, *The Tragic Era*, was a notable exception to his otherwise stalwart liberalism. In it he displayed racist emotions and championed the southern Democrats' successful efforts to oppress the former slaves.

Born in Westfield, Indiana, Bowers was reared in Indianapolis. He developed interests in politics and oratory, listening to campaign speeches, sermons, and lectures. In the public library he studied discourses by Irish independence leaders. At Indianapolis High School, later Shortridge, Bowers's public speaking led to presidency of the Student Senate and the Oratorical Association. In contrast to his short stature, his strong voice lent authority to his arguments. In 1898 his oration on Alexander Hamilton took first prize at the Indiana

Claude Bowers (center) poses with Congresswoman Edith Rogers from Massachusetts and House Foreign Affairs Committee chairman Sol Bloom, circa 1939.

High School Oratorical Contest.

Unable to afford college, Bowers turned to writing and political speaking. In 1900 he published two articles on Jefferson in *The Jeffersonian Democrat*, a Washington periodical. That year he became a writer for the *Indianapolis Sentinel* and backed William Jennings Bryan for president and Kern for senate, lambasting Republicans for their advocacy of "unjust privileges" for the rich. Bowers became a popular speaker, gaining the appellation "Gatling-Gun Orator of the Wabash."

In 1903 Bowers went to Terre Haute, where he wrote editorials for two newspapers and served on the Board of Public Works. A friend of Democrat boss John E. Lamb, Bowers was the Democrats' unsuccessful congressional nominee in 1904 and 1906. In the 1908 campaign Bowers campaigned for the Democratic ticket of Bryan for president and Kern as vice president.

The nation's capital was Bowers's home from 1911 to 1917. Kern was elected to the U.S. Senate in 1911 and chose Bowers as his secretary. With Woodrow Wilson's victory in 1912, the Democratic Party became the majority party in the Senate and elected Kern as its leader. Bowers ran Kern's office and handled relations with constituents. He also delivered talks to Irish American groups and wrote his first book, *The Irish Orators: A History of Ireland's Fight for Freedom*. In 1911 he married Sybil McCaslin, an Indianapolis native, and they had a daughter Pat, born in 1915.

Kern's defeat in 1916 brought Bowers to Fort Wayne, where, as editor of the *Journal-Gazette*, he excoriated the conservative policies of Warren G. Harding, "The Marionette of Marion Town." The editor also condemned the Ku Klux Klan for rejecting "Americanism." Bowers penned a biography of his Washington boss, *The Life of John Worth Kern*, and *The Party Battles of the Jackson Period* brought him national recognition. The latter lionized Jackson and reminded Democrats of their party's defense of the masses.

Bowers's move to New York in 1923 led to prominence on the national stage. Until 1931 he worked for Ralph Pulitzer's *New York World* and then for William Randolph Hearst's *New York*

Evening Journal. Republicans remained his targets. Calvin Coolidge was "the tacit tool of privilege" and Herbert Hoover displayed "ineptitude for government." Bowers's *Jefferson and Hamilton: The Struggle for Democracy in America* was his most popular work, condemning Hamilton's conservatism and praising Jefferson for organizing "the forces of democracy." Bowers believed that Jeffersonian Democrats had continued this battle to the present day. The journalist backed Robert Wagner's successful 1926 campaign for the U.S. Senate, writing editorials and helping prepare speeches.

Bowers's writings and speeches made him keynoter at the 1928 national convention, where he called his party "to wage a war of extermination against privilege and pillage." Distressed by southern Democrats who opposed Alfred E. Smith because of his Roman Catholicism, Bowers wrote *The Tragic Era: The Revolution after Lincoln* to bring them back to the fold. He lambasted Radical Republicans for depriving the white majority of its rights, while praising southerners for "fighting for the preservation of their civilization."

Bowers's most important friend was Franklin D. Roosevelt. The governor asked him in 1929 to help identify his allies, and during the 1932 presidential campaign Bowers huddled with the candidate at Hyde Park, spoke on his behalf in three states, and substituted for Roosevelt in a nationally broadcast radio speech.

In 1933 Roosevelt appointed Bowers as American ambassador to Spain, where he remained for six years. The new Spanish Republic was engaged in a battle with traditionalist factions opposed to democracy. In 1936 this led to the Spanish Civil War between leftist forces and moderate democrats on one side and large landowners and businessmen on the other. The Soviet Union came to the aid of the Republic, while Adolf Hitler's Germany and Benito Mussolini's Italy backed General Francisco Franco's forces, who were dedicated to the overthrow of the Republic. For Bowers, the Spanish fight was a replay of the early conflict in the United States between Jeffersonian democrats and reactionary Hamiltonians. The ambassador obtained U.S. aid for the Republic before the war, but despite appeals to Roosevelt to assist the government after 1936, international politics and divided U.S. public opinion prevented this. When Franco's troops won in 1939, Bowers was persona non grata, so Roosevelt named him ambassador to Chile.

In Santiago Bowers served fourteen years. When the United States joined World War II in 1941, all Latin American countries save Chile and Argentina declared war on the Axis. Given Chile's important German population, the government refused to enter the conflict. Impressed with Chile's democratic system, Bowers counseled the frustrated State Department to be patient. The ambassador's work with proallied politicians and the declining military fortunes of the Axis brought an end to Chilean neutrality in October 1943.

Chile became a focus of U.S. policy during the Cold War. Its Communist Party was the largest in the hemisphere, and Bowers spared no effort to support pro-U.S. interests. Despite disputes with North American copper and communications companies, the ambassador convinced Washington to offer substantial aid, especially public health, technical, military, and agricultural assistance. He also promoted cultural and educational exchanges. In 1952 the Chilean Congress agreed to a defense agreement with Washington that lasted for a quarter century.

Dwight Eisenhower's election in 1952 ended Bowers's diplomatic career. He spent his retirement years in Manhattan, writing and observing politics. Bowers published accounts of his ambassadorial years in both Spain and Chile and penned an autobiography. He also returned to Indiana, receiving a doctorate from Indiana University. In his eightieth year, he died of leukemia and was buried in Terre Haute.

PETER J. SEHLINGER

For Further Reading

Bowers, Claude G. *My Life: The Memoirs of Claude Bowers*. New York: Simon and Schuster, 1962.

———. Manuscripts. Lilly Library, Indiana University, Bloomington.

Sehlinger, Peter J., and Holman Hamilton. *Spokesman for Democracy: Claude G. Bowers, 1878–1958*. Indianapolis: Indiana Historical Society, 2000.

Brokenburr, Robert L.

November 16, 1886–March 24, 1974

Civil rights leader, attorney, and first African American elected to Indiana Senate.

Robert Brokenburr, born in Phoebus, Virginia, moved to Indianapolis in 1909 after receiving his law degree from Howard University. In his own words, he came with "a stylish panama hat on his head and $125 in his pocket." He had a long and distinguished legal career, but he is best known for his civil rights work, as both a lawyer and a legislator.

In 1910 Brokenburr began his legal career when he was admitted to the Indiana Bar. One of his earliest and most famous clients was MADAM C. J. WALKER, who became world renowned for her hair preparation business. Shortly after arriving in Indianapolis, he became Walker's part-time legal adviser. In 1911 Brokenburr filed articles of incorporation for the Madam C. J. Walker Manufacturing Company. Wishing to keep his private law practice, he served only as a part-time legal adviser to the Walker Company, but he still prospered from the company's financial success.

Brokenburr was the first African American admitted to the Indianapolis Bar Association. Early in his career he successfully fought and won civil rights cases, many of which preceded the civil rights era, sometimes quietly, without much notice. He won a racially restrictive residential case against the city of Indianapolis, and he also won a case that struck down the right of theater owners to separate the audience by race. He served in Marion County as deputy prosecuting attorney from 1919 to 1931. He also sat as judge pro tem for the municipal, superior, and circuit courts of Marion County. He was admitted to practice before the Indiana Supreme Court in 1953.

The work he did as a lawyer and his role as legal adviser to the Walker Company brought Brokernburr to the attention of the Republican Party. He was the Republican nominee for a seat in the Indiana Senate on three occasions: 1912, 1932, and 1934, and was defeated on each occasion. However, in 1940, he finally was elected to the Senate and held that seat continuously until 1964, except for a two-year period when Republicans lost control of the senate following a Democratic sweep in 1948 with Harry S. Truman at the top of the ticket.

In his early legislative career Brokenburr had several successes. In his first term he authored a bill to allow black schools to participate in the state basketball tournament. The bill, opposed by the Indiana High School Athletic Association, passed the Senate but failed in the House. However, the IHSAA changed its rules in 1943 and permitted black schools to participate in the state tournament. In 1943 he sponsored a bill requiring the appointment of African American policemen based on population ratio. That bill became law long before federal affirmative action plans came into being. In 1947 he introduced two other important civil rights measures that became law—an antihate bill and a bill encouraging Congress to enact an antilynching law.

Brokenburr's most significant legislative achievements came in 1961, when two bills that he sponsored were passed by both houses and signed into law by Governor MATTHEW WELSH. The first was a bill prohibiting discrimination on the basis of race in public accommodations. It was not until 1964 that the U.S. Congress passed a similar law pertaining to public accommodations. The second measure was a bill establishing the Indiana Civil Rights Commission, known as the Indiana Fair Employment Practices Act, which charged the commission with preventing or eliminating discriminatory practices in employment and other areas on the basis of race, religion, national origin, or ancestry. Discrimination in employment was not targeted by the federal government until 1964. One final measure that Brokenburr sponsored in 1963 was a bill to ratify an amendment to the U.S. Constitution that would eliminate the requirement that a poll tax be paid before citizens were allowed to vote for certain federal offices. Indiana ratified the amendment in 1963, and it became the Twenty-fourth Amendment to the Constitution in 1964.

Brokenburr was popular on both sides of the aisle, and, while bills pertaining to civil rights were his primary focus, he sponsored many other bills covering a wide range of issues that became law. These included bills pertaining to judicial reform, local government planning, removing urban blight, antinepotism, and a bill permitting Sunday baseball and ice hockey. One result of his broad support was his appointment as chair of the Senate Commission on the Affairs of Indianapolis. Freemont Powers, a writer for the *Indianapolis News*, summed up Brokenburr's style as follows: "He managed what few men ever achieved, to serve both communities, both black and white, and to do it with invariable courtesy and courage." The growing respect for Brokenburr by members of the state senate led to the adoption of a resolution urging his appointment as Hoosier delegate to Liberia for the nation's centennial celebration. The measure passed by a vote of thirty-eight to zero.

Robert L. Brokenburr

In addition to contributions made through his legislative service, Brokenburr also played an important role in the Indianapolis community. For example, he served as chair of the Better Indianapolis League, a civic organization of prominent black citizens and leaders. This organization fought the efforts, led by the Chamber of Commerce, to build a separate high school designated for African Americans only. Up until that time African Americans were able to attend any public high school in the city. Despite opposition, the board of education voted unanimously in 1922 to build a separate high school. Crispus Attucks High School opened in 1927 and remained segregated by law until 1949 when the state outlawed segregation. Other civic organizations in which Brokenburr was active included the Colored Men's Civic League, the Young Men's Christian Association, and the National Association for the Advancement of Colored People.

Although Brokenburr was well respected as a community leader, younger civil rights activists of the mid-1960s and 1970s wanted more assertive strategies, but an aggressive posture was not his way. In his own words: "A man is best off to do what he can, to be the kind of man his background makes him." In 1964 Brokenburr began to wind down his political career when he retired from the state senate.

The awards and other recognitions Brokenburr received throughout his life were testaments to a successful career as an attorney and politician. In 1949 he received an alumni award from Hampton University, in 1955 the Indianapolis chapter of the American Jewish Congress honored him with the Stephen A. Wise Memorial Citation, and in 1956 he received an honorary doctorate from Howard University. One of the highlights of his career was his appointment in 1955 as an alternate delegate for the United States to the United Nations by President Dwight Eisenhower.

Since his death in 1974, there has been a growing appreciation for Brokenburr's enduring contributions to the cause of equal rights at the local, state, and national level. He helped to lay the foundation for future civil rights initiatives and established a record that would stand the test of time. In 1975 he was posthumously elected to the Indiana Academy, which recognizes citizens for "their contributions to cultural, scientific, literary, civic, religious and educational development within the state."

STANLEY WARREN

For Further Reading

Indianapolis News. March 25, 1974, p. 12.
Warren, Stanley. "Robert L. Brokenburr: He Lived to Serve." *Black History News & Notes* 83 (February, 2001): 4–8.
———. *The Senate Avenue YMCA for African American Men and Boys Indianapolis, Indiana 1913–1959*. Virginia Beach, VA: Donning Company Publishers, 2005.

Brown, Herbert C.
May 22, 1912–December 19, 2004

Purdue University professor of chemistry who made revolutionary advances in the field of organic chemistry; Nobel Prize laureate.

A chronicle of Herbert C. Brown's life personifies the archetypal American success story. After he immigrated to the United States at the age of two with his Ukrainian parents, the "melting pot" of early-twentieth-century America served as the laboratory for the social and educational alchemy of his formative years. Overcoming obstacles in this environment inspired a strong work ethic that Brown later espoused as an important element of his success. While circumstance, serendipity, and even romance influenced his career, ultimately perseverance, intellect, and innovation—with curiosity as a catalyst—proved to be the essential ingredients for his groundbreaking discoveries within the field of organic chemistry.

Born Herbert Charles Brovarnik in London, United Kingdom, in 1912, Brown in later years often jested about his parents' foresight in giving him the initials H. C. B., foreshadowing his work with compounds containing the elements hydrogen (H), carbon (C), and boron (B). The family name was anglicized to Brown after moving to Chicago in 1914. His father, finding insufficient work as a carpenter, opened a hardware store above which the family lived. Brown made a point of noting that the family resided in a "largely . . . black neighborhood," and he attended school "with predominately black classmates" There is no evidence that he considered this anything other than a positive experience. After his father died in 1926, the fourteen-year-old Brown temporarily left school to help with the family business. However, he soon returned to finish high school on Chicago's South Side, winning a "national prize" for a humor column he produced for the school paper, an honor from which Brown stated he "never recovered."

Brown's graduation from high school roughly coincided with the onset of the Great Depression. The family business closed, and prospects for permanent employment were dim. A series of unfulfilling odd jobs helped him realize that his love of reading and studying might serve him well in the pursuit of higher education. He pooled his limited financial resources and enrolled at nearby Crane Junior College intending to study electrical engineering with the stated goal of "making a good living." After taking his first chemistry course, however, he discovered his true academic passion. At Crane he also met Sarah Baylen, his future wife. The school closed because of financial woes one semester after his arrival, but because he found his true calling and his true love there, it was perhaps the most influential experience of his life.

After Crane closed Brown enrolled at a nearby night school, financing his tuition working as a shoe clerk. At the same time, he and several students, including Baylen, accepted a generous offer from Doctor Nicholas Cheronis, a former Crane instructor who opened his private lab so that motivated students could continue to study chemistry informally under his guidance. In 1934 Brown and Baylen enrolled at newly opened Wright Junior College, where Cheronis had taken charge of the physical sciences program. Upon graduating in 1935 Baylen predicted when signing Herbert's yearbook that he would one day win the Nobel Prize.

With Cheronis's encouragement, the couple continued their studies at the University of Chicago, where Brown completed two years of study in three quarters, earning a bachelor's degree in 1936. As a graduation gift, Baylen, whom he married in 1937, presented Brown with a copy of Alfred Stock's *The Hydrides of Boron and Silicon*, selected, according to legend, because it was the cheapest book in the university bookstore. This two-dollar text triggered Brown's interest in boron chemistry so much that when encouraged by faculty to stay on at Chicago to pursue graduate work he elected to do so in that field, and received his PhD only two years later in 1938. Unable to find employment in industry, he accepted an entry-level instructor position at Chicago.

When it became clear that his instructor status would not lead to tenure at Chicago, he accepted a position as assistant professor of chemistry at Wayne State, then known as Wayne University, in Detroit, in 1943. Although he was promoted to associate professor in 1946, his wife was not satisfied because the campus lacked a true university environment. In 1947 Brown was offered a professorship in organic chemistry at Purdue University. After visiting he said of West Lafayette, "We have a nice little town here. When I . . . looked up at the sky and saw the Milky Way, I said, 'This is the place to bring up a . . . child and make my wife happy.'"

At Purdue Brown continued his research in boron chemistry. He simplified and standardized the process for the production of boranes, compounds of boron and carbon. He used these relatively simple molecules to synthesize ever more complex organic molecules. His work has been described as opening a "new continent" of compounds for exploration. Literally tens, if not hundreds, of thousands of compounds have been created using Brown's methods, a particular boon to the pharmaceutical industry. For example, discoveries led to the creation of medications such as the antidepressant Prozac and Lipitor, the cholesterol-lowering drug.

In 1979 Brown won the Nobel Prize for Chemistry for his revolutionary work in boron chemistry, which he shared with Georg Wittig of Germany. He rejected the idea that the Nobel Prize was the capstone of his career because it reminded him of a "tombstone." In his view he still had much more to do. Although he officially retired from Purdue in 1978, he continued to do research there until he died in 2004 at the age of ninety-two.

While Brown was best known to the world for his work in organic chemistry, his colleagues and former students recognized him affectionately for more than that. Two of his protégés, Ei-ichi Negishi of Purdue and Akira Suzuki of Japan received the Nobel Prize in 2010. Negishi said he could "write a book" about what made Brown a good mentor. He said Brown never quit, he just "kept going and going and growing, like a big tree." Nigishi and others lauded Brown for his optimism, patience, openness, and scrupulous attention to detail, and they credited him for "shaping their careers and lives." About five hundred graduate students and postdoctoral students benefited from his tutelage.

More than a hundred of his former colleagues and graduate students from around the world attended a three-day commemorative event sponsored by Purdue to honor Brown in 2002, the year he turned ninety. The affection for Brown was evident in the praise they had for their colleague and mentor, not only for his impact on their careers but also for his human qualities. One former student said Brown was a "great humanitarian," noting that he helped students deal with issues ranging from family concerns to medical problems. Another former student said that Brown "looked after me as if I was his own son."

Brown's influence on Purdue is still felt today in many ways. In 1984 the Browns established a Brown lecture series, a forum that today still draws top researchers in the field. In 2000 they established the Herbert C. Brown Center for Borane Research. Purdue named a chemistry lab in his honor, and there is a distinguished professorship in his name. Brown's achievements have brought distinction to Purdue through the fifty national and international awards he received in recognition for his work. Besides the Nobel Prize, he received the National Medal of Science in 1969 and in 1998 the American Chemical Society recognized him as one of the top seventy-five chemists of the previous seventy-five years. That list also included Madame Curie and Linus Pauling.

A former colleague best summed up Brown's legacy, saying, Brown's "influence is not only felt at the department level but the whole world. There are only a few Browns in the world of chemistry." The ripples of Brown's work travel throughout Indiana and the world by pharmaceutical companies delivering the practical impact of relieving the suffering of millions each year.

ALFRED L. KNABLE JR.

For Further Reading

Brown, Herbert C. Brown. Interview by James J. Bohning for the Chemical Heritage Foundation November 11, 1994. Interview transcript 0117. Purdue University, West Lafayette, IN.

Gillispie, Charles C. "Brown, Herbert C." *Complete Dictionary of Scientific Biography*. New York: Charles Scribner's Sons, 2008.

Odelberg, Wilhelm, ed. "Herbert C. Brown-Autobiography: Les Prix Nobel." *The Nobel Prizes 1979*. Stockholm: Nobel Foundation, 1980.

Weedle, Eric. "Purdue's First Nobel Prize Winner Leaves Legacy." *Scientific Computing*, December 6, 2010. http://www.scientificcomputing.com/news/2010/12/purdues-first-nobel-prize-winner-leaves-legacy

Bushemi, John A.

April 19, 1917–February 19, 1944

Newspaper and war photographer.

On February 19, 1944, two battalions of the U.S. Army's 106th Infantry Regiment, Twenty-seventh Division, hit the beaches of Eniwetok, an atoll located at the far northwest end of the Marshall Islands in the central Pacific. As the American soldiers crept toward their objectives, they were continually sniped at from the side and rear by Japanese troops cleverly hidden in a series of camouflaged foxholes.

Covering the operation that day were a correspondent and photographer from *Yank*, the army's weekly magazine produced by and for enlisted men. As the correspondent, Merle Miller, and other combat journalists stopped about seventy-five yards behind the front lines to examine a bullet-riddled chest of books, they became a target for a series of Japanese knee-mortar shells. Shrapnel from the shells hit and mortally wounded Miller's companion, Staff Sergeant John A. Bushemi, who before the war had worked as a photographer for the *Gary Post-Tribune*. Immediately after being hit, Bushemi's first concern was not for his wounds, but for his equipment. As navy surgeons frantically attempted to save the photographer's life onboard a transport ship, Bushemi, with his last words, said to Miller: "Be sure to get those pictures back to the office."

In addition to receiving a posthumous Bronze Star and Purple Heart, Bushemi was inducted into the News Photographers Hall of Fame in 1944, and two years later the Veterans of Foreign Wars named a post in Gary for him. The Associated Press bureau in Indianapolis named its award for the best news photograph of the year after him, and he was inducted into the Indiana Journalism Hall of Fame in 2001. Bushemi was considered by Gary residents their representative soldier of World War II, surpassing football star Tom Harmon and boxing champion Tony Zale.

Photography as a means of earning a living was a novelty for the Buscemi family, later Americanized to Bushemi. The family's patriarch, Pietro, had arrived in the United States from Sicily in 1906, and eventually settled in Centerville, Iowa, where he worked in a local coal mine. It was in Centerville where John was born on April 19, 1917. With the Great Depression tightening its grip on the national economy, including the coal industry, the family, now numbering nine children, moved to Gary, Indiana, in 1930, and Pietro found a job in U.S. Steel's coke plant.

For his part, Bushemi did whatever he could to earn money, from boxing in Golden Gloves tournaments to offering haircuts for twenty-five cents from a barber's chair in the basement of the family's home. After he quit school during his junior year at Gary's Lew Wallace High School, he joined his father and brothers in working at the local steel mills. With the wages from his job he purchased his first camera, a small Univex that he used to take photographs of family members and special occasions. He developed the film in a darkroom located in his mother's closet.

He left the steel mills for good in 1936 when the *Post-Tribune* hired him as an apprentice photographer. Although he covered a variety of community events for the newspaper, he earned his reputation taking sports photographs, where his "perfect timing" captured athletes at their best and he won numerous awards for his sports photography.

Five months before Pearl Harbor, Bushemi enlisted in the U.S. Army and was sent to the Field Artillery Replacement Center at Fort Bragg in North Carolina for basic training. Before long, however, the army realized that Bushemi's true skills lay not in firing a 75-mm gun but in photography. He was assigned to the post's public relations office, where he joined other privates, including Marion Hargrove, who wrote about the group's experiences in his best-selling book *See Here, Private Hargrove*, published in July 1942.

Hargrove later received orders to join the staff of *Yank*, the newly created army magazine run by enlisted men. The weekly magazine, which opened its headquarters in New York in 1942, was sold to soldiers for five cents a copy. *Yank* entertained the troops in its early days with such popular features as George Baker's "Sad Sack" cartoons and pinups of Hollywood stars. Learning of his close friend's imminent departure for *Yank*, Bushemi, according to Hargrove, "fretted and cracked his knuckles for several days" before sending a scrapbook of his best pictures to *Yank*'s New York office. Impressed by Bushemi's photography skills, *Yank*'s editors invited him to join the staff.

After a short stay in New York, Bushemi and Miller left for Hawaii to open the magazine's Pacific bureau. Both Bushemi and Miller were eager to report on the war in the Pacific, but instead spent many quiet months in Honolulu covering training stories. The tedium was broken a bit for Bushemi when he received instruction in motion picture filming from Colonel Frank Capra, the famed Hollywood director. Bushemi later shot and edited his own movies, each of which began with the words "A One-Shot Production."

In the summer of 1943 Bushemi finally had his chance to photograph combat operations in the southwest Pacific, covering the action on New Georgia, located northwest of Guadalcanal in the Solomon Islands. Hargrove said his friend turned in to *Yank* "excellent studies of jungle operations and portraits of the bearded infantrymen who had sweated out the battles of the Munda airstrip and Hastings Ridge."

In covering the invasion of Kwajalein Atoll (the largest coral atoll in the world) in the Marshall Islands in late January 1944, Bushemi was reunited with Miller. While Miller covered the operation with the army's veteran Seventh Division at one end of the atoll, Bushemi worked with the Fourth Marine Division at the opposite end. While returning from the assignment, Bushemi suffered an injury to his left hand. "I tried to urge Johnny to go back to Honolulu, but he hardly listened to me," Miller said. "He knew another operation was coming up, and he wanted to go along."

That mission was to attack Eniwetok, located about 350 miles northwest of Kwajalein. Although he had to operate his camera with one hand because of his injury, Bushemi refused to stay behind, landing on Eniwetok with Miller during the fourth wave of troops. At first there seemed to be no opposition from the Japanese. Minutes later, however, the enemy responded to the attack with rifle fire and knee-mortar shells that fell among the GIs still on the beach. Enemy units hid in foxholes and spider trenches, firing on the Americans from behind as they advanced.

Separated during the fighting, Bushemi and Miller, joined by correspondents from the *Chicago Tribune* and *Chicago Daily News* and photographers from other services, left the front for the beach early in the afternoon. Finding shelter behind an American medium tank, the group

John A. Bushemi

stopped to compare notes and smoke cigarettes. After witnessing a strafing by Gruman Avenger airplanes, the group went to survey the damage when it came under fire. Bushemi received shrapnel wounds in his left cheek, neck, and left leg. Although bleeding profusely, Bushemi joked with his companions and inquired about others also injured in the shelling before he was transported off the island. "The Navy doctors had to give him ether so they could tie some severed arteries which had caused him such serious blood loss from his neck wound," said Miller, "and it was after the anesthetic was administered that Johnny passed away—about 5:50 p.m."

Family and friends held a memorial service for the fallen photographer in Gary on March 3, 1944. Bushemi's remains did not make it home for burial at Mount Mercy Cemetery until November 1947.

RAY E. BOOMHOWER

For Further Reading

Boomhower, Ray E. "John A. Bushemi: Combat Photographer." *Traces of Indiana and Midwestern History* 14, no. 1 (Winter 2002): 4–15.

———. *"One Shot": The World War II Photography of John A. Bushemi.* Indianapolis: Indiana Historical Society Press, 2004.

Hargrove, Marion. *See Here, Private Hargrove*. New York: Henry Holt and Company, 1942.

Weithas, Art. *Close to Glory: The Untold Stories of WWII by the GIs Who Saw and Reported the War—*Yank *Magazine Correspondents.* Austin: TX; Eakin Press 1991.

Selected photographs by John A. Bushemi are in the collection of the Library of Congress in Washington, D.C.

Butler, Ovid

February 7, 1801–July 12, 1881

Lawyer, abolitionist, journalist, land developer, and founder of Butler University.

Without Ovid Butler, there would be no Butler University. The history of the man and the university are intimately and inextricably entwined. Without Butler's vision, leadership, and financial support, the university may not have come into being, or survived its early years. Butler University today is a private, not-for-profit, comprehensive university located in Indianapolis, Indiana, offering more than sixty-five majors from six colleges to four thousand students.

Ovid Butler was born in Augusta, New York. In 1817, the year after Indiana gained statehood and Butler turned seventeen, his family moved to Geneva in Jennings County. He attended common schools, but for the most part was self-educated. Between 1819 and 1825, he taught school, clerked in a store, and read law. Butler attended Vernon Seminary and lived with William Avery Bullock, a lawyer who gave him his first legal instruction.

In *The Bench and Bar of Indiana*, Butler is described as "a man of medium height, sturdy form, with a pleasant face, a very bright eye, and an expression of intelligence and kindness not to be forgotten." He was a man of "infinite patience and labor in the practice of the law, which for his firm was the most lucrative in the state." Politically he was "as independent in social, political, and religious affairs as any man could be." He liberally devoted his time, labors, and money "to further his political projects and sentiments. He largely endowed Butler University and put it into active operation."

In 1825 Butler moved to Shelbyville, Shelby County, Indiana, where he taught school and studied then practiced law. He was the first lawyer admitted to the bar in Shelby County. The Shelbyville Christian Church (Disciples of Christ) was organized in his home. Butler ran for the state legislature and for county clerk but he was defeated for both offices because of his strong abolitionist beliefs. Butler married Cordelia Cole in 1827. They had three children who survived to adulthood; three more did not survive infancy.

When Butler moved his family to Indianapolis in 1836, his father, Chauncy, moved with them and became the preacher at Central Christian Church. Cordelia died in 1838. Two years later Butler married Elizabeth Anne Elgin, a widow, and they had seven children, one dying in infancy. Three of his children—Demia, Scot, and Chauncy—went on to play important roles in the history of Butler University.

Soon after moving to Indianapolis, Butler established a law practice with CALVIN FLETCHER, Simon Yandes, and Horatio C. Newcomb. Fletcher and Butler had one of the largest, most respected, and most lucrative practices in central Indiana. In 1847 Butler went through a life-threatening illness that prompted his retirement from the law. He believed that God had spared his life to do other work, and it was possible the he took the founding of the new university as that work.

In 1846 Butler had bought land just north of the old Mile Square in Indianapolis at what is now Park Avenue and Thirteenth Street. He built a house and moved there in 1849, calling it Forest Home. Butler developed the neighborhood known as College Corner south of his home; the land to the northeast became the site of North Western Christian University.

In 1847 Butler took leadership of a Disciples of Christ proposal to found an institution of higher learning in Indiana. The closest Disciples school was Bethany College in Virginia (later West Virginia). Virginia was a slave-holding state, and Butler summed up the importance of the antislavery issue as the primary motivator in creating a new university as "an institution of learning of the highest class upon free soil, in which their children and the youth of the Northwest might receive a liberal and Christian education, removed, as far as practicable, from the pernicious influences of slavery."

In 1850 the charter Butler wrote to create NWCU was approved by the Indiana General Assembly. He offered twenty acres of his property at what is now Thirteenth Street and College Avenue. The university opened its doors on November 1, 1855, with two professors and twenty students, including several who had been expelled from Bethany College for their abolitionist beliefs. From the first day, the school admitted women and students of color, as well as students of any or no religious background, since the university was nonsectarian from its founding. NWCU was the first college in Indiana to admit women on an equal basis with men, and the second in the United States. Butler's daughter, Demia, was the first female to graduate from the school in the full four-year curriculum. After her untimely death in 1867, her father endowed the Demia Butler Chair in English Literature in 1869, the first endowed chair in the country created for a female professor. Catharine Merrill, the daughter of Civil War general Samuel Merrill, first held the chair, becoming the second woman to be named a professor in the United States.

Butler's advocacy of abolition and women's rights is clear in the draft of an essay titled "Woman's Rights," likely created after the end of the Civil War. He wrote of his desire "that the Institution of the North Western Christian University occupy a position in the front ranks of human progress and Christian civilization as the Experiment and Advocate of the common rights of humanity without distinction on account of sex, race or color." He was adamant about "absolute equity before God and before the Law of the individual members of the human family." He said that "equality of rights and duties, so far as race or color is concerned has after a long struggle and a fierce and bloody war finally obtained recognition in our National Constitution." However, he acknowledged that "there is still a controversy about its applicability where sex is concerned."

While Butler was busy helping to found the new university, he was also dabbling in politics. A dedicated abolitionist, Butler helped to organize the Free-Soil Party, which opposed the extension of slavery into the territories. He established several Free-Soil and antislavery newspapers in Indianapolis and Cincinnati. The Free-Soil Party nationally merged with the Republican Party in 1852, and in 1854 Butler called a meeting at the Indiana Statehouse that resulted in the creation of the Indiana Republican Party, the party of ABRAHAM LINCOLN.

As president of the board from 1852 to 1871 and chancellor from 1871 to 1881, he saw the new university through its founding, its first years of operation, and the move to a new campus in the Irvington neighborhood of Indianapolis in 1875. In 1877 the university was renamed Butler University over the protests of its main founder, leader,

Ovid Butler

and benefactor. Ovid disliked ostentation, but the board felt strongly about the honor, and persisted.

Butler died at his beloved Forest Home and is buried in Crown Hill Cemetery, another project he helped to develop. The cemetery is less than a mile south of the current Fairview Campus of Butler University. On the anniversary of his death, the university's board of directors declared February 7, Butler's birthday, would become Founder's Day. On the first observance of that date, Butler's son, Scot, presented to the university a life-size portrait of his father. Also on that occasion, General John Coburn, prominent Indianapolis lawyer and judge, gave an address praising Butler's mark on the school. He said: "His ambition was to make this institution as liberal, as thorough, and as beneficent as any one anywhere. . . . He believed in the equal rights of men and women; that all should be free; that all should be educated alike. . . . He put his faith and creed in the charter of the University, and upon these stones he builded."

SALLY CHILDS-HELTON

For Further Review

Butler, Ovid. Papers, 1841–1893. Indiana Historical Society William Henry Smith Memorial Library, Indianapolis.

Childs-Helton, Sally. "Ovid Butler and the Founding of Butler University." *Journal of the Butler Society* 5, no. 1 (2010): 89–105.

Waller, George M. *Butler University: A Sesquicentennial History*. Bloomington: Indiana University Press, 2006.

Cadle, E. Howard

August 25, 1884–December 20, 1942

Radio evangelist and founder of Cadle Tabernacle.

E. Howard Cadle famously experienced a conversion to Christianity after he was diagnosed with a terminal illness. When he regained his health he dedicated his life to converting others. He built the Cadle Tabernacle in Indianapolis in honor of his mother and used it as a center to promote Christianity.

Cadle found his life's calling through a much-publicized redemption. His epiphany changed his life and eventually moved tens of thousands to become his followers when he published his story in an autobiography, *How I Came Back*. Born in 1884 in Fredericksburg, Indiana, Cadle, in his early adult years, became a gambler and a drunk. He married at nineteen, temporarily quashing his vices, but eventually returned to a life of drinking, gambling, and adultery. He entered the slot machine business and became known as "The Slot Machine King." This hard living brought him to a health crisis and in 1914 he was diagnosed with Bright's Disease and given only six months to live. Cadle's mother prayed long and hard for his life and, when it became apparent that he would live, he attributed his survival to his mother's prayers, and his conversion to Christianity.

Exterior view of the Cadle Tabernacle in Indianapolis, 1923.

Cadle began to work in legitimate business, for which he seems to have had a talent. He invested in a chain of shoe repair shops and fruit stands and eventually earned a fortune. After hearing evangelist Gipsy Smith at a revival in Indianapolis, Cadle pledged to pay back his saved life. He became a fiery evangelist and channeled his newfound religious fervor to save others. Toward that goal he built the Cadle Tabernacle, a Spanish-Mission style building of whitewashed walls and red tiled roof in downtown Indianapolis. An old-time-religion revival hall, the tabernacle once occupied most of a city block across from what was then City Hall. The edifice seated 10,000 and cost $305,000 when it was built in 1921. The 1,400-person choir was the largest of its kind in the nation.

In the 1920s internal financial problems at the tabernacle caused Cadle to temporarily lose control of the property and during this time the tabernacle was used as meeting space for a number of organizations, including the Ku Klux Klan. By the 1930s, however, Cadle had regained control of the tabernacle and his revivalism business. He was able to keep the tabernacle and his radio show running as a result of contributions from the thousands of listeners who tuned into his weekly "Nation's Family Prayer Period." The program, began in 1931, was picked up by WLW in Cincinnati in 1933 and broadcast over a large multistate region. It was the most popular religious program of the period.

From the 1930s through 1942, Cadle purported to heal the sick of heart through his radio ministry. His organization distributed radios to "pastorless" churches. From within the tabernacle's stucco walls, owner and revivalist Cadle preached his message of fire and brimstone, eventually sending his sermons out over the radio waves and across the United States to 330 pastorless churches in Indiana, Ohio, Kentucky, and West Virginia, and to a vast number of at-home listeners. He preached his conversion message so successfully that he brought in four thousand letters a week.

Although Cadle's earlier jobs might have made him wealthy, his old-time religion kept him that way. A *Time* magazine article about him in 1939 was titled "Cash & Cadle." He drove a Cadillac, owned an airplane, and managed to keep up with the $100,000 a year operating expenses of the tabernacle through his own fortune and the contributions of his followers. His church's motto was "No creed but Christ, no law but love, no Book but the Bible." Flying in his own private plane piloted by his son, Buford, Cadle often visited his flock around the country, holding one-night revivals. In 1941 he published a book called *The Flying Preacher: One Night Revival Sermons*.

Cadle's preaching made good radio and good money. The *New York Times* dubbed him the "evangelist of the air," a moniker others later claimed, but one that was probably applied first to Cadle, the most famous of his generation of early radio evangelists. In 1939 *Life* magazine published a five-page photo spread about him, calling him the latest in a "long line of free-lance revivalists" who were "exhorting U.S. sinners to repentance."

In 1942 Cadle died at the young age of fifty-eight. His wife, Ola M., became president and director of the tabernacle. She and Buford, and daughters, Helen and Virginia Ann, ran the family evangelism business. In 1952 they began to air a television program based at the tabernacle. Ola died in 1955 and in 1968 the family sold the tabernacle to a local Indianapolis bank, which razed it to construct a parking lot. Cadle is buried next to his wife in his hometown of Fredericksburg, Indiana, at Kay's Chapel Cemetery.

CONNIE ZEIGLER

For Further Reading

Barlow, Fred M. *Profiles in Evangelism*. Murfreesboro, TN: Sword of the Lord, Publishers. 1976.

Slutz, Theodore. "How He Came Back: E. Howard Cadle and the Cadle Tabernacle." *Traces of Indiana and Midwestern History* 17, no. 1 (Winter 2005): 14–25.

Zeigler, Connie "Cadle Tabernacle, Indy's Home of Fire and Brimstone." *Urban Times*, March 2008.

Caldwell, Lynton Keith
November 21, 1913–August 15, 2006

Arthur F. Bentley Professor of Political Science and of Public and Environmental Affairs, Indiana University, Bloomington; internationally respected authority on environmental affairs and policy; principal architect of the National Environmental Policy Act of 1969; and originator of the Environmental Impact Statement.

The vast improvement in the quality of the environment in the United States since the early 1960s can be attributed in part to the tireless efforts of Lynton K. Caldwell, who wrote the report that led to the landmark legislation, the National Environmental Protection Act, and the well-known enforcement mechanism—the environmental impact statement. Caldwell insisted when testifying before the U.S. Congress in 1969 regarding the proposed NEPA that it include a provision that would compel executive agencies and the nation "to take the kind of action which will protect and reinforce . . . the life support of this country

In 1921 Caldwell's father, a superintendent of schools in rural Montezuma, Iowa, took up a new position in the heavily industrialized town of Hammond, Indiana. There, Caldwell developed his early love of nature, becoming a keen botanist, birdwatcher, a largely self-taught ecologist, and later a supporter of the Save the Dunes movement whose members were then attempting to thwart plans to turn the rare Dunes ecosystem along Lake Michigan into a new industrial city and deepwater port. In 1934 he completed his undergraduate degree with honors in English at the University of Chicago, where, among other areas, he took courses in the emerging fields of ecology and human ecology. For the rest of his life Caldwell stressed the importance of taking a broad-based, interdisciplinary approach to education. In the depths of the Great Depression he found a job teaching high school history in Whiting but, deeply dissatisfied, he applied successfully to Harvard, gaining a master's degree in history and government in 1938. He then returned to Chicago, where, under the guidance of the renowned constitutional scholar Leonard D. White, he completed a doctorate in government and public administration in 1943. The University of Chicago Press published his dissertation and first book, *The Administrative Theories of Hamilton and Jefferson*, in 1944.

In 1939 Caldwell was appointed assistant professor of government at Indiana University's Calumet Extension Center in East Chicago. In 1940, still only twenty-six, he became executive secretary of IU's South Bend-Mishawaka Extension Center. Soon afterward, he was elected president of the Audubon Society's new South Bend chapter. In 1941 he married Helen Walcher and they later adopted two children.

In 1944 Caldwell became head of research, inquiry, and publications at the Council of State Governments in Chicago. In this period, as executive secretary of the local Izaak Walton League branch, he began speaking out publicly about the noticeable lack of political will to solve growing environmental problems. In December 1946, during a business trip to the University of Wisconsin, he met the great ecologist Aldo Leopold and afterward spent the evening at Leopold's home. It was a conversation that later helped to change the direction of his life.

In 1947, appointed by Governor Thomas Dewey of New York, Caldwell moved to Albany as the coordinator of a new postwar program in public administration for civil servants established by New York and Syracuse Universities. In 1950 he took a two-month, 11,000-mile solo drive through the western states from which he returned determined "to be of help in the movement that wanted to change the accepted attitudes and assumptions regarding human use of the natural environment."

In 1951 Caldwell helped to establish and became president of the Nature Conservancy's first local chapter of eastern New York. In 1959 he became a founder and first president of the Conservancy's chapter in Indiana. Between 1952 and 1955, Caldwell served on public administration missions to Colombia, the Philippines, and a yearlong assignment in Turkey. In 1956, after a year at the University of California, Berkeley, he took a new position as professor of government at IU, Bloomington, directing a newly established public administration program with Thailand that, in 1958, was extended to Indonesia. During the next few years he traveled extensively in Asia, Australia, Europe, the Middle East, and Scandinavia, leading him to become increasingly concerned about the mounting levels of pollution and environmental degradation he observed.

In 1962, during a stop in Hong Kong, Caldwell made a life-changing decision to refocus his career to the pioneering development of environmental policy. In 1963 *Public Administration Review* published his first, award-winning article, "Environment: A New Focus for Public Policy?" After that, despite early criticism from some of his peers, he never looked back, going on to play a leading role in establishing research into the relationships between humans and their environment as a subfield of government and public administration studies. On a related theme, in this same period he also played a principal role in launching research into biopolitics and bioethics. In the 1960s and 1970s he helped to establish innovative programs of environmental studies across the country, including at IU. In 1972, after he had lobbied tirelessly for more than a decade, the School of Public and Environmental Affairs was established on the Bloomington campus.

In the mid-1960s, after years of increasing public demand for improved environmental quality, Senator Henry M. Jackson, concerned about the increase in environmental conflicts resulting from the lack of communication between federal agencies, determined to bring about needed change. Jackson's staff asked Caldwell—known for his then unique combination of skills in public administration and environmental affairs—to be the consultant for Jackson's proposed bill. Caldwell's subsequent report, "A National Policy for the Environment," became the basis on which NEPA was developed. At the April 16, 1969, Senate hearing on NEPA, Caldwell's arguments in favor of incorporating "action forcing" provisions resulted in the act's important environmental impact assessment clauses that require government agencies to consider the impact of government-funded projects before undertaking action. Since 1970, NEPA, widely acknowledged as the nation's "keystone" environmental law, has been emulated in one way or another by some one hundred countries.

For the next thirty years Caldwell worked tirelessly to instill environmental thinking and values, lecturing and speaking around the world at many universities, national, and international institutions, scientific and engineering bodies, and law schools. During these decades he wrote or coauthored fifteen books and more than two hundred peer-reviewed articles. He served on advisory committees of the United Nations, United Nations Educational, Scientific and Cultural Organization, International Union for Conservation of Nature, National Oceanic and Atmospheric Administration, National Academy of Sciences, the US-Canada International Joint Commission, and the World Council for the Biosphere. In 1972 he was a member of the U.S. delegation at the groundbreaking UN Conference on the Human Environment. Indiana governor OTIS BOWEN in 1980 made Caldwell a Sagamore of the Wabash, awarded for distinguished service to the state or to the governor. In 1991 he was named to the UNEP Global Five Hundred Roll of Honor for "outstanding environmental achievements." In 2002, as

Lynton K. Caldwell at his home, Cedar Crest, April 1972.

one part of his enduring environmental legacy, Caldwell and Helen willed their beloved home, Cedar Crest, and its wooded acreage to become the headquarters of the Bloomington-based Sycamore Land Trust that he had also helped to found.

WENDY READ WERTZ

For Further Reading

Caldwell, Lynton K. *Environment as a Focus for Public Policy*. Edited by Robert V. Bartlett and James M. Gladden. College Station: Texas A&M University Press, 1995.

Caldwell, Lynton K. Papers. Indiana University Office of Archives and Record Management, Bloomington, Indiana.

Wertz, Wendy Read. *Lynton Keith Caldwell: An Environmental Visionary and the National Environmental Policy Act*. Bloomington: Indiana University Press, 2013.

Capehart, Homer E.

June 6, 1897–September 3, 1979

Phonograph entrepreneur and three-term U.S. Senator.

The rotund, cigar-smoking, plainspoken Homer E. Capehart, by the end of his first term in the U.S. Senate in 1950, had become the favorite stereotype of liberal pundits and historians—a virtual caricature of Midwest, right-wing Republicanism. This image from his senatorial career concealed his remarkable faith, courage, and patriotism, as well as his earlier image of hard work, ambition, resilience, integrity, and adaptability—a story of American entrepreneurship.

Capehart was born on June 6, 1897, the eldest son of four children, in a small house in a family farm settlement of Highbanks on the east fork of White River about six miles northeast of Petersburg between Evansville and Bloomington in southern Indiana. Although his father, Alvin T. Capehart, owned seventy-one acres, he soon moved the family to the Graham farm just north of Washington in Daviess County, where to make ends meet he worked as a tenant. Young Homer learned to do the chores and do them well. Upon entering Washington High School, he returned home after school each afternoon to help his father.

In April 1917, with America's entry into World War I, having graduated from high school, Capehart enlisted in the army, rising to the rank of sergeant in supply with the task of providing forage for thousands of horses being shipped to U.S. forces assisting an international anti-Bolshevik intervention in Siberia in 1918. After his discharge at the war's end, Capehart took a job selling automatic milking machines for the Burton Paige Company and then another demonstrating tractors at farm shows put on by J. I. Case Corporation.

Capehart soon found that he had a knack for sales and moved on to the Holcomb and Hoke Manufacturing Corporation in Indianapolis, selling Butter-Kist brand popcorn and peanut roasters to owners of drugstores and movie theaters, eventually becoming the company's general sales manager. In the early 1920s, he saw the possibility of profits in recorded music, especially the popularity of the songs of Dixieland and Paul Whiteman and his orchestra. He found the inventor of a device that would turn over a stack of records, allowing the other side to be played automatically, and purchased the invention. In 1928 in Huntington, Indiana, he founded the Capehart Automatic Phonograph Corporation.

In June of the following year he moved the company into a large factory in Fort Wayne where—renamed the Capehart Corporation—it produced, along with coin phonographs, luxury "Capehart" record players to wealthy individuals around the world.

Unfortunately, the Wall Street Crash of 1929 and the Great Depression of the 1930s ended Capehart's association with his own company. The local bank that had provided funding took over when revenues declined and fired him.

Refusing to be defeated, Capehart founded another company, the Packard Manufacturing Company, and found another invention called the Simplex, which allowed selection of an individual song after insertion of a coin. He sold the Simplex along with his own services to the beleaguered Wurlitzer Corporation, the famous but failing manufacturer of musical instruments in North Tonawanda, New York. As vice president for jukebox production and sales, he brought Wurlitzer back to profitability, and by 1936 had become a millionaire. Capehart had a played an important major role in the transformation of American popular culture that grew out of the mass popularity of jukebox music and dancing. By 1939 there were some three hundred thousand jukeboxes operating in America, playing thirty million records a year.

With his newfound financial independence, faith in his country and himself, and boundless energy, he returned to his childhood location in Daviess County, Indiana, and purchased the fertile bottomland of just over a thousand acres where he had worked with his father. By this time he began to look askance at New Deal programs that he determined created "make-work" jobs, undermined private initiative, and interfered with the work ethic and with economic growth. Contacting state Republican officials, he offered to help fight New Deal programs by hosting a conference and pep rally for party workers. The Capehart Cornfield Conference of August 1938 announced the resurgence of the state GOP, which—while it accepted New-Deal assistance to farmers, free collective bargaining by workers, and unemployment compensation—labeled any further federal programs socialist and even communist. Soon thereafter Capehart became district GOP chairman.

With the outbreak of World War II, he converted the Packard Manfacturing Company that he had started in Indianapolis from producing remote coin boxes for jukeboxes to manufacturing military tank turret slip rings and cartridge magazines for the M1 carbine rifle. In the spring of 1944, at the urging of party officials, he decided to run for the U.S. Senate, narrowly defeating the popular Democratic governor, Henry F. Schricker.

Following the lead of the isolationist Senate leader, "Mr. Republican," Robert A. Taft of Ohio, Capehart was a steadfast opponent of Harry Truman's Fair Deal and Cold War foreign policy. Capehart also set the stage for the demagoguery of U.S. Senator Joe McCarthy of Wisconsin through his support of McCarthy during Capehart's campaign for a second term in 1950 and his willingness to cooperate with his fellow Hoosier senator, the sharp-tongued William E. Jenner, in attacking Democratic national security policy and refusing to support foreign aid or European defense.

With the election two years later of Dwight D. Eisenhower and Republican control of the Eighty-third Congress in 1953, Capehart became chairman of the Joint Committee on Defense Production, chairman of the Banking and Currency Committee, and member of the Foreign Relations Committee, replacing Taft in this post after the latter died of cancer that July. Abandoning his support for McCarthy, Capehart, like Democratic leaders Lyndon Johnson, Harry Byrd, Richard Russell, Walter George, and John McClellan, backed Eisenhower's policies and became a proponent of trade with Latin America, taking a large delegation of businessmen on a tour of the southern continent and hosting delegations from those countries in the United States.

Capehart reached the height of his influence by speaking on behalf of Eisenhower's programs in the areas of military servicemen, farming, and housing. Indeed, a major contribution was his committee's national investigation of fraud in the Federal Housing Administration. He won election for a third term in 1956, defeating Claude Wickard by 212,481 votes—the largest margin of his career.

Capehart did not trust Nikita Khrushchev and the Soviet Union. After President John F. Kennedy's failed invasion organized by the Central Intelligence Agecny at the Bay of Pigs in April 1961, his criticism of the president's Cuba policy grew sharper; and he made this the main issue in his 1962 Senate campaign. As Kennedy ordered a blockade and issued a public ultimatum to Khrushchev during the Cuban Missile Crisis, the young president muttered sardonically that the Hoosier senator had been correct. "Homer Capehart," he said, "is the Winston Churchill of our generation." The Soviet decision to withdraw the missiles was insufficient, however, to return the visibly aging Capehart to the Senate. The nation rallied to the president and Hoosiers elected Kennedy's choice, the youthful Birch Bayh, by a narrow margin of 11,000 votes.

When he left Washington, Capehart had served longer in the U.S. Senate than anyone elected by the people of Indiana. In retirement he made his home in Indianapolis but enjoyed supervising his farm corporation in Daviess County. He served on the boards of businesses and charitable institutions, spent time with his grandchildren, and shared memories with his biographer—the author, then a history graduate student at Indiana University. Capehart died on September 3, 1979, at age eighty-two in Indianapolis after surgery for an aortic aneurysm.

WILLIAM B. PICKETT

For Further Reading

Capehart, Homer E. Papers, 1938–1962. William Henry Smith Memorial Library, Indiana Historical Society, Indianapolis.

———. Senate Papers. Indiana State Library, Indianapolis.

Pickett, William B. *Homer E. Capehart: A Senator's Life, 1897–1979*. Indianapolis: Indiana Historical Society Press, 1990.

———. "Homer E. Capehart: Phonograph Entrepreneur." *Indiana Magazine of History* 82 (September 1986): 264–76.

Carmichael, Hoagland "Hoagy" Howard

November 22, 1899–December 27, 1981

Notable composer of popular music, pianist, singer, and actor who earned a place in the Songwriters Hall of Fame.

He was born Hoagland in Bloomington, Indiana, named after a traveling circus troupe called the Hoaglands who had lodged with the Carmichaels. He quickly became "Hoagy" as he grew up and became a composer of more than six hundred songs—some fifty of hit status—including "Stardust," an American standard recorded by hundreds of artists as well as Carmichael himself.

In his autobiography, *The Stardust Road*, he fondly recalled his birth name: "Other people call me Hoagy, but it is Hoagland that remembers the long chromatic runs my mother [Lida] played when the redskins bit the dust on the flickering silver screen. My mother played the picture-show music and I got in free." Lida not only helped family finances by accompanying silent movies and providing music at Indiana University fraternity

Hoagy Carmichael

parties, but she also taught young Hoagy the piano. That would be his only musical training, save for lessons during his teens from an Indianapolis-based African American pianist, Reginald DuValle, who instilled in Hoagy a love for jazz and ragtime and showed him the ways of jazz improvisation.

The Carmichael family moved frequently because of father Howard's unstable job situation, in earlier years as a horse-drawn taxi driver, later as electrician. Hoagy took jobs in construction, a bicycle chain factory, and a slaughterhouse. Finances and a constant draw to music slowed his education, but he entered IU to earn a bachelor's degree in 1925 and a law degree in 1926.

While an IU student, Hoagy formed his own band, Carmichael's Collegians, which gained a reputation not only on campus but also throughout Indiana and Ohio. He also turned to booking. In 1924 he booked a band called the Wolverines to play ten dates at fraternity houses. In its ranks was a gifted young cornetist from Iowa, Bix Beiderbecke, who befriended the booker. For Beiderbecke, Carmichael wrote his first piece. "Free Wheeling" he called it. Beiderbecke took the score with him to Richmond, Indiana, where the Wolverines recorded it for Gennett Records, but under a different title, "Riverboat Shuffle."

The recording was Beiderbecke's act of encouragement, but, still, the fledgling composer did not make up his mind about a music career. Could he succeed, he worried, remembering the death of his little sister, Joanne, several years earlier. On the back of her photograph he had written that Joanne had been "the victim of poverty." He later noted, "We couldn't afford a good doctor or good attention, and that's when I vowed I would never be broke again in my lifetime." Lawyer Carmichael moved to Florida and set up practice. While in West Palm Beach, however, he happened to hear a recording of his song, "Washboard Blues." Music beckoned and won out.

He moved to New York City in 1929, worked for a brokerage house by day, but at night wrote music and sought contacts. Beiderbecke was there. So were Louis Armstrong, the Dorsey Brothers, Benny Goodman, and others, including an ambitious lyricist from Savannah, Georgia, Johnny Mercer, who became a frequent songwriting partner with Carmichael.

Just as Carmichael moved, a New York firm, Mills Music, decided to publish an upbeat Carmichael instrumental, "Stardust." It aroused little interest. A Mills-connected lyricist, Mitchell Parrish, added words; again, there was no public enthusiasm. In 1930 bandleader Isham Jones recorded it as a ballad, using a slower tempo. That worked. With "Stardust," Carmichael struck gold. No longer would he need to worry about money or question his decision to give up law for music.

He remembered recording "Stardust" himself earlier, at Gennett. It brought, he remembered in his autobiography, "a queer sensation. This melody was bigger than I was. It wasn't part of me. Maybe I hadn't even written it. It didn't sound familiar in the playback. And I lost the recollection of how, when, and where it all happened. It was a complete blackout, as if for some unconscious reason, I didn't want to know, remember." But his the song was; his it remains. That Gennett recording has been inducted into the Grammy Hall of Fame and been chosen into the National Recording Registry by the Library of Congress. At century's turn, Swedish music critics voted "Stardust" the tune of the century.

A string of hits followed: "Georgia on My Mind," "Rockin' Chair," "Lazy River," " In the Still of the Night," and "Lazy Bones," his first with Mercer. In 1936 Carmichael married a fellow Hoosier, Ruth Meinardi, and they moved to Hollywood. He had his eyes on film. There, with Frank Loesser, he wrote "Two Sleepy People," "Small Fry," and "Heart and Soul." With others or on his own, he continued to produce songs, among them "I Get Along without You Very Well," and "The Nearness of You."

New York not completely out of his system, Carmichael made his only attempt at a Broadway musical comedy—*Walk with Music*, created with Mercer—and failed. Thereafter, he focused exclusively on Hollywood, not only as composer but also as character actor. A small role as a piano player in *Topper* led to more assignments: *To Have and Have Not*, *The Best Years of Our Lives*, *Canyon Passage*, and *Young Man with a Horn*, a fictionalized version of his friend Beiderbecke's life. In total, he made fourteen films. Meanwhile, the songs kept coming: "Skylark," "Ole Buttermilk Sky," "In the Cool, Cool, Cool of the Evening" (winner of an Academy Award), "My Resistance Is Low," and more. A number of the songs he himself performed, employing his unique style of pianism and sound of voice.

With the arrival of the 1950s, the Carmichael hit parade faltered. Public taste changed to rock and roll and rhythm and blues. The era of the Great American Songbook, which recognized the most significant popular songs of the day, particularly from Broadway and musical theater, was over. So was his marriage, from which came two sons, Hoagland Jr. and Randy. In 1977 Carmichael married Wanda McKay, an actress. In the meantime, he had taken a role in a television series, *Laramie*; written two classical works for orchestra, *Johnny Appleseed* and *Brown County in Autumn* that made hardly a ripple; and settled into comfortable retirement, enjoying golf, coin collecting, and two California homes, one on Sunset Boulevard the other in Rancho Mirage.

It was in Rancho Mirage that he died. He was buried in his native Bloomington. His archives were given to IU, where a Hoagy Carmichael Room was opened to honor him.

Carmichael's songs continue to delight, distinctive for their catchy, often jazz-infused melodies and nostalgic, down-home lyrics. They reflect a different aura from that of his Hoosier contemporary, Cole Porter, who moved east and turned out music of sophisticated wit and continental urbanity.

Carmichael could not forget his roots. Consider what he wrote in the *Stardust Road*: "I thought of Bloomington. I remembered the boys I knew, the circuses coming to town, and the flour sacks we collected from boardinghouses and sold to the local grocer for a cent each. Remembered the pop stands we built with the money; the quarry holes where we used to swim. I remember the kindly neighbors who suffered us with never a reproachful word, except when we smoked corn silks in their privies."

The Indiana native and the world-renowned songwriter were one.

PETER P. JACOBI

For Further Reading

Carmichael, Hoagy. Papers. Indiana University. Bloomington, IN.

———. *Sometimes I Wonder: The Story of Hoagy Carmichael*. New York: Farrar, Straus, and Giroux, 1965.

———. *The Stardust Road*. Bloomington: Indiana University Press, 1983.

Sudhalter, Richard M. *Stardust Melody, The Life and Music of Hoagy Carmichael*. New York: Oxford University Press, 2002.

Carmony, Donald

January 18, 1910–February 14, 2005

Professor of history, author, and editor of *Indiana Magazine of History.*

Donald Carmony spent most of his ninety-five years in a never-ending drive for learning, understanding, and explaining the fabric of Indiana and the events and people who weaved its pattern as the nation's nineteenth state. He became, as many have proclaimed, the acclaimed dean of Indiana history who passed his experiences and knowledge on to countless thousands of students, colleagues, and to the public at large.

Carmony found his calling quickly and it lasted a lifetime as a professor of history, a researcher, author, longtime editor of the *Indiana Magazine of History*, and a circuit rider of sorts reminiscent of Indiana's pioneer era he spent so many years researching and writing about. He often took his teaching—not preaching—on the road to service clubs, community groups, and on field trips, where he lectured on the bus. As Indiana historian James H. Madison once said of Carmony, he became a "public historian" long before the label was created by playing key roles in celebrations of the bicentennial of the American Revolution, of Indiana's sesquicentennial of statehood, of Indiana University's 150th anniversary, and in guiding an incredibly rich and detailed history of the Indiana General Assembly. By the time he retired as a full-time professor at Indiana University at age seventy, he was widely recognized as the ultimate authority on the state's history.

Carmony was born in Shelby County, Indiana, in 1910, the son of Bert and Golda Carmony, and his childhood helped shape his own understanding of place. As a boy, he lived for a long time in a log cabin, and his father farmed the horse-drawn way. As Carmony recalled in a 1995 interview, "There was no tractor, no electricity. In some respects, it was like the early history of Indiana." His father was not formally educated, but for thirty-three years he taught grades one through eight in a one-room brick schoolhouse and instilled in his son "an adventure for learning."

Carmony quickly demonstrated that spirit, graduating from high school in Rush County by age fifteen. He graduated cum laude from Indiana Central College (now the University of Indianapolis) in 1929 and began teaching there while also enrolled in graduate studies at IU. Over the next twenty-one years he earned a master's and a doctorate in history while teaching at Indiana Central, IU extensions in Fort Wayne and South Bend, and then IU's main campus in Bloomington. He spoke often about the debt he owed his parents, relating that on one occasion when he was thinking of quitting college, his mother told him, "I've given up too much. I've sold too many chickens. You're not going to quit school now."

He wrote numerous articles and essays and for twenty years was editor of the *Indiana Magazine of History*. But his most noted works were a two-volume history of Indiana coauthored with John Barnhart, *Indiana: From Frontier to Industrial Commonwealth*, published in 1954, and *Indiana 1816–1850: The Pioneer Era*, published in 1998. That latter book recounts in immaculate detail the origins and formations of Indiana's statehood "on borrowed money," its early economy and banking, its education system, its politics, and its long toils in deep debt due to its ill-fated plunge into building canals in a drive to boost commerce in an interior state. Madison called the book a culmination of a half century of scholarship that "will remain the standard reference for the period." Its 632 pages of prose are followed by 245 pages of detailed notes and citations from books, essays, and hundreds of newspaper accounts of the times.

But more than his scholarly endeavors, Carmony, his granddaughter, Diane Carmony, said he was most proud of his students. His love for history, she said, came from his affinity for educating people. "He was very much a story teller," she said.

He spoke often of the need to learn about other parts of the world, but through his teaching of Indiana, Carmony sought to give his students a greater understanding of the place they lived, and in turn, of themselves. Carmony said the primary purpose of his book *The Pioneer Era* was to explain how and why Indiana developed as it did during its formative years and also describe its role in the country as a whole. "Too often, state history has been presented mainly as a history of the United States, with a miscellany of items and episodes about the state described," he wrote. "Citizens generally should be encouraged to learn more about their communities, states, and countries."

Indeed, much of Carmony's legacy is in the passion of his teachings. Two of his former graduate students, Madison and Fred Hill, became distinguished Indiana historians and authors themselves. And Carmony helped shape countless more minds in what some have described as his "perpetually over-enrolled courses." As his obituary published in the *Indianapolis Star* on February 17, 2005, noted, "His greatest pleasure arose from teaching both graduate and undergraduate courses to thousands and thousands of students."

He was also outspoken on progressive and controversial issues of the times, including civil rights. In 1930, at the beginning of his professional career when popular adherence to philosophies of the Ku Klux Klan still lingered in Indiana, he was the only white speaker on the program at the Indiana National Association for the Advancement of Colored People conference held in French Lick. He was an outspoken advocate of public education, too, believing it crucial to a responsible citizenry.

Carmony served on numerous state committees and his awards and accolades were many. He was twice given the Sagamore of the Wabash—the highest honor Indiana governors can bestow on state citizens. Governor Frank O'Bannon, who was considered a quintessential Hoosier in his own right, presented it to Carmony the second time during a statehouse ceremony in 1998. There is also an IU chair of history endowed in his name, the campaign for it initiated and led by two of his former students, Stephen Moberly and John Worth.

Carmony was married to his wife, Edith, from 1934 until her death in 1991. They had two sons, Duane and Lowell Carmony, and he later married Mary Hiatt Crawford—a friend from his graduating class at Indiana Central—in 1993. She said Carmony left a "legacy of pioneerism," adding that he "made a great contribution to Indiana, and Indiana made a great contribution to him. And he was always a student." Said Madison: "He was the man for Indiana history, and it was for a long, long time."

MICHAEL SMITH

For Further Reading

Barnhart, John D., and Donald F. Carmony. *Indiana: From Frontier to Industrial Commonwealth*. 2 vols. New York: Lewis Historical Publishing, 1954. Reprint, Indianapolis: Indiana Historical Bureau, 1979.

Blair, Rebecca, A. James Fuller, and Michael G. Cartwright. *Profiles in Service: 1905–2005*. Indianapolis: University of Indianapolis (Crossings Project), 2006.

Carmony, Donald F. *Indiana 1816–1850: The Pioneer Era*. Indianapolis: Indiana Historical Bureau and Indiana Historical Society, 1998.

Carson, Julia

July 8, 1938–December 15, 2007

Indiana state legislator and U.S. congresswoman.

On the morning of Friday, December 21, 2007, a horse-drawn military caisson left 2530 North Park Avenue on the near north side of Indianapolis for a trip to the Indiana Statehouse. Drummers and an honor guard with rifles and a U.S. and Indiana flag led the way while about fifty friends and family members marched behind the caisson. As members of the Indiana National Guard carried the body to lie formally in the rotunda, a large gathering met them to pay their respects. Only a few dignitaries—ABRAHAM LINCOLN, JAMES WHITCOMB RILEY, and BENJAMIN HARRISON, for example—had received such a distinction in the nineteenth state's history. All of those so honored had one thing in common—they were male. The newest member of this select company, someone Governor Mitch Daniels called "the people's best friend," however, was a woman, Julia Carson.

Carson, who died from lung cancer at the age of sixty-nine on December 15, had broken barriers throughout her life. The only child of an unwed mother, Velma Porter, who had spent her life doing backbreaking work cleaning the homes, cooking the meals, and caring for children of wealthy families on Indianapolis's north side, Carson had grown up to become only the third African American woman to serve in the Indiana House of Representatives and the first black woman, along with Katie Hall of Gary, to be elected to the Indiana Senate.

After eighteen years of service with the Democratic Party in the state legislature, Carson left her secure seat to run and win election in 1990 as Center Township trustee, an office in debt. She instituted antifraud procedures and a workfare program whereby able-bodied relief recipients were required to perform community service in return for assistance. These efforts helped move the office into the twenty-first century and resulted in a $6 million surplus and won for Carson her second honor as "Woman of the Year" from the *Indianapolis Star*.

Before her own tries for public office Carson had maintained a healthy skepticism for politics and politicians. In her mind, those involved in the system were often dishonest and could not be trusted to do what was right for people in need. Carson's attitudes about politicians were altered by her work as a legislative assistant to Indianapolis congressman Andrew Jacobs Jr., who in 1965 hired the divorced mother of two away from her job as a secretary with the United Auto Workers Local 550. "We just had a lot of rapport," Jacobs remembered. "I liked what she had to say, particularly the way she said it. And I said, 'Boy, there's an awful lot of brains in that large head.'" Carson found Jacobs to be "a rare kind of politician," as he displayed a real interest in his constituents. "And I thought that perhaps those qualities could be transferred to someone like me," she said.

In 1996, urged on by Jacobs, Carson ran for the Tenth Congressional District seat being vacated by Jacobs, and became only the second African American woman from Indiana to serve in Congress, and the first woman and the first African American

Then State Senator Julia Carson talks to constituents, 1981.

to represent Indianapolis in Washington, D.C. In 2002, as a result of redistricting, she ran and won re-election to the Seventh Congressional District, which had a slight Democratic edge and a decided majority of white voters. A fiercely liberal representative, she fought off numerous challenges over the years from a variety of Republican opponents.

Carson won six terms in office with the help of a dedicated group of supporters who wielded red-and-white campaign signs emblazoned with the slogan that came to symbolize their adoration for their candidate: "I ♥ Julia." She proved time and time again, noted one Hoosier political expert, that she could "bring people to the polls who ordinarily may not participate in the political process."

In her attempts for state and national office, Carson engaged in a down-to-earth style of campaigning. She became known for wearing big hats and her unpretentious speaking style, calling young people "Baby" and older women "Mom." Until her death, Carson lived in the same house and neighborhood she had lived in before her rise to political prominence, and refused to obtain an unlisted telephone number. Her ability to connect with average citizens impressed political pundits. "She'd walk up to somebody—I've seen this at the polls—and even if she didn't know them, she appeared to, and they responded as if they knew her. And this was not just political savvy; it was, for want of a better term, 'street smarts,'" noted Brian Vargas, a former pollster and frequent commentator on politics in central Indiana.

Carson also made sure that her congressional office paid attention to what was occurring in her district, including sending letters of condolence to families whose loved ones had died and paying visits to those who were sick and in the hospital. While in Congress, Carson fought for legislation to expand a program to offer children health insurance, sponsored a measure to ensure veterans who completed prison terms would still have the right to vote, and supported a bill to help individuals and families in danger of becoming homeless. Perhaps her crowning achievement came in 1999 when she convinced Congress to pass legislation honoring Rosa Parks, the African American woman who had refused to give up her seat on a segregated city bus in Montgomery, Alabama, with a Congressional Gold Medal. Carson also opposed the war in Iraq, indicating the 2003 invasion was to protect U.S. oil interests in the region. "Julia [spoke] for those with no voice," said Dan Parker, Indiana Democratic Party chairman. "She fought for those who had lost hope in the system. She fought for and never lost sight of what she believed in."

Carson's crusade for the disadvantaged was fueled in part by her own humble beginnings growing up in the Haughville section of Indianapolis, where she lived in an African American neighborhood of mostly poor families. For a role model, Carson could look to her mother, someone who worked hard all of her life to give her daughter the opportunities she never had. "She taught me about hard work, spirituality, and trust," Carson said, adding that her mother also educated her through both word and deed that "great pride can come from work well done, even if it was not well-compensated."

Despite the underprivileged surroundings, there existed a strong sense of community in Haughville. Because her mother often had to be away from home when she was working, Carson had to rely on her neighbors to help take care of her. "Every woman on the block or in the rooming houses where we sometimes lived was my 'auntie' and every man was my 'uncle,'" Carson recalled. "Our neighbors were truly like family." This lesson from her younger days followed her throughout her political career.

Carson's final years in politics were filled with uncertainty. Bouts of illness caused her to miss a number of votes in Congress, a situation that caused fueled speculation that she might not run again. In August 2007, after her grandson, Andre, had announced that he intended to run for a seat on the Indianapolis City-County Council, Carson indicated she would run for a seventh term. On Saturday, November 24, 2007, however, Carson stunned her supporters by revealing she had terminal lung cancer.

Just three weeks after her shocking announcement, Carson died on Saturday, December 15, 2007, at her Indianapolis home on North Park Avenue with her family at her side. As she had in life, Carson's death touched the lives of a diverse group of people. At her funeral at the Eastern Star Church, approximately two thousand gathered to pay their respects, including such disparate figures as longtime Republican U.S. Senator Richard G. Lugar and leader of the Nation of Islam Louis Farrakhan. Speaker after speaker praised Carson for her kindness, her ability to remain connected to her constituents, and lifelong commitment to social justice.

RAY E. BOOMHOWER

For Further Reading

Boomhower, Ray E. "I ♥ Julia: Congresswoman Julia Carson of Indiana." *Traces of Indiana and Midwestern History* 23, no. 4 (Fall 2011): 4–11.

Carson, Julia. "A Work in Progress: 'My Neighbor as Myself.'" By Fran Quigley. *Julia Carson for Congress Committee*, Indianapolis (March 1996).

Jacobs, Andrew. *Slander and Sweet Judgment: The Memoir of an Indiana Congressman*. Zionsville: Guild Press of Indiana, 2000.

Pierce, Richard B. *Polite Protest: The Political Economy of Race in Indianapolis, 1920–1970*. Bloomington: Indiana University Press, 2005.

Carter, Vivian

March 25, 1921–June 12, 1989

Gary radio celebrity and founder of Vee-Jay Records, the first successful black-owned record label in America.

For a dozen years beginning in 1953, Vivian Carter's Vee-Jay Record Company, an independent label, released some of the most original music of the mid-twentieth century, from rhythm and blues, doo wop, and pop to jazz, electric blues, and gospel.

When Carter was a toddler, her parents moved from Tunica, Mississippi, to Gary, Indiana, hoping for better opportunities for themselves and their children. As a student at all-black Roosevelt High School, Carter excelled at the auditorium components of public speaking, chorus, and theater that were central features of Superintendent William A. Wirt's famous work-study-play system. Lifelong friend YJean Chambers described Carter as lively, extroverted, and full of fun, with a rich alto voice that seemed to have its own built-in microphone. After school let out, Carter frequently waited tables at her mother's restaurant in Midtown, Gary's black district, bantering easily with steelworker patrons.

After graduating in 1939, Carter took business college classes and during World War II joined the Quartermaster Corps as a clerical worker. She embarked on a radio career after winning a contest held by Chicago's WGES to host a segment of a program. During the early 1950s she had her own show, "Livin' with Vivian," six nights a week on WWCA, Gary's premier radio station. With future husband Jimmy Bracken she opened Vivian's Record Shop at 1640 Broadway in Midtown's black commercial district. The enterprise benefited from her popularity among young fans. Often calling female listeners "Powder Puffs" and guys "Sponges," Carter declared herself to be the "hostess with the mostest." If she particularly liked a record, especially one on sale at her record store, she might play it several times in a row and then again if a caller requested it.

Carter and Bracken borrowed $500 and recorded a local group, the Spaniels, led by James "Pookie" Hudson, who recently had won a talent contest at Roosevelt High School, Carter's alma mater. They chose Vee-Jay (sometimes spelled Vee Jay or VeeJay) from the first letters of their names. It was an immediate success. The Spaniels' first recording, "Baby It's You," rose to number ten on *Billboard*'s rhythm-and-blues charts. With no distribution capacity Vee-Jay leased the record to Chance. After that label went out of business in 1954, its accountant, Ewart Abner, joined Vee-Jay and, along with Vivian's brother, Calvin, soon took over most day-to-day operations. Opening headquarters in Chicago, Vee-Jay was poised to market the Spaniels' ballad "Goodnight Sweetheart," which reached number thirty-five on the rhythm-and-blues charts. Covered by the McGuire Sisters, the song became a million-selling crossover hit.

In 1955 another Vee-Jay act, the El Dorados, had a huge hit titled "At My Front Door" (sometimes known as "Crazy Little Mama"), which reached number one on the rhythm-and-blues chart and number seventeen on *Billboard*'s Top 100. Pat Boone's syrupy cover version climbed to number seven. By 1956, when the Dells recorded "Oh What a Night," growing numbers of teenagers were demanding original rhythm and blues versions to white imitations, and "Oh What a Night" became the label's first million-seller. The success of the Spaniels, El Dorados, and Dells enabled the independent label, now with headquarters on the city's "Record Row," to attract top harmony groups from the Chicago area and beyond, including the Impressions, featuring Jerry Butler and Curtis Mayfield, whose 1958 hit "For Your Precious Love," earned the group a gold record.

Jimmy Reed, whose "High and Lonesome" had been Vee-Jay's very first single, scored a crossover hit in 1957 with "Honest I Do." With his distinctive voice and unique blend of harmonica and guitar, he expanded the parameters of electric blues that so influenced British bands such as the Rolling Stones, as did another Vee-Jay artist, John Lee Hooker, who recorded six albums for the label and is best known for the songs "I Love You Honey" (1958), "No Shoes" (1960), and "Boom Boom" (1961).

Vee-Jay's impressive array of gospel artists included the Staple Singers, who in 1956 recorded the classic "Uncloudy Day." Another gospel group, the Highway QCs, featured such future solo artists as Lou Rawls and Sam Cooke. Vee-Jay put out a line of jazz albums that also sold moderately well.

One of Vee-Jay's most innovative artists was Delectus "Dee" Clark, who enjoyed moderate success in 1959 with "Nobody but You" and scored a monster hit with "Hey Little Girl (in the high school sweater)." Clark's 1961 ballad "Raindrops" reached number two on the *Billboard* charts. The following year, Vee-Jay had its first number one hit, "Duke of Earl" by showman Gene Chandler, the bulk of whose earnings, as with other Vee-Jay artists, came from personal appearances rather than record royalties.

Flushed with success, Vee-Jay attracted The Four Seasons, a white harmony group that subsequently had three number one hits, "Sherry," "Big Girls Don't Cry," and "Walk Like a Man," but the group's agent had negotiated for such high royalties that the company struggled to pay them. Then an apparent windfall fell its way. After achieving a Number Five hit with British singer Frank Ifield in 1962, Vee-Jay entered into a licensing agreement with EMI for the Beatles in January 1963. In 1964, after the "Fab Four" appeared on Ed Sullivan's show, Vee-Jay sold an estimated 2.6 million Beatles records in a single month. Contract loopholes, however, led to Vee-Jay losing the Beatles to Capitol Records, and the so-called British Invasion diminished the market for Vee-Jay's stable of African American performers. The label's last top-ten hit was Betty Everett's "The Shoop Shoop Song (It's In His Kiss)." Only one more release reached the top twenty-five, the 1965 single "Oo Wee Baby, I Love You" by Fred Hughes.

By 1964 Carter had delegated management responsibilities to others whose spendthrift ways and extravagant lifestyles ultimately bankrupted the company. Abner, for example, was a compulsive gambler who ran up huge debts in Las Vegas. As Chandler recalled, "He'd go to a hotel and buy up the whole floor, top floor, penthouse, and the disc jockeys would come up and party. That's how Vee-Jay got in trouble." While it lasted, Carter herself enjoyed her wealth to the hilt, riding around Gary and Chicago in a gold Cadillac and often sporting a mink coat. In 1967, a year after the company ceased production, the Internal Revenue Service seized her record store for unpaid back taxes. As Chambers put it, "Hers was a rags to riches to rags story." Her mother added that her daughter started out in her basement and ended up in her basement. Some former employees helped make Berry Gordy's Motown label in Detroit a success while Carter remained active on WWCA, hosting a late-night gospel show.

By the mid-1980s diabetes, high blood pressure, and a series of strokes had taken their toll, leaving Carter paralyzed on her left side and barely able to talk. In a nursing home Hudson, for years estranged from her over unpaid royalties, sang "Goodnight Sweetheart" at her bedside shortly before Carter passed away. Though negligent financially toward performers whose talents her company developed, she captured on vinyl arguably the musical sounds of her generation, nurturing artists who might not otherwise have had recording success.

JAMES B. LANE

For Further Reading

Farag, Henry. "The Signal: A Doo Wop Rhapsody." *Steel Shavings* 32 (2001).

Lane, James B. Lane. "Gary's First Hundred Years: A Centennial History of Gary, Indiana, 1906–2006." *Steel Shavings* 37 (2006)

Pruter, Robert. *Chicago Soul*. Urbana: University of Illinois Press, 1991.

Chambers, David Laurance
January 12, 1879–January 12, 1963

Editor, publisher, executive, Bobbs-Merrill Company, Indianapolis.

A cultivated and complex man and a remarkable editor and publisher, David Laurance Chambers was well known during his long career for both his charm and his temper. Faced with either trait, or some ingenious combination of both, the authors, editors, and salespeople who worked with him and for him over the years were generally powerless to oppose his will. His influence on American publishing was immense, not only through the many authors he cultivated and the books he published, but also through the numerous editors he trained who went on to establish successful publishing careers.

Born in Washington, D.C., Chambers was the youngest in a long line of men named David Chambers. His father, David Abbot Chambers, served as private secretary to U.S. Senator John Sherman of Ohio, and his grandfather, Doctor David Chambers, had been a physician in Zanesville, Ohio, where both Chambers's mother and father were born. Following in the footsteps of previous Davids, Chambers attended Princeton University, where he was a brilliant student. He graduated in 1900, was salutatorian of his class and a member of Phi Beta Kappa. After graduation, he earned the Charles Scribner Fellowship in English and received his master's degree in 1901. He served as secretary to Princeton's chief literary figure of the time, Henry Van Dyke.

In the spring of 1903, when Van Dyke was too busy to evaluate a manuscript for Bobbs-Merrill, Chambers took the assignment and handled it so well that he was sent more. "The work seemed

Vivian Carter

down my alley," he recalled, and he asked about an opening at Bobbs-Merrill. There was not one at the time, but the firm said it would keep him in mind. In the meantime he applied for a position at Charles Scribner's Sons and Century. "They used almost identical words," he wrote: "Young man, if you want to make money, don't go into the publishing business." He worked briefly as assistant to the managing editor at *Ladies' Home Journal*, but was unsatisfied and left when he received an offer from Bobbs-Merrill.

When Chambers joined the firm in September 1903, Bobbs-Merrill was one of the country's leading publishers, having established a national reputation with the works of Indiana authors such as MEREDITH NICHOLSON, GEORGE ADE, and JAMES WHITCOMB RILEY under the name Bowen-Merrill Company during what would later become known as the golden age of Indiana literature. It began as a bookstore owned by Samuel Merrill around 1850 that published legal decisions. The enterprise was passed down to his son, Samuel Merrill Jr., who ran it with his brother-in-law, Charles W. Moores, until the Civil War. In 1885 a merger with Bowen, Stewart and Company created Bowen-Merrill, and in 1903, with ascendancy of William C. Bobbs as president, the firm became known as Bobbs-Merrill, an imprint that remained intact after the sale of the company to Howard W. Sams in 1958 and ended in 1985 with the sales of backlist titles and rights to Macmillan Company.

Drawn by the gravitational pull of literary Indiana, Chambers came to Indianapolis at the age of twenty-four to serve as secretary to W. C. Bobbs, who had built the firm on publishing what he called "good clean fiction and corking good tales." From that point forward for the next fifty years, Chambers's role in the affairs of the company expanded by geometrical proportions—becoming vice president in 1921, editor in 1925, president in 1935, and chairman of the board in 1953. As president, Chambers continued to serve as head of the trade department, where no publishing decisions were made without his approval and where the initials "DLC" on letters and memorandums designated supreme authority.

The project files in the vast Bobbs-Merrill Collection at Indiana University's Lilly Library contain thousands of examples of Chambers's correspondence with authors and memorandums to staff, and any sampling reflects the intensity

David Laurance Chambers

with which he approached his work. Reading through them one cannot help admire the tactfulness with which Chambers could deflect unreasonable demands, suggest revisions or cuts to unwieldy manuscripts, or stifle impossible projects. In 1975 author Glenn Tucker remembered the "unbelievably large volume" of correspondence that he had accumulated in his ten years of writing under Chambers's direction. Tucker also described the "pink slips" on which Chambers wrote memorandums to staff in "a never ending stream" and that were "the controlling deity of the Bobbs office."

Perhaps the most prevalent author's complaint that Chambers faced throughout his career was that the firm did not do enough to promote books. Adhering to a standard set by the firm in 1916 of not advertising a single title until sales from multiple-title, or "list," advertisements justified the expenditure, Chambers remained adamant in his belief that word of mouth was what made best sellers, not advertising. Though his authors often disagreed, he did know something about best sellers. In the 1920s he was instrumental in finding and developing such best-selling authors as John Erskine, Bruce Barton, Richard Halliburton, and Earl Derr Biggers. In 1925, the year Chambers became editor, Erskine's *The Private Life of Helen of Troy*, Barton's *The Man Nobody Knows*, Halliburton's *The Royal Road to Romance*, and Bigger's first Charlie Chan mystery novel, *The House without a Key*, appeared, signaling the beginning of a period of soaring sales and profits for the trade department.

The Great Depression brought an end to these good times. During the 1930s the firm sought every possible means to cut expenses. As the trade and law book divisions began losing money, staff members were given forced vacations and pay reductions. Only the schoolbook division remained profitable. Historian Thomas D. Clark remembered first meeting Chambers in 1939. Describing him as someone who had "stepped fresh out of a Dickens novel" with shirt tail out and "rumpled hair," who eyed him "over pince-nez glasses as if [he] had brought a dead fish into the parlor," Clark quickly got the point that "the book business was bad and that [Chambers] had not worked his shirt tail out in anxiety to publish [Clark's] book." Chambers's weariness with author's demands surfaced on occasion. In a memo from 1926 he wrote: "One of the trials of life is the necessity of constantly showing an accommodating spirit to authors."

In his later years, the trials became more onerous, especially as tastes in literature began to change and the economics of publishing remained tenuous. Chambers's name continues to surface in the literary world as new books by and about Bobbs-Merrill authors appear, and unfortunately the unflattering portrait of him drawn by Hiram Haydn in *Words & Faces* (1974) still provides the basis for what most people outside of Indiana know about him.

Chambers's place in American publishing deserves further inquiry. While he may have had a quick temper and was unable to appreciate new trends in American literature, Chambers loved good writing. In his later years, he continued to work to bring Bobbs-Merrill back to the forefront of American publishing. Yet, despite such successes as Ayn Rand's *The Fountainhead* (1943), William Styron's *Lie Down in Darkness* (1951), Saunders Redding's *On Being a Negro in America* (1951), and Elmer Davis's *But We Were Born Free* (1954), the firm never attained the prominent position it had once occupied. After long failing health, Chambers died in Indianapolis on his eighty-fourth birthday in 1963, respected and admired by friends and authors throughout the country, but especially in Indiana.

J. KENT CALDER

For Further Reading

Calder, J. Kent. "Ordeal and Renewal: David Laurance Chambers, Hiram Haydn, and *Lie Down in Darkness*." *Journal of Scholarly Publishing* 27 (April 1996).

Clark, Thomas D. Clark. "David Laurance Chambers as I Knew Him." *The Indiana University Bookman* 8 (March 1967).

Schrader, Richard J., ed. *The Hoosier House: Bobbs-Merrill and Its Predecessors, 1850–1985; A Documentary Volume*. In *Dictionary of Literary Biography*, vol. 291. New York: Thomson/Gale, 2004.

Charleston, Oscar

October 14, 1896–October 5, 1954

African American baseball player and manager inducted into the National Baseball Hall of Fame.

During his career, sportswriters dubbed Oscar Charleston the Black Babe Ruth for his slugging power, the Black Ty Cobb for his lightning speed, and the Black Tris Speaker for his tremendous fielding. The first superstar of professional black baseball, Charleston had an amazing forty-three-year career playing for and managing segregated teams. His reputation helped establish and sustain the Negro Leagues through turbulent times.

Charleston was born in Indianapolis and grew up playing on neighborhood sandlots. In 1912 he misrepresented his age, enlisted in the military, and was assigned to the Twenty-fourth Infantry Regiment in the Philippines. There, he honed his baseball skills and became the Twenty-fourth's ace pitcher in the 1914 Manila League. Honorably discharged in 1915, Charleston returned to Indianapolis and joined C. I. Taylor's ABCs, a professional black team. In his first game, the left-hander pitched a three-hit, 7–0 shutout against a semiprofessional white team. Despite this success, Taylor shifted him to center field, where his speed, instinct, and large hands produced amazing "circus catches."

As a young player, Charleston was temperamental. During a 1915 postseason game against

Owen "Donie" Bush's All Stars that included white major and minor leaguers, the ABCs grew frustrated with biased calls. In the fifth inning, Bush was clearly tagged out stealing second, but the white umpire called him safe. When protests escalated from shouting to shoving, Charleston punched the umpire, triggering a near riot. The ABCs spent the offseason in Cuba, and in the spring, Taylor temporarily sent Charleston to the New York Lincoln Giants to avoid racial conflict about the umpire incident. Charleston returned to Indianapolis in June to help the ABCs claim "The Championship of Colored Baseball."

During World War I, after an abridged 1918 season, Charleston enlisted in the Colored Officer Training Program, served briefly, and was discharged after the Armistice. Meanwhile, several other ABCs players served in Europe and had not returned by late February, so Taylor did not field a team in 1919. That season Charleston played for the Chicago American Giants. The following winter, Taylor rebuilt his club and helped establish the Negro National League. Its success required balancing talent among teams, so Charleston returned to Indianapolis and was in center field when the ABCs defeated Joe Green's Chicago Giants in the first game of the new league at Washington Park.

As a top player, Charleston drew offers from other teams, including the Saint Louis Giants, which in 1921 paid him $400 a month, the league's highest salary. This was also his best year statistically, with an amazing .437 batting average. After the season, though, the team owner went bankrupt and Charleston returned to Indianapolis.

The 1922 ABCs were a different team after the death of its owner, Taylor, leaving ownership to his widow, Olivia, and management to his brother. Ben Taylor wanted to sign top talent, but Olivia was afraid to overspend. As a result, players began jumping to other teams, especially after the Eastern Colored League formed in 1923. Charleston stayed in Indianapolis until 1924, when he signed to play for and manage the Harrisburg Giants. Besides a hefty salary, he had another reason for moving to Pennsylvania. On November 24, 1922, he had married Jane Blalock Howard of Harrisburg. However, his nomadic baseball lifestyle did not agree with her, and the couple separated after a few years. They had no children.

Charleston was an immediate celebrity in Harrisburg. In July 1924 the city honored him with Oscar Charleston Day and presented him a wallet containing $500. That season he slugged forty-one home runs and the *Harrisburg Telegraph* tracked his progress alongside that of Ruth, who hit forty-six homers. The Harrisburg Giants thrived through 1924 and 1925, but other Eastern Colored League teams struggled financially. Fearing the league might not survive another full season, Harrisburg entered a second league in 1926. Amazingly, this Interstate League united three black teams and three white—twenty years before Jackie Robinson played his first season with a professional white team. Economics, not racism, caused this league to collapse. The black teams were overwhelmingly superior, so outcomes were predictable and fans stopped attending games.

During the 1926–27 offseason, Charleston signed with the Homestead Grays in Pittsburgh. However, as opening day approached, he returned to the Harrisburg Giants, fearing jumping to a nonleague team might jeopardize his future in organized black baseball. His job as manager had been already filled, so Charleston was only a player during his final season in Harrisburg, moving from center field to first base. The team folded at the end of 1927.

In 1928 and 1929 Charleston played for Ed Bolden's Hilldale Club outside Philadelphia, but when the team finished only third and fourth in the league, he again sought other offers. In 1930 and 1931 he managed and played for the Homestead Grays. The next shift in Charleston's career came in 1932. Pittsburgh nightclub owner Gus Greenlee had purchased a semiprofessional team with plans to develop the club. His first steps were building a new ballpark and hiring Charleston to assemble and manage a star team. Josh Gibson caught for Satchel Paige, joined by Judy Johnson and later Cool Papa Bell. With five future Hall of Famers, the Pittsburgh Crawfords became one of baseball's greatest teams.

Just weeks after the first Major League All-Star Game in 1933, Greenlee promoted a Negro League version. Fans selected participants by submitting ballots published in African American newspapers, and Charleston received the most votes. He also appeared in the 1934 and 1935 games and served as manager, coach, or umpire in other years. While the annual East-West All-Star Game thrived, individual teams struggled during

Oscar Charleston

the Great Depression. In 1937 Dominican Republic President Raphael Trujillo raided the Crawfords to assemble his own dream team, signing Gibson, Paige, and other stars. Charleston chose to remain in Pittsburgh, but in 1938 the city seized the team's home field to build public housing.

Without a facility, the Crawfords moved to Toledo in 1939 but lost many players to other teams. Failing to develop an Ohio fan base, the team moved to Indianapolis in 1940, playing at Perry Stadium when the Indianapolis Indians were away. In his mid-forties, Charleston focused on managing and rarely played. During winter of 1940–41, he planned a new Indianapolis team under his own control, but it never materialized because Charleston was hired to manage the Philadelphia Stars. He kept that position through 1944.

In 1945 professional baseball anticipated great changes as Brooklyn Dodgers general manager Branch Rickey contemplated integration. To better scout black players, he created the Brooklyn Brown Dodgers and hired Charleston as manager. Though not directly involved in signing Robinson, Charleston did help recruit other integration pioneers, including Roy Campanella. Having served Rickey's purpose, the Brown Dodgers folded midseason.

Charleston began his third military enlistment in September 1945 at the Philadelphia Depot. Officially a security guard, his primary duty was managing the depot's fully integrated baseball team. After the war, Charleston led the Philadelphia Stars for five more seasons. He retired in 1950 but remained connected to the game as a scout and occasional umpire.

In 1954 Charleston again donned a jersey of his hometown, this time to manage the Indianapolis Clowns. After claiming the Negro American League pennant, Charleston returned to Philadelphia, where he suffered a stroke and died just nine days before his fifty-eighth birthday. Charleston, who is buried in Floral Park Cemetery in Indianapolis, was inducted into the National Baseball Hall of Fame in 1976.

GERI STRECKER

For Further Reading

Debono, Paul. *The Indianapolis ABCs: History of a Premier Team in the Negro Leagues.* Jefferson, NC: McFarland and Company, 1997.

Lanctot, Neil. *Negro League Baseball: The Rise and Ruin of a Black Institution.* Philadelphia: University of Pennsylvania Press, 2004.

Strecker, Geri. "Indianapolis's Other Oscar: Baseball Great Oscar Charleston." *Traces of Indiana and Midwestern History* 24, no. 3 (Summer 2012): 30–39.

Clark, George Rogers

November 19, 1752–February 13, 1818

Revolutionary War militia officer; first chair of Clarksville, Indiana, board of trustees; and namesake of Clark County, Indiana.

The premier American military hero in the Revolutionary War in the West, George Rogers Clark led the expedition that captured the British forts at Kaskaskia, Cahokia, and Vincennes during 1778–79. The victory was the basis for American claims to the Northwest Territory during negotiation of the 1783 Treaty of Paris. The same year, the Virginia General Assembly granted Clark and his troops 150,000 acres on the north side of the Falls of the Ohio. In addition to creating the town of Clarksville, Clark's Grant forms the core of Clark County and part of eastern Floyd County in southern Indiana.

Born near Charlottesville, Virginia, Clark was the second of ten children born to John and Ann Rogers Clark, a moderately prosperous family with deep roots in Virginia's past. As a youth, he studied mathematics, surveying, history, and geography. An important element of his education was his early frontier experience. In 1772 Clark joined a surveying party that descended the Ohio River and spent two years charting wilderness land in the Kanawha River region. In the process he acquired substantial knowledge of natural history and Native American ways.

Clark's military career began in 1774 when he served as a captain in the Virginia militia during Lord Dunmore's War, which pitted the Shawnee against settlers on the Kanawha frontier. He saw little fighting and missed the final battle at Point Pleasant, yet he displayed a gift for command and learned much about Indian fighting and military organization. After the war, Clark spent several months surveying for the Ohio Company in central Kentucky and aiding the organization of Kentucky County for Virginia. Meanwhile, fighting between colonists and the British erupted in Massachusetts, and over the next two years the rebellion expanded westward. As the war intensified, Clark joined the Kentucky County militia, and by 1777 he was a major and temporary ranking officer in Kentucky. After spending several months attempting to defend scattered settlements against sporadic Indian attacks, he formulated a strategy for a long-distance strike against the British and their Indian allies in the Illinois Country.

In December 1777 Clark laid his strategy before Governor Patrick Henry. Impressed by his audacity and vision, Henry persuaded the general assembly to fund the mission. He also promoted Clark to lieutenant colonel and gave him secret orders to raise a regiment to attack the British forts at Kaskaskia, Cahokia, and Vincennes. Clark and his officers began recruiting volunteers in western Pennsylvania, upland Virginia, and the Holston valley of North Carolina. By early May, 150 men had assembled near the Forks of the Ohio south of Fort Pitt. On May 12 Clark and his troops, along with about a dozen families, departed for the Falls of the Ohio. On May 27, after picking up a few more recruits, the flotilla landed at Corn Island near the falls. After drilling for a month, Clark and his regiment departed for the Illinois Country.

By July 4 Clark was poised at the outskirts of Kaskaskia. During the night the troops broke into the fort and captured the garrison without firing a shot. The next day, a company led by Captain Joseph Bowman captured Cahokia, about sixty miles north, in a similar manner. The following month, the British-governed French garrison at Vincennes, about 240 miles east on the Wabash River, surrendered to Clark after learning of the Franco-American Alliance of 1778. Only Detroit, headquarters of Lieutenant Governor Henry Hamilton, the chief British official in the Northwest, remained in British hands.

Before marching on Detroit, Clark had to deal with the expiring enlistments of his troops. Having exhausted the funds appropriated by the Virginia legislature, he used his own resources and borrowed from friends to continue the campaign. By offering attractive inducements, he persuaded about one hundred men to reenlist and recruited several French militiamen. During the fall of 1778 Clark developed plans to take Detroit. But before he could march, Hamilton counterattacked and captured the poorly defended Fort Sackville at Vincennes in December. Having achieved his first objective, and with winter setting in, Hamilton decided to wait until spring to retake the other two posts. It was a fateful decision.

While Hamilton waited, Clark plotted a surprise attack against Vincennes. After recalling a company from Cahokia and recruiting a company of French volunteers, he crossed the Kaskaskia River on February 5 with about 170 men. For two weeks, they slogged through swamps and rain-swollen rivers. On February 23 they arrived at Vincennes and Clark delivered a surrender ultimatum. Hamilton proposed a truce, but Clark, having deployed his troops to make their number appear much larger and fearful of exposing his weakness, demanded that Hamilton accept or reject his conditions at his peril. Realizing that Clark was unmovable, Hamilton capitulated.

Clark immediately began planning to attack Detroit. But the plan collapsed for lack of troops, and he returned to the Falls of the Ohio and the new village of Louisville, where he spent most of the remainder of the war conducting the defense of the Ohio valley. The goal of taking Detroit was finally achieved through the Treaty of Paris, where American negotiators used Clark's capture of the Northwest forts as the basis for claiming the entire territory, which included the present state of Indiana.

Many of Clark's postwar activities extended his wartime service. A skilled Indian negotiator, he worked out the Treaty of Fort McIntosh in 1785 and the Treaty of Fort Finney in 1786 and joined an expedition against the Wabash Confederacy in southwest Indiana later in 1786. The campaign was a fiasco, but the pressure spurred the tribes to request a council, and peace was arranged in the spring of 1787. Clark also assumed a leading role in administering the Illinois Military Grant awarded by the Virginia legislature in 1783. As chair of the Clarksville board of trustees and the board of commissioners created by the legislation to survey the grant, he played a central role in town governance and land distribution. These responsibilities placed him in a position to advance the interests of military associates who had received large shares of the grant.

Despite his accomplishments, Clark's reputation sank quickly after 1787. Pressured by creditors for repayment of loans he had obtained for the Illinois campaign, he asked for assistance from the Virginia legislature. Turned down several times, he began drinking heavily and became involved in questionable intrigues with Spain and France that caused some to question his loyalty. Clark spent the rest of the century at Mulberry Hill, his parents' Louisville estate, supervising farm work and attempting to untangle his finances. In 1803 he built a cabin on his Clarksville land overlooking the falls. There he received numerous visitors and accomplished some competent studies in natural history. He also hosted Meriwether Lewis and William Clark, his younger brother, as they prepared for their expedition to explore the Louisiana Country in 1803 and welcomed them upon their return in 1806. Alcoholism, however, steadily undermined his health, and in February 1809 he suffered a stroke and fell into his fireplace. The burns required removal of his right leg. Rendered an invalid, he moved to Locust Grove, the home of his sister and brother-in-law, Lucy and William Croghan, outside Louisville. In 1812 the Virginia legislature presented him a sword and a pension of $400 a year in recognition of his service during the revolution. He died at Locust Grove on February 13, 1818.

Clark's name and feats are memorialized in many ways, most notably the George Rogers Clark National Historical Park in Vincennes, located on what is believed to be the site of Fort Sackville. Statues of him can be found elsewhere and a host of schools, counties and streets bear his name.

CARL E. KRAMER

George Rogers Clark

For Further Reading

Bakeless, John. *Background to Glory: The Life of George Rogers Clark*. Philadelphia: B Lippincott, 1957.

Carstens, Kenneth G., and Nancy Son, eds. *The Life of George Rogers Clark, 1752–1818: Triumphs and Tragedies*. Westport, CT: Praeger, 2004.

James, James Alton. *Life of George Rogers Clark*. Chicago: University of Chicago Press, 1928.

Clarke, Grace Julian

September 11, 1865–June 18, 1938

Clubwoman, author, newspaper columnist, editor, and tireless advocate for women's suffrage.

That Grace Julian Clarke would become one of the most politically active women in Indiana in the late nineteenth and early twentieth centuries was virtually preordained. She was the daughter of George Washington Julian, an abolitionist and the first member of Congress to introduce a resolution calling for women's suffrage, and Laura Giddings, daughter of Joshua Giddings, also a congressman, abolitionist, and advocate for women's suffrage. Clarke devoted her life to multiple reform efforts, especially to the cause of women's suffrage, and to that end she helped found and lead numerous organizations for women. Simultaneously, she was an editor and columnist for the *Indianapolis Star* for eighteen years.

Born in Centerville, Wayne County, Indiana in 1865, Grace was eight when her family moved to Irvington, an Indianapolis neighborhood her uncle, Jacob B. Julian, helped to found. She was educated in the local public schools and later attended Butler University, where she received her bachelor's degree in philosophy in 1884 and master's degree in philosophy in 1885. She married attorney Charles B. Clarke in 1887. He had been a U.S. deputy surveyor general under her father in the New Mexico Territory. Charles, a Democrat, was an Indiana state senator in 1913 and 1915.

Clarke's first exposure to women's organizations occurred when her mother and several other prominent women in 1875 established the Indianapolis Woman's Club, created to help women reconcile "intellectual and domestic work." In comments published on the club's fiftieth anniversary, Clarke wrote that her mother believed that women with families needed "to belong to a club more than women who go to college, because the young ladies have to study anyway, but the [other] ladies might not if they didn't have the club."

Organizations such as the Indianapolis Woman's Club provided training for future leaders of community affairs and the women's suffrage movement. Clarke, who became one of the leading feminists of her day, is a perfect example. Although she belonged to many women's organizations, she devoted most of her time and energy to three that she helped to found and lead: the Indiana State Federation of Women's Clubs, the Women's Franchise League, and the Legislative Council.

The Indiana Federation of Women's Clubs, founded in 1900, eventually became the Indiana Federation of Clubs. Clarke's involvement with the federation grew out of her participation in the Irvington Women's Club, basically a literary club, which she started and served as president. Concerned that literary clubs remained "too far apart from the great world issues," she became interested in the federation, an organization she thought would be "perfectly rounded" and "satisfying." Clarke served as president of the federation from 1909 to 1911. The federation included 7,000 women in 185 clubs around the state.

Initially the federation mainly supported such measures as fair housing, child labor laws, and working conditions for women, but in Clarke's first term as president the organization endorsed the idea of "municipal suffrage," meaning women would be allowed to vote in municipal and school board elections. The Indiana Constitution at the time limited voting for state elections to males. Suffrage leaders thought that left room to extend suffrage to elections not covered by the constitution.

The federation was affiliated with the national General Federation of Women's Clubs, of which Clarke served as a director and press chairman. When the issue of women's suffrage created dissension within the General Federation, Clarke worked to get Indiana and other states to endorse it, but many states, particularly southern states, were not ready to commit to the cause. Clarke did not want to drive out these women because she said they needed the education and that "they would get it much more slowly" if they left the organization.

Clarke was also a founder of the Women's Franchise League, which began as the Women's School Commission in 1909, when Clarke and other women started a campaign to elect a school principal to a local school board. Following their success in this effort, the organization adopted the name the Women's School League, with Clarke as president. The School League endorsed "municipal suffrage" because members thought partial suffrage would command more support than full suffrage. The organization changed its name in 1911 to the Women's Franchise League and quickly became one of the leading suffragist organizations in the state with sixty branches and 3,000 members. Clarke served as director for several years. Although the constitution made no mention of suffrage, Clarke optimistically wrote to Ida Husted Harper, a fellow Hoosier working for suffrage at the national level, that by changing the name they would be "free to ask for full suffrage" in the next general assembly. The Franchise League was affiliated with the National American Woman Suffrage Association.

After women failed to achieve reform proposals in the Indiana legislature in 1913, Clarke decided that women needed a statewide organization that could empower disenfranchised women to promote legislation concerning women and children. Clarke based the Legislative Council on a similar program in California. The council was essentially a lobbying organization that one scholar called "the most outstanding accomplishment of Hoosier female reformers during the progressive years [1900 to 1920]." Women enthusiastically embraced the Legislative Council and elected Clarke president. The council represented fifty thousand to eighty thousand women.

The council did not initially support women's suffrage but ended up endorsing the idea of partial suffrage. Council members spent a great deal of time lobbying for it in 1915 and felt confident they would succeed. What they did not count on was the power of the liquor interests, who defeated both prohibition and women's suffrage legislation. Despite the setbacks the Legislative Council did succeed in many ways, thanks to the organizing concept introduced by Clarke. By uniting women throughout the state, the council became a powerful lobbying force by bringing divergent groups together to work toward goals that they agreed upon.

Agreement on goals, however, did not always reduce conflict as evidenced by the virtual war that broke out in November 1915 among the members of the Federation of Clubs over the selection of a new president, and it had serious ramifications for the Federation of Clubs, the Franchise League, and Clarke. The issue arose when Stella Stimson, a member of both the Franchise League and the Federation of Clubs from Terre Haute, made a personal attack against Lenora Cox, also from Terre Haute and a member of both the federation and the league. Stimson charged that Cox was not a fit candidate to be president of the federation because her husband owned a tavern, making her a candidate of the liquor interests. Furthermore, Stimson said that Cox "smoked and served beer in her home." While the dispute initially was limited to tersely worded letters among members of both organizations, and especially between Clarke, who backed Cox for president, and Stimson, it gained public attention in 1915 when the directors of the Franchise League, including Clarke, voted to remove Stimson from their board because of her personal attacks on Cox and stories began to appear in newspapers across the state. Cox was defeated for the presidency and Caroline Fairbank of Fort Wayne was elected instead. Ironically, after Fairbank's election, federation members learned that she owned stock in a brewery and admitted that she kept beer in her home, which she drank whenever she pleased.

As Cox's campaign manager this episode was the first political defeat for Clarke. She was criticized for exercising poor judgment in letting personal friendships take precedence over larger issues. The whole episode demoralized Clarke to the point that she seriously considered withdrawing from both organizations, but many of her supporters begged her not to abandon them, and she did not.

In 1917 the general assembly passed a partial suffrage bill and a measure to call a constitutional convention to address the suffrage issue. However, the Indiana Supreme Court invalidated both measures as unconstitutional. In 1919 victory finally came when the U.S. Congress passed the women's suffrage amendment. Governor James P. Goodrich called a special session of the general assembly, and on January 20, 1920, Indiana became the twenty-sixth state to ratify the amendment. Final victory came on August 20, when Tennessee ratified the Nineteenth Amendment. More than a hundred women attended a celebration luncheon in Indianapolis and Clarke was one of the speakers.

After suffrage was achieved, many of the women's organizations began to fade away. The Franchise League voted in May 1920 to dissolve and to form a new group—the League of Women Voters of Indiana, paralleling a similar move by NAWSA at the national level. Clarke continued to work with the league, but she also became actively involved in the peace movement, supporting the League to Support Peace and the ratification of the League of Nations. Many Hoosiers were critical of her for this unpopular effort, and one denounced her as a "traitor."

After many years of poor health, Clarke died in 1938 at the age of seventy-two. She was memorialized at a meeting of the Indianapolis Woman's Club for "converting the women of Indiana to a sense of their political responsibility." It was said that she "fought for the causes in which she believed, always for the public good rather than her own private gain . . . [and] her best efforts were given to Votes for Women."

LINDA C. GUGIN

For Further Reading

Clarke, Grace Julian. Papers. Indiana State Library. Indianapolis.
Springer, Barbara. "Lady Like Reformers: Indiana Women and Progressive Reform, 1900–1920." PhD diss., Indiana University, Bloomington, 1985.

Clowes Family

Doctor George Henry Alexander, August 27, 1877–August 25, 1958; Edith Whitehill Hinkel, September 21, 1885–May 22, 1967; Doctor George Henry Alexander Jr., 1915–1988; and Allen Whitehill, 1917–2000

The family, headed by a pioneering Eli Lilly chemist, created and funded philanthropic organizations providing significant support to the arts and education in Indiana.

On Christmas Day 1921 the father of two young sons left his family to their gifts and began to make his way from Indianapolis to New Haven, Connecticut, in anticipation of a presentation by Doctor Frederick Banting. A Canadian scientist and physician, Banting was scheduled to speak about an important discovery he and another scientist had made regarding the isolation and use of insulin in the treatment of diabetes in dogs—a topic that the traveling father, Doctor George Henry Alexander Clowes, was keen to know more about. Better known to family and friends as Alec or Doc, Clowes had recently become the research director of Eli Lilly and Company and suspected that Banting's speech would represent a major opportunity for drugmakers. It also proved to be a turning point in Clowes's own life.

Clowes, who was born on August 27, 1877, studied at a number of major European universities before obtaining his PhD in chemistry from the University of Goettingen in 1899. He moved to the United States in 1901 to work as a chemist for the New York State Institute for the Study of Malignant Disease in Buffalo. In 1918, during his wartime service with the U.S. Army, he spent time at the Marine Biological Laboratories in Woods Hole, Massachusetts, studying the physiological effects of mustard gas. The next year he was hired as a research specialist by Eli Lilly and Company and moved to Indianapolis with his wife, Edith Whitehill Hinkel, whom he had married in 1910, and their two sons, George Jr. and Allen.

By October 1923, as a result of Clowes's attendance at Banting's presentation on insulin and his ensuing contact with Banting's research team, Lilly became the first drug company to test, manufacture, license, and market insulin for the treatment of diabetes—an achievement that still stands as one of Lilly's greatest. Clowes's career with Lilly continued for another four decades, including a long stint as director emeritus, during which he oversaw a number of other important pharmaceutical developments, including the mass production of penicillin and other revolutionary antibiotics.

These professional achievements allowed Clowes and his family to enjoy a comfortable life, spending summers at their second home in Woods Hole, known as Easterley, and filling their Indianapolis home, Westerley, with renowned works of European art, including those by Rembrandt Harmenszoon van Rijn, Peter Paul Rubens, El Greco, and John Constable. Clowes also became active in the Indianapolis art scene, serving as director of the John Herron Art Institute, vice president of the Art Association of Indianapolis, and president of the Indianapolis Symphony Orchestra. He was also an avid supporter of education, sitting on the board of the Orchard School and acting as a trustee of the Park School, now known as Park Tudor. With his wife, Clowes established the Clowes Fund in 1952 to support education and the fine, literary, and performing arts, a mission that the fund continues to this day. Clowes died on August 25, 1958, after suffering a stroke at Woods Hole.

Clowes's wife, Edith, who was born in Buffalo, New York, on September 21, 1885, studied for two years at Vassar College. Upon moving to Indianapolis, she worked with eight other women to found the Orchard School, which both of her sons attended. As her children grew, she took an active role in raising funds for the Park School, establishing the Park School House and Garden Tour, a popular event that served as a major source of revenue for the institution. She was also a founding board member of Planned Parenthood of Indianapolis and served and supported a number of local art and cultural groups. After her husband's death, she and her sons oversaw the transfer of the family's art collection to the Clowes Fund, and in an effort to celebrate the life of Clowes, worked to establish a permanent home for the ISO. This project resulted in the construction of Clowes Memorial Hall on the campus of Butler University.

Edith and her son, Allen, via the Clowes Fund, contributed $2 million and countless hours to the project, which celebrated its opening night on October 18, 1963, with a concert by the ISO. This gala event marked the beginning of a new era of theatrical, musical, and performance art in Indiana. As a local television station reported that night, "Clowes Hall represents the most advanced thinking in European and American design, comfort, and beauty." National and international news outlets deemed the building to be dazzling; Indianapolis "wasn't just a cow town anymore." Over the following years, Clowes Memorial Hall hosted some of the world's most famous performers and cultural icons.

In recognition of her many contributions to Indianapolis society, Edith received an honorary doctor of humane letters degree from Butler University in 1962. She died on May 22, 1967, and so did not see the departure of the ISO in 1984 from the home she built for it. Allen noted that had she, it would have been one of the greatest disappointments of her life.

Allen, who lived most of his adulthood in the family home in Indianapolis, continued his parents' philanthropic endeavors. While working as an investment counselor, he devoted much of his time to the affairs of the Clowes Fund and also established the Allen Whitehill Clowes Charitable Foundation Inc., which continues to support organizations that promote and preserve the arts and humanities. Projects of Allen's foundation include the Allen Whitehill Clowes Curatorial Fellowship and the Allen Whitehill Clowes Gallery for Special Exhibitions at the Indianapolis Museum of Art. Allen died in 2000.

Allen and his brother, Doctor George H. A. Clowes Jr., also supported the Clowes Fund's donation of artwork and money to the IMA, leading to the development of the Clowes Collection of Old Masterworks and the Clowes Pavilion in which the collection is housed. The family home, Westerley, was bequeathed to the museum and now serves as the director's residence. In total, the Clowes Fund has transferred more than $22 million in artwork to the museum, with another $32 million to be donated in the coming years; additionally, the IMA has received more than $5 million in construction and maintenance funds. While George left Indianapolis to pursue a career as a surgeon and professor of medicine, spending much of his career in Boston and dying, like his father, of a stroke at Woods Hole, his children and grandchildren play an active role in the administration of the family fund.

DORIA M. LYNCH

For Further Reading

Clowes Family Collection, 1842–1998, M 1028. William Henry Smith Memorial Library, Indiana Historical Society, Indianapolis, IN.

The Show Goes On: Clowes Memorial Hall at 50. Broadcast WFYI Television, Indianapolis, 2013. Produced and edited by Kyle Travers. http://www.wfyi.org/programs/the-show-goes-on/television/the-show-goes-on-clowes-memorial-hall-at-50.

The Coffins

Levi, October 28, 1798–September 16, 1877, and Catharine, September 10, 1803–May 22, 1881

Quaker abolitionists actively involved in the Underground Railroad and owners and operators of a free-goods store and warehouse.

Devout Quakers Levi Coffin and his wife, Catharine, left their native North Carolina in 1826, where they had seen the treatment of slaves firsthand, and came to Indiana because it was a free state. The couple settled in Newport (present-day Fountain City) and Levi established a general store that was later expanded to include the processing of flax seed for linseed oil and pork butchering. Coffin's success in business was of critical importance to his role in the Underground Railroad movement. Due to the wealth that he accumulated in his business, he became a director of the Richmond Branch of the Second State Bank of Indiana. He relied on his prominence in the community to galvanize support for the Underground Railroad and his business prosperity helped underwrite the burdensome expenses of the Underground Railroad.

Levi operated his business consistent with his abolitionist beliefs. He excluded all products made with slave labor, such as coffee, molasses, sugar, and cotton cloth. When he could not find cotton for products he wanted to sell he organized poor white farmers to sell their free-labor cotton, arranged for them to purchase a cotton gin in exchange for their cotton, and then transported cotton by free labor to be used for products such as twine, cotton yarn, and muslin.

The Coffins involvement with the Underground Railroad started during their first year in Indiana. In his *Reminiscences* Levi said he "inherited his anti-slavery principles" from his parents and grandparents, who never owned slaves and were "friends of the oppressed."

The Coffins helped on average about one hundred slaves a year escape to freedom, and approximately two thousand slaves gained freedom during their twenty-year stay in Indiana. Slaves traveling from Cincinnati, Madison, New Albany, and Jeffersonville found a safe haven in the Coffin's home. Levi kept a team ready at all times to transport slaves to places farther along the Underground Railroad. He said of Catharine, a full partner in the enterprise: "It was never too cold or stormy, or the hour of night too late, for my wife to rise from sleep, and provide food and comfortable lodging for the fugitives. Her sympathy for those in distress never tired, and her efforts in their behalf never abated." Levi was often asked by southern slave holders to aid former slaves who had been freed and moved to a free state by their white masters, including the

The Levi Coffin home in Fountain City, Indiana

masters' own children and their enslaved mothers. So many slaves passed through the Coffin house on their way to points farther north that Levi was often referred to as the "President of the Underground Railroad."

Levi's neighbors, encouraged by his example of sheltering runaways in his home, became involved with the activities of the Underground Railroad. They raised money to purchase shoes and clothing for escaped slaves, and Levi arranged for them to provide medical treatment to escaped slaves. Some neighbors hid fugitive slaves in their homes and drove them in wagons to the next depot. Young women of the town aided the cause by forming a sewing society that frequently met in the Coffin house to make clothing for the women and children.

Although some neighbors willingly collaborated in the Underground Railroad, others were more critical. Some boycotted the store. Levi's friends feared for his safety because of threats by slave hunters. Despite such threats he neither used nor carried a gun. Since his local work for temperance caused several people to leave town who were not in agreement with radical Quaker views, the community lost dissenters who might have objected to Levi's other practices.

In his *Reminiscences* Levi explained how his business influence and extensive group of acquaintances afforded him protection against legal action for his efforts to help fugitive slaves. Through his service as director of the Richmond branch of the Bank of Indiana, Levi was in a strategic position to influence whatever help his potential enemies sought from the bank. "This" he said, "seem[ed] to hold a check on some of the pro-slavery men of our neighborhood." Levi also warned that anyone who trespassed on his property trying to recapture runaway slaves without the proper paperwork would be subject to litigation and claimed that he had multiple people who would support him in his legal efforts.

Despite the openness of their activities, the Coffin home was never searched. Under the federal fugitive slave law it was a crime to harbor runaways, but enforcement of the law depended on the sympathies of the authorities. On one occasion Levi was brought before a grand jury in Centerville, Indiana, and though he freely admitted that he sheltered escaped slaves there was not enough evidence to bring charges against him in the abolitionist county seat.

In 1847 the Coffins moved to Cincinnati to operate a free-labor goods warehouse. Levi was reluctant to move, but he bowed to pressures from the Salem Free Produce Association in the East to take over the management of the Western Free Produce Association. This consisted of a warehouse that sold goods produced by free labor until 1856 and after that he operated a boardinghouse. While in Cincinnati he continued his Underground Railroad activities, helping 1,300 additional freedom seekers to safety.

When the Civil War started the Coffins were still engaged in Underground Railroad work, but they took on new responsibilities. In December of 1862 Levi traveled to Cairo, Illinois, to investigate the conditions of the people the army called "contrabands," slaves who escaped to Union territory or who were taken behind Union lines. In 1863 he was named General Agent for the Western Freedman's Aid Commission, opened an office and warehouse to coordinate the logistics of relief, and traveled the Ohio valley soliciting assistance; he sent boxes of clothing, blankets, farming tools, school books plus teachers and agents to the Freedmen. He traveled to Washington, D.C., to urge Secretary of the Treasury Salmon Chase and Secretary of War Edwin Stanton and to lobby President ABRAHAM LINCOLN to establish the Freedmen's Bureau to provide assistance to freed slaves. He remained active in Freedmen activities for the rest of his life, including making trips abroad and raising funds. In 1867 he attended the International Anti-Slavery Convention in Paris. He died in September 1877, and Catharine died four years later in May of 1881. Both are buried in Spring Grove Cemetery in Cincinnati.

In 1966, in recognition of its historic significance, the Levi Coffin house was designated as a National Historic Landmark by the United States Department of Interior. The following year it was purchased by the state and restored and opened to the public in 1970.

RONALD VAUGHN MORRIS

For Further Reading

Coffin, Levi. *Reminiscences of Levi Coffin.* Cincinnati: Western Tract Society, 1876.

Yannessa, MaryAnn. *Levi Coffin, Quaker: Breaking the Bonds of Slavery in Indiana and Ohio.* Richmond, IN: Friends United Press, 2001.

Coffin, Rhoda M.

February 1, 1826–September 28, 1909

Prominent Quaker reformer; established the first female-controlled women's prison in Indiana and the United States.

A leading figure in humanitarian and reform work in late-nineteenth-century Indiana, Rhoda Coffin was instrumental in establishing a female-controlled women's prison in Indianapolis in 1873—an accomplishment that placed her in the vanguard of the national prison reform movement, catapulted her into the national spotlight, and significantly changed the prison system in the United States. Although Coffin's reform accomplishments are substantial, her career also illustrates how nineteenth-century women reformers negotiated a blurred and evolving landscape of expectations and roles in public reform—a landscape characterized by benevolent works justified by women's inherent moral attributes, on one hand, and campaigns for legislative change and political advocacy for women's rights on the other.

Born in 1826 near Paintersville, Ohio, to a well-to-do Quaker farm family, Rhoda Johnson was raised in the strict Quaker practices of plain dress and speech and separation from the outside world. In 1845 her world broadened when she enrolled at the Whitewater Monthly Meeting School in Richmond, Indiana. A midwestern center for American Quakerism, Richmond was home to the Indiana Yearly Meeting, the largest Quaker organization in the country, which brought thousands of Quakers to the city and exposed its inhabitants to worldly religious ideas and attitudes. It was here that Rhoda met Charles Coffin, son of Elijah Coffin, the clerk (presiding officer) of IYM and a respected banker. The two were married in 1847 and began a lifelong partnership in reform work.

Although the Coffins engaged in benevolent activities in 1850s, it was a 1860s prayer meeting at IYM, organized by Charles and Rhoda and other young Quakers, that energized and enabled more organized and ambitious efforts. Subscribing to Quaker Joseph John Gurney's vision of a Society of Friends fully engaged in charitable works in the world, the Coffins and their friends defied the old guard's adherence to separatist ideals by fully embracing the Gurneyite movement.

Addressing the needs of a Richmond entrenched in poverty from economic downturns and the effects of the Civil War, the Coffins in 1864 established the Marion Street Sabbath School, designed to spread the gospel and aid the physical needs of families. Based on its success, Rhoda and other Quaker women organized a Home Mission Association in 1866 to unite Orthodox Quakers' reform efforts to hold prayer meeting, distribute religious tracts, establish Sunday Schools, and visit jails. Seven hundred women attended the association's organizational meeting and Rhoda was elected its president. In 1868 the association established the Home for Friendless Women to nurture the physical and spiritual needs of downtrodden women in the city. Through all of these benevolent activities, Rhoda gained important leadership and organizational skills while working closely with her husband to accomplish her goals.

The Coffins' work with the Marion Street Sabbath School alerted them to prison and reformatory needs and concerns. Noticing that Richmond boys with little parental supervision contributed to the city's crime rate, Charles attempted to convince Indiana governor OLIVER P. MORTON, a childhood friend, that the state needed a reformatory for boys. Morton appointed a commission to investigate and as a result the House of Refuge for Juvenile Defenders was founded in Plainfield in 1867 and Charles was appointed board president. Lobbying with Charles for this institution gave Rhoda a taste for politics and secured the Coffins' reputation as reformatory advocates. In 1868 Governor Conrad Baker requested that they visit Indiana's two state penitentiaries and report on their condition. Rhoda was disgusted by the treatment of the women inmates who were abused and mistreated by male guards and recommended that a separate female prison be constructed and managed by "God-fearing" women.

On May 13, 1869, after months of lobbying, the Indiana legislature passed the bill establishing the Indiana Reformatory Institute for Women and Girls, with the stipulation that a visiting board comprised of men and women and a managing board comprised solely of men direct it. Rhoda was appointed to the first board of visitors. Although she had not secured a female-controlled management, her success in securing the female prison brought her renown in prison reform circles and placed her squarely in a larger movement focused on the rehabilitation of female inmates. Throughout the 1870s, Rhoda traveled widely, attending the first National Prison Conference in 1870 and with Charles visiting prison systems in Europe and the Middle East.

Only a few years after its opening on October 8, 1873, the Indiana Reformatory Institute received national acclaim for its accomplishments. Its internal management, however, was problematic. Despite Rhoda's insistence that women manage all aspects of the operation, the reformatory's board of managers, comprised of men, had full financial control and sought to oversee domestic issues as well. Rhoda and the board of visitors took the matter to the Indiana legislature and in 1876 to a national audience by addressing the National Prison Conference about the importance of female-controlled women's prisons. In 1877 her efforts were successful and after an investigation of the managers' poor financial management practices, the legislature passed a bill creating a new female board. As the first prison operated solely by women in the United States, the Indiana Reformatory Institute set the standard for prison reform in the state and nation. Governor James D. Williams described it as the "best managed institution in the State" and ordered all state institutions to model their reports on those of the institute. A recognized expert on female prisons, Rhoda soon was asked to write articles and speak at prison conferences.

Although Rhoda's experiences in prison reform shaped her thinking about women's rights, a battle to secure a female physician for the Indiana Hospital for the Insane had the greatest impact. In 1880 Rhoda and others attempted to persuade the hospital's board of managers that the asylum needed a woman doctor on staff to care for female patients. The male board was uncooperative and finally demanded a recommendation from Governor Albert Porter, who tried to evade the request. However, persistence prevailed and Doctor Sarah Stockton joined the staff. Rhoda later declared, "I came out of that contest a full-fledged woman suffragist. If a vote was necessary before I could succeed in getting a woman physician to care for the helpless of my sex, I decided that I must have a vote."

Coffin believed women's Christian morality was an important force in society and through her benevolent works she promoted women's roles as wife and mother. However "combating abuses against female prisoners and fighting legislative battles shaped her increasingly progressive stance for women's equity." By the 1880s, "Coffin had recognized the need for political rights to bolster the power of moral suasion" in fighting for reform.

In July 1884 a devastating bank scandal clouded the Coffins' reform reputation. The Richmond bank Charles directed failed and was placed in receivership. Not only did the Coffins lose much of their wealth, but the community also blamed Charles and the couple's sons for the bank's demise due to extending large, unsecured loans for speculative purposes, mismanagement, and embezzlement. The city exploded with anger and the Coffins were forced to remove to Chicago. In 1886 Charles escaped conviction in the courts but was disowned by his church.

It is unclear whether Rhoda knew about the poor banking practices of her husband and children but in the public's eye she was guilty by association. For the next twenty-five years, Rhoda continued to work for prison reform, wrote articles, and served on the Protective Agency for Women and Children, albeit with less fanfare and acclaim.

Coffin died September 28, 1909. Her family brought her back to Richmond for burial in the Earlham Cemetery. Time had healed many of the old wounds and Richmond honored its daughter for the great work she accomplished for Hoosier women.

ELLEN SWAIN

For Further Reading

Charles F. and Rhoda M. Coffin Collection, 1831–1919. Friends Collection and Earlham College Archives. Earlham College, Richmond, IN.

Johnson, Mary Coffin, ed. *Rhoda M. Coffin: Her Reminiscences, Addresses, Papers and Ancestry*. New York: Grafton Press, 1910.

Swain, Ellen D. "From Benevolence to Reform: The Evolving Career of Mrs. Rhoda M. Coffin." *Indiana Magazine of History* 97 (September 2001): 190–217.

Conn, Charles Gerard

January 29, 1844–January 5, 1931

Decorated Civil War veteran, inventor, entrepreneur, politician, journalist, author, publisher, philosopher, musician, art collector, yachtsman, world-record-setting fisherman, and philanthropist.

Although not a native Hoosier, Charles G. Conn moved westward in 1848 with his parents to settle in Elkhart, Indiana. An upper-middle-class, musical family, the Conns were actively involved in the city's cultural and educational life. Gerard, as he was known, studied the violin and became a proficient cornetist under the tutelage of his father, Charles, an esteemed Elkhart educator and school superintendent.

Shortly after the Civil War began, Conn, then seventeen years old, enlisted in the Union army as a private in Company B, Fifteenth Indiana Volunteers. When it was discovered that he was not yet eighteen, he was transferred to the regimental band before being discharged. Determined to reenlist, in 1863 Conn joined Company G of the First Michigan Sharpshooters, where he was eventually promoted to second lieutenant in charge of the battalion band. The sharpshooters faced fierce combat the following year, during which Conn was superficially wounded. Days before he was to receive a field promotion to captain, the twenty-year-old was captured at the siege of Petersburg, Virginia, and spent the remainder of the war in Confederate prisons, his two attempts at escape failed. Sixty-one years later, in 1926, Conn was belatedly awarded the Silver Star for heroism at the battle of Spotsylvania.

Conn remained active in Indiana's military affairs after the war and in 1884 organized Company B of the First Regiment of Artillery in the Indiana Legion—the predecessor of the Indiana Militia and the Indiana National Guard—and served as its first major and colonel. In 1886 he was named chief of artillery and colonel of Governor Isaac P. Gray's military staff, a designation by which he was known for the rest of his life.

Conn pursued several different lines of work following the war, including helping out in his father's grocery store, making zinc collar pads for horses, selling health-care products under the name "Konn's Kurative Kream," and selling sewing machines. During the fall of 1874, he invented a rubber-rimmed mouthpiece for brass instruments. After developing a process for bonding rubber to metal, Conn added his new rubber rim to other manufacturers' mouthpieces. He obtained patents in the United States, England, France, Belgium, and Canada, and began manufacturing his own mouthpieces, using improvised machinery made from parts left over from his sewing machine business. Conn's first musical instrument, a cornet, was produced in Elkhart in April 1876 with the assistance of his new partner, the French instrument maker, Eugene Dupont. Conn and Dupont remained in business together for three years, after which Conn took over sole ownership of his growing company.

By the end of the nineteenth century Conn's company had become the largest musical instrument manufacturer in the world. The secrets to Conn's success lay in the entrepreneur's recognition of the industrial significance of Elkhart's location as a railroad hub; by his harnessing energy from the Saint Joseph and Elkhart Rivers in the city's new hydraulic system; by importing skilled French, English, and German musical instrument craftsmen to supplement a core group of local workers; by soliciting the endorsements of some of the world's leading band musicians; and by aggressively advertising his products in the United States and abroad.

Conn's success as a leader in the Elkhart business community did not go unnoticed. In 1880, at the age of thirty-six, he was elected the city's first Democratic mayor. Conn resigned during his second two-year term to attend to the rebuilding of his factory, which was destroyed by fire on January 29, 1883—his thirty-ninth birthday. He recovered quickly and, by the end of that same year, Conn's new Elkhart Lighting Company sent out the city's first electric current to illuminate the city's business district. Shortly thereafter, Conn announced his vision of establishing outlets for his musical products in large cities nationwide. His first business venture outside Elkhart was the establishment in 1887 of a distribution and instrument repair shop in Worcester, Massachusetts.

Conn served a term in the Indiana General Assembly in 1889 representing Elkhart, Noble, and De Kalb Counties and served on three committees, chairing the panel on military affairs. A strong advocate of labor, Conn supported a bill establishing an eight-hour workday.

In October 1889 Conn founded the *Elkhart Truth*, the city newspaper that continues today under that name. Even after his election to Congress as the Thirteenth District representative, Conn maintained control over the newspaper's editorial columns. When not on Capitol Hill, Conn set out on a personal mission to uncover vice and crime in the capital city. He purchased the *Washington Times* newspaper in 1894 and used its editorial pages to target corruption, beginning with the local police force. Following his acquittal from an indictment for libel, Conn sold the paper and returned to Elkhart. Numerous attempts to lure him back into public office failed despite calls for his renomination to Congress, calls for a presidential run, a motion at the Democratic National Convention in 1896 to nominate him for vice president, and several attempts to entice him to run for governor.

Conn's passion was clearly rooted in the musical instrument industry. In a voluntary move to distribute some of his company's profits among the employees, Conn introduced a widely admired profit-sharing plan in 1891. He established the Conn Conservatory of Music in Elkhart in 1896 to train music teachers. He phased out his Worcester, Massachusetts, outlet by 1898 and in its place established a retail store in New York City for the sale of his Wonder line of instruments.

In 1906, slightly more than a year after the formation of the C.G. Conn Company, it became the first industry of its kind to open its doors exclusively to union labor with the establishment of Local Number 335 of the Metal Polishers, Buffers, Platers, Brass Moulders, Brass and Silver Workers International Union of North America. The union was broken, however, in early 1910 over wage disputes. Ten days later, the company was dissolved and reverted to sole ownership by Conn.

A fire destroyed Conn's factory later in 1910. The plant burned while Conn was deep-sea fishing off his yacht near Catalina Island, California, a favorite vacation spot where he had maintained a residence since 1909. Conn's business losses amounted to $500,000, in addition to the loss of several valuable oil paintings stored in the factory. Upon his return to Elkhart four days later, Conn announced that he would rebuild his Elkhart facility on a portion of his own farmland near the edge of town. Work began on the facility in August and the Spanish Mission-style factory was in full operation four months later.

The Conn dynasty ended in 1915 with the entrepreneur's retirement and sale of the company. A corporation in which Carl Dimond Greenleaf was the principal stockholder purchased the instrument factory, as well as almost all of Conn's other Elkhart investments, including the newspaper and real estate. While Conn was wrapping up his affairs in Elkhart, another fire in 1915 destroyed virtually all of the hotels and residences in Avalon, on Catalina Island, California, including Conn's vacation home. Fortunately, local citizens managed to save the portion of Conn's art collection, valued at $460,000, on display in Avalon.

Following the sale of his company, Conn left both Elkhart and his wife in June 1916. He settled in Los Angeles with his longtime mistress and their son. Conn returned to Elkhart only once after that, to visit his sister in 1926. During his retirement, the self-made millionaire encountered many more difficulties, lost heavily in the stock market crash of 1929, and faced turbulent personal and family problems (his daughter suffered from schizophrenia). The company that Conn created, however, lived on and flourished under the leadership of the Greenleaf family. Today the spirit of the company and its indomitable founder lives on in Conn-Selmer Inc., a subsidiary of Steinway Musical Instruments Inc., purchased in 2013 by Paulson & Company, the hedge fund owned by billionaire John Paulson.

Conn died at his home in Los Angeles in 1931 at the age of eighty-seven, with his second wife and their son at his side. To help Conn's widow cover final expenses during the depressed national economy, the members of the Elkhart Masonic Lodge paid for Conn's remains to be returned to Elkhart and buried in Grace Lawn Cemetery, where a memorial headstone was erected in 1937.

MARGARET DOWNIE BANKS

For Further Reading

Banks, Margaret Downie. "Conn." In *The Grove Dictionary of American Music*. Second Edition. Vol. 2. New York: Oxford University Press, 2013.

Conn, Charles G., Ben Gordon Whitehead, and Bruno David Usher. *Charles Gerard Conn: A Brief Sketch of Life*. Los Angeles, 1926.

Deahl, Anthony, ed. *A Twentieth Century History and Biographical Record of Elkhart County, Indiana*. Chicago and New York: Lewis Publishing Company, 1905.

Conner, William

December 10, 1777–August 28, 1855

Pioneer, entrepreneur, and state legislator.

William Conner was an important figure in Indiana history, both for what he accomplished and what he represented. In many ways his was a quintessentially American story, one abounding in the icons of the American consciousness: Indians, pioneers, the foreboding frontier, even the international economy.

Conner was born on the frontier's jagged edge that was the Moravian mission town of Lichtenau, Ohio, in 1777. His father, Richard, was a sometime trader, sometime tavern keeper; his mother a one-time captive of the Shawnee who was ransomed by his father for two hundred dollars.

Caught in the crossfire of the Revolutionary War, the Conners joined the Delaware (Lenape) and the missionaries on their British-forced removal to Michigan. When the Moravians and their converts later returned to Ohio, Richard and his family remained in Michigan. Eventually purchasing more than four thousand acres of land in what became Macomb County, Richard established a trading post and facilitated settlement.

Although he acquired land from his father, William also inherited his father's sense of wanderlust and his trader's instincts. By 1795 William was trading with the Native Americans around Saginaw Bay.

Conner joined his older brother, John, in Indiana during the winter of 1801–2, with both serving as agents for a Canadian fur trader. The brothers settled among the Delaware, who had been removed to Indiana in 1795 and lived in villages strung along the White River from north of present-day Indianapolis to modern Muncie. Both married Delaware women; according to legend, William's wife, Mekinges, was the daughter of Chief Anderson. Traders often found it to their advantage to marry into the tribes with which they dealt. It eased their way into the community and helped assure a feeling of loyalty, increasing their influence and allowing them to exert some control over the actions of the tribe. Traders often became unofficial liaison officers between the "their Indians" and the white world and government.

Conner soon attached himself to the land that now bears his name. The two-hundred-acre prairie, hard by the White River, was an ideal location for both agriculture and trade. His double-pen log cabin doubled as a trading post and he began raising a family. Officially licensed traders since 1801, the brothers' activities made them a part of a complex economic network well on its way to eroding many aspects of Native American life and culture. An old pattern in which newcomers first came looking for the bounty of the land and then cast covetous eyes toward the land itself was being retraced in Indiana. The dependence engendered by the trade allowed the government to manipulate and coerce tribes into ceding their homelands. The Conners had small but vital roles in the process.

John was the first to officially perform duties for the government, serving in several capacities under the territorial governor, WILLIAM HENRY HARRISON. William appears to have eschewed any official role prior to 1811, but increasing conflict and the War of 1812 drew him into government service. The man who had lived and worked with Native Americans most of his life, who had married a Delaware woman, whose children were certainly more "Indian" than "American," became a soldier, scout, interpreter, and spy for those who were arguably his family's enemies. Among the services rendered by William were maintaining Delaware loyalty during the War of 1812 and identifying the body of Tecumseh following the Battle of the Thames.

Following the war Conner continued his trading and farming activities. His home on the White River became a gathering place for Native Americans and a stopover for white travelers. It was there that the committee tasked with choosing the site of a new state capital for Indiana met in 1820.

The years 1820 to 1823 were ones of transition. Within three months of his family's forced departure, William married Elizabeth Chapman, possibly the only young, eligible white women in the area, taking her into the home he had shared with his Delaware family. His tentative steps into the white world soon became determined strides. He was to become a primary facilitator of settlement in central Indiana.

In 1823 Conner built his brick home overlooking the White River less than one-half mile south of his log cabin. From his new home Conner entered fully into the teeming world advancing toward him, acquiring, sometimes in partnership with others, ever-increasing amounts of land—acreage that could be profitably sold to new settlers. He and Josiah Polk platted Noblesville in 1823, shrewdly donating land to make it the county seat, and later platted the towns of Alexandria, also in Hamilton County, and Strawtown in Madison County. At one point Conner owned approximately four thousand acres in Hamilton County.

In addition to farming and raising livestock he expanded his business interests by owning or investing in stores, mills, and a distillery. In many ways he may be seen as a prototype of the entrepreneur. His enterprises ranged from small country stores to a larger one in Indianapolis. By the 1830s Conner was well established in his own "new world." He had become a respected figure. He made occasional forays into politics, supporting Whig policies, and he served three nonconsecutive terms in the state legislature from 1829 to 1837. His motives were more those of a businessman seeking to advance his interests than a man wishing to be a public servant. Each of his terms saw him lobbying for interests—roads, canals, railroads—that would aid his businesses. He also was a founding member of the Indiana Historical Society.

Seven of William and Elizabeth Conner's ten children were born in their brick home. In 1837, in his sixtieth year, Conner moved his family to Noblesville, his final step into settlement. He continued to oversee his business interests, but eased into his final role as a pioneer patriarch, becoming a source for those wishing to learn about early Indiana. Life slowed considerably for the ever-active man. When he died in 1855 many of the trails he helped blaze had become roads, many of the forests he roamed had been cut away to reveal towns. The Conner house rising out of the prairie remained.

Today, thanks to the foresight of Eli Lilly, Conner and his home serve as the centerpiece of one of the nation's finest museums, one that tells not only Conner's story, but also that of generations of early Hoosiers.

TIMOTHY CRUMRIN

For Further Reading

Crumrin, Timothy. "Between Two Worlds: William Conner of Indiana." *Traces of Indiana and Midwestern History* 5, no. 1 (Winter 1993): 18–23.

Thompson, Charles N. *Sons of the Wilderness, John and William Conner*. Indianapolis: Indiana Historical Society, 1937.

Weslager, C. S. *The Delaware Indians: A History*. New Brunswick, NJ: Rutgers University Press, 1972.

Cook, William Alfred "Bill"

January 27, 1931–April 15, 2011

Built $1,500 initial investment into multibillion-dollar medical device company, nationally recognized philanthropist and preservationist.

The biography of William Alfred Cook captured his philosophy and language with its title: *Ready, Fire, Aim*. Right up until his death at age eighty from half-a-lifetime's battle with congestive heart failure, Cook operated with an approach that eschewed caution in favor of action, though reckless he was not.

A Cook quotation on the book's third page explained its title: "Ready, fire, aim. Ready means preparation. Get yourself ready to do something, then do it. If you screw up, you go back and see what happened. What I call 'aim' is hindsight you find out where you screwed up, and you can correct it much easier. A lot of people would rather sit and prepare. They can prepare all their life."

Cook did not hurry into his life's ultimate work. He was thirty-two when he sat down for a remarkably prescient self-assessment. He once planned to be a doctor; his Northwestern University degree had prepared him for medical school. Military service changed that plan. A few years of working for others convinced him that he wanted to be his own boss and own his own small company. On July 1, 1963, Cook Inc. was established in Indiana with Cook and his wife, Gayle, using a spare bedroom in their Bloomington apartment to launch a company making catheters and a few other medical devices. Without ever having to go into debt or bring outside capital into the business, Cook grew from a $1,500 investment into a $1 million sales operation, then hundreds of millions, and then billions. By 2013, its fiftieth year, Cook Inc. employed more than 13,000 people on four continents with annual sales of approximately $2 billion.

Along the way, Cook, who beginning in 1989 was labeled by *Forbes* as the richest man in Indiana, seemed to take to heart the biblical advisory: "From everyone to whom much has been given, much will be required." He treated it like a poker game and responded, "See you, and I raise." The billionaire businessman never stopped raising the stakes as a philanthropist-preservationist. He died the day before the dedication of his last big project. In true Cook spirit, that show went on, as scheduled, reintroducing what once was the leading Methodist Church in Indianapolis—reduced over time to a crumbling, decaying eyesore—as the new home of Indiana Landmarks and a handsome site for weddings, business and professional gatherings, art events, lectures, concerts, as well as a self-sustaining hub for Indiana Landmarks' preservation operations. "That was such an important part of his vision. Bill believed this could work for us, and it really has," Indiana Landmarks president Marsh Davis said. It was a $17 million gift from Cook.

That was small compared to the Cook money that achieved an even grander rescue of two hotels built to European grandeur in the early days of the nineteenth century—in two neighboring hamlets between cornfields in sparsely populated southern Indiana. Through the Roaring Twenties, the West Baden Springs Hotel and the French Lick Springs Hotel operated as rivals two miles apart. And they flourished, gems amid two strips of casinos and saloons that brought in high society (Joe and Rose Kennedy) and high rollers (Diamond Jim Brady and Al Capone) from not just nearby Louisville and Indianapolis but also railroad-linked Chicago.

Prohibition (and state government that winked) did not stop them, but the Great Depression did. The Sheraton chain kept the French Lick hotel alive, though fading, into the 1990s, but the lights at West Baden went out in the 1930s. The Cooks acquired it in the mid-1990s with plans to nurse it back to sufficient health that might then attract the interest of a hotel chain. Only after his investment had topped $30 million and there was no buyer in sight did the Cooks arrive at a wholly different decision: purchase the French Lick hotel, too; undertake massive, ultraexpensive resuscitation of both; construct a top-of-the-line golf course with master golf architect Pete Dye the designer; and do everything else necessary to convert the area into a genuine resort, complete with one of Indiana's first gambling casinos.

The grandeur there is unmatched, but the heart of Cook may be even more evident in what he took on once the hotels were done. Defying author Thomas Wolfe, he did go home again, and brought life back to Canton, the small Illinois town where he grew up.

Long before young Cook's traveling-salesman father bought a couple of grain mills and made Canton his family's base, the western Illinois town in Peoria's outskirts had international renown as the place where the world's best plows were made. A young Massachusetts blacksmith, William Parlin, settled there in 1840, went into business, and clicked with a hand-built plow. Its feature was the cutting blade set at an angle (thirty-eight degrees) that made it self-cleaning and a regional, then national, then international success—at a time when "shipping" was a literal term, down the Illinois River to the Mississippi River to Saint Louis and New Orleans and ports and points far and wide. Parlin's daughter married a man who became the Parlin operation's bookkeeper and sales director, and Parlin took him into the Parlin and Orendorff Plow Works of Canton. The town grew around the company's downtown manufacturing plant, which employed more than 2,000 people in a town of approximately 10,000 in population.

In 1919 the massive International Harvester Company bought out Parlin and Orendorff. All continued to go well at the Harvester factory until October 1983, when Canton learned of a total pull-out that left the huge downtown site barren and management and factory personnel jobless or headed out of town. Without its employment base, the town shriveled. Downtown was deteriorating buildings and declining shops. In 1997 the empty factory building burned; the site was labeled by the Environmental Protection Agency as a "brownfield," too contaminated for use without an expensive cleanup. "The demeanor of the people got bad," said a one-time Canton shop owner. "Negative. Hopeless. We lost self-respect. We lost our families. We lost our soul."

In 2007 Mark Rothert, at the time heading an economic development organization in Canton, read a magazine article about Cook that mentioned his interest and success in helping downtown development in Bloomington. Rothert, who knew of Cook's roots in Canton, wrote to ask for a chance to talk with him about how to revive his old hometown. Like a spark that became a flame, the conversation among Cook, Rothert, and future Canton mayor Kevin Meade led to a first small step, then a flurry. Cook began quietly, buying and restoring a century-old downtown square corner building that had not had a tenant, or even modest maintenance, for years. He did the same with a shopping center a block away and built the town's first hotel at another corner on the Square. Meade and the city secured an Illinois grant that helped store owners around the Square do their own restoration.

The pinnacle was reached with the announcement—at a jammed church, across the street from the ugly blight that the P&O/International Harvester factory site had become—that hometown boy Cook was going to clean up a major portion of it, complete with greenery and landscaping, and put in a factory of his own there. "The people of Canton had turned out," Meade recalled. "The looks in their eyes and tears on their cheeks were pure joy. They knew that the spark this town needed had just arrived."

Now there are two Cook factories there. The spark is still alive.

BOB HAMMEL

For Further Reading

Hammel, Bob. The Bill Cook Story: *Ready, Fire, Aim*. Bloomington: Indiana University Press, 2008.

Cornish, Clarence F.

November 10, 1898–December 22, 1995

Aviation pioneer who helped promote and develop air travel in Indiana and the country and was the first director of the Aeronautics Commission of Indiana.

After the Indiana General Assembly passed the Aeronautics Commission Act of 1945, Governor Ralph Gates called Clarence "Cap" Cornish to offer him the position as the commission's first director. At the time, Cornish was back in uniform as a lieutenant colonel with the U.S. Army Air Forces and in Washington, D.C., assisting in controlling and monitoring domestic and military air traffic in defense of the continental United States during World War II. The governor picked the right man. Cornish, who was born in Canada but grew up in Fort Wayne, Indiana, began his decades-long devotion to flying after gaining acceptance into the aviation section of the U.S. Army Signal Corps during World War I. He first took to the skies on May 6, 1918, in a Curtiss JN-4D, popularly known as a "Jenny," the famous American biplane used during the war for training and combat. The war ended before he was sent overseas, but his passion for flying never abated.

After leaving active duty, Cornish returned to Fort Wayne and opened the city's first retail radio store, selling receivers and supplies, but then was appointed a second lieutenant in the reserves of the army air service, which allowed him to continue developing his flying proficiency during annual two-week training sessions. However, beginning in 1925 and over the course of the next several decades, Cornish devoted most of his time and talents to flying and to his vision of seeing aviation develop to its fullest in Indiana and throughout the country. About the time Fort Wayne was opening its first commercial airport, Cornish was hired to be the part-time pilot of the newly established Goral Airways, formed by a local car dealer. Cornish also participated with other pilots in a number of air shows to draw people to the airport and to demonstrate to them the wonders of flight, including air races and stunts such as barrel rolls and dives.

In 1928 Cornish was named manager and chief pilot of Aereco, an aviation subsidiary created by the Auto Electric Radio Equipment Company of Fort Wayne. In addition to flying passengers and freight, the new venture also won approval to establish Indiana's first flying school. When business at Aereco faltered during the Great Depression, Cornish became chief pilot for Oscar Foellinger, publisher of the *Fort Wayne News-Sentinel*, and was then appointed manager of the Paul Baer Municipal Airport, a position he held from 1934 to 1941. By the time he was called back into the military in the summer of 1941, Cornish had packed considerable progress for the airport into his seven-year tenure. Fort Wayne was added to Trans World Airlines' nighttime route between New York and Chicago, the U.S. Weather Bureau located an observation station there, and two runways were added and two others extended.

During this period Cornish was also active in various organizations created to promote air travel and safety. Through the Indiana Aircraft Trades Association, he and other pilots regularly formed a flying armada, traveling to various cities throughout the state to showcase new aircraft, perform stunts, and generally to draw the public's attention to the marvels of aviation. One such event attracted a crowd of about 50,000.

Cornish also focused his attention on getting state and federal officials to support legislation that would further the development of air transportation. As chair of a panel to study the state of aviation in Indiana and to chart its future course, Cornish traveled throughout the state, holding meetings to solicit opinions on the needs of various communities and also to explore ways of funding increased development of aviation. At the center of his proposal was the creation of a state agency to develop and regulate air travel. "I wanted an airport in every county in the state, particularly at the county seat, if possible, and in the state parks," Cornish said in an interview. The plan was presented to and then rejected by

Governor Clifford Townsend in late 1940. Shortly thereafter, Cornish was recalled to military duty.

Recalling his time in Washington, D.C., Cornish said he noticed an obvious bias in where new airports were being built for the military. "When I saw the South being plastered with air bases, I sold the brass on building some north of the Mason-Dixon Line," Cornish said. Specifically, he thought that an area of land between Peru and Kokomo, Indiana, would be an ideal spot. In short order, construction was approved for the Bunker Hill Naval Air Station, later renamed Grissom Air Force Base, and currently known as Grissom Air Reserve Base.

With the war winding down Cornish was granted his release from active duty and became the first director of the Aeronautics Commission of Indiana and "anxious," he said, "to get the story about aviation in Indiana going." Though inadequate funding and staff hampered his fledgling agency, Cornish nonetheless charted an aggressive agenda to accelerate the growth of Indiana aviation and he traveled throughout the state to explain it and win support for his plans. At the top of his list was expanding the number of airports in the state, a goal greatly assisted by the Federal Airport Act of 1946, which pumped $500 million into grants for airport projects across the country.

Safety in the air and on the ground had been a priority for Cornish since he began flying and he made it a chief concern. Under his leadership, the agency compiled and widely distributed annual accident reports in the belief that knowing the particulars of accidents could help others avoid similar mishaps. He also conducted safety conferences in various Indiana cities to discuss safety issues with pilots, airport owners and managers, members of flying clubs, and law enforcement officials. His efforts in this area also led to the formation of local airport safety committees and the appointment of safety directors. Safety was a common topic in *Aero-Notes*, a monthly newsletter Cornish started to keep the state's aviation community informed of the state's aviation activities.

As a safety measure for cross-country navigation, Cornish placed an air marking program on the agenda. Before the days of sophisticated radar that guided pilots to their destinations, flyers relied on painted signs placed atop buildings that contained such information as the city they were over and a directorial arrow with the mileage to the nearest airport. By 1951 some three hundred air markers were in place throughout the state and with plans to eventually have one thousand.

Cornish also believed in educating the general public about the importance of aviation and he believed that process started by reaching out to elementary and secondary schoolteachers by sponsoring summer workshops to give them instruction in air transportation and showing them how to incorporate aviation materials in the subjects they taught. In addition, teachers visited airports to learn about their operations and also climbed aboard planes for brief flights.

Cornish's effectiveness and expertise leading the aviation agency was not only recognized in Indiana but also nationwide. He was elected as president of the National Association of State Aviation Officials and was also called to testify at various hearings into proposed legislative and regulatory changes to the nation's air transportation system. Although Cornish was reappointed to a second four-year term as director of the aeronautics commission by Henry F. Schricker after his election as governor in 1948, four years later Schricker's successor, George Craig, decided to appoint someone else. At that point, Cornish turned to another career, starting his own insurance agency, which he ran until retiring in 1970.

Cornish, however, never gave up his love of flying. He was still taking to the air well into his golden years, a feat that earned him a place in the *Guinness Book of World Records* as the world's oldest active pilot. His last flight on December 4, 1995, came just days before his death at age ninety-seven.

JAMES E. ST. CLAIR

For Further Reading

Cornish, Clarence F. Interviewed by Douglas E. Clanin, January 11, 1992. Indiana Historical Society, World War II Oral History Collection, William Henry Smith Memorial Library, Indianapolis.

Ingraham, Ruth Ann. *"Cap" Cornish, Indiana Pilot: Navigating the Century of Flight*. West Lafayette, IN: Purdue University Press, 2014.

Walton, Lloyd B. "Cap Cornish—On A 'High' That's Lasted Since 1918." *Indianapolis Star Magazine*, October 7, 1973, pp. 8–14.

Counsilman, James E. "Doc"

December 28, 1920–January 4, 2004

Distinguished as athlete, scholar, war pilot,

author, coach, and innovator setting records for success still unequaled as collegiate and Olympic swimming coach.

The International Scholar-Athlete Hall of Fame in Kingston, Rhode Island, included in its charter class Plato, who wrestled in the Isthmian Games, a forerunner for the ancient Olympics, and who argued for the ideal of physical training complementing philosophical education. That twenty-member charter class in 1999 also included two American presidents, Gerald Ford and George H. W. Bush; a U.S. Supreme Court justice, Byron "Whizzer" White; and others of extraordinary achievement, including Bobby Jones, Roger Bannister, Bill Bradley, Arthur Ashe, and Paul Robeson.

That first class did not include any of the college football or basketball coaches to whom America accords top rank, with seven-figure salaries and accordant fame and name recognition. But there was one U.S. college coach: swimming's "Doc" Counsilman of Indiana University. The "Doc" was genuine for James E. Counsilman, who earned a doctorate in physiology at the University of Iowa. By then he already had started the career in coaching swimmers that took him to nonpareil status.

Swimming saved Counsilman, and he more than returned the favor. Young Jim and older brother Joe were left for their mother to raise when his dad, a circus barker, left them. The swimming coach at the Forest Park Young Men's Christian Association in Saint Louis, Ernie Vornbrock, was the outsider who stepped in and gave Counsilman's life a direction. Vornbrock, a lifelong hero and role model for Counsilman, developed the young man into a breaststroker good enough to attract the attention of Ohio State swimming coach Mike Peppe, who saw Counsilman at the national Young Men's Christian Association swimming meet in Saint Louis and extended a scholarship offer.

Scholarship became more than an athletic term for Counsilman, who took to academics with as much zest as he did to swimming, and with a ceiling much higher. He had a mind that never stopped learning, observing, and experimenting. Perhaps more than anyone in any sport he wove science into physiology, blended in his knowledge of psychology, and singlehandedly changed his sport. A peer said before Counsilman, swimming advanced through experiments by coaches, but his erudition brought such things as Bernoulli's principles of hydrodynamics into play. "Doc advanced swimming a hundred years beyond where it would have been on trial-and-error," said Jack Pettinger, a one-time Counsilman assistant who built his own successful program at the University of Wisconsin.

As a coach, Counsilman repeatedly made excellent swimmers great, including Olympic triple-gold medalists Charlie Hickcox in 1968 and Jim Montgomery in 1976, and great swimmers greater, most notably with Mark Spitz, the Olympics' first seven-time gold medalist (in 1972).

Beyond that, Counsilman had a gift for bringing teams together for peak results, even in such a self-obsessed culture as the Olympic Games. Twice he served as head coach of the U.S. men's Olympic swimming team, and those two teams produced the best cumulative performances the United States has ever had in Olympic swimming. In 1964 at Tokyo his swimmers won six of a possible ten gold medals, and in 1976 at Montreal they were almost perfect: twelve of a possible thirteen golds and ten of a possible eleven silvers, plus four events where U.S. swimmers finished first, second, and third.

His Indiana teams won six straight National Collegiate Athletic Association championships (1968 through 1973), a streak unmatched in the national meet's seventy-seven-year history. His teams in that era were so dominant that at one time, in 1971, swimmers on Counsilman's Indiana team held nine of the listed twelve world individual swimming records. A *Sports Illustrated* story said that team, using officially recorded best times of each swimmer, was capable of winning a hypothetical dual meet against a composite team drawn from the rest of the swimming world, including all the rest of America. And the man himself—in that era—swam the English Channel, at age fifty-eight, the oldest at the time ever to do so.

In addition to his renown as scholar-athlete and teacher-coach, Counsilman was also a military hero. His competitive years at Ohio State were interrupted by service in World War II that included piloting one of the difficult-to-fly but tide-turning B-24 heavy bombers. On one of his bombing missions, German flak hit his plane, severing the hydraulic line. Without brakes, he crash-landed the plane and his entire ten-man crew survived. He was awarded the Distinguished Flying Cross.

The scholar part is documented, too, his readings and implementations covering Sigmund Freud as well as the classic sciences. "The most important thing in my life is to constantly do research," he said. "I never looked at it as research. I'm trying to answer questions. I've always had a tremendous curiosity about swimming. I watch a dog running along, hop in the water, and I watch his strokes. I've got a reputation as kind of a nut ." And it was fun, Counsilman said: "When you love a sport like that, it's not work."

His sport's history intrigued him. In a small, out-of-the-way London bookstore, he found a book written in 1764 on swimming. "I was shaken and incoherent; you would be, too, if you found a book for $2.50 that was worth thousands of dollars." The book advised: "Swim naturally, with the head erect toward the heavens." The wording made Counsilman smile as he said: "I don't know if it was natural in those days to walk around with your face toward the sky, but I doubt it."

Swimming history says the "Australian crawl," the "freestyle" stroke that all swimmers use today for maximum speed, was introduced in 1902 by an astute Australian who noticed some South Sea islanders were swimming that way. "I'm confident that the crawl as we know it was swum by Polynesians for thousands and thousands of years," researcher Counsilman said.

However, as Counsilman also noted, the swimming world was slow to change, and he included himself among the slow learners. In his first year coaching, as an assistant at the University of Iowa while doing doctoral work, he had an Olympic champion on the team, Wally Ris. "I was teaching the principles I learned the same way everybody else did—out of the Red Cross and YMCA handbooks," Counsilman said, adding both asserted that the most efficient way to swim freestyle was to reach out and pull the arm straight through. "Only, Wally Ris couldn't swim that way. His arms were all over the place," Counsilman said. "He was pulling with a bent elbow with sort of an elliptical pull pattern. It only took me fifteen years to see why that worked. You don't go anyplace until you're working with still water." Using what was then the standard technique, however, meant swimmers created a wall of water that limited forward movement.

"Wally Ris had the right idea all along," Counsilman said, adding that, "Mark Spitz was the best at it. He had the tremendous ability to pitch his hands exactly right through the stroke. Mark did more to give us stroke enlightenment than anyone ever has. And he did it naturally."

That kind of information came from studies Counsilman conducted by taking underwater photographs of his swimmers practicing. Those were included in instructive principles Counsilman published in his 1968 book, *Science of Swimming*. That is when "Doc started a new career. With the completion of *Science of Swimming*, Doc began to instruct every age-group, high school and college team in the world," said IU faculty colleague Joel Stager.

Counsilman's research and teaching did not just benefit swimming. For years at IU he taught a graduate-level course that brought anatomy, physiology, and psychology into a coaching focus. Coaches of all sports took it. Kay Hutsell, one of Indiana's top high school coaches, called it the most valuable course he ever took—and his sport was wrestling. Another of Counsilman's IU faculty colleagues, Wynn Updyke, recalled a conversation he had in Europe with the coach of an internationally successful national junior team. After confirming that yes, Updyke's residency at IU meant he did know Counsilman, the coach said, "Tell him the people of Bulgaria thank him for the instruction he has given us." He coached weightlifting.

BOB HAMMEL

For Further Reading

Counsilman, James E. *The Science of Swimming*. Englewood Cliffs, NJ: Prentice Hall, 1968.
Kennedy, Ray. "Go For the Gold, Doc." *Sports Illustrated*, September 24, 1979.
Whitten, Phillip. "Doc's Family." *Swim Magazine*, July/August 1966.

Crosley, Powel, Jr.

September 18, 1886–March 28, 1961

Broadcast pioneer, industrialist, inventor, entrepreneur, and owner of the Cincinnati Reds.

Powel Crosley Jr. was one of the most innovative, eclectic, and far-seeing industrialists of his time. Products that sprang from his inspired vision ranged from a baby's walker to airplanes. He was dedicated to providing quality products at a low cost aimed at the mass market. In 1947 *Life* magazine said "Crosley pioneered high volume and low price with nearly as much success as Henry Ford."

Crosley was born in 1886 in Cincinnati to Powel and Charlotte Crosley. His eclecticism likely sprang from his father, who had been a farmer, traveling salesman, lawyer, and theater owner. Young Powel was fascinated with things mechanical, particularly automobiles, from an early age. He attended the University of Cincinnati, first in the engineering school, where he failed academically, later turning to law, which could not hold his attention. Leaving school after two years he ventured into his real love, automobiles. He had ideas about building his own line of cars.

Crosley first put his ideas to work in 1907 when he founded a company in Connersville to manufacture a car he called the Marathon Six. Indiana was an automaking mecca at that time. His prototype attracted interest and a few advance orders, but the panic of 1907 spelled the end of his dream. Crosley spent the next few years working for other Hoosier automakers, including the famed CARL FISHER. He subsequently made further aborted efforts to build his own low-cost car.

With partner Ira Cooper, Crosley founded the American Automobile Accessory Company in Ohio in 1916. Also involved with the company was Powel's younger brother Lewis. They were an ideal team. Powel was the idea man, the innovator, while Lewis was the steady hand who found a way to make his big brother's ideas work. The mail-order company was huge success.

Always looking to diversify, Crosley began making phonograph cabinets. Already interested in the exciting new medium of radio, Crosley began thinking of a low-cost radio set to expand the field. It was then that he found his niche, which was to make innovative, inexpensive items for a mass market. He introduced a low-cost radio dubbed the Harko in 1921. Within a year the Crosley Radio Corporation was the largest in the world. To help spur sales Crosley turned to broadcasting in 1922, starting with a small transmitter in his home. He then began WLW radio in Cincinnati. The station had the most powerful transmitter (at one point it pushed out 500,000 watts) in the

Powel Crosley Jr. speaking before the Federal Communications Commission, October 7, 1936.

country and featured many commercials for Crosley radios. During this period he also introduced the Crosley Go-Bi-Bi, a version of a rideable baby walker so prevalent today.

Two Crosley ideas of the late 1920s show how eclectic was his thinking. He made a brief foray into the airplane business when he founded Crosley Aircraft to build a low-cost airplane. The venture was short-lived as only six of the Moonbeam planes were built. A bit more successful was the Autogym, a weight reduction device featuring a motor-driven vibrating belt placed around the waist that promised to shave off inches.

Crosley was also a sportsman and baseball fan. He bought the hometown Cincinnati Reds in 1934 and their stadium was renamed Crosley Field. In 1935 it hosted the first major league baseball night game. He was also an avid hunter (he was a founder of the American Wildlife Institute) and later bought a farm in Jennings County, Indiana, that became a quail-hunting habitat and working farm.

Radios were such a success that Crosley diversified once again when he added refrigerators to the Crosley line. The inexpensive, aptly named Shelvador refrigerator was the first one to feature shelves in the door. It too was a Crosley success, so successful that in 1938 Crosley built a mile long factory in Richmond, Indiana. That factory was also to be the site of Crosley's dream to return to car making.

Now a wealthy man, Crosley set his sights toward making the car he always hoped to. A second assembly line was set up at the Richmond plant that would produce both refrigerators and autos. His goal was to build a inexpensive auto that would get up to fifty miles per gallon at fifty miles per hour. After experimenting with several designs, including one for a three-wheeled vehicle, Crosley settled on a small, triangular-shaped car. The prototype was built at his Jennings County Farm, Sleepy Hollow.

The car debuted at the Indianapolis Motor Speedway in April 1939. Reaction was decidedly mixed with some likening it to a bathtub on wheels, while the influential *Time* magazine called it sleek and rakish. The Crosley initially came in two models that cost $325 and $350. They were considered the lowest priced vehicles on the market. A pickup truck and panel van were added later. One of the most unique aspects of the Crosley was that they were initially sold through Crosley appliance dealers and department stores, including Macys. Nearly 6,000 vehicles rolled off the line before World War II stopped auto production in the United States. During the war Crosley factories retooled to make gun turrets, fuses, and military vehicles.

Crosley was well positioned to return to auto making after the war. In 1945 he sold all of his interests except the Reds and the car company to focus on his latest effort. And a nation accustomed to gas rationing was ready for low-cost, high-mileage cars. Crosley took over a former truck-manufacturing plant in Marion, Indiana, in 1946. The first model drove off the assembly line in 1946. Within three years over 50,000 vehicles had been produced. The plant produced cars, trucks, and station wagons. As usual, Crosley gave them distinctive names—Hotshot, Crosmobile, and Gasporter. There was even an early version of a sport utility vehicle called the Farm-O-Road. It seemed that Crosley's vision was now in sync with America's needs (indeed he called his compact automobile the "Car America Needs").

His success, however, was fleeting. The release from the war's restrictions and the beginning of the "fin age" in Detroit pushed Crosley's cars off the road. After producing more than 84,000 cars Crosley shut down the plant in 1952. It was to be another decade before Americans were ready to accept compact cars. Today, Crosley cars are much prized by vintage auto collectors appreciative of its maker's vision.

His remaining years were troubled by the deaths of many of his family. He began to divest himself of some of his properties and yachts. He retained his passion for improving his beloved Reds, but did not live to see them reach the World Series. Crosley died on March 28, 1961, having left his permanent mark on many areas of American life: autos, broadcasting, sports, and manufacturing.

TIMOTHY CRUMRIN

For Further Reading

Banks, Michael A. "Big Dream, Small Car: Powel Crosley, Jr.'s Indiana Automobile." *Traces of Indiana and Midwestern History* 19, no. 2 (Spring, 2007): 26–37.

McClure, Rusty, David Sterns, and Michael Banks. *Crosley, Two Brothers and a Business Empire That Transformed the Nation.* Cincinnati: Clerisy Press, 2006.

Piel, Gerard. "Powel Crosley Jr." *Life,* February 17, 1947, pp. 47–52.

Crowe, Ray P.

May 30, 1915–December 20, 2003

Basketball coach, player, educator, legislator, city official, and civil rights leader.

It was a Hoosier basketball tradition. The team that won the high school state championship proceeded triumphantly through the streets of Indianapolis to celebrate its victory. The team, their fans, and city residents crowded into cars and drove to Monument Circle at the heart of downtown. In 1955 the triumphal process, however, took a different route than the traditional one. The champions hailed from Crispus Attucks, an African American high school, and racial tensions seethed beneath the polite surface of congratulations offered from the broader community. Segregation required the parade to avoid downtown and go through a black neighborhood. Ray Crowe, the head coach of the Crispus Attucks basketball team, understood the situation well.

Born and raised on a farm near Franklin, Indiana, Crowe was one of ten children. At Whiteland High School, he was the only black player on the basketball team. Recruited by the basketball coach, Crowe went to Indiana Central College (now the University of Indianapolis) in 1935. After graduation, he began his career as an educator, teaching math and coaching basketball at School Number 17 in Indianapolis. His success as an eighth-grade coach led to his appointment in 1950 as head coach at Crispus Attucks, which opened in 1927 as the city's only black high school. Despite a 1949 state law that outlawed school segregation, separation remained the reality in Indianapolis for years afterward.

Unlike in other cities, where racial confrontation and mass protest became the norm in the struggle for civil rights, black leaders in Indianapolis tried the moderate approach of political exchange, or negotiation, to achieve incremental victories in their fight for equality. Working with whites within the power structure created an environment that often allowed white leaders to ignore racial problems, and the policy of give and take pursued by African Americans was certainly not a negotiation between equals. But the methods of what historian Richard B. Pierce called "polite protest" did bring considerable progress, especially at times when the city was concerned about its image.

Crowe came to embody those methods while coaching at Attucks. On the floor, he adopted an aggressive style of play that became the hallmark of his teams. In his first season, the Attucks Tigers lost only one game in the regular season and advanced to the state tournament. Since Indiana had not yet divided high school athletics into different classes according to size for tournament play, the state finals could conceivably be a David and Goliath match, a fact made famous by tiny Milan High School's championship in 1954. While the "Milan Miracle" story became the stuff of legend, Indiana largely ignored the road taken by Attucks. Yet, that story was just as dramatic and more significant historically.

Indianapolis mostly ignored the 1951 Attucks team. Although the capital city had not yet produced a state champion, the community was reluctant to embrace the African American school. But the Tigers went to the fieldhouse at Butler University and won the sectional tournament, the first rung of competition. Some whites feared that if Attucks won the state title, blacks would riot. But African Americans embraced their team with joy. The sectional victory brought a huge celebration in the streets as thousands flocked to Indiana Avenue in the heart of one of the city's major African American neighborhoods. Despite white ambivalence, many blacks hoped to make high school basketball another arena for the struggle for civil rights. Indeed, many black leaders saw the team's success as an opportunity to advance race relations by bringing the city's policy of segregation to the forefront. The community urged the players to behave themselves and repeatedly reminded them that they represented not only their school but also their race.

Crowe worried about the pressure and joined some other black leaders who feared that winning might hurt race relations because whites were not ready to have an all-black team represent the city. The most dramatic moment of the 1951 sectional came in the game against Anderson High School. The crowd at the Butler Fieldhouse cheered along racial lines as the white team took a ten-point lead with four minutes to go. Throughout the game, Attucks suffered from bad calls by the white officials, as racial prejudice interfered with the contest. The Tigers came back, scored on a last-second shot, and won by a single point, making it one of the most dramatic games in tournament history.

Indianapolis broadcaster Tom Carnegie (left) interviews Coach Ray Crowe following Crispus Attucks victory in the 1956 high school state basketball championship.

Attucks went on to reach the final four. Crowe talked continually to his team about sportsmanship—a decision that he came to believe was a mistake. There had been no trouble with discipline, but the coach felt the weight of carrying the hopes of the whole community. If the team won and acted politely, they would become living symbols of why blacks deserved civil rights. Throughout his career, Crowe emphasized sportsmanship and urged his players to serve as black ambassadors, but in this situation, he worried that this might have hurt his team, because it reined in its aggressive style of play. Attucks lost their semifinal game and, years later, Crowe lamented that, "We were not ready, and that was my fault. I made up my mind right then that we would be back, and the next time we would be ready."

Four years later, in 1955, Crowe's team returned and won the state championship. Many Indianapolis whites embraced the Attucks team led by Oscar Robertson, but the championship was not a clear victory for civil rights. In the intervening years, Crowe's team dominated the city and white residents adjusted their thinking. When Attucks did win it all, sports no longer carried the same weight of race. Whites were now able to compartmentalize sports, allowing themselves to cheer for a black team while also continuing to support segregation.

Thus, the championship was an ambivalent victory, as blacks celebrated the symbolic confirmation of their worth and identity on the one hand, but, on the other hand, they were marginalized in the midst of their celebration. That same ambivalence reigned when Attucks won the state championship again the following year. Robertson won the vote for Indiana's Mr. Basketball award, but Crowe did not win Coach of the Year.

In 1957 Crowe retired from coaching and became the school's athletic director. In 1966 he won election to the state legislature, where he served two terms. Later, he served as the chair of the House Education Committee, and worked for school integration in Indianapolis. Crowe continued his public service career as director of the city's Department of Parks and Recreation and, later, he won election to the City-County Council.

Crowe died in December 2003 at the age of eighty-eight. His memorial service drew a large, diverse crowd and included a procession that drove along the traditional route taken by Indiana State Basketball Champions. As the cars made their way around Monument Circle, Crowe again became a symbol of race and sports in Indiana. Unlike in 1955, however, this time whites and blacks traveled the road together.

A. JAMES FULLER

For Further Reading

Marshall, Kerry. *The Ray Crowe Story: A Legend in High School Basketball*. Indianapolis: High School Basketball Cards, 1992.

Pierce, Richard B. *Polite Protest: The Political Economy of Race in Indianapolis*, 1920–1970. Bloomington: Indiana University Press, 2005.

Roberts, Randy. *"But They Can't Beat Us": Oscar Robertson and the Crispus Attucks Tigers*. Indianapolis: Sports Publishing, 1999.

Cummins, Clessie Lyle

December 27, 1888–August 17, 1968

Founder of Cummins Engine Company and a prolific inventor.

The day Clessie Lyle Cummins died can be seen as a reflection of his life. He spent August 17, 1968, working on yet another of his inventions, a diesel engine based on a barrel design. It was meticulous work in which the seventy-nine-year-old carefully clamped a cylinder on one of the shop benches in his Sausalito, California, retirement home to measure its incremental distortion as he tightened the bolts with a torque wrench. Finished for the night he went to bed. He died in his sleep.

Cummins—part inventor, part entrepreneur, part showman—is best known for the company he cofounded in 1919 and still bears his name, Cummins Inc. in Columbus, Indiana, the country's leading diesel engine manufacturer. Not bad for a fellow who dropped out of school in the eighth grade.

Born on December 27, 1888, at Honey Creek in Henry County, Indiana, to Francis Marion and Almira Josephine Eddleman Cummins, he was the oldest of five children and much of his childhood was spent moving with the family from one community to another in Indiana and Ohio. The moves took their toll on his interest in a formal education. By the time the senior Cummins moved the family to Columbus in 1904, Clessie was sixteen and was told that he would have to repeat the eighth grade for the second time. Although he persevered for a semester, he eventually told his parents he could take no more, ending his formal education after having completed only seven grades.

By that time he had already developed a keen interest in mechanical things and found work at a number of production facilities and machine shops in and around Columbus. Eventually he came to the attention of Columbus banker W. G. Irwin, who hired him as a driver for the wealthy family in the fall of 1908. It turned out to be a partnership that had a profound effect on Columbus and the entire country.

Cummins was given considerable leeway in the new position by his employer. He was able to pursue other job opportunities and was even allowed use of the family garage to begin his first business, the Cummins Machine Works. His business grew and eventually he obtained contracts with the U.S. government during World War I. It was during this period that he entered the diesel engine business, securing manufacturing rights from an American licensee of a Dutch technology.

For his business to grow Cummins needed financial support and he gained it from Irwin and a group of early investors. That support led directly to the incorporation of Cummins Engine Company in 1919. The early years of the company were somewhat of a roller-coaster ride with more dips than rises. One of the high points in the company's first year of operation was an order from Sears Roebuck to build 3,500 small engines, which were advertised in the company's famous catalog. Responses to the advertisement were strong because Sears offered the engines to customers for $10 down, ten months to pay, and a thirty-day free trial. The offer was quickly accepted by hundreds of customers, especially farmers who used the engines for thirty days and returned them to the company without incurring any expense. Many asked that their $10 down payment also be refunded. The initial success of the promotion had an immediate effect on the Cummins workforce, which increased from nine to eighty-five over a short period of time. The massive returns had the opposite effect; Cummins was forced to lay off more than seventy of the newly hired employees.

Disastrous as the experience might have been in the short term, it also had positive long-term effects, mainly that Cummins became a familiar name to potential users. It took time to build on that initial exposure. In fact, it would be eighteen years before the company could produce a profit. Irwin, the banker, subsidized the operation in those lean years, investing hundreds of thousands of dollars in a venture dependent on Cummins's selling ability. Cummins was definitely a salesman, sometimes using unorthodox methods. One of his most noteworthy ventures was in 1930 when he drove from Indianapolis to an auto show in New York City in a Packard automobile powered by a diesel engine. He wanted to demonstrate the engine's durability and efficiency, promoting the trip through a well-planned media blitz. The car covered a distance of 792 miles on thirty gallons of fuel. Total fuel cost was $1.38.

Cummins built upon that success by introducing the diesel engine to the world of auto racing. He entered a car built by Cummins workers in the 1931 Indianapolis 500. The endeavor was a twofold undertaking, one purpose being to test the endurance of the engine and the second being to make Cummins a household name. It was not an easy task as the inventor had to challenge the traditions of the auto racing fraternity. Despite numerous roadblocks erected by the establishment, the Cummins entry not only started the 1931 race but completed it, setting a record believed unattainable. Driven by Dave Evans, car number 8 completed the 500-mile distance without making a pit stop.

The 1931 experience marked the beginning of a long relationship between Cummins and the Indianapolis 500. The company entered two cars in the 1934 race and followed that up with an entry in 1950. A Cummins car driven by veteran Fred Agabashian won the pole position in 1952.

Although there were some close calls during the Great Depression, the company emerged from the 1930s on sound financial footing. During World War II, Cummins stepped away from day-to-day duties to take a position on the War Production Board. His position at the company was again altered after W. G. Irwin died unexpectedly in 1943 and his nephew, J. IRWIN MILLER, assumed his management role. Cummins remained as president but only in a limited capacity, actually leaving Columbus for California in 1945. He formally resigned as president in 1947. His retirement was only from the engine company. In 1955 he began work on a problem he confronted in 1931 on the test drive of a truck down a mountainous terrain in California. The drive turned out to be a near-death experience as the truck's red-hot brakes gave out entirely.

Determining that the problem was not in the brakes but the diesel engine, Cummins set out to find an answer in the basement of his California home in 1955. His answer was a "diesel brake control device." The product was first offered to Cummins Engine but was rejected because the company believed it could produce its own system. Eventually Cummins offered the device to the Jacobs Manufacturing Company, a small manufacturing concern in Connecticut. The company lent its name to the product, the Jake Brake. Later, after the success of Cummins's invention, Miller acknowledged that his firm had made a mistake.

Cummins's pioneering achievements were widely honored. In 1969 the Society of Automotive Engineers recognized him posthumously with its Horning Medal, one of the organization's highest awards. He was inducted into the Indiana Academy in 1973 and the Automotive Hall of Fame in 1976. In 1985 his Jake Brake was designated by the American Society of Mechanical Engineers as a "National Historic Mechanical Engineering Landmark." A citation on his induction into the Automotive Hall of Fame best summed up his importance to his state, country and industry, noting that he "had introduced the automotive diesel to the United States."

HARRY MCCAWLEY

For Further Reading

Cruikshank, Jeffrey, and David B. Sicilia. *The Engine That Could: Seventy-Five Years of Values-Driven Change at Cummins Engine Company*. Boston: Harvard Business School Press, 1997.

Cummins, C. Lyle, Jr. *The Diesel Odyssey of Clessie Cummins*. Lake Oswego, OR: Carnot Press, 1998.

Cummins, Clessie. *My Days with the Diesel: The Memoirs of Clessie Cummins*. Philadelphia: Chilton Books, 1967.

———. Papers. Lilly Library, Indiana University, Bloomington, IN.

Cushman, Charles Weever

July 3, 1896–June 8, 1972

Financial analyst and amateur color photographer.

Charles W. Cushman was raised in rural Posey County, Indiana. Leaving for college in 1914 and never returning to live in southern Indiana, Cushman built for himself a career (first in Chicago, then in San Francisco) as a financial writer and analyst, but gained greater recognition—long after his death—for an avocation known, during his lifetime, only to his family and friends: color photography.

Cushman's matriculation at William Lowe Bryan's Indiana University brought him into the same orbit of ideas and opportunities that attracted ERNIE PYLE, HOAGY CARMICHAEL, and other upwardly mobile and ambitious small-town Hoosiers in the early twentieth century. Cushman studied English and business, gaining both a practical aptitude for figures and a skill for telling stories. As a sportswriter for the *Indiana Daily Student*, he established himself as a gifted watcher—an observer more than a doer.

A brief stateside hitch in the U.S. Navy during World War I took Cushman to Chicago, the city in which he remained for most of the next three decades. Once there he found work as a traveling salesman for the Addressograph Corporation, which pioneered the technology of image reproduction with its machines for mass-producing business correspondence. After a few years on the road, he became a researcher for the *LaSalle Business Bulletin*, a financial publication produced by a business college located near Cushman's home on Chicago's South Side. At the *Bulletin*, he assisted senior analysts as they forecast trends in the nation's financial sectors. Those trends looked quite positive; consumer spending, homebuilding, and automobile ownership all seemed capable of climbing forever—and the market for smart financial forecasters grew apace. In 1929 the Standard Statistics Company (later Standard and Poor's) invited the young analyst to come to New York to edit a new magazine designed, like the *Business Bulletin*, to assist everyday investors in taking advantage of plentiful investment opportunities. *Your Money*, like the prosperous economy that it documented, lasted less than a year. Cushman returned to Chicago to face the Great Depression.

With him was his young wife, Jean. Her father, Joseph R. Hamilton, was a prominent Chicago advertising executive who had made his name, before arriving in that city, as director of advertising for Philadelphia's pioneering retailer John Wanamaker. Hamilton helped the couple financially, providing Cushman with the opportunity to serve as treasurer of a newly incorporated American branch of Canada's Drewry's Ale, which he launched at the end of Prohibition in 1933. Hamilton and Cushman sold the business after a few years, when the older man left for Washington, D.C., to serve as director of information for the Works Progress Administration. Just as important as his financial and political connections, Hamilton also provided Cushman with entrée into a world of culture, ideas, and personalities. Chief among those personalities was Hamilton's nephew (and Jean's first cousin), the writer John Steinbeck. Like Cushman, Steinbeck looked to Hamilton for advice and professional assistance throughout his early career.

Steinbeck's cross-country travels made him a regular guest at the Hamilton home in Chicago. While the particulars of the relationship between the two young men who each vied for Hamilton's mentorship are unknown, what is clear are their oddly parallel lives: in the late 1930s, as the writer, armed with his typewriter, took to the highway to create novels such as *The Grapes of Wrath*, Cushman traveled equal distances, sometimes to the same places, with a different creative tool: his Contax IIA 35-mm camera.

Cushman's photographic interest went back at least as far as the mid-1920s. There is no evidence that he ever studied photography or aspired to make it anything more than a hobby, but he was clearly serious about his equipment (the Contax, similar to its near-relation the Leica, was one of the expensive, high-quality "minicameras" that in the 1930s began to find favor with photojournalists and serious amateurs) and he further distinguished himself as one of the earliest to make substantial use of Eastman Kodak's new Kodachrome color film.

In 1938 Cushman loaded his first Kodachrome roll into the Contax. His initial color photographs showed his red Ford Deluxe coupe as it sat parked at a dusty brown turnout in the Marin Headlands, with a new (and very orange) Golden Gate Bridge looming in the background and the San Francisco skyline rising beneath a pale blue sky in the distance. This preview of a world turned suddenly colorful captured the photographer's imagination, and he soon gave up black-and-white film entirely.

As Cushman's financial comfort increased (thanks to shrewd investing and, after 1941, his and Jean's inheritance of her father's estate), so did the frequency of his cross-country trips—always with Jean by his side. They traveled for nearly thirty years, driving some half million miles in the process—from Puget Sound to Miami Beach; from San Diego to Maine. After each trip he labeled his hundreds of new slides, placed them in secure boxes, and filed them away beside the small notebooks in which he had recorded the subject, frame number, and exposure details of each image. They were striking pictures: images of small-town, big-city, and farm life in the United States that parallel the famous photographs commissioned by the Farm Security Administration (which Cushman surely knew via Hamilton's WPA connections), but that lack the political agenda or the stark gray tones that we have since come to associate with midcentury documentary photography. Cushman's view was that of a traveler—one who saw the connection among resources, business, and culture, but who remained, unlike his famous cousin, apolitical in his outlook. Nor was he artistically ambitious: there is no evidence that he ever printed any of the images or that he intended anyone to see them beyond his immediate circle of friends.

As compelling as Cushman's road pictures are his images of everyday life in the city—first Chicago, then after 1951, San Francisco, the city where he and Jean spent the remainder of their lives. An amateur street photographer, he did not seek out human subjects with any frequency, although he retained a soft spot for attractive women and cute children. More typical of his city work are images of age and decay—of old neighborhoods slated for redevelopment, of corner stores and street markets and turn-of-the-century rooming houses. Cushman's pictures of his hometown help to remind us of how present, still, was the past, even in a postwar era noted for its eagerness to invest in the future.

Cushman's 14,000 color slides, his equipment, and his logbooks passed to his alma mater on his death in 1972. They remained, unseen, in the Indiana University Archives until the late 1990s, when curator Bradley Cook and photographic historian Rich Remsberg jointly discovered the collection. IU received a grant to digitize the images, and their appearance online in 2003 brought sudden international recognition to the previously unknown collection. Today, the Charles W. Cushman Photograph Collection website, a published biography of Cushman, and countless appropriations of his works for commercial and scholarly purposes have given this hitherto unknown Hoosier photographer the respect and recognition that he never sought in his lifetime.

ERIC SANDWEISS

For Further Reading

Cushman, Charles W. Photograph Collection. Indiana University Archives, Bloomington, IN. http://webapp1.dlib.indiana.edu/cushman/index.jsp.

Sandweiss, Eric. *The Day in Its Color: Charles Cushman's Photographic Journey through a Vanishing America.* New York: Oxford University Press, 2012.

———. "'A Fair Collection of Interesting Pictures': Charles Cushman's Indiana, 1938–1966." *Traces of Indiana and Midwestern History* 24, no.2 (Spring 2012): 14–25.

Davis, Elmer

January 13, 1890–May 18, 1958

Newspaper and network radio journalist, author, and director of the U.S. Office of War Information during World War II.

Elmer Davis is sometimes vaguely and mistakenly recalled as simply a Will Rogers-like, down-home wag. However, Davis was a highly educated media man of great erudition who combined Hoosier common sense with a scholarly drollness; a combination that took the Indiana native into meetings at the White House, into (via radio) the homes of Americans from coast to coast, into (via his novels and nonfiction) bookstores and libraries across the country, into propaganda wars against the Nazis, and into battle against McCarthyism.

Davis was a newspaper journalist, a freelance writer, a radio broadcaster, and a public relations pioneer. He was so well known in his day that he appeared in a brief cameo role as himself in the 1951 classic science fiction film *The Day the Earth Stood Still*.

Davis was born in 1890 in Aurora, a town on a nook of the Ohio River in southeastern Indiana. His father was a banker, his mother a teacher. Davis attended Franklin College, where wrote and edited for student publications. A member of Franklin's class of 1910, Davis earned a Rhodes Scholarship, which afforded him the opportunity to study at Oxford University in England.

After Oxford, Davis taught briefly at Franklin High School and then launched a career as a writer, first at *Adventure* magazine. It did not take Davis long to hit the big time in the big city. In 1914 he began working for the *New York Times*, eventually serving as both a reporter and editorial writer. Much of his work for the newspaper focused on news interpretation and analysis rather than on the matter-of-fact reporting of hard news. At the *Times*, Davis created the fictional persona Godfrey

Gloom, a plainspoken everyman who commented bemusedly on political conventions. Readers were in on the joke, knowing Davis was playing off his Indiana roots to comment as Gloom. Davis also served on the newspaper's editorial board. In 1921 he wrote the official *History of the New York Times, 1851–1921*, a 434-page book.

After a decade with the *Times*, Davis quit the nation's "newspaper of record" to focus on freelance writing. His essays and short stories appeared in numerous magazines, including *Collier's, Harper's, Red Book*, and *The New Yorker*. A collection of his essays, *Show Window*, was published in 1927. A collection of short stories, *Morals for Moderns*, was published in 1930.

The prolific Davis wrote a string of novels: *Times Have Changed* (1923), *I'll Show You the Town* (1924), *Friends of Mr. Sweeney* (1925), *The Keys of the City* (1925), and *Strange Woman* (1927). His novels were well received by critics, but never considered important literature, as his fiction tended toward light entertainment. The possible exception was 1928's *Giant Killer*, a hefty historical novel set in the Old Testament Middle East, and which imagines a ruthless, lying King David who did not really slay Goliath, yet took credit anyway, hence the irony of the novel's title. Novelist Sinclair Lewis saw *Giant Killer* as "a lively, well-colored and sometimes ribald restoration of King David the Psalmist, Joab who was his field marshal, his other sanguinary and difficult relatives, and their innumerable girls. As such, the book is brilliant entertainment." But Lewis also saw the novel as reflecting early 1900s America, and felt that Davis was "telling us our own story under the guise of David's true chronicle." Two of Davis's novels were made into movies: the 1925 silent comedy *I'll Show You the Town*, and the 1934 film *Friends of Mr. Sweeney*.

Davis gained national fame in 1939 when he combined his writing with his reading for CBS radio. He often did five-minute newscasts in the prime radio listening slot between entertainment programs at 8:55 p.m. But he became best known for the fifteen-minute *Elmer Davis and the News* broadcasts that often aired three nights a week at 6:30 p.m. In 1940 and 1941 many Americans settled in for a Saturday night of radio entertainment by first listening to Davis's popular weekend news analysis at 6:30 p.m. Fifteen minutes was then, and is now, a long block of time to fill on the radio, and Davis wrote his own scripts.

Elmer Davis at his desk at the Office of War Information, circa 1940s

Edward R. Murrow biographer Philip Seib noted that in 1939 the most famous radio news voices in America included Raymond Gram Swing, William L. Shirer. H. V. Kaltenborn, and Davis, whose not-quite-southern, but definitely not New York or Los Angeles, resonant twang became iconic and trusted to many listeners. *Radio Guide* magazine neatly summed up the combination of voice, intellect, and fairness that would be the legacy of Davis's radio journalism, noting that he had "an Oxford brain and Indiana twang that reeked of neutrality" and that was "exactly the kind of homey down-to-earth manner needed in a moment of crisis."

It was after the crisis at Pearl Harbor and subsequent American entry into World War II that the nation turned to Davis as the official storyteller of the nation's war effort. President Franklin D. Roosevelt hired Davis in 1942 to develop and direct the Office of War Information, a massive global public relations endeavor aimed at both foreign and domestic audiences. Davis oversaw communication efforts that involved extensive use of every mass medium of the time, from brochures to Hollywood movies. On the domestic front, OWI focused on boosting home-front morale and on delivering key messages intended to support the war effort. On the international front, OWI focused on explaining American values and actions to foreign audiences, often using country/language-specific foreign radio broadcasts to do so.

Davis walked a couple treacherous tightropes as OWI director. First, he had to satisfy the insatiable news media and public demand for war news, yet work closely with military leaders to ensure that OWI was not providing specific and timely information that might aid enemy forces. Second, he fought constantly mainly with politically powerful colleagues inside OWI to maintain the integrity of the agency's information so that even though it was indeed one-sided, government-sponsored, and pro-United States, it was also based on facts and "truth" and not distorted, nasty, over the top, or false.

In that respect, Davis can be seen as helping to define the modern differences between the phrases "public relations" and "propaganda." Public relations—albeit one-sided, interpretative, and promotional—involves communicating factually and fairly. Propaganda involves lies, distortions, and misappropriation of images (such as the Ku Klux Klan's use of religious imagery). Davis and his approach as OWI director was in direct opposition to that of Nazi propagandist Joseph Goebbels, who, by the way, kept a file on Davis.

After the war, Davis moved backed to radio news, this time with the ABC network. He became an early and frequent on-air critic of the red-baiting tactics of U.S. Senator Joseph McCarthy of Wisconsin. Davis's 1954 book, *But We Were Born Free*, is a collection of essays that are both anti-McCarthyism and anti-Communist. In his final book, *Two Minutes till Midnight*, published in 1955, Davis brought his scholarship and news analysis skills to tackle no less a subject than nuclear war.

Davis was married and had two children. He died in 1958 in Washington, D.C. In a 1958 speech to radio and television news directors, legendary broadcaster Murrow summed up the impact of the loss of Davis to radio news: "In this kind of complex and confusing world, you can't tell very much about the why of the news in broadcasts where only three minutes is available for news. The only man who could do that was Elmer Davis, and his kind aren't about anymore."

RAY BEGOVICH

For Further Reading

Dunning, John. *The Encyclopedia of Old-Time Radio*. New York: Oxford University Press, 1998.

Murrow, Edward R. *In Search of Light: The Broadcasts of Edward R. Murrow, 1938–1961*. Edited by Edward Bliss Jr. New York: Da Capo Press, 1997.

Seib, Philip. *Broadcasts from the Blitz*. Dulles, VA: Potomac Books, 2006.

Deam, Charles "Charlie" C.
August 30, 1865–May 29, 1953

Indiana's first state forester and a pioneer in protecting the state's soil and forests, as well as documenting its trees and plants.

By 1900 Indiana's extensive woodlands had been decimated by settlers, farmers, and the lumber industry. Forests had sunk to a new low of 7 percent of lands. Better management of natural resources was badly needed in Indiana and elsewhere in the nation. President Theodore Roosevelt helped raise awareness about the need for conservation. In response to these developments, Governor Thomas R. Marshall appointed Charles Deam as Indiana's first state forester in 1909. Although Deam had no training in forestry, neither did anyone else. The practice of forestry and conservation was just beginning in the early twentieth century.

Born in 1865, Deam grew up on his parent's farm near Bluffton, Indiana. As a boy, he collected Indian relics he found on the farm. Throughout his life, Deam remained a collector of the unusual and mundane. Eventually he directed his curiosity to the study of Indiana's plants and trees.

Deam attended DePauw University in the fall of 1885. Two years later, when his money ran out, he sold his books and walked home to Bluffton. He took up shop keeping and purchased a drugstore in Bluffton in 1891. He worked grueling hours and was sometimes abrupt with customers. A doctor advised him to get out and take a walk each day. About this time he also met a young schoolteacher, Stella Mullin. The two married in June 1893.

Deam developed a strong interest in botany. He read and talked about it whenever possible. He found a kindred spirit in a young zoology student, Bruce Williamson, who taught Deam about scientific methods. Deam was drawn to taxonomy, the identification and classification of plants.

During 1896 Deam started collecting plants as he hiked country lanes and meadows. Williamson helped him identify plants using *Gray's Manual of Botany*. The ability to identify plants opened a new world for Deam and set him on a lifelong path, and his thriving drugstore allowed him increasingly to pursue his interest in plants. By 1897 Deam was corresponding with other botanists, including Stanley Coulter, a biologist from Purdue University. Coulter and his brother, John, had written a book on the flora of Indiana in 1891, followed by

Forest Trees of Indiana in 1892. Coulter mentored Deam as an aspiring botanist.

Studying plants helped Deam notice subtle changes in the environment. For example, he noticed wild soldier rosemallow had multiplied rapidly and become common in wetlands and streams. He attributed the rapid increase to careless land management. "In the early history of our state our streams were clear," Deam noted. "But when the forests were removed, the streams became muddy and sediment was deposited on the shores and on the gravely and rocky bars that made a suitable habitat for this species."

By 1910 Deam turned his attention to plants native to Indiana. He first began collecting plant specimens during his walks, but he soon took to the road by horse and carriage, bicycle, and even motorcycle, which allowed him to cover more ground and collect more species. His field trips usually began in April and continued to mid-October each year. Stella often accompanied him on his travels.

About 1913 Deam became acquainted with a young botanist teaching at Indiana University, Paul Weatherwax, who often joined Deam in his fieldwork. Weatherwax said that while Deam complained of infirmities each morning, by the end of the day he was "still going strong long after most of the party had had enough."

During his lifetime, Deam gathered more than 78,000 plant species, which he identified with great care. In his botanical work he discovered twenty-five new plant species. Another forty-eight species were named for him, including the Deam Oak, a natural hybrid discovered in Wells County by Williamson.

In 1915 Deam purchased a Ford Model-T touring car. He customized the truck bed for sleeping, with a frame and mounted canvas tarps to keep out the rain. The roving field laboratory stored plants, books, and camp necessities. Deam nicknamed the vehicle the Weed Wagon. Deam traveled more than 125,000 miles, visited every township of the state's ninety-two counties, and collected thousands of specimens each year.

Deam put his collections and knowledge to work by publishing several reference works on Indiana's plants and trees. Deam's *Trees of Indiana* appeared in the state forestry's annual report in 1911. The work was so popular it was reprinted several times. His next book, *Shrubs of Indiana*, was published in 1924. An article that year by Deam appeared in *Proceedings of the Indiana Academy of Science* and urged a study of the state's indigenous plants before the opportunity was lost. He also asked that nature preserves be established. Another work, *Grasses of Indiana*, appeared in 1929. Deam's last book, *Flora of Indiana*, tackled plants native to Indiana and took him eight years to complete. Deam's prolific authorship laid a solid foundation for Indiana's botanical, natural history. Referring to Deam's impressive list of publications Weatherwax said, "Deam's particular service was to leave an accurate and detailed record of what plants were here and what happened to them."

Another of Deam's important legacies was the impact he had on Indiana's forests. By 1900 Indiana was the leading hardwood producer in the country, yet the state's forests were in pitiful shape. The land, stripped of trees and loosened by plows and domestic animals, quickly began to erode. Mountains of soil were washed into Indiana's streams for years. Deam warned, "If we lose our trees we can still live off the soil, but if we lose the soil, we will surely perish."

Deam worked tirelessly at reforestation. In 1903 the Indiana forestry board had purchased 2,000 acres of worn-out land in Clark County. At the site, Deam investigated what species worked best in reforesting the land. He found the area's poor soil could not support replanted hardwood, but pines or conifers prospered. At the Clark State Forest, which is among the nation's first state forests, Deam created and managed a tree nursery. The seedlings were planted on state property and sold at cost to farmers.

Deam worked as a state forester from 1909 to 1913. He took a brief hiatus, but resumed the post in 1917. He also wanted to educate farmers about managing forests as a resource. Deam developed educational materials to improve woodland management on farms. He also wrote a conservation bill that provided a tax break to farmers who classified parts of their land as forests, and agreed to protect the trees from fire and livestock grazing. As a result of the Forest Tax Classification Act, passed in 1921, four hundred acres of wooded lands on private property are now protected.

In 1928 Deam, then sixty-three years old, retired as state forester. However RICHARD LIEBER, the director of the Indiana Department of Conservation, wished to keep him and appointed Deam

Charles Deam at breakfast in his Weed Wagon at Marble Hill, Jefferson County, Indiana, June 20, 1923.

state forestry researcher. This post allowed Deam to continue his publications for the next twenty years. He eventually sold his herbarium and reference library to Indiana University.

Although Deam was awarded honorary degrees by DePauw, Wabash College, and Indiana University, he always thought of himself as an amateur botanist. Yet Deam accomplished more than many college-trained naturalists. Deam's forestry experiments and conservation work helped replenish Indiana's woodlands. As a result of the work begun by Deam, Coulter, and Lieber, 4.5 million acres in Indiana are now wooded, compared to 1.5 million acres in 1900. This early passion for conservation continues to protect Indiana's soil and woodlands today.

JENNFER YANTIS HARRISON

For Further Reading

Charlie Deam Papers. Indiana University Archives, Bloomington, IN.

Harrison, Jennifer. "Naturalist Charlie Deam: Forestry and Conservation Pioneer." *Traces of Indiana and Midwestern History* 22, no. 4 (Fall 2010): 46–55.

Kriebel, Robert C. *Plain Ol' Charlie Deam: Pioneer Hoosier Botanist*. Lafayette, IN: Purdue University Press, 1987.

Weatherwax, Paul. "Charles Clemon Deam: Hoosier Botanist." *Indiana Magazine of History* 67 (September 1971): 197–267.

Dean, James

February 8, 1931–September 30, 1955

Iconic pop-culture film star.

On September 30, 1955, young actor James Dean died recklessly in a car crash, just a month before the release of his signature movie, *Rebel without a Cause*. The star of only two other films, *East of Eden*, released earlier in 1955, and another yet-to-be released picture, *Giant*, which came out in 1956, he would almost immediately become one of Hollywood's most enduring legends. How does this happen after only three pictures? While several explanations are possible, it begins with him playing angst-ridden youth forever flirting with death throughout his early television work and aborted film career—a persona he encouraged fans to believe was based in reality. So his death at only twenty-four, *Forever Young*, seemed to be tragic theater of the real youth mourning itself ad infinitum.

As with many icons, his beginnings were modest. He was an unplanned baby, causing Winton Dean and Mildred Wilson to marry only six months before his birth in Marion, Indiana. Given that Dean's father dragged his feet on the union is a fitting foundation to the lifetime of indifference he showed his son. Conversely, Mildred was the most nurturing of parents, enrolling the boy in a smorgasbord of cultural activities even before he started school. The family lived in a series of dwellings in both Marion and nearby Fairmount, before Winton's job as a dental assistant took the family to Santa Monica, California, in 1936. For the entertainment-starved Mildred, Southern California was a secular mecca. But soon she found movie land too artificial for raising a son.

Perversely, Mildred's 1940 death from cancer resulted in her wish coming true—Winton sent his son back to Fairmount to be raised on the farm of his sister and brother-in-law, Ortense and Marcus Winslow. Naturally, for a child essentially to lose both parents would be devastating, even though his father had long been figuratively dead to him. This was the source from which Dean drew his long-suffering persona of the disenfranchised and misunderstood youth, an angst card he sometimes later played in reality. Yet, the Winslows were the most loving surrogate parents imaginable, and they provided him with an almost spoiled idyllic midwestern upbringing. He was popular, active in many organizations, and even starred in Indiana's favorite sport, basketball. Most important, his high school drama teacher, Adeline Nall, helped steer the teenager toward acting, with Dean periodically returning to guest lecture.

His stops on the way to stardom included a 1949 return to California and an attempt to both reconnect with his father and enter college. While neither endeavor was particularly successful, he managed to occasionally act (ranging from a panned performance in a University of California at Los Angeles production of *MacBeth*, to a Pepsi-Cola commercial), as well as make industry contacts, though these connections were radically different in nature. Along traditional lines, he was greatly influenced by off-campus acting lessons with the nurturing Oscar-nominated James Whitmore. In contrast, the opportunist bisexual Dean entered into a relationship with an older sophisticated industry player named Rogers Brackett, who performed a *Pygmalion*-like makeover of Dean. This led to small unbilled parts in such Hollywoods hits as the Dean Martin and Jerry Lewis comedy *Sailor Beware* in 1952.

Yet, to make it on the West Coast, Dean realized he had to polish his craft on the East Coast. The Hoosier was soon a struggling young actor in New York, but after being accepted into the acclaimed Actors Studio, under the leadership of Lee Strasberg, Dean began to have a career. With his performances in small but much-praised parts in two Broadway plays in 1952, *See the Jaguar* and *The Immoralist*, Dean's life changed. Elia Kazan, arguably then America's hottest stage and screen director (with direct ties to the Method Actor's Studio), was adapting John Steinbeck's best-selling 1952 novel *East of Eden*, and he wanted Dean for a screen test.

From this sprawling multigenerational work, Kazan was keying upon a Cain and Abel story set in World War I era California, with Dean's Cal as Cain the unappreciated son. The director was impressed with Dean's acting, but what really sold him on the young Hoosier was how Kazan could use Dean's Method acting and his real disconnect with his own father to enhance the story. As in the Bible, Cal's father Adam, played by Raymond Massey, also manages to reject his son's surprise birthday gift of money earned from his success as a bean farmer. The director further fueled the antagonism by manipulating Massey, the traditional actor. For example, with the Hoosier's assistance, Kazan had Dean deviate from the script and even use improvised language. Massey was properly incensed, but Kazan got the cinema conflict he was after. As with many directors, the means justified the end. Regardless, Dean's playfulness in *Eden*'s fields seemed most like his family's boy, and it remained their favorite Dean film.

The movie was a greater critical and commercial hit than expected, so more money and attention was focused upon Dean's next movie, *Rebel without a Cause*. Though played in a contemporary setting, the heart of *Rebel*'s story paralleled *Eden*—another dysfunctional family has a son trying to forge a relationship with his father. Even more than Kazan, *Rebel* director Nicholas Ray all but collaborated with Dean on a tale about yet another troubled teen. With Dean's death all but paralleling the opening of Rebel, the actor's mythic movie status had begun.

Dean's final film, from yet another epic novel, Edna Ferber's *Giant*, was frequently an unhappy production for him. Veteran director George Stevens called the shots; and Dean missed having more creative input. Plus, Stevens took his larger-than-life Texas characters through two generations, with Dean initially playing yet another troubled youth. He steals this portion of the picture from costars Elizabeth Taylor and Rock Hudson. However, his character's jump in age from teenager to his mid-forties by the close is jarring in part because Dean, the Method actor, made the effort to "age," while the others merely seemed to acquire blue-gray hair. Though a critical and commercial success, *Giant* is the least liked by Dean fans.

The movie also poses the question: Had Dean lived, would he have remained riveting in ruin, as did his Method actor hero Marlon Brando, or would he have been unable to move beyond playing struggling youngsters? Of course, that remains another portion of Dean's "what if" mystique. As a darkly comic Humphrey Bogart observed at the time, "Dean died at just the right time. Had he lived, he'd never have been able to live up to his publicity." Whatever the reason for Dean's deification, he remains a young "rebel" symbol, preserved in cinema amber, for all frustrated lonely youth.

WES GEHRING

For Further Reading

Bart, James. *James Dean: A Biography*. New York: Ballantine Books, 1956.

Gehring, Wes D. *James Dean: Rebel with a Cause*. Indianapolis: Indiana Historical Society Press, 2005.

Hofstede, David. *James Dean: A Bio-Bibliography*. Westport, CT: Greenwood Press, 1996.

Debs, Eugene Victor

November 5, 1855–October 20, 1926

National labor organizer, socialist leader, and five-time candidate for U.S. president.

Eugene Debs had what appears on the surface to be a longtime friendship with the Hoosier Poet, JAMES WHITCOMB RILEY. Debs was a founder of the Occidental Literary Club in Terre Haute in 1874. The club invited speakers, and Riley came several times. Riley was hardly known at the time of his first visit. Like Debs, Riley was building his career, working at the *Indianapolis Journal* and just starting to publish his distinctive dialect poems about life in Indiana. The two men liked each other immediately and, though they rarely met, each maintained a deep respect for the other. Riley wrote in his poem about Debs's hometown, "Regardin' Terry Hut,"

> And there's 'Gene Debs—man 'at stands
> And jes' holds out in his two hands
> As warm a heart as ever beat
> Betwixt here and the Jedgment Seat—!

Debs was born in Terre Haute to parents who had emigrated from the Alsace region of France. He attended both private and public schools but dropped out of high school at fourteen and took a job as a locomotive degreaser and, later, a locomotive painter, giving him a harsh introduction to the life of the working classes. In the late 1870s he was promoted to locomotive fireman. At the same time, he took night classes at a business college in Terre Haute. At his mother's insistence, he gave up his dangerous railroad job and went to work for the Terre Haute firm of Hulman and Cox as a billing clerk. Here, he began making contacts with businessmen and other community leaders. He also became active in local Democratic Party politics. In 1879 Debs was elected to the first of two terms as Terre Haute city clerk, and in 1884 won election as state representative from Terre Haute and Vigo County. His path toward being a leader in certain Terre Haute social circles seemed to be set.

In 1875, however, he began to veer onto another path. He joined the newly established Vigo Lodge of the Brotherhood of Locomotive Firemen as a charter member, and was elected secretary. Much of his salary from Hulman and Cox was devoted to his union work. In 1878 he was appointed assistant editor of the BLF's *Locomotive Firemen's Magazine*. Two years later, he became grand secretary of the national BLF and editor of the magazine. He served in that post until 1891, when he retired as grand secretary, but he was persuaded to continue editing the magazine.

Amid these activities, Debs married Katherine Metzel in June 1885, although Kate's family considered Debs to be beneath her socially. Debs undoubtedly foresaw some advantages for his career in marrying Kate. Despite the belief of some biographers that the marriage was unhappy, it endured extraordinary strains that many unions would not: the increasing demands on Debs's time even when he was at home in Terre Haute, the almost unbelievable amount of traveling he did for speaking engagements, and at least one serious extramarital relationship on his side.

In 1893 Debs organized the American Railway Union, the first industrial union in the United States. The union had the first test of its strength the following year, when it struck the Great Northern Railway. After a three-week strike, the union emerged victorious, which led to appeals to Debs for the ARU to support the action against the Pullman Palace Car Company the following year. After some reluctance, Debs did approve the ARU's participation in the Pullman strike, though he made every attempt to avoid violent confrontation and to keep all union activities transparent to avoid charges of subversive actions. In spite of these efforts, he and fellow ARU leaders were jailed—charged with contempt of court for refusing to obey an injunction issued by a federal judge to end the strike. The federal government sought the injunction because of its claim that the Pullman strike was interfering with moving the U.S. mail. Debs was convicted of contempt in 1895 and served a six-month sentence at the McHenry County jail in Woodstock, Illinois.

Following the Pullman strike, Debs joined the Socialist Party. Between 1907 and 1912, Debs was associate editor and prolific writer for the party organ, the *Appeal to Reason*. He also was an indefatigable speaker on behalf of the socialist cause, attracting large and wildly enthusiastic crowds wherever he appeared. On the strength of this popularity the Socialist Party chose Debs to run as its candidate for president in the 1900, 1904, 1908, and 1912 elections. The adulation he attracted at the podium did not, however, translate into electoral success, as he had a modest showing in each of those contests. The best was in 1912, when he garnered approximately 900,000 votes. His next run as a socialist candidate was in 1916 for member of Congress from his home district in Terre Haute, which earned him another defeat.

He did not cease his political activity, however. In 1918 Debs made what is probably his most famous speech—an impassioned protest against U.S. involvement in World War I delivered in Canton, Ohio. The speech was vintage Debs, including his scathing reference to "the gentry who are today wrapped up in the American flag, who shout their claim from the housetops that they are the only patriots, and who have their magnifying glasses in hand, scanning the country for evidence of disloyalty."

As a result of this speech, Debs was indicted by a federal grand jury on June 29. Arrested in Cleveland, Ohio, the next day, he was charged with violating the Sedition Act of 1918 and convicted on September 12. He was sentenced to ten years in prison. Debs spent most of his time served at the federal prison in Atlanta. While serving his time, he was nominated for his fifth run as candidate for president, the first American to run for that office as a federal convict.

Though Debs's incarceration was unconventional—with regular visits from delegations and a close relationship with the warden—it took a serious physical and emotional toll on him. Already looking haggard by the time of his nomination, he was to serve another eighteen months before his sentence was commuted by President Warren G. Harding and he was released on Christmas Day,

Eugene V. Debs

1921. Debs never fully recovered either his health or his zest for the causes to which he had devoted all his waking thoughts and energies for decades. On October 20, 1926, he died in Lindlahr Sanitarium, near Chicago. He is buried in Highland Lawn Cemetery in Terre Haute.

Debs could be egotistical, certainly understandable in light of the hero worship he experienced as he traveled around the country giving speeches. On the other hand, he was selfless with his time and money, perhaps to the detriment of his marriage and certainly at the cost of his health. And, though wildly popular on a personal level, he was never able to translate that into political and electoral success. But he was straightforward in his dealings, a faithful friend to all who would meet him halfway, and a constant champion of the underdog.

LEIGH DARBEE

For Further Reading

Debs, Eugene V. *Letters of Eugene V. Debs*. Edited by J. Robert Constantine. Urbana: University of Illinois Press, 1990.

Ginger, Ray. *The Bending Cross: A Biography of Eugene Victor Debs*. New Brunswick, NJ: Rutgers University Press, 1949.

Salvatore, Nick. *Eugene V. Debs: Citizen and Socialist*. Urbana: University of Illinois Press, 1982.

DePauw, Washington C.

January 4, 1822–May 5, 1887

Industrialist, philanthropist, and benefactor of DePauw University.

While perhaps best known as the benefactor of the university in Greencastle, Indiana, that bears his name, Washington C. DePauw is not as famous for leading Indiana into the industrial age after the Civil War. He became the state's most influential entrepreneur and richest man in the postwar period through his various business enterprises, which included manufacturing, banking, railroads, and grain trading.

DePauw's energetic, purposeful life had its genesis in earlier generations. His grandfather, Charles, came to America from France with the famous French friend of the colonies, Marquis de Lafayette, serving with him through the Revolutionary War, including the decisive victory at Yorktown. His father, John, a lawyer and judge, surveyed and platted the town of Salem, Indiana, was a delegate to the state's first constitutional convention in 1816 in Corydon, was a general in the state militia, and served in both houses of the general assembly.

Washington, who was born in Salem in 1822, was already working in his father's grain business at age thirteen, once transporting merchandise for a hundred miles by wagon through the Indiana wilderness. John died when his son was just sixteen, but he had laid the foundation on which Washington's future successes would be built—with education, sending him to the two-room Washington County Seminary, which attracted students from as far away as Louisville, Kentucky, and with the best inheritance: wisdom and business skills.

DePauw briefly detoured into politics at age twenty-two when he was elected Washington County Clerk and also handled the duties of county auditor. Soon, however, his entrepreneurial spirit overshadowed political ambitions. He began working at a saw and gristmill, eventually owning it and then added other mills while also starting a bank and investing in the Second State Bank of Indiana. He also ventured into grain trading, farming, and merchandising, as well as building the Salem depot of the New Albany and Salem Railroad and constructing one of the earliest brick buildings in Salem.

In the early 1850s DePauw turned his attention south to New Albany, building a hotel and making substantial investments in banking. He later controlled a majority of shares in three of the six New Albany financial institutions. With the outbreak of the Civil War, DePauw became a major supplier of grain and feed for the Union army. He also bought government securities, redeeming them after the war for investment capital. By 1864 he was considered to be the richest man in Indiana with an income of about $300,000.

Following the war DePauw made New Albany his home and began an aggressive and successful push into manufacturing, either acquiring or investing in plants making such varied products as textiles and railroad spikes. His major success in manufacturing came in plate glass. His entry into glassmaking started in partnership with a cousin, John Ford, who had taken over the Star Glass Works in New Albany. DePauw bought out Ford and other investors in 1879 and increased the value of annual production to more than a $1 million a year and had a workforce that eventually exceeded 2,000, making the DePauw American

Plate Glass Works New Albany's largest employer. Profitability was harder to achieve because of competition from cheaper European imports, but by 1881 DePauw's company, aided by a tariff, was thriving, producing plate glass for windows and other products such as bottles, fruit jars, and apothecary jars.

Three key character traits—careful attention to detail, perseverance, and initiative—propelled DePauw's business successes, according to biographer Michael O'Brien. Historian Gerald Haffner, in his chronicle of New Albany's glass industry, wrote, "Washington C. DePauw possessed an acumen for investment. He seemingly could invest in projects no one would touch and, in the end, made the projects pay."

DePauw's commitment of capital to the glass business was praised by the *Louisville Courier-Journal*, which called him New Albany's best job creator. "Constantly improving his manufactories, never curtailing their capacity, he is, beyond doubt, a great benefactor to New Albany and the nerviest businessman in Indiana," the newspaper's editor wrote, adding that DePauw "invests his money as fast as he earns it, giving the workman employment and remuneration for his services." However, another view of DePauw was expressed by the *Jeffersonville Evening News* during a strike by plate glass workers in the winter of 1880, denouncing DePauw as a "heartless capitalist" who "rolls in fatness while they [the strikers] want food."

DePauw's wealth and success did make him controversial, like other nineteenth-century industry titans such as John D. Rockefeller and Andrew Carnegie, but beside an occasional strike nothing happened that compared to the tragedy at Carnegie's Homestead, Pennsylvania, steel plant when Pinkerton's armed guards hired by company officials killed and wounded many strikers. DePauw, on the other hand, lived where he did business and went to church with his workers and joined them in civic work such as the temperance movement. Some union leaders were strong opponents of alcohol, having seen drinking ruin the families of fellow workers.

DePauw's civic service also cut across potential social divisions. He started the Kingsley Mission Sunday School class for poor children, and it grew so large—seven hundred young people—that it met Sunday afternoons in the downtown New Albany Opera House. He led flood relief efforts in 1884 and established a fund for children in need.

Such accomplishments in the corporate and civic worlds made him politically attractive. In 1872 Democrats nominated him for lieutenant governor, but he declined. "I have neither the time nor the inclination for politics," DePauw explained. "I have found full work in endeavoring to assist in promoting the religious, benevolent and educational interests of Indiana."

His Christian faith grew stronger in response to tragedies such as the loss of his first two wives and five children. His first wife, Sarah Malott, died when she was just twenty-seven, in 1851, not long after the deaths of two of their three children. He married Catherine Newland in 1855 and they had nine years together and three children. Her death in 1864 contributed to his move to New Albany, to avoid the heartaches of their Salem years.

DePauw never kept a journal, but made this revealing comment at a Methodist conference in 1881: "The most joyous thing that ever came into my heart is the religion of Christ." He called for renewed dedication to Christ, noting, "We must come back by consecrating ourselves and our homes, our lives, our pocket books, our business, everything we have to Christ."

Obviously, he also had a zeal for higher education, helping rescue and expand a seminary for women in New Albany. Started in 1852, it was renamed the DePauw College for Young Ladies and lasted until the early twentieth century. DePauw also served two terms as a trustee of Indiana University.

His lasting link to higher education resulted from his service on the board of Indiana Asbury College, a school his sons attended and that faced closing because of the 1883 recession. When it became known that DePauw had included in his will a clause to start a new college under his name, Asbury officials asked him to transfer that intent to the struggling Methodist school in Greencastle. He agreed, pledging substantial support, with the stipulation that the school expand and become a university. As board president, DePauw immersed himself in the details of expansion, but did not live to see the full fruits of his contributions to the university. He died unexpectedly in 1887 on a trip to Chicago.

His son, Newland, was promptly named chairman of the DePauw board, and he and another son, Charles, continued to manage the businesses, which suffered crippling losses in the 1893 recession. DePauw's widow, Fannie, his third wife, carried on another part of the family legacy in starting rescue homes for prostitutes in New York City and Los Angeles. What has survived longest is his name on one of the top academic institutions in the Midwest.

RUSSELL PULLIAM

For Further Reading

Haffner, Gerald O. "The Glass Industry of New Albany," New Albany, IN: Indiana University Southeast Bookstore, 1982.

Lipin, Lawrence M. "Producers, Proletarians and Politicians: Opposition and Accommodation in the Small Industrializing City, 1850–1887." PhD diss., University of California, Los Angeles, 1989.

O'Brien, Michael. "A Nineteenth Century Hoosier Businessman, Washington Charles DePauw." Thesis, DePauw University, 1966.

Dillinger, John H. Jr.

June 22, 1903–July 22, 1934

Bank robber, gangster, and declared Public Enemy Number One by the Federal Bureau of Investigation.

By the time the city fathers of Goshen, Indiana, dedicated their bulletproof police booth strategically located opposite two banks on the corner of Main and Lincoln Avenues, the state's most infamous bank robber had already been dead for five years. The excitement of the event, however, was not lost on the locals as the mayor and police officials emphasized the booth could help lower rising insurance rates for the banks in Goshen and help protect the city. The booth worked; a Goshen bank was never robbed again and the booth, unused since 1969, has stood on the city's main corner as a lasting monument to the impact of John Dillinger on 1930s Indiana.

Dillinger's short but deadly ascent to the FBI's Public Enemy Number One was deeply felt in Indiana cities and towns—big and small. He focused the majority of his bank robberies on Hoosier soil—targeting banks in Daleville, East Chicago, Greencastle, Indianapolis, Montpelier, and South Bend, as well as overtaking police stations at Auburn, Peru, and Warsaw to steal machine guns and bulletproof vests. He also managed to embarrass law enforcement officials in Lake County by walking out of the "escape-proof" jail at Crown Point. Historian William Beverly anoints Dillinger as the best-known gangster of the Depression era, noting that while some of Dillinger's associates "had longer sheets . . . none had longer reputations."

Born on the east side of Indianapolis on June 22, 1903, John suffered the loss of his mother, who died just before his fourth birthday and he was raised primarily by a stern father (a neighborhood grocer by trade), his older sister, and eventually a stepmother. An unremarkable student, Dillinger began showing signs of delinquency by his teen years and dropped out of school before ever enrolling in high school. Dillinger's father moved the family southwest from Indianapolis to Mooresville in adjacent Morgan County in about 1920. The move to the country did little to curtail Dillinger's emerging antisocial behaviors—he was arrested on suspicion of auto theft in 1922; joined and later was dishonorably discharged from the U.S. Navy. In September 1924 Dillinger and an accomplice robbed a local merchant and were quickly arrested. Dillinger was sentenced to ten to twenty-one years in the Indiana State Penitentiary at Michigan City, which he entered on September 16, 1924. While incarcerated, Dillinger was a quick study and made friends with some of the era's most notorious criminals, gaining an education in criminal activity.

He was paroled in 1933 after serving more than eight years for a fifty-dollar take. The Great Depression and a poorly prepared law enforcement community combined to create an ideal environment for Dillinger to quickly pursue his new life of crime. Within a month after leaving prison, he and an accomplice were suspected of robbing the Commercial Bank at Daleville in Delaware County of $3,500. Days later and just forty-five miles north, Dillinger was identified as part of a small gang that robbed the First National Bank of Montpelier in Blackford County of about $7,000. A subsequent robbery followed in tiny Bluffton, Ohio, in August—and the next month Dillinger and his gang broke their established modus operandi and robbed their first "big city" bank in downtown Indianapolis, netting $24,800. Dillinger escaped to the compact working-class neighborhoods on the east side of Indianapolis that he knew well and eluded capture.

Dillinger's luck ran out, however, later in September when he was arrested by police in Dayton, Ohio, and returned to the Allen County Jail in Lima, Ohio, for the previous Bluffton bank robbery. Some of Dillinger's friends, who had escaped from the state prison in Indiana, went to Ohio in October 1933 and, posing as Indiana law enforcement officials, sprung him from jail. However, the sheriff was shot and killed in the escape, and for the first time, Dillinger was directly linked to a murder.

Back on the streets, Dillinger returned to two things he knew well—Indiana and robbing banks. First, however, Dillinger and his associates raided two police station arsenals. Days later, his gang pulled its most successful heist ever—walking out of the Central National Bank of Greencastle with $144,000 in cash and bonds. In the weeks and months that followed, smaller robberies occurred out of state, but in early 1934 Dillinger was again linked with murder in a gun battle following the robbery of $15,000 at the First National Bank in East Chicago. Witnesses identified Dillinger as the gunman who fatally shot patrolman William Patrick O'Malley.

John Dillinger Jr.

When Governor PAUL V. MCNUTT turned up the heat by activating Indiana National Guard troops, Dillinger and his gang fled to Florida and then to Arizona. Dumb luck intervened in January 1934 when a fire broke out at the Tucson motel where Dillinger and his gang were hiding out. A firefighter recognized Dillinger and the local police caught the criminals and Dillinger was extradited to Indiana for O'Malley's murder.

A massive fleet of police transported America's most wanted criminal back to Lake County—with local officials insisting that Dillinger be jailed in Crown Point rather than the state prison at Michigan City. Inside the county jail, a surreal scene played out as county prosecutor Robert G. Estill and Sheriff Lillian M. Holley (who had assumed the office after her husband was killed while trying to arrest a murder suspect) were goaded by local, state, and national reporters, photographers and cameramen to "pose" with Dillinger inside the jail. No handcuffs were in sight for Dillinger, who looked relaxed in his pressed white shirtsleeves and vest, striking a friendly pose by gently leaning his forearm over the shoulder of a peevishly smiling Estill. Holley appeared less enamored with the display and she, along with Estill, were severely criticized after Dillinger escaped the jail on March 3, 1934, one that Holley had declared as "escape proof." Compounding the embarrassment, Dillinger even stole the sheriff's Ford. Estill, voted from office in the subsequent election, had attempted to get Dillinger transferred to the state prison, but was rebuked by a Lake County judge.

Federal authorities finally entered the hunt for Dillinger. His theft of Holley's car and its subsequent dumping in Illinois violated the federal Dyer Act, springing the fledgling FBI into action. A $25,000 reward was offered for the dead or alive capture of Dillinger, who continued his crime spree in Illinois and Wisconsin. Dillinger surfaced again in Indiana in the spring of 1934, this time overpowering a city police officer at Warsaw and getting away with more guns, ammunition, and bulletproof vests. Not surprisingly, another bank robbery followed shortly—this one a poorly executed robbery of $28,000 from the Merchants National Bank in downtown South Bend on June 30, 1934. In the ensuing shoot-out on a busy Saturday afternoon sidewalk, South Bend patrolman Harold Wagner was killed, and four others were injured.

Time was running out for Dillinger, however, as law enforcement continued to gain in its professionalism with state and federal officials taking the first steps toward shedding patronage systems that had long been the hallmark of police agencies in Indiana and elsewhere. Other advances included the development of crime laboratories, extending training of fingerprint identification, use of photography, and comprehensive efforts to obtain and maintain criminal records of criminals in each state. In Indiana, the general assembly approved legislation to fund more officers and equipment. The added professionalism and resources coincided with efforts by the Indiana Bankers' Association and others to purchase the very first police radios for the Indiana State Police in 1934. The one-way radios allowed dispatches to go out to patrol officers in the field, but they still had to stop at local stores or elsewhere to telephone back to headquarters. However, radio communications *between* police agencies, local and state, remained far out of reach in this era. These limitations gave distinct advantages to Dillinger and his ilk, as did the 1932 introduction of the first widely available V-8 engine from Ford, putting small-town police departments and state police officers at a distinct disadvantage as criminals eagerly stole the popular and fast new Fords.

While Indiana's law enforcement community had just begun improving, police in Chicago and federal authorities were already quite sophisticated, including their use of cash and other favors to extract information from sources. Informant tips from prostitutes and others allowed police to track Dillinger to the Biograph Theater in the Lincoln Park neighborhood of Chicago. Ultimately, Dillinger's love of women, movies, and a desire to escape the stifling summer heat led to his death, shot down by federal agents as he left an "air conditioned" showing of *Manhattan Melodrama* on July 22, 1934. Bizarre details followed—thousands strolled by a Chicago funeral parlor to see Dillinger's body being prepared for transport back to Indiana and eventually to his sister's bungalow outside Indianapolis. There, *Time* magazine reported, 2,500 mourners filed past the casket. The next day, the article added, a "cortege set off for Indianapolis Crown Hill Cemetery where President Benjamin Harrison and three Vice Presidents rest in peace."

ANDREW E. STONER

For Further Reading

Beineke, John. *Hoosier Public Enemy: A Life of John Dillinger.* Indianapolis: Indiana Historical Society Press, 2014.

Beverly, William. *On the Lam: Narratives of Flight in J. Edgar Hoover's America.* Jackson: University Press of Mississippi, 2003.

Matera, Dora. *John Dillinger: The Life and Death of America's First Celebrity Criminal.* New York: Carroll & Graf Publishers, 2005.

Olsen, Marilyn. *Gangsters, Gunfire and Political Intrigue: The Story of the Indiana State Police.* Indianapolis: .38 Special Press, 2001.

Dillon, John Brown

1808?–February 27, 1879

Lawyer, journalist, and the "Father of Indiana History."

On August 8, 1838, readers of the *Indiana Democrat* in Indianapolis were greeted by a special correspondence from the northern Indiana community of Logansport, which had been originally printed in the *Logansport Telegraph*. The article, signed "A Visitor to the Lake," reported on the sighting of a sixty-foot-long creature sliding through the once quiet waters of Lake Manitou, located near Rochester in what is now Fulton County. The article quoted one eyewitness, who viewed the monster from the safety of the shoreline, as describing the beast's head as "being about three feet across the frontal bone . . . but the neck tapering, and having the character of the serpent; color dingy, with large bright yellow spots." The monster inhabiting what came to be celebrated as "Devil's Lake" received attention nationwide, with reports on its existence published in Buffalo, Boston, and New York.

The man responsible for the *Telegraph*'s publication of this unlikely story was a person who, in all other respects, seemed to be the least likely to come up with such a whopper of a tale—John Brown Dillon, who became known as the "Father of Indiana History" for his much respected *History of Indiana*, which went through four editions between 1843 and 1859 and helped save the state's past for future generations through his work with a number of early Hoosier historical organizations. His writings won praise from Indiana historians who came after him, with one, EMMA LOU THORNBROUGH, commending Dillon for being the "only person in the state in this period whose writings deserved to be called history by modern standards of historical scholarship."

Details about Dillon's early life are sketchy at best. Born sometime in 1808 in Wellsburg, Brooke County, in present-day West Virginia, Dillon and his family soon moved to Belmont County, Ohio. After the death of his father, nine-year-old Dillon was apprenticed to a printer in Charleston. At the age of seventeen Dillon moved to Cincinnati, where he displayed literary skill, having his poems published in several local newspapers. Sometime in his life Dillon had suffered a visual malformity, and always could be seen wearing dark-green eyeglasses equipped with side mirrors. A shy man, he never removed his eyeglasses, even among his friends.

By 1834 Dillon had settled in Logansport, where he studied law and was admitted to the Cass County bar in 1840. However, he never established a law practice, preferring instead, noted his friend, fellow attorney Horace P. Biddle, to spend his time on "hoary border legends, traditional story, but more especially local history." Dillon pursued these interests through a career in pioneer journalism, starting work as an editor for the *Logansport Canal Telegraph* in August 1834. A year later he purchased an interest in the newspaper, which, by 1836, had changed its name to the *Logansport Telegraph*.

Dillon's work as a historian soon usurped his journalism career. He started his research on a history of Indiana in 1838, receiving assistance from U.S. Senator John Tipton, a close friend. Dillon left Logansport in 1842, moving to Indianapolis to pursue his historical studies and find funding for his history. Although he could rely on materials from the state library and private collections, Dillon lamented that "many interesting facts, connected with the early settlement of Indiana, have been perverted, or lost forever, because they were never recorded, and the stream of tradition seldom bears to the present, faithfully, the history of the past." Still, his *Historical Notes on the Discovery and Settlement of the Territory Northwest of the Ohio*, appeared in 1843, and was followed sixteen years later by his *History of Indiana*. Fellow Hoosier historian George S. Cottman, founder of the *Indiana Magazine of History*, praised him as the first in the state to enter the field "with any seriousness of purpose, and his contributions exceed in value any that have come after." In his writing Dillon displayed "immense industry, unflagging perseverance and an ever-present purpose to find and state the truth," said Cottman.

Dillon himself wrote that in his work he was striving to give an "impartial" recording of history. He noted in his preface to his *History of Indiana* that in writing the book he attempted to keep his mind free from such influences as "ambitious contentions between distinguished men, or from false traditions, or from national partialities and antipathies, or from excited conflicts between the partisans of antagonistic political systems, or from dissensions among uncharitable teachers of different creeds of religion."

In 1845 the state legislature elected Dillon as state librarian, a post he held until 1851, when a Democratic legislature replaced him with Nathaniel Bolton. Dillon later served as assistant secretary of state, secretary to the State Board of Agriculture and held a number of offices with the Indiana Historical Society, including secretary and librarian. He proved indefatigable at adding books and manuscripts to the Society's early collection. In addition to state offices, Dillon served on a variety of Indianapolis governmental bodies, including being a member of the Marion County Library Board and a school trustee.

In 1862 Dillon left Indianapolis for Washington, D.C., where he first worked as clerk to the Department of the Interior and then as clerk with the House Military Affairs Committee. Civic leaders in Indianapolis remembered Dillon's contributions to the state, with noted attorney CALVIN FLETCHER calling upon the state legislature to bring the historian back to Indiana to write a history of the state's contribution to the Civil War. Dillon finally returned to Indianapolis in 1875, living in a room on Washington Street. He struggled to make a living, even having to sell his beloved library in order to make ends meet. Dillon died at age seventy-one and was buried at Crown Hill Cemetery.

RAY E. BOOMHOWER

For Further Reading

Coburn, General John, "Life and Services of John B. Dillon, *Indiana Historical Society Publications*. Vol. 2, no. 2. Indianapolis: Bowen-Merrill Company, 1895.

Cottman, George S. "John Brown Dillon: The Father of Indiana History." *Indiana Magazine of History* 1 (1905): 3–8.

Ruegamer, Lana, *A History of the Indiana Historical Society, 1830–1980*. Indianapolis: Indiana Historical Society, 1980.

A collection with John Brown Dillon's notes and material on his histories of the state, and correspondence concerning the Indiana Historical Society, is in the Manuscript and Rare Books Division of the Indiana State Library in Indianapolis.

Dreiser, Theodore

August 27, 1871–December 28, 1945

Author of more than twenty novels, plays, short story collections, and autobiographies, including *A Hoosier Holiday, Sister Carrie, Jennie Gerhardt, The Financier,* and *An American Tragedy*.

In 1999 Random House published a list of the one hundred best English-language novels of the twentieth century. Two of the novels listed were *An American Tragedy* and *Sister Carrie*, both written by Theodore Dreiser, one of the most important novelists in American literary history. He was closely associated with early-twentieth-century literary naturalism, which depicted the harshness of everyday life. Dreiser consistently challenged basic assumptions of American literature and thought regarding moral and ethical choices and the relevance of traditional middle-class values during a time of rapid industrialization, large-scale immigration, and the birth of American consumer society. Dreiser's writing instead adopted a much more deterministic narrative stance, illustrating the absence of free will. He created characters deprived of autonomy, ruled by inescapable laws of heredity and environment, marked by an inability to resist their desires, their "innate animality," characters "who were not responsible in a world they had not made."

But Dreiser's work and life contradict themselves. For in spite of his commitment to the deterministic ethos of naturalism, his numerous assertions that the "strong" will inevitably, rightfully, rule over the "weak," his rejection of American optimism and its belief that the future will automatically be an improvement on the present, Dreiser also demonstrated a lifelong sympathy for the underdog, the poor, the workingman and woman, the immigrant, and the "losers" in the struggle for survival. Separating himself from the prevailing Social Darwinism of the 1890s, Dreiser never believed that the "survival of the fittest" entailed the inherent and permanent superiority of the privileged classes. Even though they were imprisoned by forces outside their control, he always insisted that the helpless should be helped. Indeed in one of his earliest published newspaper articles, "Cheyenne, Haunt of Misery and Crime," describing one of the poorest, roughest Chicago neighborhoods of his day, written in 1892 for the *Chicago Daily Globe*, we hear for the first time that "deterministic yet compassionate narrative voice that leads us through his greatest works." It is this voice that defines Dreiser as both a determinist and a reformer, as "simultaneously the observer of nature's law of survival and the apologist for its victims."

This identification with the American underclass is directly related to Dreiser's Indiana childhood. Born in Terre Haute to a devoutly Catholic, German immigrant father and a Mennonite mother of Czechoslovakian ancestry, the twelfth of thirteen children, Dreiser grew up poor, knowing both hunger and cold from an early age. Because of his father's inability to earn a living and the family's subsequent economic hardships, Dreiser spent little time with his father, moving in 1879 from Terre Haute to Vincennes to Sullivan with his mother, Sarah, and the two other youngest children.

In 1882 they relocated once again, this time to Evansville, after being rescued financially by the sudden appearance of Dreiser's oldest brother, PAUL DRESSER, the popular songwriter and entertainer. Then, one year later, following a brief stay in Chicago, they moved to Warsaw, where Dreiser graduated from high school.

Theodore Dreiser

Clearly, this migratory, somewhat fragmented, and impoverished childhood conditioned Dreiser's views on the poor and poverty. It also affected his later, hard fought but finally successful efforts to gain acceptance by the American literary establishment, dominated as it was and had always been by white, male, Anglo-Saxon East Coast Protestants. Walt Whitman's archetypal "shaggy outsider," Dreiser was the first major American writer raised on the wrong side of the tracks, the first great German American writer, and the first great American writer brought up in the Roman Catholic Church.

Dreiser left Warsaw for Chicago in 1887, spending two difficult years there, first as a dishwasher in a Greek restaurant and then as a clerk in a large hardware store. But in 1889 he discovered that for $200 he could attend Indiana State College, now Indiana University, in Bloomington, for one year. He arrived at an auspicious moment in the school's history, near the beginning of David Starr Jordan's tenure as president, a period when the campus was expanding, the curriculum was being modernized, and new, younger faculty were being hired. Never academically inclined, Dreiser did not do especially well in the classroom and for financial reasons did not stay for a second year, but his time in Bloomington was important to his development as a man and as a writer, if only because "his year away from working class strife had lifted him out of his milieu long enough to see it emotionally or objectively for the first time." At Bloomington he had broadened his social horizons and his intellectual and professional ambitions had grown. He began to understand that his future might hold more potential than he had previously thought possible.

Moving back to Chicago in 1890, just months before the death of his beloved mother, Dreiser did not return to Indiana for twenty-five years. He spent most of the 1890s as a newspaper reporter and editor (a career path common to many of the naturalists) in Chicago, Saint Louis, Pittsburgh, and finally New York, where he settled permanently in 1894. During this time he published his first novel, *Sister Carrie*, in 1900. Although that novel became an American classic and "changed the course of American letters," it was initially disastrously reviewed and harshly criticized for its alleged immorality and scandalous portrayal of human sexuality. Selling only a handful of copies, Dreiser did not write another novel for over a decade, not publishing his masterpiece, *An American Tragedy*, until 1925.

In the summer of 1915, Dreiser met his friend Franklin Booth, the Indiana artist and illustrator, at a party in New York. Booth had just bought a new automobile and he proposed that Dreiser travel back with him to Indiana by car. Dreiser instantly agreed and thus was born that uniquely American literary genre—the road novel. During the trip Dreiser visited all of the towns of his Indiana boyhood, meeting and observing a variety of people along the way and describing all of it in detail in the subsequent travel book *A Hoosier Holiday*. A celebration of not only his youth but also "the youth of a great country," the book is quite simply one of the best portrayals of the people, towns, and natural environments of Indiana ever written. The book, with the "Hail, Indiana!" chapter especially, extols the generative power of Indiana's soil and light, and eloquently declares that the state has "established its freedom from isolation and mere locality and accomplished here a quite vital contact with universal thought," thus dismissing forever H. L. Mencken's scornful labeling of the "Indiana peasant." Ultimately, that may prove Dreiser's greatest contribution to the state he always remembered as truly his own, his "native land."

DAVID L. GUGIN

For Further Reading

Dreiser, Theodore. *Dawn: An Autobiography of Early Youth*. Santa Rosa: Black Sparrow, 1998.
———. *A Hoosier Holiday*. Bloomington and Indianapolis: Indiana University Press, 1998.
Loving, Jerome. *The Last Titan*. Berkeley and Los Angeles: University of California Press, 2005.

Dresser, Paul

April 22, 1858–January 31, 1906

Songwriter, comedian, actor, and author of the state song "On the Banks of the Wabash, Far Away."

> Oh, the moonlight's fair tonight
>   along the Wabash,
> From the fields there comes the
>   breath of new mown hay.
> Through the sycamores the candle
>   lights are gleaming,
> On the banks of the Wabash, far away.

Had Paul Dresser done nothing more than pen the song "On the Banks of the Wabash, Far Away," his legacy as a major figure in American musical history would be secure.

When published in 1897 it became an immediate hit, yielding more than $50,000 in sheet-music royalties within a year. In 1913 the Indiana General Assembly adopted it as the state's official song. And more than a century later its yearning nostalgic strains still tug at the heartstrings of Hoosiers and lovers of sentimental songs. Dresser wrote more than one hundred songs, twenty-five of which landed a spot in the Billboard Top 25.

For the last two decades of the nineteenth century, Dresser was a dominant figure and his songs retained their popularity for decades after his death. But in 2003, when music historian Clayton W. Henderson published his magisterial On the Banks of the Wabash: The Life and Music of Paul Dresser, he lamented that Dresser's music had fallen into cultural oblivion. Although the songs had still been sung well into the 1950s, he noted, by the turn of the twentieth century they had faded from memory. "Now most would be hard-pressed to sing much from the late nineteenth and early twentieth centuries," he wrote.

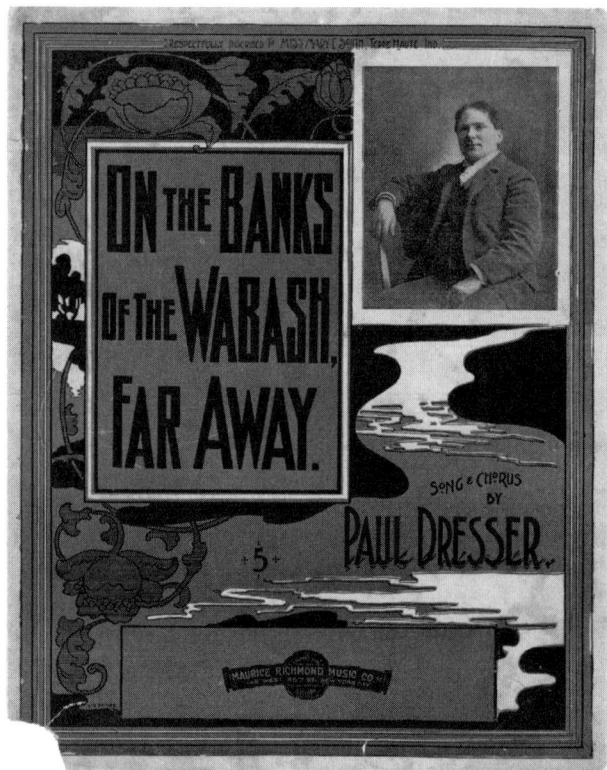

Sheet music to Paul Dresser's classic "On the Banks of the Wabash, Far Away."

True enough at the time. But in the years since, Dresser's legacy has seen a digital revival. Search Youtube.com and you will find dozens of period recordings of Dresser tunes: a digitized version of a scratchy 1898 wax cylinder recording featuring the famed Irish tenor George Gaskin singing "On the Banks of the Wabash" on an early Columbia recording; Al Jolson singing the same song in 1935; a smooth quartet version from the Mills Brothers from 1943; and, most tellingly, a twenty-first century recording by popular singer-songwriter Rufus Wainwright. And in the fall of 2014, the city of Terre Haute paid tribute to Dresser by erecting a six-and-a-half-foot tall bronze sculpture by artist Teresa Clark in a park on the banks of the Wabash River.

"On the Banks of the Wabash" has never really fallen out of favor with Hoosiers. In fact, the complex, contested story of how and where it came to be written has fascinated Indiana and music historians for more than a century. One oft-repeated account has it that Dresser's younger brother, novelist THEODORE DREISER, actually wrote the first verse and chorus. Another, arguably more plausible account, holds that Dresser finished the song during a restorative visit to the West Baden Hot Springs. And there are a handful of competing tales that place the composition in places such as Chicago or the Mudlavia springs in Warren County, Indiana.

Just as the source of the song is shrouded in controversy, so is its legacy. In 1917, just three years after Indiana adopted Dresser's song as its own, James Hanley and Ballard MacDonald wrote a song called "Back Home Again in Indiana" that lifted liberally from the lyrics, images, and melody of "On the Banks of the Wabash, Far Away." Over the years, the Hanley-Ballard piece, commonly referred to simply as "Indiana," has surpassed Dresser's in popularity. It was featured in the 1940 Hollywood movie Remember the Night with Fred McMurray and Barbara Stanwyck, was often performed by Louis Armstrong, and for decades has been part of the opening ritual at the Indianapolis 500 auto race, where Jim Nabors's version was a staple for decades, and at the Little 500 bicycle race in Bloomington.

In the 1940s Dreiser pressed an unsuccessful allegation of copyright violation against the publishers of "Back Home Again in Indiana," but his effort was thwarted by a counter claim that the owners of Dresser's song had granted permission for the reuse of the melody with revised lyrics.

All of these competing claims speak to the fascinating nature of Dresser's career and the hold it has had on generations of music lovers, and if further evidence is needed, Dresser's life received a Hollywood treatment in the 1942 movie musical *My Gal Sal* starring Victor Mature and Rita Hayworth. But Dresser's legacy is as expansive as his famous waistline. A man of immense appetites, who made and spent more than one fortune during his lifetime, he reputedly weighed some three hundred pounds at his death.

In many ways, Dresser was the embodiment—figuratively and literally—of the gilded age in which he lived. The oldest of ten children, he was born in Terre Haute to a struggling working-class family. His father, a German immigrant, was a weaver and dyer of wool and a sometime wool mill manager. Dresser was raised in western Indiana, in Terre Haute and Sullivan, and was an indifferent student who spent a couple of years at Saint Meinrad Academy.

But by the time he was eighteen, Dresser had decided to pursue a career in show business. Starting around 1876, he was apprenticing on the minstrel and medicine-show circuits. In 1880 he made a splash in Evansville, building a burgeoning reputation as a performer, songwriter, humorist, and actor whose comic essays appeared in area newspapers. Over the next few years, he worked as a singer, comedian, and actor on a regional vaudeville circuit extending to Chicago, Indianapolis, and Louisville, with occasional forays to the northeast. In 1886 Dresser scored his first hit as a songwriter with a melancholy ballad about a Civil War veteran who dies while awaiting "The Letter that Never Came." He continued acting on stage, but increasingly it was his songwriting that caught the public's attention.

At the beginning of the 1880s, music publishing was a widespread regional business. But by the end of the decade that had changed. New approaches to marketing and distributing songs led to a concentration of publishing houses in a Manhattan neighborhood that came to be known as Tin Pan Alley. It was a change that transformed the American music business—and Dresser was one of the founding figures in the new model.

Dresser came to understand that his songs were more profitable for his publisher than for himself. So in 1893 he leapt at the opportunity to become a partner, silent at first, in a new publishing house called Howley, Haviland and Company. He wrote songs, pitched them to performers, and recruited other songwriters into the fold. It was a move that made him a music magnate.

Over the next decade, what had been a fragmented cottage industry developed into a progressive modern industry that understood and capitalized on the great urban migration that saw millions of Americans move from the countryside to the city, as Dresser himself had, bringing with them a surging appetite for nostalgic ballads, sentimental love songs, and patriotic anthems. And Dresser, by all accounts, was master of the genre. One critic described him as the musical heir to Stephen Foster, "the only worthy successor," arguing that while his contemporaries focused on "catchy, easily memorable tunes," Dresser was special because he "persisted in writing songs dependent for their appeal on the effectiveness of human dramas sketched in their verses, their invocation of painful nostalgia, grief, and the burden of lost happiness and hope." Another critic wrote that Dresser was "less disposed toward clichés than so many of his rivals, less inclined to stretch an emotion to the point of a maudlin and cloying sentimentality," and described him as "a composer whose finest ballads have a winning charm and a lingering fragrance."

It's that "lingering fragrance" that pervades "On the Banks of the Wabash" and many of Dresser's other songs, and thus helped shape American musical tastes for the first half of the twentieth century, and beyond.

C. MARTIN ROSEN

For Further Reading

Dowell, Richard W. "'On the Banks of the Wabash': A Musical Whodunit." *Indiana Magazine of History* 66 (June 1970): 95–109.

Dreiser, Theodore. *Theodore Dreiser—Sister Carrie, Jennie Gerhardt, Twelve Men.* New York: Library of America, 1987.

Ewen, David. *Panorama of American Popular Music.* Englewood Cliffs, NJ: Prentice Hall, 1957.

Henderson, Clayton. *On the Banks of the Wabash: The Life and Music of Paul Dresser.* Indianapolis: Indiana Historical Society Press, 2003.

Digitized recordings of Dresser's songs can be heard at the following websites:

Irish tenor George Gaskin https://www.youtube.com/watch?v=KKwjgea53Io/.

Al Jolson https://www.youtube.com/watch?v=ROxPuI5Unkw/.
Rufus Wainwright http://www.youtube.com
/watch?v=kpZgIY5Zg18/.

Dudley, Frank V.
November 14, 1868–March 5, 1957

Artist and advocate for the preservation of the Indiana Dunes.

Frank V. Dudley is an artist widely viewed in the Midwest as a legendary figure who depicted the Indiana Dunes and its flora in an impressionist style and with vivid color. In addition to creating beautiful paintings of the Dunes, he was also a tireless advocate for its preservation as state and national parks.

Born in 1868 to deaf parents in Delavan, Wisconsin, Dudley was the oldest of three boys, all with normal hearing. He left home at nineteen to take classes at the Art Institute of Chicago with his brother, Clarence, an aspiring photographer. During this time the Dudley brothers promoted various inventions of their craftsman father such as scaffolding and wallpaper cleaning compound before Frank established his own photography studio, where he enlarged and retouched portraits. By the early 1900s both brothers were exploring Chicago's environs looking for subjects for Frank to paint and Clarence to photograph. Their discovery of the Indiana Dunes, a wasteland for many, inspired Clarence first, but over time Frank learned to appreciate the barren dunes, evoking his aesthetic appreciation for an ever-changing landscape.

Dudley established himself as an exhibiting artist at the Art Institute of Chicago in 1902. Two years later his wife, Mahala Boxwell, died of tuberculosis. He immersed himself in the Chicago art world, joining the Palette and Chisel Club and the Chicago Society of Artists, painting outdoors in various locations many canvases concerned with the tonal effects of snow and moonlight. As a charter member of the Cliff Dwellers Club in 1907, Dudley came into contact with a wide range of professionals, including Jens Jensen, a conservationist who later helped to establish the Chicago Park District. Jensen's wide-ranging concerns with landscape preservation led him to the Indiana Dunes and the founding of the Prairie Club in 1908 and the Friends of Our Native Landscape in 1913, the same year that Dudley married his second wife, Maida Lewis. He joined Jensen's new organization just as the Dunes began to haunt his mind and challenge him to capture the natural grandeur of its timeless landscape.

Dudley painted the Dunes landscape almost exclusively for more than forty years. He and Maida participated in the growing conservation movement to save the Dunes. His paintings memorialized the 1917 Dunes Pageant, sponsored by the Prairie Club and numerous other civic organizations. The following year he exhibited thirty paintings in a one-man show at the Art Institute, under the auspices of the Friends of Our Native Landscape and the twelve organizations of the Conservation Council. In 1921 he received the Art Institute of Chicago's Logan Medal for his painting, *Duneland*, now in the permanent collection of the Brauer Museum of Art at Valparaiso University, a gift from the Art Institute of Chicago. Funds from this Logan Prize enabled Dudley to build a cottage in the Dunes, which he and Maida named Duneland Studio, bringing a wide range of Dunes visitors to open houses on Sundays.

In the ensuing four decades Dudley attracted a following of loyal art collectors who sought out his paintings at the Chicago Galleries Association and the Hoosier Salon, his two most popular venues. The Indiana Dunes State Park was established in 1923 and was open to visitors by 1929. Dudley's 1931 exhibition at the Chicago Galleries celebrated the ten-year anniversary of the Duneland Studio. From 1934 to 1952 Dudley gave one painting a year in lieu of rent for Cottage 108 to the state of Indiana, on whose property his Duneland Studio now stood. Dudley died in 1957, and in 1967 Maida sold the state of Indiana fifty-three paintings. These paintings are now in the collection of the Indiana State Museum, the largest public collection of Dudley paintings. Federal protection came when the Indiana Dunes National Lakeshore, surrounding the state park, was dedicated in 1966.

The Brauer Museum of Art, located just south of the Indiana Dunes State Park, owns twenty paintings by Dudley, including *Sandland's Even Song* and *Land of Sky and Song*, both among the larger paintings that Dudley created. James Dabbert, a collector and Dudley scholar, was the driving force behind the Brauer Museum's 2006 retrospective exhibition of Dudley's work that included more than seventy paintings from all phases of the artist's long career. Additionally, Dabbert was the editor of the accompanying book *The Indiana Dunes Revealed: The Art of Frank V. Dudley*, the first book on the artist, with a thorough biographical essay by Dabbert and additional essays by founding Brauer Museum director Richard H. W. Brauer, historians J. Ronald and Joan Gibb Engel, and art historians Wendy Greenhouse and William H. Gerdts. The Brauer Museum continues to exhibit its Dudley collection as well as works from numerous collectors and donors, not only from Porter County but also from throughout the Great Lakes region. In this way the Brauer may serve the greater good of extending Dudley's own purpose of bringing attention to preserving the fragile Lake Michigan dunes environment.

Today, Dudley paintings are enjoying a lively market and widespread general appreciation, impressing all who see them as they proclaim the beauty of a primeval landscape beloved by many, bordered by steel mills to the west. Greenhouse described the enduring appeal of Dudley's art by saying, "The early success of Dudley's Dunes paintings was due to more than a straightforward realism, however. Striking a balance between subject and sentiment, Dudley satisfied traditionalist expectations for art to be at once accessibly representational and inspirational."

Dudley's works have delighted the public with their blend of a reverent treatment of the landscape and a lovely sensitivity for color and light. While more modern forms of expression interested art enthusiasts beginning in the early twentieth century, Dudley turned his artistic insights to a place of unique character to record his impressions that were based equally on observation and on imagination, as he let his feelings for the place act upon him and drive his creativity. His influence is such that many Dunes visitors who have seen his paintings, as they stand among the dunes and look out toward Lake Michigan, notice perhaps for the first time the many colors and natural wonders that surround them.

GREGG HERTZLIEB

For Further Reading

Dabbert, James, ed. *The Indiana Dunes Revealed: The Art of Frank V. Dudley*. Champaign: University of Illinois Press, 2006.

Engel, J. Ronald. *Sacred Sands: The Struggle for Community in the Indiana Dunes*. Middletown, CT: Wesleyan University Press, 1983.

Schoon, Kenneth J. *Dreams of Duneland: A Pictorial History of the Indiana Dunes Region*. Bloomington, IN: Quarry Books, 2013.

The Duesenberg Brothers

Friedrich, December 6, 1876–July 26, 1932,
August, December 12, 1879–January 18, 1955

Automotive pioneers and builders of successful racecars and ultraluxury motorcars.

With their complementary automotive talents, the Duesenberg brothers, Friedrich (Fred), an engineering genius, and August (Augie), a tireless worker with a passion for speed and competition, were destined to combine forces to create winning racecars and the world's finest passenger cars. The German-born brothers immigrated with their family to America in 1885 and settled in Iowa. At an early age, both exhibited great aptitude for things mechanical, and it was not long before they were building, repairing, and racing bicycles. Fred learned that racing his product created interest and sales, and before he parted company with two-wheelers, he had established two world speed records with his bicycles. Intrigued with the internal combustion engine, Fred and Augie built a small one of their own design around 1900 and mounted it onto one of their bicycles. It was their first motorized vehicle and was exhibited at a show in Chicago.

Soon thereafter, Fred was exposed to the various aspects of automobile production when he began working for Rambler in Kenosha, Wisconsin. He later opened an automobile repair business in Iowa and became acquainted with local attorney Edward Mason. With Mason's backing, Fred designed and built a successful two-cylinder automobile. The Mason Motor Car Company, incorporated in April 1906, began production in August. The car was marketed as "The Fastest and Strongest Two-Cylinder Car in the World." It soon proved itself as an impressive hill climber and racecar.

Fred and Augie started their racing activities in earnest by entering Masons in many races. Their new four-cylinder engine design featured long vertical rocker arms that controlled the horizontally situated valves. The unique arrangement, patented by Fred, was noted for its simplicity, reliability, and high performance. In 1913 Eddie Rickenbacker joined the Duesenberg racing team and racked up important victories, spurring on the brothers' fame. They then established the Duesenberg Motor Company after a move to Saint Paul, Minnesota, and soon received a request to build engines for a racing boat for Commodore James

A. Pugh of Chicago. The craft was fitted with two inline twelve-cylinder power plants producing an amazing 800 horsepower each. The boat set a new world speed record of sixty miles per hour. With this success, the Duesenbergs attracted the attention of the Loew-Victor Company of Chicago. With war brewing in Europe, an agreement was reached with Loew-Victor for the Duesenbergs to produce aircraft and marine engines for the military forces of England, Italy, Russia, and the United States. A new factory was built in Elizabeth, New Jersey, for this purpose, and by 1918 its workforce numbered 1,200 people.

Fred and Augie withdrew from the large corporation after the war to concentrate on the development of racecars for the 1919 season. The brothers rented a small space in Newark, New Jersey, where they built their first overhead cam straight-eight engine. They gained national attention in April 1920 when a racecar powered by twin Duesenberg straight-eight engines set a world speed record of 156 miles per hour on the sands of Daytona Beach. In addition to their racecar efforts, the brothers and their backers set in motion plans to manufacture a technically advanced passenger car with racecar features. To that end, a new corporation was formed in March 1920: the Duesenberg Automobile and Motors Company. Duesenberg was cast into the international spotlight in 1921 when hard-charging Jimmy Murphy drove a Duesenberg racecar to victory in the French Grand Prix at Le Mans.

The first passenger car to bear the Duesenberg name appeared at the New York Auto Salon in November 1920. The car featured an inline eight-cylinder overhead cam engine and four-wheel hydraulic brakes, both firsts on an American car. A quote in the sales catalog read, "Out of the crucible of racing has come commercial perfection." A factory to produce the new car was built in Indianapolis, which was chosen for its proximity to the famous motor speedway, where it could be utilized as a test track. The brothers became permanent Indiana residents. With great expectations, production began in 1921, however, by the end of 1922 a meager total of 150 cars had been sold. This was far short of the projected 2,400 figure that had been touted to investors. With little working capital available and an inadequate dealer network, the days of the company appeared to be numbered

A classic Duesenberg convertible.

as the firm went into receivership in 1924. Victories at the Indianapolis 500 in 1924, 1925, and 1927 made Duesenberg a household name, but did little to boost sales. However, the greatest days for the Duesenberg marque were yet to come as industrial genius and entrepreneur extraordinaire Errett Lobban Cord entered the picture.

Cord, flush with his success as president of the Auburn Automobile Company, was determined to expand his company's product line in 1926. Looking for an offering with more speed and prestige, Cord cast his eye on Duesenberg. He obtained control of the financially troubled company through an exchange of Auburn stock. Not only did Cord acquire one of America's most respected luxury models, but the deal also included Fred. Augie was not part of the new Duesenberg Inc., and he continued to run the racing team in second-floor quarters across the street from the factory. Cord challenged Fred to start with a clean slate and create the world's finest motorcar, regardless of cost. Fred was up to the challenge, and the result was the magnificent and incomparable Duesenberg Model J. The car was announced in the fall of 1928 with orders being filled in the spring of 1929. The list price was $8,500 for a running chassis, with complete cars starting at $13,500 and eventually reaching over $20,000. All Model Js carried custom coachwork. For these astronomical prices, customers got one of the largest, fastest, and most luxurious and technologically advanced automobiles in the world. There was nothing else like it in America. The heart of the car was a 420-cubic-inch, 32-valve, dual overhead cam straight eight engine that generated 265 horsepower. The chassis was built on a choice of either a 142 ½- or 153 ½-inch wheelbase. The car featured adjustable power brakes, automatic chassis lubrication, and a top speed of approximately 115 miles per hour.

A calamity befell the company and the automotive engineering world in July 1932 when Fred died from medical complications resulting from an automobile accident. He was driving a Duesenberg equipped with a prototype supercharged engine along the Lincoln Highway on a trip from New York to Indianapolis. His car went out of control when he swerved to avoid an oncoming car. Fred was thrown from the car, and his injuries were relatively minor. However, he developed pneumonia while recovering in the hospital and passed away several days later. At the age of fifty-five, the life of the great automotive genius was over. He held many patents including four-wheel hydraulic brakes, the pressurized cooling system with recovery tank, and an early version of the automatic transmission.

The Great Depression obviously had a devastating effect on automobile sales, particularly on luxury brands. Accordingly, Duesenberg was hard hit as poor economic conditions lingered into the 1930s. Ultrawealthy and famous individuals were eager Duesenberg purchasers, but their numbers were too small to sustain the ailing company. However, Duesenberg did not just fade into oblivion without an attempt to win customers. New body styles and supercharged engines were developed to attract buyers, but sales continued to decline, and by the mid-1930s the Model J was falling behind the times. The last of the fabulous Model Js were built in 1937. A total of only 481 of the highly coveted masterpieces had been produced by the time Duesenberg closed its doors.

Augie, however, continued with his automotive career, serving as a consultant to the Auburn Automobile Company. He developed land-speed and endurance racers with Ab Jenkins into the 1940s. Augie retired to a farm near Indianapolis after World War II. He died in 1955 at the age of seventy-six, ending a career that witnessed some of the greatest automotive engineering achievements, many for which he and Fred were responsible. Together, they were a rare combination of brains and talent whose contributions to automobile racing and passenger car history are truly remarkable.

The Auburn Cord Duesenberg Automobile Museum, opened in 1974 in the building that housed the headquarters of the Auburn Automobile Company, has on exhibit more than 120 cars built from 1894 through 1999, including the most extensive collection of Auburn, Cord, and Duesenberg cars.

JON M. BILL

For Further Reading

Bill, Jon M. *Duesenberg Race Cars and Passenger Cars*. Hudson, WI: Iconografix, 2005.

Butler, Don. *Auburn Cord Duesenberg*. Minneapolis, MN: Crestline Publishing, 1992.

Roe, Fred. *Duesenberg: The Pursuit of Perfection*. Second Edition. New York: Dalton Watson, 1982.

Dunn, Jacob P. Jr.
April 12, 1855–June 6, 1924
Journalist, historian, and political reformer.

In the early summer of 1924 a reporter for the *Indianapolis News*, preparing an obituary on the life and career of Jacob Piatt Dunn Jr., asked for a comment from U.S. Senator Samuel M. Ralston. The former Indiana governor had nothing but praise for the man who worked as his private secretary in Washington, D.C. Expressing his admiration for Dunn, Ralston noted that when the two had returned to Indianapolis from the nation's capital he could tell that something was wrong and that death was near.

Characteristically, Ralston's friend and fellow Democrat was convinced he would be all right. "His will power was strong," Ralston said of Dunn, "and he was slow to admit that he could not accomplish anything he undertook. The idea of his having to surrender to the will of any man or even to physical troubles was to him apparently a preposterous thought."

This stubbornness, even in the face of the illness that killed him, stood Dunn in good stead throughout his life as he battled to reform Indiana's wayward electoral system during the Progressive Era and struggled to save Indiana's history from being carelessly lost. During his career Dunn produced riveting firsthand accounts of the state's past, improved the Indiana State Library and the state's public library system, and helped preserve the language of the Miami Indians through support from the U.S. Bureau of Ethnology.

Dunn was born in Lawrenceburg, Indiana, the third of five children raised by Jacob and Harriet Louisa Tate Dunn. Dunn's father was the son of Isaac Dunn, one of the first settlers in the Whitewater valley as well as a judge, bank president, businessman, and postmaster in Lawrenceburg. Jacob Piatt Dunn Sr., a cattle trader for a time and a lifelong Democrat, was one of many who traveled to California in 1849 seeking his fortune in the goldfields. Jacob Sr. returned to Lawrenceburg in the spring of 1854, moving his family to a farm on the Ohio River. In the summer of 1861 he moved his family to Indianapolis, where he opened a slaughterhouse and pork-packing business in partnership with James McTaggert.

After attending private schools for several years, the junior Dunn entered the public schools in Indianapolis in 1867. Four years later he enrolled at Earlham College in Richmond, graduating in 1874 with a bachelor's degree in science. Two years later he received a University of Michigan law degree. After returning to Indianapolis, he continued studying law with the firm of McDonald and Butler. Like his father, however, Dunn headed west to seek his fortune, as he and his brothers looked after a stake in a silver mine owned by their father and also did some prospecting. While in Colorado Dunn worked as a reporter and wrote articles for such newspapers as the *Denver Republican, Denver Tribune, Leadville Chronicle, Maysville Democrat,* and *Denver Rocky Mountain News.*

Dunn returned to Indianapolis in 1884 and, four years later, became head of the Democratic State Central Committee's literary bureau. This was the beginning of his long career as a "political man of letters" who earned his living as a "professional Democrat." The legislature elected Dunn as the state librarian in 1889 and 1891, he served on the Indiana Public Library Commission for twenty years, and he was Indianapolis city controller for two terms (1904–06 and 1914–16). Even while serving in these posts, Dunn continued to contribute to newspapers. He wrote and served as editor for at time at the *Indianapolis Sentinel,* and later produced articles for the *Indianapolis News, Indianapolis Star,* and *Indianapolis Times.* In 1902 he lost to Republican incumbent Jesse Overstreet in the race to represent Indiana's Seventh Congressional District. On November 23, 1892, Dunn married Charlotte Elliott Jones, and they had two daughters, Caroline and Eleanor. The couple lived for much of their married life in a house at 914 North Pennsylvania Street that had been built in 1868 by Charlotte's father.

Political animal though he was, Dunn wrote more than just partisan journalism. Described by a fellow Indiana historian as possessing "a versatile mind and a facile pen," Dunn combined his interest in history and his western experiences to produce *Massacres of the Mountains: History of the Indian Wars of the Far West* (1886), which received a glowing review from a New York amateur historian named Theodore Roosevelt. In 1886 Dunn also helped reorganize what had been a dying Indiana Historical Society—an institution he served as recording secretary until his death. Other historical publications by Dunn included

Indiana: A Redemption from Slavery (1888), *Documents Relating to the French Settlements on the Wabash* (1894), *The Mission to the Ouabache* (1902), the two-volume *Greater Indianapolis* (1910), and his five-volume state history *Indiana and Indianans* (1919).

Dunn merged his political, reform, and historical interests throughout his career. His daughter, Caroline, who followed in her father's footsteps by pursuing a career in a number of Indiana libraries, noted that her father was fascinated with politics. Much of his writing, she said, was "political or politico-economical." In an article titled "Duty of the State to Its History," which appeared in the December 1910 issue of the *Indiana Magazine of History*, Dunn set out his philosophy about the blending of history and politics. He agreed with the Roman historian Tacitus that the "chief use of history is to promote good government." Dunn noted that the democracy of his own day was a far cry from the absolute monarch of the Roman historian's time. He theorized: "History in our times is the record of progress in civilization and government. It is the record of the experience of the state, and a state should profit by its experience just as an individual does. But there is this difference: An individual carries the memory of his experience with him, while the governing powers of a state are frequently changed, and the experience of one generation is lost to following ones, unless it be recorded in some permanent way."

Disturbed by election chicanery in Indiana, especially a scandal regarding the buying of votes in the 1888 presidential election of Republican Benjamin Harrison and Democrat Grover Cleveland, Dunn used his writing and political skills to push for reform, and saw the state legislature enact an Australian ballot system in 1889 that served as a model for other states to follow. In 1891 he played a key role in reforming the Indianapolis city charter. During Democrat Thomas R. Marshall's term as governor in 1911, Dunn, working once again to secure honest elections in the state, attempted to circumvent the cumbersome amending process for the state constitution by drafting a new document that included such reform measures as granting the legislature the power to fix requirements for admission to the bar, increasing the size of the Indiana Supreme Court and Indiana House of Representatives, and toughening eligibility requirements for voters. Although the measure received approval from the legislature and Marshall signed the bill into law, the Indiana Supreme Court struck it down as unconstitutional.

In 1921 Dunn, well into his sixties, journeyed to the island of Hispaniola, which included the present-day countries of Haiti and the Dominican Republic, with the intention of finding the lost gold mine of Christopher Columbus. Dunn was exercising his well-known wit by spreading such a story. Actually, the main purpose of his journey to the tropics was to prospect for a mineral potentially as valuable as gold—manganese, used in steel production, glassmaking, fertilizers, and paints. His trip ended in failure and, upon his return to Indiana, Dunn accepted a position as private secretary to Ralston in Washington, D.C.

Unfortunately, during his travels in Haiti Dunn had contracted a tropical disease that left him susceptible to jaundice. He died on June 6, 1924. Dunn's death received front-page coverage in both the *Indianapolis Star* and *Indianapolis News*. Commenting on his fellow Democrat's death, Ralston expressed his "great admiration" for Dunn. Ralston noted that the first time he

Jacob P. Dunn Jr.

heard Dunn make a speech its subject was the value of circulating libraries to citizens. "It was characteristic of him to be most interested in those things that most benefited the people," said Ralston. Dunn was not only loyal to the truth, at whatever the cost, Ralston added, but also loyal to his friends. "And trustworthy—absolutely so," said Ralston. "I shall miss him."

RAY E. BOOMHOWER

For Further Reading

Boomhower, Ray E. *Jacob Piatt Dunn, Jr.: A Life in History and Politics, 1855–1924*. Indianapolis: Indiana Historical Society.
———. "To Secure Honest Elections: Jacob Piatt Dunn, Jr. and the Reform of Indiana's Ballot," *Indiana Magazine of History* 90 (December 1994): 311–45.
Ruegamer, Lana. *A History of the Indiana Historical Society, 1830–1980*. Indianapolis: Indiana Historical Society, 1980.
———. "History, Politics, and the Active Life: Jacob Piatt Dunn, Progressive Historian," *Indiana Magazine of History* 81 (September 1985): 265–83.

The Efroymson Family

Gustave A., January 21, 1870–1946; Clarence W., November 1, 1897–March 5, 1988; Robert A., September 27, 1905–December 30, 1988; and Daniel, September 28, 1941–November 30, 1999

Businessmen, philanthropists, and civic leaders.

Noted for both their philanthropy and civic engagement, members of Indianapolis's Efroymson family have been involved in public service in the city for more than a century and through numerous endowments their generosity now reaches across Indiana and beyond.

In 1877 Jacob Efroymson, who owned a dry goods store, moved his family from Evansville, Indiana, to Indianapolis. It was his son, Gustave A., however, who established the family fortune. At age fourteen, he began working in a one-room dry goods shop in Indianapolis. In 1896 he married Mamie W. Wallenstein, with whom he had two children, Robert A. and Clarence W. In 1912 Efroymson and his brother-in-law, Louis M. Wolf, formed a partnership and purchased H. P. Wasson and Company, a department store located in downtown Indianapolis. Turning the store into one of the city's most successful retail venues, Efroymson served as both its president and general manager until he retired in 1930. In 1932 he purchased a controlling interest in the near-bankrupt Real Silk Hosiery Mills. By the time of his death in 1946 Real Silk was a thriving concern due, in no small part, to its lucrative government contract for manufacturing parachute bomb sleeves and hosiery for male and female soldiers during World War II.

In addition to being a successful businessman, Gustave also left his family a tradition of civic commitment through public service. He helped start the Public Welfare Loan Association in 1912, lobbied the state legislature to regulate moneylenders in an effort to protect borrowers, was one of the founding members of the Indianapolis Foundation when it was created in 1916 to support community-wide issues and needs, and served as both its vice president and on the board of trustees. Additionally, over time, both he and other members of his extended family established a number of charitable funds that were managed through the foundation. In the 1920s Efroymson helped organize Jewish, African American, and Catholic civic leaders against the Ku Klux Klan's influence in Indianapolis, and in the 1930s he aided Jews fleeing Nazi Germany. He also served as president of the William E. English Foundation, which supports nonprofit organizations, and as director of both the Jewish Federation of Indianapolis and the Union of American Hebrew Congregations.

In 1945, after serving in World War II, Harvard-educated Robert A. Efroymson returned to Indianapolis and accepted a vice presidency with Real Silk. He succeeded his father as president of the company in 1946, but was forced to shut down the company's manufacturing operations in Indianapolis and Dalton, Georgia, in the early 1950s due to declining profits as synthetic fibers, such as nylon, replaced silk in hosiery. After gradually liquidating the assets into a closed-end investment trust, he registered Real Silk Investments Inc. with the Securities and Exchange Commission in 1957 and served as its president until his death in 1988.

Like their father before them, both Robert and his brother, Clarence, an economist who taught at Butler University for more than thirty years, shared a deep commitment to public service. Named as one of the thirty-two most influential people in the city in 1976 by the *Indianapolis Star*, Robert served as chairman of the board of the Indianapolis Foundation from 1946 to 1988. In 1955 he became the first president of the Civic Progress Association and played a pivotal role in the downtown redevelopment plan that became known as the Riley Center. As president of Community Hospital from 1952 to 1959, he oversaw a campaign that raised $15 million for local hospital construction. Robert helped found the Greater Indianapolis Progress Committee in 1964 and chaired the Indianapolis Housing Authority from 1964 to 1973, a period during which most of the city's public housing projects were built. Robert also served on the boards of the Marion County Child Guidance Clinic, the English Foundation, the Jewish Welfare Federation, Planned Parenthood, and as president of the United Way. Clarence worked on behalf of the United Negro College Fund, serving as the first chairman of its fund drive in Indianapolis, and the Indiana Mental Health Association. He was also instrumental in bringing the Nature Conservancy to Indianapolis.

In 1985 the brothers established the Moriah Fund as a private charitable foundation. Seeded by an initial contribution of about $40 million from both brothers, the fund was established in order to insure the continuation of their family's philanthropic commitment, as first established by their father. Reflecting the interests and concerns of the brothers, as well as their father, the fund initially provided grants in five areas: promoting the well-being of Jewish people, improving the quality of life in Indiana, stabilizing population growth and promoting reproductive health, conserving natural resources, and fighting the causes and effects of poverty.

Succeeding his father, Robert, as president of Real Silk Investments Inc. in 1988, Daniel R. Efroymson oversaw its conversion into a regulated investment company (similar to a mutual fund or real estate investment trust) the following year. In addition to serving as president of Real Silk Investments, he was also a managing partner of SEE Investors. Like his father and grandfather before him, Daniel served on the board of the Indianapolis Foundation, assuming his father's seat in 1988 and serving until his own death in 1999. In addition to his role with the Indianapolis Foundation, Daniel was a trustee at Butler University and also served as chairman of the Nature Conservancy. In the 1980s he was instrumental in designing pioneering legislation that established a public-private partnership to protect Indiana's natural resources. Indeed, working through the Indiana Heritage Trust, which he helped to create in 1992, more than 26,000 acres of land across the state had been purchased for the purpose of preservation by the time of his death.

Working with the Indianapolis Foundation and the Legacy Fund (which serves Hamilton County, Indiana), Daniel and his wife helped craft a partnership between the two organizations to form the Central Indiana Community Foundation in 1998, to which they then donated $90 million to establish the Efroymson Fund. The fund, which was designed to be used to help disadvantaged people, the environment, historic preservation, the well-being of Jewish people, and the general viability of Indianapolis, was the single largest gift of its kind to a philanthropic organization in the history of the state. The gift, which increased the assets of the Central Indiana Community Foundation to about $325 million, making it one of the largest community foundations in the nation, was expected to create about $4.5 million in new grant dollars yearly. By the mid-2000s it was estimated that the Efroymson Foundation had already awarded $47 million in grants and donations to a variety of social and cultural organizations, most of which were based in Indiana.

Since 2000 the Efroymson family has continued its commitment to philanthropy not only by working through the both the Moriah Fund and the Efroymson Foundation, but also through direct giving such as a $12.5 million gift to the Indianapolis Museum of Art for the construction of a new entrance pavilion as well as an additional donation of $2.5 million to the museum to commission a series of artworks to be installed on a rotating basis within the pavilion.

JEFFERY A. DUVALL

For Further Reading

Albert, Barb. "Family Donates $90 million: Gift to Foundation Targets Needy People, Environment, Preservation, Jewish Causes." *Indianapolis Star*, July 10, 1998.

"Success of Gustave A. Efroymson Graphically Told in Trade Paper." *Indianapolis Star*, June 28, 1914.

Swiatek, Jess. "Gustav Efroymson Started Fortune in One-Room Dry Goods Store: Success Included H.P. Wasson & Co. Store, Real Silk, Launching of Welfare Loan Endeavor." *Indianapolis Star*, July 10, 1998.

Emrick, Paul "Spotts"

March 30, 1884–July 28, 1965

Purdue band director whose innovations for marching bands forever changed college halftime shows.

It was October 1935, the middle of the Great Depression, and Purdue and Northwestern Universities were playing the first night football game in the history of the Big Ten. The lights at Northwestern's Dyche Stadium had been turned down for Purdue's halftime band show that stunned people and brought them cheering to their feet. When it was done, fire dripped from the baton of the Purdue drum major. Behind him the uniforms and instruments of Purdue Band members sparkled with tiny lights. Spotlights beamed from inside the World's Largest Drum. It was a lighted halftime show and it surpassed anything the world had ever seen.

At the front of it all, basking in the applause and cheers that rumbled through the stadium, was Paul "Spotts" Emrick, Purdue's band director. An electrical engineer in his training and a musician in his heart, Emrick had already revolutionized college marching bands and now he was doing it again. It was a pivotal moment in the history of Purdue and in the story of its legendary band that has produced university icons for generations. It was also a pivotal moment in the life of the patriotic man from Rochester, Indiana, who brought music to Purdue.

Born in 1884 and known to most as Spotts, his mother's maiden name, Emrick grew up in a family of musicians. His father and uncle played in the Rochester Citizens Band and he followed quickly in their footsteps, eventually becoming director. "[A] fine young man, a chip off the old block is Paul Emrick," wrote William W. Rannels, in a Rochester publication titled *Home Town Folks* published in 1911. "[He] grew up in the band. He is full of music enthusiasm and capable of blowing any part."

Emrick enrolled at Purdue in 1904, eager to join the fledgling university band and show his leadership as well as his musical ability. Without a school of music, students had created the band in 1886, mostly to perform for Reserve Officer Training Corps marching drills. But football was introduced to Purdue in 1887 and everyone quickly realized the natural affinity between marching bands and the game that included a long halftime break. In 1905, as a sophomore clarinetist, Emrick was elected band president and director. It was a position he held, with only a few months interruption, for the next forty-nine years.

His longevity at the front of the Purdue Band alone would establish him as a legend. But Emrick was not satisfied with following the marching styles of other bands. He dreamed and innovated and played a major role in creating the college marching bands we know today that thrill people throughout the nation and have become a staple of autumn American Saturday afternoons.

Emrick's record of innovations started in 1907 while he was still an undergraduate. Bands at that time were military units. They stood on the football field in straight, rigid lines, like soldiers. Emrick changed all that. As a boy he had loved watching geese fly over a lake in Rochester, he told the *Lafayette Journal and Courier* in 1953. They formed a V formation. "But once in a while," he said, "they'd change formation and fly in various figures. I used to wonder if you could do that with men drilling." So he tried it. He had his band break its straight lines and form the letter P on a football field. Other universities quickly copied it and soon the Purdue band was taking the lead in the formation of words as it marched down the field. Other marching band firsts introduced by Emrick included carrying the colors of all schools in the Big Ten and playing the opposing university's fight song.

As he innovated and invented, Emrick also gained a reputation as a taskmaster, always striving for excellence. In his senior year, 1908, the student yearbook, the *Debris*, joked that he had grown tougher in his third and fourth years as director. "Emrick has made Purdue famous with his military band," the yearbook said. "Of course, his band boys all loved music—for the first two years. But just the same they produced music the kind which made everybody sit up and take notice."

In a 1986 interview, C. W. Hemmer, Purdue class of 1921, talked about his tryout with the band. "I was nervous," he said. "Spotts didn't spend much time with me. He left in his typical way and said, 'I think we can use him.' He (became) a real buddy of mine. I loved that man. Whenever anyone couldn't play something right, I remember him showing how it should be done. I remember him once playing the cymbals. You could almost see smoke coming out of them the way he played."

In rehearsal Emrick once complained a timpanist was not hitting the drums hard enough. He pushed the student and pushed him until finally the student hit the drum so hard he broke his mallet. "Now you've got it," Emrick shouted. And practice went on.

When freshmen played at an armory rehearsal early in their first year Emrick enjoyed frightening them by walking to the back of the band as it played and firing his .38 caliber pistol filled with blanks. The freshmen hit the floor while the older students, and Emrick, roared with laughter.

The band grew in size, year by year, quickly becoming one of the largest in the nation. In addition to playing for ROTC functions and football games, the band also traveled around the state of Indiana and to Chicago, gaining a large and loyal following. In 1919 the Purdue Band performed at the Indianapolis Motor Speedway before the 500 race and it continues that unbroken tradition today.

By 1920 Emrick had reached the conclusion that what his band needed next was a big bass drum—and not just any big bass drum. He wanted the "World's Largest Drum." He took his idea to the Leedy Drum Company, then of Indianapolis, and the firm went to work. The first challenge in determining how big the drum could be was finding cattle hides large enough to form the heads. As progress continued, Emrick became concerned that the company was building the drum too big. It would not fit in railroad baggage cars so it could be taken with the band when it traveled, he complained in a letter to U. G. Leedy, the company's president. Leedy responded by telling Emrick that the process was very complicated and he only intended to build one big drum. He said the one he built had to be the world's largest. He then pointed out to Emrick that people at Indiana University were also interested in a drum, they were not concerned about baggage cars, and if Emrick did not want the drum Leedy would sell it to IU. Emrick told Leedy to make the drum as big as possible, and it would be Purdue's drum. He solved the baggage car problem by transporting the drum on a flatbed railcar. The drum debuted in Indianapolis in 1921 and remains in use today.

Through the decades the young people whose lives Emrick influenced included popcorn king ORVILLE REDENBACHER, who said he learned to "toot his own horn" while in the band, and first man to walk on the moon, Neil Armstrong, who called Emrick "an icon, easily the most colorful of all my professors."

Among all his success was that October evening in 1935 at Dyche Stadium and the first college halftime lighted band show. At the end of

Paul "Spotts" Emrick

the crowd-thrilling performance, famed sportscaster Ted Husing from the broadcast booth told his nationwide CBS radio audience, "this is a real All-American" Band. And that's what it's been ever since, the Purdue "All-American" Marching Band.

A reluctant retiree in 1954, Emrick returned to Rochester, where he died on July 28, 1965, at the age of eighty-one. But he is not forgotten. His bust is at the entrance to band rooms outside of the Elliott Hall of Music on the Purdue campus and students learn of his legacy and innovation and carry on the traditions he started. The excitement he initiated in college marching bands continues throughout the nation to this day—he was the "All-American" leader of the band.

JOHN NORBERG

For Further Reading

Norberg, John. *Hail Purdue*. Lafayette, IN: The All-American Ball Club, 1987.

———. *Heartbeat of the University: 125 Years of Purdue Bands*. West Lafayette, IN: Purdue University Press, 2011.

Topping, Robert. *A Century and Beyond: The History of Purdue University*. West Lafayette, IN: Purdue Research Foundation, 1988.

Esarey, Logan

January 3, 1873–September 24, 1942

Noted Indiana historian, prolific author, and first history PhD at Indiana University.

Logan Esarey's life and career spanned periods of significant change in both Indiana and the profession of history. Although the circumstances of his birth were modest, the trajectory of Esarey's life mirrored that of his state. Among other noteworthy achievements, he produced the first scholarly history of Indiana and taught generations of students to appreciate their Hoosier roots. Esarey's professional accomplishments—and conflicts—paralleled those occurring in the field of history as a whole during his years as an active historian. While he aimed his historical output at a wide audience, he also focused much of his writing on helping teachers of history become better educators. His generally informal appearance and fondness for cigars, coupled with his shrewd, rustic wit and encyclopedic knowledge of Indiana history, ensured that Esarey made a singular and enduring impression on both students and colleagues.

During Esarey's lifespan—the Gilded Age to World War II—both Indiana and the United States experienced immense changes as a result of industrialization, urbanization, and immigration. Quantum leaps in technology, manufacturing, and science all meant that the days of rural, cabin-dwelling frontier farmers would soon vanish. Esarey was born in a two-story log cabin in southern Indiana in 1873, one of nine children. Esarey started common school at the age of four in nearby Branchville, went as far academically as he could as quickly as possible, and began teaching at the age of sixteen. After three years, he had earned enough money to enroll in the Central Normal College, a private teacher's college in Danville, Indiana. Esarey alternated between teaching and attending classes at the Normal College, year by year, for five years until he became superintendent of the schools in Perry County in 1897. By then, Esarey had married a woman he had met in Danville and would soon have a family—four children were born between 1898 and 1903, and another in 1906.

These family obligations meant that Esarey could not follow one of his older brothers to Harvard to study law; instead, in 1903 Logan and his wife, Laura, moved their young family to Bloomington, where he enrolled in Indiana University as an undergraduate—at the age of thirty.

Once he finished his undergraduate work, Esarey again turned to teaching to support his family—briefly in Tell City, and then for a longer duration in Vincennes. At the same time, though, Esarey continued with his graduate studies and earned his master's degree in 1909. In 1912 his master's thesis was published as *State Banking in Indiana, 1814–1873*. With this work, Esarey launched his formal career as a bona-fide historian of Indiana. Esarey, at the age of forty, wrote both the thesis and his doctoral dissertation, *Internal Improvements in Early Indiana*, while teaching a variety of high school subjects at Vincennes. Esarey, at the age of forty, achieved the most advanced degree possible and become the first person to earn a PhD in the history department at IU.

With that singular accomplishment, Esarey continued the professional work to which he would devote the rest of his life: teaching history, writing history, and collecting and cataloging various elements of Indiana history. Upon conferral of the PhD, Esarey was appointed to the post of secretary of the Indiana Historical Survey—a position that enabled him to amass, index, and edit important documents in the state's background, and to preserve them for generations. He was also made a professor of what was then called "western" history at IU, specializing in Indiana and midwestern history. Esarey's attainment of the PhD was emblematic of the professionalization of history in the United States in the early twentieth century—a move away from devoted amateurs toward graduates of universities with credentials and "scientific" expertise. Indeed, when historian Peter Novick characterized the professionalization movement as "a dramatically successful ladder of personal social and economic mobility for dozens of small-town boys of lower middle-class backgrounds" in the "rapidly expanding" prewar American universities, he could have been writing of Esarey's life.

Esarey also began his tenure as editor of the *Indiana Magazine of History* in 1913. IU had just taken over control of the *IMH*, which had been founded by George S. Cottman in 1905 and had recently encountered financial difficulties. Esarey's selection as editor proved to be a wise choice on the part of the university—under his leadership the *IMH* grew in professionalism (he instituted the practice of footnotes), circulation, and influence, and became nationally recognized as a leading publication of its kind. Esarey presided over some fifty-nine issues of the *IMH* in an editorial career that spanned nearly fourteen years. His resignation from the post of editor in 1927 was not entirely voluntary, but rather something he felt compelled to do as a result of a contretemps with Christopher B. Coleman, the director of the Indiana Historical Commission, ostensibly about editorial differences relating to Esarey's work on the papers of former Governor James Brown Ray. Coleman, a Butler University history professor and urbane Ivy Leaguer with midwestern roots, was Esarey's opposite number in many respects, and the two scholars differed on an issue that was in fact much larger than editing—whether the commission should be transferred to IU and placed under Esarey's direction.

When Esarey lost that battle, the commission remained in the state capital and merged with the Indiana State Library to become the Indiana Historical Bureau, with Coleman as its head. Coleman was also the secretary of the Indiana Historical Society, which helped sponsor the *IMH* and was largely responsible for the journal's increasing financial stability. Thus, once he lost his bid to have the base of operations for state history transferred to his jurisdiction, Esarey's position as editor of the *IMH* grew untenable. In a sense, the power struggle between the two men in Indiana foreshadowed the growth of state historical societies nationwide—from 313 in 1926 to 1,378 in 1944—in both numbers and influence. When faced with a choice to align with the academy or the state historical society, Esarey chose the former.

His choice was not surprising, because at his core Esarey was an educator and historian first and foremost. Just as the fields of midwestern and Indiana history did not exist when Esarey began his studies, before Esarey there was no complete survey of Indiana history—in fact, no midwestern state could boast of one. But Esarey, in anticipation of the Hoosier State's centennial, produced volume one, *A History of Indiana from Its Exploration to 1850*. In 1918 he presented volume two, *A History of Indiana from 1850 to the Present*. By 1924 these works were already in their third edition. He also created *Readings in Indiana History* in 1914 and *Indiana Local History: A Guide to Its Study, with Some Biographical Notes* in 1916 for the IU Extension Division. Esarey wrote articles for the *Mississippi Valley Historical Review*, including "The Literary Spirit among the Early Ohio Valley Settlers," as well as numerous reviews, in addition to his many contributions to the *IMH*. As part of an effort to make the state's history come alive for the public at large, he published a regular series of articles on Indiana state history for the *Indianapolis Star* during the years-long run-up to the centennial celebration in 1916. Esarey was committed to helping history teachers at all levels excel, regularly penning historiographic and methods pieces in the *IMH*, such as "Some Suggestions for Teaching Civil Government (1913)," "The Approach to History (1921)," and "The Outlook for History," his final piece for the journal, in 1927.

The Indiana Home, published posthumously, was and still is one of Esarey's most popular books. While he may have intended the series of essays recollecting daily pioneer life as nothing more than a means of preserving a long-vanished heritage for his grandchildren, the *Indiana Home* has been in continuous publication since 1953. In it, Esarey debunked the myths that the early settlers in the Indiana Territory were "poor white trash" who "wasted" the land's dense forests, and his celebration of the common folk and their influence on the course of history presaged the sociocultural revolution of "history from the ground up" by several decades. Esarey's work as a teacher and historian touched the lives of many people, and his legacy is apparent every time a reader opens a book on Indiana history.

RUTH D. REICHARD

For Further Reading

Buley, R. Carlyle. "Logan Esarey, Hoosier." *Indiana Magazine of History* 38 (December, 1942): 337–81.

Esarey, Logan. *A History of Indiana from Its Exploration to 1850*. Fort Wayne, IN: The Hoosier Press, 1918.

———. *A History of Indiana from 1850 to the Present*. Third Edition., Fort Wayne, IN: The Hoosier Press 1924.

———. *The Indiana Home*. Bloomington and Indianapolis: Indiana University Press, 1953.

Feuerlicht, Morris Marcus

January 15, 1879–November 30, 1959

Rabbi of the Indianapolis Hebrew Congregation (1904–46) and leader in Jewish and community organizations.

A dynamic rabbi both in his words and deeds, Morris M. Feuerlicht not only spent more than forty years devoted to his congregants but also strove to better the lives of all Hoosiers, regardless of religion, race, or socioeconomic status.

Feuerlicht, a rabbi's son born in Tokay, Hungary, came to the United States while an infant and spent his early years in Chicago and Boston. He graduated from the University of Cincinnati and in 1901 was one of ten graduates of Hebrew Union College, Reform Judaism's rabbinic seminary in Cincinnati, having served as student rabbi in Muncie, Indiana.

After ordination, Feuerlicht became rabbi in Lafayette, conducting biweekly services in Kokomo and Logansport as well as taking advanced courses at the University of Chicago. In 1904 Feuerlicht was appointed associate rabbi at the Indianapolis Hebrew Congregation. He had to stop his formal academic studies in 1906; nevertheless, he later became a professor and lecturer at the School of Religion at Butler University where, for twenty-three years, he taught Judaism to Protestant ministers. Often asked how he preferred to be called, "Rabbi or Doctor," he responded "officially and professionally . . . 'Rabbi,' but personally, socially and generally, I prefer plain 'Mr.'"

Feuerlicht succeeded Rabbi Mayer Messing at IHC on November 17, 1907. Many Reform congregations at that time were seeking American-trained rabbis to be spokesmen to their secular communities. Young and energetic, Feuerlicht more than fulfilled expectations for the approximately two hundred IHC families, becoming a frequent speaker and active leader throughout Indiana. In May 1944 congregational membership was about four hundred families, yet he maintained a full schedule, for example, addressing nine religious and civic associations within a two-week period.

Feuerlicht observed that when he became rabbi in Lafayette, Jewish and Christian clergy emphasized "the highest service to God was best reflected and expressed in a corresponding service to man." His social-service efforts started in rabbinic school, where twice weekly he taught English to immigrants. Helping others based on mutual justice for all was his vision.

The Marion County Juvenile Court's volunteer probation system, which placed delinquents under the supervision of qualified volunteers, provided Feuerlicht entry into decades of Indiana community service. The presiding judge, George W. Stubbs, asked Feuerlicht to travel Indiana promoting the juvenile court's virtues. Feuerlict was president of the Children's Aid Association, which was affiliated with the court, and served in that capacity for twenty-one years until it merged with other organizations. This position led to Feuerlicht's appointment to the County Board of Welfare, becoming president of the Indiana State Conference of Charities, and his being the first Jew to serve on the Indiana State Board of Charities.

None of these responsibilities prevented Feuerlicht from performing his duties at IHC or for the Indianapolis Jewish community. In 1904 he and several Hoosiers representing national Jewish charitable organizations formed a "Jewish Federation of Indianapolis, the first of its kind in the land among cities of comparable size." Feuerlicht wrote the constitution and the bylaws, emphasizing that the federation was for all Jewish organizations, not just charities. He also was secretary and a longtime board member. In June 1906 Feuerlicht and IHC proudly hosted the annual Central Conference of American Rabbis. In the 1920s Feuerlicht served as president of the conference's Alumni Association.

To support the Sephardic community (Jews of Spanish and Portuguese descent), in 1916 Feuerlicht and IHC helped purchase land for their cemetery; in 1919 the rabbi, IHC, and the Jewish Federation contributed toward their acquiring a former church for use as a synagogue.

During World War I Feuerlicht was chairman of the Jewish Welfare Board and also worked with the Relief of Jewish War Sufferers. In addition, he was a civilian chaplain at Fort Benjamin Harrison and joined the American Red Cross. An early foe of Nazi Germany, Feuerlicht supported the American troops during World War II. In particular he, along with Rabbi Maurice Goldblatt, assistant rabbi at the IHC, visited many army camps conducting and supervising religious services for Jewish men and women in the armed services.

Feuerlicht's activities went beyond service to the Jewish community. For example he also played host to visiting dignitaries. Wong Kai Kah, the Chinese ambassador to the Louisiana Purchase Exposition in 1904, spoke on the history and status of Jews in China during a December Friday night service, receiving a copy of Heinrich Graetz's

History of the Jews, with the rabbi's inscription, "From a Congregation of Jews to a Buddhist on Christmas Day!" Feuerlicht invited Chaim Weizmann, chemist and future first president of Israel, who passed through Indianapolis on business trips to the Commercial Solvents Company in Terre Haute, to a Friday night service where he could speak freely, though most congregants, including Feuerlicht, were not Zionists.

Feuerlicht was also active in the interfaith and civic communities. In 1911 he vigorously encouraged contributions for a "colored" Young Men's Christian Association in Indianapolis for which Julius Rosenwald of Sears, Roebuck and Company had pledged funds. In 1913 Mayor Samuel Shank appointed Feuerlicht to the Citizens Relief Committee, established to help Indianapolis residents who suffered during the 1913 flood. The rabbi resolved several labor and management disputes, once being the only arbiter selected by both union and company representatives from a list of ninety-seven prospects.

During Indiana's centennial year, the National Conference of Jewish Charities met concurrently with the National Conference of Charities in Indianapolis. The IHC sanctuary was the site of the opening meeting addressed by Samuel M. Ralston, governor of Indiana, and Francis H. Gavisk, president of the National Conference of Charities, the first time either had been in a synagogue.

Several years after his 1909 marriage to Mildred M. Mayerstein, whose family had owned the *Lafayette Evening Courier*, Feuerlicht was asked by the Lafayette Chamber of Commerce to become the newspaper's manager and return as temple rabbi. Though tempted, he stayed in Indianapolis, responding similarly to other invitations to leave for "larger fields of action." His literary abilities were affirmed in 1922 when he was named editor in chief of the *Indiana Jewish Chronicle*, a weekly publication. He was a member of the Indiana Literary Club, and of the Indiana Library and Historical Board (1942–1956; president, 1950–56), and he wrote a research article, "Influence of Judaism on the Foundation of the Republic." He also wrote an essay on his early life as a rabbi that was included in the publication *Lives and Voices*.

As a member of the State Board of Charities during the time when the Ku Klux Klan had a hold on the state, Feuerlicht readily spoke out in opposition to the Klan, appealing to people's better judgment of what it meant to be an American patriot. He coordinated two mass meetings at Cadle Tabernacle to demonstrate that Indianapolis opposed Klan theories and tactics. For his efforts, he was described as "the single most important spokesman for the Jewish community against the Klan. His charming personality, sense of humor, a genuine tolerance for others, and public-speaking abilities, catapulted him into the public eye during the twenties as a defender of minority interests."

A highlight of Feuerlicht's career occurred on October 17, 1928, when he and Clarence Darrow debated "Is Man a Machine?" Darrow, an agnostic, took the positive and Feuerlicht took the negative viewpoints. Posters on numerous telephone poles heralded the debate, word spread, and several thousand people attended the event at Cadle Tabernacle. Asked in 1954 to reflect on the debate, Feuerlicht, "a small, compact man with a lively mind and tongue," said he felt as he had years before, "without a soul, man would not be a man, but only another species of animal."

Feuerlicht became Rabbi Emeritus in 1947 and after his death in 1959 was buried at the IHC cemetery on Kelly Street. A testimonial to Feuerlicht on his seventy-fifth birthday expressed the affection and esteem with which he was held for a lifetime of service, "you have been a blessing to our city, state, and country, to Jewry, and to all mankind."

EVELYN POCKRASS

For Further Reading

Endelman, Judith E. *The Jewish Community of Indianapolis, 1849 to the Present*. Bloomington: Indiana University Press, 1984.

Feuerlicht, Morris M. "A Hoosier Rabbinate: Memoirs of Morris M. Feuerlicht." In *Lives and Voices*. Philadelphia: Jewish Publication Society, 1972.

Rosenberg, David, and Ethel Rosenberg. *To 120 Years! A Social History of the Indianapolis Hebrew Congregation (1856–1976)*. Indianapolis: Indianapolis Hebrew Congregation, 1979.

Fisher, Carl

January 12, 1874–July 15, 1939

Entrepreneur, promoter, automobile executive, and cofounder of the Indianapolis Motor Speedway.

Fifteen-year-old Jane Watt was walking along Meridian Street in Indianapolis one fall afternoon in 1908 when she noticed something strange. All traffic on the street had stopped, and people were craning their necks upward. Following their lead, Watt halted, gazed skyward, and saw a giant hot-air balloon floating by with, instead of the usual wicker basket, a Stoddard-Dayton automobile, the engine removed to make it lighter. Sitting in the car she saw, for the first time, the man she would marry—Carl G. Fisher.

Wild stunts were a regular feature of Fisher's career. Regarded as a promotional genius for most of his life, Fisher, responsible for turning Miami Beach from a mangrove swamp into America's favorite resort, also played an important role in Indiana's early automotive history. His stamp had been placed on such impressive automotive achievements as the Prest-O-Lite Storage Battery Company, the Indianapolis Motor Speedway, and the Lincoln and Dixie Highways.

The man Will Rogers described as doing "more unique things even before he had heard of Florida than any man I ever met" was born on January 12, 1874, in Greensburg, Indiana. His parents separated when Fisher was young, and his mother moved the family to Indianapolis. Suffering from severe astigmatism, Fisher quit school at twelve. According to family lore, Fisher got a job in a grocery store, took a bundle of food home to his mother, and boldly announced: "From now on, I'm supporting this family."

In the coming years, Fisher held a number of jobs, everything from clerking in a bookstore to hawking newspapers, candy, and other products on trains leaving Indianapolis. In 1891 he and his two brothers opened a bicycle shop in Indianapolis, where they repaired flat tires for just twenty-five cents. Fisher convinced a leading Ohio bicycle manufacturer to supply him, on credit, $50,000 worth of merchandise. To sell his products, he turned to promotional stunts for attention, wearing a padded suit to ride a bicycle across a tightrope stretched over Washington Street and operating a twenty-foot-high bicycle.

As the bicycle craze faded at the turn of the twentieth century, Fisher embraced a new means of transportation—the automobile. "I don't see why the automobile can't be made to do everything the bicycle has done," he said. Fisher converted his bicycle shop into an automobile repair/sales facility and barnstormed through the Midwest with his friends putting on automotive races.

The product may have been different, but Fisher used gimmicks similar to his bicycle stunts to promote car sales. In addition to his balloon trip, he turned to an Indianapolis rooftop as the stage for his unusual advertising. While his brothers waited on the street below, Fisher shoved a seven-passenger car off a building's roof. When the car safely reached the street, one of Fisher's brothers climbed into the car, started it up, and drove away with the crowd's cheers ringing in his ears.

In 1904 Fred Avery, holder of a French patent for a method using compressed gas as headlights for automobiles, convinced Fisher (who brought in his friend, JAMES ALLISON) to market his invention. The result was the Prest-O-Lite Company, which soon had factories in Indianapolis (later moved to Speedway), Cleveland, Omaha, New York, Boston, and Chicago. An idea man who was often fuzzy when it came to details, Fisher had a simple method for doing business: "I have a great many men working for me who I consider have more brain power than I have, and I always try to get this type of men to aid me. It pays well in any sort of business to know all your employees, from the truck drivers up—and to stick by them in any sort of trouble." With Fisher's ideas and Allison's good business sense, Prest-O-Lite prospered. In 1911 Union Carbide bought the company for $9 million.

On a 1905 trip overseas to compete in the Gordon Bennett Cup Series in France, Fisher was stunned by the European cars' superiority over the American models. To help improve the American automotive industry, he conceived of a proving ground where cars could be tested and raced. In 1909 Fisher, Allison, Arthur Newby, and Frank Wheeler pooled $25,000 in capital to form the Indianapolis Motor Speedway Company, transforming the Pressley Farm on the city's west side into a two-and-a-half-mile oval that became synonymous with automobile racing.

When a crushed stone track proved to be unsuitable for racing, Fisher returned to the drawing board. He persuaded Newby to pay for repaving the track with more than three million ten-pound bricks, and "The Brickyard" was born. The new surface stood up well in the 1910 racing season, and Fisher promised bigger things to come the next year. On Memorial Day 1911 the Speedway hosted the first in a long line of 500-mile races. Ray Harroun, driving an Indianapolis-made Marmon Wasp, won the race with an average speed of 74.59 miles per hour. Fisher had helped inaugurate an event

Carl Fisher

that became "the greatest spectacle in racing."

Fisher next turned his relentless energy to a problem that had plagued the automotive industry for years—bad roads. "The highways of America," wrote Fisher, "are built chiefly of politics, whereas the proper material is crushed rock or concrete." He often told the story about an automobile trip he made out of Indianapolis with a few friends. Caught in a rainstorm at night, Fisher and his companions had reached a fork in the road and were unsure about which way to proceed. Sighting a white sign on a telephone pole, Fisher stopped the car and climbed up the pole. The sign offered no assistance; its message read: "Chew Battle Ax Plug."

At a September 1, 1912, dinner for automobile executives in Indianapolis, Fisher unveiled his plan for a highway spanning the country from New York to California. "A road across the United States! Let's build it before we're too old to enjoy it!" he urged the auto executives. With financial aid from Henry B. Joy, Packard Motor Company president, the Lincoln Highway Commission was formed on July 1, 1913.

As work progressed on completing America's first transcontinental highway, Fisher turned his sights to other projects, especially improving a jungle of swamps to be known as Miami Beach. Florida, as Fisher envisioned the state, could be the perfect spot for auto executives and their families from the Midwest tired of frigid winter weather. But in order to get vacationers to his resort, Fisher had to use his promotional talents once again to nurture another highway's birth. On December 4, 1914, he wrote Indiana governor Samuel M. Ralston suggesting that an interstate highway be built from Chicago to Miami.

A strong believer in good roads, Ralston quickly acted on Fisher's proposal. The Indiana politician invited his fellow governors from the affected states—Illinois, Ohio, Kentucky, Tennessee, and Georgia—to a meeting in Chattanooga, Tennessee, on April 3, 1915. The other governors warmed to the idea and pledged their support. In September 1916 Fisher and Ralston attended a celebration in Martinsville opening the roadway from Indianapolis to Miami.

Fisher's grand dreams for continued success came crashing down with those of many other businessmen in the 1929 Wall Street crash. He had sunk millions of dollars into a new development at Montauk on Long Island's eastern tip and, with the Great Depression's onset, had to sell his Miami Beach property in order to satisfy Montauk bondholders' claims. He died from a gastric hemorrhage on July 15, 1939, in Miami Beach.

RAY E. BOOMHOWER

For Further Reading

Fisher, Jane Watts. *Fabulous Hoosier: A Story of American Achievement.* New York: R. M. McBride and Company, 1947.
Fisher, Jerry M. *The Pacesetter: The Untold Story of Carl G. Fisher.* Fort Bragg, CA: Lost Coast Press, 1998.
Foster, Mark S. *Castles in the Sand: The Life and Times of Carl Graham Fisher.* Gainesville: University Press of Florida, 2000.

Fletcher, Calvin
February 4, 1798–May 26, 1866

Attorney, banker, farmer, community leader, landowner, and state legislator.

Calvin Fletcher, who helped to create the new city of Indianapolis, became an essential figure in its economic development during a half century of profound changes, and he recorded his experiences in one of the most important diaries of early Indiana history.

Born in Ludlow, Vermont, in 1798, Fletcher left home in his teens, and moved through Pennsylvania and Ohio. He was admitted to the practice of law in Urbana, Ohio, where he married his first wife, Sarah Hill. In 1821 they moved to the recently platted city of Indianapolis. He first appeared in public records as a prosecuting attorney for Marion County in 1822 and 1823, and for the state in 1825 and 1826. He subsequently formed partnerships with OVID BUTLER, Simon Yandes, and Horatio Newcomb. In 1825 Fletcher was elected to the Indiana State Senate, serving until he resigned to pursue other interests in 1833.

Chief among these interests was a growing involvement in the mechanisms of state government finance. Like other western states, Indiana was caught up in the passion for what were called internal improvements: toll roads, canals, and particularly railroads. Through the issue of state bonds Indiana hoped to find capital to support these enterprises and needed to find revenues to "sink," or pay off, debt. Fletcher, who became a member of the state Sinking Fund Commission in 1833, worried about the enormous debt the state was accumulating and wrote presciently in his diary in early 1836 of the great danger of a possible economic crash, which did occur the following year. In the 1840s Fletcher put his connections and experience to work helping to organize the State Bank of Indiana, serving for a time as Indianapolis branch director and then as branch president until 1858.

Preferring to identify himself as a farmer, Fletcher filled his diaries with records of livestock, crops, weather, and soil. He first owned a 269-acre farm at Wood Lawn, southeast of the Mile Square, and later other farms, including a 1,400-acre plot located northeast of the city. As a large landowner he was always interested in markets for agricultural commodities, and many of his other interests flowed from his desire to find ways to make the route to those markets faster, cheaper, and more direct. His most notable involvement was as a stockholder, director, and (briefly in 1855) president of the Indianapolis and Bellefontaine Railroad, a primary route to early Ohio.

Fletcher regularly recorded the events of his life, and frequently included his opinions about himself and others as part of his personal record. The resulting diary has become an important primary source for the study of antebellum Indiana, and especially of Indianapolis. Available today in a nine-volume edition, it is a significant and revealing source. The survival and publication of the diary is itself an instructive story of the survival and access to local records. Fletcher probably began the diary about the time he moved to Indianapolis, but only the volumes from 1832 and beyond survived into the twentieth century.

Bound in a dozen volumes, they were donated by his descendants to the Indiana Historical Society in the 1920s. There they attracted the attention of ELI LILLY, who clearly saw in Fletcher a kindred spirit: a successful businessman of broad interests, a respectable reformer whose interests focused upon his state and community, and a literate individual who viewed his wealth within a context of self-awareness and stewardship. In the early 1930s Lilly set in motion the initial transcription of the manuscript.

Intervening events delayed the actual publication of the diaries for about thirty years. Then a series of experienced editors, led by GAYLE THORNBROUGH, Dorothy Riker, and Paula Corpuz, brought the project to completion. In the published form, the diaries themselves are

Calvin Fletcher

supplemented by the letters and diaries of Fletcher's wife, Sarah, and by family letters that extend the narrative back into the 1820s and into the Fletcher connections in Vermont.

His significance in Indianapolis continues, in part, because one of the city's important historic preservation districts bears his name and reflects his imprint. The Fletcher Place historic neighborhood lies on the near southeast side of the city, at the site of his original 269-acre farm. Ever the entrepreneur, Fletcher began subdividing the farm to residential lots as the city's boundaries expanded. The earliest structures of Fletcher Place date from his tenure. The Fletcher Place Methodist Church building is on the site of land that Fletcher donated to encourage his denomination.

Fletcher has also attracted the attention of contemporary historians because his career fits readily within the interpretive paradigm of Indiana as a melting pot of regional cultures. As commonly summarized, this approach begins by noting that Indianapolis did not attract many foreign-born residents. Yet, the interpreters continue, the state still enjoyed a remarkable diversity based upon the influx from three older regions of the country: the upland South, the Middle States, and New England. Representatives of the first two are numerous and easy to locate. But New England migrants were far smaller in number.

Fletcher exemplified the "improving" spirit that many identified with Yankee migrants. He valued work, admired personal effort, and sought to use public offices and institutions as tools for community improvement. He encouraged others to follow a moral compass that encouraged Christian morality and republican virtue. In his diary entry of August 26, 1850, Fletcher wrote: "I think a young man . . . unworthy of a place a home a good character who can act like a man feel like a man able to battle with world as the most distinguished men of our nation have done beginning in poverty gradually going forward to wealth and usefulness. May the Lord impress the lesson." Fletcher was a devout and active Methodist layman and a friend to Sunday schools and charity. Although a member of the city's elite, he often spoke in a language of stewardship. Seldom doctrinaire, he used a language of persuasion that encouraged other community members to help produce better individuals through such reforms as free public schools and temperance. A political pragmatist, he undertook challenges that had a chance of succeeding and shunned lost causes.

Fletcher opposed slavery, instead supporting free-soil issues and interests. He admired the Northwest Ordinance with its prohibition of slavery north of the Ohio River, and associated with such men as Butler in opposing the fugitive slave laws of his time. One of the more revealing moments in his diary is his expression of deep resentment at the treatment of John Freeman, a freed slave who was materially impoverished in a court fight with a corrupt slave taker. "I have had a call from his wife. I would turn out at once but counsel are employed. I have already had some unpleasant words with our officers who have taken secretly a part with the Slaveholders," he wrote on June 21, 1853. Fletcher moved easily from the Whig Party to the Free-Soil movement, and then to the new Republican Party, and supported the Union cause in the Civil War.

GEORGE GEIB

For Further Reading

Geib, George. "The Diary of Calvin Fletcher and the Historians." *Traces of Indiana and Midwestern History* 10, no. 1 (Winter 1998): 23–25.

Fletcher, Calvin. *The Diary of Calvin Fletcher.* 9 vols. Edited by Gayle Thornbrough, Dorothy Riker, Paula Corpuz. Indianapolis: Indiana Historical Society, 1972–84.

Huffman, Harry V. "The Diary of Calvin Fletcher, Volume One: A Lawyer's Appreciation." *Traces of Indiana and Midwestern History* 10, no. 1 (Winter 1998): 26–28.

Fletcher, William B.
August 18, 1837–April 25, 1907

Physician, administrator of mental health facilities, professor of medicine, and one-term Democratic state senator from Marion County.

As an advocate for public and mental-health reforms, William B. Fletcher is renowned for abolishing the use of physical restraints at the Indiana Hospital for the Insane in Indianapolis in 1883. A proponent of "moral treatment" for mentally ill patients, Fletcher burned more than 500 straightjackets, covered cribs, restraint chairs, and similar devices in an enormous bonfire. Fletcher also influenced generations of physicians as a professor of medicine.

Born to pioneer Indianapolis residents CALVIN and Sarah Hill Fletcher, William studied at Indiana

Asbury University (today DePauw University). He then attended the College of Physicians and Surgeons in New York City, completing a medical degree in 1859.

Following graduation, Fletcher returned to Indianapolis. There he established the first of several private medical practices, and he considered working at the Indiana Hospital for the Insane. However, the Civil War intervened, and in April 1861 he joined the Sixth Indiana Regiment, serving as a fife major and spy. Captured by the Confederates while scouting near present-day Mingo, West Virginia, Fletcher spent several months as a prisoner of war, narrowly escaping execution for spying. Although weak from his incarceration at Libby Prison in Richmond, Virginia, he cared for Union soldiers at a nearby hospital while on parole.

In 1862 Fletcher returned to the Hoosier capital to resume civilian life. He married Agnes O'Brien and went back to private medical practice. Fletcher also continued to help the war effort by visiting Confederate prisoners in Terre Haute, briefly taking charge of the Confederate prisoners at a military hospital in Indianapolis, and traveling to the battlefields of Perryville, Stones River, and Vicksburg to care for the wounded.

Postwar, Fletcher spent two years studying in famous European hospitals, where the most advanced western medicine was being taught and practiced. After returning home, he cofounded the Indiana Medical College in 1869. The school eventually allied itself with Indiana University and is considered a forerunner to the IU School of Medicine. Fletcher also taught at the Central College of Physicians and Surgeons and the Medical College of Indiana. Throughout his career, Fletcher wrote and published numerous papers on various medical subjects.

To aid public health in his hometown, Fletcher helped to establish a city dispensary in the mid-1870s. The dispensary treated and supplied medicines to inmates from the city jail and to the "worthy" poor, using a blend of public and private funds. Fletcher served as its superintendent from 1875 to 1879.

In 1882 the residents of Marion County elected Fletcher, a Democrat, to a term in the state senate. His personal interests were reflected in his committee assignments, including those concerned with benevolent and reformatory institutions, temperance, and public health. Fletcher also introduced bills intended to improve public health and safety, prisons, and common schools. In addition, he presented petitions that favored the prohibition of alcohol, advocated the employment of female doctors for the women's department at the Indiana Hospital for the Insane, and opposed the repeal of the act that created the state board of health.

The following year Fletcher accepted an appointment as superintendent of the Indiana Hospital for the Insane. Having considered the post on more than one occasion, he wasted no time in implementing reforms. Within the first few months Fletcher reduced the amount of "medicinal agents" (namely whiskey) given to patients, and he appointed a hospital chaplain, who offered weekly services and the first public burials in the institution's history.

Fletcher also employed more women staff during his tenure. Believing that patients responded better to female voices and influence, he appointed women teachers, selected married couples to supervise some of the wards, and even assigned matrons to wards where violent patients were housed. Moreover, Fletcher hired Doctor Sarah Stockton as an assistant physician in the women's department, the first female to hold the position. She looked after the reproductive and general health of female patients, since gynecological ailments were linked to insanity during the late nineteenth century.

The reform that garnered Fletcher international attention, the burning of restraints, placed him in the avant-garde of mental health care. Nationally, hospital superintendents debated the merits of physical restraints, since few effective medications were available to treat the mentally ill, who might be dangerous to themselves and others. Fletcher reportedly was the first to destroy physical restraints so dramatically, and the episode received wide coverage in outlets from local newspapers to medical journals, including the *American Journal of Insanity* and the *British Medical Journal*. Years later, a description of Fletcher's bold act appeared in *One Hundred Years of American Psychiatry, 1844–1944*, a volume published to celebrate the centenary of the American Psychiatric Association.

Moral treatment, the regimen that Fletcher and like-minded superintendents employed, included firm but kind discipline, a structured schedule, and mental and physical diversion. Daily activities for patients included recreation, classroom lessons, religious services, and work. In his annual reports Fletcher claimed that moral treatment, along with additional staff training and lack of physical restraints, contributed to an increased number of cures, a decreased number of deaths, and improved health among both staff and patients.

A true reformer, Fletcher lost the superintendency in 1887 after calling attention to political abuses at the hospital. The position depended on political favor, and he was rousted after calling attention to what he claimed were corrupt practices in hiring and food procurement that were encouraged by the hospital trustees. Soon after, he established Doctor W. B. Fletcher's Sanatorium, later known as Neuronhurst. The facility specialized in treating mental and nervous diseases in women. Here, Fletcher continued to employ female doctors and staff. Doctor Mary A. Spink, who worked for him at the state hospital, joined him immediately, followed by her sister, Doctor Urbana R. Spink. Advertised nationally, the facility offered individualized attention, exercise, baths, electrotherapy, massage, and phototherapy.

In the late 1880s and even into his later years, Fletcher worked toward reform of mental health laws. He supported an 1889 statute requiring a woman attendant to accompany any woman being transported to a state mental hospital. In 1901, after complaints that state commitment laws enabled collusion among justices of the peace, police, and physicians for monetary gain, the Indiana Medical Society appointed him to lead a committee that would recommend wide-ranging reforms to the Board of State Charities.

Fletcher died in 1907 at his second home in Orlando, Florida. His death was noted by many, including mentions in medical journals in the United States and abroad. Hoosier Poet JAMES WHITCOMB RILEY memorialized him in "The Doctor," which repeats the line "Why not idealize the doctor some?"

RACHAEL L. DRENOVSKY

For Further Reading

Brigham, Loriman S., ed. "The Civil War Journals of William B. Fletcher." *Indiana Magazine of History* 57 (March 1961): 43–76.

Rachael L. Drenovsky, "Humanity's Bonfire: William B. Fletcher, M.D.: 1837–1907." *Traces of Indiana and Midwestern History* 13, no. 2 (Spring 2001): 19–25.

Forsyth, William Jefferson

October 15, 1854–March 29, 1935

Artist, Hoosier Group painter, and teacher at Herron Art Institute.

William Jefferson Forsyth, the most experimental of the noted Hoosier Group of painters, taught many of the following generation's best-known Indiana artists. Forsyth's forty-two years as an art instructor left a legacy of devoted students in addition to his prolific output of disparate artworks.

The five artists known as the Hoosier Group included Forsyth, T. C. STEELE, J. OTTIS ADAMS, OTTO STARK, and RICHARD GRUELLE. Their enthusiastic belief that Indiana was "as beautiful, characteristic and worthy of being interpreted as anything else in the world" helped to promote a tradition of landscape painting that has influenced local artists and collectors for generations.

Forsyth moved from the riverside town of California, Ohio, to Indianapolis with his family as a teenager in 1869, and was expected to help with his father's house-painting business. His general education was not a priority, but he was the initial student to enter James F. Gookins and John Love's first Indiana School of Art in the fall of 1877.

During his two years of study, Forsyth was inculcated with the importance of mastering drawing skills, which he later emphasized to his own students. Following the lead of Steele and Adams, Forsyth secured funding to study further in Germany. He found a sponsor in his friend and fellow student, Thomas E. Hibben Sr., whose family owned a local dry goods store. Hibben offered to finance Forsyth's studies abroad in exchange for half of his paintings created while a student.

On Christmas Eve day, 1881, Forsyth sailed for Munich to join Steele and Adams at the Royal Academy of Art. Forsyth spent two years in drawing school under Professor Gyula Benczur, then advanced to painting school with Professor Ludwig Von Löfftz, allegedly the best of the painting instructors at the art academy.

The big event for Munich artists during the summer of 1883 was the triennial Ausstellung International exhibit. Forsyth called the paintings by Hollanders "the most promising of any in the exhibition." The Dutch artists had used their formal training to effectively paint what they knew best. Steele and Adams shared Forsyth's opinion, and the Indiana painters were inspired by the idea of expressing a national identity.

Forsyth won a bronze medal for his portrait of a model, *Kathie*, in the 1885 exhibition of student work. Despite discontinued financial support from his sponsor Hibben, Forsyth studied at the Academy until the fall of 1886, when he opened a Munich studio with Adams. In addition to head and figure studies, the Indiana artists enjoyed excursions into the Bavarian countryside to paint landscapes.

By the time Forsyth returned from Munich in 1888, Steele had become the premiere portrait painter of Indiana. Although Forsyth had planned to paint portraits for income, he did not possess the diplomatic personality required for such work. He had earned a reputation for his temperamental personality, rarely censoring his opinionated comments to others.

Both Steele and Forsyth preferred to paint landscapes, but the market for landscape paintings was practically nonexistent in the early 1900s. They each spent much time and energy creating that market by writing, lecturing, teaching, and serving on art juries locally and internationally.

Their big break came in November 1894, when Steele and Forsyth, along with Gruelle and Stark, participated in an Exhibit of Summer Work, sponsored by the Art Association of Indianapolis. Knowing the sympathies of the Central Art Association in Chicago for the idea of a uniquely American "Western" art, Steele sent a letter to the president, Hamlin Garland, inviting the Art Association's officers to come see the exhibit. Although the letter arrived too late for their attendance, Garland's brother-in-law, sculptor Lorado Taft invited Steele to bring the show to his studio in the Chicago Athenaeum Building. The Central Art Association sponsored the exhibition, called *Five Hoosier Painters*, with the addition of paintings by Adams.

The exhibition enjoyed unprecedented critical acclaim. The exhibit catalog, written by the self-named Critical Triumvirate of Taft, Garland, and painter Charles Francis Brown, stated that the Hoosier Five artists were significant for their ability to create excellent artwork from unpromising material, and that the history of the Hoosier artists "exemplifies all the difficulties in the way of original western art and foreshadows its ultimate victory."

While Steele's primary income was always from painting commissioned portraits, Forsyth became an art instructor. His commitment to teaching began in 1889 with the Muncie Art School, founded by himself and Adams, along with weekend classes in Fort Wayne. He then taught at Steele's Capitol City Art School of Indiana from 1891 to 1897; gave private classes and organized student plein air (outside) painting jaunts for several years; and finally became the painting instructor at Herron Art Institute from 1907 to 1933, with seven summers of classes at Winona Lake. He wanted students to be well trained and prepared for lives dedicated to Art with a capital "A."

Known for his ruthless criticisms and lifelong loyalty to his serious students, Forsyth taught many significant artists, including Robert Selby, Ruth Pratt (Bobbs), Grant Christian, Randolf Coats, Floyd Hopper, Dorothy Morlan, and Julia Graydon Sharpe, to name a few.

While teaching six days each week, Forsyth always made time for his painting and exhibited internationally. He won numerous major awards, such as bronze and silver medals at the 1904 Louisiana Purchase Exposition in Saint Louis, Missouri, for *Late Afternoon* and *In the Afternoon*, respectively; the Mary T. R. Foulke Prize for *A Woodland Brook* at the Richmond Art Museum's 1907 annual exhibition; a bronze medal for *Moonrise and Twilight* at the 1910 Buenos Aires International Exposition; the Fine Arts Building Prize for *The Last Gleam* in the Fifteenth Annual Exhibition of the Society of Western Artists; bronze and silver medals for *The Red City* and *Sunny Corner*, respectively, in the 1915 Panama Pacific International Exposition in San Francisco, and a second Mary T. R. Foulke prize for *The Smoker* at the Richmond Art Museum's 1923 annual exhibition.

By 1933, in the depths of the Great Depression, Donald Magnus Mattison became director of the Herron Art Institute. In an effort to make the school solvent, he fired nine of Herron's fifteen teachers, including Forsyth. After losing his job, Forsyth participated in the federal government's Public Works of Art Project. A congratulatory form letter from the Treasury Department pointed out that the program "is the finest gesture that this or any other country has ever made to its artists."

When money ran out from the Public Works of Art Project, Herron Art Museum Director Wilbur Peat saw to it that Forsyth received the much-reduced Governor's Commission for Unemployment Relief, which required the creation of art panels for public schools and state-owned buildings.

Forsyth died of kidney failure on March 29, 1935. As the last venerable member of the Hoosier Group, his prolific output of original artwork became part of his legacy. Unlike the four other artists of the noted group, however, Forsyth bequeathed his strong belief in a life committed to serious creative effort to the next generation of Indiana artists.

RACHEL BERENSON PERRY

For Further Reading

Forsyth, William. Papers. William Henry Smith Memorial Library Papers. Indiana Historical Society, Indianapolis.

———. *Art in Indiana*. Indianapolis: H. Lieber Company, 1916.

Krause, Martin. *The Passage: Return of Indiana Painters from Germany, 1880–1905*. Indianapolis: Indianapolis Museum of Art, 1990.

Newton, Judith Vale. *The Hoosier Group: Five American Painters*. Indianapolis: Eckert Publications, 1985.

Perry, Rachel Berenson. *William J Forsyth: The Life and Work of an Indiana Artist*. Bloomington: Indiana University Press, 2014.

William J. Forsyth

Fox, Lillian Thomas

November 1854–August 29, 1917

African American journalist and community activist.

From the late nineteenth century into the early twentieth century, Lillian Thomas Fox was a leader in the struggle for black survival and advancement in Indianapolis. The *Indianapolis Freeman*, a prominent black newspaper, called her "an original thinker and one who dare[d] to flout" popular dogma or philosophy that went against her cardinal principles of justice and right." Fox's life reflects the myriad ways that black women crossed the boundaries of gender and race in the early Jim Crow Era.

Fox belonged to the "fruit of emancipation" generation, that first group of African Americans who came of age after slavery ended. Born in 1854 in Chicago to the Reverend Byrd Parker, pastor of Quinn African Methodist Church, and Jane Janette Johnson, Lillian was raised in Oshkosh, Wisconsin. Her father, who also established an elementary school in Chicago in 1852 for black children, was a noted orator and he lobbied Wisconsin legislators for the cause of civil rights. After his death in 1860, his widow married Robert E. Thomas and Lillian continued using the name Thomas throughout her life.

Lillian's education began at home with her parents, and she was reading and writing at an early age. In the 1880s she moved with her mother and brother to Indianapolis, where she learned dramatic reading and dialect at Hattie Prunk's Indiana-Boston School of Elocution. By the 1890s, Lillian had become an established speaker.

Like most educated middle-class women of her generation, Lillian actively sought and acquired a range of skills that exalted respectability and enabled her to earn a living. At one point Lillian lived in Louisville, Kentucky, where she worked as a stenographer. In Indianapolis she supplemented income from professional speaking by taking in sewing at home. Lillian successfully sat for the civil service clerk's exam in 1891. She also freelanced for black newspapers and then was hired by the *Freeman* as an assistant correspondence editor, the paper noting that she "already . . . had considerable experience in that line."

Two years later, trusting the idea that the home was a respectable married woman's true sphere of influence, Lillian left her job at the *Freeman* to marry James E. Fox, a Jamaican merchant tailor who relocated his business from Pensacola, Florida, to Indianapolis to be with her. Shortly after her marriage, Fox's mother and brother died of tuberculosis within two days of each other.

Fox subscribed to black nationalistic values of uplift and self-help. After her marriage, Fox continued to speak and organize programs about those values for women's clubs. Participation in national gatherings opened her eyes to the experienced resources available in those networks as she tried to effect social change in Indianapolis. Fox attended an Atlanta Congress of Colored Women meeting in December 1895 and shared the speaker's podium with black women activists from twenty-five states and the District of Columbia. The Negro Building at that year's Cotton States and National Exposition drew the attendance of black activists such as Fannie Barrier Williams, Frances Harper, Victoria Earle Matthews, Lucy Laney, Frederick Douglass, Lucy E. Moten, and Margaret (Mrs. Booker T.) Washington.

On the train ride from Indianapolis to Atlanta, Fox challenged Jim Crow segregation by refusing to move from her first-class coach seat into the smoking car that had a partitioned compartment for blacks. Like fellow journalist Ida Wells-Barnett, who in 1884 had been removed from a train when she refused to change seats, Fox sued the railroad when she returned home. Wells-Barnett's won her suit, but Fox's outcome is unknown. Neither woman allowed that experience to proscribe further travel.

When Fox's husband, James, died in 1898, she turned her grief to activism and returned to journalism. In 1900 she spoke to black newspaper editors from across the county who had convened in Indianapolis for the Afro-American Press Association's annual meeting. Addressing the topic of "Women in Journalism," Fox said, "No human device holds a more exalted place in mankind's regard than the pen" and when considering epoch periods in the world's history, that pen "has been most efficiently wielded by women." Fox also helped draft the resolution that closed that year's convention, which read in part that schools are "the greatest agency in life for the uplift of any people. The race will make more advancement when it reads more and thinks more."

That same year, the *Indianapolis News*, a white-owned newspaper, hired Fox as a correspondent to write weekly columns about local black organizations and articles about the successes of black mutual-aid societies nationwide. Her columns informed white Indianapolis about black community life, and she used the *News* as a vehicle to remedy black Indianapolis's lack of healthcare delivery systems.

Fox joined with Indianapolis's first black female physician, Beulah Wright Porter, in 1903 to found the Woman's Improvement Club, a literary society aimed at self-education. The next year, she led the drive that brought fourteen black women's clubs together across the state into the Indiana Federation of Colored Women's Clubs. The pooling of assets statewide enabled individual clubs to undertake larger projects.

Led by Fox, the WIC launched an attack on tuberculosis in 1905 by forming a nurses' training class and creating one of the country's first outdoor "fresh-air" camps. WIC women also worked with community organizations such as Flanner Guild settlement house to hold classes on sanitation, mothering, childcare, and nutrition; the Phyllis Wheatley Young Women's Christian Association to offer domestic science and nutrition programs for young women; and the Alpha Home for Aged Colored Women to provide geriatric care. For nine years, Fox wrote reports and appeals in the *News* that connected black community organizations to resources in the larger Indianapolis community.

Chronic illness forced Fox to end her activism in 1914. In the summer of 1917 she suffered a stroke and died of a heart attack at the home of friend and clubwoman, Florence Wayne.

In 1919 the WIC presented the Marion County Health Commissioners with statistics that persuaded them to open a tuberculosis inoculation clinic at Flanner Guild and to provide beds for incurable black patients at Sunnyside Sanatorium. In the decades that followed Fox's death, WIC women extended her legacy by providing direct hospital care. The organization opened a six-bed hospital on Agnes Street in 1924 and by 1938 WIC women persuaded the Flower Mission Hospital to open a ward for black patients at its new site on Fall Creek Boulevard. In 2014 Fox was inducted into the Indiana Journalism Hall of Fame.

EARLINE RAE FERGUSON

For Further Reading

Ferguson, Earline Rae. "Lillian Thomas Fox: Indianapolis Journalist and Community Leader." In Wilma L. Gibbs, ed. *Indiana's African-American Heritage: Essays from* Black History News & Notes. Indianapolis: Indiana Historical Society, 1993.

———. "The Woman's Improvement Club of Indianapolis: Black Women Pioneers in Tuberculosis Work, 1903–1938." *Indiana Magazine of History* 84 (September 1988): 237–61.

Hine, Darlene Clark. *When Truth Is Told: A History of Black Women's Culture and Community in Indiana, 1875-1950.* Indianapolis: National Council of Negro Women, Indianapolis Section, 1981.

Garrett, William

April 4, 1929–August 7, 1974

Broke the color barrier in Big Ten basketball and opened the door to the widespread integration of college basketball.

In the spring of 1947, Bill Garrett led his Shelbyville High School basketball team to the state championship, set a new state tournament scoring record, and was named Indiana's "Mr. Basketball." But no coach of a white college team even tried to recruit Garrett. For in 1947 college basketball was segregated, in Indiana and in much of the country.

But the times were changing. Here and elsewhere groups and individuals were standing up to segregation with a restlessness that soon coalesced into the civil rights movement. The best-known example in that summer of 1947 was Jackie Robinson's integration of Major League Baseball. To many African Americans, Robinson's breakthrough was an example of sports as a wedge for possible broader integration.

Some saw the integration of college basketball as another opportunity for such a wedge. Except on the two coasts college basketball was segregated, and many athletic conferences had unwritten "gentleman's agreements" not to play African Americans. One of the most important of those agreements was the one among the athletic directors and coaches of the Big Ten, to which Indiana and Purdue Universities belonged. Segregation in Big Ten basketball was practically absolute. Only one African American, Dick Culberson, who saw limited action for the University of Iowa in part of one season during World War II, had ever played for a Big Ten team.

The segregation in Big Ten basketball was symbolically important nationally. At a time when basketball was the country's most popular amateur sport, the Big Ten was by many standards the most dominant college basketball conference, drawing the biggest crowds and stretching across the geographic and psychological heartland from Ohio to Iowa. As long as the Big Ten's "gentleman's agreement" held, others could hide behind it. And if it fell, others would be next in line.

Indiana in the 1940s seemed an unlikely place for a racial breakthrough. Sometimes called "the most Southern state in the North," it was mostly rural and lacked a progressive tradition. But in 1947 Indiana had four things that existed in combination nowhere else: an all-consuming passion for basketball, a commanding black leader who was pushing sports as a wedge for integration, a university president of great vision and finesse, and a talented teenage basketball player suited for his time and role.

Throughout the summer of 1947, as white newspapers described the college choices of lesser white players and ignored Garrett, black newspapers, led by the *Indianapolis Recorder*, speculated about his prospects. In early September, as classes were starting, Faburn DeFrantz, executive director

Bill Garrett

of Indianapolis' Senate Avenue Young Men's Christian Association, led a delegation to Bloomington to meet with Indiana University president Herman B Wells about giving Garrett a chance to play at IU. It was a meeting of formidable figures. DeFrantz had built the Senate Avenue Y into the largest black YMCA in the world and had made its "Monster Meetings" into one of the preeminent black forums nationally. Wells had built IU into a great university and (often with DeFrantz) had been working quietly to integrate the IU campus despite opposition from Ora L. Wildermuth, the IU board of trustees chairman.

Persuaded by DeFrantz, Wells, who also was worried about lawsuits and bad publicity, made a deal with IU basketball coach Branch McCracken: if McCracken would give Garrett a chance, and if Garrett was good enough to make the IU team, Wells would back McCracken regardless of the reactions. All summer McCracken had also been hearing from his friend Nate Kaufman, a prominent businessman from Shelbyville and top basketball referee, who wanted Garrett to play for IU. With Wells and Kaufman's backing, McCracken agreed.

Garrett was already at Tennessee Agricultural and Industrial College (now Tennessee State University) in Nashville. A few months earlier he had expressed to a reporter for the *Recorder* his fears of being a racial trailblazer, saying, "Too much in the spotlight. What if I didn't make good?" Reminded of Robinson's example, he replied, "That's right. Jackie is preparing a way for others, and I guess I could do that too." With Kaufman's encouragement and help, Garrett boarded a bus for Bloomington.

Playing center at six feet two, Garrett led his IU team in scoring and rebounding in each of his three varsity seasons (freshmen were not eligible for the varsity in 1947). He set a new IU career scoring record. He endured taunts from opposing fans and bigotry from hotels and restaurants. He won the respect of his teammates, including some who initially opposed integration. Garrett also became a favorite of IU fans, who gave him a long, heartfelt standing ovation after he played his final home game. In his senior year, he was a consensus All-American, his teammates voted him IU's Most Valuable Player, Big Ten coaches and sportswriters voted him onto the All-Big Ten first team, and he received IU's Balfour Award as the basketball player exhibiting outstanding performance and conduct. He graduated in 1951 with a degree in physical education and business, married his college sweetheart, Betty Guess, and was drafted by the Boston Celtics.

But he was also drafted by the U.S. Army. By the end of Garrett's two-year army hitch, the Celtics had released him and the Harlem Globetrotters offered him a contract. Never a showman, Garrett soon left the Globetrotters and moved with Betty to Indianapolis. There, Garrett led all-black Indianapolis Crispus Attucks High School to the 1959 state basketball championship, making him the only Indiana Mr. Basketball to play on an Indiana boys' state championship basketball team and coach one, a record that still stands. He became athletic director at Crispus Attucks, director of continuing education at Indiana Vocational College, and an assistant dean at Indiana–Purdue University at Indianapolis. Twice he ran for the IU board of trustees, seeking to become the first African American member, but each time lost by narrow margins.

Bill and Betty, who became dean of girls at Indianapolis Shortridge High School, raised four children—Tina, Judith, Laurie, and Bill. In August 1974, after a heart attack, Garrett died at age forty-five.

Worried at first that he might not be up to the task, Garrett bore the spotlight and fulfilled the responsibilities of a trailblazer so smoothly and well that his legacy goes almost unnoticed. After he arrived on the IU campus, black newspapers all over the country wrote of his breaking the Big Ten's color barrier, often alongside stories about Robinson. During his years at Indiana, dormitories, dining halls, and other facilities became integrated. By his junior year, after he had proved the experiment to be a success, coaches all over the Midwest were looking for "a Bill Garrett." In 1952, the year after Garrett graduated, there were six African Americans on five Big Ten teams. Unlike anyone before him, Garrett opened the door a crack, making possible opportunities for a stream of black players to enter college basketball between 1951 and 1955, before superstars such as Bill Russell, Wilt Chamberlain, Oscar Robertson, and Elgin Baylor opened the door more widely.

Reminded of Robinson's example, the eighteen-year-old Garrett had mused that maybe he, too, could "prepare a way for others." IU's second black basketball player, Wally Choice, expressed how well he had done that: "Bill Garrett left such a strong legacy that it could never be reversed. African Americans made me aware that I was following an icon—not just in basketball but in personality too. I became aware that I couldn't mess up at IU, or I would mess up the legacy. I would be letting him down. As I've grown older, I've realized that he paved the way—showed an example. Bill Garrett made it a pleasant situation for me."

Garrett's progeny has continued making strides in college basketball. His grandson, William L. Garrett II, or "Billy," a point guard for DePaul University and coached by his father, senior assistant coach Bill Garrett, was named the Big East Conference Freshman of the Year in 2014.

RACHEL GRAHAM CODY
TOM GRAHAM

For Further Reading

Cody, Rachel Graham, and Tom Graham. *Getting Open: The Unknown Story of Bill Garrett and the Integration of College Basketball.* New York: Atria Books, 2006.

Thornbrough, Emma Lou, and Lana Ruegamer. *Indiana Blacks in the Twentieth Century.* Bloomington: Indiana University Press, 2000.

Thomas, Ron. *They Cleared the Lane: The NBA's Black Pioneers.* Lincoln: University of Nebraska Press, 2002.

Warren, Stanley. *The Senate Avenue YMCA for African American Men and Boys, Indianapolis, Indiana, 1913–1959.* Virginia Beach, VA: Donning Company Publishers, 2005.

Gennett Family

Henry, September 13, 1852–June 3, 1922; Fred, December 20, 1885–November 27, 1964; Harry, July 11, 1877–November 5, 1952; Clarence, August 25, 1879–January 14, 1953

Owners and executive management of Starr Piano Company and founders of Gennett Records.

During the early twentieth century, Henry Gennett and his three sons operated the massive Starr Piano factory secluded in a glacial gorge along the Whitewater River in Richmond, Indiana. It was among America's largest piano manufacturers and an industrial cornerstone in Richmond. Then, in 1916, the Gennett family created a sideline business by entering the new, brash frontier of phonographs and music recording. Within a few years, their upstart Gennett Records label left a lasting impact on American music.

It is a legacy the Gennett family could not have imagined for themselves. After all, Henry and his sons, Harry, Fred, and Clarence, were Indiana piano makers and retailers who introduced their "Starr" brand-name phonographs and 78-rpm records (soon renamed "Gennett Records") simply to increase sales in their national network of Starr Piano retail stores.

From 1916 to 1934, the small, but prolific, Gennett Records produced thousands of 78-rpm discs (called 78s), first at a Manhattan recording studio, and beginning in 1921, from a second studio at the Starr Piano factory in Richmond. Far from the major cities, the primitive Richmond studio often halted recording sessions due to the noise from slow-moving trains in the factory and by trains roaring along the ridge of the gorge. The studio mostly waxed obscure musicians passing through rural Indiana, ranging from vaudeville singers, hotel orchestras, and brass bands to sacred choirs, country blues wailers, and backwoods fiddlers. However, interspersed in the long parade of forgotten musicians were several future icons of early jazz, blues, and country music. The small Indiana record company promoted and preserved a remarkable musical era when America's original sounds would be embraced by the world.

The son of a grocery wholesaler in Nashville, Tennessee, Henry married into the music business through his father-in-law, John Lumsden, and his brother-in-law, Jesse French, who operated a chain of piano retail stores in the South. In 1893 the three men acquired control of the highly respected Starr Piano Company in Richmond. Within a decade, Henry assumed full ownership of Starr Piano, appointing his three young sons as company officers.

Henry was a distinctive, tan-skinned Italian with a black moustache, and he was a dynamic leader. Though he was short and slightly built, he more than compensated for his small physical stature with an outgoing, confident personality and a reputation among employees as a bold decision maker. He developed Starr Piano into one of the nation's largest mass producers of pianos. By 1915 Starr Piano's factory complex in Richmond produced 15,000 pianos annually and had sold 100,000 pianos nationwide.

After Henry died in 1922, his eldest son, Harry, was named president of Starr Piano, and the youngest son, Fred, managed the Gennett Records division. On the guidance of Fred Wiggins, manager of the Starr Piano store in downtown Chicago, Fred in 1922 began recording white and black Chicago jazz musicians, and promoted the releases with both white and black consumers. A diminutive man with receding hair and horn-rimmed glasses, Fred resembled a bookish professor more than an entrepreneur in the radical new world of jazz music. But he identified a business opportunity. New Orleans jazz blossomed in Chicago speakeasies and dance halls in the early 1920s, and Gennett Records became its Rosetta Stone, debuting King Oliver, Louis Armstrong, Johnny Dodds, Bix Beiderbecke, Earl "Fatha" Hines, Freddie Keppard, Leon Roppolo, and other jazz pioneers. Piano solos recorded in Richmond by Jelly Roll Morton captured the genius of one of jazz's first significant composers. The development of Bloomington's HOAGY CARMICHAEL from an obscure jazz player to a polished songwriter is documented almost exclusively on Gennett. From 1925 to 1928 Carmichael recorded in the Richmond studio several times, including the first ever recording of his classic "Stardust."

When Fred aggressively produced 78s in the late 1920s for various discount labels, the Richmond recording studio became a lightning rod for early American rural music. Hundreds of rare Gennett country (called "old-time" and "hillbilly"), sacred, and blues recordings preserved regional songs and music styles, from Appalachia to the Deep South. Musicians recorded at the Richmond studio—Charley Patton, Blind Lemon Jefferson, Uncle Dave Macon, Lonnie Johnson, Bill Broonzy, Scrapper Blackwell, William Harris, Gene Autry, and Fiddlin' Doc Roberts—are part of the early development of country and rock music.

While not a musical visionary, Fred focused on how to best turn a dollar by releasing discs as diverse as songs by Hopi Indian tribes, to speeches by politician William Jennings Bryan, to hymns with new politically charged lyrics sung by members of the Ku Klux Klan, whose membership peaked in Indiana in the early 1920s. The Gennett family never supported the Klan, nor did they market KKK records. They custom recorded and pressed the discs for cash payment from the Klan membership.

The 1920s was a remarkable decade for the recording industry. Small record labels proliferated, in large part because of the triumph by the Gennett family over dominant Victor Records in a landmark patent infringement case that made key recording technologies controlled by Victor available to everyone. As America's jazz, blues, and country music styles developed, the Gennett studio in Richmond might record a black jazz band in the morning and a white Appalachian string band in the afternoon. Despite the social barriers imposed between races, the cross-pollination between white and black approaches to jazz, blues, and country music is evident on the Gennett releases.

This wonderful era in music recording quickly collapsed. By 1934 the Great Depression forced the Gennett family to close its record division, joining several record labels that disappeared. Starr Piano survived by producing pianos and refrigeration supplies. By the late 1930s bitter disputes within the Gennett family ultimately led to Fred's departure from Starr Piano. Finally, in 1952, his brother, Harry, closed the piano factory, which had struggled for several years. By then, the Gennett family's prominent place in Richmond society had long faded. Gennett family members continue to this day to operate a successful refrigeration supply company in California.

However, the music they preserved lived on. As early as the 1930s, jazz enthusiasts pursued the old Gennett 78s by Oliver, Beiderbecke, and Morton in secondhand stores. Beginning in the 1950s, classic Gennett recordings appeared on jazz, blues, and country anthologies on long-playing vinyl records, and by the 1980s, on cassette tapes and compact discs.

Today, Gennett's landmark music captured on primitive equipment in a piano factory along the river has never sounded better, nor has it been more accessible. With the advent of Internet music downloads, hundreds of digitally remastered Gennett records are just a credit card and a click of a computer mouse away for a listening audience that now spans the globe.

RICK KENNEDY

For Further Reading

Kay, George W. "Those Fabulous Gennetts! The Life Story of a Remarkable Label." *The Record Changer* (June 1953).

Kennedy, Rick. *Jelly Roll, Bix & Hoagy: Gennett Records and the Rise of America's Musical Grassroots.* Revised Edition. Bloomington: Indiana University Press, 2013.

Schiedt, Duncan. *The Jazz State of Indiana.* Pittsborough, IN: Published by the author, 1977.

Gilbreth, Lillian Moller

May 24, 1878–January 2, 1972

Purdue University professor, time-and-motion study researcher, industrial psychologist and engineering consultant, and the mother to twelve children featured in the book *Cheaper by the Dozen*.

President Herbert Hoover declared Lillian Gilbreth, who had created a successful jobs program at the outset of the Great Depression, "the most heroic woman in America," and commended her children who authored *Cheaper by the Dozen*. "Your book" he said, "should make her an immortal in the life of our country." Unfortunately the memoir that brought her much fame downplayed Lillian's life's work and her internationally acclaimed professional accomplishments as a scientist.

Lillie Evelyn Moller (she changed to Lillian in college) was born in Oakland, California, the second of ten children born to Annie and William Moller. Lillian described herself as descending from entrepreneurial German immigrant grandparents: the Delgers, on the maternal side, struck it rich during the gold rush, supplying boots to the miners, and reinvested in California land; and the Mollers owned a New York sugar refinery.

Lillie was a bright child who spoke early, but was also shy, nervous, and easily frightened, having nightmares of dying. Her upper-middle-class family had servants and her parents were strict and protective. Older siblings served as caregivers for the younger children—a practice Lillian employed with her own children. Lillian thought she was unattractive and committed herself to academics saying, "If I couldn't be pretty, then instead I could be clever." She took pleasure in reading, piano lessons, and dramatic training. At Oakland High School she enjoyed her teachers and poetry, composing poems her entire life.

Her father opposed Lillian attending college, thinking degrees were for schoolteachers and workingwomen, and also perhaps out of fear of losing his oldest daughter. Her mother, however, persuaded him that college could be a sort of finishing school, protecting Lillian's health from having children too young. At the University of California, Lillian took Latin, advanced German, science, and math. Her German professor told her father that his daughter was "one of the best minds in the freshman class." She majored in English, studied psychology, and took enough education classes to earn a teaching certificate. She graduated from Berkley in 1900 and became the first woman to deliver the commencement address.

Lillian pursued a master's degree at Columbia, where a literature professor refused to allow her to take his class because she was a woman. She developed pleurisy and returned home to the University of California, earning her master's in literature in 1902. She started PhD courses in the fall but dropped out for the spring semester to prepare for a European tour. On the way to Europe she stopped over in Boston, where she met her future husband, Frank Gilberth.

Ten years Lillian's senior, Frank was outgoing and loved to tease people. He was already a famous building contractor known for his work speeding the productivity of employees. His widowed mother had moved her family from Maine to Boston for better educational opportunities, but instead of attending the Massachusetts Institute of Technology, Frank apprenticed in the construction industry, studying the efficiency of bricklaying by eliminating fatigue and excess motions of workers.

Shortly after she returned from Europe, Frank proposed to Lillian, and while they were engaged, she indexed an instruction book, *Field System*, that he had written for his employees. Together they adopted the slogan that became the hallmark of the Gilbreth System: "The one best way to do work." Frank and Lillian began married life in October 1904 as a fifty-fifty partnership and planned on having six boys and six girls. Their first child arrived in 1905, the last in 1922. They settled in New York, and Lillian started researching, writing, and editing the first of many books about construction and engineering. She persuaded Frank to close the construction business, and together they started their business as consulting engineers and efficiency experts.

With Lillian's education in psychology and the humanities and Frank's experience in construction, they applied a human, individual, approach to scientific management. They developed a new technique for what were known as time-and-motion studies that were integral to theories of scientific management made famous by Fredrick Wilson Taylor. Instead of using a stopwatch to record a worker's motions, the

Gilbreths used a movie camera to observe a work cycle. Through their observations they were able to decrease worker fatigue and thereby increase efficiency by redesigning machinery to fit the worker. These studies were the forerunner of today's ergonomic studies.

The Gilbreths moved to Providence, Rhode Island, to consult for the New England Butt Company, a manufacturer of machines for various products. In 1914 Lillian's book *The Psychology of Management* was published, encouraging scientific management and engineering communities to be concerned with the human psychology of workers. The following year, Lillian earned her PhD in applied psychology from Brown University. Their next move was to Montclair, New Jersey, where they established a business called Gilbreth Incorporated and continued their productive lives together. They frequently lectured to engineering and business schools and published in professional journals and magazines. They coauthored five books about their research between 1912 and 1920.

Their lives changed significantly when the United States entered World War I. They began pioneering work with amputees. A medical expert in the field credited them with laying "the basis for modern rehabilitation services for the physically handicapped." The war had a very personal impact as well. Frank volunteered and soon developed several illnesses, including rheumatic fever, uremic poisoning, and pneumonia. The damage to his heart was such that he died five years later of a heart attack in 1924 at the age of fifty-six.

Frank and Lillian had scheduled a tour of Europe with professional lectures booked, and despite her grief, Lillian filled in for her husband. She also continued the work that she and Frank had done together. Although many in the engineering community respected Lillian's contributions to the field, sex discrimination remained. Using her knowledge of women and management experience, she consulted with Macy's, Green Line lunch rooms, and Johnson and Johnson on female sanitary products. Lillian created model kitchens with a circular work plan, adjusted counter heights, and a household management desk designed with International Business Machines Corporation. Financially challenged, Lillian sold her jewelry, and the children delayed or changed universities; the eleven surviving children all earned degrees.

Lilian's fifty-year association with Purdue University began in 1925 when the university asked Lillian to continue Frank's annual lectures. Ten years later, Purdue president Edward C. Elliott appointed Gilbreth professor of management in the School of Mechanical Engineering, making her the first person to hold such a position, not only at Purdue but in the entire country. In 1940 Lillian became a full professor. Her contributions to Purdue and to Indiana were numerous. Her teaching and research responsibilities included home economics, industrial engineering, industrial psychology, and women's careers. Gilbreth began working at Purdue about the same time as Amelia Earhart, and they became good friends. Both resided in Windsor Halls, the women's dormitory. Just before leaving on her last flight, Earhart said that her association with Gilbreth was "the most rewarding part of her time at Purdue."

Gilbreth supervised the creation of a time-and-motion study laboratory in the School of Industrial Engineering, and she applied her work simplification research studies in the kitchen and also to the field of agriculture. During World War II, she consulted with defense manufacturers, improving work for "crippled soldiers." Homemakers today owe much to Gilbreth because of her scientific kitchen designs. Her son, Frank, commenting on his mother's impact on American households, said that "every washing machine, kitchen stove, and refrigerator that rolls off the assembly line today bears the imprint of her research."

Gilbreth generously gave Purdue hundreds of volumes of her husband's original research notes, now part of the Gilbreth Engineering Library, and she also donated her own professional and personal correspondence and other items, which are now in the Lillian Gilbreth Collection in the Department of Special Collections and Archives. She retired from Purdue at age seventy.

Gilbreth continued working, volunteering with the Girl Scouts, consulting with hospitals, and creating the Heart Kitchen for "handicapped homemakers." She traveled the world lecturing on household and industrial engineering, psychology, and lifelong learning, encouraging older people to stay engaged.

In 1968, battling skin cancer and heart disease, she retired. Gilbreth suffered strokes, broke her hip, and was placed in a nursing home. Her brilliant memory faded. She passed away at the age of ninety-four, having lived her strenuous life's quest to the fullest.

MELANIE E. HUGHES

For Further Reading

Gilbreth, Lillian, and Frank Gilbreth Papers. Purdue University Libraries, Archives and Special Collections, Lafayette, IN.

Graham, Laurel. *Managing on Her Own: Dr. Lillian Gilbreth and Women's Work in the Interwar Era.* Norcross, GA: Engineering and Management Press, 1998.

Lancaster, Jane. *Making Time: Lillian Moller Gilbreth, A life Beyond "Cheaper by the Dozen."* Boston: Northeastern University Press, 2004

Weber, Catherine E. Forrest. "Dr. Lillian Gilbreth and the One Best Way." *Traces of Indiana and Midwestern History* 9, no. 3 (Summer 1997): 38–45.

Gingold, Josef

October 28, 1909–January 11, 1995

Prominent violinist, orchestral concertmaster, teacher, and founder of the Indianapolis International Violin Competition.

A portrait of Josef Gingold hangs in the lobby of the Musical Arts Center on the Indiana University campus in Bloomington. A spotlight shines upon it. He is holding a violin, his violin, the Martinelli Stradivarius of 1683, and he is smiling. The painting symbolizes how Joe, as friends referred to him, how Mr. Gingold, as students addressed him, is remembered at the institution where this beloved teacher spent thirty-five years, from 1960 right up to his death. He was the genial professor with a smile, in later years a grandfather figure, and throughout his long tenure a frequent and welcomed presence at musical events.

His students insisted that during lessons their Mr. Gingold was demanding, but the stories that come from their experiences indicate he was a gentle master and that they loved him. William Preucil, concertmaster of the Cleveland Orchestra, called each lesson "an event. We'd deal with bow and fingering and phrasing and being in tune, and then he'd read Shakespeare, and there'd be lighter moments with jokes and laughter. If I had trouble staying in tune, he'd turn Biblical, saying, 'Seek, and ye shall find.'"

Gingold's distinguished colleague at IU, cellist Janos Starker, a legendary teacher in his own right, once told David Blum in *The New Yorker*: "I consider Josef Gingold the greatest violin teacher I have ever known. His background is almost unparalleled; he has done practically everything that a string player can do in music—even played in Broadway shows. He's the only teacher I know who is equally qualified to teach the instrument, solo repertoire, orchestral repertoire, and chamber music. He also happens to be one of the most genuine human beings I've ever met."

The "greatest violin teacher" was born in Brest-Litovsk, then part of the Russian Empire, now in Belarus. He was the youngest of six children in a family that encouraged music. His own violin lessons began at age four. "I can't remember ever not playing the violin," he once said. Fascination set in on hearing his older brother play. Given an instrument of his own, he puzzled over what made it play. "My father said, 'When you put the bow on the strings, there's a little man inside, and he starts to dance because he's happy.' Well, I wanted to see the little man, so I smashed the violin, and my father began screaming, and my mother came to my rescue saying, 'Why do you tell him such fairy tales? He's only three!'"

Josef smashed no more violins. He was not yet six when he gave his first public performance, this to German soldiers stationed in the area during World War I. They rewarded him with food. But German occupation led to the family's displacement into an internment camp. Such wartime experiences and political turmoil caused the Gingolds to come to the United States in 1920. There, in New York City, Josef's studies continued with Vladimir Graffman, of whom Gingold said "You couldn't play a note out of tune in front of this man," and at the Third Street Settlement, where instructors "taught me free of charge, gave me an instrument, bought me music, and even saw to it that I received complimentary tickets to important musical events."

In 1927 Gingold played a debut recital in New York's Aeolian Hall. He then moved to Brussels for two years of study with the legendary virtuoso Eugene Ysaye whose influence, he said, "remained with me all my life. . . . He believed in the beauty of sound. Never was the violin treated brutally. . . . Just being around him, one got a tremendous feeling that you must be a human being."

Back in New York, with the nation in economic depression, Gingold began jobbing on Broadway and wherever he could find opportunities to eke out a living. In 1937, dared to by his wife, Gladys, he auditioned for Arturo Toscanini and the NBC

Symphony Orchestra. He won and spent seven years with the fabled ensemble, "the most inspiring time in my life," said Gingold. About the maestro, Toscanini, he said: "We all adored him for his honesty to music making, his faithfulness toward the intentions of composers." Gingold later told his own students that composers "are the heroes. We as performers serve the music given us."

He left the NBC Symphony Orchestra to become concertmaster of the Detroit Symphony Orchestra and then to spend thirteen years as concertmaster of the Cleveland Orchestra. Its music director, George Szell, was, said Gingold, after Toscanini, "second among the major musical influences of my life. As a musician, no one had his knowledge. He was a man of enormous natural ability. . . . He made demands, but he knew what he wanted and why. . . . He taught me much about the violin and about teaching."

It was for teaching that Gingold left Cleveland in 1960. Wilfred Bain, dean of IU's School of Music, seeking to add more professionals to a faculty whose ranks already included cellist Starker and pianist Menahem Pressler, set his sights on Gingold who, while with the Cleveland Orchestra, had been teaching part time at Case Western Reserve University. "I was looking for someone who could supply the sort of discipline Szell brought to his orchestra," said Bain.

Gingold brought the discipline but also a generous personality that attracted students, including the most gifted. At IU, in master classes most everywhere, and during summers at the Meadowmount School in Westport, New York, he guided several generations of young violinists to lives in music, some—such as Jaime Laredo, Miriam Fried, Leonidas Kavakos, and Joshua Bell—to solo stardom, but many others to successful careers in orchestras and chamber groups and as teachers.

When, in 2009, IU remembered Gingold with a 100th birthday celebration, Laredo said he "touched more people than anyone I've ever known. To me, he was my teacher, my mentor, my colleague, my friend, and I always think of him as my second father."

Joshua Bell recalled: "Mr. Gingold made the most beautiful, the sweetest sounds on his violin. To hear him play was an inspiration. His love for

Josef Gingold and pupil, September 1967

music was infectious. When I left his studio after a lesson, I never felt intimidated but always excited. He taught each student differently because each of us had different needs. He was so generous of his time. I'd come to him at the end of the day and never know how long I'd stay. But every moment—when I played, when I listened, when we talked—was an adventure. To me, he was a grandfather figure, the warmest person and the most significant in my musical life."

Regrettably, Gingold's "sweetest sounds" can be heard on all too few recordings. But his striving for them has been imbued in former students who, as performers and teachers, pass the tradition along. As for the violin that helped produce the sounds, the Martinelli Strad, it is now owned by the prestigious Indianapolis International Violin Competition, which Gingold founded in 1982. Winners of the competition earn use of the instrument, so, in his memory, they can entertain audiences with their individual augmentation of that sweet Gingold sound.

PETER P. JACOBI

For Further Reading

Jacobi, Peter P. "Josef Gingold: A Life in Music." *Traces of Indiana and Midwestern History* 8, no. 1 (Winter 1996): 14–21.
Saslay, Isidor. "Josef Gingold Turns 100." *Swans Commentary*, December 28, 2009.
Logan, George M. *The Indiana University School of Music: A History*. Bloomington: Indiana University Press, 2000.

The Glicks

Eugene Biccard, August 29, 1921–October 2, 2013, and Marilyn, March 8, 1922–March 23, 2012

Real estate developers and philanthropists.

For many, the eleventh hour of the eleventh day of the eleventh month carries great significance, as at that moment in 1918 World War I finally shuddered to an end. On the twenty-sixth anniversary of the armistice, while World War II raged, November 11 took on new meaning for a young man from Indianapolis. At 10:50 on that bitterly cold morning, Eugene B. Glick found himself facedown in an icy slit trench in France, with shells decimating the earth around him. The twenty-five-year-old graduate of Indiana University made a vow: "If I get out of this alive, anytime in the future, if it gets tough, I am going to remember November eleventh, 1944." Around 11:00 a.m., the shelling stopped. Glick survived, and after helping liberate the concentration camp at Dachau, where he witnessed and documented the aftermath of the Holocaust, he returned to Indianapolis.

Gene, as he was known, was born and raised in Indianapolis. He graduated from Shortridge High School in 1939, where he had honed his entrepreneurial skills selling advertisements for the school newspaper. He continued to build his business acumen at Indiana University, setting up charter buses to take students home for the holidays and establishing a credit service at a toy store. After being discharged from the army, and in spite of his lack of experience, Glick convinced an officer at Peoples Bank to hire him to establish a GI loan department to assist returning veterans obtain mortgages. While working for the bank, he began dating a young woman he had met once before the war, and once again while home on leave: Marilyn Ruth Koffman.

Marilyn lived in an apartment with her mother just a stone's throw from Glick's house. Marilyn had moved to Indianapolis from Detroit in 1939, following a childhood that saw the loss of her father when she was eleven. Like Glick, she attended Shortridge and graduated a year after him, in 1940. Prior to meeting her husband, she worked for the Indianapolis Life Insurance Company, advancing from her starting position as a clerk to head of the reinsurance department and secretary to the vice president. Following a brief courtship, the two were engaged to marry in January 1946; their wedding followed a year later, on January 7, 1947.

Before their wedding, the young couple went into business together, first selling existing houses, then building new ones. They used their combined savings to finance their business, which became the Gene B. Glick Company, one of the largest privately held real estate development firms in the country. For the first few years, Marilyn played a leading and vital role in the company, creating a crucial filing system to track potential clients and hounding suppliers for materials needed to keep projects on schedule. After the birth of the first of four daughters, in November 1949, Marilyn slowly began to devote less time to the business, which was growing at an impressive rate. She soon became involved in a number of civic and religious organizations, including the National Council of Jewish Women and the United Way.

As the Gene B. Glick Company developed and managed more properties (both single family homes and apartment and subsidized housing complexes), the family accumulated significant wealth; however, the Glicks did not live an extravagant life. Instead, Marilyn and Gene preferred that their savings be put toward causes that would benefit others, as Gene reflected in his autobiography, *Born to Build: The Story of the Gene B. Glick Company*: "We've all received so much; we can ill afford not to share." In 1982 the couple established the Eugene and Marilyn Glick Family Foundation, which follows the philosophy that the highest level of giving is teaching others to take care of themselves. This approach was reflected in Gene's PRO-100 program, a summer internship experience for economically disadvantaged youth. The Glicks also placed an emphasis on supporting causes that promote education, art, and creative expression, and the alleviation of human suffering.

As the Glicks grew older and their company's profits grew larger, their devotion to civic causes reached new heights. Both Marilyn and Gene spent countless hours serving on a variety of boards and committees, raising funds and contributing their own wealth. Of particular note is their funding of the Arthur M. Glick Jewish Community Center, named in honor of Gene's brother, who died as a teenager. Gene also established the Gene B. Glick Family Housing Foundation, which acquires and maintains affordable housing and operates as a not-for-profit, as well as the Gene Glick Family Support Center. In recognition of his contributions to the community, Gene received an honorary doctorate of law degree from Butler University in 1989, one of many state and local honors bestowed upon him.

Marilyn spearheaded additional causes. She first began supporting blindness prevention initiatives in 1980, establishing an auxiliary of Prevent Blindness called People of Vision. Her passion for eye health culminated in a gift, via the Glick Family Foundation, of $30 million to the IU School of Medicine's eye institute, which was renamed in the couple's honor. The Indianapolis Cultural Trail was another legacy project, receiving a donation of $15 million, and the family name is also attached to the Eugene and Marilyn Glick Indiana History Center, which is home to the Indiana Historical Society; the Indiana Authors Award; and the Glick Fund of the Central Indiana Community Foundation. In 2001 Marilyn received an honorary doctorate of humane letters degree from IU, and, like her husband, numerous other public recognitions and awards.

Marilyn also had an abiding passion for contemporary art glass, which she collected on her travels to various shows and galleries. Art glass was perhaps the one indulgence the Glicks allowed themselves, but it is of no surprise that Marilyn made arrangements to give her collection to the Indianapolis Museum of Art. In 1991 the Eugene and Marilyn Glick Gallery opened and continues to display pieces that were hand-selected by Marilyn. Via the Glick Fund, Marilyn also donated $5 million to Ball State University to create the Glick Center for Glass.

Despite their exceptionally full and busy lives, Gene and Marilyn both agreed that the best decision each of them had made was marrying the other, and their marriage endured until Marilyn's passing on March 23, 2012. Gene died a year and a half later, on October 2, 2013. Between the two of them, Gene and Marilyn amassed, and then gave away, a fortune, making them two of the most generous philanthropists the state has known. Their devotion to bettering their community has made a lasting impact that, through their family's foundation, scholarship programs, and myriad other organizations, will endure and benefit generations of Hoosiers.

DORIA M. LYNCH

For Further Reading

Glick, Eugene. *Born to Build: The Story of the Gene B. Glick Company*. Carmel, IN: Guild Press of Indiana, 1997.
Glick, Marilyn. *Once Upon a Lifetime: Marilyn's Story*. Carmel, IN: Hawthorne Publishing, 2007.

Goth, (Jessie) Marie

August 15, 1887–January 9, 1975

One of Indiana's premier portraitists and the first woman artist to paint a portrait of an Indiana governor (Henry F. Schricker) to hang in the Indiana Capitol.

In 1909 twenty-two-year-old Marie Goth left Indianapolis to study art in New York City. When she returned ten years later, she moved to Brown County, lived alone in a cabin on the family property, and dedicated her life to painting. V. (Varaldo) J. (Giuseppe) Cariani, whom she had met in

New York and later became her lover, eventually joined her, staying nearby in his art studio. This lifestyle was bold for the time, but independence and bravery were fundamental to Goth's character throughout her long life. With an ironclad will, this charming, yet shrewd, woman even managed to guarantee her legacy along with the legacies of Cariani, her sister, her brother-in-law, and the Brown County Art Guild.

Goth's ancestors passed down to her their grit and tenacity. Three of her four grandparents were immigrants: one from Bavaria, another from the border between France and Germany, and a third from Ireland. Irish grandmother Mary Powers Meck, often outspoken about her noble lineage, was the likely role model for Goth's patrician demeanor. Goth's love of music came from her parents. Her mother, Jessie, had been groomed for a musical career as a singer but changed her plans when she met Charles Goth, who played bass violin for an operetta in which she performed. The couple offered piano lessons to Goth as a young girl, and she grew up to be an accomplished musician. Painting, however, was her passion.

It may have been Charles Goth's cousin, OTTO STARK, a member of the Hoosier Group of five nineteenth- and twentieth-century impressionist painters in Indiana, who inspired Goth to cultivate her artistic gifts. Her talent was evident by the time she entered Indianapolis's Manual Training High School, where Stark headed the art department. She focused on drawing and painting and, by the time she was sixteen, won twenty-five dollars in her first competition. After graduation Goth was working at Manual as an assistant art instructor when she saw a notice for a scholarship to the Art Students' League of New York. She entered several small sketches of heads, including a large charcoal drawing of a friend, and received a scholarship for one of the drawings. A letter of congratulations from a friend said, "(Y)our future seems pretty plain to me. . . . I'll be saying 'oh, yes, I knew her years ago—before she became famous.' And yet 'It is so hard for girls to succeed.'"

Though she entered the Art Student's League with the goal of becoming an illustrator, she changed her plans after taking classes with portraitist Frank Vincent DuMond, with whom she studied for ten years. Goth may have been too good a student. As one Indianapolis art critic observed "all of her portraits reflect [the] ideas on lighting and design" of DuMond.

Goth's mentor certainly influenced her painting techniques, and she used them to create luminous portraits that broke new ground for women artists in Indiana. Before she joined the competition for Indiana's prestigious commissions, men had dominated the genre of adult portraiture. By choosing to ignore one expectation for women artists of the era—that they confine themselves to children's portraits—Goth ultimately increased the opportunities for all who followed.

Through most of her New York years, Goth had lived at the Three Arts Club on West Fifty-eighth Street. It was a residence for young women from the United States and Canada pursuing careers in music, dance, or visual art. Cariani was among the many students Goth met and the one who affected her most profoundly. "[E]veryone called him 'Cari.' I remember the first time I ever saw him . . . at the Art Students' League . . . surrounded by girls," Goth wrote in her diary. She said that he was he was very handsome and that she "fell in love with him at once, as everyone did . . . somehow we were drawn together. . . . Even when it was very cold winter weather we would take these walks and it was wonderful just being near him."

Reflecting on those New York days in later years, Goth remembered the burning desire to paint like Rembrandt after repeated viewings of an exhibition of his work at the Metropolitan Museum. "But that was fanciful thinking to be quickly dismissed," she said. "For it took 20 years of long-hour days of experimenting just to control my oils, so they wouldn't be too runny, nor too tacky. This cannot be taught. You must keep working until you get it absolutely right."

Goth returned from New York to her parents' Indianapolis home in 1919. Within a couple of years she had moved into a four-room cabin in Brown County bought with the help of her sister, Genevieve, an Indianapolis schoolteacher who later became a painter herself. Cariani came to help move Goth's belongings to Nashville. Though he had been honorably discharged from the military, he was having trouble adapting to civilian life. The entire Goth family welcomed him, but it was Marie and Genevieve who gracefully guided him back to normalcy. Though unconventional at the time for couples that were not married, Goth and Cari lived a circumspect life together in Brown County, where both were prolific painters. Her career was built primarily on portraiture and his on florals and landscapes. "You couldn't help but see her love for him," said artist Amanda Kirby, "but they were of a vintage that they were discreet."

"I think Marie was interested in marrying Cari," said journalist Abe Eyed, "and he was in love with her. But he was a devout Catholic and wouldn't marry out of his religion." So closely associated were Goth and Cari that some newspapers referred to her as Mrs. V. J. Cariani of Nashville.

In 1926 Chicago artist Charles Dahlgreen encouraged Goth to enter the portrait she painted of him in the Hoosier Salon exhibition. *Charles W. Dahlgreen* won the two hundred-dollar prize for Best Portrait in Oil. With the passing years, the awards mounted, as did the "sitters," who included Goth's neighbors as well as countless Indiana icons. On her list of celebrities were poet JAMES WHITCOMB RILEY, Pulitzer Prize–winning cartoonist John T. McCutcheon, and artists ADA WALTER SHULZ, Adolph Robert Shulz, Genevieve Goth Graf, and, of course, Cariani. She also painted PAUL V. MCNUTT (a future governor of Indiana) when he headed Indiana University's School of Business. Her portrait of Governor Henry F. Schricker was the first by a woman to hang in the statehouse. Indianapolis Symphony conductors Fabien Sevitzky and his successor, Izler Solomn, also were among Goth's sitters.

So close were the Goth sisters, it was just a matter of time before Genevieve began painting as well. Marie was her first teacher, but Genevieve went on to study with Cariani and his friend Carl C. Graf, whom she married in 1928. For years the two couples hiked the hills of Brown County together, setting up their easels at picturesque spots. These days usually ended with a spaghetti dinner prepared by Cari in Goth's cabin.

As Brown County artists grew in stature, galleries in the area opened their doors. Goth became a charter founder of the Brown County Gallery and served as its president for two years; but, in the mid-1950s differences dividing Gallery artists became insurmountable. Goth left to cofound the Brown County Art Guild, which thrives to this day because of her ingenuity. A lifetime of thriftiness added up to an estate valued at more than $600,000, which included two thousand paintings by Goth, Cariani, Genevieve and Carl Graf. The bulk of the estate was willed to the Guild with stipulations that safeguarded the memory of the four artists.

Goth was eighty-seven when she entered two paintings in the fifty-first Hoosier Salon, but she never made it to the gala. The week before, she fell down a short flight of stairs in her cabin and suffered head injuries. Some suspected the fall was triggered by a bite from a poisonous brown recluse spider, which had infected her leg. Her entry *Neighbor* was awarded a Hoosier Salon Jury Prize of Distinction, a lovely grace note in this distinguished life.

CAROL WEISS

For Further Reading

Eyed, Abe. "Musical Marie." *Brown County Democrat*, July 15, 1971.
Goth, Marie. "Marie Goth Autobiography." Unpublished manuscript. Brown County Art Guild, Nashville, IN.
Newton, Judith Vale, and Carol Ann Weiss. *Skirting the Issue: Stories of Indiana's Historical Women Artists*. Indianapolis: Indiana Historical Society Press, 2004.

Gougar, Helen
July 18, 1843–June 6, 1907

Lawyer, women's suffrage orator and writer, newspaper owner, and one of the first women to argue before the Indiana Supreme Court.

Helen Mar Jackson Gougar was a passionate advocate of temperance, prohibition, and women's rights during her lifetime. She was a much sought-after speaker and traveled around the country giving speeches on these topics while sharing the platform with the likes of Susan B. Anthony and MAY WRIGHT SEWALL. She was one of the first women lawyers in Tippecanoe County and also one of the first to argue before the Indiana Supreme Court. Gougar is a woman whose name was recognized by most Hoosiers during her lifetime, but is little known today.

Helen Jackson was born near Litchfield, Michigan, in 1843. In her teens she attended Hillsdale College and moved to Indiana around 1860 to teach school in Lafayette. In 1863 she married local attorney John Gougar. He had an eye condition that limited his ability to read. As a result, Helen often helped him with his work and essentially served a legal apprenticeship. Over time, she became as familiar with the law as any practicing attorney.

The Gougars were active members of the intellectual and social life of Lafayette. Together they organized a Parlor Club to study literature with friends and family. Newspapers noted when they attended local cultural events. Helen served on the committees of numerous organizations including the Young Men's Christian Association, Lafayette Home Association, Ladies Benevolent Society, Second Presbyterian Church, and a committee to build an opera house in Lafayette. However, it was activities related to temperance, especially an April 1878 speech at a Blue Ribbon temperance rally, and women's suffrage that brought her to the public's attention on a much larger stage.

By the late 1870s, Gougar was regularly invited to speak in both literary and political settings. She campaigned for state and national figures who shared her beliefs, including William Jennings Bryan. She worked tirelessly in Indiana for the passage of various suffrage bills. In 1887 Gougar helped to organize suffrage conventions in thirteen Indiana cities, and was influential enough to attract Anthony to deliver the keynote address. While women achieved little success in Indiana, the municipal suffrage bill she helped to draft in Kansas was enacted. Gougar's efforts on behalf of women's suffrage and temperance brought her to the attention of the National Prohibition Party, which nominated her for Indiana attorney general in 1896.

During the same period that Gougar was gaining national prominence as a speaker, she was also busy writing a regular column, "Bric-a-Brac," for the *Lafayette Daily Courier*. Her column generally appeared in the paper on Saturday and was not limited to the usual women's topics. She wrote on anything that captured her interest, but especially on suffrage and temperance topics. In 1881 she took her writing skills to *Our Temperance Herald*, acting initially as its editor and eventually purchasing the paper.

As a public figure during a time when men still dominated the headlines, especially in the political world, Gougar was often the target of harsh criticism for her strong views. She fought for equality for women at every level. In 1882 Gougar was in court suing the Western Union Telegraph Company for sending later arriving telegrams from male customers before her own. The court awarded Gougar $100.

Never one to run from a fight, she twice found herself in court to defend and protect her reputation. In 1883 she sued Lafayette police chief Henry Mandler for slander, and in 1893 sued Massachusetts congressman Elijah Morse for libel. She did not back down from what she thought was right, not just for herself, but against the double standard applied to women in public life. While Gougar undoubtedly helped prepare these cases for trial, someone else represented her in court.

Under the 1851 Indiana Constitution, the only requirement to become a lawyer in Indiana was to be a voter and of good moral character. There was no standardized exam or education requirements, and each community determined its own requirements for admission. As a result, when Helen applied for admission to the Tippecanoe County bar in 1895, she was admitted despite her lack of formal training and was likely its first female member. Years working alongside her husband and familiarity with court proceedings prepared her well for her own appearance in court as a member of the bar arguing for women's suffrage in Indiana.

The Indiana Supreme Court ruled in 1893 that a qualified woman could be admitted to the practice of law even though they could not vote because it was not prohibited by the constitution (*In re Leach*). Hoping to build on this same logic—that women were not expressly prohibited from voting by the constitution—in 1894 Gougar tried to vote in Tippecanoe County. She was turned away, and she took the case first to her local court before eventually heading to the Indiana Supreme Court (*Gougar v. Timberlake*, 1897).

Gougar made her first appearance as an attorney before Judge F. B. Everett of the Tippecanoe Superior Court on the same day she was admitted to the bar in January 1895. Despite her lengthy and well-researched argument in favor women's right to vote, Everett ruled in favor of the local election board. Gougar's four-hour presentation was later published in pamphlet form under the title "The Constitutional Rights of the Women of Indiana." Gougar appealed to the state supreme court and the case was heard in Indianapolis on February 19, 1897.

Newspaper coverage described the case as friendly. This claim seems to be accurate since Alexander Rice, attorney for the local election board, spoke only for a few minutes, yielding the rest of his time to Gougar. Encouraged by the Court's opinion *In re Leach*, Gougar presented a carefully organized and detailed argument as to why women should be allowed to vote. Two of her many points focused on the natural rights of men and women using the Constitution and the Declaration of Independence as points of reference and that the Indiana Constitution did not specifically prohibit women from voting. Local newspapers quoted Judge James McCabe praising Gougar's skillful presentation: "Mrs. Gougar made one of the most forcible, logical and concise legal arguments ever made before this court. Not one man in a hundred acquits himself so well." In its opinion, however, the Court rejected Gougar's argument, specifically designating voting as a political instead of a natural right. Indiana women did not achieve the vote until the Nineteenth Amendment to the U.S. Constitution took effect in 1920.

For several years following her appearance in front of the Indiana Supreme Court, Gougar continued her public speaking career, and in 1900 campaigned once again for Bryan in his bid for the presidency. However, this was her last major speaking tour. Helen and John traveled extensively between 1901 and 1906, sending frequent letters to their hometown newspaper. She published a travel memoir in 1905. Gougar died, unexpectedly, in 1907 at her home in Lafayette.

ELIZABEH R. OSBORN

For Further Reading

Anthony, Susan B., and Ida H. Harper, *History of Woman Suffrage*. Vol. 4. Indianapolis: Hollenbeck Press, 1902.

Adams, Jennifer. "The Scandal, Rumor, and Politics of Helen M. Gougar." *Traces Magazine of Indiana and Midwestern History* 23, no. 2 (Spring 2011): 39-45.

Kriebel, Robert C. *Where the Saints Have Trod: The Life of Helen Gougar*. West Lafayette, IN: Purdue University Press, 1985.

Grissom, Virgil I. "Gus"

April 3, 1926–January 27, 1967

U.S. Air Force test pilot and one of the Original Seven Project Mercury astronauts.

At the beginning of February 1959, U.S. Air Force veteran Virgil I. "Gus" Grissom, a test pilot at Wright-Patterson Air Force Base in Dayton, Ohio, was shocked to learn that he had received top-secret orders to report to Washington, D.C., and to wear civilian, not military attire. Grissom's wife, Betty, thinking of the wildest possibility, prophetically asked him: "What are they going to do? Shoot you up in the nose cone of an Atlas?"

After an arduous selection process, Grissom became one of seven members of qualified military test pilots to serve as America's original Project Mercury astronauts. Although bedeviled by a balky hatch on his suborbital mission aboard *Liberty Bell 7*, Grissom went on to a distinguished career with the National Aeronautics and Space Administration, becoming the first person to fly in space twice when he commanded the first Gemini mission, as well as being selected by NASA to test the Apollo spacecraft designed to take American astronauts to the moon and back. He, along with crewmates Ed White and Roger Chaffee, died in a fire during a ground test of the Apollo 1 command module.

Grissom, born and raised in Mitchell, Indiana, reportedly possessed an IQ of 145, though he later admitted, he was not a "whiz" in school. He did complete one year of precadet training in the U.S. Army Air Corps while in high school and following graduation was inducted into the Air Corps. After basic training, he was stationed at Brooks Field in San Antonio, where he spent much of his time as a deskbound clerk before his discharge in November 1945. He made it back to Mitchell for his marriage on July 6, 1945, to Betty Moore.

After his discharge, Grissom worked installing doors on school buses at Carpenter Body Works, but with the help of the GI Bill, left Mitchell to enroll at Purdue University as a mechanical-engineering student. His wife joined him during his second semester in West Lafayette, and helped pay for his education by working as a long-distance telephone operator. Grissom, who worked after class as a short-order cook, finished his degree early and graduated in 1950.

Grissom then rejoined the armed services and became an air cadet. After basic training, he moved on to Williams Air Force Base in Arizona, where his wife and six-month-old son, Scott, joined him. In March 1951 Grissom was commissioned a second lieutenant in the Air Force and saw his pay skyrocket to $400 a month. Just nine months later Grissom received orders for Korea where he joined the 334th Fighter-Interceptor Squadron at Kimpo Air Force Base, just twelve miles from the front lines.

Grissom flew more than one hundred combat missions in Korea and received the Distinguished Flying Cross for his actions on March 23, 1952, during a photoreconnaissance mission. In August 1955 Grissom took a vital step toward becoming a test pilot, and consequently an astronaut, when he enrolled at the Institute of Technology at Wright-Patterson Air Force Base in Dayton, where he met and became friends with Gordon Cooper, another future space explorer. Both also attended test-pilot school at Edwards Air Force Base in California. After completing his test-pilot training, Grissom returned to Wright-Patterson and was there testing aircraft when the Soviet Union shocked the world on October 4, 1957, by announcing it had successfully launched the first satellite, *Sputnik*, into space.

After a few failures, scientists managed to put the first American satellite, *Explorer 1*, into orbit nearly four months after the Soviets' space success. As the public and politicians clamored for action, the government initiated in 1958 the United States' first man-in-space program, Project Mercury. When he arrived in Washington in early 1959, Grissom learned that he was one of thirty-nine test pilots who would undergo exhaustive testing, both physical and mental, to determine America's first space corps. From this process NASA picked seven men to serve as Project Mercury astronauts and presented them to the public in April 1959. The American astronauts were John Glenn, from the U.S. Marines; Walter Schirra, Alan Shepard, and Malcolm Scott Carpenter, from the U.S. Navy; and Donald "Deke" Slayton, Cooper, and Grissom, from the Air Force.

Shepard was the first American into space with his suborbital flight aboard *Freedom 7* on May 5, 1961, less than a month after the Soviet Union became the first nation to put a human being into space.

Though the country's initial manned mission into space went well, the same could not be said of Grissom's flight, which blasted off from Cape Canaveral on July 21, 1961. His fifteen-minute, thirty-seven-second flight seemed to have gone off without a hitch, as his *Liberty Bell 7* spacecraft made a successful splashdown in the Atlantic Ocean. From that point on, however, everything that could go wrong did go wrong.

According to the recovery plan, a helicopter pilot from the aircraft carrier *Randolph* was supposed to radio Grissom when he had successfully hooked on to the capsule and lifted it from the water. At that point, Grissom would remove his helmet, hit the switch to blow off the hatch, and exit the capsule. "I had unhooked the oxygen inlet hose by now and was lying flat on my back and minding my own business," Grissom recalled, "when suddenly the hatch blew off with a dull thud. All I could see was blue sky and sea water rushing in over the sill."

The recovery helicopter could not handle the weight of the waterlogged spacecraft and had to cut it loose; it was the first time in his long flying career that Grissom had ever lost an aircraft. (In July 1999 the *Liberty Bell 7* was raised from the Atlantic and is now part of the Kansas Cosmosphere and Space Center collection.) Meanwhile, Grissom was struggling to keep from drowning. Finally picked up by another chopper, the now exhausted astronaut had strength enough to grab a life jacket and put it on for the flight back to the recovery aircraft carrier.

Although an accident review panel cleared Grissom, and the other astronauts supported him, unanswered questions about the hatch dogged him for the rest of his career. Still, he remained a valuable member of the astronaut corps, becoming so involved in the design of the two-man Gemini spacecraft that fellow astronauts dubbed it "the Gusmobile." He and John W. Young were selected to make the first manned flight in the Gemini program. Grissom, playfully, christened his Gemini

Gus Grissom in his Apollo 1 spacesuit.

craft *Molly Brown* after the character from the musical, *The Unsinkable Molly Brown*. Grissom and Young made a successful three-orbit Gemini flight on March 23, 1965.

In March 1966 NASA named Grissom as commander of the first manned Apollo mission, along with crewmates White, a veteran of the Gemini program, and Chaffee, a rookie astronaut. Troubles plagued the Apollo program from the start, especially with the scheduled first manned vehicle. Grissom expressed some misgivings, saying to a reporter, "We've had problems before, but these have been coming in bushelfuls. Frankly, I think this mission has a pretty damn slim chance of flying its full fourteen days."

Grissom's premonition of trouble came tragically true during the January 27, 1967, test of the Apollo spacecraft and Saturn 1B rocket. Shortly after 6:30 p.m., under Grissom's commander seat, a frayed wire sparked, causing a fire. Fueled by the pure-oxygen atmosphere that permeated the Apollo spacecraft's pressurized crew cabin, which caused even fire-resistant material to burn at a furious rate, the fire also fed itself on a host of combustible materials in the command module, especially the Velcro and nylon netting used by the crew as a means of holding items that would float around the capsule if not secured while in space. As the material burned, it released poisonous gases that eventually suffocated the three astronauts.

Grissom was given a hero's burial at Arlington National Cemetery in Virginia, with the service broadcast nationwide on television. Neighbors from Mitchell joined President Lyndon Johnson, members of Congress, and fellow astronauts at the funeral. In an interview before his death, Grissom summing up the feelings of the astronauts, many of them test pilots used to losing friends in the line of duty, said: "If we die, we want people to accept it, and hope it will not delay the space program. The conquest of space is worth the risk of human life." On July 20, 1969, the crew of *Apollo 11*, flying in a totally redesigned spacecraft, touched down on the moon.

RAY E. BOOMHOWER

For Further Reading

Boomhower, Ray E. *Gus Grissom: The Lost Astronaut*. Indianapolis: Indiana Historical Society Press, 2004.

Catchpole, John. *Project Mercury: NASA's First Manned Space Programme*. London, New York: Springer/Praxis, 2001.

Newport, Curt. *Lost Spacecraft: The Search for Liberty Bell 7*. Burlington, Ontario: Apogee Books, 2002.

The Gruelle Family

Richard Buckner, "R. B.," February 22, 1851–November 14, 1914; John Barton "Johnny," December 24, 1880–January 9, 1938; Justin Carlisle, July 1, 1889 – April 20, 1979; and Prudence, August 14, 1884–February 13, 1966

Acclaimed creative family headed by one of the Hoosier Group of artists whose progeny included the creator of the Raggedy Ann and Andy dolls and stories, a renowned muralist and painter, and a popular writer and illustrator.

Richard B. Gruelle was a self-taught artist who inspired Hoosiers by interpreting the beauty of nature through watercolor and oil paintings, descriptive writings, and inspirational lectures. He became one of the five nationally acclaimed artists who were known as the Hoosier Group. He was the father and art instructor of three children who gained recognition on their own for their creative accomplishments.

A descendant of French immigrants, Gruelle was born in 1851 in Cynthiana, Kentucky, into a large family that later moved to Arcola, Illinois. Gruelle took advantage of available schooling and worked as farmhand, railroad construction crew member, and apprentice to a house painter. His ability to mix and match colors, combined with an intense interest in studying art books, led to recognition of his natural talent for drawing and painting. A Cincinnati firm hired him to paint landscape scenes on doors of heavy, cast-iron safes. Years later he established his first studio in Decatur, Illinois, where he painted signs, portraits, and landscapes, and married the local photographer's assistant from New England.

In 1882, at age thirty-one, Gruelle and his wife, Alice, chose Indianapolis, with its many cultural opportunities, as the ideal place to raise their three children: Johnny, Prudence, and Justin. They taught their children the art of drawing, painting, music, and storytelling. Gruelle believed that to possess talent required a sense of responsibility toward the younger brother artist creating a brotherhood of art.

His downtown studio-gallery became a gathering place for a wide circle of friends, artists, musicians, and writers, including poet James Whitcomb Riley. Some of Gruelle's friends worked in the administration of President Benjamin Harrison, an Indiana native, and arranged successful exhibitions of Gruelle's watercolors and oil paintings in Washington, D.C. While there, Gruelle visited museums, galleries, and the private collection of Baltimore businessman William T. Walters. Gruelle returned home with hundreds of pages of handwritten descriptions of paintings he had studied and was invited to write five articles for publication in early issues of *Modern Art*, a new Indianapolis quarterly with national distribution.

Gruelle's articles were read by Walters, who invited him to create a catalog with "word pictures" of his collection of paintings, sculptures, and porcelains. That work, *Notes: Critical and Biographical, Collection of W. T. Walters* (1895), "proved to be one of the most highly prized and unusual books published in America at that time." wrote Mary Q. Burnet in *Art and Artists of Indiana*.

In 1894 forty-three-year-old Gruelle and four other Indiana artists exhibited in Chicago and became known as the Hoosier Group. They were highly praised across the nation for having "helped the people of Indiana to see the beauty in their own quiet landscapes." A good example of this claim is one of Gruelle's most famous works, *The Canal, Morning* (1894), which depicts a "pale distant vision of the urban panorama, featuring the dome of the State Capitol in the distance."

In the late 1890s Boston lithographer Louis Prang, who had purchased *Modern Art* quarterly, challenged the Hoosier artist to paint marine impressions along rocky Massachusetts coastline. On summer painting trips to the fishing village of Gloucester on Cape Ann, Gruelle studied movements of the ocean and captured its many moods in sketches and paintings. His marine images were popular at annual Indianapolis studio and gallery shows and when exhibited at the Hoosier Group Pavilion at the 1904 World's Fair in Saint Louis (Louisiana Purchase Exposition). Upward of one hundred of Gruelle's pencil-and-charcoal drawings of nature are in archives of the Indiana State Museum.

During the years 1906 and 1907, Richard and Alice moved to New York. Son Justin later wrote, "I believe that R. B. (age fifty-five) felt the need of a little artistic rejuvenation and that he realized a visit to Manhattan, with its art galleries and museums would contribute to my aesthetic development." Following their short residence in New York, the Gruelle family was attracted to the Silvermine community of artists in Connecticut and in 1910 purchased property along Silvermine River. Gruelle and his sons became members of the Knockers, a group of Silvermine area artists who enjoyed criticizing each others' work before its annual exhibitions. The Knockers became the Silvermine Guild of Artists and Art School, one of the largest and oldest arts centers in New England.

Richard Gruelle died in Indianapolis in 1914 at age sixty-three, surrounded by his three children. Shortly before his death he wrote, "No matter where I may be, Indianapolis is my home, the place where my heart is." Gruelle believed in the gospel of encouragement and helpfulness, seeking always to express that which appealed to him as being beautiful. There was always religious significance in his work, the thought of God's work expressed on earth through man.

Richard's oldest son, Johnny, was taught drawing by his father and had an early career of creating political and sports cartoons for the *Indianapolis Star*, the *Indianapolis Daily Sentinel*, and the *Cleveland Press*. In 1911 he won first place in a competition to create a full-page children's comic strip in color for the *New York Herald*. Titled *Mr. Twee Deedle*, it was syndicated nationwide weekly until 1918.

Johnny is best known for his design of a rag doll for commercial manufacture. The doll, modeled on one with which his daughter, Marcella, played, became a legendary icon worldwide with her red yarn hair, painted face with black eyes, a teardrop nose, and intriguing happy smile. His 1915 patent application for a doll was followed three weeks later with an application for the trademark logo name, "Raggedy Ann," a combination of two poems, "The Raggedy Man," and "Little Orphant Annie," written by Gruelle family friend Riley.

After Marcella died in 1915, at age thirteen following a long illness, Johnny wrote down the stories he had told her about the fanciful adventures of Raggedy Ann and other dolls left alone in the nursery after she went to sleep. Starting in 1918, with publication of *Raggedy Ann Stories*, the dolls were marketed along with more than thirty books. In 1920 Johnny created sequel stories about Raggedy Andy, decked out in a sailor suit and hat.

In the late twentieth century, Internet sales, a musical, and a movie with worldwide distribution expanded the market for collectors of Raggedy Ann dolls, costumes, books, games, and memorabilia. A recent Raggedy Ann trade show attracted more than a hundred dealers from throughout the United States, Japan, England, Canada, and South America. In 2002 Raggedy Ann was inducted into the National Toy Hall of Fame in Rochester, New York, and in 2007 Raggedy Andy joined her.

Justin was trained as a painter by his father and later studied at John Herron Art Institute in Indianapolis and the Art Students' League of New York. He received wide acclaim in the 1930s because of fourteen large murals that he painted for the Works Progress Administration. Inspiration came from stories of Mark Twain, *Aesop's Fables*, *Aladdin and the Lamp*, and *The Chinese Nightingale*. His murals are on permanent exhibition in the schools of New Canaan, Connecticut, and in libraries and City Hall of Norwalk, Connecticut. Justin collaborated on three pavilion murals at the 1939 New York World's Fair.

During the 1940s Justin was commissioned to research and paint eight large murals that featured American scientists and their inventions. One of these murals, *The Early Birds*, an eighteen foot by seven foot painting on canvas, featured seventeen portraits of aviation pioneers, including the Wright Brothers, and more than twenty early aircraft against a visualized background of how the earth might appear from outer space. The painting was formerly in the collection of Smithsonian National Air and Space Museum, Washington, D.C. After an extended exhibition at the Indiana Historical Society in Indianapolis during the centennial celebration of the Wright Brothers first flight, it is now permanently installed at Museum of Flight, Seattle, Washington.

In 1955 Justin moved to Alpine, California, where he continued painting landscapes and portraits. He completed two large murals about the history of naval aviation and fourteen large religious paintings on stations of the cross. Pencil-and-chalk drawings to scale were completed for five murals to depict the *Mythology and History of Flight*, for a proposed Museum of Air and Space that never happened. Before his death in 1978 he compiled a Gruelle family memoir and archive scrapbook.

Prudence received a scholarship to study voice in New York, sang with a New York opera company and later in vaudeville theaters, using the stage name Prudence Gru, the Singing Cartoonist. She wrote and illustrated a children's textbook, *The Meadow Folks Story Hour*, and was author and illustrator of a syndicated newspaper column for children, "Good Night Stories" by Blanche Silver, another pseudonym. In her later years in Florida she painted landscapes and made rag dolls as gifts, just as her mother had made for her. She was pleased with the Gruelle family legend that her childhood rag doll had been the inspiration for her brother's later creation and success with Raggedy Ann and Raggedy Andy dolls and books.

PAUL WILLIAM SMART

For Further Reading

Burnet, Mary Q. *Art and Artists of Indiana*. New York: The Century Company, 1921.

Gerdts, William H., and Judith Vale Newton. *The Hoosier Group: Five American Painters*. Indianapolis: Eckert Publications, 1985.

Hall, Patricia. *Johnny Gruelle, Creator of Raggedy Ann and Andy*. Gretna, LA: Pelican Publishing Company, 1998.

Krause, Martin. *The Passage: Return of Indiana Painters from Germany, 1880–1905*. Indianapolis: Indianapolis Museum of Art, 1990.

Grutka, Andrew Gregory

November 17, 1908–November 11, 1993

First Bishop of the Roman Catholic Diocese of Gary, Indiana, and active in support of ethnic communities, civil rights, and labor unions.

Born in Joliet, Illinois, Andrew Grutka spent the majority of his life in northwest Indiana, where he was a respected leader in the communities he served. Ordained to the priesthood for the Catholic Diocese of Fort Wayne in 1933, he was consecrated a bishop in 1957 for the new Diocese of Gary, consisting of Lake, Porter, La Porte, and Starke Counties. Grutka's contributions to the history of Indiana revolved especially around his work within ethnic communities, approach to labor relations, and pursuit of racial justice. To Grutka these issues were deeply interrelated and came together in the episcopal motto he chose when he became a bishop: "Where there is charity, there is God."

Grutka's involvement with Hoosiers of eastern European ancestry began in his childhood. His

Slovak immigrant parents attended the Joliet, Illinois, parish of Saints Cyril and Methodius, which promoted the Slovak culture of many of its parishioners. There Grutka was steeped in the culture of his ancestors and gained an appreciation of Slovak history and the lives of Slovaks who had immigrated to the United States. In his parish assignments before being made a bishop by Pope Pius XII—Sacred Heart in East Chicago, Indiana, and Holy Angels in Gary—Grutka shepherded Hoosier Slovaks in the twilight of ethnic communities' dominance of American Catholicism. While his service to the Slovak community in the Midwest was lifelong, he presented himself as a leader for other Eastern European Catholics in the United States as well. He celebrated Masses for the Croatian Catholic Union in 1941 and for the one thousand year anniversary of Polish Christianity in 1963. These events were all the more significant in the ongoing context of the Cold War, as Catholic Christians in Soviet-controlled Europe enjoyed far less religious freedom than their relatives and friends in the United States.

The Bishop also fostered Slovak culture in an international context, working vigorously to establish and maintain the Institute of Saints Cyril and Methodius in Rome. The institute served as a seminary to train men of Slovak descent for the priesthood. Grutka's pastoral ministry to the eastern European heritage of Hoosier Catholics thus had worldwide ramifications, enhancing a transnational sense of ethnic identity beyond the Diocese of Gary.

Eastern European immigrants played an important role in Northwest Indiana's industrial labor force, and Grutka was active in the union efforts of laboring Hoosiers within his diocese due to his own experience—he had been a steelworker himself before becoming a priest. His father had been a steelworker during the Great Depression. As he was only able to find work for a few days each month at the local mill, the Grutka family suffered financially in Andrew's childhood.

Grutka's support for local unionization did not extend, however, to one of the most significant components of his own diocese: Catholic education. When some lay teachers in the diocese's Catholic schools—men and women who were not in religious orders or members of the clergy—attempted to unionize in 1976, the bishop prohibited them from holding an election to decide whether the educators wanted to come under the auspices of the National Labor Relations Board. The NLRB sued on behalf of the teachers when a meeting between diocesan officials and the teachers' leader was begun with a passage from Saint James that emphasized "humility and fidelity," which the NLRB charged was an attempt to spiritually cow the teachers. In any case, employees eventually voted 260 to 172 against unionization, and the NLRB case was decided on appeal in favor of the diocese. National, secular authority over a local, religious institution such as the diocesan Catholic schools likely pushed Grutka away from supporting this union effort. He explained the problem in thoroughly Catholic terms, writing in a public letter to the Catholics of his diocese that "the right to govern our schools according to the mind of the Church and in them—to teach as Jesus did—is being threatened. This is the real reason why we are struggling to prevent anyone from interfering with ecclesiastical jurisdiction over our schools."

In addition to labor, race relations played a formative role in the history of northwestern Indiana in the middle of the twentieth century. Grutka felt a responsibility to contribute toward a more harmonious community in Gary, and served on a commission established by Mayor A. Martin Katz intended "to see that no individual or group is the victim of unfair treatment by reason of religion, place of birth, or race." Grutka became a life member of the National Association for the Advancement of Colored People in 1964 and introduced Doctor Martin Luther King Jr. when King addressed a Gary meeting of local clergy in 1966. Additionally, the only pastoral letter that Grutka authored and published during his episcopate, "How Good a Neighbor Am I?" specifically addressed the problem of racial prejudice, and he republished the letter in 1968 after the citizens of Gary elected their first black mayor, Richard Hatcher.

Advancing a more just vision of race for the Diocese of Gary and indeed all of the United States was enormously important to Grutka. He made it the topic of his public speech on the floor of the great Basilica of Saint Peter during the Second Vatican Council, the series of meetings in Rome between 1962 and 1965 that introduced momentous reforms to the Catholic Church worldwide. Addressing nearly all the bishops of the Catholic Church, the bishop of the tiny diocese in northern Indiana said, "Discrimination and segregation because of color, country of origin, or creed must not be condoned for any reason.... Some form of degradation, some form of hate, some form of disrespect is invariably involved in every act of segregation and discrimination. Every human being regardless of color, origin or creed should be afforded equal opportunities for housing, education, culture and employment."

While race relations and justice for laborers formed two of the largest components of Grutka's vision of the ideal society, he was involved in numerous other organizations and projects that catered to specific needs. He was a leader among American bishops in ministry to the incarcerated. Among his voluminous correspondence with prisoners is a request, apparently fulfilled, for Grutka to send a photograph of himself to a prisoner in need of prayer. Also, Grutka accompanied several Protestant ministers on a tour of North Vietnam to assess the situation of the Vietnamese people in 1974. In the final assessment, however, it was Gary to which Bishop Grutka was most dedicated. At his death in 1993, the pastor of Holy Angels Church, which Grutka himself served before becoming bishop, said that Grutka was a "bishop who loved Gary. And the people of Gary, in turn, black and white, loved him."

MICHAEL SKAGGS

For Further Reading

Banks, Nancy. "Remembering Bishop Grutka." *Northwest Indiana Times*, November 12, 1993.

Bonta, Anthony. "Where There is Charity, There is God." PhD diss., Marquette University, 2009.

Johnson, Janice. "Catholic Bishops Squirming on Horns of Labor Dilemma." *Washington Post*, October 17, 1976.

Guérin, Saint Theodora

October 2, 1798–May 14, 1856

Founder of the Sisters of Providence at Saint Mary-of-the-Woods and Indiana's first canonized Catholic saint.

She was the slight French sister who was called to serve God by devoting her life to educating young children and caring for the poor, sick, and dying. She left her homeland and traveled to a new world, where she founded a ministry that mushroomed in the decades that followed and remains a strong presence in the nation today. She was called a "timely gift from God to renew the Church in its infancy in Indiana" by Indianapolis Archbishop Emeritus Daniel M. Buechlein, and her life serves as a blueprint for us all. She is Indiana's first Catholic saint, Mother Theodore Guérin.

Born in the village of Etables-sur-Mer in Brittany, France, Anne-Thérèse Guérin was a lively, precocious child who felt called to religion early in life. The death of her father when she was fifteen curtailed her plans as she shouldered the responsibility of caring for her younger sister and a grief-stricken mother, but thoughts of a religious vocation were never far from her mind or her heart.

With her mother's blessing she entered the convent of the Sisters of Providence in Ruillé-sur-Loir when she was nearly twenty-five years old and was quickly recognized as a talented postulant with plenty of potential. She was given important jobs throughout the community and, after teaching and caring for the sick in France, was selected to lead a small band of women religious to the United States. The mission was to create a ministry that would serve the growing number of Catholics settling throughout the Diocese of Vincennes in Indiana. Guérin felt unworthy of the awesome responsibility that came with establishing a motherhouse and schools throughout such a large area and, given her chronic health issues, she was not even sure she would make it through the first winter. After much prayer and meditation, she agreed to go.

On July 15, 1840, Guérin and five companions left France, embarking on a harrowing two-month journey across the ocean, through the heart of the United States, and to the small community of Saint Mary-of-the-Woods. Guérin was unimpressed by the primitive surroundings she encountered as she stepped from her carriage on October 22, 1840, and wondered how she would ever turn a forest into a functional institution. There were no families. There were no people. She wrote that her future convent was "so deeply hidden in the woods, that you cannot see it until you come up to it." However, with a reliance on faith, her own ingenuity, and a belief in providence, she persevered through the good times and bad.

Accorded the name "Mother Theodore" by the Bishop of Vincennes, Guérin arranged for the purchase of a local farmhouse to serve as a convent and began to carve a life for herself and her congregation of sisters out of the hilly, ravine-cut land. In her first year, she opened her first academy (Saint Mary-of-the-Woods College), which is the oldest Catholic women's liberal arts college in the nation; recruited new women to the order; and established schools in Jasper, Indiana, and Saint Francisville, Illinois. In spite of her successes, she endured a number of trials and tribulations, including prejudice, betrayals, misunderstandings with a cantankerous bishop, fires, and the feeling of being torn between the wishes of her superiors in Indiana and edicts established by her motherhouse in France. In one of her letters she wrote, "If ever this poor little community becomes settled, it will be established on the Cross; and that is what gives me confidence and makes me hope, sometimes even against hope."

Before she died, Guérin established several schools throughout Indiana, earned the respect of her peers and superiors, and left behind a strong legacy of love, justice, and mercy that permeates the Sisters of Providence community to this day. Those who knew her testified that her holiness and humility was evident in everything she did, and she had a knack for being able to draw out the best in people in order for them to attain more than they ever believed possible. "She practiced virtue without affection," said Sister Marie Antoinette Buchanan in her testimony. "When she was ridiculed or insulted, she remained patient. When she was praised, she tried to persuade herself of the contrary."

In 1909 Bishop Francis Silas Chatard formally opened Guérin's Cause for Canonization and began the long, arduous process of examining her life and writings and awaiting evidence that she was in heaven and able to intercede with God for the living. That evidence came in the form of two miracles, both of which occurred to members of the Saint Mary-of-the-Woods community and came in the form of healings. Sister Mary Theodosia Mug was cured of an abdominal tumor and partial paralysis after praying for another sister near Guérin's crypt in 1908 (paving the way for Guérin's beatification on October 25, 1998) while an employee of the Congregation was cured of a degenerative eye condition in 2000 after praying to Guérin for assistance inside the Church of the Immaculate Conception.

After both cases were examined for any "scientific" explanation and passed through the Vatican chain of command, Pope Benedict XVI announced that Guérin would be canonized on October 2, 2006. More than 1,200 people from the Archdiocese of Indianapolis, the Sisters of Providence, graduates and students of the schools founded by or named in her honor, as well as a delegation from France were on hand to witness the event as Guérin was officially renamed Saint Theodora Guérin and honored by his Holiness. "With great trust in Divine Providence, Mother Theodore overcame many challenges and persevered in the work that the Lord called her to do," Pope Benedict XVI said, as he announced that Guérin was inscribed into the Catalogue of Saints as a role model for the universal Church and where she is remembered with pious devotion by Catholics everywhere.

JULIE YOUNG

For Further Reading

Guérin, Mother Theodore. Journals and Letters. Sisters of Providence, Saint Mary-of-the-Woods, IN.

Young, Julie. *A Belief in Providence: A Life of Saint Theodora Guérin*. Indianapolis: Indiana Historical Society Press, 2007.

Saint Thedora Guérin

Hamilton, Alice

February 27, 1869–September 22, 1970

Hoosier reformer and "Mother of Occupational Medicine" in America.

During the first half of the twentieth century, little was known of the hazards of the workplace and the threats of industrial diseases in America. At century's end, conditions for workers had improved dramatically. The social reforms and science needed to improve their health and safety were pioneered by Alice Hamilton of Fort Wayne, Indiana, a physician, scientist, and a visionary social reformer. Hailed as the mother of industrial medicine, Hamilton was an unlikely blend of crusader and scientist.

Born in New York City in 1869 and raised at the Hamilton Homestead in Fort Wayne, Alice enjoyed a protected childhood in one of Indiana's privileged and cultured families. She was surrounded by a large extended family with many cousins, aunts, and uncles. Homeschooled in the humanities and science, she learned to be self-sufficient, a critical thinker, and accepting of religious values.

Her grandmother and family matriarch, Emerine Hamilton, was raised at Veraestau in Aurora, Indiana, the daughter of JESSE L. HOLMAN, one of the first three justices of the Indiana Supreme Court, as well as a Baptist minister and abolitionist. Alice was enthralled by Emerine's vivid stories and reciting of Sir Walter Scott's poems. A passionate supporter of temperance and women's suffrage, Emerine established the first African American church congregation and free public library in Fort Wayne. Alice learned of pioneer life from her grandfather, Allen Hamilton, through his experiences as a land speculator, fur trader, U.S. Indian agent, sheriff of Allen County, and an Indiana state senator. Her father, Montgomery, taught her language and theology and her mother, Gertrude, raised in Europe "free from Victorian prudery," taught her about personal liberty, privacy, and the responsibility to right injustices in society.

As a young girl, Alice dreamed of becoming a medical missionary to Teheran, having been fascinated by Edmond O'Donovan's *The Merv Oasis*. She attended the Fort Wayne College of Medicine but graduated from the University of Michigan Medical School in 1893, after which she studied in Germany, at the Pasteur Institute in Paris, and Johns Hopkins University. Her life changed in 1897 when she became professor of pathology at Northwestern University and also a resident of the Hull House Settlement in Chicago after hearing a lecture on social reform by Jane Addams, a leader of the Progressive Era in the United States.

At Hull House, Hamilton saw how dangerous trades affected the lives of workers. She witnessed carbon monoxide gassing in steel mills, lead poisoning among potters, and pneumonia and rheumatism in stockyard workers and began to consider how to meld medical science with social reform into a career that would improve workers' health and provide her "a life full of human interest."

Hamilton's career in health and safety began when the governor of Illinois asked her to study industrial diseases resulting from exposure to lead and other toxins. Hamilton's seminal report, the *Illinois Survey* in 1911, prompted passage of the first worker's compensation laws in Illinois in 1911, in Indiana in 1915, and then in several other states. The U.S. Commissioner of Labor asked Hamilton to replicate this work, and she investigated hazards in the dye, rubber, and pottery industries, as well as hazardous worksite chemicals at the Indiana Woolen Manufacturing Company in Mishawaka.

Combining science and reform advocacy, Hamilton created the specialty of industrial medicine in America. Emerging from her late-Victorian life in Fort Wayne, she became a brilliant reformer and pragmatist who used science to advance progressive policies. Her successes were attributed to her unique upbringing and her serene and ingratiating manner that inspired cooperation. Never prolabor, procapital or progovernment, she had the credibility of a scientist and the stature of a diplomat. To Hamilton, good intentions of parties, fair debate, and publicity with compelling stories would change attitudes and laws to protect workers—a "peculiarly American" approach in her view.

As World War I loomed, Hamilton, Addams, Emily Balch, and women from warring countries traveled to Europe to promote peace through the process of continuous mediation. Their mission failed but their model of diplomatic negotiations among hostile nations is used today. Ironically, when Hamilton returned from her peace mission, the government put her to work in the vital munitions industry, where she reformed worker safety.

At the end of World War I, Hamilton returned to Europe with Addams, Herbert Hoover, and representatives of Quaker Relief, where they were among the first to bring humanitarian aid to war-torn countries.

Now a well-recognized scientist, Hamilton became the first female faculty member at Harvard in 1919 as an assistant professor of industrial medicine, though with the stipulation of President Abbott Lawrence Lowell that she not enter the Harvard Union or receive the quota of football tickets offered to Harvard men. For sixteen years, Hamilton's scholarship brought recognition to Harvard, but when she retired from the "jealously guarded masculine world at Harvard," she was still an assistant professor, having never received a faculty promotion.

Between the great wars, Hamilton divided her time between research and social reform. She published landmark reports for the U.S. Department of Labor, one of which was based on her research in Arizona copper mines. She used "shoe leather epidemiology," with first-hand interviews and on-site inspections, where she donned miner's clothes, helmet and lamp, and rode open elevators to shafts eight hundred feet below. In Bedford, Indiana, Hamilton researched workers' injuries that resulted from use of air hammers. The stonecutters had demanded a federal investigation of the cause of their "dead fingers," painful, discolored, and numb digits. Her research improved worker safety there.

Hamilton's social activism also led her to take on controversial subjects, including birth control, civil liberties, opposition to war, and protective labor legislation for women. Called a "radical" and "subversive" by some, she was followed by agents from the Federal Bureau of Investigation from the 1920s to the 1960s, when she was in her nineties. Ironically, Hamilton was one of the first prominent citizens in America to accurately predict the dangers of the Third Reich in a prescient article: "Hitler Speaks: His Book Reveals the Man," in an April 1933 issue of the *Atlantic Monthly*. Though a pacifist in World War I, Hamilton rejected radical antiwar sentiments.

When she was eighty, Hamilton published a revision of her acclaimed textbook, *Industrial Toxicology*. Her many accomplishments earned her the Lasker and Chi Omega Awards. Her likeness adorned a 1955 U.S. postage stamp and a National Institute of Occupational Safety and Health laboratory was dedicated to her memory. Bronze statues of Hamilton, her sister Edith, and cousin, Agnes, were erected in Headwaters Park in Fort Wayne.

Alice and her four sisters never married. Remaining close throughout their long lives, they established a retirement home at Hadlyme, Connecticut. EDITH, was a preeminent classicist and author of *The Greek Way* and Greek translations used by Robert F. Kennedy in his speech in Indianapolis on April 4, 1968, after Martin Luther King Jr.'s assassination. Margaret was a prominent educator and Nora an artist. Their brother Arthur, also known as Quint, was an esteemed professor of language at the University of Illinois, Urbana. He married but had no children.

Hamilton corresponded into her nineties with prominent Americans, including her lifelong friend U.S. Supreme Court Justice Felix Frankfurter. When she turned one hundred, Hamilton received accolades from around the world; President Richard Nixon praised her work at Harvard and Hull House and her role in bringing workmen's compensation to America. Three months after Alice died at 101, Nixon signed the Occupational

Alice Hamilton

Safety and Health Act, the first federal law to enforce healthier workplaces in America. Hull House, a center for social reform modeled after Toynbee Hall in London and Hamilton's home and inspiration for her remarkable professional career, closed in 2012, 123 years after it was founded.

STEPHEN J. JAY

For Further Reading

Hamilton, Alice. *Exploring the Dangerous Trades: The Autobiography of Alice Hamilton*. Boston: Little, Brown and Company, 1943.

Sicherman, Barbara. *Alice Hamilton: A Life in Letters.* Champaign: University of Illinois Press, 2003.

Hamilton, Edith

August 12, 1867–May 31, 1963

Educator, writer, and classical scholar

Edith Hamilton is often identified as a "classicist," indeed as the most renowned American classicist of her time. After all, her lucidly written, easily accessible, best-selling books on classical antiquity—chief among them *The Greek Way* (1930), *The Roman Way* (1932), and *Mythology* (1942)—illuminated the ancient Greco-Roman world for a wide and diversely constituted readership. These books were, moreover, noteworthy for representing the Greeks in particular as a prestigious source of cultural inspiration for American society during the decade before and the two decades after World War II.

Hamilton was born in Dresden, Germany, but she grew up in Fort Wayne, Indiana, where her father's father had settled in the early 1820s. In 2000 that city recognized her, her younger sister ALICE, a physician and social activist who became the first woman appointed to the Harvard University faculty, and their cousin, Agnes, by erecting statues in their honor, now displayed in its Headwaters Park. She was homeschooled by her father because her parents did not approve of the emphasis on American history and math in the public-school curriculum. Her obituary in the *New York Times* referred to her recollection of her early education in Fort Wayne. It was her father, she said, who steered her toward the classics. He taught her Latin and Greek at an early age.

Edith left Fort Wayne in 1884 to spend two years at Miss Porter's School in Farmington, Connecticut, following a Hamilton female family tradition. There she concentrated on Latin rather than Greek. She came back home again to Indiana in 1886 to prepare for the Bryn Mawr College entrance exams. It took her four years to prepare for majoring and specializing in classics there. She entered Bryn Mawr in Philadelphia in 1890 and earned her bachelor's and master's degrees in Latin and Greek in 1894. She pursued graduate work in Latin there through the spring of 1895, when she won Bryn Mawr's Mary E. Garrett European fellowship. It enabled both her and Alice to study in Germany, first in Leipzig and then in Munich, for the next academic year. In 1896 she returned to the United States to assume the post of headmistress at the Bryn Mawr School, a newly created college preparatory school located in Baltimore. Hamilton remained in that job, and in Baltimore, for the next twenty-six years.

Immediately before retiring in 1922, Hamilton adopted Dorian Fielding Reid, the four-year old grandson of her Baltimore friends Harry Fielding and Edith Gittings Reid. Edith and Dorian moved, first to Maine for a winter, and then to New York City, with the Reids' daughter, Doris Fielding Reid, a former Bryn Mawr School pupil twenty-seven years Edith's junior who had by then become Edith's lover and life partner. From 1923 onward, Edith and Doris resided in New York, summered in Maine, and raised Dorian and two of the Reids' granddaughters. A few years after they settled in New York, when she was still homeschooling Dorian, Edith—by then nearly sixty— launched her second career as a popular writer, first with essays on Greek tragedy and comedy in *Theatre Arts Monthly*, and then the series of books about ancient Greek and Roman civilization for which she is most famous.

In 1943 Edith and Doris moved to Washington, D.C., where the Wall Street investment firm of Loomis, Sayles, that had hired Doris in 1929 placed her in charge of its office in the nation's capital. It was in Washington that Edith died in May 1963 at nearly ninety-six. Four years after her death, Doris published a memoir, *Edith Hamilton: An Intimate Portrait*, that remains, despite its serious omissions and inaccuracies, Edith's "official" biography. Edith and Doris are buried alongside Alice; Edith's mother; Edith's sisters, Margaret and Nora; and Margaret's life-partner, Clara Landsberg, in Hadlyme, Connecticut, where the other three Hamilton sisters had retired.

Hamilton's ties to Indiana remained after her death. Her adopted son, Dorian, who graduated from Amherst College with a degree in chemistry in 1938, decades later relocated from California to Indiana, living in West Lafayette, the home of his daughter, Alice Reid Abbott, until his death, at age ninety, in January 2008. And it was in Indiana, indeed in its Greek-named state capital of Indianapolis, that one of Hamilton's most prominent disciples, U.S. Senator Robert F. Kennedy, twice quoted, from memory, her renditions of ancient Greek and Roman writers, in what is perhaps his most memorable speech.

RFK delivered these words, with their two quotes from Hamilton's works, on the evening of April 4, 1968, while campaigning for the Democratic presidential nomination, and in breaking the news that Doctor Martin Luther King Jr. had been assassinated to an anguished audience who had gathered to hear him at an outdoor campaign rally. One of these quotes was Hamilton's translation of a choral passage from Aeschylus' tragedy *Agamemnon*: "He who learns must suffer. And even in our sleep pain that cannot forget, falls drop by drop upon the heart, and in our own despair, against our will, comes wisdom to us by the awful grace of God." The other was her representation of an ancient Greek inscription, embedded in Kennedy's exhortation: "Let us dedicate ourselves to what the Greeks wrote so many years ago—to tame the savageness of man and to make gentle the life of this world."

Although Hamilton's reputation is related mostly to writings about Greece, she concentrated much of her professional life on Latin. Even after leaving Bryn Mawr College with undergraduate and graduate degrees in both Latin and Greek, Edith focused on Latin at the expense of her Greek, spending a further year at Bryn Mawr as a fellow in Latin, and studying Latin during her year in Germany. In her twenty-six years at the Bryn Mawr School in Baltimore, she taught only Latin to the senior girls, yet she claimed special expertise in Greek. Other than in *The Roman Way*, she lavished all her energies and affections on what she referred to as "ancient Greece," although she wrote almost exclusively about fifth and fourth century BC Athens, giving short shrift to earlier and later eras, and other parts of the Hellenic world. Her writings about Greece, moreover, frequently and unfairly disparage Roman culture.

In so doing, Hamilton embraced a distinctly late-nineteenth-century-German vision of classical antiquity, an attitude difficult to espouse publicly here in the United States, especially during the period of the two world wars—her heyday as an educator and spokesperson for the classics.

Greece repaid the honor Hamilton had given to that country's history and culture in 1957, when King Paul of Greece awarded Hamilton the Golden Cross of the order of Benefaction, the highest honor of Greece. The mayor of Athens made her an honorary citizen of the city. Speaking after that proclamation she said: "I am an Athenian citizen. This is the proudest moment in all my life."

JUDITH P. HALLETT

For Further Reading

Hallett, Judith P. "Edith Hamilton." In Ward W. Briggs Jr., ed. *Biographical Dictionary of North American Classicists*, 253–54. Westport, CT: Greenwood Press, 1994.

———. "Edith Hamilton and Greco-Roman Mythology." In Gregory A. Staley, ed. *American Women and Classical Myths*, 105–130. TX: Baylor University Press, 2008.

Hamilton, Edith. *The Greek Way*. New York: W. W. Norton and Company, 1930.

———. *The Roman Way*. New York: W. W. Norton and Company, 1932.

———. *Mythology*. Boston: Little Brown and Company, 1942.

Hapgood, Powers

December 28, 1899–February 4, 1949

Social radical, union activist and organizer, and prominent figure in the Socialist Party of America.

Scion of a solidly upper-middle-class but progressive-minded Indianapolis family, Powers Hapgood spent his fairly brief life attempting—with mixed success—to become a de facto member of the working class. His life was devoted to the cause of labor organization as a means for the working classes to gain control of their working conditions.

Powers was the only child of WILLIAM POWERS HAPGOOD, founder of the Indianapolis worker-cooperative Columbia Conserve Company, and Eleanor Page Hapgood. Powers's education was typical of his social stratum; he attended Phillips Exeter Academy in Andover, Massachusetts, graduating in 1917, and earned a bachelor's degree from Harvard University in 1921. But unlike a majority of his classmates, who would have entered professions such as law and business, Powers pursued nontraditional jobs even before he finished college. He worked in an iron mine in Minnesota, a sugar beet processing operation in Montana, and coal mines in Montana and Colorado. This marked the beginning of what would become a lifelong quest for credibility and influence in the national labor movement.

He began in late 1921 to work for the American Bureau of Industrial Research, based at the University of Wisconsin in Madison. He investigated working conditions in the Pennsylvania coalfields. Finding that research alone did not satisfy his aspirations, in early 1922 he became a miner in Pennsylvania and, later that year, a labor organizer for the United Mine Workers of America. His organizing and leadership abilities were tested during the Somerset County, Pennsylvania, coal strike in 1922–23, when he devoted himself to organizing nonunion mines. The strikers' goals were to achieve recognition for miners' unions, to protect their pay rates, and to make sure they were paid fully and fairly for the coal they extracted. The unionized miners needed the nonunion workers to walk out with them, or the strike would have no hope of succeeding. Even better, however, would be to increase union representation significantly, and Hapgood and his friend, John Brophy, strove to organize as many union locals as possible. The contract that settled the strike preserved many of the unionized miners' gains, but excluded many of the nonunionized labor force.

During the strike, many locals felt abandoned by the UMWA. Because of that, and with perhaps an inflated belief in the strength of their newfound power, Brophy and Hapgood challenged John L. Lewis's leadership of the UMWA in the aftermath of the strike. Both were ultimately ousted from the UMWA, leading Hapgood to go to Europe and work in mines in Russia, France, Germany, and Wales.

Upon his return to the United States in the late 1920s, Hapgood joined the Socialist Party of America. He was also allowed to rejoin the UMWA and at the group's annual convention in 1927 he was elected as a delegate from the Cresson, Pennsylvania, local. At that convention, he headed Brophy's campaign to replace Lewis as head of the UMWA. This confrontation with Lewis led to Hapgood being lured into a hotel brawl. As a result, Hapgood was once again a pariah to the UMWA, and he left the Pennsylvania coalfields behind to work as a longshoreman. This was also a particularly active period in which he made speeches to middle-class audiences. He had a little more success in convincing these people of the community of interest he saw between social classes in achieving social justice than he did the working classes.

In 1927 Hapgood joined the Nicola Sacco-Bartolomeo Vanzetti defense committee, which was organized both to keep the case in the public eye and to raise funds for the two defendants' legal expenses. This period was also of personal significance to Hapgood, as he met his future wife, Mary Donovan, who served as secretary of the defense committee. Both gave a number of speeches on behalf of the committee, and both were arrested several times during public demonstrations relating to the case. Neither was convicted of a crime, and the next year Mary accompanied her husband as he returned to work in the Pennsylvania coalfields. Hapgood in turn campaigned for her when she ran for governor of Massachusetts on the Socialist ticket in 1927.

In 1930 Powers worked for a time at his father's Columbia Conserve Company in Indianapolis, but the two reached an impasse over Powers's prounion ideas and William's nonunion stance. Hapgood ran as the Socialist candidate for governor of Indiana in 1932, finishing far behind Paul V. McNutt. Hapgood later left the Socialist Party.

On the move again after leaving Indianapolis, he became a union organizer between 1930 and 1936 for the Amalgamated Clothing Workers and the Textile Workers Union of America, and tried to organize tenant farmers in the South. In 1935 he returned briefly to organizing mine workers. After that, he became active in the Congress of Industrial Organizations and was assigned to work with a number of CIO unions, including auto, steel, shoe workers, and shipbuilders. He rose in the CIO ranks, serving as the regional director for Indiana from 1941 to 1947 and in 1948 becoming a national vice president and assistant to the national director of organization.

The continuing breakneck pace of his organizing efforts took its toll. On February 4, 1949, he suffered a fatal heart attack while in his car on the way back from consulting his physician, who had ordered a period of complete rest. He was cremated and his ashes were scattered over the graves of

Sacco and Vanzetti. Like many activists before him (such as EUGENE V. DEBS), Powers discovered that his aspirations for the advancement of workers far outstripped their own. Where he believed in the benefit of collective action, workers tended to pursue individual, self-interested goals and accepted traditional relationships between workers and management. His life was dogged by his unrealistic expectations that the working classes would be able to grasp his own expansive vision of the goals of labor organization. He was as much a victim of the labor movement as he was its champion.

LEIGH DARBEE

For Further Reading

Bussel, Michael Robert. *From Harvard to the Ranks of Labor: Powers Hapgood and the American Working Class.* University Park: Penn State University Press, 1999.

Hapgood, Powers. Papers. Lilly Library Manuscript Collection, Indiana University, Bloomington, IN.

Hapgood, William Powers

February 26, 1872–July 30, 1960

Businessman and pioneer in workplace democracy.

Three days before Christmas in 1917, workers at the Columbia Conserve Company, an Indianapolis canning plant that manufactured condensed soup, catsup, boned chicken, and other items packed and sold under private brands of customers throughout the country, gathered in the firm's dining room to hear the annual report from the company's president. Instead of a bland rendition of profit and loss, however, Columbia employees learned they were to be part of an experiment in workplace democracy, an effort to create "an industry of the worker, by the worker and for the worker." The employees were to be responsible for determining the length of time they worked, how much they were paid, their share of production, and all other policies involved in running a business. They also shared in any profits and eventually used them to buy, through stock held collectively, the firm for which they toiled.

Initially, the plan met with, at best, skepticism from those who would be its chief beneficiaries. "Those [workers] who understood did not believe me, and very few understood," noted the plan's architect, Columbia president William Powers Hapgood. "Why should they? Their own experiences, as well as those of their forefathers, told them it was all a lie." Hapgood, part of a trio of remarkable brothers that included Norman, journalist and editor at *Collier's National Weekly* and *Harper's Weekly*, and Hutchins, author and bohemian, struggled mightily over the next few years to convince the company's workers of his sincerity and to inspire confidence in their own abilities. His efforts, including lending a hand on the shop floor by assisting the head cook, produced dividends; by 1930 the company's approximately 150 employees collectively controlled the majority of the firm's voting stock.

Born in Chicago on February 26, 1872, William Powers Hapgood was the youngest of three sons (a fourth child, a daughter, died at age ten) raised by Charles H. and Fanny Louise Powers Hapgood. A successful plow manufacturer, Charles Hapgood moved his family to Alton, Illinois, in 1875. An admirer of agnostic freethinker Robert G. Ingersoll, Charles attempted to instill in his offspring "an acute distaste for moral softness," noted eldest son Norman.

A sickly child, William received special attention and indulgence from both his parents. Growing into a lively, athletic young man who termed sports as "the most interesting activity of my early life," William, like his brothers, received his education at Harvard University. Unlike his brothers, who had worked on the editorial side of the *Harvard Monthly* while students, Norman as editor and Hutchins as a writer, William served as the periodical's business manager. His interest in the commercial realm continued after his graduation when he became an assistant shipping clerk in November 1894 at Franklin MacVeagh Wholesale Grocery in Chicago. In 1899 he married Eleanor Page and their son, POWERS, was also born that year.

Seeking new challenges, in 1903 William convinced the then-retired Charles to buy the Mullen-Blackledge Canning Company, located on South Meridian Street in Indianapolis. The new Columbia Conserve Company, with brothers William, Norman, and Hutchins as stockholders, had an inauspicious start; by 1910 the firm had left Indianapolis because of financial difficulties and moved its operations to an abandoned factory purchased by Charles for $5,000 in Lebanon, Indiana. Reincorporated with $125,000 in capital stock, the company returned to Indianapolis in 1912.

Buoyed by an upturn in business, William

William Powers Hapgood

decided that the time seemed favorable to unveil his plans for moving Columbia from "an autocratic to a democratic form of government." For a number of years, he had discussed and debated with his brothers and friends the idea of installing democracy in the workplace. He had been troubled by the fact that complete control of the company had been vested in him "not by superior ability necessarily, but by property rights," since the Hapgood family owned all of Columbia's stock.

His initial plan for Columbia's employees involved creating a ten-person committee, three appointed by the firm's owners and seven elected from the plant, to oversee such issues as wages, hours, hiring (including supervisory personnel such as foremen), and other plant policies. Hapgood retained the authority, withdrawn a year later, to veto the committee's decisions, but such an action could be overruled by a two-thirds vote by that body.

Pay at the canning plant became based on need. The maximum salary, received by Hapgood, was set at $100 per week with the minimum salary in 1917 set at $15 per week. By 1931 the latter figure had increased to $22 per week for all unmarried salaried employees. Those workers with families to support received more money, with the minimum salary for married staff established at 50 percent higher than the minimum for unmarried workers. Fringe benefits included: a pension plan; medical, dental, and hospital care; accident insurance; free meals in the company's cafeteria; free classes in various subjects at the plant; and reimbursement to workers hired from out of town for their traveling expenses to move to Indianapolis.

Realizing that the Columbia experiment could be checked or destroyed as long as control by the workers was only given to them voluntarily, and not by a definite contract, Hapgood, in 1925, set about to create a way employees could eventually own the business. Approved by the workforce, the plan called for net profits, after dividends had been paid, to be distributed to the employees to buy common stock in the company at $150 per share. Stock was not held on an individual basis, but owned collectively by the workers and overseen by three trustees elected by the council.

With the Great Depression draining business, however, Columbia began to experience problems. Pledged to keep employees on the job even if there were no orders to fill, the firm attempted to stem the flow of red ink by cutting salaries. At the end of May 1931, with sales shrinking, salaries were reduced by 50 percent. As the economy worsened, that figure grew to 75 percent. Seeking to increase business, the company in late 1932 embarked on a far-ranging plan to market its product under its own label. Workers, who in some instances had gone without pay, balked at the expense of such a program, including the $2,000 a year paid to Norman for publicity and advertising work. Among the most vocal critics were former union leaders brought into the firm by William's son, Powers, who had spent his life fighting for the rights of working men and women as a union organizer.

The experiment in workplace democracy survived until 1942, when workers, who still controlled approximately 60 percent of the company's stock, went on strike over wages. Shortly after they returned to work, twenty-four of the two hundred salaried workers filed suit for receivership against Columbia and its management in Marion County Superior Court. The trustees responsible for holding the commonly held stock in the firm filed a countersuit to dissolve the trust. On July

8, 1943, Superior Court Judge Hezzie B. Pike refused to name a receiver for the company, but did rule that the worker ownership plan had to be dissolved and the firm must distribute stock to individual employees who could do with it what they wanted. In 1953 William, who had become blind from trachoma, sold Columbia to John Sexton and Company, a Chicago wholesale grocery chain.

Tragedy plagued the Hapgood family in later years. Powers, who had continued to work for the union's cause as a regional organizer for the Congress of Industrial Organizations, died in 1949 due to a coronary blockage as he was driving to the family's farm. He was forty-nine years old. William, who died in 1960, did live long enough to see the fringe benefits enjoyed by his Columbia employees become a common fact of life for workers in other industries.

RAY E. BOOMHOWER

For Further Reading

Boomhower, Ray E. "'A Business without a Boss': William Powers Hapgood and the Columbia Conserve Company." *Traces of Indiana and Midwestern History* 13, no. 1 (Winter 2001): 4–13.

Bussel, Robert. *From Harvard to the Ranks of Labor: Powers Hapgood and the American Working Class*. University Park: Pennsylvania University Press, 1999.

Hapgood, William P. *An Experiment in Industrial Democracy: The Results of Fourteen Years of Self-Government*. Indianapolis, 1931.

Maraccio, Michael D. *The Hapgoods: Three Earnest Brothers*. Charlottesville: University Press of Virginia, 1977.

McQuaid, Kim. "Industry and the Co-Operative Commonwealth: William P. Hapgood and the Columbia Conserve Company, 1917-1943." *Labor History* 17 (Fall 1976).

Hardrick, John Wesley

September 21, 1891–October 18, 1968

Artist best known for his portraits, landscapes, and still lifes.

It was said of the remarkable painting *A Little Brown Girl*, created by John Wesley Hardrick that "this picture radiates a moral beauty that should be preserved eternally." That could easily have been used to describe the numerous other works produced by Hardrick.

A lifelong resident of Indianapolis, Hardrick earned recognition for his artistic ability early in life. A teacher encouraged him to pursue his natural talent in the arts while he was a student at Harriet Beecher Stowe School. She introduced him to Herman Lieber, owner of the leading art supply store and gallery in Indianapolis. Leiber persuaded his parents to enroll Hardrick in children's classes at the John Herron Art Institute. At the age of thirteen, Hardrick had the first exhibition of his art at the Negro Business League convention. He attended Emerich Manual High School, where he became a student of OTTO STARK, one of the famous Hoosier Group of painters.

In 1910, following his graduation from high school, Hardrick returned to Herron to continue his studies in art. There he studied under WILLIAM FORSYTH, another of the Hoosier Group of painters, as well as Stark. Forsyth's influence is seen in Hardrick's many landscape paintings, while Stark had an important influence on his skill in portraiture. Hardrick submitted more than fifty drawings at the Indiana State Fair in 1911 and won eight awards.

For Hardrick, 1914 was an important year, professionally as well as personally. While he was still a student at Herron, he had the first major exhibition of his art at the Allen Chapel Church. The *Indianapolis Star* noted that he was "a young local artist whose paintings have attracted the attention of art critics and have won their favorable comment." That same year he married Georgia Howard, with whom he had four daughters and a son. To care for his family and to support his art education classes Hardrick took other work besides his art. He worked at the Indianapolis Stove Company, sold newspapers, drove a truck, cleaned carpets, and drove a cab. His daughter, Rachel Buckner, recalled that her father gave his children "an appreciation for fine art and fine music." She also said that her father used a somewhat unconventional method to find models for his portraits. She said her dad "would be driving down the street and see someone who had character. He'd stop, get out and say 'Pardon me, I'm an artist, and I'd like for you to pose for me.'"

The Indiana Association of Colored Men commissioned Hardrick to paint portraits of ABRAHAM LINCOLN and Frederick Douglass for the February 20, 1916, Lincoln-Douglass Memorial held at Tomlinson Hall in Indianapolis. In a February 26, 1916, letter, the executive secretary wrote that the group hoped that "those who see these likenesses of God's noblemen may be inspired to larger usefulness in the cause of human uplift." In 1917 Hardrick's work was featured in the Tenth Annual

Exhibition of Works for Indiana artists held at the Herron Art Institute, and he graduated the following year.

Hardrick's subject matter mostly included portraits, especially African Americans, and landscapes. His 1927 oil painting titled *A Little Brown Girl* captured the innocence and beauty of people, of nature, and of his Indiana home and brought acclaim for Hardrick's artistry. The painting received a bronze medal from the Harmon Foundation, an organization dedicated to the nurture and promotion of black artists, and recognition from the Indiana State Fair with a second-place award. In 1929 African American citizens raised money to purchase this painting of a young girl, Nellie Henderson, surrounded by flowers. A March 1929 article in the *Indianapolis Recorder* identified "lodges, churches, fraternities and sororities" as organizations called upon to contribute funds so that the work could be part of the permanent collection at the John Herron Art Institute. Today, it is part of the Indianapolis Museum of Art's collection. Bret Waller, former director of the IMA, described the artist and the particular piece: "Hardrick was a significant African American artist, and this painting won national awards. From our judgment, based on the paintings by Hardrick we've seen, this is certainly one of his finest" Additional works by Hardrick can be found in the IMA, the Indiana State Museum, the Hampton University Museum in Hampton, Virginia, and in private collections.

During the Great Depression in 1934 Hardrick received a commission from the Works Project Administration to paint a mural for Crispus Attucks High School, an all-black high school. *The Workers* portrayed three African American workers pouring molten metal at a foundry. The school principal refused to display it because he thought its representation might dampen the aspiration of students. Hardrick's daughter later said that she thought the principal had failed to grasp the meaning her father intended. She thought he was trying to portray "life without education and therefore the importance of staying in school." Indeed, Hardick defined his role as a black artist in the brochure he wrote for his Allen Chapel Church art exhibit in 1914. He said then that the object of the exhibition was "an attempt to stimulate an interest among the colored citizens of Indianapolis to encourage art, to inspire, if possible, some young talented boy or girl to realize that 'Life without labor is crime, and labor without art is brutality.'"

William Taylor, artist, teacher and African American art historian, concluded that Hardrick had succeeded in his goal. "Hardrick," he said, "was a model for the younger generation of aspiring African American artists and endeavored to pave the way for their progress. His ability to succeed as an artist, sometimes in the face of daunting odds is vividly apparent in the abundant landscapes and portraits he produced, expressing his passion for nature and his love for his people."

Parkinson's disease eventually brought an end to Hardrick's career. His unique talent allowed for a dignified presentation of African American life in Indianapolis. Lucille E. Morehouse, art critic for the *Indianapolis Star*, writing about the fine quality of Hardrick's art in 1913 said, "John Hardrick. Just remember the name, will you please? . . . I have put John Hardrick's name down in my little memorandum book as the name of a future great artist." She was correct.

KISHA TANDY

For Further Reading

Taylor, William E., Harriet G. Warkel, and John Geiser. *A Shared Heritage: Art by Four African-Americans*. Indianapolis: Indiana Museum of Art, 1996.

Thompson, Bryan. "John Wesley Hardrick's 'Little Brown Girl' Returns." *Indianapolis Recorder*, April 9, 1994.

Warkel, Harriet G., Martin F. Krause, and S. L. Berry. *The Herron Chronicle*. Bloomington: Herron School of Art, IUPUI, in Association with Indiana University Press, 2003.

Harper, Ida Husted

February 18, 1851–March 14, 1931

Journalist, writer on women's issues, and leading figure in the national women's suffrage movement.

Soon after her marriage in 1871, Ida Husted Harper wrote the first of scores of columns she would produce for the *Terre Haute Saturday Evening Mail*—initially, like many female authors before her, under a pseudonym, "Mrs. John Smith." Her column was first titled "A Woman's Thoughts," and later "A Woman's Opinions," and she expressed those opinions on a wide variety of topics—including women's rights. Starting in 1882 her own name appeared on her pieces. In addition, the editor of the paper was willing to pay for her work, which she accepted. Her husband did not believe this appropriate, and indeed it was a departure for a married woman of her class at the time. This divergence of views may have been a contributing factor in Ida's divorce in 1890.

Ida Husted gave hints of her future prominence from a fairly early age. Born in Franklin, Indiana, she moved to Muncie with her family around 1861. She was in the first class to graduate from Muncie High School in 1868. She attended Indiana University in Bloomington for a year, enrolling as a sophomore the year after women were first allowed to matriculate, then left to become a teacher and the principal at the high school in Peru, Indiana, in 1869.

Her administrative career was brief, ending with her marriage to Thomas Winans Harper on December 28, 1871. Harper was a veteran of the Civil War from Ohio, who attended the University of Michigan law school in 1867–68, though he did not graduate. Thomas and Ida set up housekeeping in Terre Haute, and he practiced law while she ran the household. For nearly twenty years, Thomas was chief counsel to the Brotherhood of Locomotive Firemen, the railroad union established by Eugene V. Debs. In 1879 Thomas was elected city attorney on the same ticket on which Debs secured the position of city clerk.

The couple's Terre Haute social circles and Debs enabled Ida to make the contacts that initiated her newspaper career and her involvement in the suffrage movement. In 1878 Debs courted controversy when he sponsored a visit by Susan B. Anthony in spite of her activist role in women's suffrage, which was not an issue embraced by organized labor or the general public. It was at this meeting that Ida met Anthony. From 1884 to 1893 Ida edited the "Woman's Department" in the *Locomotive Firemen's Magazine*, the organ of the BLF. In addition, Harper became secretary of a statewide suffrage association in 1887

In the middle of this editorial tenure, in February 1890, Ida divorced Thomas. Later that same month she accepted the position of editor-in-chief of the *Terre Haute Daily News*, from which she resigned in May 1890. She moved to Indianapolis,

Ida Husted Harper

where her only child, Winnifred, was attending the Girls Classical School, founded in 1882 by MAY WRIGHT SEWALL and her husband, Theodore. Ida joined the editorial staff of the *Indianapolis News* and wrote articles for the paper for many years. By 1893 Ida had moved to California and enrolled along with her daughter at Stanford University. She ultimately did not receive her degree.

Harper's contact with Sewall in Indianapolis further fed her interest in the women's suffrage movement, a natural outgrowth of her interest in women's issues in general. In 1896 Harper joined the National American Woman Suffrage Association and became head of press relations. In that position, Harper was intimately involved with the group's efforts to see a suffrage amendment pass in the California state legislature. Though that effort failed, Harper's relationship with Anthony flowered. The two developed a personal friendship and professional collaboration that lasted until Anthony's death in 1906.

Harper moved into Anthony's home in Rochester, New York, in 1897 after Anthony selected Harper to be her official biographer. Harper produced an exhaustive study of Anthony's life, the three volumes of which appeared in 1898 and 1908 under the title *The Life and Work of Susan B. Anthony*. The work was assessed at the time as "exhaustive, if somewhat pedestrian." This contribution to women's history was unfortunately counterbalanced by Harper's destroying most of Anthony's personal papers so that no other biography could eclipse hers.

Harper and Anthony traveled to many women's rights events together in the years around the turn of the century, and both were in demand as lecturers. Harper was far more comfortable writing about than speaking on women's issues, however, and during this period she also produced a women's column in the *New York Sunday Sun* and contributed a regular column titled "Votes for Women" to *Harper's Bazar*. Hers was an increasingly familiar name in papers published in major cities nationwide. Harper also continued working for passage of an amendment to the U.S. Constitution to gain the vote for women.

In the early years of the twentieth century Harper was active in the International Council of Women and in 1916 was made head of national publicity for the Leslie Bureau of Suffrage Education by the bureau's founder, Carrie Chapman Catt. This work contributed directly to the passage of the Nineteenth Amendment in 1919, by which time Harper had outlived many of her suffragette colleagues. The final major achievement of Harper's life was her revision of the massive *History of Woman Suffrage*, published between 1881 and 1922. She and Anthony had originally coauthored volume four. Harper was sole author of volumes five and six.

In 1931, at the age of seventy-nine, Harper suffered a fatal cerebral hemorrhage. She is buried in Muncie, Indiana.

While Harper wrote about domestic matters in many of her early columns, in others she was hinting at the possibilities for expanding women's roles in public life. While communicating with women about how to improve their marriages, she was leaving her own unsatisfactory union and striking out on her own. As much as Harper achieved in words, she accomplished much more for the cause of women's rights in the way she chose to live her life.

LEIGH DARBEE

For Further Reading

Jones, Nancy Baker. "A Forgotten Feminist: The Early Writings of Ida Husted Harper, 1878–1894." *Indiana Magazine of History* 73 (June, 1977): 79–101.

Phillips, Clifton J. "Ida A. Husted Harper." *Notable American Women, 1607–1950: A Biographical Dictionary*. Cambridge, MA: Belknap Press, 1971.

Harrison, Benjamin

August 20, 1833–March 13, 1901

Served as reporter of the Indiana Supreme Court, colonel of an Indiana regiment during the Civil War, U.S. senator, and twenty-third president of the United States.

The only person elected from Indiana to the White House, Benjamin Harrison squired an impressive legislative agenda through Congress, deftly piloted the nation's foreign relations, and effected significant change in the nation's highest office. Nonetheless, an electorate wary of government activism turned him out after four years, and his important legacy soon faded from public consciousness.

Born in southern Ohio, the son of a congressman and grandson of President WILLIAM HENRY HARRISON, Benjamin received a classical education that honed his powerful intellect and religious training that imparted a strict sense of duty and service. He graduated from Miami University in 1852 and turned to reading law in Cincinnati. He married Caroline Scott in 1853, won admission to the bar in early 1854, and soon thereafter moved to Indianapolis, which he called home for the rest of his life. His skill at the bar not only attracted clients but, along with his famous name, also earned him notice in his adopted state's politics. Embracing the new Republican Party, he rose quickly in its ranks, and in 1860 won election as the reporter of the state supreme court.

In the spring of 1862, Harrison left editing and publishing the court's opinions to take command of the Seventieth Indiana Volunteer Infantry Regiment. A tough disciplinarian and an eager student of military tactics, he led his thousand Hoosiers ably in the western theater and saw hard fighting in the Atlanta campaign. In 1865 he mustered out as a brevet brigadier general. In 1864 he had won election again to the reporter's office, and when he returned to Indianapolis he resumed that work and also pursued his lucrative private practice.

Over the next several years, Harrison became known as "one of the state's leading lawyers," and as an adept expositor of Republican doctrine on the stump, achieving prominence in the Hoosier party and beginning to win notice from Republican leaders across the nation. In 1876, when scandal forced the party's gubernatorial nominee to withdraw, Harrison stepped in and fought a hard campaign, which he lost narrowly to James "Blue Jeans" Williams. During the great railroad strike of 1877, Harrison assembled a citizen militia to help preserve peace in Indianapolis and another group to negotiate with the strikers, although some workers thought the sharp lawyer showed them scant sympathy.

Hoosier Republican boss U.S. Senator OLIVER P. MORTON, a former governor, viewed Harrison's political rise warily, but the senator's death in late 1877 opened the way for Harrison to take control of the party. In 1881 he easily won a seat in the U.S. Senate, where once again his speaking talents earned him admiration from his fellow Republicans, who invited him to campaign in their home states. In 1884 the Indiana delegation at the Republican National Convention toyed with presenting him as a candidate for president but concluded that the time was not yet right. In 1887, largely because of a Democratic gerrymander of state legislative districts, Harrison lost re-election to the Senate, but his gallant struggle in a rigged fight catapulted him into the circle of presidential prospects for 1888.

At the national convention that year, Harrison faced a large field of candidates, several more prominent than himself. But his Hoosier managers skillfully touted his distinguished lineage, war record, speaking ability, Republican orthodoxy, and residence in the swing state of Indiana. After three days of balloting he won the nomination.

Indiana became the hub of the 1888 Republican presidential campaign. In an era when most presidential candidates said little in their own behalf, Harrison, determined to pull his own weight, launched a highly effective front-porch campaign. Day after day he spoke to visiting delegations of voters who streamed into Indianapolis from around Indiana and from other states. He emphasized the benefits of a protective tariff, generous pensions for Union military veterans, and civil rights for African Americans. He slept each night in his own bed on North Delaware Street, but newspapers carried his message next morning

Benjamin Harrison

to the breakfast tables of voters across the land. The suppression of African American voting in the South enabled incumbent Democrat Grover Cleveland to amass a popular vote plurality over Harrison, but the Hoosier candidate won the two key states of Indiana and New York and an electoral vote victory of 233–168.

The Republicans also won control of the House and the Senate, ending an era of divided government that had existed for more than a decade. Seizing the opportunity, Harrison pushed his legislative agenda in his state of the union messages and in special communications to Congress, as well as by privately cajoling individual or small groups of legislators. The Fifty-first Congress posted an extraordinary record: the McKinley Tariff Act, the Sherman Anti-Trust Act, the Sherman Silver Purchase Act, the Dependent Pension Act, the Meat Inspection Act, increased naval construction, subsidies to revitalize the merchant marine, internal improvements, the Forest Reserve Act, and antilottery legislation. The one major failure was the defeat of voting rights legislation after virulent opposition by Democrats from the North as well as the South and the apostasy of a few western Republicans. In the midterm elections of 1890, the Democrats frightened voters with the specter of an intrusive activist government, and the Republicans lost control of the House of Representatives by a wide margin, thereby ending Harrison's forward-looking agenda.

In foreign affairs Harrison negotiated reciprocal trade agreements with several countries, achieved an agreement with Great Britain for arbitration of the Bering Sea fur-seal dispute, created a condominium with Britain and Germany for the management of affairs in Samoa, and fashioned a treaty for annexation of Hawaii, which failed to win Senate passage before his successor withdrew it. Casting aside the tendency merely to react to incidents, Harrison pursued a more activist involvement in foreign affairs, especially in quest of economic advantage overseas.

Harrison traveled widely and gave more presidential speeches than any of his predecessors. Advocating the Republican program as well as highlighting general ideals such as equality and economic growth, Harrison foreshadowed Theodore Roosevelt's use of the presidency as a "bully pulpit." Nonetheless, Harrison's essentially reserved personality that some saw as coldness, coupled with his inability to satisfy all the patronage requests for offices that flooded his desk, won him few friends among Republican Party bosses. He managed to win renomination in 1892, but party disaffection, economic discontent in various sectors, and suspicion of Republican activism dealt Harrison a loss to former president Cleveland.

Harrison returned to Indianapolis in 1893. His wife had died in October 1892, and in 1897 he married her niece, Mary Lord Dimmick. Harrison resumed his legal practice and made a few political speeches as ex-president. After an economic collapse made a disaster of Cleveland's term, voters swept Republicans back into power under William McKinley, who adopted many policies and governing techniques that Harrison had fashioned. But in historical retrospect it was McKinley and even more his successor, Roosevelt, who won acclaim for transforming the presidency, while many came to regard Harrison's term as an undistinguished interlude between Cleveland's two terms.

CHARLES W. CALHOUN

For Further Reading

Calhoun, Charles W. *Benjamin Harrison*. New York: Times Books, 2005.

Benjamin Harrison Papers. Library of Congress, Washington, D.C.

Sievers, Harry J. *Benjamin Harrison: Hoosier President*. Newtown, CT: American Political Biography Press, 1996.

———. *Benjamin Harrison: Hoosier Statesman*. Newtown, CT: American Political Biography Press, 1996.

———. *Benjamin Harrison: Hoosier Warrior*. Newtown, CT: American Political Biography Press, 1997.

Harrison, William Henry

February 9, 1773–April 4, 1841

Indiana territorial governor, general in the War of 1812, and ninth president of the United States.

Few men had as large an impact on Indiana during the pioneer era as William Henry Harrison, although he also had a knack for irritating people on the frontier. Nevertheless, Harrison's accomplishments in Indiana distinguished him on the national stage. Building on his successes, Harrison eventually attained the highest office in the land—president of the United States.

Harrison was born to a prominent Virginia family. One of his paternal ancestors served on Jamestown's governing council during the 1630s.

His father, Benjamin, who owned a vast plantation, signed the Declaration of Independence. William attended Hampden–Sydney College in Virginia for three years where he received a classical education. His parents then sent him to study medicine in Richmond, Virginia, and later in Philadelphia, Pennsylvania.

When Harrison's father died in 1791, his family could no longer pay for his education. He joined the army at age eighteen, becoming knowledgeable about Indians and the state of affairs on the western frontier. In 1794 he served as General Anthony Wayne's aide-de-camp at the Battle of Fallen Timbers—the final battle of the Northwest Indian War that determined U.S. control of the Northwest Territory. From that point forth, Harrison was on the fast track to success.

In 1795 Harrison met Anna Symmes, the twenty-year-old daughter of Colonel John Symmes, a distinguished Revolutionary War colonel. Anna and Harrison married soon after, in spite of Colonel Symmes's disapproval; he did not want his daughter to marry a soldier. Nevertheless, it was a happy marriage and the couple had ten children.

President John Adams appointed the twenty-seven-year-old Harrison to be the first governor of the Indiana Territory in 1800. Harrison and his family, which by now included three young children, settled in Vincennes, a settlement with around a thousand residents, many of whom were of French and/or Indian descent. By 1805 the Harrisons had built a thirteen-room brick mansion, which Harrison named Grouseland. He staffed it with former slaves with whom he signed indentured servitude contracts. This conspicuous show of wealth came back to haunt Harrison as the local population marked him as an elitist and outsider.

Harrison's proslavery stance also made him unpopular with the majority of residents in the Indiana Territory. In 1802 he used his clout to call a territorial convention to consider repealing Article VI of the Northwest Ordinance, which prohibited slavery. Although this attempt failed, in 1805 Harrison and the territorial judges passed a law that allowed slaves to be brought into the territory as indentured servants. In time, however, the antislavery movement in Indiana proved to be stronger than Harrison and the proslavery forces. In 1810 the general assembly repealed the indentured servitude law; and when the territory gained statehood five years later, slavery and involuntary servitude were banned.

Even though his elitism and proslavery stance alienated many people in the Indiana Territory, Harrison continued to please his superiors in Washington, D.C., especially in the area of Indian relations. Between 1803 and 1809 Harrison served President Thomas Jefferson by shrewdly negotiating many treaties with Miami, Potawatomi, Delaware, Shawnee, and other tribes, opening millions of acres of land to white settlement in what would become Indiana and Illinois. Harrison was skillful at identifying the most persuadable chiefs and using them to divide and conquer more resistant ones. When necessary, he rewarded chiefs who agreed to cede land on his terms with gifts and bribes. He also reminded them of American invincibility.

Harrison's negotiating tactics worked with many Indian chiefs, but not TECUMSEH, the powerful Shawnee chief, who defiantly refused any terms Harrison offered. These two men—arguably the most powerful in the West—met several times, including at Grouseland in August 1810. Tensions always ran high at their meetings; Tecumseh once called Harrison a liar, and Harrison responded by drawing his sword. No blood was shed then, but it soon would be.

William Henry Harrison

In fall 1811 Harrison felt an urgency to squelch the Indian rebellion fueled by Tecumseh and his brother TENSKWATAWA, the Prophet. When he knew that Tecumseh was away from their village, Prophetstown, recruiting Indians to join their growing anti-American confederation, Harrison acted. On November 6 Harrison's militia of about a thousand men camped along the Wabash River, planning to strike Prophetstown at daybreak. Instead, the Indians attacked before dawn, ineptly led by the Prophet. Two hours of fierce fighting concluded with an Indian retreat. Although Harrison proclaimed the Battle of Tippecanoe a total victory, it was far from it. Almost one-fifth of his men were dead or wounded. Harrison, though, escaped unscathed.

When the War of 1812 between the United States and Great Britain broke out, Harrison resigned his post as governor of the Indiana Territory. Rejoining the army, he swiftly attained the rank of brigadier general. In fall 1813 Harrison successfully retook the fort at Detroit, which had been surrendered to the British the previous year. Then he and his army pursued British troops working in collaboration with Tecumseh in Ontario, Canada. There, at the Battle of the Thames, Tecumseh died, and Harrison emerged a hero. In May 1814 Harrison resigned from the army and left for Ohio, where his family had been living in his absence, but returned to the army to negotiate postwar treaties with the Indians at the request of President James Madison.

From his farm and large home (which he named North Bend) on the Ohio River, Harrison earned a reputation as an advocate for veterans, a generous host, and a civic leader. In 1816 he filled the seat of an Indiana congressman who had resigned, marking the launch of a new political career. In 1819 he won a seat in the Ohio Senate. In 1825 Harrison traveled to Washington, D.C., as one of Ohio's two U.S. senators.

After serving as ambassador to Colombia for a brief time in 1829, Harrison returned to Ohio, where he tried various business ventures, many of which failed. In 1831 he ran again for the U.S. Senate, but lost. Five years later, however, Harrison was in the thick of national politics.

Harrison's 1840 presidential campaign proved a brilliant public relations model that is still emulated today. His famous slogan, "Tippecanoe and Tyler, too," was a catchy phrase remembered long after his short presidency. "Tippecanoe," of course, referred to Harrison's victory in battle against the Indians. "Tyler" referred to John Tyler of Virginia, who was Harrison's vice presidential running mate on the Whig Party ticket.

The Whigs promoted Harrison's "pioneer virtues" with symbols such as log cabins and hard cider, knowing they would appeal to the primarily rural and hard-working American populace. In contrast, his opponent, Martin Van Buren, was portrayed as a wine-drinking rich man and a Washington insider. A glance at recent presidential campaigns shows how enduring this marketing ploy of appealing to the electorate through emotive symbols turned out to be.

Finding out who won the 1840 presidential election took several weeks. Voting began on October 30 and continued until November 18. When all of the votes were counted, the result was an Electoral College landslide for Harrison, who won 234 votes to Van Buren's 60. The Whigs also gained control of Congress.

Harrison rode his favorite horse, Whitey, to his inauguration in Washington, D.C., on March 4, 1841. Although it was a cold, wet day in the capital, Harrison wore no overcoat and waved his hat at the crowds. At age sixty-eight, he was the oldest president sworn into office (a record he kept until Ronald Reagan in 1980). Harrison set another record with his nearly two-hour inauguration speech—the longest of any U.S. president as of 2013. The many hours Harrison spent in the cold and slush on inauguration day took its toll. He soon contracted pneumonia. Harrison died exactly one month after he took office.

Harrison had a grand and dignified funeral, a credit to the American people who had not mourned a sitting president before. His body lay in state in a glass-topped coffin at the White House, where thousands of citizens filed past to pay their respects. In the funeral procession, Harrison's horse trotted without a rider to symbolize the fallen leader. At Anna's request, Harrison's final resting place was near her father's grave in North Bend, Ohio.

LEE ANN SANDWEISS

For Further Reading

Clanin, Douglas, et al., eds. *The Papers of William Henry Harrison, 1800–1815*. Indianapolis: Indiana Historical Society, 1994.

———. *A Guide to the Papers of William Henry Harrison,*

1800–1815. Indianapolis: Indiana Historical Society, 1999.

Cleaves, Freeman. *Old Tippecanoe: William Henry Harrison and His Time*. 1939. Reprint, Newton: CT, American Political Biography Press, 1990.

Collins, Gail. *William Henry Harrison: The American Presidents Series*. New York: Times Books, 2012.

Horsman, Reginald. "William Henry Harrison: Virginia Gentleman in the Old Northwest." *Indiana Magazine of History* 96 (June 2000): 125–49.

Haynes, Elwood

October 14, 1857–April 13, 1925

Inventor, metallurgist, and businessman. Invented one of America's first automobiles in 1894 and the superalloys Stellite and stainless steel.

Elwood Haynes is best known as an automobile pioneer, having invented what seems to be the first successful self-propelled vehicle in America, although others, upon scant evidence, also claim that distinction. The case is much clearer for Haynes, a metallurgical genius, regarding his discoveries of an incredibly hard and durable heat- and stain-resistant alloy he named Stellite because of its permanent star-like brilliance. The basic ingredients of Stellite were cobalt (or nickel) and chromium, but the later addition of tungsten (or molybdenum) added more hardness and toughness to the alloy, which instantly replaced "high-speed steel" as a tool used to cut other metals and it found great usefulness in the industrial world, particularly in aeronautical manufacturing and in the space age. Today there is Stellite on the surface of the moon.

After creating the highly profitable Stellite, further experimentation led Haynes to discover that adding chromium to steel renders that combination stainless. A later similar discovery in Sheffield, England, of "rustless iron" that was also patented in this country resulted in Haynes and Harry Brearley, a Sheffield metallurgist, sharing the royalties on all the stainless steel produced in America during the life of their combined patents.

Haynes was born into a remarkable family in Portland, Indiana, in 1857. He was the sixth of ten children of Judge Jacob M. and Hilinda Haines Haynes, eight of whom lived to maturity and became prominent citizens. Elwood was considered by one of his siblings "slow," and another feared that their father "would always have to keep Elwood."

But the rather dreamy Elwood had no concerns about making a living—his early drive was for an education. When a high school was finally established in Portland in 1876, Elwood, even though he was nearly nineteen, enrolled there. His two years of study at Portland High School

Elwood Haynes with his 1904 Haynes Pioneer automobile at a historical marker commemorating his achievement.

qualified him for admission to the Worcester County (Massachusetts) Free Institute of Industrial Science, now Worcester Polytechnic Institute, where continued his education at minimal expense to his family. As its original name indicates, the institute was free to residents of Worcester County, so Haynes moved there in 1878 and completed its rigorous three-year program on schedule.

Returning home to Portland in 1881, Haynes became a teacher, first in a one-room district school, then at Portland High School (where he also served as principal), and finally as professor of science at the Eastern Indiana Normal School, also in Portland. Highly successful and popular as a teacher at all levels, Haynes once confided to his special friend, Bertha Lanterman, then living in Alabama, that "I like school teaching first rate, and the more I teach, the better I like it."

Upon the discovery of natural gas in Indiana in 1886, a discovery in which scientist Haynes had assisted, the economy of Indiana was transformed and Haynes was soon persuaded to begin working full time in the gas industry. As the inventive superintendent of the Portland Natural Gas and Oil Company, Haynes not only managed the local office and supervised the drilling of new wells and the piping of the city, but he also invented gas meters and "an automatic gas regulator" or thermostat. His larger income at this time permitted him to marry, at age thirty, the aforementioned Lanterman.

Haynes's superior talent as a gas man brought him to the attention of the Chicago-based Indiana Gas and Oil Company, directed by "urban corruptionist," Charles T. Yerkes, who was seeking to monopolize the supply of gas to Chicago. Yerkes hired Haynes to build what became the first long-distance high-pressure gas pipeline in America. This line, actually two parallel eight-inch pipelines that extended 120 miles from Greentown, Indiana, to the Illinois state line, utilized another Haynes invention, now universally used, of dehydrating the gas prior to transmission and also was a factor in Haynes's decision to seek a better way to journey long distances via mechanized travel. His gas company work, following completion of the pipeline, took him to Kokomo in 1892 and he lived there the rest of his life. In addition to managing the gas company office in Kokomo, he began concentrated research on developing both a new means of mechanical travel and new and better alloys, first for use in his automobiles and then for use in general manufacturing.

As early as 1890, Haynes was investigating whether steam-, electricity-, or gasoline-powered automobiles would be best. He finally decided on gasoline when he saw a gasoline engine for use in boats exhibited at the Chicago World's Fair in 1893. Haynes decided to buy one and try to adapt it to his planned vehicle. He received a small one-cylinder, one-horsepower Sintz engine in November 1893, and then hired the Apperson brothers, Elmer and Edgar, to build the vehicle he had designed at their machine shop.

After months of work, the little machine was ready for a test drive on, of all days, July 4, 1894, and the men immediately tried it out. Because of the crowd in Kokomo that holiday, Haynes and the Appersons had their little machine towed by horses to the edge of town. There, where the twisting Pumpkinvine Pike led into the countryside, the men push-started the engine and then, with Haynes at the controls, drove into history.

"The Pioneer," as Haynes named his invention, reached a speed of seven or eight miles per hour, traveled about a mile or two down the road and then coasted to a stop (no brakes yet). They turned the machine around, and then Haynes drove it all the way back to the brothers' shop.

Delighted with their test drive, Haynes and the Appersons soon built a second car, with a larger engine of their own design, and entered the first automobile race in America—in Chicago on November 28, 1895. There was only one other gas-powered American automobile entered, the Duryea, which had first been tested, unsuccessfully, in 1893—three other domestic entrants were battery or steam powered. Unfortunately, on the wintry race day, while en route to the starting line, the Haynes car had an accident on the snow-covered streets and broke a wheel. Without a spare, they watched Frank Duryea slowly complete the course and win the race, but Haynes and the Appersons won a prize for their "balanced" engine. They decided at once to begin large-scale production. Haynes subsequently manufactured automobiles for the next thirty years.

Recognized throughout his lifetime as the inventor of the automobile in America, it was a particular joy for Haynes, driving his 1894 Pioneer, to lead the historical section of a two thousand-car parade down Broadway in New York City in 1908, part of a celebration commemorating the first ten years of the automobile there. Soon thereafter Haynes donated his first car to the Smithsonian Institution, where it is on permanent display.

By this time, having turned over active management of the car company to others, Haynes was primarily involved in his metallurgical research and soon patented both of his major discoveries—Stellite in 1912 and stainless steel in 1919, the former of which he manufactured for eight years before selling his company to others, who still manufacture Stellite. As his daughter, Bernice, remarked in 1970, "Father hated business, deciding who should do what, he much preferred his research." He also devoted considerable time to his cherished causes or reforms in America, the chief of which were Prohibition (he once ran for the U.S. Senate on the Prohibition ticket), having the United States adopt the metric system, and American entry into the League of Nations. A lifelong Presbyterian, Haynes also supported various charitable organizations.

Haynes was primarily an intuitive inventor, but he was well trained (at Worcester and Johns Hopkins University) and extraordinarily diligent. Neither exceptionally bright nor a fast learner, Haynes had the capacity to retain that which he learned, and good fortune, happy circumstance, and timing enabled him to place himself in the forefront of the most exciting and significant technological and industrial breakthroughs of his lifetime.

RALPH D. GRAY

For Further Reading

Gray, Ralph D. *Alloys and Automobiles: The Life of Elwood Haynes*. 1979. Reprint, [Zionsville, IN]: Guild Press Emmis Publishing, 2002.

———. *Stellite: A History of the Haynes Stellite Company*. Kokomo, IN: High Technology Materials Division, Cabot Corporation, 1974.

Griffey, Dave. *Beyond the Pioneer: The Impact of "America's First Mechanically Successful Automobile."* Oxford, England, 2006.

Hays, William (Will) Harrison, Sr.

November 5, 1879–March 7, 1954

Postmaster General of the United States and first president of the Motion Picture Producers and Distributors of America.

Profiles of Will H. Hays described him in 1919 as "a boyish-looking man" who was "alert, quick moving" and part of the progressive wing of the Republican Party. He was optimistic about America, and had "an unholy capacity for work," but was also cautious by nature. He liked to quote a fellow Hoosier, former President BENJAMIN HARRISON, who had said, "The length of the step is not so important as the direction in which it is taken."

Hays was then chairman of the National Republican Party and preparing to manage Warren G. Harding's successful campaign for the presidency in 1920. After the election, Harding appointed Hays as postmaster general. In that office from 1921 to 1922, Hays worked to modernize the nation's communication network, an effort that included extending rural-free delivery and promoting the use of air mail.

But Hays's time in the Harding administration was brief, and he is best remembered for being the head of the movie industry from 1922 until 1945. Movie producers hired him to be the first president of the Motion Picture Producers and Distributors of America, with a starting annual salary of more $100,000, at that time more than earned by the U.S. president. Under his leadership, the MPPDA simply became known to the public as the "Hays Office."

William Harrison Hays Sr. was born in Sullivan, Indiana, in 1879, the son of John Tennyson and Mary Cain Hays. After graduating from Wabash College and being admitted to the bar in 1900, he practiced law in Sullivan. Fascinated by politics from an early age, he rose quickly through the political ranks in Indiana. His interest in politics began in 1896, when he traveled with his father to attend the Republican National Convention in Saint Louis where William McKinley was nominated to run for president. Hays later came to like Theodore Roosevelt who, he felt, bridged the progressive wing of the party with its more conservative factions.

Hays was naturally inclined toward compromise, strongly probusiness, and favored such reforms as women's suffrage and prohibition. In Indiana politicians recognized his political acumen and made him head of the state's Republican Party. In 1916 he was able to unite the state's divided Republicans behind James P. Goodrich, who was elected governor. During World War I, Goodrich appointed Hays to head Indiana's State Council of Defense. Hays's work in Indiana won him a national reputation that culminated in his being named head of the National Republican Party in 1918, a post he held until 1921.

Hays's conservative credentials and his powerful political connections appealed to movie producers who hired him to lead the MPPDA. They wanted Hays to refurbish Hollywood's image at a time when the film industry had been roiled by sex scandals, and the producers hoped that his political ties would help them fend off government censorship. A number of cities and states had already instituted censorship boards and there were calls for federal legislation. Moreover, following the Bolshevik Revolution in Russia, there were growing fears that motion pictures might be used to inspire revolution.

In background and appearance, the slender Hays seemed ideally suited for the task at hand. Hollywood's moral critics were reassured by the fact that he was an elder in the Presbyterian Church. Businessmen liked Hays because he was a staunch believer that films should be used to promote capitalism and the American way of life. Cinema was a great "international salesman," Hays said, and movies were "animated catalogs" that advertised American products worldwide.

If Hays's name became synonymous with the MPPDA, it also became identified with censorship and moral prudery. During the 1910s and 1920s, filmmakers came under increasing attack by religious leaders, women's organizations, educational leaders, and civic groups for undermining morality and social order. Hays sought to appease such critics by convincing the public that Hollywood was capable of regulating itself. To this end, he tried a couple of plans, the "Formula" in 1924, and the "Don'ts and Be Carefuls" in 1927. Both of these strategies, which lacked adequate means to enforce their rules, failed to quell criticism of Hollywood.

When studios began producing talking films during the late 1920s, calls for government regulation increased and Hays was forced to undertake stronger measures. The result was the Production Code, a document that was strongly influenced by Roman Catholic theology and which attempted to bind movies to the Ten Commandments. Movie producers adopted the Production Code, often referred to as the Hays Code, in 1930 and strengthened its enforcement in 1934 with the creation of the Production Code Administration. Contrary to popular belief, Hays did not write the Production Code but oversaw its enforcement. To help him in that job, Hays brought to Hollywood a Roman Catholic layman, Joseph I. Breen, to head the PCA. Nearly all mainstream movies made from the mid-1930s through the early 1960s were censored by the PCA. Hays and Breen interpreted the Code to support Judeo-Christian values but they also often went beyond the letter of the Code to endorse social and political ideas that were strongly conservative.

While Hays's name became inextricably linked to this censorship, it should be remembered that his primary job was to promote the interests of the movie producers who had hired him. In this regard, Hays became one of the most powerful practitioners of public relations during the 1920s and 1930s, building a vast publicity apparatus that was used to advance the entertainment industry. In 1925 Hays created a Committee (later Department) of Public Relations and he used every form of communication and mass advertising—newspapers, magazines, pulp fiction, photography, sound recording, radio, billboards—to create an entertainment complex of unprecedented dimensions. The MPPDA attempted to extend its reach into virtually every community by cultivating local merchants, editors, women's groups and anyone else who might be considered a leader of opinion. Hays offered a glimpse of this communication complex in his annual reports. If we take him at his word, by the time he retired in 1945, the MPPDA could count on about 600,000 people "doing something on an organized basis."

With such powerful weapons of publicity at his disposal, Hays deflected much criticism aimed at Hollywood. Calls for government censorship diminished. Critics of movies and film stars did not disappear, but the PCA placated enough of them to secure cinema's acceptance in mainstream entertainment. When social scientists warned during the 1930s in the Payne Fund Studies that movies might have damaging effects on children, Hays put such scholars as Mortimer Adler on his payroll to discredit the research. When war clouds gathered and Hollywood was accused of warmongering during the late 1930s, Hays understood that patriotism was one of the best ways to transcend criticism of the industry. During World War II, under Hays's leadership, the motion industry became a powerful arm of U.S. propaganda. "We are going to sell America to the world," he said, "with American motion pictures."

Will Hays, 1941

The critics of Hollywood morality never fully trusted Hays. At one point, his private life became an issue. He was married twice. In 1902 he wed Helen Louise Thomas and the couple had one son, William Harrison Hays Jr. This marriage ended in divorce in 1929, and in 1930 Hays married Jessie Herron Stutesman, the widow of the former U.S. minister to Bolivia.

Hays retired in 1945 but remained as an adviser to the MPPDA (which changed its name to the Motion Picture Association of America) until 1950. Despite his prudish reputation, few people did more to make Hollywood and America's celebrity culture respectable during the first half of the twentieth century. He died in Sullivan in early 1954, at the age of seventy-four.

STEPHEN L. VAUGHN

For Further Reading

Black, Gregory D. *Hollywood Censored: Morality Codes, Catholics, and the Movies*. New York: Cambridge University Press, 1994.

Hays, Will H. Papers. Manuscript and Rare Books Division. Indiana State Library, Indianapolis.
———. *Memoirs*. Garden City, NY: Double Day, 1955.
Vaughn, Stephen. "The Devil's Advocate: Will H. Hays and the Campaign to Make Movies Respectable." *Indiana Magazine of History* 101 (June 2005): 125–52.

Hendricks, Thomas Andrews

September 7, 1819–November 25, 1885

Attorney and Democratic Party leader during the Civil War years and afterward and the only Hoosier to have served as governor, senator, and U.S. vice president.

Thomas A. Hendricks, the major Democratic politician in Indiana during and after the Civil War, was his party's counterpoint to the dynamic leader of the Republicans at that time, OLIVER P. MORTON. Both of these men, in different order, served as governor and U.S. senator. Hendricks alone added to those high offices the honor of twice being nominated by his party for the vice presidency of the United States. Probably the people's choice by popular vote both times, only his second such campaign in 1884 ended victoriously. Earlier too, in 1872, when Hendricks was elected Indiana governor, he became the first northern Democrat to be so honored after the Civil War. The keys to Hendricks's success were his skills as an orator, his empathy for his fellow man, and his firm belief in the democratic process.

Hendricks, a nephew of Indiana's third governor, William Hendricks, was born in Muskingum County, Ohio, in 1819, and moved to Indiana with his family in 1820 at the urgings of soon-to-be governor Hendricks. Settling first in Jefferson County, the John Hendricks family moved to Shelby County in 1822 where the elder Hendricks became a farmer and businessman. There young Thomas grew up amid countless visitors to the spacious Hendricks home, which included circuit-riding ministers, attorneys, and judges, whose lively discussions of politics and current events fascinated the young boy and inspired him to seek a career in law and politics.

After attending the local schools, Hendricks enrolled in tiny Hanover College, class of 1841, where, according to a classmate, "he excelled as a debater . . . and exhibited much of the urbanity that characterized him through life." Immediately following his graduation, Hendricks undertook the study of law in attorney offices in Indiana and Ohio, married Eliza C. Morgan from North Bend, Ohio, and began both a law practice and a life in public service back home in Indiana.

Elected to the Indiana House of Representatives in 1848, Hendricks served a single term. Then he was elected to the state's constitutional convention of 1850–51, which produced Indiana's second and current constitution, and to the U. S. House of Representatives in 1851. When the key issue of slavery in the territories arose, Hendricks supported the principle of popular sovereignty written into the Kansas-Nebraska Act of 1854, which theoretically opened those territories to slavery. This stance, however, led to his defeat in a re-election bid. But Hendricks was not out of public life long. Immediately afterward, he was appointed by President Franklin Pierce as commissioner of the General Land Office, a highly significant post at that time given the enormous number of land sales in an era of vigorous western expansion.

Hendricks spent four years at the land office, returning to his law practice in Shelbyville in 1859. The following year he moved to Indianapolis and established, with Oscar B. Hord, a new law firm, Hendricks and Hord. That firm later evolved, after Hendricks and Governor Conrad Baker essentially traded positions in 1872, into the large and distinguished firm of Baker and Daniels, which became in 2012 the huge multistate firm of Faegre Baker Daniels LLP. Hendricks also made the first of his three races for Indiana's gubernatorial office in 1860, which featured ABRAHAM LINCOLN and Stephen Douglas-style debates between Hendricks and Republican candidate Henry S. Lane, the eventual victor. By prearrangement, if Lane's election also resulted in a Republican majority in the state legislature, he would be elected by that body to the U.S. Senate. This happened, so Lieutenant Governor Morton moved into the executive office in January 1861 and thus became Indiana's powerful Civil War governor. In the meantime, the elections of 1862 having returned a Democratic majority to the state legislature, Hendricks was elected to join Lane in the U.S. Senate in 1863.

The Indiana Democrat's membership in the next three congresses, known respectively as the

Thomas Hendricks

Civil War, the Reconstruction, and the Impeachment congresses, featured his leading role among the tiny number of Democratic senators in those years, and Hendricks's principled opposition to the so-called Civil War Amendments, the Thirteenth, Fourteenth and Fifteenth, and to the removal of President Andrew Johnson from office on impeachment charges. Hendricks is also remembered for his widely quoted remark during one of the amendment debates, that "this is the white man's Government, made by the white man, for the white man." Obviously, Hendricks was no friend of the African American, but that did not mean, as his political opponents often charged, that he favored slavery, that he was a Copperhead (a northern Democrat opposed to the Civil War), and that he was anti-Lincoln and pro-South in his outlook. Instead, Hendricks was absolutely devoted to the Union and he always fully supported measures leading to the defeat of the Confederacy.

During his final years as a senator, after having been denied a second term, Hendricks made another run for the governor's seat in 1868. He was narrowly defeated by his friend and future law partner Baker, but in 1872, upon his third attempt, Hendricks was elected, also narrowly, over his opponent, General Thomas M. Browne, a Civil War veteran. Hendricks's gubernatorial years were marred by a severe national depression in the 1870s and unsettled conditions at home, but he was untouched by even a hint of scandal in the scandalous years of post-Civil War America generally.

Hendricks, although frequently called upon to run for president, saw his political career peak in two races for the vice presidency. In the first one in 1876, he was paired with New York Governor Samuel J. Tilden, and they were opposed by the governor of Ohio, Rutherford B. Hayes, and his running mate, William A. Wheeler, a congressman from New York. Tilden and Hendricks clearly won the popular vote, but their Electoral College votes were one short of the needed 185. On the other side, Hayes and Wheeler were twenty short of that number, with twenty votes in four states in dispute. A specially appointed fifteen-member Electoral Commission, composed of an equal number of senators, representatives, and Supreme Court justices, in a partisan vote of eight to seven, awarded all twenty of those votes to the Republican ticket.

Things were different in 1884 when Hendricks reluctantly, because of recurring health problems, again accepted second place on the Democratic ticket, headed by New York Governor Grover Cleveland. This time the Democratic ticket prevailed, but Hendricks served only eight months as vice president. He died in Indianapolis in the fall of 1885.

Hendricks's long years of service, his fame as an orator, his skill as a debater, and his principled dedication to his party and his country were such that an impressive monument, a towering bronze statue labeled simply "Hendricks," was erected on the statehouse grounds in 1890. Appropriately, this monument in the southeast corner of the grounds faces Hendricks's adopted hometown of Shelbyville.

RALPH D. GRAY

For Further Reading

Gray, Ralph D. "Thomas A. Hendricks: Spokesman for the Democracy." *Gentlemen from Indiana: National Party Candidates, 1836–1940*. Indianapolis: Indiana Historical Bureau, 1977.

Holcombe, John W., and Hubert M. Skinner. *Life and Public Services of Thomas A. Hendricks: With Selected Speeches and Writings*. Indianapolis: Carlon and Hollenbeck, 1886.

U.S. Congress. *Memorial Addresses on the Life and Character of Thomas A. Hendricks*. Delivered in the Senate and House of Representatives Forty-ninth Congress. First Session. Washington, DC: Government Printing Office, 1886.

Hesburgh, Theodore Martin, CSC
May 25, 1917–February 26, 2015

Roman Catholic priest, president of the University of Notre Dame, founding member of the U.S. Commission on Civil Rights, and recipient of Presidential Medal of Freedom and Congressional Gold Medal.

Father Theodore Hesburgh led the University of Notre Dame as its president from 1952 to 1987, raising the profile of Catholic education in the United States and putting Notre Dame at the forefront of American Catholic universities. He was an integral member of numerous commissions, initiatives, and other projects, bringing a Catholic perspective to American problems. His major contribution to Indiana was the growth of Notre Dame both physically and symbolically. During his presidency the school became a major economic engine in northern Indiana, employing thousands and drawing millions of dollars to the South Bend economy through tourism, especially as fans of the Fighting Irish flocked to Notre Dame stadium for football games—even though Hesburgh himself criticized excessive focus on university athletics.

The school also raised Indiana's educational profile, drawing students from the state, across the country, and around the globe to study under the university's iconic golden dome. Hesburgh's service to both the university and the nation stoked debate on the role of religion in American society, especially as Catholics became more involved in politics and the intellectual life of the nation as the twentieth century progressed.

Hesburgh was born in Syracuse, New York, to Pittsburgh Plate Glass executive Theodore Bernard and Anne Murphy Hesburgh. The younger Theodore, one of five children, followed a traditional path for Catholic boys at the time, with parochial school and altar service marking his daily life. Hesburgh claimed to have wanted to be a priest from the age of six. Priests from the Congregation of Holy Cross, which owned Notre Dame, visited Hesburgh's parish when the was twelve and made note of his enthusiasm for the priesthood. One of the priests, Father Thomas Duffy, helped steer him to Notre Dame for study after high school. Hesburgh attended both Notre Dame and the Jesuit-founded Pontifical Gregorian University in Rome, graduating in 1939. Hesburgh was ordained a priest for the Congregation of Holy Cross by Fort Wayne bishop John F. Noll in June 1943.

After receiving his doctorate in sacred theology from the Catholic University of America in 1945, Hesburgh joined the Notre Dame faculty and became head of the religion department in 1948. University president John J. Cavanaugh appointed Hesburgh executive vice president in 1949; he was promoted to president three years later at only age thirty-five. He remained in this capacity until his retirement in 1987, ending what was then the longest presidency in American higher education.

Hesburgh was a key force behind the 1967 Land O'Lakes Statement, issued by North American representatives of the International Federation of Catholic Universities. The brief document arose out of the idea "that the Catholic university not only can and must be a university in the authentic sense of the word . . . but that, in fact, a Catholic university properly developed can even more fully achieve the ideal of a true university." As such the federation sought to construct a system of higher education that would be of service

Father Theodore Hesburgh stands in front of the library later named in his honor.

both to global scholarship and the worldwide Catholic Church.

Hesburgh's vision for Notre Dame required implementing the Land O'Lakes statement to its fullest, which was not without controversy. The statement declared that Catholic universities should be free from all authority, including that of the Catholic Church, thus initiating a controversy that has continued to this day. Outside of the conflict, however, Hesburgh's commitment to excellence in Catholic higher education transformed Notre Dame into one of the most recognizable and prestigious Catholic universities in the United States.

Hesburgh's career extended far beyond Notre Dame and into numerous other American and international initiatives. His influence within the world of higher education helped him convince the Indiana Conference of Higher Education to support a pilot project for President John F. Kennedy's Peace Corps in 1961. When he was profiled by *Time* magazine in 1962 at the age of forty-five, Hesburgh was already serving as a founding member of the U.S. Civil Rights Commission, a member of the National Science Board and Rockefeller Foundation, and the Vatican's representative on the International Atomic Energy

Agency. He later served on President Gerald Ford's Presidential Clemency Board, the Select Commission on Immigration and Refugee Policy, and initiatives dedicated to eliminating nuclear weapons and fostering world peace.

His activism both on and off campus sometimes courted controversy. Hesburgh limited protests against the Vietnam War, inviting criticism from the student body. Although President Richard Nixon congratulated Hesburgh for his handling of the protests, the White House later pressured the priest to resign from the Civil Rights commission for his criticism of Nixon's antibusing policy.

Despite the criticism that Hesburgh faced over the course of his career, he was lauded by many Americans, Catholic and otherwise, for his contributions to ecumenism, civil rights, and world peace. His achievements in life were recognized with the awarding of the Presidential Medal of Freedom and the Congressional Gold Medal.

Hesburgh presided over numerous, and far-reaching, changes to Notre Dame. He worked diligently to address the contemporary lag of Catholic universities behind their secular counterparts: in his first ten years as president, the university added $12 million in new construction, tripled its endowment, almost doubled faculty salaries, and began construction on the $8 million library now bearing the famous "Word of Life" mural more commonly known as "Touchdown Jesus." In 1967 he shepherded the university's governing board to include lay trustees and fellows, ending the school's century-long leadership solely by clergy from the Congregation of Holy Cross. Remaining in the statutes was the requirement that the university's president be a priest from the Indiana Province of Holy Cross. Five years later, he oversaw the beginning of women's admission to the university. Even after his retirement in 1987, "Father Ted" came to Notre Dame's campus almost daily. He maintained an office on the thirteenth floor of the library that eventually bore his name and wrote his autobiography.

Hesburgh wrote that on the day he was ordained by Bishop Noll, he paused at the east entrance to Sacred Heart Church on Notre Dame's campus. "I read the dedication above the door: GOD, COUNTRY, NOTRE DAME. I would dedicate my life to that trinity, too." After a lifetime of service as a priest, educator, and public citizen, he celebrated Mass until the day of his death in 2015.

MICHAEL SKAGGS

For Further Reading

"God and Man at Notre Dame," *Time*, February 9, 1962.
Hesburgh, Theodore M. *God, Country, and Notre Dame* (New York: Doubleday, 1990).
———. *The Hesburgh Papers: Higher Values in Higher Education* (Kansas City, KS: Andrews and McMeel, 1979).

Hinkle, Paul D. "Tony"

December 19, 1899–September 22, 1992

Legendary coach of basketball, football, and baseball, and athletic director at Butler University.

Nearly everything about Paul Daniel "Tony" Hinkle brings to mind more innocent times. He earned his nickname in college because he liked spaghetti. He called everyone "kid," or by the name of their hometown. He recruited players with longhand, personal letters—like the one he wrote to Milan High School basketball star Bobby Plump on April 5, 1954, which is on display in the field house named for Hinkle in 1965.

> Bob,
> I want you to come to Butler. We have a swell school, and I know you will be satisfied here. We have a bunch of good boys. Also I have a man who has taken an interest in you and wants to help you through school financially.... Many schools probably will be after you, but just make up your mind to be with us. You can't go wrong.

Hinkle joined the Butler University athletics staff as an assistant coach with no fanfare in 1921, and his appointment as athletic director merited a one-paragraph mention in the March 20, 1926, *New York Times*. But by the time he retired at the end of the 1969–70 school year—as athletic director; football, baseball and basketball coach; director of physical health and full professor—he had created Butler's athletic reputation.

Hinkle's teams won a combined 1,060 games—560 in basketball, 335 in baseball, and 165 in football. In 1929 his Bulldogs basketball team won the national championship. (In another example of more innocent times, they received a letter notifying them of this achievement.) The *Butler Collegian* reported that Hinkle "was so overwhelmed that he was not in a talkative mood.... [H]e bore the honor in silence but had the happiest smile that has been seen around the fieldhouse for many days."

By all accounts, Hinkle always conducted himself simply and honorably. In 1948, when one of his basketball players was offered a bribe to keep Butler's victory under nine points, the player notified Hinkle, who immediately called the police. Butler won that game, 59–35. His stock line was, "The team that puts the ball in the basket the most times is going to win."

In his book *Tony Hinkle: Coach for All Seasons*, Butler alumnus and longtime Indianapolis broadcaster Howard Caldwell called that quip "pure Hinkle: subtle, uncomplicated and true." Caldwell added, "He had a knack of keeping his athletes from getting bogged down in complexity. By stressing fundamentals he was saying, let's keep to the basics and remember the uncomplicated purpose of what we're doing."

Hinkle could have left Butler for bigger opportunities, but, as he noted, "I love this school. A lot of people want to advance, advance, advance, advance and change jobs for a little extra money. I had chances to go other places and I could have made more money. But I didn't look at it too much as an advancement. I had everything here—a wonderful city, a good university."

Hinkle was born on December 19, 1899, in Logansport, Indiana. He earned nine letters in football, basketball and track from 1918 to 1920 at the University of Chicago, where he was assistant basketball coach alongside coaching great Amos Alonzo Stagg and studied for a degree in oil geology.

At Butler, Hinkle's football teams went undefeated in 1936, 1939, 1959, and 1961. In basketball, he led Butler to its first National Invitational Tournament berth in 1958 and to its first National Collegiate Athletic Association Tournament bid in 1962. He coached in the East-West College All-Star game, the Indiana-Kentucky College All-Star game and in the first game between the United States all-star team and the Soviet Union all-stars.

The only time Hinkle left Butler was during World War II—he served as a U.S. Navy lieutenant from 1942 to 1945 and coached at the Great Lakes (IL) Naval Training Center. In 1943 he coached the Great Lakes football team to a memorable upset of previously unbeaten University of Notre Dame.

Hinkle also served as the color analyst for the Indiana boys' high school basketball tournament broadcasts. "The thing about Hinkle," longtime Indianapolis sportswriter Bill Benner said, "is the breadth of the coaching tree. You can go to every corner of Indiana today and find a coach who can be traced to Hinkle or the Hinkle system. Postwar till the time he retired, there was a legion of players who were good enough to play for Butler but not to go into the pros. Most of them ended up coaching, and many of them ended up coaching in Indiana. He's been gone for a long time, but the Hinkle system and tree are very much alive."

Hinkle's influence extended to many other areas. He originated the orange basketball. Until the late 1950s, basketballs were dark brown, but he wanted a ball that could be better seen by players and fans. He worked with the Spalding Company to come up with a new ball, which was tested at the 1958 NCAA Finals in Louisville. The NCAA was impressed, and the new orange ball was adopted.

In the early 1930s, he initiated the Butler Relays, one of the leading track events in the nation. He was a founder of the Hoosier Classic, which brought together Indiana University, Purdue University, Notre Dame, and Butler in basketball. He introduced the Butler season-ticket plan, which helped make Butler basketball popular. He was a longtime member of the NCAA Rules Committee that helped the game evolve. In 1955, for example, the committee voted to widen the free-throw lane from six feet to twelve feet.

By the time his career was over, Hinkle had been inducted into the. Naismith Memorial Basketball Hall of Fame, the Helms Foundation Football Hall of Fame (as a coach), the Helms Foundation Basketball Hall of Fame (as player and coach), the Indiana Basketball Hall of Fame, the Indiana Football Hall of Fame and the National Association of Collegiate Directors of Athletics Hall of Fame.

"I am deeply grateful to Butler for having given me the rare opportunity to coach in a manner and to a degree that hardly exists anywhere else in the United States," Hinkle said when he announced his retirement. "I have had a wonderful life. I have always had the betterment of the school, the community and the kids in mind in anything I tried to do. After about fifty years of it, I believe it is time to step down and give others a chance." Hinkle never actually retired, though. He stayed on with Butler, as special assistant to the university president, until his death in 1992.

Alexander Jones, Butler's president at the time Hinkle stepped down from coaching, said this: "'Hink,' as he is known to his many colleagues and friends, is a truly remarkable person because of his tremendous physical ability, his exhaustive knowledge of sports, and his amazing ability to win against tremendous odds. Above all, he is a fine gentleman with rare insight into young men, whose welfare he has placed above victory."

MARC ALLAN

For Further Reading

Caldwell, Howard. *Tony Hinkle: Coach for All Seasons.* Bloomington: Indiana University Press, 1991.

Belzer, Jason. "Why Butler basketball holds the key to organizational success." *Forbes*, February 7, 2013. http://www.forbes.com/sites/jasonbelzer/2013/02/07/why-butler-basketball-holds-the-key-to-organizational-success/

Hohenberger, Frank

January 4, 1876–November 15, 1963

Photographer and journalist known for his images of Brown County and his *Indianapolis Star* column, "Down in the Hills o' Brown."

No one raised the public awareness of Brown County more than photojournalist Frank M. Hohenberger. His iconic photographs shaped outsider perceptions and expectations of the county as a place of rustic beauty and a land where pioneer life persisted. For more than forty years, he fixed to film the county's striking landscapes, bucolic buildings, and portraits of rural residents, making his photographic catalog an unrivaled snapshot of Indiana history. Arguably Indiana's best-known photographer, Hohenberger's black-and-white images continue to garner attention from historians, collectors, and enthusiasts fifty years after his death. He was approaching middle age when he began his life's work of photographing Brown County.

Born in Defiance, Ohio, in 1876 and orphaned at the age of five, Hohenberger was raised by his grandparents. He learned to work as a printer from his uncle, but in 1904 took up photography. He worked for a time as a composer at the *Indianapolis Star*, but lost his job when the paper came under new management. At the age of forty-one, he quit a job managing an Indianapolis camera shop and moved to the rolling hills of Brown County to pursue his passion for photography. It was 1917 and the desire to artistically capture the county's picturesque scenery and log cabins proved to be a life-changing decision. He set up his first studio in the old Odd Fellows Lodge in Nashville in a room once used by famed wood-block artist Gustave Baumann. Hohenberger combed the countryside practicing his craft and perfecting his talents; however few of his earliest Brown County images remain.

By 1923 Hoh, as his friends called him, had his own periodic column in the Sunday edition of the *Star*, titled "Down in the Hills o' Brown." Usually anchored on one of his photos, the column either focused on an interesting encounter between the photographer and a local or it read as a running commentary about humorous happenings in the county. His fictionalized accounts of real people often contrasted the old-time ways of Brown County with modern activities in Indianapolis—fueling the belief that the county was a place frozen in time.

The photographer captured nostalgic images of Brown County's abandoned log buildings, rural landscapes, and people engaged in practices associated with Indiana's "pioneer" past. He crafted

Frank Hohenberger

striking snapshots of people making brooms, playing fiddles, weaving rugs, and swapping stories and these images came to represent the idealized "Brown County Natives."

Hohenberger, however, was not the first to cast his gaze toward Brown County. Humorist FRANK MCKINNEY "KIN" HUBBARD's character Abe Martin had already piqued the appetite of urban dwellers for strange stories and odd saying from the county. However, while Hubbard rendered the place in simple line drawings and short captions, Hohenberger 's images offered the "Hills o' Brown" in photographic realism. Nevertheless, both Hubbard and Hohenberger created a Brown County shaped by their antimodern sentiments. Hohenberger's images struck a chord with customers who desired nostalgic images of the county. The entrepreneur confided to his diary, "Photograph the old things which are fast disappearing. . . .When you picture something that takes the observer back to boyhood days on the farm, you have hit the vital spot in the region of their pocketbook."

Although the journalist often changed the names in his humorous accounts, many locals took offense at his characterization of the county as backward; some especially disapproved of his use of the term "native," thinking it a pejorative expression. Nevertheless, after decades of living in and writing about the county, Hohenberger became as much a fixture in the community as any of his rural characters.

Hohenberger's best-known photograph, *The Liars' Bench*, was taken in 1923 and shows six locals relaxing on the bench in front of the courthouse, presumably engaged in swapping tall tales. The iconic image sold well both locally and by mail order, but Hohenberger's stories about local men lazing around town, pitching horseshoes, and exchanging yarns caused many to feel he presented the county in a bad light. Perhaps his stories conjured the way he thought life should be in Brown County. Known to frequent the liars' bench from time to time, Hohenberger pitched horseshoes most days in the summer and enjoyed his life as a bachelor, having left his estranged wife, Grace, to live in Nashville.

Hohenberger not only photographed people and places near his Brown County home, but also captured pictures from throughout the state and beyond. However, he often sought the same subject matter for his images wherever he went. For example, while in Brown County he photographed Dick Griffith at the wheel throwing pottery, but he also shot images of potters on his South Carolina trip in 1929 and during his tour of Mexico in 1940. He also took photos of run-down buildings and nature's beauty everywhere he traveled.

Hohenberger's photographic collection contains more than 17,000 prints and negatives, which the photographer donated to the Lilly Library at Indiana University. He also left them his 573-page diary that contains his notes and writings from October 1, 1917, to April 27, 1957. In addition, many of his images are now available online at the Frank M. Hohenberger Photograph Collection. In 1952 Hohenberger published a book of his writings and images using the same title as his *Star* column. The small, privately published book highlights his many talents, since he also composed and printed the collection. After his death in 1963, his work was the topic of two additional books, Dillon Bustin's *If You Don't Outdie Me* (1982) and Cecil Byrd's *Frank M. Hohenberger's Indiana Photographs* (1993).

Perhaps, however, the best place to see his work is the Old Country Store, adjacent to the Nashville House in Brown County. On the south wall dozens of portraits hang, each hand printed by the photographer. An assemblage he called his "nativity" the collection contains the best of his portraits of locals, including Valentine Penrose, a 100-year-old fox hunter; Allie Ferguson, the proprietor of one of the old inns in town; and Grandma Barnes, the 1929 Spring Blossom Festival Queen. Among the last of the images printed by Hohenberger, the sepia-toned pictures are the culmination of decades of work in Brown County. The collection reflects both the photographer's talent and artistic vision, but moreover it represents the rich and complex visual legacy Hohenberger left to Indiana.

JON KAY

For Further Reading

Bustin, Dillon. *If You Don't Outdie Me: The Legacy of Brown County*. Bloomington: Indiana University Press, 1982.

Hohenberger, Frank M. Frank M. Hohenberger Photograph Collection. Indiana University Digital Library Program, http://webapp1.dlib.indiana.edu/hohenberger/index.jsp.

Sylvester, Lorna Lutes. "'Down in the Hills o' Brown County:' Photographs by Frank M. Hohenberger." *Indiana Magazine of History* 72 (September 1976): 189–249.

Holman, Jesse L.

October 24, 1784–March 28, 1842

Indiana Supreme Court Justice, member of the Indiana Territorial General Assembly, state and federal judge, county prosecutor, minister, and builder of historical home Veraestau.

Jesse L. Holman, often called a "Renaissance Man" because of his wide-ranging fields of endeavor, made numerous contributions to the development of Indiana from its territorial status through its first quarter of a century of statehood. He served the state in numerous positions at critical times in the its evolution, including judge of the first Indiana Supreme Court and representative in the territorial general assembly. He was active in the founding of Franklin College and served on the Indiana University Board of Trustees in its early years. Perhaps his most long-lasting legacy is Veraestau, the home he built on the banks of the Ohio River in Dearborn County.

Holman moved to the Indiana Territory from Kentucky in 1810 and settled in Dearborn County. There he built his now-famous home Veraestau on a hill overlooking the Ohio River. He created the name from the Latin words for spring, summer, and fall, omitting the word for winter because he did not want the "winter outside to be reflected within." The two-story home has been described as "sturdy and unpretentious," the same words often used to describe Holman himself. From its humble beginnings, Veraestau has undergone three major restorations in the Greek Revival style, carried out by heirs of Holman and subsequent owners. It is listed in the National Register of Historic Places and is owned and operated by Indiana Landmarks.

Holman became a leader in the social and political life of Dearborn County, and it was there that he began his life in public service. In 1811 territorial governor WILLIAM HENRY HARRISON appointed him prosecuting attorney for Dearborn County. Eighteen months later Holman received a pro tempore appointment as prosecuting attorney for Jefferson County. In 1814 Holman filled the vacancy of Isaac Dunn, Dearborn County's representative to the territorial general assembly, and was elected to the Fifth General Assembly in August 1814. At the close of the first session, Holman was appointed by territorial governor Thomas Posey to be the presiding judge of the Second Judicial Circuit, comprised of Clark, Harrison, Jefferson, and Washington Counties. He served in that capacity from 1814 until 1816, and during part of that time he was also the presiding judge of the Third Judicial Circuit, comprised of the counties of Dearborn, Franklin, Wayne, and Switzerland.

Simultaneously, the movement for Indiana statehood was occurring. On June 10, 1816, the new Indiana Constitution was ratified and sent to Congress. Indiana was admitted to the Union on December 11, 1816, and in the ensuing months the framework of the newly established government began to take shape. The Supreme Court was the last of the three branches of government to be formed, and on December 28, 1816, the state's first governor, JONATHAN JENNINGS, appointed Holman as one of the first three judges to the Indiana Supreme Court.

During his tenure Holman was confronted with two important cases relating to slavery. In 1820 the court heard the contentious case of *State v. Lasselle*, which raised the issue of the legal status of slaves owned prior to Indiana's statehood. The Supreme Court ruled that the language of the constitution, "there should neither be slavery nor involuntary servitude in the State," meant that "slavery could have no existence in the State of Indiana." One year later, in the case of *In re Clark*, Holman wrote an opinion ruling that contracts for personal services, i.e. indentured servitude, could not be enforced by the state because they would produce a condition of servitude equivalent to a "state of absolute slavery." Holman's term on the court ended in 1830 when Governor James B. Ray refused to appoint him to a third term, ostensibly for political reasons. Ray delayed the appointments to the court hoping to gain support for his election as U.S. senator, which would be made by the state legislature. He eventually replaced Holman and James Scott with two members of the state senate who were more likely to lend support to his election to the U.S. Senate seat two years later.

Holman's judicial career, however, did not end. In 1835 Benjamin Parke, the first federal district judge of Indiana, died. Holman wrote to friends to intercede on his behalf with President Andrew Jackson, and the president gave Holman an interim appointment until the end of the next session of Congress. Opposition to a permanent appointment arose, however. Holman's opponents accused him of being anti-Jacksonian because he cast his presidential electoral vote for John Quincy Adams. There was also an issue as to whether Holman was an abolitionist because he freed his slaves upon entering Indiana from Kentucky, where Holman had been born. However, Holman freed the slaves because it was illegal to transport slaves into Indiana. Holman was only a moderate abolitionist who believed in establishing a colony in Africa for ex-slaves. Holman was also accused of being an unqualified religious fanatic, which he successfully disputed. Despite the opposition, Jackson appointed Holman to the judgeship on March 29, 1836, and he held the position until his death on March 28, 1842.

Although not a religious fanatic as claimed, Holman was a man of strong faith and played an active role in his Baptist religion. In 1820 Holman and other elders and laymen organized a Baptist church in Aurora in 1820. In 1834 Holman was ordained a minister by the church, and he preached at the church without pay when he was available. Even when Holman was sufficiently entrenched in his public duties, he frequently addressed his fellow citizens on biblical and religious topics.

His involvement with the Baptist religion was responsible for one of Holman's important contributions to higher education in the state. He believed education was key to overcoming opposition by fellow Baptists to the missionary movement and other benevolent projects that Holman strongly supported. He believed that this resistance was largely due to the poor scholastic attainment of Baptist ministers. In 1835 the Indiana Baptist Education Society in Indianapolis chose the town of Franklin as the location for the Indiana Manual Labor Institute that later became Franklin College. Holman helped write the first constitution for the institute, was named to the first board of trustees, and was elected as one of two vice presidents of the board. He served in that capacity from 1835 until 1839. Holman was invited to become the principal of the institute in 1837 but declined because of his responsibilities on the federal bench to which he had recently been appointed. Holman remained on the board until his death.

Holman also had a role in IU's development. When Indiana College, originally known as Indiana Seminary, was renamed Indiana University in 1838, Holman was named to the board of trustees. His support for these two prominent institutions of higher education in the state was due to his progressive philosophy that led him to encourage others to seek higher scholarly pursuits and to think for themselves. Holman endeavored to merge his deep Baptist faith with his pursuit of secular knowledge and commitment to public service.

It was fitting that Holman died at his beloved Veraestau, in Dearborn County, in the town of Aurora, which he was responsible for naming. Aurora means dawn, which comes before the rising sun, and he reportedly did this to spite the town of Rising Sun just a few miles downriver. It was in Dearborn County that he started his career in public service, and where he had contributed much to the advancement of the community—from creating the plat for the town to serving as town trustee, and later as superintendent of public schools. In his fifty-eight years, Holman achieved a distinguished record of public service to his community and to the state. At his memorial service, U.S. Supreme Court Justice John McClean said of Holman, "he had no motive but to discharge his public duty uprightly. He has left behind him the influence of high moral example."

JOHN G. BAKER

For Further Reading

Baker, John G. "Jesse L. Holman." In *Justices of the Indiana Supreme Court*. Edited by Linda C. Gugin and James E. St. Clair. Indianapolis: Indiana Historical Society Press, 2010.

Blake, George. "Jesse Lynch Holman: Pioneer Hoosier." *Indiana Magazine of History* 34 (March 1943):25–51.

———. *The Holmans of Veraestau*. Oxford, OH: Mississippi Valley Press, 1943.

Hopper, Floyd

November 1, 1909–July 2, 1984

Artist, businessman, and teacher who painted in the Regionalist style and was later known as "Dean of Indiana Watercolorists."

At the beginning of World War II, Floyd Hopper, one of Indiana's most promising Regionalist painters, left his studio and entered the noisy, smoke-filled world of the foundry. Almost twenty years later, he left his successful business to begin again as an artist. Never looking back, Hopper became Indiana's best-known and most-loved watercolorist. In each distinctive part of his career, he made significant contributions.

Born in Martinsville, Indiana, he graduated from West Baden High School in 1929. He had planned to go to Purdue University to study engineering, but the availability of a scholarship led him to the John Herron School of Art in Indianapolis (also known as the John Herron Art Institute). Founded in 1902, Herron offered classes in drawing, painting, design, and composition that were originally taught by Hoosier Group artists J. Ottis Adams, William Forsyth, and Otto Stark. By the time Hopper entered the school in 1929, a number of endowments, including the Mary Milliken Fund, provided scholarships, and a new Beaux Arts-style building had just opened that offered increased studio, lecture, and exhibit space. Hopper studied fine art, commercial art, and scenic design with such teachers as Wayman Adams, Clifton Wheeler, and Paul Hadley.

After receiving a four-year certificate from Herron in 1933, Hopper attended the Pennsylvania Academy of Fine Arts summer school at Chester Springs, studying with Eliot O'Hara and Francis Schoonover, after which he returned to Indianapolis and Herron, where he continued his studies and began making a living through art commissions, odd jobs, and selling paintings at very modest prices. In 1933 Donald M. Mattison was appointed director of Herron, and a bachelor of fine arts degree was created. Hopper received his BFA from Herron in 1940 along with a Mary Milliken Travel Scholarship. Unable to travel in Europe because of the onset of World War II, he toured the Northeast, the West, Canada, and Mexico.

As a young artist, Hopper was greatly influenced by Regionalist painters of the "American Scene": Thomas Hart Benton, Grant Wood, John Steuart Curry, and others. He was twenty-three in 1933 when Benton came to Indiana to create his monumental mural cycle *The Social History of Indiana*, which would bring Regionalism to the attention of thousands of visitors to the Chicago World's Fair. Benton painted in an empty dance hall in Indianapolis, and Hopper would have had opportunities to see the master at work.

Hopper was among a number of young Indiana artists who set out to paint the "Hoosier Scene" in realistic terms. Painting primarily in oil, Hopper depicted in his work such themes as the resiliency of rural life during tough times, the nobility of common folk, and the sterility of the urban environment. His best-known paintings in the genre include *Thirteenth and Roosevelt* (1935), *A Summer Rain* (1935), *Red Bandana* (1937), *Our Alley* (1939), and *The Stone Quarry* (1940). Along with their thematic depiction of workers, small towns, farms, and bleak urban environments, these paintings also revealed Hopper's facility with shadow, light, and ominous skies, which would become his trademark.

World War II brought about an end to Regionalism by discrediting what was perceived as its implicit isolationism and nationalism. It also brought an end to the first chapter of Hopper's career. In 1941 Hopper joined the firm Hetherington and Berner, an Indianapolis steel fabricator, as a pattern maker, no doubt helped by his Herron training and a government sponsored pattern-making class. A few years later, with coworkers, he founded Noblesville Casting Company, which manufactured auto and hydraulic parts.

Hopper made a decision in 1958 to devote the rest of his life to his art. He sold his interest in the company he had founded and began teaching classes and entering exhibitions again. In 1966 Hopper told a reporter for the *Indianapolis Star*: "I thought I could paint during that twelve-year period, but as the business got bigger the less painting I could do." A self-portrait he painted at this time reflects the clarity and deliberateness of his decision. Staring squarely at the viewer, past what appears to be a newly stretched canvas, he displays a calm sense of purpose in his decision to face the future as an artist. This 1958 painting is Hopper's only self-portrait.

Although Hopper continued throughout his life to accept commissions for oil painting, he chose to make his living primarily as a watercolorist, and it was as such that he would make his most significant contribution as an artist. He had displayed a special skill with watercolor since he had taken classes in the 1930s with O'Hara and Francis Chapin. In 1973 Hopper said: "I like the facility of the medium. You can push colors around and tell almost immediately whether you're right or wrong." Working from slide photographs that he took on trips with his wife, Hazel, head of the Indiana Room at the Indiana State Library for many years, he painted Indiana scenes as well as scenes from Michigan, Wisconsin, and the East Coast. He was always looking for an arrangement of shapes and colors that reflected a mood, and that mood was generally revealed through dramatic lighting and changing skies. A retrospective exhibition, held at the Indianapolis Art League in 1986 after Hopper's death, featured primarily oil paintings of his early work from the years 1934 to 1944. A reviewer commented: "His skies are patterned with dark clouds and patches of blue: we sense the light could change instantly." The reviewer also stated: "In most cases, Hopper's later paintings are not as strong as his early works. Some of the watercolors from this period are formally strong, but they are thematically weak."

The exhibition, like the review, missed the point regarding Hopper's later work in which the themes of his earlier days gave way to technique and mood. Watercolor allowed him to paint faster, do more paintings, teach a wider variety of techniques, and sell paintings at reasonable prices that even his students could afford. He taught out of his Cherry Tree Hill Studio in his home in Noblesville and also at the Indianapolis Art League and developed a loyal following of students. Hopper won many awards during his career, one place listing 143 prizes in 232 competitive exhibitions, but he made his greatest impact through the paintings that hang in homes around the country and through the work of his students who carry on his tradition and philosophy.

In 1990 the Anderson Fine Arts Center mounted a retrospective exhibition of more than fifty of Hopper's watercolors, bringing to a fitting conclusion the second phase of his remarkable artistic career. Hazel attended, as did a number of Hopper's students. Former student Irene Tucker remembered Hopper saying to her, "You should establish a tone and make everything go with it. Values and color should reflect mood." He also told her, "You create your mood, but you live with what happens to the watercolor." Hopper deliberately chose to "live with what happens to the watercolor," and Indiana is the richer for it.

J. KENT CALDER

For Further Reading

Calder, J. Kent. "Floyd D. Hopper: Dean of Indiana Watercolorists." *Traces of Indiana and Midwestern History* 3, no. 1 (Winter 1991): 34–39.

Nagler, Katherine C. *Floyd D. Hopper Retrospective Exhibition, 1935–1969.* Indianapolis: Indianapolis Art League, 1986.

Owings, Frank, and Patte Owens. *The Edge of Town: Painting the Indiana Scene, 1932–1948.* Indianapolis: Indianapolis Art League, 1989.

Simons, Richard S. "From Pigments to Pig Iron." *Indianapolis Star Magazine*, March 25, 1951.

Hovey, Edmund Otis
July 15, 1801–March 10, 1877

A principal founder of Wabash College and long-time trustee.

Wabash College was Edmund Otis Hovey's life's work. One of the college's first trustees, Hovey was responsible for hiring Wabash's first three presidents; for persuading CALEB MILLS, the father of public education in Indiana, to become Wabash's first faculty member; and for raising the lion's share of the funds that were necessary for the college to survive its early years. A man of varied interests, Hovey taught at Wabash for more than forty years and served as the college's librarian, treasurer, and in many other capacities. He also preached on occasion and wrote an early history of Wabash.

Hovey was born on July 15, 1801, in Hanover, New Hampshire, to Roger Hovey, a blacksmith, and Martha Freeman. At age eight his family moved to Thetford, Vermont. Hovey attended the Thetford academy and in 1821 he joined the Thetford Congregational Church. Church members, and then later a local judge, sponsored Hovey's studies and gave him boarding for a period of time.

In 1828 Hovey graduated, with Phi Beta Kappa honors, from Dartmouth. According to one account, Mills, Wabash's first instructor, was Hovey's "most intimate friend of all" at Dartmouth. In 1831 Hovey graduated from Andover Theological Seminary, a Congregationalist institution in Massachusetts. During his time at Andover, he supported himself doing mission work and working as a carpenter and a blacksmith. On July 16, 1831, Hovey wrote to Mary Carter, a friend in Vermont, regarding his meeting with a representative of the American Home Missionary Society that he was ready to devote his life to serving as a missionary in the Mississippi Valley. In the same note, he offered a marriage proposal: "The question arises, dear Mary, whether you can on so short notice join your interests with mine & in that sacred union which time alone can dissolve, consecrate life to the service of Christ in that interesting field of labor." Thereafter, Hovey signed a contract with the AHMS and he entered into an agreement of a different sort with Mary.

The Hoveys were married on October 5, 1831, in Andover, Massachusetts, and soon moved to the Coal Creek settlement in Fountain County, Indiana, where Hovey was a missionary. Their son, Horace C., was born in Fountain County on January 28, 1833.

On November 21, 1832, Hovey and a group of Presbyterian ministers and elders met in James Thomson's home in Crawfordsville, Indiana. The following day they traveled together to inspect the land that had been given to what would become Wabash College and to select the site where its buildings would be constructed. According to an early history of Indiana, after making the selection, "they all knelt down in the snow, and by prayer dedicated the ground to liberty and to God." One year later, on December 3, 1833, Mills and his twelve students gathered for the college's first class.

On April 19, 1834, an advertisement appeared in the *Crawfordsville Record* for what was then known as the Wabash Manual Labor College and Teacher's Seminary. The ad, which provides perspective regarding Wabash when it was still in its infancy, advised readers that an instructor had been procured for the preparatory and teachers' departments, that both departments were "regularly organized," and that qualified teachers would be required to pass "an honorable examination in the studies of this course" to graduate. The ad noted that board was one dollar per week "exclusive of washing," that room rent was one dollar per session (students being required to bring their own bed and bedding), and that tuition ranged from five dollars to $7.50 per session depending upon the department. The notice said that "[t]he Trustees have made arrangements by which students can labor from one to three hours daily, and thus preserve their muscular energy and contribute very essentially to lessen the expense of their education." The college's name was shortened to Wabash College in 1839, and the emphasis on manual labor was eliminated as well.

Hovey's imprint on the evolution of the institution began in 1832, with his service as one of the original trustees. Hovey and the college presidents with whom he worked for more than four decades built the reputation of the institution while securing funding, hiring qualified instructors, and dealing with issues relating to administration. It was generally conceded by the eight other founders of the college "that it was Hovey who did the most for the college."

In 1834 Hovey became the second faculty member of the college when he was appointed professor of natural and moral science and of mathematics. He reportedly taught nearly every class Wabash offered other than "the calculus." He was also noted for his large collection of shells and minerals. He brought an extensive collection with him to Wabash, and he added a large number of specimens that he discovered in the famous crinoid beds of Crawfordsville. Four years before his death, the college managed to house his entire collection in one building. Along with the addition of some notable and large collections more room was needed, and in 1833 the college remodeled the gym to house all of the collections. The remodeled building was named Hovey Museum. In 1899 the collection was scattered to various sites on campus and eventually sent to other museums.

Simultaneously with his faculty duties, Hovey in 1834 was appointed the college agent to the East with responsibility for raising money and recruiting a president—someone who was a "good administrator and a money getter." His mission was partially fulfilled when he succeeded in

Edmund Hovey

persuading Elihu Baldwin, a Presbyterian minister from New York, to accept the position of president. Hovey and Baldwin set to work to raise funds. With support from various religious groups and congregations in the northeast they were able to raise a substantial amount of money.

The first faculty meeting with Baldwin as president was held on October 28, 1835. Hovey was appointed clerk of the faculty, and for thirty-nine years his signature was the only one to appear on records of faculty proceedings.

On September 23, 1838, the same year that Wabash celebrated its first graduating class of two students, a fire destroyed the college's new building and its contents. Five days after the fire, the Hoveys' daughter, Mary Freeman, was born in Crawfordsville. The Hovey children ultimately chose to become educators. Mary Freeman served as Wabash's first female professor and thereafter as a language professor at Kansas Agricultural College. Horace C., often described as the "father of modern cave exploration," became a home missionary, a Presbyterian minister, and a geologist with a national reputation. His *Hand-Book of the Mammoth Cave of Kentucky* notes that he "imbibed" his early taste for science from his father.

In addition to his devotion to Wabash, Hovey was passionate about certain societal reforms, which he viewed as critical to the country and the church. In 1843 Indiana's Presbyterian Synod formed an Anti-Slavery Committee that was chaired by Hovey's brother-in-law, Wabash College president Charles White. Two years later, on October 14, 1845, Hovey and a number of other Presbyterian ministers and church elders of the Constitutional Presbyterian Church published a notice in the *New Lisbon Anti-Slavery Bugle*, an Ohio newspaper, that called for a convention of the ministers and elders of the United States who believed "slaveholding is a sin" and for those who attended the convention "if possible to devise a remedy for the evil." While the movement did not gain significant traction and the "remedy for the evil" would be nearly two decades in coming, the message in the call to action was powerful and says a great deal about Hovey and his colleagues.

On March 10, 1877, Hovey died at his home in Crawfordsville, after suffering for two weeks from a bilious-intermittent fever. Mills, Hovey's friend and colleague of many years, was at his bedside. The *Crawfordsville Star* reported that Hovey's funeral services, which were held at the Center Church, "were attended by a great concourse." Another report noted that "every church bell in the city was tolled and all places of business were closed as the long procession wound its way to Oak Hill [cemetery], led by the officers and students of the institution."

DONALD B. KITE SR.

For Further Reading

History of Montgomery County, Indiana: With Personal Sketches of Representative Citizens. Indianapolis: A. W. Bowen and Company, 1911.

Hovey, Horace. "Edmund O. Hovey." *The Indianian* 5 (1900): 159–65.

Osborne, James I., and Theodore G. Gronert. *Wabash College: The First 100 Years, 1832–1932.* Crawfordsville, IN: R. E. Banta, 1932.

Swift, Beth. Dear Old Wabash, Wabash College Archivist Blog postings, www.wabash.edu/blog/.

Vanderstel, David G. "To Outfit Destitute Young Men for the Ministry: Thetford's Response to the Call for Evangelism." *Vermont History* 69 (2001): 79–80.

Hubbard, Frank McKinney "Kin"

September 1, 1868–December 26, 1930

Journalist, cartoonist, and creator of Abe Martin.

Irvington, a planned community on Indianapolis's east side, has been home to a number of famous Hoosiers through the years. One day in the 1910s, a camera-laden tourist was searching through the area for the home of Frank McKinney "Kin" Hubbard, creator of cracker-barrel philosopher Abe Martin, whose folksy brand of humor graced the *Indianapolis News*'s back page for twenty-six years.

Finally finding Hubbard's home, the visitor approached a disheveled-looking gardener working on the author's lawn and asked him if he thought Mr. Hubbard would mind if he took a few snapshots of the house. "What if Mr. Hubbard does care?" the man asked the tourist. "How will he ever know?"

The tourist was closer to his favorite author than he knew. The man he questioned was Hubbard himself, who was involved in two of his favorite hobbies: gardening and being mischievous. His behavior with the tourist merely reinforced a fellow *News* employee's observation that Hubbard was "a genial Dapper Dan with the soul of an imp."

Operating out of the fictional town of Bloom

Center in Brown County, Abe Martin delighted millions of readers across the country with such sage wisdom as "It ain't no disgrace t' be poor, but it might as well be," and "When a feller says, 'It hain't th' money, but th' principle o' th' thing,' it's the money." Hubbard, the *News* noted upon his death in 1930, possessed the uncanny ability "of seeing life clearly, and touching it kindly in the places where it should be touched." Although biting at times, Hubbard's humor could always be counted on to produce a laugh and leave behind no trace of bitterness.

Hubbard displayed an artistic flair at an early age. He recalled that from the time he was old enough to hold a pair of scissors, he could "cut from blank paper any kind of an animal with a correctness and deftness that was almost creepy." This artistic talent, however, did not translate into classroom success, as Hubbard dropped out of school in his hometown of Bellefontaine, Ohio, before the seventh grade and took a job in a paint shop.

With the election of Democrat Grover Cleveland to his first term as president in 1884, Hubbard's father, Thomas, was rewarded for his lifelong devotion to the party with an appointment as postmaster. Kin clerked at the post office for a time, but it did not cure his ambition for the theatrical life. During his employment, he made trips to the South as a silhouette artist and even enrolled in the Jefferson School of Art in Detroit for a time before quitting.

Frank McKinney "Kin" Hubbard at his drawing board

Hubbard's love for the theater paid off in a way that set the course for his future career. After witnessing a local performance of the Grand Bellefontaine Operatic Minstrels and Professor Tom Wright's Operatic Solo Orchestra, Hubbard wrote to a friend in Indianapolis about the show, embellishing his remarks with some drawings. Impressed with Hubbard's artwork, the friend showed the drawings to John H. Holliday, *Indianapolis News* owner and editor. The friend then urged Hubbard to come to Indiana and try for a job on the *News*. Hubbard agreed, but once in the city he waited for nearly a week before gaining enough courage to approach the newspaper for work. Finally given a job, Hubbard remembered the editor remarking as a salary was agreed upon ($12 a week), "I reckon you've got to live."

Hired in 1891, Hubbard remained at the *News* for three years. During that time he produced a number of works for the newspaper, but, as he remembered, was "always handicapped by not knowing how to draw. I could execute rude, sketchy caricatures that were readily recognized, but I knew nothing of composition, light and shade, and perspective." Although apprehensive about his position, Hubbard did manage to enjoy his life in Indianapolis. Given an annual pass to local theaters, he never missed a show or, when they came to town, a circus.

The end of his first stint at the *News* came with the hiring of a new managing editor who wanted, according to Hubbard, "a real artist who could draw anything." Asked by the editor to produce a drawing of an angel for Easter, Hubbard did not panic, but hurried to the city editor and asked for his help. The sympathetic editor found an art student to furnish the needed illustration (described by Hubbard as a "production that would have made a circus wagon woodcarver turn green with envy") and Hubbard's job was saved for a time.

His time at the *News*, however, would be short. Called upon to draw pictures of the intricately restored interiors for a number of city banks, Hubbard threw up his hands and departed Indianapolis for the safety of the family home in Bellefontaine. During the next few years, Hubbard kept busy by again visiting the South, driving a mule team in Chattanooga, serving as a gatekeeper for a Cincinnati amusement park, and working as an artist for the *Cincinnati Tribune* and *Mansfield News*. In 1899 Hubbard was hired by the *Indianapolis Sun* and during the two years he worked at the *Sun* "really made more progress as an artist . . . than I had in all the years before," he said. Hubbard rejoined the *News* as an artist in the fall of 1901 and worked there for the rest of his life.

Upon his return to the *News*, Hubbard became well-known for his caricatures of state political figures, particularly Indiana legislators. In working with politicians as subjects, he preferred to draw those with whiskers and hair, as caricaturing bald lawmakers was "just like drawing a cocoanut." Although a collection of these drawings was published in 1903, Hubbard's lasting fame came not from politicians, but from a rustic character that made a habit of commenting on legislators' foibles all the way from the wild country of Brown County.

In 1904, while traveling on trains during campaign trips by Democratic presidential candidate William Jennings Bryan and Republican vice presidential candidate Charles Fairbanks, Hubbard found that at campaign's end he had some extra material. After first experimenting with such names as Seth Martin, Steve Martin, and Abe Hulsizer, Hubbard finally hit on the right one—Abe Martin. On December 17, 1904, the Abe Martin character made his first appearance. The drawing showed a smiling, whiskered gentleman staring at a playbill featuring a scantily clad (for those days) woman. At the drawing's bottom, the character commented: "If I thought that blamed troupe done everything it has pictures fer, I'd stay over this evening and go home on the interubin." The feature, Hubbard laconically recalled years later, "caused some favorable comment and it was decided to continue it."

On February 3, 1905, Hubbard moved Abe Martin to Brown County, where he remained for the rest of his career. Finding that sometimes he had things to say that Abe Martin would be unlikely to utter, Hubbard added to his cast with such delightful country neighbors as spinster Miss Fawn Lippincut; senior citizen Uncle Niles Turner; teacher Professor Alexander Tansey; editor and publisher of the *Bloom Center Weekly Sliphorn* the Hon. Ex-Editor Cale Fluhart; businessman Tell Binkley; and many others. In 1910 Hubbard signed with the George Matthew Adams Syndicate and Abe Martin was soon appearing in newspapers in approximately two hundred cities.

On December 26, 1930, at his new North Meridian Street home, the sixty-two-year-old Hubbard died from a heart attack. Tributes to Hubbard flooded the *News* following his death. Although touted as "the humorists' humorist" by David Laurance Chambers of Indianapolis's Bobbs-Merrill Company, Hubbard probably would not have let the praise go to his head, preferring to remember what Abe Martin once said: "Flattery won't hurt you if you don't swallow it."

RAY E. BOOMHOWER

For Further Reading

Boomhower, Ray. "A 'Dapper Dan with the Soul of an Imp': Kin Hubbard, Creator of Abe Martin." *Traces of Indiana and Midwestern History* 5, no. 4 (Fall 1993): 38–45.

Hubbard, Kin, and David S Hawes. *The Best of Kin Hubbard: Abe Martin's Sayings and Wisecracks, Abe's Neighbors, His Almanack, Comic Drawings*. Bloomington: Indiana University Press, 1984.

Kelly, Fred C. *The Life and Times of Kin Hubbard, Creator of Abe Martin*. New York: Farrar, Straus and Young, 1952.

Hulman, Anton Jr. "Tony"

February 11, 1901–October 27, 1977

Businessman, civic leader, philanthropist, and savior of the Indianapolis Motor Speedway.

Meeting Tony Hulman could be quite a disarming experience. In spite of his immense wealth, power, and influence, the owner of the Indianapolis Motor Speedway (among numerous other entities) was a most pleasant, soft-spoken, bashful, and unassuming individual. There was no entourage, no limousines, no sirens, no barking orders, and no tension. He typically wore business attire bearing telltale traces of dropped cigarette ash, parted his hair (until about 1970) down the center, never raised his voice, had a great weakness for chocolate, and always seemed to be grinning and shyly thanking everyone for coming.

While formally Anton Hulman Jr., he was simply "Tony" rather than Mr. Hulman, and it was almost as if the Indianapolis Motor Speedway was the manor, Hulman the beloved lord of the realm, and all of the people in the surrounding neighborhoods of Eagledale and the town of Speedway his adoring subjects. They even spoke as if he did everything himself with comments such as, "Tony's going to have to build some new grandstands," "Tony's going to have to paint that fence," and so on.

Born in Terre Haute on February 11, 1901,

Hulman was the grandson of a German immigrant who had landed in Cincinnati, created a very successful wholesale grocery concern, and then moved to Terre Haute. By the time young Tony came along, his family was affluent enough to send him to Worcester Academy and then to Yale University, from which he graduated in 1924 with a degree in engineering from its Sheffield Scientific School. Very much the star athlete, he had been named the most outstanding high school pole vaulter in the United States for 1919 by the Amateur Athletic Association, and he was a member of Yale's undefeated football team in 1923. Also a standout in track and field, he took part in several intercollegiate meets in 1923 and 1924, even traveling to the then brand-new Wembley Stadium in England in 1923, where he won the high hurdles event. Even before going to Worcester, he had undergone a real character-building experience at seventeen by serving in France in the waning days of World War I as an ambulance driver for the American Red Cross.

Anton Hulman Sr., a stern disciplinarian, insisted that his son learn the business of Hulman and Company from the bottom up, but within a couple of years Tony was named the company's sales manager. One of his tasks was to market a then little-known product the company had owned for some time called Clabber Girl Baking Powder and insiders have given him much credit for building up what eventually became an immensely popular and internationally known product. By 1931 he was entrusted with the entire Hulman concern.

In 1926 Hulman married Mary Fendrich, whose upbringing was remarkably similar to his own. She was an only child and granddaughter of a German immigrant whose La Fendrich Cigar Company was a flourishing concern in Evansville. The couple had one daughter, Mary (later Mari) Antonia Hulman, born in 1934.

As great as were the fortunes at Hulman and Company, they were about to multiply. Longtime company treasurer and family confidant (of more than six decades) Joseph R. Cloutier recommended an aggressive acquisition plan in 1938 that involved buying companies that held high potential but had temporarily fallen on hard times, building them up, and then selling them. This resulted in Hulman acquiring power and utility companies, newspapers, radio and television stations, a brewery, real estate, and a number of Coca-Cola bottling concerns. Because several deals were made with an Indianapolis real estate broker, Homer Cochran, Hulman ended up with what became his prized possession. One of Cochran's colleagues at that time was three-time Indianapolis 500 winner WILBUR SHAW, and Cochran arranged the historic meeting between Shaw and Hulman when Shaw was attempting to save the shuttered Indianapolis Motor Speedway from potential demise during World War II.

Shaw was delighted to discover that the shy and retiring forty-four-year-old Hulman had been attending the 500-mile race on a fairly regular basis ever since being taken there as a boy of thirteen. Once the deal had been made to purchase the track from World War I flying-ace Eddie Rickenbacker, Shaw pretty much became the front man, serving as president and general manager on a day-to-day basis, while Hulman—who was barely known in Indianapolis at the time—typically remained on the sidelines, even at the track on race morning. It was only after Shaw perished in a private plane accident on October 30, 1954, that Hulman began to emerge, naming himself as IMS president. Even then, his style was extremely

Anton "Tony" Hulman Jr.

gentle, even to the point of commending security guards when he would be stopped at the pits or garage area for not being properly credentialed (a frequent occurrence).

Even as the years went by, all he needed to say in any endeavor—track related or not—was, "Gee, don't you boys think it would be kind of nice if we did so-and-so?" in order for that to be construed as the direction to be taken.

The late Bob Collins, sports editor of the *Indianapolis Star*, was greatly amused while attending the first PGA 500 Open at the Speedway's golf course in 1960 and Tony asking him, "Do you think it would be okay if I went over there to meet some of the golf boys?"

"Tony," replied the incredulous Collins, "you OWN the golf course!"

Tony was just so thoughtful and courteous. It was not at all unusual to see him at a function carrying a tray of drinks back to his table, while anybody in the place would have been happy to have done it for him. He once wandered into a banquet hall while the cocktail hour was still in full swing outside and, upon encountering a half a dozen ladies stuffing the evening's printed program with an insert, sat down and proceeded to assist them.

The fact that to this day the cars are pushed back and forth during practice between the pits and garage area is a Hulman legacy. He wanted the fans to have an opportunity to see the cars at close quarters.

It has been unfairly suggested that Hulman was always so nervous and preoccupied on the morning of the 500-mile race that he had to read the four words "Gentlemen, start your engines!" from a card. That is not entirely accurate. It is true there was a card, but it was the result of longtime radio announcer Luke Walton feeling Hulman's much-anticipated delivery could "use something." Walton built in some drama by underlining and "stretching" portions of the words on a card and coaching Hulman to the point where the eventual interpretation became the stirring, never-to-be-forgotten, "GENNELLMENNNNNN, START YOURRRRRRRRENGINES!"

When A. J. Foyt became the first four-time Indianapolis 500 winner in 1977, he invited Hulman to join him in the pace car on the victory lap, something Hulman had never before done. It was one of the truly great moments in the history of the Indianapolis Motor Speedway as thousands upon thousands of devoted fans ran onto the track to wave and yell their approval at the iconic pair as they rode past.

In fact, this was the last time most people would ever see Hulman, as he passed away following an operation in Indianapolis five months later on October 27. The standing-room-only funeral was held at Saint Benedict Church in Terre Haute. The church had been financed by Herman Hulman, Tony's grandfather, who wanted to duplicate the church he had attended as a boy in Lingen, Germany.

Over the years, the extraordinarily philanthropic family, with virtually no fanfare, has donated millions of dollars to a wide range of charities and educational institutions. In recognition of this generosity, Rose Polytechnic Institute was renamed Rose-Hulman Institute of Technology, and Indiana State University established the Hulman Center Arena and Hulman Memorial Student Union.

DONALD DAVIDSON

For Further Reading

Kramer, Ralph. *The Indianapolis 500: A Century of Excitement.* Iola, WI: Krause Publications, 2010.

Shaplen, Robert. "Hoosier Pied Piper." *Sports Illustrated*, May 26, 1958.

———. "Savior of the Speedway," *Sports Illustrated*. June 2, 1958.

Hurty, John Newell
February 21, 1852–March 27, 1925

Pharmacist, public-health advocate, secretary of the Indiana State Board of Health, and state legislator.

John Newell Hurty served the state of Indiana for more than twenty-five years as secretary of the state board of health and two years as a member of the general assembly. In these roles, he led reform initiatives intended to improve the health of Hoosiers. The influence of his views extended well beyond the state's borders. Hurty's passionate convictions about well-being resulted in numerous accolades and national recognition. His work, however, was sometimes controversial in Indiana, and while many lauded his efforts, more recently there has been attention to the ways that some of his convictions failed to respect the rights of his fellow citizens. Hurty was nonetheless a connected, well-traveled man whose humanity and sense of wonder are often regarded as less interesting than his enduring public health pronouncements, though the two aspects of his life are interrelated.

Hurty was born in Lebanon, Ohio, in 1825. His father was an educator whose work to improve communities in which he lived had an important influence on his son's professional career choice. From 1871 to 1873 Hurty trained to be a pharmacist at the Philadelphia College of Pharmacy and then the Franklin Institute before coming to Indiana in 1873. He went to work as a chemist for the corporation that became Eli Lilly and Company. Hurty left Lilly in 1879 and opened his own drugstore, where he set up a chemistry lab in the basement, said to be one of, if not the first of its kind, in Indiana.

Hurty received his medical degree in 1891 from the Indiana Medical College, although he never practiced medicine. In fact, some of his critics questioned whether he did have a medical degree, but in 1979, fifty-four years after his death, his actual diploma was found. He taught at the Indiana Medical College from 1883 until his death. Hurty also had a long history with Purdue University, where he assisted in the founding of the School of Pharmacy, and later served as dean. It was from Purdue that he received his doctor of pharmacy degree in 1882.

From 1890 to 1893 he worked as a chemist for the Indianapolis City Board of Health, where he aggressively fought to improve the city water supply to eradicate typhoid fever. It was his success in this position that led to his appointment in 1896 as secretary of the Indiana State Board of Health, a post in which he served for twenty-six years. In this capacity much of his signature work was done. For his leadership in key areas of public health, such as combating typhoid fever, smallpox, and tuberculosis, Hurty has been remembered as Indiana's "most useful citizen" and someone with a broader, significant influence as well.

Hurty initially achieved recognition as someone who established standards for water purification and for the safety of food and medicine. He first proposed a comprehensive pure food and drug law 1897, which was adopted by the state in 1899, making Indiana among the first states to have such a law. Another Hoosier, Harvey Wiley, who became chief chemist for the U.S. Department of Agriculture, used the Indiana law as his model for the federal Pure Food and Drug Act passed in 1906. For Hurty's work on the pure food and drug measure and other achievements, including the enactment of birth and death registration laws, the Indiana Department of Environmental Management named an award for him. In 1922, after resigning from the State Board of Health, Hurty was elected to one term in the Indiana House of Representatives, where he proposed legislation to strengthen the agency he had just left.

Hurty was equally influential in the emerging areas of public health concerned with reproduction and childhood development as the foundations of well-being in later life. This innovative work, much of which was deeply controversial at the time, intersected with social movements outside the state, with its origins in medicine and in eugenics. His efforts to create and carry out a state-level infant health program following the foundation of the federal Children's Bureau and the subsequent passage of the Sheppard-Towner Act of 1921, which provided aid to states to establish programs to enhance the health of pregnant women and infants, produced considerable publicity. He was involved in instituting a program for the sterilization of prisoners and others regarded as inferior. The attention garnered by his conviction that sexually transmitted infections were preventable diseases like any other, however, proved to be a veritable lightning rod.

According to the 1907 issue of the *Indiana Medical Journal*, Hurty was one of "thirteen gentlemen" who "responded to a call to organize the Indiana Society of Social Hygiene" in October of that year. Although Doctor William Wishard was identified as the presiding officer for this meeting, Hurty himself chaired the society's organizing committee. Even at this initial meeting, it was clear that Hurty and his collaborators understood the challenge that their subject represented in an era long before sex education. The fact that the Reverend George D. Wolf was among its members gave the organization confidence that "all ministers of the gospel everywhere would favor the work proposed by the society, which was to combat the venereal plagues and to teach and advocate social purity." Its stated aim of "social purity" hints at the eugenic underpinnings of social hygiene and foreshadows the elements of the effort that eventually compromised Hurty's reputation.

Records of Hurty's life demonstrate that he was a busy man who understood that carrying out his agenda of improving the health of Hoosiers committed him to activism and outreach. He maintained a considerable correspondence with those who shared his sense of the seriousness of health problems. He spoke regularly at professional meetings and, as time permitted, a local literary society. He authored articles, pamphlets, and books, including the 250-page *Life with Health: A Text-book on Physiology, Hygiene, and Sanitation*. In any venue, how to bring about a better life, which to Hurty meant a more healthful one, seemed to be a constant theme.

It is simple, when looking back at a man like Hurty, whose fierce determination to improve the world resulted in applause and approbation alike, to see only the public figure who was at times out of sync in his own era and whose work has been increasingly recognized as distant from our own. It is worth considering, too, how far he traveled in order to bring his notions of good health and a life well lived to Indiana.

JENNIFER BUREK PIERCE

For Further Reading

Bennet, Jeff, and Richard D. Feldmam. "The Most Useful Citizen of Indiana: John N. Hurty and the Public Health Movement." *Traces of Indiana and Midwestern History* 12, no. 3 (Summer 2000): 34–43.

Pierce, Jennifer Burek. *What Adolescents Ought to Know: Sexual Health Texts in Twentieth Century America*. Amherst: University of Massachusetts Press, 2011.

Stern, Alexandra Minna. "Making Better Babies: Public Health and Race Betterment in Indiana, 1920–1935." *American Journal of Public Health* 92 (March 2002): 742–52

———. "'We Cannot Make a Silk Purse Out of a Sow's Ear': Eugenics in the Hoosier Heartland." *Indiana Magazine of History* 103 (March 2007): 3–38.

Jackson, Michael

August 29, 1958–June 25, 2009

Singer and entertainment icon.

Michael Jackson was a thrilling artist who redefined popular music. His albums became the soundtrack of a generation, his videos were the gold standard of the early MTV era, and he won more awards and accolades than any other performer in music history. His forty-five-year career earned him a double induction into the Rock and Roll Hall of Fame and his name is synonymous with iconic entertainers such as Frank Sinatra, Elvis Presley, and the Beatles. "Michael Jackson doesn't just come along once in a century or once in a lifetime," Motown founder Barry Gordy said. "He only comes along once."

Born into a large, working-class family from Gary, Indiana, Michael was the little boy with a big voice and the showmanship of James Brown. At the age of five, he became the front man of the Jackson 5 and by the time he was ten, he and his brothers were among the biggest recording artists on the Motown record label with hits such as "I Want You Back," "ABC," "The Love You Save," and "I'll Be There." While at Motown, Michael also launched a solo career that included four albums and a string of hit songs including "Got To Be There," a remake of "Rockin' Robin" and the Oscar-nominated "Ben."

After leaving Motown in 1975, Michael began to look for opportunities that would stretch him creatively and artistically while still working with his famous family. He began writing his own material, helped produce the Jacksons albums *Destiny* and *Triumph*, and took the role of the Scarecrow in the film adaptation of *The Wiz* starring his former Motown mentor Diana Ross.

Although the movie itself was a box-office failure, the venture proved to be fortuitous for Jackson. He received critical praise for his performance and while on the set he also met the man who would be instrumental in shaping the next phase of his career: Quincy Jones. In Jones, Jackson found a musical soul mate and the two began laying down the tracks that would become his breakthrough solo effort, *Off the Wall*.

With hits such as "Don't Stop 'til You Get Enough," and "Rock with You," *Off the Wall* was a sonically perfect dance record released at the height of the disco era. However, despite critical and popular appeal, *Off the Wall* was snubbed by the industry during the 1980 Grammy season. Jackson won the Best Male Rhythm and Blues Performance for "Don't Stop 'til You Get Enough," but he was disappointed that *Off the Wall* had not been nominated for album of the year. He vowed that he would record an even better record in the future. "Just wait," he said. "They won't be able to ignore the next album."

The "next" album, 1982's *Thriller,* was more than a hit, it was a global phenomenon. *Thriller* spent more than two years on the charts, boasted seven top-ten singles, won seven of Jackson's eight Grammys in 1984 and went on to become the biggest selling album of all time. His videos such as "Beat It," and "Thriller" broke through the color barrier on the infant MTV channel and went into heavy rotation. However, it was his performance of "Billie Jean" on the Motown Twenty-fifth Anniversary Special that sent the twenty-five-year-old into superstardom with a little dance move that was out of this world. "When Michael did his iconic Moonwalk . . . it was magic," Gordy said. "Michael went into orbit and never came back down."

On the heels of *Thriller*, Jackson teamed with Lionel Richie in 1985 to pen "We Are the World," the anthem for the USA for Africa famine relief effort, and he filmed *Captain EO* for Disney before returning to the studio to record the follow-up to his musical masterpiece. The result was *Bad*. Produced once again by Jones, *Bad* topped the *Billboard* charts for six weeks, spawned five number-one singles and sold 30 million copies worldwide. The subsequent tour, Jackson's first as a solo artist, shattered audience attendance records and proved that even if he could not top the success of *Thriller*, his "failures" were most impressive.

It would be four years before Jackson released his next album, but during that time, he was rarely out of the spotlight. With 1991's *Dangerous*, he hoped to recapture his eighties glory days while incorporating the new sounds of the nineties. He replaced Jones with new jack swing producer Teddy Riley and laid down seventy-seven minutes of material that included "Black or White," "Remember the Time," "Jam" and "In the Closet." *Dangerous* debuted at number one, but dark days were ahead for Jackson that would haunt him the rest of his life.

Jackson released three more albums, all of which sold well, but could not come close to shattering the records set by *Thriller*. In 1995 *History: Past, Present and Future Vol. I* was a two-CD set designed to be part greatest hits compilation and part new material. The album had a few standout moments including "Scream" a duet with sister Janet, "They Don't Care About Us," and "You Are Not Alone" but rock critics felt that it lacked consistency. "It's his most pained record, and sadly, his hardest to love," said Jon Dolan of *Rolling Stone* magazine.

As Jackson transitioned from his place as the biggest star in the world and into a tragic cautionary tale, his albums *Blood on the Dance Floor* (1997) and *Invincible* (2001) failed to make much of a ripple in the industry and it appeared that his best days were behind him. He returned to Gary in 2003, visited with family, community officials and attended ceremonial events throughout the city. Jackson made plans to partner with Gary on a performing arts center, but a fresh round of legal troubles curtailed all business endeavors for the time being.

After living abroad for several years with his children, in 2009 Jackson announced a fifty-concert engagement at London's O2 Arena. Tickets sold out within hours, but unfortunately, the show did not go on. On June 25, 2009, Jackson was pronounced dead at the UCLA Medical Center of a cardiac arrest resulting from an acute overdose of the surgical anesthetic Propfol.

As reports of Jackson's death hit the news wires, search engines and social media, the Internet crashed, and within forty-eight hours, his name surpassed "Jesus Christ" as the most Googled search term of all time. Sales of his albums and merchandise skyrocketed and more than a billion people saw his memorial service. In death, Jackson had finally achieved the comeback he craved.

Jackson was the Indiana boy who grew up to be a global icon and whose name is associated with both triumph and tragedy. Though there were highs and lows throughout his incredible career, Jackson himself said that if he had to do it all over again, he would not have done it any differently. "He was driven by his hunger to learn, to constantly top himself," said Gordy, during his eulogy at Michael's memorial service. "He studied the greats and became greater . . . he was simply the greatest entertainer that ever lived."

JULIE YOUNG

For Further Reading And Viewing

Jackson, Michael. *Moonwalk*. Revised edition. New York: Harmony Books, 2009.

Lemon, Don. *CNN Live Event/Special* broadcast June 27, 2009. "Micheal Jackson: Man in the Mirror." http://www.youtube.com/watch?v=PPN9STmOGmQ

Fox News broadcast July 7, 2009. "Michael Jackson Memorial: Barry Gordy's Eulogy." http://www.youtube.com/watch?v=6OpQql8vm3A

Jenckes, Virginia Ellis
November 6, 1877–January 9, 1975

Indiana's first congresswoman, served as U.S. representative for Indiana's Sixth Congressional District.

Virginia Jenckes

A farmer, an ardent anticommunist, and an advocate for women, Virginia E. Jenckes made her mark in Washington, D.C., during the depths of the Great Depression. As a farmer, she learned firsthand of the problems caused by the periodic flooding of her land and sought public funds for adequate flood control along the Wabash and White Rivers. She championed the cause of defending America from the threat of communism in its schools and government, going so far as to claim that the Communists had thwarted the placement of flagpoles on government buildings in the nation's capital. She urged women to join with men as equal partners in solving the nation's problems and acting as "the first line of defense of the home."

Virginia Ellis Somes was born in Terre Haute, Indiana, where she attended public schools and then Coates College for one year. In 1912 she married Ray Jenckes, a Terre Haute grain dealer thirty-four years her senior, calling herself "an old man's darling." They had one daughter, also named Virginia. Upon her husband's death in 1921, Virginia inherited his business and his 1,300-acre farm, experiencing firsthand the problems caused by the repeated flooding of her land. In response, she joined with others to form the Wabash-Maumee Valley Improvement Association dedicated to protecting more than two million acres of farmland from floods.

Her local success as a farmer and civic leader led Jenckes to the realm of politics. In 1932 Indiana had a newly drawn Sixth Congressional District and she secured the nomination of the Democratic Party to run for the seat. While railing against the economic policies of President Herbert Hoover, Jenckes supported veterans' benefits and the repeal of Prohibition, arguing that it had destroyed farmers' markets for wheat, corn, rye, barley, and other grains. Presenting herself as strong and independent, she won the election easily, carried by a strong showing in Vigo County in the normally Republican district. While only four women nationwide ran for Congress in 1932, Jenckes's gender turned out to be a nonissue with voters.

On her first day in the House of Representatives, Jenckes caused a stir, which was reported in the national press, by wearing a hat onto the floor of the House, violating a longstanding unwritten rule against such apparel. Despite that rocky beginning, she effectively represented her district by promoting congressional action to further greater uses of farm wastes and other materials, such as making paper products from corn stalks and motor fuel from corn alcohol. She fought vigorously for a federal flood control program for the Wabash valley, asking for $18 million under the Recovery Act and getting the support of the U.S. Army Corps of Engineers. The money was eventually included in an appropriations bill that was enacted into law. While supporting most of President Franklin Roosevelt's New Deal initiatives, she astonished her Democratic colleagues by casting her first vote in Congress against the President's Economy Act, which included a 15 percent across-the-board cut in government expenses, saying, "I promised the veterans back home I wouldn't reduce their benefits."

In 1934 Jenckes handily won re-election, receiving strong labor support and the endorsement of the new National Women's Party, which claimed that "women owe her a deep debt of gratitude for her splendid work for them in Congress. During her second term, she spoke out more on so-called women's issues, stressing their role as "the caretakers of the home, the fireside and the children," and claiming "it is fitting and proper that women should take a special place in the councils of the people in the Congress." Jenckes urged Congress to reduce taxes on cosmetics, protesting against such "discriminatory taxes on the cosmetics which American women use and consider part of their everyday dress," and calling such taxes a "genuine hardship" to working women often judged by their personal appearance.

During her tenure in Congress, Jenckes spoke out frequently about the perceived threat of communism, claiming later that she was the most active anticommunist in the House of Representatives during that period. She charged that the lack of flagpoles atop government buildings in Washington, D.C., resulted from architectural plans devised by Communists. In a 1937 speech to the Women's Patriotic Conference on National Defense, she claimed that, due to the lack of flags, "there is a very marked similarity of our new buildings on Pennsylvania Avenue and the buildings in Red Square, Moscow." Such statement and others about "secret propagandists" being responsible for the failure of the flag to be displayed on top of government buildings exposed Jenckes to public ridicule since American flags still flew prominently in front of buildings in the nation's capital, just not atop them. Jenckes particularly called on women to become informed about national defense, declaring, "I am calling on every American woman regardless of her status in life or regardless of her political affiliations to stand shoulder to shoulder in repelling that horrible menace called 'Communism.'" At one point, she called on schools to stop distributing *Scholastic Magazine*, calling it subversive and communist.

Due in large part to the landslide victory of Roosevelt in 1936, Jenckes won re-election to a third term. She continued to spark controversy and draw ridicule in Washington when she suggested in 1937 that the capital's famous Japanese cherry trees by replaced with American cherry trees as a protest against the Japanese invasion of China. The trees represented "a symbol of traitorism and disloyalty" that she could not tolerate even though they had been a gift of friendship in an earlier time. Another favorite topic during her third term was her dislike of the reciprocal trade agreements championed by Roosevelt, objecting to them because of their effect on local farmers and calling them "almost a calamity." In 1938, despite opposition in the primary election, Jenckes secured her fourth nomination for Congress. Nationally, the New Deal had ebbed in popularity and a number of Democrats in the House of Representatives failed to win re-election, including Jenckes, who blamed her defeat on ballot tampering.

Jenckes remained in Washington, D.C., after her defeat, becoming involved with the International Red Cross. She remained an ardent anticommunist and, in 1956, worked on behalf of the Hungarian Freedom Fighters, assisting five priests to enter the United States after escaping from Budapest prisons. In 1969 she moved back to Indiana and died in Terre Haute in 1975. A friend of Jenckes, Terre Haute newsman Lawrence E. Sawyer said of her, "She was strong-willed and independent up to the end—a women's libber sixty years before the fad became popular."

SUZANNE S. BELLAMY

For Further Reading

Jenckes, Virginia E. Papers. Manuscript Division, Indiana State Library, Indianapolis.
Spann, Edward K. "Congresswoman Virginia E. Jenckes." *Traces of Indiana and Midwestern History* 17 (Winter 2005): 36-43.
———. "Indiana's First Woman in Congress: Virginia E. Jenckes and the New Deal, 1932–1938." *Indiana Magazine of History* 92 (September 1996): 235–53.

Jenkins, Charles Francis

August 22, 1867–June 6, 1934

One of America's greatest inventors awarded hundreds of patents and the pioneer inventor of television and a motion picture projector.

A pioneer in early film and television technology, Charles Francis Jenkins developed his gift for invention on a farm near Richmond, Indiana, after the Civil War. As a professional inventor, Jenkins was both prolific and diverse in his creations, amply supported by his record of having been awarded at least 280 patents, though some sources credit him with an even higher number. His many achievements include the early development of television and a movie projector, and a mechanism to start cars to replace the old unwieldy hand cranks. "He was the only inventor who participated in the birth of both motion-picture photography and television," noted his biographer Donald Godfrey.

Born on a farm near Dayton, Ohio, in 1867, Jenkins was two years old when his parents, who met during the Civil War at Earlham College (then known as Friends Board School), moved to Indiana to be near his mother's parents. Farming gave Jenkins an ideal setting to prepare for a lifetime of invention.

From his maternal grandfather, Jenkins learned practical mechanics, which he then applied by wiring a telephone connection between the barn and house. In charge of maintaining the family farm equipment, he also gained a reputation among neighbors for repairing mechanical devices. Perhaps fearful it would give him a swelled head, his father warned him: "That is thy gift, and to thee it is no great credit." The son never forgot his father's comment, a paraphrase of a Bible passage, 1 Corinthians 4:7: "What do you have that you did not receive?" Jenkins no doubt retained many other Scriptures since he was raised in a household where reading and reciting Bible passages was a daily ritual before breakfast.

After hearing stories of pioneers from his grandfather, Jenkins took his talents West at age sixteen, finding work in sawmills, mines and lumberyards, and even became a skilled repairman in the Sierra Nevada mines.

On one of his annual trips home Jenkins had taken a civil service examination and learned several months later, while in Mexico, that he passed and had received an appointment as a clerk in Washington, D.C. He eventually worked as secretary to Sumner Kimball, founder of the U.S. Life Saving Service, the forerunner of the Coast Guard. Jenkins found his job interesting, especially learning of heroic rescues in turbulent seas, and he also enjoyed the historical attractions and vibrant nightlife in the nation's capital. He had also been smitten by a new hobby, photography, which started him toward inventions in film and television technology. He invented the forerunner of the movie projector, the phantoscope, which he demonstrated in Richmond in 1894 by projecting on the wall of a downtown jewelry store scenes of a vaudeville dancer performing a "butterfly dance." He then teamed up with Thomas Armat, a classmate at the Bliss Electrical School in Washington, D.C., to make improvements to the "motion picture projecting box." They showed the new device at the Cotton States and International Exposition in Atlanta in 1895 and, encouraged by the positive reception, Jenkins left government service to work full time as an inventor.

When his partnership with Armat dissolved in a dispute over who invented the phantoscope, Jenkins sold his rights to Armat, who then in turn teamed with Thomas Edison, selling him the rights to market the movie projector as the Vitascope. However, the dispute was settled in a sense by the Franklin Institute and Science Museum that awarded Jenkins the Elliott Cresson Medal in 1897 for his invention of the phantoscope and in 1913 bestowed the Scott Medal, citing Jenkins as inventor and Armat as investor.

In 1902 Jenkins married Grace Love, a descendant of an old established Maryland family and one also steeped in the Bible. Her parents, however, did worry how someone with so nebulous an occupation as inventor could adequately support their daughter. Perhaps their apprehensions were short-lived as Jenkins continued applying his fertile mind to conceiving and producing a myriad of innovations.

Following his invention of the movie camera, Jenkins, like many other mechanics, launched into the early automotive business, creating the Jenkins Automobile Company, producing the first horseless carriage in Washington, D.C., in 1898. His cars had the engine in the front instead of under the seat, used steam, and reached eight miles per hour at top speeds. Although his venture into this industry did not last long, Jenkins felt he did "contribute his bit" to the infant industry.

Jenkins's creations ranged widely and included a container for more sanitary milk delivery, a cap for milk bottles, a pocket calculator, and a lawn mower. His interest in aviation led him to become a pilot after World War I and to innovations in that field, including a high-speed camera and a two-day radio transmission device. The Professional Golf Association asked Jenkins to use the camera to take high-speed pictures of the golfing great Bobby Jones to help golfers improve their swings. Another of his inventions provided the U.S. Navy with radio weather maps to send to ships at sea.

Although innovative in many fields, Jenkins kept coming back to motion pictures and the challenge of sending pictures through airwaves. In 1921 he established Jenkins Laboratories to transmit movies by radio, or what he called radiovision, which propelled the development of television. In the 1920s he developed prismatic rings that scanned images continuously for viewers, another key step in television technology. The Federal Radio Commission granted Jenkins the first experimental television station license, with the call letters W3XK, and he started transmitting radio movies, or images of motion pictures, on the East Coast in 1928. Jenkins began selling television sets equipped with a mechanism for viewing images on a six-inch square mirror for $85 to $135. He also joined his new company, Jenkins Television Corp., with the old Lee DeForest radio company.

The Great Depression contributed to the bankruptcy of Jenkins Television in 1933, with the assets becoming part of the Radio Corporation of America. Before his death in 1934, Jenkins had been moving away from the slower system of mechanical scanning to one he called electro-optical. This technology, had Jenkins lived to develop it, might have been competitive with the purely electronic television system pioneered by Philo Farnsworth, who demonstrated his invention to the public in 1934 and established the Farnsworth Television and Radio Corporation in Fort Wayne in 1938.

Despite his impressive record of innovations, Jenkins is not as well known as he deserves to be, perhaps explaining the delay in his induction into the National Inventors Hall of Fame until 2011. Still, the name Jenkins resonates with industry insiders because of the influential organization he founded, now known as the Society of Motion Picture Engineers and Television Engineers, and the Charles F. Jenkins Lifetime Achievement Award, an Emmy presented annually to honor a person's contributions to advancing television technology and engineering.

Additionally, knowledge of his achievements may spread with the publication of the first biography of Jenkins, which was written by historian Donald G. Godfrey and chronicles how Jenkins more than held his own competing against giants such as Edison and David Sarnoff of RCA.

RUSSELL PULLIAM

For Further Reading

Godfrey, Donald G. *C. Francis Jenkins Pioneer of Film and Television*. Champaign: University of Illinois Press, 2014.

Jenkins, C. Francis. *The Boyhood of an Inventor*. Washington, DC, 1931.

Lachenbruch, David. "They Called It Radiomovies," *TV Guide*, July 3, 1971, 5–10.

Jennings, Jonathan
1784–July 26, 1834

Indiana territorial representative, first state governor, and member of the United States House of Representative.

As the state of Indiana's first governor, Jonathan Jennings faced the challenges of placing the state on a sound financial foundation, implementing a court system, and developing rudimentary educational and internal improvements systems. During his career, Jennings vigorously defended the rights and equality of white men against the forces of aristocracy and corruption, symbolized in his mind by Territorial Governor WILLIAM HENRY HARRISON and others whom he believed used government to advance their own wealth and position at the expense of the average citizen.

Jennings was born in 1784, probably in Hunterdon County, New Jersey, and was the sixth child of Jacob and Mary Kennedy Jennings. His father was a physician and Dutch Reformed minister. In the early 1790s the family moved to Dunlap's Creek, Pennsylvania, where the elder Jennings accepted a pastorate. After receiving his elementary education at home, Jonathan studied Greek, Latin, and mathematics at a grammar school in Canonsburg. He subsequently read law with John Simonson in Washington, Pennsylvania. After a brief stay in Steubenville, Ohio, he moved in 1806 to Jeffersonville, the seat of justice for Clark County, Indiana Territory.

Eager to enter politics, Jennings relocated to Vincennes, the territorial capital, where he was admitted to the bar in April 1807 and appointed clerk of the land office. In September 1807 he was elected clerk of the Vincennes University board of trustees, of which Harrison was president. They quickly crossed swords, and Jennings resigned in May 1808.

Recognizing that his conflict with Harrison limited his chance for advancement in Vincennes, Jennings returned to Clark County and settled in Charlestown. He had assumed that his political fortunes would be greater in the eastern part of the territory and that the capital would be

Jonathan Jennings is paired with Governor Samuel M. Ralston for Indiana's centennial celebration in 1916.

relocated to Clark County. But his action proved even more propitious when in February 1809 Congress divided Indiana to create the new Illinois Territory and mandated that Indiana's congressional delegate be elected by the voters. Meanwhile, southeastern Indiana residents were growing increasingly resentful of Harrison's efforts to open the territory to slavery. Meshing his own resentment against Harrison with those of the electorate, Jennings declared for congressional delegate. As important as his message was his style. He courted voters directly, treating them like friends and often drinking with them before mounting the stump. Whether it was his message, his style, or a combination of the two, he won a plurality in a three-way race and took his seat in late November. He was reelected in 1811, 1812, and 1814.

On August 8, 1811, Jennings married nineteen-year-old Ann Gilmore Hay, daughter of a prominent Charlestown politician. After her death in 1826, he married Clarissa Barbee on October 19, 1827. Although a gregarious politician, Jennings suffered periods of despondency, and his personal insecurity, combined with his casual drinking and campaign camaraderie, probably fostered his alcoholism. Nevertheless, Jennings closely attended to his constituents' concerns. He supported relief measures for those at risk of losing land purchased under the Land Act of 1800, secured passage of a bill to strengthen frontier defense, and promoted road development. He also worked to undermine Harrison's gubernatorial powers. After arriving in Washington, D.C., Jennings failed in an attempt to block the governor's reappointment. But he successfully championed measures to block most gubernatorial appointees from serving in the territorial assembly and to broaden white male franchise rights. Meanwhile, the governor's control of the political process was further weakened by the legislature. By the time Harrison resigned in late 1812 to resume military service, his political hold on the territory was in decline, in part due to the rise of democratic leaders such as Jennings.

In December 1815 Jennings presented a petition from the legislature asking Congress to authorize a constitutional convention to determine if Indiana should become a state. The next month he introduced a statehood Enabling Act, which Congress passed on April 11, 1816. Jennings was one of five Clark County delegates to the convention, which met in Corydon in June. As a reward for pushing through the Enabling Act, he was elected the convention's president. Under Jennings's leadership, the delegates crafted a constitution that embodied the democratic values he had supported and created a structure of governance that exalted the legislature at the expense of the governor.

In August Jennings defeated Territorial Governor Thomas Posey and took office as state governor in November. During his tenure, he concentrated on six broad goals: establishing a court system, organizing an educational system that reached from the common schools to a state university, creating a state banking system, preventing illegal efforts to capture and enslave free blacks, organizing a state library, and implementing an internal improvements plan. His limited success in achieving these objectives was as much a reflection of the governor's limited powers and the state's weak financial position as it was of his political skills and knowledge of the issues.

Jennings's powers were most constrained in the area of justice, where his main responsibility was to nominate the three judges of the state supreme court. He urged the legislature to implement the constitution's ambitious educational vision, but the document conditioned action on the capacity of counties to finance such a system. Thus the general assembly gave little more than lip service to the subject. It was a similar story for his state library proposal. In 1817 he signed legislation creating the State Bank of Indiana, with headquarters in Vincennes and branches in Brookville, Corydon, and Vevay. It soon became a federal depository, but it was then engulfed in the speculative wave that triggered the panic of 1819 and was forced to suspend specie payment. Soon thereafter the federal treasury suspended deposits and by 1821 the system was insolvent.

Faced with a "road system" that consisted mainly of Indian and buffalo trails, Jennings made internal improvements one of his highest priorities. The first legislative session empowered county commissioners to layout roads, appoint township road supervisors, and compel men between ages eighteen and fifty to provide labor for road construction. In 1821 he persuaded the assembly to provide $100,000 from a pool of money received from federal land sales for roads and canals to build twenty-two state roads that would link most of the state's larger communities with Indianapolis, the proposed capital. But the plan's scale far exceeded the available resources, and few roads were built during Jennings's tenure. A fierce opponent of slavery, Jennings urged the legislature in November 1816 to make it illegal to seize free blacks and sell them into slavery. But he also objected to efforts by people in other states to make Indiana a refuge for runaways. In response, the legislature approved fines on anyone who knowingly aided escaped slaves.

Jennings faced his greatest political crisis in 1818 when President James Madison asked him to serve as a commissioner to negotiate the Treaty of Saint Marys, in which the Miami relinquished most of their lands in Indiana to the United States. But the state constitution prohibited any federal officeholder from serving as governor. When Jennings returned to Corydon, Lieutenant Governor Christopher Harrison, a political rival, urged the legislature to institute impeachment proceedings on the grounds that the governor had abandoned his position. But the legislators demurred and in 1819 Jennings defeated Harrison by a large majority in his bid for re-election.

Jennings resigned as governor in September 1822 after being elected to represent the Second Congressional District in the U.S. House of Representatives. In Congress he successfully advocated appropriations for the National Road and the Wabash and Erie Canal and favored an Indiana canal around the Falls of the Ohio. By the late 1820s he had become increasingly addicted to alcohol, and in 1830 he lost a re-election bid to Clark County politician John Carr. He lived with his wife, Clarissa, on their farm outside Charlestown until his death on July 26, 1834. He is buried in the Charlestown cemetery.

CARL E. KRAMER

For Further Reading

Cayton, Andrew R. L. *Frontier Indiana*. Bloomington: Indiana University Press, 1998.

Mills, Randy K. *Jonathan Jennings: Indiana's First Governor*. Indianapolis: Indiana Historical Society Press, 2005.

Riker, Dorothy. "Jonathan Jennings." *Indiana Magazine of History* 28 (December 1932): 223–39.

Julian, George Washington

May 4, 1817–July 7, 1899

Lawyer, writer, state legislator, U.S. congressman, and surveyor general of New Mexico.

George Washington Julian's political career spanned some of the most turbulent times in the history of the state and the nation—from the heated debate in Indiana about internal improvements and the subsequent colossal debt owed by the state, to the onslaught and conduct of the Civil War, to the period of Reconstruction. Although he belonged to five different political parties during the course of his public service, Julian was persistent in his stance against slavery, his effort to bring about land reform, and his support for women's suffrage. Accused by some of switching his positions to suit his whims, he claimed that it was the parties that changed position, while he remained true to his principles—the primary being his opposition to slavery.

Born in Centerville in Wayne County on May 4, 1817, Julian's views about the social and political issues of his time were shaped from an early age by the convictions of his Quaker parents, Isaac and Rebecca, who had moved to Indiana from North Carolina because of their strong opposition to slavery. His father was one of the first trustees of Centerville. In 1823, the beginning of an unsettled period for young George, his father moved the family to what is now Tippecanoe County. Shortly thereafter, when George was only six, his father died. A year later his mother moved the family back to Centerville. A woman with a deep Quaker faith and a strong personality, Rebecca left a strong imprint on her son, who embraced her Quaker values.

Julian got a rudimentary education in local schools, but he was a voracious reader, and supplemented his education through books. At the age of eighteen he became a schoolteacher in the area around Centerville and later in Illinois. His increasing dissatisfaction with the teaching profession led him to pursue the study of law. In 1840 he was licensed to practice law and began his legal career in Greenfield, Indiana. In 1843 he joined his older brother, Jacob, in his law practice. At this stage of his life, Julian was already developing an interest in politics. Centerville, the county seat of Wayne County at this time, was a center of culture, education, and business. Julian organized a debate group of young men that included future Indiana governor OLIVER P. MORTON. Later Julian and Morton became bitter enemies.

Julian was drawn to the Whig Party, the dominant party in Centerville at the time, largely because of its opposition to slavery, and in 1845 he won election to the Indiana House as a Whig candidate. The most prominent issue at that time was the large debt that the state had accumulated as a result of an internal improvements plan that included building the Wabash and Erie Canal. The state failed to set aside funds to pay for these improvements, and in order to deal with the debt problem the general assembly passed the Butler bill, which was strongly opposed by the Whig Party. Julian, however, voted for that bill, and as a result lost the support of the party. Consequently, he failed to secure the party's nomination for state senate in 1847. The following year Jacob, concerned about George's political independence and antislavery positions, ended their law partnership.

After failing to gain the Whig Party nomination for state senator, Julian became more involved with the antislavery movement and in 1848 helped to form the Free-Soil Party based on strong opposition to slavery and the overlapping issue of land reform, a policy Julian thought would allow slaves to become property owners. He eagerly traveled and gave speeches to promote the Free-Soiler stand against slavery. In 1850 he

George Julian

successfully ran as the party's candidate for the U.S. House of Representatives. Two years later, however, he was defeated for re-election. Politics in Wayne County and the state had changed significantly in the two-year interim, and the Democratic Party, and the state in general, had become less supportive of congressional restrictions on slavery. A new state constitution had been drafted barring blacks from migrating to the state. Morton, a leader of the Democrats at that time, led the local opposition to Julian.

In spite of his defeat, Julian did not waiver in his campaign against slavery, but he and his fellow abolitionists were subjected to slurs, slander, and threats of physical harm. His law practice suffered and former friends in his hometown ostracized his family. Newspapers called Julian a fanatic and a radical abolitionist and derided his speeches.

The Free-Soil Party nominated Julian as its vice presidential candidate in 1852, but the party's candidates won no electoral votes. Within two years the Free-Soil Party ceased to exist. Out of the ashes a new Republican Party was formed in 1854 made up of Whigs, Free-Soilers, and Democrats, all united in their opposition to the Kansas-Nebraska Act, which allowed settlers in the two territories to determine for themselves whether to permit slavery. This in effect repealed the Missouri Compromise of 1820, which would have banned slavery in the territories. The Republican Party also wanted to repeal the Fugitive Slave Law of 1850 that provided for the return of slaves who escaped to free states or territories. Julian and Morton were among the first members of this new political party.

In 1860, the same year that the Civil War began, Julian returned to Congress and became one of the Radical Republicans, pushing for aggressive conduct of the war and tough punishment for southern states. He served on the Joint Committee on the Conduct of the War and called for the removal of General George B. McClellan for his failure in battle. He was even critical of President ABRAHAM LINCOLN, doubting his true commitment to emancipation and opposed Lincoln's Reconstruction plan. Julian called for the hanging of Jefferson Davis and General Robert E. Lee. He proposed several resolutions to repeal the Fugitive Slave Act, which was finally accomplished 1864. In addition to being a strong advocate for giving former slaves the right to vote, Julian proposed a constitutional amendment giving women the right to vote in 1868, but it was defeated.

Among his most important achievements in Congress was the significant role he played in the passage of the Homestead Act in 1862—a policy Julian had advocated since his days as a Free-Soiler. The Homestead Act gave public land free to any adult citizen or potential citizens such as slaves if they had never borne arms against the United States.

While Julian saw himself as a man of principle who sometimes acted and voted against the wishes of his party, many of his Republican cohorts did not always take kindly to his independence. He alienated many in the state party as well as Congress, including Morton. Then the governor of Indiana, Morton worked to prevent his re-election through a gerrymandering scheme in 1868, but Julian hung on to win another term. However, in 1870, opposition in the party was too strong, and he was defeated in the primary.

After being defeated for Congress, Julian joined the Liberal Republican Party, which opposed what it considered the corrupt politics in the administration of President Ulysses S. Grant. The party called for the removal of federal troops from the South because of corrupt practices there, and promoted civil service reform. Julian continued to support women's suffrage, temperance, and land reform. He moved to the Indianapolis suburb of Irvington in 1873 and resumed his law practice. He switched parties once again and became a Democrat. In 1885 President Grover Cleveland appointed him surveyor general of New Mexico, a position he held until 1889. He returned to Irvington, where he lived until his death in 1899.

CAROLYN R. LAFEVER

For Further Reading

Clarke, Grace Julian. *George W. Julian*. Indianapolis: Indiana Historical Society, 1923.

Julian, George W. *Political Recollections: 1840 to 1872*. Chicago: Jansen, McClure and Company, 1884.

Riddleberger, Patrick W. *George Washington Julian, Radical Republican*. Indianapolis: Indiana Historical Bureau, 1966.

Kinsey, Alfred Charles
June 23, 1894–August 25, 1956

Entomologist, zoologist, pioneer sex researcher, and founder of the Institute for Sex Research at Indiana University.

Where do birds go during rainstorms? This question framed New Jersey-born adolescent Alfred Kinsey's first scientific essay, displaying already his fascination with organisms' adaptations to environments. Entranced by discovery and classification of diversity within organism communities, eventually he applied the same approach to human sexuality. "A clinic is no place to get incidence data," he quipped, criticizing distorted and norm-bound sexology derived from patients, inmates, or clients. Sex needed scrutiny across its full natural variations in its specific habitats.

Instead of mechanical engineering, Kinsey disappointed his domineering Methodist father and majored in biology at Bowdoin College. He earned a doctorate at Harvard University, where his adviser was William Morton Wheeler, famous for his research on the social behavior of ants. In 1917 Kinsey's congenital spinal curvature and heart disorder nixed military service. He became professor of zoology at Indiana University in 1920, and he and his spouse, Clara Bracken McMillen, had four children. A world expert on the North American gall wasp, he located more than two hundred new species. An avid gardener, he hybridized new irises, also publishing *Edible Wild Plants of Eastern North America* (1943). Field biologist rather than modern laboratory scientist, Kinsey perhaps closed a scientific arc stretching back to Charles Darwin. Were he just the "Indiana Jones" of gall wasps, the popular lecturer might have been unknown beyond colleagues, students, family, and friends sharing this fine pianist's enthusiasm for classical music.

At the age of forty-four, however, Kinsey changed his trajectory. He began quantitative, nonclinical interview studies of sexual behavior and, in 1947, he founded the Institute for Sex Research at IU. Soon, to substantial acclaim, he published *Sexual Behavior in the Human Male* (1948). With the second bestseller Kinsey report, *Sexual Behavior in the Human Female* (1953),

Left to right: Alfred Kinsey, Clyde Martin, and Wardell Pomeroy at Indiana University's Institute for Sex Research, 1947.

a portrait of Kinsey graced the cover of *Time* magazine. The only two other Hoosiers ever so featured—Democrat governor Paul V. McNutt in 1939 and Charles A. Halleck, Republican minority whip in 1959—never, however, became subjects of Hollywood movies. The movie *Kinsey* (2004) deployed original materials from the extraordinary collections held in his institute, posthumously renamed The Kinsey Institute for Research in Sex, Gender and Reproduction. Kinsey was, and remains, Indiana's most famous and frequently cited natural scientist.

Today a researcher shifting from entomology to sexology would be unusual. After World War I though, scientists and clinicians often researched sexual issues. Their studies of reproduction, overpopulation, birth control, divorce, prostitution, venereal diseases, erotic maladjustments, and "varietism" (engaging in a variety of uncommon sexual activities) offered more scientific methods than the anecdotal works of earlier European pioneers. None matched Kinsey's dedication to placing sex research on unimpeachably empirical and behavioral bases while expanding the areas that typically monopolized external research support: marriage and animal sex behavior. Instead, his quest was sexual behavior at large.

Necessarily, he ditched normative presumptions in his three hundred-question interview schedule that he piloted with marriage-course students responding to his lectures on biology, reproduction, and birth control. He refined it with Indianapolis and Chicago interviewees. Declining to treat marital coitus as the norm and marginalizing other erotic behaviors, Kinsey quantified the orgasm as his proxy measure of sexual behavior. Calling sources of orgasm "outlets," he planned on 100,000 sex histories, from which he would analyze patterns in reported orgasms from various outlets—masturbation, nocturnal emissions, petting, coitus, same-sex contacts, and animal contacts.

Ultimately, the completed histories numbered only 18,000. Still, this total was unprecedented and remains unsurpassed, documenting considerable behavioral diversity, not only between different sociological groups, but also during individual lifetimes. Obstructed from interviewing black Americans in segregated regions, however, his team also disagreed about sampling adequacy and interpretation, making the research fall short on representative samples of African Americans. The same held for working-class women and some regions. Nonetheless, Rockefeller Foundation grants, book contracts, and associated researchers made "the Kinsey Reports" from thousands of accounts.

The 1948 male volume outlined the project's methodology and key findings. Interviewers established rapport by assuring confidentiality in dealing with a subject delicate and taboo, and often beset by shame, guilt, or fear. Necessarily, certain interviewee answers evaded, exaggerated, misled, or lied, needing redress. Kinsey stressed subcultures in hypothesizing sexual behavior as learned. Erotic preferences matched pleasurable early reinforcement of some sexual releases, while disapproval of others produced aversion. Once established, and reinforced, preferred sources of sexual gratification proved defiant of social norms. Hence adolescent experiences shaped adult patterns.

That said, interviewees' wide range of experiences debunked theories that early erotic behaviors always shaped sexual behaviors. The six point "Kinsey Scale" (0–6) graphed this range: "0" for the majority exclusively heterosexual, and "6" the minority exclusively same-sex, all others 2, 3, 4 or 5, by outlet range and ratio. Moreover, class, as measured by level of education, predicted differential male erotic patterns. Least educated men proved least restrained, having frequent coitus from age fourteen, with earliest marriages, and were often adulterous during the childbearing years of marriage. Unnatural and counterproductive criminalization of nonmarital sexuality—including unwed motherhood—imposed needless hardship on the sexually active young. If adultery was a majority male pattern, Kinsey found that inhibited "upper level" men began coitus late, making their infidelity a middle-aged pattern. He deplored medical men's authority over sexual problems as well as the narrow range of "upper level" sexual outlets leading to condemnation of other sexual subcultures, universalizing their minority mores to restrain the majority.

The 1953 female volume differed from its predecessor. Kinsey jettisoned the male volume's class analysis, perhaps because the female data diverged inexplicably. University-educated women had the most diverse orgasmic outlets and more lifelong orgasms than least-educated women. A quarter of women admitted adultery, and for most women masturbation remained important lifelong. The most orgiastic informants had pursued teenage sexual experiences, especially petting. Women had greater erotic variation than men, invalidating deterministic explanations for higher male lifelong orgasm counts.

The female data challenged Kinsey's basic assumptions. He undertook new research, advised by expert gynecologists, obstetricians, marriage counselors, psychiatrists, and lawyers, many of them women and friends of Kinsey. Several held orgasm a poor proxy for women's sexual experience, given women's frequent failure to achieve orgasm in marital coitus, for example, but not in other forms of sexual gratification. He called the alleged "vaginal orgasm" an anatomical impossibility that led to the myth of mass female frigidity. Instead, he found the sexes analogous in both structure and function, without anatomical, physiological, or hormonal distinctions sufficient to explain the orgiastic differences between the sexes. His achievement here was in exposing these explanatory gaps in theories about sex differences in sexual behavior. Yet, the limits of his zoological training forestalled adequate explanation of these sexual differences and their cultural habitats, making the female volume uncertain and unfinished, if arguably more intriguing than the 1948 volume.

The Cold War context proved more hostile to the 1953 female volume. Criticism of Kinsey's project and findings by clinicians with antithetical approaches sharpened. Psychoanalysts, his most vehement opponents, considered interviewees as patients incapable of true testimony. Negative reviews, as well as a McCarthyistic public enquiry that threatened the Rockefeller Foundation's tax-exempt status for funding Kinsey's "Communist" research, resulted in the termination of his grants in 1954. Stress took its toll as he sought funding to continue the work. He presented his data on criminal abortion at a Planned Parenthood Conference in April 1955, shortly after commencing his next book titled "Abortion." In October he testified for the Wolfenden enquiry into Homosexual Offenses and Prostitution, urging repeal of draconian British sodomy sentences and those for other sex offences. A planned book on sex offenders had him interviewing at Alcatraz and other prisons, as well as testifying against sadistic calls for castration of offenders.

Unsurprisingly, Kinsey's legacy remains debated. Both canonized and demonized in late postwar sexual politics, some depict him as the father of the sexual revolution or of liberation movements promoting legalization of virtually all sexual practices. Conversely, others draw him as a voyeuristic, masochistic, misogynist, and amoral accessory to criminal perversion. Both assessments are superficial, anachronistic, selective, and disproportionate—as well as singularly inattentive to Kinsey's historical context and actual scientific work. At his untimely death in 1956, obituaries nationwide and worldwide noted that not only Indiana, but the United States, also had lost a momentous figure, who at a minimum had changed the discourse about human sexual behavior.

JUDITH A. ALLEN

For Further Reading

Drucker, Donna. "Creating the Kinsey Reports: Intellectual and Methodological Influences on Alfred Kinsey's Sex Research, 1919–1953." PhD diss., Indiana University, 2008.

Garton, Stephen. *Histories of Sexuality*. New York: Routledge, 2004.

Irvine, Janice M. *Disorders of Desire: Sexuality and Gender in Modern American Sexology*. Philadelphia: Temple University Press, 2005.

Robinson, Paul. *The Modernization of Sex: Havelock Ellis, Alfred Kinsey, William Masters and Virginia Johnson*. New York: Harper and Row, 1976.

Knox, George Levy
September 16, 1841–August 4, 1927

Escaped slave, innovative entrepreneur of luxury barbershops, active Republican Party member in a time when blacks were not represented in the party, and newspaper owner and writer.

The story of George Levy Knox is the stuff of Hollywood biopics, an epic American tale that traces events impacting black life between antebellum America and the Jazz Age. Enslaved from birth, Knox escaped from a plantation near Nashville, Tennessee, during the Civil War and found refuge with the Fifty-seventh Indiana Infantry Regiment, then stationed a short distance away in Murfreesboro. He made his way north in 1864 when he was allowed to accompany an officer of the Fifty-seventh going home on leave to Indianapolis. Knox first labored at menial jobs before finding his calling as a "tonsorial artist," or barber, a skill the illiterate former slave used to transform himself into a highly successful businessman. His acclaim in the business community in turn led to influence and leadership roles in political and religious organizations, locally, statewide, and nationally.

Knox began his career as an apprentice with Reuben Gibbs, a prominent "colored tonsorial artist" of the city, and then ventured out on his own only to go broke. Believing his future was elsewhere, he started over in the barbering business in Greenfield, Indiana, most likely because it was home to many of the soldiers from the Fifty-seventh he had befriended. He was soon joined in Greenfield by his bride, Aurilla Harvey, a member of Indianapolis's "mulatto elite" or "colored aristocracy," who was to play no small role in his success in Greenfield and beyond. She taught him how to read and write and used her "brains and education" to help him prosper.

When he arrived in Greenfield in the fall of 1865, as Knox acknowledged in his autobiography, "prejudice was very high," not surprising in a city where only one other black family lived. Over the course of nearly twenty years, though, Knox, through hard work and making strong impressions and connections with his prominent white clientele, became so respected and revered that even the local Democratic newspaper, which had frequently made him a target of its racist rants, ended its harassment. Beyond his obvious business success, Knox had gained stature in other arenas as well. For example, he became an ally of local Republican leaders, who came to value his political instincts and insights, and he spearheaded the organization of a black congregation, affiliated with the Methodist Episcopal Church, and the establishment of a public school for black children. By the time he and his family, which by now included three children, left for Indianapolis in 1884, Knox was well prepared to build upon his successes in Greenfield as well as add others.

In less than a year after returning to Indianapolis, a barbershop he opened with a partner, which employed six barbers, had already expanded its facilities and he leased the Bates House Barbershop in the hotel where he had worked as a porter years earlier. In time it came to be called "the second finest barber shop in the world," exceeded only by Chicago's Palmer House Barber Shop. Knox's Oriental pleasure palace, employing fourteen barbers, five porters and several laundry men, was magnificently furnished and upholstered, conjuring "the harem of an eastern Caliph." The women's salon offered haircuts, shampoos, and "chiroposdistry" (bunion, callus, corn, and blister treatments). He introduced the manicure, the "bob" hairstyle and "facial," then unknown in Indianapolis. Beneath the parlors, were fifteen ornate baths. Although Knox's "whites only" policy drew criticism from blacks, the *Indianapolis Freeman*, a "colored illustrated newspaper," which Knox eventually purchased, called his establishment "the finest barbershop in America."

Knox continued expanding, adding barbershops at the Young Men's Christian Association, Grand Hotel, and the Denison Hotel. He also ventured into the growing hair-care industry, convinced by his wife to buy an interest in a product known as Soft, Straight, and Silky, a "nutritive pomade," which focused on black women. He also began manufacturing Skin Clear cosmetics, which sold at Knox Hair Parlors.

As he had in Greenfield, Knox continued combining business with politics and religion. Through his friendship with such prominent Republicans as BENJAMIN HARRISON and LEW WALLACE, who were patrons of his barbershop, Knox ultimately was considered Indiana's leading black Republican, though his stature in this regard was not universally accepted. In fact, some critics in the black community of Indianapolis called him the leader of blacks chosen by whites. Although he never held public office, Knox was a member of the Republican State Committee and in 1892 Harrison invited him to accompany him to the Republican National Convention in Minneapolis, where Knox was the only black delegate-at-large from northern states.

Church and civic activities also continued to be central to Knox's life in Indianapolis. For more than forty years he was a leader of the Simpson Chapel Methodist Episcopal Church, active in Sunday school and spearheading the construction of a new church building. In addition, he was elected a delegate to national conferences of the denomination. His civic involvement included service as president of the Douglass Literary Society, participation in the Anti-Lynching League, Colored Benevolent Society, and a founder of the Colored Branch of the Indianapolis YMCA.

Knox was also active in the Afro-American National Business League, holding a number of offices, including first vice president. It was through this organization, formed to encourage business development, that he and Booker T. Washington, the league's president in 1902 and 1903, became close friends. The league argued that "Negroes must become producers and a useful and necessary factors in the community." Black Americans, in Washington's view, had to free themselves from the "suffrage sellers." Similarly, Knox, while not denying racial discrimination existed, believed blacks could overcome such barriers through ambition and perseverance. He believed one promised land to be Guthrie, Oklahoma, a city "where colored men prospered as the white," he said after a visit. Knox purchased land there and began promoting a development called College Heights.

In 1892 Knox ventured into the newspaper business with the purchase of the *Freeman* and by 1900 had infused new life into his national newspaper, giving extensive coverage to show business and baseball. The "Stage" column was to black theater what *Variety*, started in 1905, was to white theater. Black patrons followed performers and their touring schedules and the column provided aspirants and veterans opportunities to communicate directly with theatrical companies. The *New York Age* concurred, writing, "The newspaper became the chief organ of the theatrical profession." Knox's son, Elwood, who assisted in managing the paper, devoted more column space to the national pastime, covering black baseball on all levels, college, amateur, semiprofessional, and professional, providing significant coverage of the Negro Baseball League in particular.

The *Freeman* also published Knox's autobiography in regular installments, which came out in 1895 as the book, *Life as I Remember It: As a Slave and a Freeman*. The newspaper ceased publication in 1926 and Knox died a year later of a stroke he suffered while on a business trip to Richmond, Virginia. His wife, Aurilla, died in 1910 and two of their children preceded them in death: William in 1892 at age twenty-five and Nellie in 1904 at age thirty-six.

In its illuminating account of Knox's life, the *Indianapolis News* wrote, "Those who knew him best will remember him most pleasantly in connection with the barber shops he owned, and over which he presided with rare dignity," adding that he "embraced the opportunity and made the most of it."

JAMES BRUNSON

For Further Reading

Bristol, Douglas Walter. *Knights of the Razor: Black Barbers in Slavery and Freedom*. Baltimore: John Hopkins University Press, 2009.

Cimprich, John. *Slavery's End in Tennessee, 1861–1865*. Tuscaloosa: University of Alabama Press, 2002.

Knox, George L. *Slave and Freeman: The Autobiography of George L. Knox*. Lexington: University of Kentucky Press, 1979.

Taylor, Lynette. "Uncle Sam's Landlord: Quartering the Union Army in Nashville in the Summer of 1865." *Tennessee Quarterly* (Fall 2002): 242–65.

Koch Family

Louis J., June 12, 1882–September 14, 1979; William A., Sr., January 10, 1915–September 17, 2001; William A., Jr., October 22, 1961–June 13, 2010; Philip J., October 11, 1965–April 9, 2013

Founders and developers of Holiday World and Splashin' Safari and Lake Rudolph Campground and RV Resort.

Mention to almost any family in Indiana names such as the Raven, the Voyage, the Legend, Bakuli, Kimba Bay, Pilgrims Plunge, the Wildebeest, and the Mammoth and immediately they recognize these as features at the famous Holiday World and Splashin' Safari in Spencer County, Indiana. With more than 1.2 million visitors a year, Holiday World is known not only in southern Indiana but also in places throughout the state and country. This popular family attraction is due to the vision and hard work of three generations of the family of Louis J. Koch, grandson of German immigrants who came to Evansville, Indiana, in 1843. The family was blessed with an entrepreneurial gene and a strong sense of community obligation. Together they developed over seven decades a nationally recognized and award-winning theme park and also transformed the tiny hamlet of Santa Claus, Indiana, into a thriving community and tourist mecca.

Louis J. Koch was the second oldest son of George Koch, who founded a company in Evansville that specialized in metal products, known today as George Koch Sons Inc. Louis served as managing director of the company. In a foreshadowing of his future endeavors, Louis once built a small amusement park in his backyard. In 1930 he bought property in Santa Claus. He became concerned that children came to Santa Claus expecting to see Santa but were disappointed to find he was not there, only a giant Santa statue. After retiring in 1940 he devoted his time and energy to the development of a park for children. On August 4, 1946, Santa Claus Land, the first theme park in the world opened—nine years before Disneyland in California. The original park consisted mainly of a few themed children's rides, some Mother Goose characters, a miniature train, a live Santa, a toy shop of elves, and a restaurant. Admission was free.

Shortly after opening the park, Louis turned operations over to his son, Bill, who had recently returned from World War II. Bill, a man with a big vision, undertook a major park expansion. A deer farm was added, with deer named, Donner, Blitzen, Comet, and Cupid. Over the years he built new rides for children such as the Jeep go-round, the first of its kinds in the country; a merry-go-round; rides with airplanes and rockets; bumper cars; flying scooters; and a tilt-a-whirl. Live attractions included a ski show on Lake Rudolph. In 1955 the park began charging fifty cents for adults, but children were still free. As more themed sections, such as Halloween and Fourth of July were added, Koch changed the name to Holiday World. By the early 1980s, Holiday World had become a major tourist attraction.

In 1960 Bill married Pat Yellig, the daughter of the park's longtime Santa Claus, Jim Yellig. Together they had five children—Will, Kristi, Dan, Philip, and Natalie; all of them grew up working in the park. Pat worked as a full partner with Bill in running the park. She became the public face of the park in its advertisements.

Bill's vision for development included much more than the theme park. He wanted the community of Santa Claus itself to grow and prosper. He wanted a community where families could live and raise their children, so he built a 2,300 acre gated subdivision at Christmas Lake Village. Many doubted the wisdom of this venture, and lots sold slowly at first, but today Christmas Lake Village has 2,200 home sites.

As the Koch enterprises grew so did the town of Santa Claus. Koch worked to establish the first bank in Spencer County, create a town government, build a town hall, improve roads, install a water and sewer system, and develop a shopping center and a supermarket. The town became incorporated in 1967. When Koch first began his investment in Santa Claus, the community had only thirty-five residents. Today there are 2,500, which includes Christmas Lake Village and Holiday Village, another subdivision developed by Koch. In 1984 the Koch family became independent of George Koch and Sons in Evansville when it formed the Koch Development Corporation, which owned and operated Holiday World and Splashin' Safari, Christmas Lake Village, Holiday Village and Lake Rudolph Campground and RV Resort.

While building a town, Koch also helped establish the Lincoln Boyhood National Memorial in nearby Lincoln City, Indiana. For years the site was a poorly funded state memorial, and Koch wanted it to become a national memorial in order to obtain better funding and attract more tourists. He was present in 1962 when President John F. Kennedy signed the legislation making the former state site into a national memorial.

One of Koch's most significant projects involved the rerouting of the planned Interstate 64, which was originally supposed to go from Louisville to Vincennes, bypassing much of southern Indiana and the Evansville metropolitan area. Koch lobbied hard with the federal Bureau of Public Roads, got the Indiana and Illinois governors to agree to the more southern route, and enlisted the support of community groups across the region. In 1976 Interstate 64 was completed, and the economic ripple effects soon followed, including the AK Steel Plant in Rockport and the Toyota plant in Princeton. Holiday World benefited as well—the interstate is only seven miles from the park.

Koch dabbled in other significant road changes. He had a role getting the Indiana Department of Transportation to relocate and expand U.S. Highway 231, which now runs within three miles of Santa Claus. A year after he died in 2002 the state legislature designated Indiana 162, from the rerouted Highway 231 at Gentryville to its intersection of Interstate 64, as the William A. Koch, Sr. Memorial Highway. Fittingly, Highway 162 runs through the Lincoln Boyhood National Memorial and Santa Claus.

About twelve years before his death, Koch had turned the operation of Holiday World over to his oldest son, Will. Like his father, Will had a vision. In 1993 the park added the Splashin' Safari water park as well as numerous rides and water features. These included the wooden roller coasters the Raven, the Legend, and the Voyage, all of which have won annual awards for being the best and or the tallest. After the water park was opened came ZOOMbabwe, the world's largest enclosed water slide; Pilgrim's Plunge, the world's tallest water ride; and the Wildebeest, the world's longest water coaster. Will initiated the policy of giving unlimited free soft drinks to visitors in 2000 and free sunscreen at the water park in 2002. Aside from winning awards for its big roller coasters and giant water slides, the park won recognition year after year for being "the cleanest" and "the friendliest." In 2004 it won the prestigious Applause Award, the smallest park to ever win the industry award, given every two years by a theme park in Sweden. It is considered to be the Academy Award of the theme-park industry.

On June 13, 2010, the Koch family suffered a major blow when Will drowned at the age of forty-eight in the family swimming pool, a tragedy believed to be due to complications from diabetes. His brother, Dan, who at the time was a lawyer in Florida, was summoned to take over the operations of the park. He continued the family tradition of building more spectacular rides and water features. But in 2013 a legal dispute arose between Dan and Will's widow, Lori, about who had legal control over the Holiday World enterprise. The dispute resulted in lawsuits and countersuits. Ultimately, Lori won the legal battle and named Mack Eckert, a longtime employee and former chief financial officer of Holiday World, as CEO and president, the first person outside of the Koch family to hold that title. Despite the dispute, the park has continued to expand and grow. In 2015 Holiday World debuted the Thunderbird, the nation's first launched-wing coaster and the park's first major steel roller coaster.

On April 9, 2013, the Koch family experienced another loss. Philip J. Koch, who had continued his father's 1958 investment in Lake Rudolph, died unexpectedly at the age of forty-seven following cardiac arrest. In 2002 he had formed with his sister, Kristi Koch George, HO HO HOldings, LLC, the parent company of Lake Rudolph Campground and RV Resort Park, a shopping center and various other real estate, including Santa's Land. At the time of Philip's death, the campground and park that his father started on a limited scale had 272 family rental RVs and cabins, 188 hookup sites, forty tent sites with water and electricity, and averaged 3,000 to 3,500 guests a day during the summer. In 2011 the campground was named one of the top ten in the country in a guest survey by Woodall's Campground Directory.

When Louis Koch first began his Santa Claus venture in 1946, no one could have fully appreciated the legacy that he was starting. The Koch family put Indiana on the map in the world of theme parks, transformed Santa Claus into a thriving town, and helped turn the surrounding area into a prosperous economic region.

LINDA C. GUGIN

For Further Reading

Koch, Pat, and Jane Ammeson. *Images of America: Holiday World*. Charleston, SC: Arcadia Publishing Company, 2006.

Koch, Pat, and Emily Weisner Thompson. *Images of America: Santa Claus*. Charleston, SC: Arcadia Publishing, 2013.

The Koch's Recipe for Success. Produced by Parri O. Black. Evansville, IN. WNIN Public Television Station, 2013.

Lambert, Ward Lewis "Piggy"
May 28, 1888–January 20, 1958

Basketball coach at Purdue University from 1917 to 1946, member of Naismith and Indiana basketball halls of fame, and commissioner of National Basketball League from 1946 to 1949.

In the shadows of Mackey Arena on the campus of Purdue University in West Lafayette stands Lambert Fieldhouse, a monument to "a little man who was well over 7 feet tall." Legendary *Lafayette Journal and Courier* sports editor Gordon Graham wrote that tribute to Ward "Piggy" Lambert, exaggerating his height to illustrate his giant-sized impact on basketball that can be traced from the peach basket games as a child in his adopted hometown of Crawfordsville, Indiana, to the tenth and final National Collegiate Athletic Association championship won by his prize pupil, University of California at Los Angles coach JOHN WOODEN in 1975.

Lambert's importance to the success of Boilermaker basketball was such that from the time he resigned as coach in 1946 until eleven years after his death, Purdue failed to win a Big Ten championship; it had won or shared only two crowns before Lambert became coach in 1917.

Born in Deadwood, South Dakota, Lambert got his nickname because his hair poked out of his stocking cap like a pigtail while riding his sled. At an early age, Lambert and his family moved to Crawfordsville, just about the time when the game of basketball had migrated west from Massachusetts, the game's birthplace. As a ten-year-old, Lambert got the job of knocking the ball out of a peach basket with a stick. He watched basketball grow from a gymnasium game to seven-man teams to the game we all know today.

At five feet, six inches tall and 114 pounds, Lambert led Wabash College in scoring as a sophomore. The next year, while still playing for the Little Giants, his coaching career began at Crawfordsville High School. A natural as a coach, Lambert took over the reins of the Little Giants as player/coach his senior year before graduating in 1911.

Basketball, however, was never first in Lambert's life. Few know that he held a postgraduate degree in chemistry from the University of

Purdue University coach Ward "Piggy" Lambert instructs two of his players from his 1934 basketball team.

Minnesota, which he applied as a chemistry and physics teacher at Lebanon High School. But his coaching experience led school officials to name him coach of the school's athletic teams in 1912.

In a move that would make headlines today, but little noticed at the time, Lambert left Lebanon in 1916 to take over a Purdue program that had gone 14–27 the three previous seasons. The Boilermakers went 11–3 in his first season, and for twenty-five of the next twenty-six seasons (not counting 1917–18 when Lambert was a field artillery lieutenant in the U.S. Army during World War I), Purdue won considerably more games than it lost.

Purdue peaked under Lambert from 1928 to 1932, when two of the greatest players in basketball history—Charles "Stretch" Murphy of Marion—who at six feet, seven inches stood more than a foot taller than Lambert—and Wooden, from Martinsville, Indiana, led the Boilermakers to seventy victories in eighty-four games and a national championship in 1932.

Wooden so revered his coach that, even in his nineties, he still referred to him as Mr. Lambert. "He was a man of extremely high principles," Wooden said of Lambert in 2006. "And I think my basic coaching philosophy came more from him. At the heart of my pyramid I have three things: condition, skill and team spirit. And I think that came from Mr. Lambert, as much as anybody else."

While high-scoring basketball games are common today, they were not in Lambert's time, something he changed by installing the fast break, which quickly gained widespread acceptance. His teams smashed Big Ten scoring marks year after year with an exciting "run, run, run" style. But Lambert also believed in defense.

More than once, Wooden spoke of Lambert's moral character, which perhaps saved Purdue from being engulfed in the point-shaving scandals that occurred in the decade following his retirement. After watching a game at Madison Square Garden in New York during the late 1930s, Lambert refused to schedule any games there and urged his Big Ten peers to do the same. "There are gamblers all over the place, even around the hotels," Lambert said, adding, "Somebody is going to get hurt if we don't keep the game where it belongs—on the college campuses."

Lambert also had a wicked sense of humor, which he demonstrated in an exchange with the Bob Knight of his day, Wisconsin coach Walter E. "Doc" Meanwell, who had a basketball named after him, as did Lambert. Meanwell, worried about what tricks Lambert might come up with for an upcoming game in West Lafayette, wired Lambert to ask what type of ball would be used in the game. Lambert wired back, "A round one."

His final Big Ten championship team in 1940 finished one game ahead of Indiana University at 10–2. Legend has it that Lambert refused to play in the second-ever NCAA tournament, opening the door for the Hoosiers to represent the Big Ten and claim the university's first NCAA title. Another version says the selection was based on Purdue losing twice to Indiana in the regular season.

Before retiring during the 1945–46 season due to failing health, Lambert led Purdue to eleven Big Ten Conference championships, which at the time of his death was more than any other coach in league history. Lambert remains second in Big Ten winning percentage behind Knight's mark of .685 (228 wins and 105 losses) and third in conference victories behind Knight and one of Lambert's successors at Purdue, Gene Keady.

True to his frenetic coaching style, Lambert was active in retirement. He served as commissioner of the National Basketball League from 1946 to 1949, when the league merged with the Basketball Association of America to become today's National Basketball Association.

Unable to sit still, Lambert returned to Purdue to coach freshman basketball and baseball in 1950. He was still freshman baseball coach at the time of his death. A month before he died, Lambert told sports editor Graham that Wooden and Jewell Young were the best players he ever coached. "They had something extra," Lambert said. "If Jewell and Johnny were playing the way the game is played today, they'd average over 25 points per game."

Two years after his death, Lambert was enshrined in the Naismith Memorial Basketball Hall of Fame. "My respect for coach Lambert has grown even stronger over the years as I've come to recognize his authentic ability to transform individuals in a positive way, both for their own good and for that of the team," Wooden said in 2004. "He genuinely cared about those under his supervision. For me he is the model of what a great coach and teacher can be."

KEN THOMPSON

For Further Reading

"Most Memorable Moments in Purdue Basketball History." *Lafayette Journal and Courier*, 1998.

"Ward 'Piggy' Lambert." CBS Interactive, 2014. http://www.purduesports.com/sports/mbaskbl/spec-rel/legends-wardlambert.html

Lanier, James Franklin Doughty

November 22, 1800–August 27, 1881

Lawyer, banker, and financier.

Although James F. D. Lanier spent only a portion of his life in Indiana, his contributions to the state were indelible. In the 1830s and 1840s he played an integral part in salvaging Indiana's failing banking system, as well as assisting in rescuing the Madison and Indianapolis Railroad. But it was during the Civil War, years after he had moved to New York City, that Lanier made his most significant contribution to Indiana history. By lending funds to the state twice during the war he insured that Indiana remained a mainstay of the Union cause.

Lanier was born in Washington, North Carolina, in 1800, the son of Alexander Chalmers Lanier, a struggling farmer and storekeeper, and Drusilla Doughty. Due in large part to his father's financial difficulties, Lanier spent his childhood on the move. In 1807 his father moved the family to Eaton, Ohio, where he freed his slaves. The family moved one last time in 1817, settling in Madison, Indiana, where Lanier's father opened a dry goods store. The venture was unsuccessful and after Alexander's death in 1820 the family was left deep in debt. In spite of his father's financial difficulties, Lanier was able to attend an academy in Newport, Kentucky, where he received a solid education. He began to read law in 1819 with General Alexander A. Meek in Madison. Later that same year he married Elizabeth Gardiner, with whom he had eight children.

After completing his legal training at Transylvania University in Lexington, Kentucky in 1823, Lanier returned to Madison and went into private practice. Although his business thrived, riding the circuit across southeastern Indiana proved to be too much of a strain on his health, and Lanier left private practice to seek steadier employment elsewhere. He accepted the position of assistant clerk of the Indiana House of Representatives in 1824 and then served as chief clerk of the House from 1827 to 1830. He was elected prosecuting attorney for the third district in 1830 on an anti-Andrew Jackson ticket. That same year he was also hired to settle the accounts of the closed Farmers' and Mechanics' Bank in Madison. It was during this time that Lanier began investing heavily in real estate, both in Madison and in the frontier counties of northern Indiana. Having become president and chief shareholder of the Madison branch of the new State Bank of Indiana in 1833, he left both politics and the law in order to concentrate solely on business. Even so, Lanier remained engaged in Madison's civic life by serving as an officer of both the local Grand Lodge of Indiana and the Temperance Society.

So successful was he in his new career that just four years later in 1837, when the state banking system was near collapse, it was Lanier who was selected to go to Washington, D.C., with $80,000 in gold, to persuade the Treasury Department to continue federal deposits in the State Bank. The success of this mission, which allowed the bank to survive the panic of 1837, was largely credited to Lanier, who was then appointed a pension agent by Treasury Secretary Levi Woodbury for part of the western region. In the following decade Lanier played an instrumental part in salvaging Indiana's financial credit by brokering a deal with European creditors to restructure the state's interest payments on bonds that were badly in arrears.

By the 1840s Lanier was one of the most successful bankers and land speculators in Indiana and it was at that time that he commissioned noted Hoosier architect Francis Costigan to design and build a mansion for his family residence in Madison. Completed in 1844, the Classical Revival house, overlooking the Ohio River, was the largest and most expensive home built in Indiana up to that time. In 1848, two years following the death of his first wife, he married Mary McClure, with whom he had three children.

While involved with the struggling Madison and Indianapolis Railroad, Indiana's first railroad, in the mid-1840s, Lanier became intrigued with the investment possibilities presented by expansion of railroads across the West. As a result, in late 1848 he moved to New York City where, along with partner Richard H. Winslow, he formed Winslow, Lanier and Company in January 1849. As a private bank, the firm specialized in railroad securities and worked for railroads regarding local county and city issues. A pioneer in the industry of floating railroad securities, the firm was a major success from the outset and Lanier later wrote that they "not unfrequently negotiated a million dollars in bonds daily."

At the time Lanier and Winslow formed their partnership there were fewer than seven hundred miles of railroad in the West. Between 1849 and 1854 more than 10,000 miles of new rails were constructed and Winslow, Lanier and Company was involved (in some fashion) with every mile of new track that was laid. The company withdrew from underwriting railroad securities in 1854 and in 1859 Winslow retired, leaving Lanier in control of what was now a flourishing Wall Street bank specializing in acting as both the financial and transfer agent for railroads across the United States. That same year Lanier took charge of reorganizing the Pittsburgh, Fort Wayne and Chicago Railroad, which had come perilously close to bankruptcy following the panic of 1857, and transformed it into one of the nation's premier lines.

For all his success both in Indiana and New York, it was not until the Civil War that Lanier provided the service upon which, more than any other, his remarkable reputation for public service is based. In 1861 Indiana's finances were once again in disarray. The state was heavily in debt, the treasury was empty, and Governor OLIVER P. MORTON was unable to raise the funds necessary to equip the thousands of Hoosier recruits that the federal government called upon the state to provide for the war effort. Unable to raise money through the sale of bonds, the governor turned to Lanier, who advanced the state $420,000, which was repaid the following year. Then in 1863, after the Democratic-led legislature refused to pass any appropriations to cover the necessary expenses of the state, Lanier once again stepped in and loaned the state (entirely without security) an additional $629,000 over a two-year period. These loans were repaid, with interest, in their entirety in 1865.

Lanier's actions were not seen as entirely unselfish by all observers, including the *Indianapolis Sentinel*, which took a dim view of Lanier's motives, and the question of repayment even became an issue in the 1864 gubernatorial race. However, Lanier's efforts were largely credited with not only ensuring that Indiana's first regiments were better equipped than many of their peers, but also with ensuring that the state would not only continue meeting all of its ongoing military obligations, but also could keep its institutions such as hospitals and prisons open.

Following the end of the war, despite increasing health problems, Lanier continued to play an active role on Wall Street, serving as president of the Third National Bank of New York. In his later years, Lanier eschewed both politics and society, although he did provide financial assistance for his distant cousin, the poet Sidney Lanier. Following years of declining health, Lanier died in New York City in August 1881, leaving behind a personal estate reportedly worth almost $10 million and an outstanding reputation for public service based upon his efforts on behalf of the state of Indiana during a time of national crisis.

JEFFERY A. DUVALL

For Further Reading

Bruggen, Bill, and R. David Cart. *JFD Lanier: America's Forgotten Patriot and Financier.* Carmel, IN: Lanier Mansion Foundation, 2000.

Lanier, James F. D. *Sketch of the Life of J. F. D. Lanier.* New York: Hosford and Sons, Printers, 1871.

Leach, Antoinette Dakin
April 3, 1859–June 11, 1922

Campaigner for women's suffrage and lawyer whose lawsuit opened the Indiana bar to women.

If Antoinette Dakin Leach could look around a modern courtroom, she might be a little surprised, but she would surely be pleased. As the person credited with formally opening the Indiana Bar to women attorneys, Leach could easily find herself watching a female judge preside over a case argued by two women lawyers or the first female chief justice of Indiana presiding over oral arguments before the state supreme court.

Women now play leading roles in law firms large and small. They also preside at all levels of state and federal courts in numbers so substantial that even close observers would be hard-pressed to summon up the totals at any given moment. Finally, with women having achieved rough parity with men in the state's law schools, the whole profession continues to grow rapidly toward representing the society it serves.

This ongoing development is certainly good for both women and men, but not everyone realizes how much of it must be credited to the leadership of a thirty-four-year-old former court reporter from the small town of Sullivan, Indiana.

Antoinette Dakin Leach was born in Wooster, Ohio, but moved to Gosport in Owen County, Indiana, and later to Sullivan, Indiana, with her mother and stepfather when she was about twelve. Her classmates at Sullivan's Ascension Academy knew her as Nettie Brighton, having taken her stepfather's last name. Around 1875 she was hired to teach school in Sullivan, remaining there for several years, but returned to Ohio in 1878 to attend Ohio Wesleyan University in Delaware, Ohio. There she met and married George W. Leach. In an unusual move, Antoinette and George signed a prenuptial agreement specifying that Antoinette could pursue educational and work opportunities as she chose.

The couple took up residence in Sullivan and had two children: Hortense Eugenia, born in 1880, and George Jr., born in 1882. The 1880 census lists Leach's mother, Lydia Dakin Brighton, as a part of their household. Perhaps it is because she had her mother's help at home that in 1884 Leach was able to leave Sullivan to attend law school in Knoxville, Tennessee. She continued her legal training in Detroit. There are no journals or letters from this time indicating how long Leach was away from home at any one time, but in 1887 she was back in Sullivan working in the law office of John S. Bays. She served as the court reporter for the Greene-Sullivan Circuit Court at the same time, instituting the use of stenography at a time when many courts did not even have typewriters. Being an astute businesswoman as well as a lawyer, she opened a stenography school in addition to her other activities.

Despite being a law school graduate and a veteran court reporter, Leach's attempt to become an attorney was blocked by her employer, Judge John C. Briggs. He denied Leach's petition for admission to the bar, relying on a provision in the Indiana Constitution that declared voters of good moral character eligible for bar admission. In 1893 Indiana women did not have the right to vote and thus did not appear to qualify under this provision. Nevertheless, at least one woman, Bessie Eaglesfield, had been admitted to the bar in Vigo County.

Hoping to achieve a ruling that might apply statewide, Leach appealed the denial of her application, an appeal necessarily filed for her by a male lawyer. The Indiana Supreme Court reversed the trial court's ruling, and ordered Leach admitted to the bar, saying that the Indiana Constitution should not be read as disqualifying nonvoters from becoming lawyers (*In re Petition of Leach*). Writing for a unanimous Supreme Court, Justice Leonard J. Hackney, a jurist with just a few months experience on the court, rejected the "fiction" that women should remain at home. He wrote:

> If nature has endowed women with wisdom, if our colleges have given her an education, if her energy and diligence have led her to a knowledge of the law, and if her ambition directs her to adopt the profession, shall it be said that forgotten fiction must bar the door against her?

The Indiana ruling was especially progressive for the age given decisions issued by other courts. The Illinois Supreme Court had denied a similar petition brought by Myra Bradwell, observing that the "strife" of the bar would surely destroy femininity. And the Illinois decision was affirmed by the U.S. Supreme Court, with three justices going out of their way to say that "the natural and proper timidity and delicacy which belongs to the female sex evidently unfits it for many of the occupations of civil life."

Following her victory before the Indiana Supreme Court, Leach was sworn in as a member of the bar October 10, 1893, and Indiana coincidentally became the first place in the nation where courts admitted women to the profession without being commanded to do so by legislation. By 1897 women were arguing for women's suffrage before the Indiana Supreme Court. Emboldened by Leach's win, HELEN GOUGAR brought litigation asking the court to extend voting rights to women. Her case did not meet with the same success. This time, Justice Hackney's opinion indicated that the court felt bound by the very specific provision in the constitution that voting was for "every male citizen," though he spent several paragraphs suggesting that women's suffrage might be beneficial and declaring that the result in Gougar's case did not reflect the justices' personal views on the question of granting women the vote.

For many years, Leach herself pushed for women's suffrage and became a national leader in the movement, a prominent ally of Susan B.

Anthony. She chaired the Sullivan County Progressive Party in 1912 and became the first woman president of the county bar association. Besides breaking the gender barrier, Leach also injected new technology into the practice of law. She typed her petition for admission to the bar, and it is believed to be one of the first typewritten documents filed in the Indiana Supreme Court.

Leach practiced law in Indianapolis and Sullivan until 1907 when ill health forced her to retire. She died in 1922 at the age of sixty-three—two years after Indiana women won the right to vote. Fortunately, she lived long enough to hear the many celebrations of her work. Alva Belmont of New York, for example, president of the National Suffrage Association, called her "the most capable advocate of the equal suffrage movement since Susan B. Anthony."

The legacy of her bar admission victory lives on. Each year, the Indiana State Bar Association names one of Indiana's most respected women attorneys as the recipient of the Antoinette Dakin Leach Award—a fitting tribute to the former court reporter from Sullivan whose lawsuit firmly established a woman's right to practice law in Indiana.

ELIZABETH R. OSBORN
RANDALL T. SHEPARD

For Further Reading

Farmer, James. "Women in the Law: A Centennial Legacy of Antoinette Dakin Leach." *Res Gestae* 37 (September, 1993): 106–11.

In re Petition of Leach 134 Ind. 665 (1893).

McCarty, Virginia Dill. "From Petticoat Slavery to Equality: Women's Rights in Indiana Law." In *The History of Indiana Law*. Edited by David J. Bodenhamer and Randall T. Shepard. Athens: Ohio University Press, 2006.

Shields, Sue Vivian, "Antoinette Dakin Leach: A Woman Before the Bar." *Valparaiso University Law Review* 28 (Summer 1994): 1,188–230.

Lieber, Richard N.

September 5, 1869–April 15, 1944

An ardent conservationist who was known as the father of the Indiana Park System and the first director of both the Indiana Department of Conservation and the Indiana State Parks Commission.

An early conservation visionary, Richard N. Lieber championed the acquisition of pristine wilderness areas for state parks. He believed natural areas could provide quiet and respite to "refresh and strengthen and renew tired people" and should be preserved for generations. Lieber became interested in public parks after coming to the United States from England in 1891. He explained, that he "could not help notice the many wasted opportunities in proper land use, such uses as Parks, Forests, Land & game Refuges, all of which would be of great scenic & economic value."

Born in Duesseldorf, Germany, in 1869, Lieber was the first son of an upper-class family. After a fall down the family's circular staircase, he spent his first eight years in poor health, requiring private tutoring. Later, he attended the Municipal and Royal Lyceum followed by two years at the University of Bonn. An outstanding language scholar, he mastered Greek, Hebrew, Latin, French, and Italian. In 1890 he went to England to learn English, and with financial support from his father, he enjoyed the life of a gentleman—traveling, attending lectures, and visiting museums. When he returned to Germany at Christmas with liberal views, his concerned parents promptly sent him to America to live with two uncles in Indiana in hopes of tempering their son's political ideas.

Richard Lieber in his military dress uniform during World War I.

In Indianapolis Lieber fell in love with Emma Rappaport, daughter of the publisher of the *Indiana Tribune*, but needed a steady income before he could marry her. In 1892 he borrowed $3,000 from his Uncle Herman Lieber and with two friends formed the Western Chemical Company. The company suffered three disastrous fires between January 1892 and March 1893. A frustrated Lieber resigned from the company in 1893. As a result of this experience, he became passionate about civic reforms, specifically fire prevention and affordable fire insurance. Through his efforts the Indiana General Assembly passed legislation in 1913 creating the office of State Fire Marshall. Stricter building codes and regulations for handling flammable materials resulted.

In 1893, at age twenty-three, he married eighteen-year-old Rappaport. For the next eight years he wrote witty and informative columns on music and art for the *Indiana Journal* and the *Tribune*. He served as city editor of the *Tribune* until 1900. His interest broadened and he was elected president of the Indianapolis Trade Association, a position he held from 1910 to 1912.

Disgusted with inept government practices Lieber worked to establish a merit system for public employees in Indianapolis. In December 1912 the city implemented a civil service commission plan to test job applicants. Lieber was elected the commission's president. However, in 1914 the newly elected mayor disbanded the commission. Perhaps in response to this action, Lieber told the *Indianapolis News* that "the difference between a cheap politician and a real statesman is the willingness, courage and ability of the man to stake his temporary popularity against higher patriotic duties." In spite of repeated attempts, a state merit plan was not enacted until 1936.

In 1900 Lieber became an ardent proponent of conservation after a tour of Yosemite National Park and later that year a trip through the Rocky Mountains of Idaho and Montana, where he saw the ravages of commercialization. During a 1910 visit to Brown County, Indiana, Lieber fell in love with natural beauty closer to home. He built a summer residence there in 1911 and christened it Whip-Poor-Will Lodge.

About this time Lieber became active in the growing national conservation movement and attended a White House conference on conservation sponsored by President Theodore Roosevelt. He returned to Indiana and became an advocate for conservation in the state. In 1912 Indianapolis hosted the Fourth Conservation Congress. As chair of the conference Lieber seized opportunities to highlight Indiana's natural heritage. In a press interview, he spoke eloquently about the environmental damages that had beset the country and concluded, "The cure lies . . . in prevention and in conservation."

An opportunity to promote the cause of conservation in the state arose in 1915 with the death of John Lusk, who owned a tract of land in Parke County known as Turkey Run. This situation eventually led to Lieber's role in establishing the state park system. Lusk allowed people to camp and hike on the property, which was filled with sandstone cliffs, magnificent canyons, and huge stands of giant trees, and he steadfastly resisted all entreaties by timber companies to purchase it. When he died, Juliet V. Strauss, who delighted in the property as a child, became concerned that the towering pines would fall to the axes of the timber companies.

Strauss, who wrote articles extolling the virtues of rural life that appeared in *Ladies' Home Journal* and the *Indianapolis News*, sought Governor Samuel M. Ralston's support to preserve this virgin forest. Her initiative was timely because Ralston had established the Indiana Historical Commission to plan for ways to commemorate the state's centennial. The commission's members saw Strauss's proposal to save Turkey Run as a state park as a way to establish a statewide centennial memorial. The IHC formed a special parks committee, named Lieber as its chairman, and raised $20,000 to purchase Turkey Run. Unfortunately, the Hoosier Veneer Company outbid the commission and announced plans to remove "all merchantable trees." Nonetheless, through further negotiations, and the support of public and private contributions, in November 1916 the state acquired Turkey Run from the Hoosier Veneer Company for $40,200.

Meanwhile, property at McCormick's Creek in Owen County was about to be auctioned, and the state, along with Owen County residents, raised $5,250—enough to win the bid, and McCormick's Creek became Indiana's first state park. With two parks entirely paid for by donations, thanks in large part to Lieber's role, Indiana had the beginnings of its state park system. Today there are twenty-eight state parks and fifteen state forests.

Leiber enjoyed a close relationship with Ralston's successor, James P. Goodrich. A few days after the United States entered World War I, Goodrich appointed twenty-four individuals to his military staff including Colonel Lieber, a designation he carried thereafter. In 1919 Goodrich appointed Lieber as director of the new Department of Conservation. In that capacity, Lieber also became superintendent of the Division of Land and Water. During a lifetime of service, he worked tirelessly to establish more state parks. As a nationally recognized authority, he advised many states interested in acquiring and maintaining land for parks, and in 1932 was elected president of the National Conference on State Parks. In 1934 the National Park Service recognized Indiana, New York, and California as having the nation's three top state park systems.

Lieber recommended moderate user fees for park maintenance to reduce the necessity for government support. He firmly believed that paying visitors were more apt to appreciate and care for this natural beauty, which he dubbed "the dietetics [nutrition] of the soul." He built inns at some of the parks to encourage longer visits and stated that natural surroundings provided "revitalization and recreation." He asserted that "the selection of park lands is akin to the work of the artist. It is a form of creation; a vision. Park planning is a technical job and park management a business enterprise. If these items are harmoniously balanced they produce, as a result, park service."

Lieber's service to the state ended in 1933, when he was demoted by Governor PAUL V. MCNUTT to the position of director of the Division of State Parks and Lands and Waters. He resigned shortly thereafter.

Lieber died unexpectedly on April 15, 1944, at McCormick's Creek Canyon Inn, while on a visit there with his wife. His will requested burial at Turkey Run, his favorite park. His ashes, and those of his wife and oldest son, rest at the base of the lifelike bronze sculpture erected in 1932 during Lieber's lifetime to honor this visionary man. The *Indianapolis Times* editorialized, "it is as the father and creator of the state parks that he will be remembered." In 1957 the state announced that Cagles Mill Recreation Area in Putnam County would be named for Lieber, and in a ceremony on July 12, 1958, Richard Lieber State Park was dedicated.

CAROLYN HARSTAD

For Further Reading

Frederick, Robert. A. "Colonel Richard Lieber Conservationist and Park Builder: The Indiana Years." PhD diss., Indiana University, Bloomington, 1960.

Lieber, Emma. *Richard Lieber*. Indianapolis: Privately printed, 1947.

Lieber, Richard N. Papers. Lilly Library, Indiana University, Bloomington.

Lilly Family

Eli, *July 8, 1838–June 6, 1898.* **Founder of Eli Lilly and Company, 1876; Indianapolis leader. Josiah K. Sr.,** *November 18, 1861–February 8, 1948.* **President of Eli Lilly and Company, 1898–1932; cofounder of Lilly Endowment. Eli,** *April 1, 1885–January 24, 1977.* **President of Eli Lilly and Company, 1932–48; cofounder of Lilly Endowment. Josiah, K. Jr.,** *September 25, 1893–May 5, 1966.* **President of Eli Lilly and Company, 1948–53; cofounder of Lilly Endowment.**

In the course of three generations the Lilly family built a world-class pharmaceutical business and a pattern of philanthropic giving that reached deep into Indianapolis and Indiana.

The first prominent Lilly was a Greencastle druggist who at the age of twenty-four formed a Civil War cavalry unit and rose to the rank of colonel. Eli Lilly engaged in several business ventures before establishing a small pharmaceutical company in Indianapolis in 1876. In a few years Colonel Lilly, as he was then known, employed a hundred workers and moved to McCarty Street on the industrial south side. Eli Lilly and Company grew to one of the largest businesses in the city. The Colonel also played a leading role in organizing the Commercial Club and other civic and charitable projects.

The Colonel's only son, Josiah K. Lilly, entered the business at age fifteen. In 1880 his father sent him to the Philadelphia College of Pharmacy, an important step in bringing more scientific expertise to the family business. J. K. soon became the de facto head of the company and the formal head when the Colonel died in 1898.

J. K. and his wife, Lilly Ridgely, named their first-born Eli. Four years later came a second son, Josiah K. Lilly Jr., known as J.K. Jr. or Joe. The two brothers developed respect but not close fraternal affection, perhaps because Eli believed his mother always gave more attention to Joe. The

Lilly brothers began working at the pill factory, as they called it, as young boys. Both obtained good educations. Eli graduated from his father's alma mater, the Philadelphia College of Pharmacy in 1907, and Joe completed his pharmacy degree at the University of Michigan in 1914.

Young Eli and Joe took on more responsibilities in the 1910s as their father spent more time traveling and then pursuing his collection of Stephen Foster memorabilia. The family triumvirate worked well together, keeping very tight control of the family business and rejecting offers for mergers with other companies. None of the Lillys was a playboy even as their wealth grew. Each avoided the limelight, seldom putting their name on buildings or projects, preferring quiet hobbies and a few close friends.

Eli and Joe brought to the business a passion for scientific management and efficiency. At the McCarty Street complex they pushed through new manufacturing and research buildings. They built massive assembly lines to produce high-volume output at lower prices. They stocked a new capsule plant with machines that replaced hand labor, making it perhaps the largest capsule factory in the world. Some of their colleagues, including sometimes their father, thought the young Lillys moved too quickly.

In addition to streamlining the manufacturing process, the Lillys addressed scientific research. At the beginning of the century the company still relied mostly on the nonefficacious patent medicines the Colonel produced at the start. One best seller was Succus Alterans, supposedly made from a secret Creek Indian formula and sold as treatment for all manner of maladies, from rheumatism to syphilis.

In the late 1910s the Lillys carefully prepared for the future of pharmaceutical research. One of their early steps was to hire GEORGE HENRY ALEXANDER CLOWES, an Englishman with a German PhD in chemistry. Clowes made the first contacts with University of Toronto scientists who had developed a treatment for diabetes. Eli understood the potential. He built the team that brought the university laboratory experiments to Indianapolis and created the manufacturing capability to turn small samples into large-scale production. In 1923 Lilly's insulin began to raise diabetics from their deathbeds and rapidly increase company profits. The Indianapolis pill factory joined the small circle of first-class, research-based pharmaceutical manufacturers.

Eli succeeded his father as president of the company in 1932. He carried forward scientific research and development, including production of penicillin and other antibiotics in the 1940s. With his brother, he also instituted new employee relations programs that raised morale and that included a refusal to lay off any worker during the Great Depression. Under Mr. Eli's leadership, Hoosiers came to know that Lillys, as many called it, was one of very best places to work in central Indiana.

In 1948, following the death of J. K. Sr., Joe succeeded Eli as president, although Eli stayed closely involved in the business. By then the brothers had begun to plan for the next generation. No young Lilly stepped up, however, so that planning necessitated bringing nonfamily members into leadership positions, as when Eugene Beesley succeeded Joe as president in 1953.

As the economy boomed and profits rose in the postwar years, both brothers drifted into nonbusiness pursuits. Joe became a collector of rare books. His superb collection was the foundation for the Lilly Library at Indiana University, Bloomington. Eli developed an interest in archeology

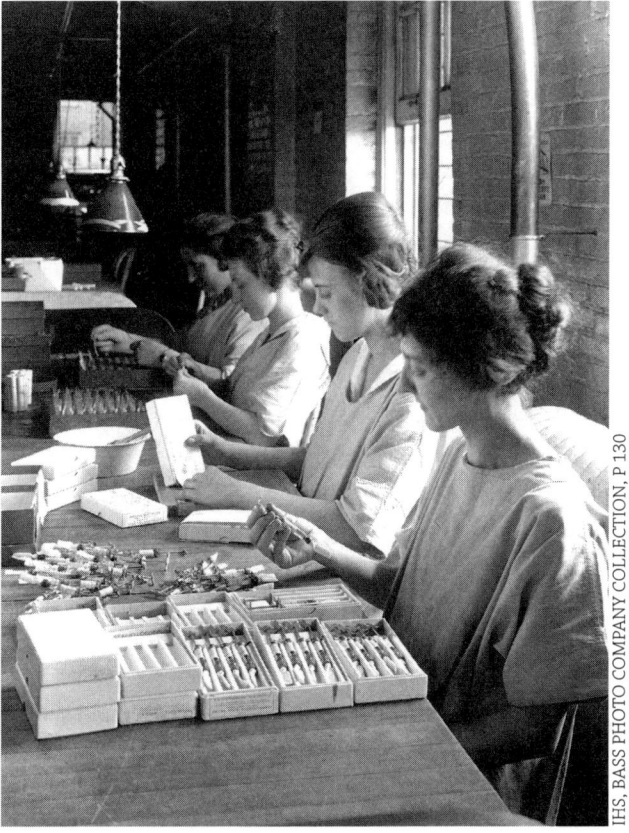

Eli Lilly and Company employees, 1919.

and history that had many consequences, including the Angel Mounds archaeological site on the Ohio River; preservation of William Conner's 1823 home, which became the seed for today's Conner Prairie Interactive History Park; and support of Indiana Landmarks and the Indiana Historical Society.

As their fortunes accumulated the family began to give. The Colonel and his son initiated a tradition of giving to Indianapolis. Eli and Joe followed. The predecessor to the city's United Way was among the first, while Christ Church on the Circle was always a family favorite. Eli became a major benefactor, giving millions to the Indianapolis Museum of Art, several universities, the IHS, and the Children's Museum of Indianapolis.

Much of the family's giving was personal, often anonymous, and seldom with conditions. J. K. Sr. joined Eli and Joe to move toward more formal philanthropy with the founding in 1937 of the Lilly Endowment. They wanted to continue their giving tradition and also reduce their tax burdens while maintaining family control of the business. The Endowment's assets consisted almost entirely of company stock from the three men. Eli led the organization, operating it out of one desk drawer. Like the business, it was a family-run operation.

The Lilly Endowment focused on education, religion, and community service, mostly in Indianapolis and Indiana. Among the largest beneficiaries were the state's liberal arts colleges and churches. In the early 1960s Joe pushed some giving into conservative anti-communist, free market, and evangelical religious organizations. Eli, though conservative himself, was lukewarm or nonsupportive of these right-wing initiatives and soon moved the organization in broader directions following his brother's death in 1966.

After Joe's death, when the Endowment was among the nation's five wealthiest foundations, Eli led a transition toward more professional operation. He added board members outside the family and new staff and giving procedures. Eli's personal interests and style nonetheless remained a part of the Endowment's culture long after his death. One of his last initiatives was to push the Endowment in the early 1970s toward massive contributions to rebuilding downtown Indianapolis. Joe's daughter, Ruth Lilly, continued the family tradition of local giving.

In business and philanthropy over three generations the Lilly family was among Hoosier royalty. At the end of the twentieth century the *Indianapolis Star* named Eli the man of the century. He would have modestly turned away from such visibility and perhaps quoted Oliver Wendell Holmes, as he often did, that "every man is an omnibus in which our ancestors ride." Colonel Eli Lilly, J. K. Lilly Sr., and brothers Eli and Joe made a handsome Hoosier omnibus.

JAMES H. MADISON

For Further Reading

Bodenhamer, David J., and Robert G. Barrows, eds. *The Encyclopedia of Indianapolis*. Bloomington and Indianapolis: Indiana University Press, 1994.

Madison, James H. *Eli Lilly: A Life 1885–1977*. Indianapolis: Indiana Historical Society, 1989.

Lincoln, Abraham

February 9, 1809–April 15, 1865

President of the United States during Civil War who engineered passage of the Thirteenth Amendment to the U.S. Constitution.

Within days of Indiana's becoming a state—on December 11, 1816—a family crossed the Ohio River from Kentucky to create a new life on the frontier. Abraham Lincoln, one member of this family, was influenced by this new state of Indiana; and he, in turn, influenced Indiana. The Thomas Lincoln family, in many ways, typified the new state's residents. Originating in the upper South, these pioneers strongly believed in the American promise of individual freedom, and Indiana was a land of opportunity free from both slavery and antiquated land laws that threatened economic security.

In what became Spencer County, Thomas and Abraham built a primitive, three-sided shelter, and later a strong log cabin to protect the family from the elements. In 1818, just as life was becoming more comfortable, the nine-year-old Lincoln experienced hardship and great sorrow when his mother, Nancy, died of milk sickness. As the wifeless, motherless family struggled, Thomas understood he must act. He returned to Kentucky, already aware that Sarah Bush Johnston, an acquaintance, had recently lost her husband. In December 1819 Thomas returned from Kentucky with a new wife and her family. Years later, Lincoln said of his stepmother, "She proved a good and kind mother." No doubt, she was a genuine comfort to Lincoln when, in 1828, his beloved sister, Sarah, died in childbirth. Certainly thoughts of his Indiana years came to mind when, on December 23, 1862, Lincoln wrote young Fanny McCullough after the wartime death of her father:

> It is with deep grief that I learn of the death of your kind and brave Father; and, especially, that it is affecting your young heart beyond what is common in such cases. In this sad world of ours, sorrow comes to all; and, to the young, it comes with bitterest agony, because it takes them unawares. The older have learned to ever expect it.

Young Lincoln's formal schooling totaled about a year, including short terms at three different Indiana schools. In addition to this instruction, his education included conversations at Gentry's Store and Baldwin's blacksmith shop, observations of travelers while he worked at the Ohio River town of Troy, reading neighbors' newspapers, and occasionally court sessions he attended. Indeed, in Indiana Lincoln borrowed his first law book, *The Revised Laws of Indiana, 1824*, which included the Declaration of Independence.

Gentry's Store, an important stop for local and state politicians, nurtured his interest in politics, particularly with the newly emerging party politics in the 1820s. Lincoln's Spencer County presidential vote went for Henry Clay in 1824, but for Andrew Jackson in 1828. By the time his family moved to Illinois in 1830, Lincoln's political thought—perhaps under the influence of his friend, William Jones—was firmly in line with Clay, a rising star in the soon-to-be formed Whig Party. In Illinois Lincoln became a leader in the Whig Party, and in 1844 he returned to his Spencer County neighborhood to campaign for Clay in his quest for the presidency against James Polk. Although the political impact of Lincoln's efforts for Clay remains unclear, he renewed acquaintances with old friends and even wrote poetry about his Hoosier memories.

By the 1850s the nation's political structure had changed over the issue of slavery, something Lincoln said he always opposed. His father was antislavery, and one reason for the 1816 move to Indiana was so farmer and woodworker Thomas need not compete with slave labor. But Lincoln's first exposure to large-scale plantation slavery and slave auctions occurred during his 1828 flatboat journey with Allen Gentry down the Ohio and Mississippi Rivers to New Orleans. Even if we cannot judge with certainty the long-term impact of that visit on the young Lincoln, certainly he always remembered the experience.

Like Lincoln, most Indiana residents opposed slavery. Though not abolitionist, they did not want slavery extended to western territories, and as seen in the 1851 Indiana Constitution, neither did they welcome freedmen in the state. In fact, freed slaves were prohibited from moving into the state. By 1860 the new Republican Party had become a force in the state, and Indiana played a major role in selecting the party's candidate for president. With his moderate image, Lincoln ultimately became Indiana's choice and won the nomination.

In the election of 1860, Hoosiers not only helped to elect Lincoln president, but also gave control of state government to the Republican Party. However, by the time of the state elections in October 1862, war stalemate, use of the draft, and Lincoln's preliminary Emancipation Proclamation allowed the Democrats to win control of Indiana's General Assembly. This control led to two years of a dysfunctional government that was unable to secure passage of legislation, leading Republican governor OLIVER P. MORTON to circumvent the legislature, in part to raise money to operate the state. Then, in the election of 1864, Republicans regained control of the Indiana House while the Senate was divided with each party having twenty-five members.

Lincoln led the country during a war that influenced the political, economic, and social activity of Indiana like no other event to that time—and perhaps since. In the Civil War, only one Northern state contributed a higher percentage of military-age men to the war than did Indiana. Sadly, of the more than 200,000 Hoosier men who fought in the war, 12.6 percent never returned, and scores more returned without limbs or with life-changing injuries. Indeed, the war's impact remained long after the war itself ended.

Lincoln was reelected president in 1864, and his top legislative priority was to secure passage of an amendment to abolish slavery in the United States. The proposed Thirteenth Amendment was first passed by the U.S. Senate in April of 1864, but passage in the House was not certain. Lincoln maneuvered mostly behind the scenes to obtain the votes needed to approve the amendment. Largely through his efforts, the House finally passed the amendment on January 31, 1865, and it was sent to the states for ratification. It won approval in the Indiana House fifty-seven to forty-two. Victory in the Indiana Senate, however, was not assured. Through spirited debate the opponents raised concerns about future racial equality and states' rights. Finally, on February 10, 1865, one Democrat, Paris C. Dunning, voted with Republicans and the resolution won approval twenty-six to twenty-four.

Less than three months later, on April 15, 1865, Lincoln was assassinated. His funeral train crossed Indiana, carrying the slain president to Illinois. On April 30, 1865, at least 50,000 people viewed the president's open casket in the rotunda of the Statehouse in Indianapolis. Next, the train stopped briefly in Michigan City before traveling on to Illinois.

Lincoln's presence in the state remains, especially in Spencer County. Since the erection of a monument at the gravesite of his mother Nancy Hanks Lincoln in 1879, visitors have come to visit where Lincoln lived for one quarter of his life. By the early twentieth century, efforts of local residents, county officials, and state-appointed commissions resulted in Nancy Hanks Lincoln Park, a favorite reunion site for Civil War veterans. Major development began in 1925 when a partnership between the Indiana State Department of Conservation and the Indiana Lincoln Union, a private group of 125 influential citizens appointed by Governor Edward Jackson, joined to build a national shrine that "will express both our deathless devotion as well as our indefinite gratitude to the soul of the great departed and his Mother."

Over the next twenty years the state acquired much of the land that once constituted the Lincoln farm, erected a cabin-site memorial, designed a park with formal landscaping leading to Nancy Hanks Lincoln's grave, and constructed an imposing memorial building made of Hoosier limestone, sandstone, and native Indiana timber. Interest in the site increased during the 1959 sesquicentennial observances of Lincoln's birth. On February 19, 1962, President John F. Kennedy signed an act creating Lincoln Boyhood National Memorial, Indiana's first National Park Service unit. Today this memorial helps approximately 150,000 visitors per year appreciate the formative years of Abraham Lincoln and his lasting impact on the state of Indiana.

WILLIAM E. BARTELT

For Further Reading

Bartelt, William E. *"There I Grew Up": Remembering Abraham Lincoln's Indiana Youth.* Indianapolis: Indiana Historical Society Press, 2008.

Basler, Roy P., ed. *The Collected Works of Abraham Lincoln.* By Abraham Lincoln. New Brunswick, New Jersey: Rutgers University Press, 1953.

Warren, Louis Austin. *Lincoln's Youth, Indiana Years, Seven to Twenty-one, 1816–1830.* New York: Appleton, Century, Crofts, 1959.

Link, Goethe

May 20, 1879–December 31, 1980

Physician and astronomer.

During the 1930s, Indianapolis physician Goethe Link had achieved great prominence in his field, earning the respect of his fellow doctors with his skill as a surgeon. "I had several lucky breaks in my practice," Link noted. "In fact, it seemed that if I got ready for something, opportunity soon knocked on my door." With his medical practice a success, Link, born in Selvin, Warrick County, Indiana, sought escape from the busy city life of Indianapolis. He purchased more than fifty acres in northern Morgan County, building a country home on land that had formerly been an apple orchard. "When I got here, like Brigham Young I said, 'This is the place!'" Link recalled. He named his property Tanager Hill after the scarlet tanagers and summer tanagers that flocked to the area.

Although he continued to hone his surgical skills, Link believed that pursuing other activities "rested me intellectually and thus aided progress in my life's work." As a young boy in Petersburg, Indiana, Link had become fascinated by a book on astronomy he found in his father's library. "I used to watch large birds that could fly across a valley without moving their wings," he recalled, "and I became fascinated by ascending currents of atmosphere and astronomical facts."

Years later, Link renewed his interest in the subject through a class taught by K. P. Williams, a professor of mathematics, through an Indiana University extension program in Indianapolis and membership in the fledgling Indiana Astronomical

Society, founded in 1933. Planning a honeymoon to the West with his new wife, Helen (his first wife died in 1930), Link also took with him on the trip a letter of introduction from Williams to three former IU students—Earl C. Slipher, Vesto M. Slipher, and Carol O. Lampland—who worked as astronomers at the Lowell Observatory, a privately owned astronomical research institution in Flagstaff, Arizona. Link later joked that he received so much information from the astronomers that he suffered "intellectual indigestion." During the trip Link also met with Russell W. Porter, an amateur astronomer who had helped design the Mount Palomar Observatory near San Diego. Porter sketched out plans for Link so he could build an observatory close to his Morgan County home.

Establishing the Goethe and Helen Link Foundation for Scientific Research, Link began construction on his observatory in 1937. The facility received support from a variety of members of the Indianapolis Astronomical Society and was supervised by Victor E. Maier, a noted Indianapolis amateur astronomer who had previously advised other enthusiasts on how to build telescopes. The facility immediately attracted the attention of members of the IU astronomy department, who visited the site along with groups from Indianapolis. One fellow physician told Link after seeing the partially completed observatory: "Goethe, you are going to have to operate in all doubtful cases to pay for this."

Work at the observatory centered on building a facility to securely house a telescope equipped with a thirty-six-inch mirror that had been a test pouring for the 200-inch mirror provided by the Corning Glass Works for the Hale Telescope at Mount Palomar. It took ten months and the building of a special machine by Carl D. Turner, an Indianapolis engineer, to grind and polish the ribbed Pyrex mirror, which cost $385.

To support the 400-pound mirror and its cross-axis German equatorial mounting, which weighed 5,000 pounds, crews using wheelbarrows and shovels constructed a concrete pier resting on bedrock. After the pier had been competed, workers used wood from a nearby forest to construct the building's frame made of oak posts and beams, with an interior of oak hardwood floors and knotty-pine walls. The lower floor included a large auditorium that could seat 150 people, a darkroom, library, sleeping quarters, and a kitchen.

To keep the large dome housing the telescope the same temperature as the outside air, the building had no central heating system; those who worked there had to rely instead on portable electric heaters. The dome itself measured thirty-four feet in diameter and included an eight-foot-wide shutter opening through which the telescope could peer into the heavens. The entire dome could be moved to different positions by using only a half-horsepower electric motor that could be operated by the push of a button. In a second, smaller dome, located on the flat roof over the auditorium, Link placed his own personal telescope, a five-inch Zeiss refractor.

With the observatory ready to begin operations in early January 1939, Link made the facility available to scientists at local colleges and universities. IU President HERMAN B WELLS quickly took advantage of the offer for the university's astronomy department. In October 1938 the university announced it would establish a postdoctoral fellowship (first awarded to Doctor James Cuffey, a graduate of Harvard University) to conduct research at the observatory on a year-round basis. Cuffey took the first celestial photograph from the observatory in August 1939.

In addition to the research work, the observatory also hosted field trips from IU astronomy students and regularly scheduled visitor nights open to the general public. On those nights the auditorium became jammed with people listening to presentations on the stars while another group crowded up the circular staircase waiting their turn to mount an observation platform for a glimpse through the 5,200-pound telescope at the evening sky.

Cuffey continued his research into star clusters at the observatory until World War II intervened, and he left in June 1941 to serve in the navy, teaching navigation at the U.S. Naval Academy in Annapolis, Maryland. He returned to the Bloomington campus in 1946 as an assistant professor. Following the war, IU astronomers, in cooperation with the International Astronomical Union, used the observatory to track the orbits of asteroids (called minor planets in those days) that had been lost track of during the war years. For the asteroid observations, Link and the university reached agreement with the University of Cincinnati for the permanent loan of a ten-inch diameter astrographic lens. Link funded the construction of a separate building for the telescope. From 1948 to 1967, astronomers at the observatory took more than six thousand photographs and discovered more than a hundred new asteroids.

Shortly after arrangements had been made for the installation of the new astrograph, Link decided in 1948 to donate the observatory along with twelve acres to IU. He later told a reporter that as he got older he could no longer do as much work in astronomy as he wanted to because of the late hours involved. Doctor Frank K. Edmondson, chairman of the IU astronomy department, noted that Link's generous gift greatly expanded the scope of the department's activities. "It gave us a large telescope, a vital element which we lacked and which is necessary to support a graduate program in astronomy leading to a Ph.D. degree," Edmondson said. The university made some alterations to the facility, adding photoelectric and spectrographic equipment to the thirty-six-inch telescope, overhauling the main dome's turning gears, and moving by crane the small dome from the roof over the auditorium to a site on the ground south of the main building. In 1978 IU, with financial help from the National Science Foundation, added a control room to the main dome for the use of researchers.

By the 1980s light pollution from Indianapolis's urban sprawl had hampered use of the Link observatory's telescopes and IU had to move its research activities to other locations. The public, however, continued to visit the site whenever possible for programs given by the university and the state astronomical society, as well as to marvel at the numerous varieties of daffodils planted on the grounds by Helen—a pastime she started with a gift of bulbs from her husband. The couple continued to enjoy the beauties of Tanager Hill until their deaths; Goethe, at age 101, in 1981, and Helen, at age ninety, in 2002.

RAY E. BOOMHOWER

For Further Reading

Boomhower, Ray E. "The Doctor and the Stars: Goethe Link and His Observatory." *Traces of Indiana and Midwestern History* 19, no. 4 (Fall 2007): 16–23.

Edmondson, Frank K. "Dr. Goethe Link—Astronomer." *Journal of the Indiana State Medical Association* (July 1970): 758–59.

Link, Goethe. "Personal Observations of Medicine and Surgery in Indiana." *Journal of the Indiana State Medical Association* (February 1968): 252–57.

The Lynds

Helen Merrell, March 17, 1890–January 30, 1982, and Robert Staughton, March 17, 1892–November, 1, 1970

Social scientists and authors of two Middletown books on Muncie, Indiana.

Writing about *Middletown*, Robert and Helen Lynd's 1929 study of Muncie, Indiana, economist and social critic Stuart Chase proclaimed, "who touches this book touches the heart of America" Chase's enthusiastic response was common among readers of the Lynd's pioneering social investigation that went onto become both a bestseller and a landmark in American sociology. It launched the scholarly careers of the Lynds and established for Muncie a reputation as a representative American community.

Robert Staughton Lynd was born in 1892 in New Albany, Indiana. Helen Merrell was born in 1896 in LaGrange, Illinois. Robert graduated from Princeton University in 1914, worked in publishing, and briefly served in the U.S. Army during World War I. After his discharge he enrolled at Union Theological Seminary and earned a divinity degree in 1923. Helen studied philosophy at Wellesley College, graduating in 1919, and she began her career teaching at a girl's boarding school in New York City. After two years she left teaching to enroll at Columbia University, where she earned a master's degree in the History of Ideas in 1922. The pair met on vacation in New Hampshire and married in New York City in 1921.

The Lynds were a surprising choice to conduct the "Small City Study" conceived by the Institute for Social and Religious Research. John D. Rockefeller Jr. had funded the institute to investigate ways for religious agencies to address social problems arising from industrialization. Robert Lynd came to the attention of Rockefeller when he wrote an article based on his summer work as a divinity student organizing a church in Elk Basin, Wyoming, site of oil camps owned and run by Rockefeller's Standard Oil. The article fiercely criticized the company for working and living conditions in the camps. Although angered at first, Rockefeller eventually agreed to let the institute hire Lynd as the head of its investigation into religious activity in a small industrial city. Helen soon joined her husband as coinvestigator.

The choice of Muncie as the site for the project

Robert Lynd (back row, left) was part of a delegation from the Consumers National Federation seeking the establishment of a Central Consumers' Agency by President Franklin D. Roosevelt in February 1938.

arose from a desire to simplify the research. Initially, the Lynds planned to study South Bend, Indiana. But that city's size and ethnic diversity made an in-depth investigation too complex. Ultimately, they chose Muncie because, as they noted, it was "compact and homogenous enough to be manageable." The decision to focus on a largely white and Protestant community, and to dismiss the significance of its rapidly growing African American population, fueled its initial popularity, as well as subsequent debates about whether Muncie should be considered a truly representative American community.

The Lynds relocated to Muncie in early 1924 and, with the support of a three-person staff, conducted their investigation over eighteen months. During that time the scope of the project expanded dramatically, encompassing not only religious activity but also all aspects of the community's life. The Lynds worked chiefly as participant observers, partaking in local social and institutional life. They also administered surveys, conducted historical investigation, and interviewed key informants. The result was a massive examination of the city's social life filled with acute observations and arguments about work life, gender roles, the impact of mass consumption, and other topics.

Drawing on anthropological categories devised for the study of primitive societies, the Lynds divided human experience into six categories: getting a living, making a home, using leisure, engaging in religious practices, training the young, and engaging in community activities. They framed the book as a comparison between the supposedly preindustrial Muncie of 1890 and its fully industrialized counterpart of 1924. In its broadest outlines, the book argued that although Middletown residents had experienced extraordinary economic and material change, they still had not adjusted their values and perceptions to the new realities of industrial life. This cultural lag left them bewildered.

Although the Institute for Social and Religious Research rejected the book, largely because it went so far beyond the initial idea for a religious investigation, it was soon published to great acclaim. Reviewers praised its careful research and its scientific character, but the key reason for its initial success and strong sales was the prevailing impression that the Lynds had captured the essence of American life. This propensity to read the book as an authoritative examination of a mainstream American community helps explain its popularity, although the Lynds' failure to address racial and ethnic experiences has also been the basis for sharp critiques of the book.

The success of *Middletown* propelled Robert and Helen into prominent academic careers. Robert submitted portions of the *Middletown* book as his dissertation and received a PhD in sociology from Columbia in 1931. Helen became a charter member of the faculty at Sarah Lawrence College and she earned a doctorate in history and philosophy from Columbia in 1944.

The Lynds completed a second study of Muncie as Middletown during the mid-1930s. Robert (but not Helen) spent the summer of 1935 in Indiana updating some facets of their earlier research. Upon his return to New York City, the couple wrote the second volume jointly. Although titled *Middletown in Transition*, the book noted the absence of meaningful cultural change. It argued that community values and attitudes stubbornly persisted even in the midst of the Great Depression. The book had a sharper tone than its predecessor and was especially critical of the heavy influence of the Ball family on local affairs and of what the Lynds described as the "Middletown spirit"—an individualistic attitude that emphasized self-help and limited government even during an economic crisis. Resting on a thinner base of evidence and evincing a more critical tone, the book received respectful reviews but failed to capture the popular interest that the first Middletown study had earned.

The couple contemplated a third Middletown book but it never materialized. Instead they pursued other academic interests during their remaining careers. Robert was a prominent social scientist, best remembered for *Knowledge for What?* (1939), a critique of value-free social science. Helen worked in several disciplines, publishing *England in the 1880s: Toward a Social Basis for Freedom* (1945) and *On Shame and the Search for Identity* (1958). During the McCarthy era, both Lynds faced accusations that they were members of the Communist Party. Helen testified before Congress in 1953 and published essays on academic freedom. Robert died in 1970 and Helen died in 1982. They were survived by two children, Staughton, a prominent historian, and activist, and Andrea.

Although both Lynds were important academics, their legacy stems largely from the success of their Middletown studies. They captured the nation's imagination with their portrait of a small city whose residents were reluctant to adjust to modern life. Their work reinforced the sense that Indiana and the Midwest were the true American heartland. The success of their research inaugurated a tradition of studying Muncie as Middletown that continues to the present. Scholars following the Lynds' lead have produced hundreds of books, articles, and films examining life in one small city in Indiana, all in the hopes of better understanding modern American life.

JAMES J. CONNOLLY

For Further Reading

Hoover, Dwight W. *Middletown Revisited*. Muncie, IN: Ball State University, 1990.

Lynd, Robert S., and Helen Merrell Lynd. *Middletown: A Study in Contemporary American Culture*. New York: Harcourt Brace Jovanovich, 1929.

———. *Middletown: A Study in Cultural Conflicts*. New York: Harcourt Brace Jovanovich, 1937.

Maclure, William
October 27, 1763–March 23, 1840

Eighteenth-century Scottish immigrant and businessman and nineteenth-century statesman, geologist, and educational reformer.

William Maclure is known as the "father of American geology" and "patron saint of Indiana libraries." He produced the first widely available geologic map of the United States in 1809, and played a key role in establishing the Owenite utopian community at New Harmony, Indiana, in 1826. He left a will that bequeathed funds to provide books for libraries in every county in Indiana, and it also ensured the continuation of his Working Men's Institute and Library, Indiana's oldest continuously operated free public library, founded in 1838 at New Harmony.

Maclure was born to wealth and privately educated in Ayr, Scotland. At age nineteen, he began working for an American mercantile business. Based in London, he traveled to and from America, and frequently worked in France and Ireland, two countries supportive of the American Revolution. He accumulated a great fortune and retired in 1796 to a life of travel. Maclure immigrated to Philadelphia and became a naturalized U.S. citizen in 1800. Continuing his travels in Europe, he conducted geological observations in France and Spain. He served in Paris in 1803 on a U.S. Commission for American citizens with losses resulting from the French Revolution, and he consulted with educational leaders in Switzerland, where he became a proponent of Johann Heinrich Pestalozzi's educational methods, which focused on the whole child, going beyond intellectual development and emphasizing hands, heart, and head.

Starting in 1808, Maclure began to focus on the United States after he had received a rare color copy of a geological map of the eastern United States by French philosopher and historian Count de Volney (Constantin-François de Chasseboeuf), and became fascinated with making a geological map of the whole country. Such a map, Maclure thought, would be the basis for evaluating economic potential—minerals, agriculture, and transportation. Maclure's map was published in 1809 and accompanied his *Observations on the Geology of the United States*, published in the *Transactions of the American Philosophical Society*. It became the first generally available geological map of the United States, and thus had strong influence on subsequent American geology.

Maclure's classification of strata was based on the simple schemes developed by European geologists of the mid-eighteenth century. These classifications assumed that most rocks had formed by precipitation or sedimentation from a primordial ocean and from later seas, rivers, and lakes, the so-called Neptunian concept. Maclure's original map included only four categories of rocks, from oldest to youngest: primitive, transitional, flötz or secondary, and alluvial.

A revised map and expanded *Observations* were published in 1817. The only notable geologic addition was the volcanic class derived from magma, the so-called Plutonic concept. The Neptunian rocks of supposed aqueous origin were thus reduced but not completely eliminated. Besides his maps and two editions of *Observations*, Maclure published several other works on West Indies, European, and Mexican geology, as well as economic and igneous geology, and stratigraphy. Maclure's many notable scientific contributions led to his election in 1791 as a Fellow in the prestigious American Philosophical Society, founded in 1743 by Benjamin Franklin. Also, Maclure joined the Academy of Natural Sciences of Philadelphia in 1816. He was a benefactor and served as president from 1817 to 1840.

Maclure was dedicated to promoting educational reform, and he was an early advocate for schools that taught science applied to industry and agriculture. He believed the vast American interior would become a great agricultural region supporting a largely agrarian society. In these views, he was not alone for the early nineteenth century. During the next few years, Maclure traveled widely and resided in several countries of western Europe. In 1819 he decided on Spain, where a new constitution held much promise to test his experimental agriculture school for poor children. However, his educational plans failed, the constitutional government was overthrown, and he returned to the United States.

William Maclure

In 1824 Maclure visited ROBERT OWEN, a wealthy Scottish industrialist and social reformer. He was intrigued with Owen's utopian experiment, and together they purchased land and structures at New Harmony, Indiana, from GEORGE RAPP, the Harmonist's leader. Maclure and Owen convinced several prominent intellectuals to accompany them, and they traveled from Pittsburgh down the Ohio River in the keelboat *Philanthropist*, later called "The Boatload of Knowledge," arriving in New Harmony in January 1826.

Maclure believed in universal education for all, including women, the poor, and workers, as crucial for a new society, and he transformed New Harmony into a mecca for natural scientists and Pestalozzian teachers. The social experiment lasted only two years, after which Owen returned to Scotland, and Maclure journeyed to Mexico. His direct association with New Harmony, although brief, proved quite fruitful. His educational scheme was a forerunner of the successful federal, land-grant college system. He continued his financial support for New Harmony, and nine other Owenite communities were established between 1825 and 1843.

The founding of the Working Men's Institute and Library at New Harmony in 1838, which continues as Indiana's oldest, continuously operating library, was a fulfillment of his educational vision. When Maclure died in Mexico in 1840, a provision in his will supported the institute and led to establishment of 143 additional libraries across Indiana and sixteen in Illinois. The original Working Men's Institute and Library at New Harmony is the only one remaining today; most of the others were taken over by township or Carnegie libraries.

Because of Maclure's input, New Harmony became a center for geological studies in the United States during the mid-nineteenth century. He inspired David Dale Owen and Richard Owen, both sons of Robert Owen, to successful careers in geology. In fact, David Dale is now regarded as the pioneer geologist of the Midwest. He conducted geological surveys in Indiana and westward beginning in 1837 until his death in 1860. During this period, New Harmony was David Dale's base of operation and became the first headquarters of the U.S. Geological Survey from 1839 to 1856. The geological laboratory and museum were housed in the Rapp Granary. David Dale's final geology laboratory occupied a smaller adjacent building. Many of the New Harmony geological specimens were later transferred to the Smithsonian Institution and became the basis of its geological collection, an indirect legacy of William Maclure.

JAMES S. AND SUSAN W. ABER

For Further Reading

Douglas, J. "William Maclure and the New Harmony Working Men's Institute." *Libraries and Culture* 26 (1991): 402–14.

Faul, Henry, and Carol Faul. *It Began with a Stone: A History of Geology from the Stone Age to the Age of Plate Tectonics*. New York: John Wiley and Sons, 1983.

Kimberling, C. "William Maclure (1763–1840) geologist, educational reformer." http://faculty.evansville.edu/ck6/bstud/maclure.html.

Working Men's Institute. "Welcome to the Working Men's Institute." http://www.workingmensinstitute.org.

Marshall, Thomas R.
March 14, 1854–June 1, 1925

Governor of Indiana and vice president of the United States.

"What this country needs is a good five-cent cigar." A century of mystique now surrounds this quip by Thomas Riley Marshall when he was Woodrow Wilson's vice president, but nobody has established its accuracy or the context in which it was delivered. The twenty-seventh governor of Indiana and twenty-eighth vice president of the United States deserves to be remembered for more than whimsy. His legacy as governor was the adoption of numerous progressive measures. As vice president he helped keep the government functioning while Wilson recovered from a debilitating stroke.

The only surviving child of Doctor Daniel Marshall and his wife, Martha, Thomas was born March 14, 1854, in North Manchester, Indiana. He attended public schools in Pierceton, Warsaw, and Fort Wayne; graduated from Wabash College with honors in 1873; and studied law under experienced preceptors. Admitted to the bar at age twenty-one, he practiced in partnership with William F. McNagny until 1909.

Marshall married Lois I. Kimsey, eighteen years his junior, on October 2, 1895. Up until then, he had a reputation as a bachelor who could not resist a good cigar or a stiff drink. In time, a drink of whiskey did not satisfy; he "wanted a barrel." His drinking problem persisted until he "took the cure" at Lois's insistence. Thereafter he did not drink.

An ardent Democrat, Marshall ran unsuccessfully for prosecutor in 1880, his only attempt at public office until he was elected governor. In spite of his loss, Marshall's reputation grew as a talented lawyer and public speaker, though he would not have advanced in politics without the support of his wife and the influence of Democratic boss THOMAS TAGGART. During the mid-1890s Marshall and Taggart served on the Democratic State Central Committee. Louis Ludlow, who at the time was the Washington, D.C., correspondent for the *Indianapolis Star*, began touting Marshall for the governorship in 1907 after Marshall expressed interest in that office.

Liquor issues plagued Democrats at their 1908 state convention, where the party would choose its nominee for governor. Neither a "dry" in his politics nor controlled by liquor interests, Marshall favored local option. To head off a temperance candidate, Taggart swung enough votes to Marshall to secure the nomination for him.

During a vigorous campaign Marshall advocated such progressive measures as direct election of U.S. senators, primary election laws, tariff reform, and control of trusts. When opponents labeled Marshall a drunk, his Republican pastor and a Columbia City Roman Catholic priest countered that "Tom" was all the stronger for having defeated demon rum. Marshall prevailed over Republican James E. Watson.

Following his January 11, 1909, inauguration, Marshall used a new State Board of Accounts to cut costs and to hold state employees accountable. He brought the selection of U.S. senators closer to the people. At the time U.S. senators were elected by state legislatures, but Senate nominees were chosen in smoke-filled caucuses. Under Marshall's plan, the state party chose and announced its nominee in advance of elections for the state legislature. The party pledged that if they gained a majority of the legislative seats they would elect their party nominee as Senator. This plan was adopted three years before the Seventeenth Amendment that established direct election of U.S. Senators. In other actions, Marshall pardoned 3,000 prisoners, throttled down a sterilization program at the state reformatory, and deployed the militia not only to protect corporate property but also workers' rights.

In 1910 Democrats won majorities in both houses of the legislature, which facilitated passage of a local option liquor law and enabled Marshall

Vice President Thomas R. Marshall throws out the first pitch on opening day, April 22, 1920, for a game between the Washington Nationals and Boston Red Sox.

to sign reform legislation regarding child labor, drugs, hygiene, employer's liability, voter registration, corrupt practices, railroad safety, and public utilities. Concluding that Indiana's 1851 constitution was obsolete, Marshall engaged his close friend and adviser JACOB PIATT DUNN JR. to draft a new one. It passed both houses with the provision that it be submitted to the voters in 1912. The "Marshall Constitution" attempted to meld progressive panaceas with restrictive voter eligibility requirements. It did not, however, address women's suffrage. Republicans labeled the document unconstitutional and revolutionary. The Indiana Supreme Court blocked its submission to the voters, reasoning that the process would violate the existing constitution. Marshall appealed to the U.S. Supreme Court, but the Court dismissed the case, thus killing the Marshall Constitution.

In the meantime, with solid progressive credentials, the appeal still pending, and the battle over the constitution advertising his name from coast to coast, Marshall attended the National Democratic Convention in 1912 with the goal of being nominated for president. Democrats smelled victory in 1912. The GOP fractured when Theodore Roosevelt divided the party base by forming the "Bull Moose" Progressive Party and becoming its nominee for president. Hoosier strategists saw possibilities for Marshall if the Democratic national convention deadlocked. With Taggart wielding the gavel, the delegates cast forty-six ballots before choosing Wilson to head the ticket. The best Taggart could finagle for Marshall was the vice presidential nomination. Only at his wife's insistence did Marshall accept.

Wilson and Marshall campaigned separately in a three-way race, but appeared together in the earliest known use of celluloid in a presidential campaign. A silent film, *The Old Way and the New*, castigated moneyed interests and asked each laborer to give an honest dollar to the Democratic cause. Their ticket won decisively.

Marshall poked fun at his office but mastered Senate rules and presided over that body with fairness and good humor during a flowering of progressive legislation that changed the course of American history. He left his mark on the Senate by refusing to bring forward petitions from individual citizens that bogged down the legislative process.

People close to Wilson, including his private secretary Joseph P. Tumulty and the second Mrs. Wilson (Edith Galt), regarded Marshall as shallow minded. Nevertheless, Wilson again accepted Marshall as his running mate in 1916. Coupled with the slogan "He Kept Us out of War," the strategy worked. They won in a close race but Marshall never became influential in the administration he faithfully served.

Upon American entry into the World War Marshall traveled the country in support of Liberty Loan drives. When Wilson went to Paris after the armistice, Marshall became the first vice president to preside over a cabinet meeting.

During the waning days of the Sixty-fifth Congress, acrimonious debate erupted in the Senate regarding Wilson's League of Nations. That body adjourned without accepting the League or the peace treaty. A disappointed Marshall banged down the gavel March 4, 1919 "sine deo" (without God) rather than the traditional sine die (without a day).

During a cross-country tour to explain the League to the people, Wilson suffered a cerebral thrombosis that left him a physical and mental invalid. Some of Wilson's close advisers and his wife kept Marshall in the dark about his health for fear that he would try to assume the presidency. Many agreed with the president's intimate adviser Edward M. House that Wilson should have resigned. Edith would have none of it. Her stewardship probably went so far as to guide Woodrow's hand as he signed documents. Influential people urged Marshall to seize the presidency but he refused because there was no precedent for doing so. He mostly attended to ceremonial functions. With dignity and restraint he kept the executive branch functioning until March 4, 1921, when Wilson's term ended.

The Marshalls returned to Indianapolis, where he spent much of his time writing. He accepted President Warren G. Harding's appointment to the U.S. Coal Commission, established to investigate and report on the causes of a prolonged coal strike, and paid off campaign debts with earnings from Chautauqua speeches.

While on a visit to Washington, D.C., Marshall died of a heart attack on June 1, 1925, at the Willard Hotel. He was reading his Bible with Lois at his side. She lived until 1958. They are buried at Crown Hill Cemetery in Indianapolis. "What this country needs is more Tom Marshalls," was Will Rogers's response to his friend's death. An early political assessment of Marshall as "a liberal with the brakes on" has stood the test of time.

PETER T. HARSTAD

For Further Reading

Brown, John E. "Woodrow Wilson's Vice President: Thomas R. Marshall and the Wilson Administration." PhD dissertation, Ball State University, 1970.

Marshall, Thomas R. Papers. Indiana State Library, Indianapolis.

Marshall, Thomas R. *Recollections of Thomas R. Marshall Vice-President and Hoosier Philosopher: A Hoosier Salad.* Indianapolis: Bobbs-Merrill, 1925.

Thomas, Charles M. *Thomas Riley Marshall: Hoosier Statesman.* Oxford, OH: Mississippi Valley Press, 1939.

Martin, John Bartlow

August 4, 1915–January 3, 1987

Journalist, diplomat, and political consultant and speechwriter.

The March 1948 issue of *Harper's* offered its readers the periodical's usual literate blend of fact and fiction. The magazine contained a poem from John Ciardi titled "Hawk," a feature from William Harlan Hale on former vice president Henry Wallace's independent presidential campaign, and a report by Eric Bentley on the previous year's theatrical offerings. The bulk of the issue, however, was given over to a lengthy examination of a coal mine explosion in Centralia, Illinois, that resulted in the death of 111 men. The piece, which the *Harper's* editors called a "top-notch reporting job, to be compared . . . with John Hersey's 'Hiroshima,'" shocked the nation. The 18,500-word tale of helpless miners and an uncaring system, the longest ever printed in *Harper's* at that time, brought about the downfall of the governor of Illinois and prompted the federal government to

John Bartlow Martin in his office at his home in Highland Park, Illinois.

enact a stricter safety code for mines.

The Centralia article was just one in a score of pieces that flowed from the busy typewriter of Hoosier author John Bartlow Martin. In the 1940s and 1950s Martin's work appeared frequently in the "big slicks," mass-circulation magazines printed on glossy paper such as the *Saturday Evening Post, Life, Look*, and *Esquire*. The former *Indianapolis Times* reporter became, as his son John Frederick Martin recalled, one of but a few freelance writers in the country able to support himself from his work. Martin's peers considered him "the best living reporter" and "the ablest crime reporter in America." What set Martin apart, however, was a deep and abiding concern for the common man. "Most journalists," he noted, "make a living by interviewing the great. I made mine by interviewing the humble—what the Spaniards call *los de abajo*, those from below."

Martin, whose career also included stints as a speechwriter and adviser for the presidential campaigns of Adlai Stevenson, John F. Kennedy, Lyndon Johnson, Robert F. Kennedy, Hubert Humphrey, and George McGovern—was born on August 4, 1915, in Hamilton, Ohio, the eldest son of John W. and Laura Bartlow Martin. The family moved to Indianapolis when Martin was three years old. Derisively dubbed "the bookworm" by his father, the scholarly young Martin had a difficult childhood. His father, who had dreams of moving the family to a better neighborhood on the city's north side, suffered severe financial setbacks during the Great Depression. Martin's two brothers, Dickie and Billy, died at a young age. These tragedies helped to tear apart his parents' marriage (they later reconciled). "Most people who write their memoirs," Martin reflected in his autobiography, "seem to have had happy childhoods. I hated mine."

At an early age, Martin knew what he wanted to do in life. "Throughout high school, and even in grade school, I wanted to write," he said. Graduating early from Indianapolis Arsenal Technical High School at age sixteen, Martin, with financial support from his grandmother, attended DePauw University. By his own admission he "behaved like a fool" during his freshman year in college. Expelled from the university because of a drunken incident, he returned home to join his father in walking the streets looking for work. Martin kept alive his dreams of becoming a writer by finding work with the Associated Press's Indianapolis bureau as a "stock gummer," taking stock market quotations off a ticker tape and pasting them onto sheets of paper containing the names of stocks for nine dollars a week.

When Martin asked Sam Ochiltree, Indianapolis AP bureau chief and the father of one of his high school friends, for a job as a reporter or editor, Ochiltree turned him down, telling Martin he would hire him only if he returned to DePauw and finished his college degree. Readmitted to the university in early 1935, Martin buckled down to his studies and continued to hone his writing skills, becoming editor of the school newspaper and working as a stringer for the *Times*.

While still in school, Martin accepted a full-time job as a reporter with the *Times* (he completed his courses at DePauw in absentia). Rising up through the ranks, Martin covered city hall for the newspaper and eventually ended up doing rewrite, taking information over the telephone from reporters and turning it into stories for the *Times*.

Martin decided to try his hand at freelance writing, setting up his home base at the Hotel Milner in Chicago with but one suitcase and a portable typewriter. During those early years, Martin's livelihood consisted mainly of writing articles for such magazines as *Official Detective* and *Actual Detective*. In August 1940 Martin married Frances Smethurst (an earlier marriage to his college sweetheart had ended in divorce in 1939) and published articles with *Harper's* on such Indiana-related subjects as the downfall of Ku Klux Klan leader D.C. Stephenson. In 1944 Knopf published the first of Martin's numerous books, *Call It North Country*, which explored the history of Michigan's Upper Peninsula. Following a short stretch in the army, Martin resumed his writing career by traveling the Midwest to research a story for *Life* on the postwar mood and producing a history of the Hoosier State for Knopf in 1947 titled *Indiana: An Interpretation*.

Martin's life changed in the early 1950s when a friend asked him to edit a book of speeches by Illinois governor Adlai Stevenson, who had used the Centralia story as an effective tool to strike at his opponent, incumbent governor Dwight Green. With Stevenson's capture of the 1952 Democratic presidential nomination, Martin went to work for the governor as a speechwriter in his 1952 race against Republican Dwight D. Eisenhower. In Stevenson's 1956 presidential campaign, and in John Kennedy's 1960 run for the White House,

Martin discovered his niche—editorial advance man. "I would talk to the local Democratic leaders, businessmen, newsmen, taxi drivers, waitresses, bartenders anybody I could find," he said. Martin would produce a report and rejoin the campaign party as it traveled through the state he had just visited.

After working for Kennedy's presidential effort, Martin was appointed U.S. ambassador to the Dominican Republic, the Caribbean nation he had first visited as a young man. The following years were busy, and often tragic, for Martin. As ambassador, he worked tirelessly to support the Dominican Republic's first democratically elected government, but saw his hopes dashed by a military coup. Just two months after Martin returned to the United States to discuss with the administration what to do next, Kennedy was assassinated in Dallas. A heartbroken Martin resigned his ambassadorship. Still, he believed that his political experience contributed to making him, in the long run, a better reporter.

The gloom that had fallen over Martin lifted in the spring of 1968, when Robert Kennedy decided to become a candidate for the Democratic presidential nomination. Kennedy's decision to run in the Hoosier primary against Eugene McCarthy and Indiana governor Roger Branigin "was in many ways the climactic event of my life, bringing together writing, politics, and Indiana," Martin said. He settled into the familiar task of serving as an editorial advance man for the campaign. Martin advised Kennedy to visit Hoosier historic sites honoring heroes such as ABRAHAM LINCOLN and JAMES WHITCOMB RILEY, to conduct a railroad whistle-stop trip on board the Wabash Cannonball, and make more campaign appearances at Kokomo and other factory cities. Kennedy took Martin's advice. The result on May 7 was a win for Kennedy. A month later in Los Angeles, Kennedy was shot and killed following his win in the California primary.

Kennedy's assassination, according to Martin's son, "broke the back of my father's spirit." Martin went on to work on behalf of the eventual Democratic presidential nominee Humphrey, but found himself moving away from politics and spending more and more time in later years on writing. Instead of magazine stories, however, Martin produced a number of books. He explored his time in the Dominican Republic in the book *Overtaken by Events: The Dominican Crisis from the Fall of Trujillo to the Civil War* (1966), and his entire career in his memoir *It Seems Like Only Yesterday: Memoirs of Writing, Presidential Politics, and the Diplomatic Life* (1986). He also found time to teach journalism at Northwestern University. Martin died of throat cancer on January 3, 1987.

RAY E. BOOMHOWER

For Further Reading

Boomhower, Ray E. *John Bartlow Martin: A Voice for the Underdog.* Bloomington: Indiana University Press, 2015.

Martin, John Bartlow. *It Seems Like Only Yesterday: Memoirs of Writing, Presidential Politics, and the Diplomatic Life.* New York: William Morrow and Company, 1986.

Martin, John Frederick. "John Bartlow Martin." *American Scholar* (Winter 1990): 95–100.

Maxwell, David Hervey

September 17, 1786–May 24, 1854

A delegate to the Indiana Constitutional Convention in 1816, state legislator, and dubbed the father of Indiana University for his critical role in the founding of the university.

Described as the father of Indiana University, Doctor David Hervey Maxwell was a tireless advocate for locating a public university in the state. As a member of Indiana's 1816 constitutional convention and a dedicated public servant for many years, Maxwell was intimately involved in crafting Indiana's first constitution, giving his particular attention to the adoption of Article 9 pertaining to education, and to state and local affairs. Maxwell's dream came to fruition in the mid-1820s with the opening of what was to become IU.

Maxwell was born on September 17, 1786, at Maxwell's Station in Lincoln (now Garrard) County, Kentucky Territory, to Bazaleel and Margaret Anderson Maxwell. His grandfather and his father both fought in the Revolutionary War. Educated at what schools were available in Danville, Kentucky, and at home, Maxwell studied medicine under Doctor Ephraim McDowell, a noted surgeon. On September 21, 1809, Maxwell married fellow Kentuckian Mary E. Dunn, and the following year they moved from the Kentucky Territory to the Indiana Territory, settling on the Ohio River six miles below Hanover.

During the War of 1812 Maxwell was a private and a surgeon in the Mounted Rangers of Captain Williamson Dunn, his brother-in-law. Maxwell lost his surgical instruments at a time of high water during the war and had to petition Congress for compensation, which he eventually received. Maxwell treated eighty-five sick soldiers of the 106 who were stationed at the fort. He and several other men were discharged from the service at Vincennes because of a service-related illness.

As a delegate to the first Constitutional Convention of Indiana in 1816, one of Maxwell's chief goals was to use his influence to establish a state university. In part because of his efforts, Article 9 of Indiana's first constitution called for the general assembly to establish a general system of education that would include a state university where tuition would be free and "equally open to all."

In May 1819 the Maxwell family moved from Madison to Bloomington, where he practiced medicine. Several months later, the first meeting of the First Presbyterian Church, with nine charter members, was held in the Maxwell's log cabin. About the same time, two opportunities allowed Maxwell to continue his quest to secure a state institution of higher education that would be located in Bloomington. In 1819 he was chosen as a state representative to the Indiana General Assembly, giving him an ideal chance to promote his cause among fellow legislators. In 1820 he was named one of six trustees for the Board of Indiana Seminary who were authorized to select a site for the institution. They chose a site on June 24, 1820, that was about a quarter mile south of the Bloomington courthouse.

Maxwell served in the legislature as a state representative from 1821 through 1826, and as a state senator from 1826 through 1830. He served as speaker from 1823 to 1824. Maxwell was a trustee of IU, including its predecessor institutions—Indiana Seminary and Indiana College—from 1820 through 1837, and then from 1839 through 1852, and for the majority of his tenure served as president of the board. One university historian said that his efforts in behalf of the university were "unselfishly directed" and that his labors were "so unremitting . . . and directed to such good purpose" that it could be said of him and no other person that he was "the father of Indiana University."

The exact date that classes started at Indiana Seminary is in dispute, but relevant letters and reports indicate that the date was most likely April 3, 1825. In a February 17, 1825, letter signed by Maxwell and the other trustees, published in the *Bloomington Indiana Gazette*, announced that the State Seminary of Indiana would begin accepting students by the first Monday of April. The letter noted that the admission fee for each scholar would be five dollars per year, that "good boarding" was available "in town, or country," and the institution "will for the present be strictly classical . . . each scholar [being] required to furnish himself with a supply of classic books." The letter also noted that the campus buildings were erected on an elevated level, "affording a handsome view of Bloomington the county seat of Monroe County."

In its brief history, the seminary was barely operating when, in 1828, the state legislature renamed it Indiana College to elevate its status. It had hired two faculty members and had only a few dozen students. What the institution lacked was leadership. To address this pressing need, on October 25, 1828, the board of trustees elected Reverend ANDREW WYLIE to be the first president. Wylie, who at the time was president of Washington College in Pennsylvania, was unaware of the board's decision until he received a letter from Maxwell advising him of his election. Maxwell and others understood that convincing an easterner to move to Indiana at the time would be a hard sell.

Maxwell, along with the two existing faculty members, wrote a series of letters to Wylie. Maxwell's letters document his deftness and his persistence. On May 7, 1828, he wrote that the board believed that under Wylie's guidance, the college "will flourish and become a praise and a glory to our young and rising state." Noting that he had lived in Indiana for sixteen years, Maxwell closed his letter by observing that "Bloomington is as healthful a situation as any in our state, or in any of the western states." In another letter sent on June 5, 1828, Maxwell observed that Indiana was "rapidly populating," that its population had more than doubled since 1820, and that "in a short time our settlements will extend north to the borders of Michigan." Maxwell invited Wylie to visit in October 1828. Just prior to that visit, a row occurred involving the board's election of a new faculty member. The strong criticism aimed at the school, the board, and the faculty member in question by supporters of other candidates troubled Wylie. On December 18, 1828, Maxwell responded explaining the facts of the dispute and assured Wylie that his concerns were unfounded. He encouraged Wylie not to let his feelings about the matter deter him from accepting the presidency.

Apparently Wylie's wife did not favor moving to the frontier. In spite of these obstacles, Maxwell's persistence, along with others who corresponded with Wyle, paid off. On April 11, 1829, Maxwell acknowledged receipt of Wylie's letter accepting the presidency. As to when Wylie should move to Indiana, Maxwell wrote that the "moderately cold weather of our winters has the effect of bracing the human system so as to enable us in a great degree to withstand the debilitating and relaxing effects of the summer's heat." Wylie arrived in due course, and served with distinction as IU's first president for more than twenty years.

As Maxwell's term on the board was coming to an end, he entered a new phase of public service. In 1836 Governor Noah Noble nominated him to serve as a member of Indiana's Board of Internal Improvement, which presided over significant infrastructure projects such as the construction of roads and canals. Maxwell served on the board, and as its president, for one year.

In 1841 Maxwell was appointed postmaster of Bloomington, a position that he had held in 1825. The *Bloomington Post* observed at that time that the "Post Office in Bloomington is now kept at Doctor Maxwell's Medicine Shop." In April 1848 Maxwell was elected mayor of Bloomington. The *Bloomington Indiana Tribune* described Maxwell's election as well as that of other local officeholders as "an excellent selection." After a one-year stint as Bloomington's mayor, Maxwell again accepted the position of postmaster. On May 24, 1854, Maxwell passed away at the home of his son, Doctor J. D. Maxwell.

DONALD B. KITE SR.

For Further Reading

Clark, Thomas D. *Indiana University: Midwestern Pioneer. Vol I: The Early Years.* Bloomington: Indiana University Press, 1970

Houston, Florence, et al. *Maxwell History and Genealogy: Including the Allied Families of Alexander, et al.* Indianapolis: Press of C. E. Pauley, 1916.

Maxwell, Louise. "Sketch of Dr. David Maxwell." *Indiana Magazine of History* 8 (September 1912): 101–8.

McCulloch, Oscar Carleton

July 2, 1843–December 10, 1891

Congregational minister in Indianapolis whose views on causes of poverty influenced on a broad scale charitable giving to the poor.

Oscar Carleton McCulloch, noted Hoosier minister and reformer, was born on July 2, 1843, in Fremont, Ohio, to Carleton and Harriet McCulloch. The oldest of five children, McCulloch was educated in Wisconsin and New York before finding employment in Illinois as a clerk and then as a salesman for a drug firm. His father hoped he would pursue a career in business, but McCulloch felt called to the ministry.

In 1867 McCulloch entered Chicago Theological Seminary, which was affiliated with the Congregational Church. Here he was exposed to the early social gospel and its calls for reforming society. Three years later, he accepted appointment to the pulpit of First Congregational Church in Sheboygan, Wisconsin. It was there that he married. McCulloch and his wife, Alice, eventually had five children.

After several years of fruitful ministry McCulloch came to Indianapolis in 1877 to head the city's Plymouth Congregational Church. His new congregation was located on the city's famed Circle. The reverend, sensing that the city's war-related growth was bound to continue, eventually moved the congregation a bit farther north, to Meridian and New York Streets, in 1884. His sermons were "straightforward" in their language, and often composed the night before or the morning that they were given. He eased the membership process, dropping even the requirement that there be a confession of faith. His efforts transformed a congregation on the decline into one with a growing membership that served as a thriving community partner.

It was in his new hometown that McCulloch's social gospel bent became more pronounced, especially in the areas of education and philanthropy. His ministerial style, coupled with his interest in reform, helped attract new members to the congregation. His business background made him a great organizer, and his flair for administration helped spur him to leadership positions beyond the pulpit. One of his early initiatives was to organize his congregation to support the Plymouth Institute, an educational outreach to the city's young people.

But it was McCulloch's interaction with the city's poor that soon garnered him national recognition. Doing home visits as part of his pulpit ministry turned into fact-finding trips for the city's philanthropic circles and institutions that cared for the indigent. McCulloch became convinced that how people provided aid to the poor needed to be dramatically revised. Influenced as much by Social Darwinism and the growing field of eugenics, as by the social gospel and faith, the reverend undertook a decadelong study (1878 to 1888) that produced a report titled *The Tribe of Ishmael*. In it McCulloch argued that genetics influenced a wealth of decisions that created a downward spiral of people becoming dependent upon and addicted to public charity. It was through his eventual work on the *Tribe* that McCulloch began his interest in halting degenerates from reproducing and thus becoming a drain on charitable giving. He referred to this phenomenon as "biological pauperism," and as a result of his research he became a leading figure in the "scientific charity movement."

In 1888, at the annual meeting of the National Conference of Charities and Correction, McCulloch for the first time discussed his findings. Shocking his listeners and bombarding them with diagrams showing how nearly 1,700 people in thirty families interrelated over the course of just six generations, the reverend asserted that pauperism was a genetic trait bred into the individuals and fostered by indiscriminate philanthropy that allowed them to live an "idle and wandering life." He was confident that society was full of degenerates, and that paupers were little more than social parasites destroying the American way of life. Paupers were a separate category of poor people, as distinct from the "worthy poor."

While the report caused a stir, giving steam to the burgeoning eugenics movement as well as spurring debate to the present as to just who McCulloch had been studying in the city to base his assertions on, the reverend's larger goal with discussing the *Tribe* was to argue for more scientific philanthropy by individuals, the church, and the state. He helped to organize or reorganize both the Indianapolis Benevolent Society and the Indianapolis Charity Organization Society, the latter of which he led from 1882 until 1891. Through these ventures, McCulloch helped create a variety of other private charities and philanthropic organizations in the city that also made him a driving force behind the creation of such state-level organizations as the Board of State Charities. His work in the field, much more than from the pulpit, garnered him national attention, eventually helping him to be elected as president of the National Council of Charities and Correction.

As a result of a personal political awakening in the late 1880s, McCulloch began to move away from biological pauperism toward a more encompassing view of the causes of poverty. Instead of the view that biology determined intergenerational poverty, he came to focus on the systemic social and economic causes and to believe that solutions to ending poverty required systemic progressive reforms. McCulloch was the first of the members of the scientific charity movement to adopt this view, but others followed. As a result, a new policy agenda began to take shape, one that called for social and economic justice for all of the poor. While these views helped to reshape the approaches to poverty at the national level, this new perspective was not widely accepted in Indiana at the time.

After a brief illness, McCulloch died on December 10, 1891. Indianapolis honored his memory by naming a public school for him. McCulloch's true legacy as a reformer came mainly after his death. His was an important influence in moving the scientific charity movement to a new perspective on the history of American poverty: "that all of the poor could potentially be raised from the depths."

JASON S. LANTZER

For Further Reading

Kramer, Elsa F. "Recasting the *Tribe of Ishmael*: The Role of Indianapolis's Nineteenth-Century Poor in Twentieth-Century Eugenics." *Indiana Magazine of History* 104 (March 2008): 36–64.

McCulloch, Oscar C. *The Tribe of Ishmael: A Study in Social Degradation*. Indianapolis: Charity of Organization Society, 1888.

Ruswick, Brent. "The Measure of Worthiness: The Reverend Oscar McCulloch and the Pauper Problem, 1877–1891." *Indiana Magazine of History* 104 (March 2008): 3–35.

Weeks, Genevieve C. *Oscar Carleton McCulloch, 1843–1891: Preacher and Practitioner of Applied Christianity*. Indianapolis: Indiana Historical Society, 1976

McNutt, Paul V.

July 19, 1891–March 24, 1955

Dean of the Indiana University School of Law, state and national commander of the American Legion, governor of Indiana, U.S. High Commissioner to the Philippines, head of the Federal Security Agency, chair of the War Manpower Commission, and ambassador to the Philippines.

Paul V. McNutt was born in Franklin, Indiana, the only child of John Crittenden McNutt, a lawyer and minor state official, and Ruth Neely. He grew up in Martinsville, where he was the academic standout in high school. In 1913 he received a bachelor's degree from Indiana University, where he majored in English, edited the student newspaper, acted in plays, and participated in campus politics. After earning an LLB from Harvard Law School in 1916, McNutt became a partner in his father's law firm and joined the faculty of law at IU as an instructor. In 1917 he enlisted in the army and attained the rank of captain. During World War I, McNutt trained soldiers at army bases in South Carolina and Texas, where he met Kathleen Timolat, whom he married in 1918. The couple had a daughter, Louise, in 1921. The war ended before McNutt could be sent overseas. Shielded from the horrors of mechanized warfare, he retained a romantic perspective on patriotic sacrifice. After the war, he returned to Bloomington to teach law, becoming a professor in 1919.

McNutt's ambition turned to politics during the 1920s. In 1925 he became dean of IU's law school, where he worked on faculty recruitment and retention, founded a law journal, and advocated greater appropriations for public education and the continuation of reserve officer training on campus. McNutt's stand on that last issue coincided with the program of the American Legion, which he joined in 1919. In 1925 McNutt became commander of his local post and then commander of the Indiana Legion in 1926. He boosted membership in the organization and pushed its agenda of military preparedness, antipacifism, and antiradicalism in speeches across Indiana and beyond. In 1928 McNutt secured the office of national commander at the Legion's annual convention.

Involvement in veterans politics proved shrewd, for the 1920s was an era of Republican ascendancy and McNutt was a Democrat. The American Legion also provided him with valuable contacts, the foremost of which was Frank M. McHale, who became his political strategist. The onset of the Great Depression reversed Democratic fortunes, and McNutt was elected governor of Indiana in 1932, along with large majorities in both houses of the state legislature.

McNutt became one of the strongest governors in Indiana history. Two months before

Paul V. McNutt gives the principal address at Memorial Day ceremonies at Arlington National Cemetery in Washington, D.C., May 30, 1940.

President Franklin D. Roosevelt inaugurated the New Deal, McNutt pushed an extensive set of reforms through an obedient legislature. His administration reorganized the state's government and reformed its tax system, tightened regulation of banking and of liquor, passed pensions for the aged, centralized control over poor relief, and worked alongside Roosevelt's administration to provide jobs to the unemployed and Social Security for the elderly. In so doing, McNutt solidified Indiana's finances, established the precedent that the state agencies must yield to periodic regrouping, and inspired Hoosiers with his rhetoric about the promise of a skillfully led government. But he also used his power for less exalted purposes. He sent Indiana National Guard troops to break strikes, and he formed a potent political machine based on an unrepentant system of patronage, the distribution of liquor licenses to favored associates, and the Hoosier Democratic Club, an organization to which state patronage employees donated 2 percent of their annual incomes. The so-called Two Percent Club proved McNutt's most enduring "contribution" to state politics, for it lasted until the governorship of Evan Bayh. Overall, McNutt's policies made him a popular governor, as Democrats prevailed in the state elections of 1934 and 1936. Yet his stand against strikes, machine-style methods, and thirst for national office led members of Roosevelt's White House to regard him as an arrogant opportunist and insincere liberal.

Roosevelt dealt with McNutt delicately. He never trusted the Hoosier, who had resisted Roosevelt's nomination for president in 1932. But the president deemed McNutt a rising political star whose talents could be utilized. In 1937 he named McNutt as U.S. high commissioner to the Philippines, an American colony that had achieved internal self-government as it prepared for independence in 1946. McNutt established rapport with Philippine president Manuel L. Quezon, and the two men worked to bring 1,300 European Jews to Manila between 1937 and 1939—a remarkable act given the world's indifference to the plight of refugees. McNutt also lobbied unsuccessfully for reexamination of the timetable for Philippine independence in order to keep the archipelago under U.S. sovereignty and prevent its absorption by Japan. In 1939 he returned home to head the newly established Federal Security Agency and launch his presidential campaign.

McNutt's quest for national elected office proved phantom. His presidential bid suffered from a cash shortfall, negative press coverage, a Treasury Department probe of the Two Percent Club, and Roosevelt's refusal to quell talk of a third term. In 1940 the Democratic Party renominated Roosevelt, who then chose Secretary of Agriculture Henry A. Wallace as his running mate. In spite of considerable support in the galleries and among delegates, McNutt withdrew from the race for vice president—a prize he might have won had he fought for it. Thereafter, he campaigned for Roosevelt's re-election and continued to head the FSA throughout World War II. Although McNutt seldom became involved in the details of FSA policy, he tailored the agency's mission to defense-related needs. One result was that the agency became home to the government's top-secret biological warfare program. Beginning in 1941, McNutt headed a related agency, the Office of Defense Health and Welfare Services that combated venereal disease, policed prostitution, provided child-care centers for women workers, and wholesome recreation for service personnel. To that end, McNutt helped organize the United Service Organizations.

Although McNutt performed ably as head of the FSA, he struggled at his other wartime assignment, as chair of the War Manpower Commission. In this position, McNutt became a familiar figure on the home front, "Uncle Sam's Personnel Boss," as the *Kansas City Star* dubbed him. In truth, he lacked the unstinting support of the president and Congress that this difficult assignment required. Pressure by the civilian and military sectors for scarce human resources proved constant, and McNutt was unable to master the manpower situation.

Such problems, along with McNutt's personal distance from the president, meant that he received no consideration for the vice presidential nomination in 1944, when Democrats replaced Wallace with Harry S Truman. In 1945 McNutt returned to Manila to serve as the last U.S. high commissioner and first ambassador to the Philippines. In those positions, he negotiated agreements that gave the Philippines preferential trade with the United States and Americans property rights and military bases in the Philippines—policies that a later generation denounced as neo-imperialism. In 1947 McNutt returned to the United

States to practice law and engage in business ventures. While he never again held public office, he continued to give speeches. He died in New York of esophageal cancer in 1955.

McNutt was one of Indiana's most distinguished political leaders. He cut an impressive figure with his angular face, platinum-blonde hair, dark eyebrows, tanned complexion, eloquent speeches, and well-advertised ambition. Although the White House eluded McNutt, his accomplishments were numerous. He was an energetic promoter of the American Legion, the architect of Indiana's welfare state, an Oscar Schindler-like savior of more than a thousand Jews, a competent steward of the wartime FSA, and an author of America's close postwar relationship with the Philippines. The concept of "security" defined McNutt's career. Shy and insecure by nature, he pushed policies to protect Americans from economic privation, internal subversion, and predatory dictatorships. An antipathy to totalitarian governments abroad and laissez-faire economics at home transformed McNutt into an early purveyor of the so-called Welfare-Warfare State and one of America's first Cold War liberals.

DEAN J. KOTLOWSKI

For Further Reading

Kotlowski, Dean J. *Paul V. McNutt and the Age of FDR*. Bloomington: Indiana University Press, 2015.

Madison, James H. *Indiana through Tradition and Change: A History of the Hoosier State and Its People 1920–1945*. Indianapolis: Indiana Historical Society, 1982.

McNutt, Paul V. Papers. Lilly Library, Indiana University, Bloomington.

———. Papers. Indiana State Archives, Indianapolis, IN.

Meredith, Virginia Claypool

November 5, 1848–December 10, 1936

President of the Indiana State Federation of Clubs, Indiana representative to and vice chairman of the Board of Lady Managers for the 1893 World's Columbian Exposition (Chicago World's Fair), pioneer in home economics education at the University of Minnesota and Purdue University, and first female member of the Purdue Board of Trustees.

Virginia Claypool Meredith watched as Shorthorn cattle and sheep grazed across the pastures of Oakland Farm near Cambridge City, Indiana. Following the unexpected death of her husband in 1882, the thirty-three-year-old had assumed the management of the farm, a pivotal decision that shaped her life's work in agriculture and higher education. It also led her to overcome gender barriers in both fields and to become an advocate for expanding women's opportunities in agriculture, as well as elevating their status as homemakers.

She was born on a prosperous Connersville farm in 1848. Her father taught her to farm just like his boys, taking Virginia with him "on countless drives to pastures and fields, talking with her meanwhile on farm subjects." She earned a bachelor's degree from Glendale College in 1866 and four years later married Henry Meredith, the son of Civil War General Solomon Meredith. She met influential politicians, agriculturists, and civic leaders who visited the general at his Oakland Farm home.

Virginia learned the finer points of breeding purebred Shorthorn cattle and Southdown sheep at Oakland Farm. Her husband and father-in-law had earned respect as livestock breeders, but their farm had suffered from mounting debt. When Virginia assumed management responsibilities in 1882, she upheld the tradition of Oakland Farm quality as her cattle brought top dollar, but her business acumen made the farm profitable as well.

Meredith became one of the nation's first women to speak regularly at Farmers' Institutes, the county-based meetings organized by Purdue University that were forerunners to the Cooperative Extension Service. While the male speakers were paid for this work, Meredith spoke as a volunteer since a Purdue trustee had objected to paying women for any kind of work.

From 1889 to 1920 Meredith faced a grueling six-day work week during the winter, traveling on trains and by horse and buggy to meeting halls. As a woman speaking on agricultural topics, she encountered her fair share of prejudice. However, she earned the respect of her audiences as the men learned that this livestock manager was a remarkable and knowledgeable businesswoman.

Meredith's practical advice made her a sought-after speaker around the country. After speaking on "Profitable Sheep Husbandry" at a Farmers' Institute in Vicksburg, Mississippi, Meredith was honored with a medallion inscribed with "Queen of American Agriculture"—this despite the feeling in the South that it was "not quite nice for a woman to speak in public."

Meredith knew that women faced inequalities and discrimination in the workplace but nonetheless advocated that farming was a suitable vocation for them. "Work," she said, "is not discounted on account of sex. A bushel of wheat brings market price; a cow makes as many—or more—pounds of butter when owned by a woman, as when owned by a man."

Meredith's life took an unexpected twist in 1889 when she promised a terminally ill friend that she would raise her children, seven-year-old Mary Matthews and two-year-old Meredith Mathews. This experience caused her to think differently about what it meant to be a caretaker at home. Realizing that farming and home management were closely intertwined, she continued to focus on farming as a career for women, but the science behind a healthy home became the subject of her speeches and writings. She once said, "If a woman can make bread and direct someone else how to make bread she can do the infinitely simpler things—make hay. . . . If she can take care of boys and girls, how easy is it in comparison to maintain the health and promote the growth of cattle, horses, and sheep." Meredith became active in the Indiana Union of Literary Clubs and Indiana State Federation of Clubs, two organizations that challenged women to speak up for issues important to the home and community. By 1900 this club work helped earn her recognition as one of the hundred most influential Indiana citizens.

Meredith's political connections, popularity as a speaker, and involvement with club activity secured her a prestigious appointment in 1890 to the Board of Lady Managers for the World's Columbian Exposition, more commonly known as the Chicago World's Fair. For three years, Meredith worked tirelessly to help plan and manage the women's exhibitions, where inventors, manufacturers, artists, and writers from around the world showcased their work to large crowds in 1893.

As articles in *Harper's Bazaar*, the *Chicago Daily Tribune*, and the *Atlanta Journal* brought her story to the public, the University of Minnesota hired forty-eight-year-old Meredith in 1897 as the first ever preceptress of the University of Minnesota School of Agriculture. She split her time between teaching there from September to March and managing Oakland Farm during the remaining months. She helped establish the university's first home economics program and became the first professor of home economics there.

Meredith left the University of Minnesota in 1902 to return to full-time farming, but daughter Mary stayed on to become the first graduate of the home economics program in 1904. Meredith sold Oakland Farm that same year but purchased a 159-acre farm just a mile away. Meredith continued speaking across Indiana, the United States, and Europe on farm and home topics. At the Lake Placid (New York) Conference in 1900, she spoke on "What Agricultural Colleges May Do for the Farmer's Daughter." She had become part of a group that was instrumental in encouraging colleges across the country to offer home economics as a field of scientific study.

Closer to home, Meredith pressed the somewhat reluctant Purdue administrators to offer a curriculum in home economics. She leveraged her political connections when asking the Indiana State Board of Agriculture in 1904 to support the home as a worthy field to study. Meredith said, "by agricultural pursuits I am going to include not only those things that have to do with plant and animal life, but I will also include a very important part of agriculture, and that is the home and the farm, and the need for special training for the one who makes that home." Purdue created a Department of Household Economics in 1905, which eventually became the School of Home Economics in 1926 with Mary as its first dean.

Meredith was sixty-seven when she left the farm in 1916 to live with Mary in West Lafayette. She kept busy writing for the press, accepting speaking assignments, and actively participating in the newly established Indiana Home Economics Association as well as the Indiana Federation of Clubs.

In 1921 Indiana governor Warren T. McCray appointed Meredith as the first female member of Purdue's Board of Trustees at the age of seventy-two. There were many battles, obstacles, and setbacks during her fifteen-year tenure, but her accomplishments included spearheading the construction of the Purdue Memorial Union to honor war veterans and the first residence hall for women students.

Meredith died in 1936. Her legacy was grounded in her belief that women had the right to work outside the home while acknowledging an equally important role for women who took care of the home and family. History recalled Meredith as "the most remarkable woman in Indiana" and "Indiana's most widely known farmer," which aptly described a woman who was also dubbed the Queen of American Agriculture.

FREDERICK WHITFORD

For Further Reading

Whitford, Frederick, Andrew G. Martin, and Phyllis Mattheis. *The Queen of American Agriculture: A Biography of Virginia Claypool Meredith.* Lafayette, IN: Purdue University Press, 2008.

———. *The Grand Old Man of Purdue University and Indiana Agriculture: A Biography of William Carroll Latta.* Lafayette, IN: Purdue University Press, 2005.

Mihšihkinaahkwa (Little Turtle)

1752–July 14, 1812

War leader, village chief, and council chief of Miami Tribe in the late 1700s and early 1800s.

Mihšihkinaahkwa, or as Americans called him "Little Turtle," was a leader of the Myaamiaki (Miami) people who have lived along the northern stretches of the Waapaahšiki Siipiiwi (Wabash River) since time immemorial. His exact year of birth, location, and parentage have long been debated among tribal and U.S. historians. At the time of his birth, his people's territory primarily included the lower Great Lakes region and was shared with many other indigenous groups, some who spoke the same language and others who were distinctly different in language and culture. This ancestral place was called Myaamionki, the place of the Miami people, and became contested during Mihšihkinaahkwa's life. His story is representative of a part of Indiana history that continues to challenge many today

Mihšihkinaahkwa was born in the mid-eighteenth century, sometime between 1747 and 1752. At the time of his birth, his people had already been in contact with the French for a hundred years. European trade transformed many aspects of Miami culture, and European religious groups, such as the Jesuits, had introduced new concepts of spirituality. He grew to adulthood in an ever-shifting social-political landscape where multiple groups interpreted and used the land for different purposes. Balancing the needs of these diverse groups sometimes produced conflicts, but this still was a period of relative peace and stability.

At the end of the American War of Independence in 1780, Miami villages became locked in a new violent struggle with Americans, who wanted to force British traders out of the Great Lakes in hopes of establishing settlements along the Ohio River on lands lived on and utilized by all the tribes of the region. Mihšihkinaahkwa first rose to prominence in this period of rising violence. He helped lead the military efforts that defeated forces under Augustin de La Balme in 1780 and General Josiah Harmar in 1790.

In 1791 another invasion of Miami homelands was launched by General Arthur St. Clair. Mihšihkinaahkwa, together with Shawnee and Delaware leaders, organized an attack on the U.S. forces before they could reach their villages. The surprise assault occurred where the city of Fort Recovery, Ohio, sits today. After hours of difficult fighting, the Americans broke into disorganized retreat south to Fort Jefferson. More than 900 of St. Clair's 1,400 men were killed or wounded. To this day, the allied Indians' victory on the Wabash River remains one of the largest defeats ever suffered by the U.S. Army.

Little Turtle

Between 1792 and 1794, Major General Anthony Wayne led the Legion of the United States on a third invasion of Miami homelands. Wayne, or Eelaamhsenwa (wind), as the Miami called him, was new to this conflict, but his tenacity and organizational preparation made the campaign into a methodical battle of attrition rather than the fast-paced war of raids and surprise attacks that so benefited the allied Indians. During this campaign, Mihšihkinaahkwa and his son-in-law, Eepiihkaanita (William Wells), concluded that the allied tribes could not defeat Wayne and decided that peace was a better option. However, Mihšihkinaahkwa could not convince his allies to pursue peace and he stepped down as intertribal war leader. At the battle of Fallen Timbers, where Wayne's forces prevailed, Mihšihkinaahkwa led only a small group from his own community.

In the summer of 1795 the allied tribes gathered at Fort Greenville in Ohio to negotiate with Wayne as the representative of the United States. At this negotiation, Mihšihkinaahkwa accomplished two important things. First, he helped establish peace between his people and the United States and declared that he would hold to that peace indefinitely. Secondly, Mihšihkinaahkwa requested to have Eepiihkaanita serve as the Indian Agent to the Miami at Fort Wayne. This turn toward peace and the placement of Wells as Indian Agent was a strategic attempt to lay the foundation for significant changes that followed the end of the war. Peace came at a steep price; the ten tribes who signed the Treaty of Greenville had to relinquish the use and control of most of Ohio to achieve this end.

Mihšihkinaahkwa's commitment to peace and his attempts to actively respond to the political, economic, and ecological changes his people experienced led many opponents to disparage him as an "accommodationist." In 1797 Mihšihkinaahkwa, explaining his understanding of these economic changes to a French visitor, said, "you whites have found means of collecting at hand and in a small space a certain and abundant supply of food. We on the contrary, require a vast extent of ground to live on." He added that because of these differences, Euro-Americans "spread like oil on a blanket," while Natives "dissolve like the snow before the vernal Sun." Mihšihkinaahkwa concluded by arguing that his people had to change their course if they were going to survive.

Just as peace had its price, so too did change. In 1801 Mihšihkinaahkwa stated, "There are more of us dead since the Treaty of Greeneville, than we lost by the years of war before." He blamed the alcohol trade, which targeted a people struggling to adjust to the push for European-style agriculture, and the decrease in hunting and trapping. In addition, the Miami struggled to develop a new form of government that would meet the needs of their new circumstances. Despite these attempts at change and adaptation, American leaders, such as Lewis Cass, maintained that the Miami "cannot live in the neighborhood of the white people," and should be forcibly removed west of the Mississippi River.

Over time Mihšihkinaahkwa has been feared, respected, honored, and violated. Following his death in 1812, he received full military honors, yet one hundred years later his remains were unceremoniously disinterred and desecrated during a construction project in Fort Wayne. The objects his family lovingly placed into the earth with him were distributed to interested collectors and eventually gathered and put on public display, while the disposition of his bones remain unclear. During the middle twentieth century the site of his grave became a memorial with the help of local citizens and members of the Miami tribe.

Mihšihkinaahkwa left a legacy of both resistance and cooperation in order to preserve the political and cultural distinctiveness of his people. He died four years before Indiana became a state in 1816. Mihšihkinaahkwa's life must be viewed from an informed contemporary perspective, for his historical legacy is not marked with great accomplishments or achievements for Indiana—he was not considered an American citizen. Instead, his life exposes the unfortunate circumstances for his people that led to Indiana statehood, which serves as an important history lesson. Hoosiers can learn something about equality, diversity, conquest, manifest destiny, tribal and state sovereignty, and lessons in humanity by examining the life of Mihšihkinaahkwa.

His legacy survives and can be seen in the lives of his descendants and Miami people today who are active, as was Mihšihkinaahkwa, in preserving the political and cultural distinctiveness of the Miami Nation. Though the Miami

Nation now resides in Oklahoma, feelings for the historic homelands of Indiana are still as strong among Miami people today as they were for Mihšihkinaahkwa during his time. To many Hoosiers, Mihšihkinaahkwa is a symbolic figure of the frontier past while for many Miami he is an important leadership link to the present.

DARYL BALDWIN
GEORGE IRONSTRACK

For Further Reading

Carter, Harvey Lewis. *The Life and Times of Little Turtle: First Sagamore of the Wabash* Urbana: University of Illinois Press, 1987.

Cayton, Andrew R. L. *Frontier Indiana*. Bloomington: Indiana University Press, 1996.

Sword, Wiley. *President Washington's Indian War: The Struggle for the Old Northwest, 1790–1795*. Norman: University of Oklahoma Press, 1985.

White, Richard. *The Middle Ground: Indians, Empires, and Republics in the Great Lakes Region, 1650–1815*. Cambridge Studies in North American Indian History. New York: Cambridge University Press, 1991.

Miller, J. Irwin

May 26, 1909–August 16, 2004

Longtime chairman of Cummins Engine Company, patron of modern architecture, and a leading national figure in religion, equal rights, and social responsibility.

The influence of J. Irwin Miller spanned the country and reached across the world. In his ninety-five years the Columbus, Indiana, native had a lasting impact in business, social justice, arts, architecture, religion, and ethics. He led the National Council of Churches through one of the most tumultuous and influential periods in American history—the civil rights struggle of the mid-twentieth century. At least three presidents considered him for appointment to cabinet positions. He was also one of the prime movers in establishing business ties between the United States and China.

The editors of *Esquire* held Miller in such regard that they put his image in profile on the cover of one of its issues over the headline, "This man ought to be the next President of the United States." Impressive as those credentials are, his greatest influence was on the community in which he was born, lived his entire life, and died—Columbus. Under his leadership and example, the town was transformed into an economic and architectural showplace, achieving national fame while at the same time shedding the reputation of a provincial Hoosier community rooted in the social inequities of the nineteenth and early twentieth centuries.

Joseph Irwin Miller was born May 26, 1909, into a family of wealth and influence. His father, Hugh, was a lieutenant governor of Indiana. His mother, Nettie Sweeney, was the daughter of a leading theologian, Zachary Taylor Sweeney, who served as president of the American Christian Missionary Society and was appointed by President BENJAMIN HARRISON as consul general in Constantinople. Miller's great uncle, W. G. Irwin, was cofounder and chief financial investor of Cummins Engine Company (now Cummins Inc.). His great-grandfather, Joseph Ireland Irwin, started a bank that bore the family name and grew to be a major financial institution in the twentieth century.

Miller's education, at Taft School in Watertown, Connecticut; Yale University; and Oxford University, exposed him to thoughts and ideas outside Columbus. After obtaining a master's degree from Oxford in 1933, he returned home and began work at the diesel engine manufacturer his great uncle and CLESSIE CUMMINS started in 1919. After serving in a variety of roles he was eventually named general manager.

At the time, Cummins Engine was still struggling to stay in business. It had yet to earn a profit since its incorporation in 1919 and Miller's family had invested heavily to keep it afloat. Conditions changed in 1937 when the company recorded its first profit. It continued to do well through the end of the Great Depression and World War II. In 1947 Miller was elected the company's president and became chairman of the board in 1951, a position he held until 1977.

By then Cummins had become a Fortune 500 company and had established a footprint, not only in the United States but also worldwide. One market that was to have enormous importance was in China, which had been opened to the international community by President Richard Nixon's historic meetings with Mao Zedong in 1972. Two years later, Miller was part of a delegation that visited there and established a business relationship. In addition to leading Cummins, Miller also directed the bank started by his great-grandfather, serving as chairman until 1976. He also was the key figure in other family operations, most notably Union

J. Irwin Miller inspects an engine at the Cummins Engine Company, Columbus, Indiana, circa 1950.

Starch and Refining Company and the Irwin Management Company.

Despite enormous business responsibilities, Miller became committed to other callings, most notably arts, architecture, religion, equal rights, and social responsibility. Although a key figure in Cummins management, he championed the rights of workers to organize at a time when the union movement was under fire. That commitment was recognized years later when, upon his retirement as chairman, members of the Diesel Workers Union elected him as an honorary member.

Miller also became a leader in the world of religion, helping to establish in 1950 the National Council of Churches. Just over a decade later, he became the first layman to be elected president of the organization. Miller became deeply involved in civil rights and was one of the key figures in the eventual enactment of the Civil Rights Act. His commitment to equality included Columbus. As recently as the 1960s, African Americans found it extremely difficult to obtain basic necessities in Columbus. Newcomers were often rebuffed in finding housing and even national figures visiting Columbus, such as Louis Armstrong, were refused service at local restaurants.

Miller joined with other Columbus activists, including Reverend William Laws, in an effort to change that attitude, using his influence as head of the city's leading employer to force landlords to rent to people of color. He carried that personal ethic into his business life. He instilled in his companies a code of "doing the right thing," regardless of whether it had a negative impact on the bottom line. That approach has been followed by the companies he led long after his departure. The name Cummins regularly appeared on the list of the most ethical businesses in the United States. Typical of this honest approach was an incident in 1994 in which a disgruntled employee at a competing business sent Cummins engineers copies of a new engine design. The engineers rewrapped the package and sent it back to the competitor.

Miller's greatest impact on his hometown was in architecture. He developed an interest in the field early in life and saw an opportunity to further it in Columbus. In the 1950s he persuaded the Cummins' board of directors to allocate 5 percent of its pretax domestic profits to charitable causes. At about the same time he developed a program supported by the Cummins Foundation to pay the architectural fees for public buildings built in Columbus, particularly schools.

Under this program, such internationally known architects as I. M. Pei, Harry Weese, Eero Saarinen, Cesar Pelli, and Robert Venturi designed buildings that put Columbus on the national map when it came to architecture. Witnessing the success of this program, other businesses and institutions in the community followed his lead in commissioning noted designers for their properties. Seven Columbus buildings are today National Historic Landmarks and Columbus is regarded as the sixth most influential city in the country in contemporary design.

Miller carried that commitment to social betterment from his business life to his personal one. In 1952 he joined with his mother; his wife, Xenia; his sister, Clementine Tangeman; their aunt, Elsie Irwin Sweeney; and family friend George Newlin to create the Irwin Sweeney Miller Foundation. Over a period of sixty-two years the foundation donated more than $57 million to projects throughout Bartholomew County, including the Commons (a community gathering place), works by such artists as Dale Chihuly and Jean Tinguely, and a memorial to Bartholomew County veterans.

The legacy of Miller, who died on August 16, 2004, is both lasting and widespread. It can be best summed up in his remarks in 1964 at the dedication of Otter Creek Golf Course in Columbus, a gift to the city by Cummins: "Why should an industrial company, organized for profit, think it a good and right thing to take a million dollars and more of that profit and give it to this community in the form of this golf course and clubhouse?

"Why, indeed, isn't Cummins, the largest taxpayer in the county, spending the same energy to get its taxes reduced, cost of education cut, cost of city government cut, less money spent on streets, utilities, schools? The answer is that we would like to see this community come to be, not the cheapest, but the very best community of its size in this country."

Miller's desire was that Columbus be a "community open in every respect to persons of every race, color and opinion; one that makes them feel welcome and at home here; a community which offers their children the best education; a community of outspoken churches, genuine cultural interests, exciting opportunities for recreation and a community whose citizens are themselves well paid and who will not tolerate poverty for others."

HARRY MCCAWLEY

For Further Reading

Cruikshank, Jeffrey, and David B. Sicilia. *The Engine That Could: Seventy-Five Years of Values-Driven Change at Cummins Engine Company*. Boston: Harvard Business School Press, 1997.

Cummins, C. Lyle Jr. *The Diesel Odyssey of Clessie Cummins*. Lake Oswego, OR: Carnot Press, 1998.

"This man ought to be the next President of the United States." *Esquire*, October 1967.

Milligan, Lambdin Purdy

May 24, 1812–December 21. 1899

Leader of secret conspiratorial society sympathetic to the Confederate cause during the Civil War; convicted by a military tribunal for conspiracy; won famous civil liberties case *Ex parte Milligan* (1866), when the U.S. Supreme Court ruled civilians could not be tried in military tribunals as long as civil courts were still functioning.

Lambdin P. Milligan was from his youth a doctrinaire state-sovereignty adherent and follower of South Carolina proslavery apologist John C. Calhoun. During the American Civil War, Milligan opposed the federal government's efforts to reunite the Union. Ultimately, he chose to join and lead a secret conspiratorial organization that aimed to subvert the war effort. Detected, arrested, and tried by military tribunal, he was found guilty and sentenced to death. However, after the end of the war, the U.S. Supreme Court decided in *Ex Parte Milligan* (1866) that military trials of civilians in places where the civil courts remained open were unconstitutional. While the ruling struck a blow for civil liberties, Milligan remained an unrepentant lifelong believer in state sovereignty and an opponent of strong central government.

Milligan was born in rural Belmont County in southeastern Ohio on March 24, 1812, the son of farmers who had moved to the region from Maryland. Raised a Protestant in the Methodist Church, in 1870 he converted to Roman Catholicism, the faith tradition of his grandfather. Raised on a farm and afforded little formal education, he studied law and was admitted to the Ohio bar in 1835, practicing law in Belmont and Harrison Counties and the surrounding region until 1845.

Evidence shows that Milligan participated in

politics from an early age, counting himself an "original Jacksonian" and ultimately a member of the Democratic Party. However, in the early 1830s, he broke from President Andrew Jackson amid the nullification crisis that pitted the president against South Carolinians, led by former Vice President Calhoun, who opposed the federal government's efforts to enforce federal law. In 1834 Milligan joined a group of Belmont County Democrats to oppose Jackson's efforts to promote Vice President Martin Van Buren as his successor. The group cited the Kentucky and Virginia Resolutions of 1798 and 1799 as their models to promote the supremacy of the states over the federal government. Milligan left the Democratic Party to follow Calhoun into the anti-Jackson opposition, which formed into the Whig Party. He became active in Whig Party affairs in Ohio. But when President Van Buren wooed Calhoun back into the Democratic Party with promises to protect slavery, Milligan turned his back on the Whigs and followed his ideological leader out of opposition, taking a prominent role in local Democratic affairs. He was a proslavery northern "Doughface" who espoused Calhoun's belief that slavery was a positive good for society and the rightful status for African American men and women.

In 1845 Milligan left behind his Ohio law practice and moved his family to frontier Huntington County, Indiana. Evidence suggests that he did not enjoy the practice of law and instead wished to speculate in real estate and run for political office. Swearing off the law, he entered Indiana politics but failed to win election in races for state representative and senator and congressman. His attempt to edit a Democratic newspaper in Huntington also failed. Many of his setbacks in politics and journalism may be ascribed to his unattractive personality. Vindictive, litigious, and unpleasant, voters found little reason to support his frequent candidacies. In the 1860s he did win election to be township trustee in Huntington, the highest post he ever attained. His lack of success as a candidate did not preclude influence as a back-room operative in partisan affairs, however, as with a handful of other Democrats he was a prominent party leader in the region. Forced to fall back on practicing law in 1853, Milligan found professional and pecuniary success as an able litigator.

The election of Republican ABRAHAM LINCOLN to the presidency in 1860 and the resultant secession of several southern states brought the national crisis to Huntington. Milligan led a faction of local Democrats who voiced support for the Southerners' constitutional right to secede. When the newly formed Confederate government fired on Fort Sumter, South Carolina, and started the Civil War, Milligan and Huntingtonians denounced the federal government's efforts to preserve the federal Union, preferring to let the South break away. He thought the federal government's war effort to coerce the southern states back into union was unconstitutional and unjust. Milligan spoke widely throughout northeastern Indiana to enunciate his prosecession views, based on his Calhounite state-sovereignty, proslavery ideology.

As the war dragged on into 1862, war weariness began to settle on the North; Democratic Party fortunes rose. Lincoln's Emancipation Proclamation policy of directly tying the war effort to the abolition of Southern slavery brought howls of protest from conservative Democrats in Indiana and elsewhere. As chairman of the county party apparatus, Milligan excoriated the Lincoln administration's war measures as "tyranny, anarchy, misrule, plunder, corruption, disunion, usurpation and despotism." He sought again to run for Congress on the Democratic ticket but failed. As a lawyer, in 1863 he defended an Indiana Democratic state senator who had been arrested by military order and tried by military commission for speaking against the war. The tribunal found the prisoner guilty but the army released him. Indiana Democrats believed, mistakenly, that Milligan's defense had been successful and lionized him. Newspapers soon began to suggest him as a possible candidate for governor.

In 1863 opposition to the war in Indiana and the Midwest grew increasingly violent, with armed and organized groups subverting the war effort by harboring deserters and draft dodgers. The organized groups sometimes acted in concert with Confederate agents. Violent incidents occurred in Huntington and surrounding counties. Evidence shows that by 1863 Milligan had joined and taken a leading role in the secret organization, called at the time the Order of American Knights that later renamed itself the Sons of Liberty. Milligan spoke publicly to armed groups that paraded through Huntington in defiance of government authority.

In July 1864 Milligan made his bid for the gubernatorial nomination at the Democratic state convention in Indianapolis, backed by members of the secret conspiratorial organization. Mainstream, establishment Democrats, however, fearful of the direction that the radicals were taking the party, successfully warded off Milligan's attempt. Unbowed, he continued to voice strenuous opposition to the war, and in an August speech in Fort Wayne called on followers to rise up against the government at a time when the secret organization planned an uprising to free Confederate prisoners of war at Camp Morton in Indianapolis. During that year, spies working for U.S. Army commanders in Indianapolis infiltrated the secret organizations and identified Milligan as one of its leaders. In October commanders ordered the arrest of Milligan and several other leaders of the Sons of Liberty. Placed on trial for conspiracy before a military commission in Indianapolis, he and two others were found guilty and sentenced to death.

Milligan awaited his execution while friends took legal steps to block it and lobbied Lincoln and, after his murder, President Andrew Johnson, who commuted the sentence to life in prison. A habeas corpus case slowly wended its way to the U.S. Supreme Court in early 1866, which decided in April in favor of Milligan and the others. The court said in its *Ex Parte Milligan* ruling that the prisoners had been tried in the wrong court; authorities should not resort to military tribunals when the civil courts are open.

Returning home, Milligan ignored the fact that he had been implicated in conspiracies and brought federal civil suit against the officers and others involved in his arrest and trial. In 1871 the civil trial affirmed that he had been illegally arrested; however, the result was a moral victory for the defendants, who showed that Milligan and others had fomented revolutionary plots. He also tried and failed to purify the Democratic Party according to his Calhounite state sovereignty views. He restored his lucrative law practice, became general counsel for a major railroad line, and ran unsuccessfully for office. He retired from the law in 1898 and died in Huntington on December 21, 1899.

STEPHEN E. TOWNE

For Further Reading

Towne, Stephen E. *Lambdin P. Milligan and Dissent in the Civil War.* http://www.in.gov/history/4040.htm.

———. "The Persistent Nullifier: The Life of Civil War Conspirator Lambdin P. Milligan," *Indiana Magazine of History* 109 (December, 2013): 303–54.

———. "Worse than Vallandigham: Governor Oliver P. Morton, Lambdin P. Milligan, and the Military Arrest and Trial of Indiana State Senator Alexander J. Douglas during the Civil War,." *Indiana Magazine of History* 106 (March, 2010): 1–39.

Mills, Caleb

July 29, 1806–October 17, 1879

First faculty member at Wabash College who was later called "the father" of the Indiana Public School System and elected as state superintendent of public instruction.

Described by generations of Hoosiers as the father of public education in Indiana, Caleb Mills engaged in a prolonged campaign to persuade voters to support, and legislators to pass, legislation establishing a system of free common schools. Significantly, Mills exerted influence with regard to the provision in Indiana's constitution of 1851 that pertained to education. He is also remembered as the first teacher at and a driving force behind the success of Wabash Manual Labor College and Teachers' Seminary, which later became Wabash College.

Mills and his twin sister were born in Dunbarton, New Hampshire, on July 29, 1804. After

Caleb Mills

growing up on a farm where he was raised with a strict Calvinist upbringing, Mills was educated in the eastern common schools. He attended the Pembroke Academy in Pembroke, New Hampshire. In 1828 Mills and EDMUND O. HOVEY, the Wabash trustee with whom Mills spent four decades of his professional life, graduated together from Dartmouth College. After graduation Mills attended Andover Theological Seminary in Massachusetts for one year before beginning what would prove to be an important two-year stint as an American Sunday School Union home missionary in Kentucky and Indiana. During this period Mills learned firsthand of what was then the poor state of Indiana's schools. Mills received his master of arts degree from Andover in 1833.

On March 18, 1833, Mills responded to an advertisement in the January 1833 edition of the *Home Missionary* for a teaching position at the classical school that was opening in Crawfordsville, Indiana. His application letter foreshadowed his interest in public education. Mills wrote that public sentiment needed to be changed regarding free schools and "the public mind awakened to the importance of carrying the means of education to every door."

On July 18, 1833, Mills, who was then a Presbyterian minister, accepted the position in the English Department and as principal of the Preparatory Department and Teacher's Seminary, the school then being known as the Crawfordsville English and Classical High School. Shortly thereafter, the school's name became Wabash Manual Labor College and Teacher's Seminary. Mills was appointed Wabash's professor of languages on September 23, 1834.

Less than two months after he accepted his new position, Mills married Sarah Marshall, from Ipswich, Massachusetts. He and Sarah and four teachers then headed to Indiana, arriving in early November. On Monday, December 3, 1833, Mills offered a prayer, enrolled twelve students, and began teaching Wabash's first class.

On Founder's Day 1904, H. J. Milligan, a member of the Wabash class of 1873, described Mills as "a direct, energetic, practical man, plain in dress and manner, original and striking in speech." Wabash President Joseph F. Tuttle later observed that Mills, who reportedly walked seven miles to and from his Sunday morning preaching appointments, was known as a fast walker. According to Tuttle, "it was sometimes said [Mills's] forward motion was so fast as to suggest that he was fleeing from his own coat-tails."

Mills played a critical role in the establishment of free public schools in Indiana. It was a long and arduous journey that began in earnest in December 1846 when he sent an address to the Indiana General Assembly under a pseudonym "one of the people" about the importance of addressing the poor quality of education in Indiana. At that time only one in seven adults in the state could read or write, and the illiteracy rate was higher than all northern states and three slave states. Educational funds were woefully inadequate and were not allocated on an equitable basis, with poor and rural counties receiving very little support. To address these problems, Mills proposed that educational funds be distributed equally throughout the state and he insisted that taxation was essential to provide adequate support for a system of free public schools. Governor James Whitcomb, echoing Mills's plea, urged the legislature to revise the entire school system and to establish a "superintendent of public instruction" to oversee the system.

That effort failed but Mills was not deterred. He sent another address to the legislature in 1848 reiterating many of the same points, and again emphasized the need for taxation as the best way to support public schools. The legislature authorized a referendum to assess public support for a tax-supported free-school system. Following a favorable vote the legislature passed a new school law that adopted taxation as the way to fund public schools. The law, however, had a serious flaw—counties were allowed to opt out, and many did. Also the law did not consolidate school funds or require equal distribution of funds. This prompted Mills to send yet another address to the legislature highly critical of the law.

In 1850 the political landscape changed when a convention was called to draft a new constitution. Mills directed his next appeal to the convention delegates in the form of four letters published in the *Indiana Statesman* (Indianapolis). He called for directing school funds into three parts—a common school fund, a literature fund, and university fund. While the education provision adopted in the new constitution did not follow Mills's proposal exactly, it did reflect some of his ideas. It called for a "general and uniform system of common schools, wherein tuition shall be free of charge and equally open to all." It also established a perpetual school fund and created the office of Superintendent of Public Instruction.

The constitution left it to the legislature to work out the details of the new school system, and to that end Mills wrote his last appeal to the general assembly that met in 1852. He cited the embarrassing statistics from the 1850 census that again revealed Indiana as having the largest illiterate population of any northern state. Once again Mills's efforts were buttressed by actions of the state's governor, Joseph Wright. The legislature responded by passing the Comprehensive School Law of 1852. The influence of Mills was apparent in the provisions. It included a taxation provision with no escape clause, and it called for the consolidation of school funds, distributed equally throughout the state. It gave local control of schools to townships under the supervisions of a State Board of Education headed by the superintendent of public instruction. As one observer noted: "In the long war for effective free schools, ultimate victory was Caleb Mills's."

In October 1854 Mills was given a golden opportunity to influence the direction of the public school system when he was elected superintendent of public instruction. He served from November 8, 1854, through February 1857.

As a result of Mills's substantial efforts, the Indiana State Teachers' Association came into being on Christmas Day 1854. The organization focused initially on universal public education and other educational issues. Years later, in late December 1867, Mills was attending an evening function at a meeting of the association in New Albany, Indiana, when his fellow attendees recognized "all who were present of the old 'Fifty four Guard,' who first organized the Indiana State Teachers' Association, fourteen years ago." Mills and six other "venerable and honored gentlemen" rose to their feet acknowledging the recognition. An emotional Mills had been "taken completely by surprise" earlier the same year during the Wabash Preparatory Department's commencement when the class presented him a gold-headed cane as a token of their affection and appreciation. In 1875 Mills was elected Wabash professor emeritus of languages and the curator of the Wabash Library.

On October 16, 1879, Mills passed away of pneumonia at home. A member of the class of 1842 recalled visiting Mills a few hours before his death, at which time Mills was "still planning for future labors, saying that he hoped to be spared as there was work for him still to do."

With Wabash faculty serving as pallbearers, President Tuttle delivered the sermon at Mills's funeral. Tuttle's sermon included mention of Hovey, Mills's colleague and an original Wabash trustee, as he and Mills were "so closely intertwined." Wabash students led the funeral cortege to Crawfordsville's Oak Hill Cemetery where Mills was buried.

One of Mills's former students later wrote that "[w]hile [Mills's] hair grew silvered with the frost of more than three-score years, time did not [diminish] his sympathies nor make him forgetful of his boys, scattered as they were over many states."

DONALD B. KITE SR.

For Further Reading

Gregg, Orpheus M. "Caleb Mills." *The Wabash College Record* 19 (January 1916): 144–49.

"Indiana Monographs: The Indiana Common School System." *Indianapolis News*, August 8, 1893.

Nolan, Val, Jr. "Caleb Mills and the Indiana Free School Law." *Indiana Magazine of History* 49 (March 1953): 81–90.

Sherockman, Andrew A. "Caleb Mills, Pioneer Educator in Indiana." PhD diss., University of Pittsburgh, 1955.

Minton, Sherman

October 20, 1890–April 9, 1965

U.S. Senator, judge of the U.S. Seventh Circuit Court of Appeals, and justice of the U.S. Supreme Court.

From the early 1930s to the mid-1950s, when the great political issues of the day in Indiana and the nation were being debated and decided, Sherman Minton was often in the middle of the action and at the right hand of such powerful figures as Franklin D. Roosevelt, Harry S Truman, and Indiana governor PAUL V. MCNUTT. As a U.S. Senator from 1935 to 1940, Minton fought vigorously on behalf of Roosevelt and New Deal legislation designed to lift the nation from the upheaval of the Great Depression. As a Supreme Court justice from 1949 to 1956, Minton was just as steadfast in his support of Truman's efforts to cope with another national emergency—the perceived threat of communism.

Minton, known widely as "Shay," the nickname he acquired in childhood, remained unassuming regardless of office or title and true to

Sherman Minton

his upbringing in rural, small-town America. "It doesn't rub off when you're born in the Southern Indiana hills," he once said.

After serving with the U.S. Army overseas in World War I, Minton resumed his law practice in New Albany and set his sights on a political career. Despite two failed attempts to win the Democratic Party nomination for Congress, Minton remained active in the party and also became involved with the American Legion, an organization that helped young men with political ambitions to establish valuable statewide contacts. One of the most politically prominent members of the Indiana Legion was McNutt, whom Minton had known at Indiana University. With allies such as Minton, McNutt used the power of the Legion to challenge and depose the old guard of the state Democratic Party. In 1932 McNutt was resoundingly elected governor and with it came the dawning of a new era of Democratic dominance. Of all the measures devised by the "McNutt Machine" to ensure party loyalty and success none was more effective or received more notoriety than the infamous Two Percent Club, which collected from all state employees 2 percent of their wages or salaries for party coffers to pay for political campaigns.

McNutt appointed Minton public counselor to the Public Service Commission, a newly created position to represent consumers in rate cases. Minton, who was ideally suited for the job, wasted little time in challenging utilities to reduce rates as their customers suffered through the depths of the Great Depression. In a matter of months utilities made settlements that resulted in annual rate reductions of $3 million and McNutt publicly gave Minton credit for the savings.

Minton's success in this effort, which was front-page news throughout Indiana, helped propel him to his next achievement, election to the U.S. Senate in 1934. Running solidly on a New Deal platform and fending off criticisms that Roosevelt's programs were a violation of the Constitution, he defeated incumbent Senator Arthur Robinson with 52 percent of the vote.

In the Senate, which prides itself as being the world's most deliberative body, Minton's competitive nature and his considerable skills as a spirited debater could be exercised to their limits. The Senate was also the ideal place for the combative and assertive Minton to demonstrate his knowledge of the law, grasp of the issues, homespun wisdom, dramatic flair, quick wit, and biting humor. He relished a good fight even when his opponents were the powerful press and the lofty Supreme Court. Minton's voice and views also frequently reached across the country on radio, then a relatively new medium of communication.

Minton particularly enjoyed his fights with the anti-New Deal press lords. He believed them to be nothing more than propagandists for the Republican Party. The Supreme Court, which had invalidated many of Roosevelt's New Deal initiatives, also came in for a lashing from Minton. In his first major speech in the Senate, he called the court's decision ruling the Agriculture Adjustment Act unconstitutional "the most strained, forced construction of the Constitution, and the most highly flavored political opinion to come from that court since the Dred Scott decision."

As a freshman senator Minton achieved an unusual degree of prominence and power, but his rise was double-edged. His standing with the White House helped him win election in 1939 as majority whip, the second-in-command position that normally went to a senior legislator. His close allegiance to Roosevelt led him to be branded a rubber stamp. He became a key player in pushing the president's infamous court-packing scheme that resulted in an embarrassing failure and his assaults on critical news coverage of the administration were interpreted as attempts to hammer the press into subservience.

Minton's prospects for re-election in 1940 also were damaged when the Republican Party nominated another Hoosier native, WENDELL WILLKIE, as its candidate for president. With the popular and charismatic Willkie at the head of the ticket, Hoosiers returned to their normal pattern of voting Republican, except in the governor's race, and Minton, who had won his 1934 race by nearly 60,000 votes, lost by 23,000 votes.

The defeat ushered in a period of transition for Minton. Roosevelt, rewarding his loyalty, named him an administrative assistant in the White House and then, in May 1941, appointed him to the U.S. Court of Appeals for the Seventh Circuit in Chicago. He served there for eight years, writing more than 250 opinions, on par with his fellow judges on the Seventh Circuit and better than average for an appellate court judge. He managed to keep up the pace despite poor health and special assignments from Roosevelt and Truman.

Minton's approach to cases before the appeals court reflected his legislative experience and his populist temperament. His judicial style was characterized by restraint, pragmatism, and common sense coupled with deference to the will of the majority expressed in legislative enactments. The style of opinion writing Minton crafted on the Seventh Circuit became his trademark. He was good at coining phrases, often with a touch of humor, but his opinions were not the kind of phrases that had enduring qualities or a broad application.

When Truman became president in 1945, speculation heightened that bigger things were in store for Minton, but Truman bypassed Minton for a cabinet position in the new administration and the Supreme Court when vacancies occurred because of concerns about his health; Minton had been diagnosed with pernicious anemia in 1943 and suffered a massive heart attack in the fall of 1945.

By 1949, however, when another vacancy occurred on the Supreme Court, Truman, satisfied that his old friend's health had been restored, named Minton to be the nation's eighty-seventh justice. During Minton's seven years on the Court, the justices dealt with a range of highly visible and divisive issues against the backdrop of the Cold War. Among the most prominent were cases pertaining to freedom of speech, subversive activities, loyalty programs for government employees, and treatment of aliens. In cases involving the rights of individuals versus the government, Minton almost always sided with the government.

On the Court Minton remained faithful to his philosophy of judicial restraint. He was loathe to invalidate state or congressional statutes. His experience with the New Deal Court left him with the conviction that the Court should not undo the actions of the political branches of government unless there was a clear prohibition in the Constitution against such action.

Minton felt that his most important legacy on the court was his role in civil rights cases. He helped to lay the foundation for ending racial discrimination in public schools in the landmark *Brown v. Board of Education* decision (1954) and in his *Barrows v. Jackson* opinion (1953), which made racially based restrictive covenants in housing virtually unenforceable in state courts. "Segregation is incompatible with democracy," he once said.

By 1956 Minton had concluded that it was time to "be going home to Indiana and its hills and people I love . . . to enjoy my remaining days doing as I damned pleased." In the early morning hours of April 9, 1965, Sherman "Shay" Minton, age seventy-four, died in his sleep at a New Albany hospital.

The most enduring tribute to Minton, and one that has made his name a household word to motorists for decades, came in 1962 when the double-deck bridge over the Ohio River between New Albany and Louisville was named in his honor.

JAMES E. ST. CLAIR
LINDA C. GUGIN

For Further Reading

Gugin, Linda C., and James E. St. Clair. *Sherman Minton: New Deal Senator, Cold War Justice.* Indianapolis: Indiana Historical Society Press, 1997.

Minton, Sherman. Papers. Lilly Library, Indiana University. Bloomington.

Neff, Robert Rex. "The Early Career and Governorship of Paul V. McNutt." PhD diss., Indiana University, 1963.

Solomon, Rayman L. *History of the Seventh Circuit, 1891–1941.* Washington, D.C.: Published under the auspices of the Bicentennial Committee of the Judicial Conference of the United States, 1981.

Monks, Leander J.

July 10, 1843–April 19, 1919

Associate and chief judge of the Indiana Supreme Court, scholar, and author of the seminal work, *Indiana Courts and Lawyers*.

A meticulous lawyer, savvy politician, diligent trial judge, indefatigable state supreme court justice, and industrious editor, Leander John Monks was also a tireless student of jurisprudence. Throughout his life, Monks devoted his considerable energies to the calling of law and legal history of Indiana's burgeoning Industrial Age, insistent in his measured, conservative approach on the principles of precedent and their application.

Monks was born July 10, 1843, in Winchester, Randolph County, Indiana, the eldest son of George Washington Monks and his second wife, Mary A. Irwin Monks. George was one of Randolph County's early settlers, its first Republican state representative (1855–56), clerk of the court for fourteen years, and a very successful attorney as well as a prosperous farmer.

Following in his father's footsteps in the law, Leander attended Indiana University's Department of Law classes from 1861 until 1864, but left Bloomington after his junior year and returned to Winchester, possibly to assist his father who, by all accounts, was devastated by his wife's sudden death that same year. From 1864 to 1865 Leander worked as an insurance agent and was admitted to the bar by the time of his father's death in April 1865. Monks entered into a partnership with Colonel Martin Boots Miller. On August 2, 1865, Monks married a young widow, Elizabeth White Teal, whose family had been lifelong neighbors in Winchester. The couple had four daughters: Margaret, Mary, Alice, and Agnes.

Monks quickly rose in both his profession and the Randolph County Republican Party, which produced a number of noted Hoosier attorneys, judges, and political leaders, including James P. Goodrich, eventual governor of the state and a longtime associate of Monks. From 1871 to 1875 Monks practiced law with Enos L. Watson, and from 1875 until his election to the circuit court in 1878 he practiced law with William A. Thompson. He also served as Republican county chairman during the elections of 1870 and 1872, the Republican district chairman in 1874 and 1876, and was also a member of the Republican state executive committee in 1876. Through Monks's comprehensive knowledge of the law and his tireless labors on behalf of his party, he garnered the 1878 Republican nomination at the relatively young age of thirty-five as judge of the Twenty-fifth Judicial Circuit (then comprising Randolph and Delaware Counties) in which he ran unopposed. Reelected for two additional terms, Monks quickly developed a reputation for running an efficient and well-organized court, and for demanding that attorneys appearing before him be as thoroughly prepared and versed in the law as himself. Although contemporary methods of reporting appellate cases during this period do not allow for a complete tally, available data suggest that Monks's opinions were upheld on appeal more often than they were reversed.

By 1894 Monks's performance on the circuit bench earned him a place on the ballot for the Indiana Supreme Court, which was an elected position under the 1851 Indiana Constitution. Monks defeated his Democrat incumbent foe in the midst of an overwhelming Republican off-year victory. From his inauguration on January 7, 1895, until January 7, 1913, Monks served longer than any other elected Indiana Supreme Court justice and wrote an astonishing 802 opinions over the course of his tenure on the bench. His longevity record was broken after a constitutional amendment in 1970 changed the method of selection from partisan elections to merit-based gubernatorial appointments. Monks quickly established himself as a meticulous expert of legal authority and procedure, especially in the areas of property and contract. He was considered such an expert in the law of contracts, in fact, that authors of treatises on that subject sought his endorsement.

During Monks's tenure on the state supreme court, the U.S. Supreme Court was breaking unchartered territory on the subject of substantive due process. Under this doctrine the Court established for itself the power to invalidate state laws regulating economic activity by the private sector, such as working hours and minimum wage. The application of this power in the late nineteenth and early twentieth centuries usually resulted in the invalidation of such regulations as a violation of the liberty of the business owner protected under the due process clause of the Fourteenth Amendment. However, laws could be upheld if the court determined that state economic regulation was reasonable and met a legitimate state objective.

Monks's view of constitutional review did not condone the Court reading into the Constitution rights authorized by statute that were not clearly delineated there. His theory of constitutional review was stated definitively in the 1896 decision *Fesler v. Brayton*. Monks wrote, "It is not the judgment of a court that renders a statute unconstitutional, but the fact that it is in conflict with some provision of the constitution. A statute, therefore, that is repugnant to any provision of the constitution is void before, as well as after it is so adjudged." He placed his high regard for property and contracts over new rights enshrined in statutes, no matter how worthy they might be. Throughout his time on the Indiana Supreme Court, the only three cases in which Monks dissented involved cases where he thought his fellow judges had erred in declaring a statue unconstitutional. Given the number of cases Monks wrote, it is astonishing that his brethren on the court dissented from his opinions only once.

Aside from his gift for clear, concise, and persuasive opinion writing, Monks continued to be recognized for his leadership of both bench and bar. Beginning in 1904, Monks served several terms as chief judge, which at that time was a rotating office among senior members of the court. He also was the first signer of the 1896 Articles of the Association of the State Bar Association of Indiana, and served as vice president of the organization in 1899.

Monks sought an unprecedented fourth term in 1912 but was defeated as Woodrow Wilson and the Democrats swept a number of Republicans out of office. The former judge wasted little time in helping create the firm of Monks Robbins Starr and Goodrich, which occupied the ninth floor of the Indiana Pythian Building in Indianapolis. During the next four years, Monks and his partners argued numerous cases before the local and appellate courts. While the former justice listed his permanent home as Winchester, he was living in boardinghouses in Indianapolis year-round. The firm was dissolved in 1916 when founding member and fellow Randolph County Republican Goodrich was elected governor. Monks then maintained a solo practice on the sixth floor of the Pythian Building, occasionally assisting with his former partners in appellate cases.

Despite his extensive service to the bench and bar of Indiana, Monks will be most remembered for is his role as editor in chief of the monumental *Courts and Lawyers of Indiana*, a three-volume work published in conjunction with the state's centennial in 1916. Monks began his labors on this set shortly after leaving the bench and was given only a few short years to compile both a historical and biographical guide to the practitioners of law in Indiana's first century. Assisting him in this massive effort were noted historians LOGAN ESAREY, who was already the editor of the *Indiana Magazine of History*, as well as Logan's brother, Solomon Esarey, assistant reporter of the Indiana Supreme Court during Monks's time on the bench, and Ernest V. Shockley. Often the only source detailing the lives and activity of hundreds of Indiana attorneys, this set, collectively known as "Monks" quickly became a staple of library reference shelves across the state and remains one of the most authoritative works on early Indiana legal history.

Monks maintained a rigorous legal practice throughout and after the publication of *Courts and Lawyers of Indiana*. He was still representing clients before the Indiana Supreme Court shortly before his death. While living with his eldest daughter, Margaret Monks Kizer, in Indianapolis, Monks suffered a stroke and died on April 19, 1919. He was buried beside his wife, who had predeceased him in 1908, in Fountain Park Cemetery in Winchester.

KEITH BUCKLEY

For Further Reading

Adams, Wendy L,. and Elizabeth R. Osborn, eds. *In Memoriam: Glimpses from Indiana's Legal Past*. Indianapolis: Indiana Supreme Court, 2006.

Baude, Patrick L., "Leander J. Monks." In *Justices of the Indiana Supreme Court*. Edited by Linda C. Gugin and James E. St. Clair. Indianapolis: Indiana Historical Society Press, 2011.

Monks, Leander J., ed. *Courts and Lawyers of Indiana*. Indianapolis: Federal Publishing Company, 1916.

Monroe, William "Bill" Smith

September 13, 1911–September 9, 1996

Country music pioneer credited with giving birth to the subgenre known as bluegrass music.

Bill Monroe, generally regarded as the father of bluegrass music, was born in Rosine, Kentucky, and naturally is most closely associated with his native state. His band, The Blue Grass Boys, took its name from the state's motto and the term bluegrass music in turn was derived from Monroe's band.

Indiana, however, is where Monroe launched his career and where his music and legacy continue to be celebrated during the annual bluegrass festival at Bean Blossom in Brown County. Held since 1967 on land Monroe purchased in 1951, it is the longest continuously running bluegrass festival in the world and continues to attract thousands of fans each summer.

The Bill Monroe Music Park and Campground is today owned by Dwight Dillman, who played banjo in Monroe's Blue Grass Boys in the 1970s. He purchased the property from Monroe's son, James, in 1998, and has made a number of improvements to the fifty-five-acre facility.

Monroe, the youngest of eight children, grew up working hard on a thriving farm and surrounded by music. His mother played fiddle, accordion, and harmonica; his father was a step dancer; and his mother's brother, Pen Vandiver, was a prolific fiddler and the inspiration for Monroe's song "Uncle Pen." Monroe wanted to play guitar or fiddle but settled for mandolin at age nine because his brothers had claimed those instruments.

His mother died in 1921 when he was ten years old, and his father died six years later. After some shuffling between family members, he ended up with Uncle Pen. Their musical collaborations left a fortuitous impression on the younger partner, and in 1929, at age seventeen, Bill set off for Whiting, Indiana, to join his brothers, Birch and Charlie. He worked four years at a Sinclair oil refinery, playing music on the side for other southerners who had made similar moves in search of work.

The brothers and their girlfriends joined a team of dancers in 1932 for a traveling country-music revue organized by Chicago radio station WLS, which ran a popular program called *The National Barn Dance*. Next, the brothers were playing music on local radio stations in Hammond and Gary, and by 1934 Bill was ready to quit the refinery to play music full time. Birch opted out, and Charlie and Bill continued as The Monroe Brothers, enjoying substantial success behind Charlie's strong singing and guitar playing and Bill's high tenor harmonies and propulsive mandolin playing.

Bill was soon ready to go out on his own. He was hearing something different in his head, the sorrowful, rapid fiddle strokes of his Uncle Pen and the country blues influence of Arthur Schulz, the black fiddler and guitarist who used to make the rounds in Rosine. Monroe said his uncle had the best bow movement with a fiddle and that "he could really shuffle." Monroe wanted some blues in his own music and tried to borrow what he could use from Schultz, who used a pick while playing guitar and could "just run from one chord to another, the prettiest you ever heard."

After a stalled effort known as The Kentuckians, Monroe formed a band he called The Blue Grass Boys. The group was distinct for its instrumental makeup—mandolin, guitar, fiddle, and bass (and later, banjo)—and for its quick tempos and high tenor singing. A style was taking shape, though it would not be labeled bluegrass for nearly another decade.

Bill Monroe and The Blue Grass Boys debuted on the *Grand Ole Opry* in 1939, performing their version of "New Muleskinner Blues" and initiating a presence that continued for fifty years. Monroe became a headlining act, and he and his crew traveled widely and in style.

Monroe loved competition and often described playing music in those terms. He was known, for example, to speed up songs and transpose keys to test the prowess of his musicians. He expected a lot from them and he drove them hard, but he was known as fair and disciplined boss. The Blue Grass Boys' heyday came with the arrival of guitarist and singer Lester Flatt in 1945 and banjoist Earl Scruggs in 1946. Scruggs played in a so-called three-finger style that was new at the time, and his addition raised the band's profile. Monroe's influence on other musicians was spreading, and by 1948 there was enough of it to give it a label—bluegrass.

Flatt and Scruggs went out on their own early that year, irking Monroe but pointing out an inherent flaw in his system: Talented newcomers are grateful for the exposure but want to lead their own band. At the same time, Monroe had an eye for talent and usually had someone waiting in the wings. Over the nearly sixty years that he performed, more than 150 musicians played in his band.

Rockabilly came along in the early 1950s and presented the first of many musical challenges to come for bluegrass. Monroe did not follow trends, and he kept doing what came naturally. It was a lean time as most of country music dried up and

Flatt and Scruggs dominated what was left of the market. Elvis Presley recorded a version of Monroe's well-known song "Blue Moon of Kentucky" in 1954 and included it as the B side of his first hit, "That's All Right, Mama."

Monroe and Presley met that year at the Grand Ole Opry when Elvis made his only appearance there. The nineteen-year-old sensation played his raucous version of Monroe's song and drew a lackluster response from the Ryman Auditorium audience that was used to hearing the song as a waltz. Monroe watched from backstage and afterward told the young singer that he liked it. Monroe later altered his arrangement of the song, starting as a waltz before turning it into a musical sprint fueled by fiery mandolin and banjo. "He learned something from young Elvis as much as young Elvis had learned from him," John Dowell, musical supervisor of the Ryman, said in a 2010 YouTube interview "He liked Elvis' version of the song, because, as he said, 'It made me far more money than my version or anybody else's.'"

By the late 1950s, rock and roll was fully ascendant, and country artists began finding new popularity among a crowd of young urban folk music fans. Flatt and Scruggs capitalized by playing on television and at folk festivals, but the stubborn Monroe only came around to the idea of expanding his reach in 1962 when he met Ralph Rinzler. The young musician, who cofounded the annual Smithsonian Folklife Festival, published the first known interview with Monroe and later became his manager.

The connection proved fruitful as Monroe found new fans who were interested in authenticity and drawn to his steadfast traditionalism. His folk festival debut came in 1963 at the University of Chicago, and he played a key role in a major Roanoke festival in 1965. His Bean Blossom festival began two years later.

Although he never hit the charts again, Monroe remained a popular and prolific live performer into the 1990s, including appearing with Willie Nelson, Neil Young, and John Mellencamp at a Farm Aid concert in Indianapolis. Monroe's honors include a Grammy Lifetime Achievement Award and a National Medal of Honor. He is a member of the Rock and Roll, Country Music, and International Bluegrass Musicians halls of fame, and he is singularly recognized for his instrumental prowess and his impact on musical style. Monroe is one of only a few musical figures to create a genre.

In the 1960s his style extended to youth bands such as The Grateful Dead, and musicians including Del McCoury, Bylon Berline, Peter Rowan, and Vassar Clements each launched solo careers after playing with Monroe.

The property in Bean Blossom, which Monroe purchased during the height of his popularity because it reminded him of the rolling hills of his youth, remains a touchstone of the bluegrass world, celebrating its forty-ninth consecutive festival in June 2015.

CARY STEMLE

For Further Reading

Ewing, Tom. *The Bill Monroe Reader*. Urbana: University of Illinois Press, 2000.
Goldsmith, Thomas. *The Bluegrass Reader*. Urbana: University of Illinois Press, 2004.
Rooney, Jim. *Bossmen: Bill Monroe and Muddy Waters*. New York: Da Capo Press, 1991.

Montgomery, John Leslie "Wes"
March 6, 1923–June 15, 1968

Jazz guitarist, composer, and bandleader.

When he died in 1968 at age forty-five, Wes Montgomery was a commercial success and an artistic pariah. After being discovered by the jazz saxophonist Cannonball Adderley in 1959, he recorded some nineteen albums for the Riverside record label of New York City under the direction of bandleader and accompanist Orrin Keepnews. Some of those recordings are now considered classics, and it is this period from 1959 to 1964 that jazz aficionados consider the apex of Montgomery's career.

When Riverside went out of business, the self-taught guitarist, who unconventionally plucked the guitar with the fingers on his large right hand instead of a pick, signed with Verve Records. There he came under the direction of producer Creed Taylor, who had different ideas about how to elevate him from niche legend to mainstream popular music artist. The plan worked as the public responded to Taylor's highly produced recordings and Montgomery won a Grammy in 1967 for his version of "Goin' Out of My Head."

For the previous twenty years, Montgomery had looked at his guitar playing as something of a hobby and certainly nothing he could count on to provide for his family. That changed with his

Wes Montgomery

commercial success, but it came with a price, as noted by critic J. R. Taylor reviewing Montgomery's instrumental cover of the Little Anthony and the Imperial's 1964 hit: "We must regret that Montgomery's gifts were turned so completely toward the radio industry's idea of what a good record was, for that idea allowed little room for large areas of his talent."

That such a heated debate would exist in the first place seemed unlikely.

Montgomery was born in 1923 in Indianapolis. His parents separated early, and in 1935 Wes and his two older brothers moved to Columbus, Ohio, to live with their father. His brother, Monk, who later became known for his pioneering technique on the Fender electric bass guitar, noticed Wes's interest in music and bought him a four-string "tenor" guitar. Monk has said his brother quickly became proficient on the instrument, although Wes said he only came into his own after he acquired his first six-string guitar for $350.

After returning to Indianapolis Montgomery was determined to justify the expense of the instrument and practiced vigorously. After hearing the solos of jazz guitar great Charlie Christian, who had pioneered electric guitar solos as a member of Benny Goodman's bands, Montgomery focused on learning exactly how Christian elicited those sounds. Montgomery apparently never thought he could learn to play in the style of Christian, but with his natural ear, he soon figured it out. "I listened to them real good," Montgomery said of Christian's records, "and I knew that everything done on his guitar could be done on mine, because I had a six-string, so I just determined that I would do it."

By age twenty Montgomery secured a gig to play Christian solos at the 440 Club in Indianapolis. He also worked a variety of day jobs that he often lost by leaving for short stints on the road. With a growing family—Montgomery and his wife, Serene, eventually had seven children—he sought a steady job and found one at Polk Sanitary Milk Company, but continued playing at various Indianapolis nightclubs.

His first break came in 1948 when he auditioned for bandleader Lionel Hampton, who hired him on the spot and took him on the road. But

Montgomery became disillusioned because he was rarely highlighted amid the myriad soloists in Hampton's band, and he also was homesick. Quitting Hampton was an unsound career move, but Montgomery resigned after two years and returned to his hometown, where he eventually began collaborating with various local musicians, including brothers Monk and Buddy, who played piano and vibes in a band called the Montgomery-Johnson quintet.

That quintet made some recordings and had a two-year residency at Tropics Club. In 1957 Buddy and Monk left for the West Coast, where they formed a band called the Mastersounds and signed a record deal with Pacific Jazz Records.

Despite his growing profile in the jazz world, Wes remained in Indianapolis and worked as a welder during the day and performed by night. After playing from 9:30 p.m. to 2:00 a.m., he hustled across town to an after-hours club called The Missile Room, where he would jam from 2:30 a.m. until dawn. That's where Adderley saw him and urged Keepnews to sign him to the Riverside label.

Montgomery took his regular trio—organist Melvin Rhyne and drummer Paul Perkins— to New York to record his first album. After twenty years, he was a bandleader and, in short order, a jazz sensation. *Down Beat* magazine critics named him their best new artist in 1960, and Montgomery followed up by winning the magazine's best jazz musician award in both the readers' and critics' polls in 1961 and 1962. Not bad for someone who could not read music. He was surprised by the acclaim because he thought he had peaked as a player around 1952.

Montgomery recorded three albums for Verve between November 1964 and September 1965 before Taylor persuaded him to do "Goin' Out of My Head." He was initially reluctant to follow the producer's big-band approach, which included adding strings and horn sections, in part because he was self-conscious about working with trained musicians who could read music in the studio. But he soon gave in and was thrilled when the 1965 recording sold in numbers to which he was unaccustomed.

Montgomery's style was defined by his use of octaves—solos where he played the same note on two strings—and block chords, in which the notes were played at once rather than strummed individually. Taylor accentuated Montgomery's octaves approach while paring his swinging jazz roots. He realized he was watering down Montgomery's talent but thought it was for a greater good. "I decided that if people were going to hear Wes Montgomery, I would have to record him in a culturally acceptable context," he said.

Like artists such as Louis Armstrong, Charlie Parker, and Nat King Cole before him, Montgomery confronted the accusation that he had sold out his art for financial gain. The reaction puzzled him. "I want to tell people—those who write about it as well as the public—not to worry about what it's called; worry about whether it pleases people," Montgomery said. "That's what it's all about anyway, people are the final judges."

There also are indications that Montgomery felt frustrated that his live audiences only wanted to hear his commercial work and not his pure jazz. He was still stuck in the debate when he died in 1968. There are varying accounts of his death from a heart attack, but general speculation that his years of relentless work, along with his chain smoking, wrecked his health.

In his relatively brief national career, Montgomery rubbed shoulders with many of the biggest names in jazz, including saxophonists Miles Davis and John Coltrane. Montgomery also inspired a generation of jazz guitarists such as George Benson, Kenny Burrell, Pat Martino, and Pat Metheny, and today ranks behind only Django Reinhardt and Christian as a practitioner of the jazz guitar. He was a natural musician who channeled deep emotion and it is said he would have excelled no matter what instrument he chose.

Montgomery is remembered as an innovator who left critics gasping for breath. Jazz musician, composer, and critic Gunter Schuller, in an article for *Jazz Review* magazine, wrote, "His playing at its peak becomes unbearably exciting, to the point where one feels unable to muster sufficient physical endurance to outlast it."

CARY STEMLE

For Further Reading

Giddins, Gary, and Scott Knowles DeVeaux. *Jazz*. New York: W. W. Norton, 2009.

Ingram, Advian. *Wes Montgomery*. Newcastle-upon-Tyne, UK: Ashley Mark Publishing Company, 1985.

Woodward, Josef. "Wes Montgomery: The Softer Side of Genius." *JazzTimes* (July/August 2005).

Morton, Oliver P.

April 4, 1823–November 1, 1877

Circuit judge, lieutenant governor and governor of Indiana, and U.S. senator.

As Indiana's governor during the Civil War, Oliver P. Morton displayed ingenuity and forcefulness in guiding the state in fulfilling its commitment to assist the federal government's efforts to preserve the Union. Though at first conservative regarding Reconstruction, as a U.S. senator he became one of the Republican Party's foremost spokesmen for civil and political rights for the former slaves. Like some other successful politicians of his time, Morton combined the zeal of a dedicated public servant with the sometimes ruthless partisanship of an effective party boss.

Oliver Hazard Perry Throck Morton was born the son of a shoemaker in Wayne County, Indiana. After his mother's death, he spent much of his childhood with her family in Ohio before returning to Indiana, where he studied briefly at the Wayne County Seminary. Apprenticed to his brother, a hatter, he tired of the work and attended Miami University from 1843 to 1845. He then read law with a leading attorney in Centerville, Indiana, where he married Lucinda Burbank, the daughter of a local merchant. After winning admission to the bar in 1846 he embarked on his career. In 1852 the state legislature chose him for a circuit judgeship. He served eight months, after which he spent a term at the Cincinnati Law School. With newly burnished credentials, he soon enjoyed a successful legal practice.

Morton began political life as a Democrat. In the 1840s he espoused Manifest Destiny, strongly favored acquisition of territory from Mexico and opposed the ban on slavery there as proposed in the Wilmot Proviso. In 1851 he supported the new state constitution that forbade blacks from entering Indiana and the following year stumped the state for Democratic presidential candidate Franklin Pierce.

For the first ten years of his political life Morton tried to avoid the issues of slavery and its expansion, believing that Democrats in the North stood to lose if these volatile issues assumed center stage. Like many other northern Democrats, he broke with the party in 1854, when the Pierce administration and other national leaders embraced the Kansas-Nebraska Act that permitted slavery to enter territories in the Louisiana Purchase previously free under the Missouri Compromise of 1820. Though reluctant to abandon the Democratic organization, Morton flirted briefly with the anti-immigrant Know-Nothings before casting his lot with the Anti-Nebraska movement, known in Indiana as the People's Party. This new organization soon adopted the label Republican, and Morton rose rapidly in its ranks. In 1856 the Republican state convention nominated him for governor. His loss by 2.6 percent to Democrat Ashbel P. Willard reflected the state's even partisan split and underscored Morton's sense that victory for his party required a gingerly treatment of sectional and racial issues.

Four years later the Republicans chose Henry S. Lane, a former Whig congressman, for governor and Morton as his running mate. Morton took the lead in campaigning, denying that he was an abolitionist, as claimed by his opponents, and focusing on the Republicans' opposition to slavery expansion. Recognizing Hoosier voters' essential conservatism, he acknowledged the moral objections to slavery but emphasized the more selfish consideration that if slavery were permitted in the territories, it would effectively preclude migration by northern free laborers. The Republicans won the governor's office and control of the state legislature in the election of 1860. In early January 1861, by a previous arrangement between Lane and Morton that was designed to assure the party's chances of electoral success, the legislature elected Lane to the U.S. Senate, and after two days as lieutenant governor Morton became governor.

When southerners sought to leave the Union in the wake of ABRAHAM LINCOLN's election as president, Morton denounced secession as an assault on the principle of democratic government and became one of the most indefatigable of the war governors assisting the federal government's struggle for preservation. Beginning with Lincoln's first call for troops, Indiana regularly exceeded its quota of new recruits. To help meet the troops' equipment needs, Morton established a state arsenal where hundreds of employees manufactured ammunition. He carefully monitored the supply and treatment of Hoosiers in the field and won their gratitude as "the soldiers' friend."

Partisan rancor continued to roil Indiana politics, and Morton did not hesitate to characterize the Democrats as willing allies or witless dupes of the Confederates. He was not above bringing charges of subversive activity against his more vigorous opponents, especially during election seasons. Recognizing the conservative racial ideas of his constituents, he early on emphasized preservation of the Union, not abolition, as the key war aim. He defended the Emancipation Proclamation as a war measure similar to the Union blockade, different in form but not in principle. He upheld the enlistment of black soldiers as a military expedient, not unlike the utilization of horses and mules.

Despite the governor's concessions to Hoosier voters' racism, dismay over casualties and the floundering Union war effort helped Democrats win control of the general assembly in 1862. During the ensuing session, the majority endeavored to curtail Morton's power and almost single-handedly the governor strove mightily to maintain the state's support for the war. When the legislature adjourned without making appropriations, he borrowed heavily from the federal government, local jurisdictions around the state in the hands of Republicans, and private banks and businesses to keep the state afloat. Portraying his political enemies as agents of treason, and aided by an upswing in the Union's military fortunes, Morton won the gubernatorial election of 1864 by 7.4 percent and carried a Republican majority into the legislature.

In the campaign of 1864 Morton embraced emancipation as an act of Christian justice, but during the early phase of Reconstruction he supported President Andrew Johnson's lenient treatment of the former Confederate states and he opposed immediate black suffrage. Before long, intransigence by southern whites convinced Morton of the futility of Johnson's program and of the necessity for enfranchisement of the former slaves. In early 1867 the Indiana legislature elected him to the U.S. Senate. He was reelected in 1873 and remained in the Senate until the end of his life.

Morton took a leading role in framing the Fifteenth Amendment that prohibited the states from denying the right to vote on the basis of race, and he even argued as well for a broader guarantee of the right to vote against discrimination on the basis of ethnic origin or religion. During the presidency of Ulysses S. Grant, Morton vigorously defended the administration's use of federal troops to protect the civil and political rights of African Americans in the South. On the currency question, he harkened to the pleas of his hard-pressed farmer

Oliver P. Morton

constituents and favored greenback inflation. A close ally of Grant, Morton deftly deployed federal patronage to maintain his firm grip on the Hoosier Republican Party.

Morton aspired to the presidential nomination in 1876 but lost to Rutherford B. Hayes, whose accession to office he assisted as a member of the Electoral Commission created to settle the disputed election outcome. Democratic candidate Samuel J. Tilden won a plurality of the popular vote, but the Republican-dominated commission gave Hayes every contested vote, making him the winner of the Electoral College by one vote—185 to 184.

Morton deserves notice as one the first handicapped individuals to achieve national political prominence. A stroke in 1865 paralyzed his legs and necessitated his use of two canes, but it did not curtail his political effectiveness. Merciless enemies ascribed his malady to dissolute habits, but he bore his infirmities with dignity. After ten years in the Senate, another stroke took his life at age fifty-four.

CHARLES W. CALHOUN

For Further Reading

Emma Lou Thornbrough. *Indiana in the Civil War Era, 1850–1880*. Indianapolis: Indiana Historical Society, 1965.

Foulke, William Dudley. *Life of Oliver P. Morton*. Indianapolis and Kansas City: Bowen-Merrill Company, 1899.

Morton, Oliver P. Papers. Indiana State Library, Indianapolis.

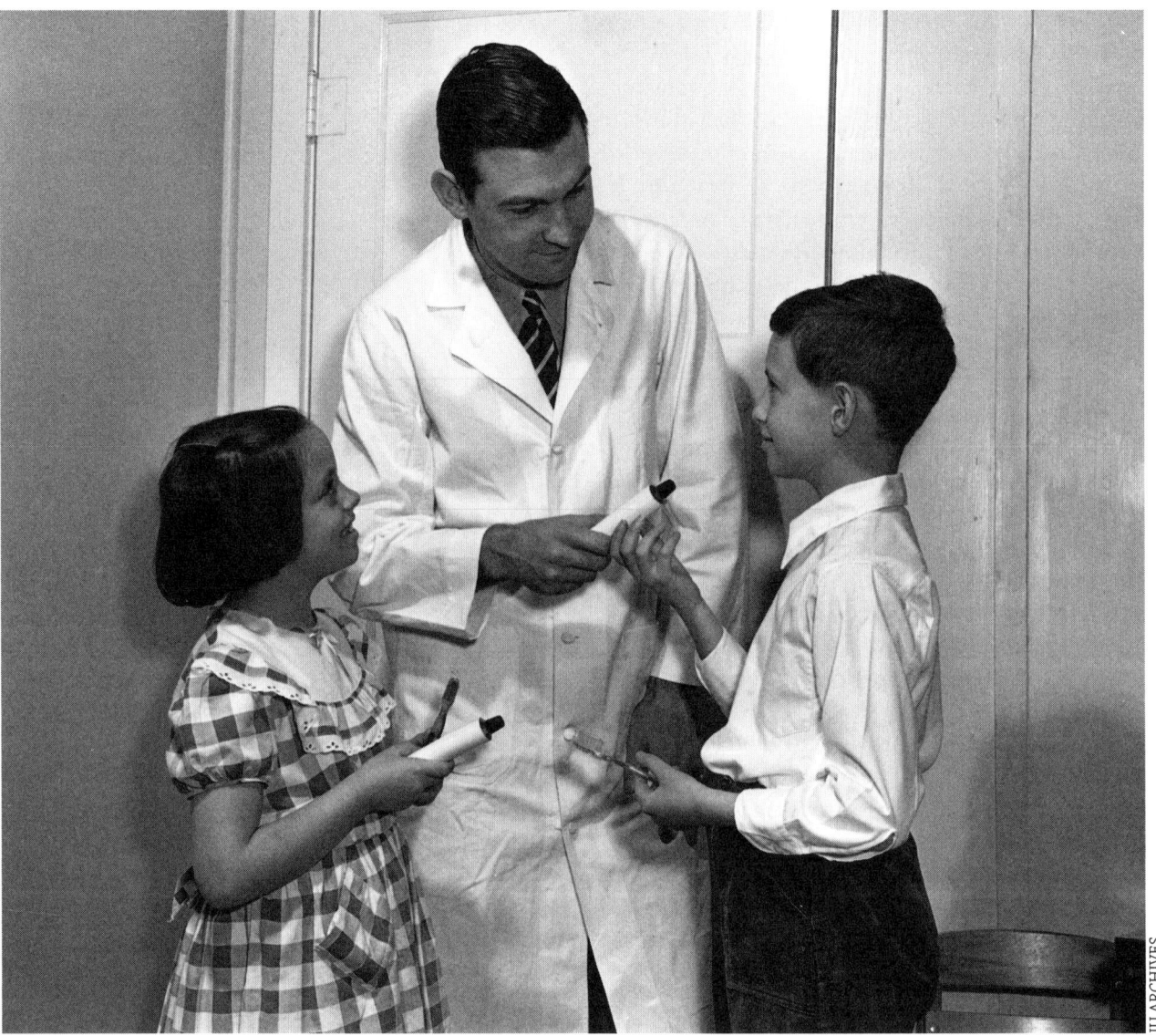

Joseph C. Muhler presents toothpaste and toothbrushes to two of the 12,000 young volunteers who took part in tests of a stannous flouride toothpaste.

Muhler, Joseph Charles

December 22, 1923–December 24, 1996

Biochemist, university professor, and author who also led the research team that developed Crest toothpaste.

Joseph Charles Muhler, who was born in Fort Wayne, Indiana, knew from an early age that he wanted to be a chemist. He had his own home laboratory and supplemented what he learned throughout high school working as a lab assistant after school and on weekends. Immediately upon graduation he began working as a machinist at the Wayne Pump Company in Fort Wayne, which produced ammunition during World War II.

Impressed with his hard work, his foreman took a personal interest in him and learned that in addition to working full time, Muhler was also taking classes through the Indiana University Extension Division. In 1943 E. J. Gallmeyer, vice president and director of sales for Wayne Pump, wrote to Indiana University president HERMAN B WELLS about how impressed he had been with Muhler and hoped Wells could help him gain admission to the IU School of Medicine.

Robert T. Ittner, assistant to the president, expressed some doubt about Muhler's decidedly average school record but conceded that if perhaps he took a lighter workload his grades would improve. A face-to-face meeting with Muhler seems to have changed his mind, however, because the following month he wrote that Muhler did not have enough credits to enter the 1944 class but if he carried a full load for three semesters he could be considered for the January 1945 class. He ended with, "I am convinced that Mr. Muhler will do superior work on our campus and that he will make an outstanding record."

In 1944 Muhler had nearly completed his undergraduate degree when he was drafted into military service. But rather than deliver him to the front line during the war, the U.S. Navy sent him to the IU School of Dentistry. "That was pretty nice except at the time I hadn't the slightest interest in dentistry," Muhler told *Collier's* magazine in 1956. His interest in entering the School of Medicine continued throughout his dental studies but it was while in dental school that Muhler began work on what he became most known for, his role in the discovery of stannous fluoride as an effective agent against tooth decay.

As a dental student Muhler studied more than 150 fluoride compounds and in 1947 he coauthored his first research results in the *Journal of Dental Research* with Doctor Grant Van Huysen. Upon completion of his doctorate of dental surgery the following year, Muhler began working as a teaching fellow, which allowed him to continue his research. While attending a dental convention in 1949, a Procter and Gamble research scientist approached Muhler and suggested the company might be able to provide research support. IU and P&G came to terms and shortly thereafter P&G began funding Muhler's work.

Muhler and his research team, which included IU chemists Harry Day and William Nebergall, tested their new toothpaste on 3,600 Bloomington schoolchildren and their families, for a total of 11,500 subjects—one-third of the Bloomington population—beginning in the early 1950s. The children were not told what they were testing, whether they received the experimental product or the control product; nor were they told how or how often to brush. They were simply provided with enough toothpaste and toothbrushes for their household and instructed to return in six months for a follow-up. The successful results of a 50 percent reduction in tooth decay led to the debut of Crest toothpaste in 1956. In 1960 the American Dental Association endorsed Crest, the first time it had backed a specific product.

In 1951 IU granted Muhler his PhD in chemistry and appointed him as a faculty member of the School of Dentistry, where he continued his research on preventative dentistry. In his chosen field Muhler was prolific in his writing and research, contributing to numerous books and journals and authoring or coauthoring several textbooks and monographs. What may be little known about Muhler, however, is that he had a wide range of interests that went well outside dentistry. He wrote detective stories and "dabbled" in farm work, which his wife called "preventive medicine," as it served as an outlet for his never-ending energy. He purchased his small northern Indiana farm with the intention of planting Christmas trees. With no experience—but abundant interest—he turned to an area farmer, Niley Wisler, who became his mentor and partner. "We have no formal agreement, nothing in writing, but it's a perfect arrangement," said Muhler. "He gets a kick out of me and I'm getting an education from him."

As with other areas of his life, Muhler was indefatigable and hungry to learn and his twenty acres of farmland eventually grew to more than 1,300 acres, where he would sometimes bring Bloomington colleagues for a spin on one of his tractors. His work on his farm coincided with his early interest in human nutrition and led to new research on the differences in regional soil and health that he worked on in the last decade of his life.

Muhler's long relationship with IU continued until his death in 1996. The university honored him with a new faculty title of research professor in 1959, established to identify individuals as superior in their field. He continued to distinguish himself throughout and beyond his career, retiring on December 31, 1983, with the title of research professor emeritus and professor emeritus of dental auxiliary education. His association with IU was mutually beneficial as portions of proceeds from his research went to the university, and in fact income from his work on Crest ultimately helped build the Oral Health Research Institute on the Indiana University–Purdue University at Indianapolis campus. Muhler was a man of his word, more than fulfilling the promise he made in a letter in 1943 to IU administrator Ittner, which read in part: "At the present time I know of no way of returning your time and efforts, but I want you to know from the bottom of my heart that if the opportunity ever presents itself whereby I may do something for you I shall do it with my whole heart and soul."

DINA M. KELLAMS

For Further Reading

Bliven, Bruce. "Next: Flouride Toothpaste." *Collier's*, January 6, 1956.

Muhler, Joseph C. *Fifty-two Pearls and the Environment*. Bloomington: Indiana University Press, 1965.

"The Double Life of Dr. Muhler." *International Harvester World* 57, no. 5 (1966).

Nicholson, Meredith

December 9, 1866–December 21, 1947

Novelist, essayist, poet, and diplomat.

A member of the so-called Big Four, along with JAMES WHITCOMB RILEY, GEORGE ADE, and BOOTH TARKINGTON, in Indiana's golden age of literature, Meredith Nicholson, primarily a best-selling novelist, produced, on average, a book a year between 1903 and 1929, after which he became President Franklin D. Roosevelt's top diplomat in three Latin American countries between 1933 and 1941.

Nicholson was the first child of two Civil War veterans (an artillery captain, Edward Willis Nicholson, and a frontline nurse, Emily Meredith), who met during the war, when Emily helped care for the ailing Captain Nicholson after the Battle of Shiloh, and married soon after the war ended. Their son was born in Crawfordsville, Indiana, on December 9, 1866. This was also John Milton's birthday, which Nicholson believed destined him to become a writer, but it was a struggle for this largely self-educated, self-made man to learn and practice the art and craft of novel writing that made him famous.

The Nicholson family (of four) moved to Indianapolis in 1872 because the elder Nicholson, suffering from the lingering effects of the Civil War, was unable to farm in Montgomery County as planned. Instead he found a series of low-paying, unfulfilling indoor jobs in the capital city and eventually moved, alone, to Washington, D.C., where he committed suicide in 1894. The son, Meredith, raised primarily by his highly literate mother (the daughter of a newspaper editor), tried hard to please her and do well in school, but, as he explained later, the regimentation of the schools just "didn't fit" and he became an early dropout during his freshman year in high school. Still, the young man venerated learning, became an omnivorous reader, and even taught himself the rudiments of several foreign languages.

Nicholson helped out the family financially through a series of odd jobs, as a soda fountain clerk, a deliveryman, and, finally, having taught himself shorthand, he became a court reporter and worked in law offices. During these apprenticeships with attorneys John T. Dye and William P. Fishback and, lastly, with William Wallace, the younger brother of famous author and diplomat LEW WALLACE, Nicholson, already trying his hand at "versifying," was thrilled to meet both Riley and Wallace, who read his poems and greatly encouraged the boy to keep writing.

Realizing that his talents were more literary than legal, Nicholson switched jobs in 1886, becoming a reporter first for the *Indianapolis Sentinel* for a year, and then for the *Indianapolis News*, where he remained until 1897. His first book, a slim volume of poetry titled *Short Flights* (1891), appeared during his years as a reporter.

A life-changing event occurred shortly afterward, when this tall, handsome, gregarious young writer gave a short talk and a reading to a Vassar College alumni group in Indianapolis. A special guest from Nebraska who was visiting her former college roommate from Indianapolis also attended this meeting. This woman, Eugenie Kountze, was brilliant, accomplished (a Phi Beta Kappa honoree at Vassar), and wealthy. When she and the guest speaker met, there was an immediate attraction and soon, in 1896, the two were married in the bride's hometown of Omaha, Nebraska. Nicholson's best man there was the still unpublished fellow writer, Tarkington.

At first, in order to provide for himself and his bride, Nicholson attempted, like his father-in-law, a career in business. After briefly working as an unhappy stockbroker in Indianapolis, however, Nicholson accepted a position with a Kountze-financed coal company in Denver, Colorado, where the Nicholsons lived from 1898 to 1901, and started a family, but this life, too, proved to be unsatisfactory.

By happy coincidence, while working in Denver, businessman Nicholson received an unlikely invitation from Professor George Woodberry, also a poet who had read Nicholson's book of poetry, to write a book for a series Woodberry was editing on the literary culture of the United States. Nicholson's assignment was to produce a volume on Indiana's literary history and culture. This book, titled simply *The Hoosiers*, appeared in 1900, was well received (eventually becoming a classic), and proved to be the most important factor in changing the homesick Nicholson from a frustrated businessman in the mountainous West into an Indiana author.

The year following publication of *The Hoosiers*, the Nicholson family, now numbering three (one daughter having died in Denver), moved back to Indianapolis, where Nicholson became a full-time writer and embarked upon an amazingly productive and successful career producing one best-selling novel after another, twenty in all, as well as a second book of poetry, three collections of essays, a volume of short stories, and a coauthored play, *Honor Bright*, based on one of his short stories of the same title.

Nicholson, unlike his Pulitzer Prize–winning friend Tarkington, never had a book manuscript rejected by a book publisher. Believing, as he had learned from his friend and role model Riley, that one should write about what he knows, Nicholson did just that and most of his novels were set in Indiana, a state that he constantly boosted in his writings. He eventually came to be recognized as the "dean of Indiana writers."

Ironically, perhaps, Nicholson's first novel was not set in Indiana. Instead, the locale for *The Main Chance* (1903) was Omaha, his wife's hometown, which of course, Nicholson also knew well. His next books, best sellers all, indeed were set in Indiana. One, his third novel *The House of a Thousand Candles* (1905), became his top-selling book, was translated and published in several foreign languages, and became the basis for a Broadway play and at least two motion picture productions.

During the stock market crash of 1929 Nicholson published two books, a great novel based on the prepresidential years in the life of Andrew Jackson, *The Cavalier of Tennessee*, and a collection of autobiographical essays, *Old Familiar Faces*. But the Nicholsons were devastated financially by the crash, and two years later Nicholson was devastated emotionally upon the death of his wife. He published no more books after this, and seemed adrift in the world. But his Democratic friends rallied around him and managed to get him an appointment from Roosevelt to be the American minister to Paraguay in 1933.

Rather than journey abroad alone, however, Nicholson abruptly married his secretary, Dorothy Wolfe Lannon, and then, only days later, the couple departed for Latin America, where Nicholson became a highly successful diplomat in Paraguay (1933–35), Venezuela (1935–38), and Nicaragua (1938–41). The Paraguayan appointment was particularly significant in that Paraguay and Bolivia were engaged in war, fighting over control of the supposedly oil-rich Gran Chaco area. Nicholson quickly became a close friend of Paraguayan president Eusebio Ayala, also a writer, and with whom he had weekly private dinners. When he was transferred to the much better (and closer to home) accommodations in Caracas, Nicholson also represented his government well, becoming known to and trusted by the aged and semiliterate dictator of Venezuela, Juan Vicente Gomez.

In 1938 Nicholson was suddenly transferred (essentially demoted) to Nicaragua, but he took up his work there with zest, befriended the country's American-educated dictator, Anastasio Somoza, and, according to Somoza, put a friendly face on Roosevelt's "Good Neighbor" policy.

Upon Roosevelt's third election in 1940, Nicholson, approaching his seventy-fifth birthday, decided not to remain in the diplomatic corps. He and Dorothy came "back home" to Indiana,

Meredith Nicholson poses with fellow Indiana author James Whitcomb Riley.

then moved to Florida, but were not happy there, either. Returning to Indianapolis, the Nicholsons quietly divorced in 1943, and for a short while Nicholson took up again a favorite pastime, writing a twice-weekly column for the *Indianapolis Star*. He retired again in 1944, lived alone in rooms at the Indianapolis Athletic Club, and died exactly sixteen years after the death of his first wife, on December 21, 1947. Among the host of obituary notices that followed, the *New York Times* writer said it best, calling Nicholson "the last leaf on a famous literary tree that grew in Indiana."

RALPH D. GRAY

For Further Reading

Gray, Ralph D. *Meredith Nicholson: A Writing Life*. Indianapolis: Indiana Historical Society Press, 2007.

———. *A Meredith Nicholson Reader*. Bloomington, IN: AuthorHouse, Marion County Historical Society, 2007.

Russo, Dorothy Ritter, and Thelma Lois Sullivan, comps. *Bibliographic Studies of Seven Authors of Crawfordsville, Indiana: Lew and Susan Wallace, Maurice and Will Thompson, Mary Hannah and Caroline Virginia Krout, and Meredith Nicholson*. Indianapolis: Indianapolis Historical Society, 1952.

Nolan, Jeannette Covert

March 31, 1896–October 13, 1974

Author, newspaper columnist, and public speaker.

A nine-year-old girl submits a poem to *St. Nicholas* magazine and is delighted to win a silver badge for her efforts. Little could she have guessed that fifty years later she would be awarded yet another prize, the Indiana University Author's Day Award for the most distinguished juvenile book by an Indiana author. But that silver badge marked the beginning of a lifetime of writing for Jeannette Covert Nolan, one of Indiana's most prolific authors.

Jeannette was born March 31, 1896, in Vanderburgh County, Indiana, to Charles G. and Grace Tucker Covert. Her father was a lawyer and active in Republican Party politics, serving terms as Vanderburgh County Sheriff and Evansville mayor. She attended Evansville public schools and at age seventeen began work for the *Evansville Courier*, reporting local news, theater reviews, and an advice to the lovelorn column, for which she felt desperately short of experience. She left journalism after three years to marry rising Evansville attorney and deputy prosecutor Val F. Nolan, who came from a Catholic Democrat family, his father having also been a former Evansville mayor. Her Protestant Republican ideals surely clashed on occasion with Val's. However, she changed allegiance to the Democratic Party in the 1920s soon after the Ku Klux Klan's increasing involvement in Republican politics.

Val served in the U.S. Army in World War I then returned to Evansville and a thriving legal career. Three children were born during the 1920s: Val Jr., Alan, and Kathleen. Val Sr. was appointed U.S. District Attorney of the Southern District of Indiana in 1933 and the family relocated to Indianapolis.

By the time of their move to Indianapolis, Jeannette was already an established author. *Barry Barton's Mystery*, written for young teenagers, was published in 1932. She had returned to writing as a means of filling her days during a time of separation for the family. Following a doctor's advice that avoiding cold weather would improve their eldest son's health, Jeannette and the children spent the winter months in Florida, while Val remained at work in Indiana. Writing occupied the lonely hours when the children were at school or asleep. The stories she constructed to entertain them became the basis for her work.

Encouraged by her success, Nolan explored other genres such as adult fiction and magazine short stories. The female sleuth Lace White was featured in several adult murder mysteries set in Indiana locales. Her adult fiction titles were categorized as light fiction. She had no interest in examining society's ills in her work and believed in the value of reading solely for enjoyment. Juvenile biographies, however, became the hallmark of her career. Nolan researched her biography subjects thoroughly and insisted on a high level of accuracy. She never underestimated a child's level of understanding and was careful to present her characters' motivations and ideals clearly. But Nolan also understood the value of a story well told and the importance of holding her young readers' attention. By re-creating dialogue based on actual letters and diaries, she wrote a fictionalized biography that read as an adventure story. Her account of the lives of people as diverse as Martha Washington and Joan of Arc to John Hancock and Roald Amundsen became a staple of school and public libraries nationwide. Nolan's captivating stories introduced countless children to the study of history and encouraged their curiosity in the world around them.

With the unexpected death of her husband in 1940, writing became a source of income and a means to educate her children. Nolan penned a thrice-weekly newspaper column, "Lines with a Hoosier Accent," for the *Indianapolis Star* from 1943 to 1944. She was a staff member of the IU Writers Conference and the University of Colorado's Rocky Mountain Writers Conference, and she taught juvenile writing courses for the IU extension program in Indianapolis.

Several of Nolan's juvenile biographies were named Junior Literary Guild Book-of-the-Month selections. Her book, *The Story of Clara Barton of the Red Cross*, was translated into German and Japanese and used in reeducation programs in Germany, Austria, and Japan following World War II. She was a popular public speaker noted for her self-effacing sense of humor and honesty, and she traveled throughout the state addressing women's clubs and writers' organizations. Nolan had little patience for artistic temperament and insisted that writing required hard work and persistence. She told a group of aspiring writers to "get a job that forces you to write. Then write and write and write."

Nolan ably tackled a different sort of project for *Hoosier City: The Story of Indianapolis* published in 1943, producing a narrative history of the city written more for pleasurable reading than scholarly study. Her 1946 novel *Gather Ye Rosebuds* had the somewhat dubious honor of being made into the 1948 Paramount movie *Isn't It Romantic?*, which bore very little resemblance to the book.

Nolan was twice honored with the IU Author's Day Award for the most distinguished juvenile book by an Indiana author, first in 1955 for *George Rogers Clark, Soldier and Hero*, and again in 1961 for *Spy for the Confederacy: Rose O'Neal Greenhow*. In 1959 she received Theta Sigma Phi's Frances Wright Award given to an outstanding female author or journalist for excellence in writing. IU granted her an honorary Doctor of Humane Letters degree in 1967.

During her lifetime, Nolan wrote more than fifty full-length books for children and adults, along with innumerable magazine articles, plays, and newspaper columns. She enjoyed a national reputation as a professional author at a time when few women could claim such a career. And she influenced a nation of schoolchildren, encouraging in them a love of reading and learning. Nolan died on October 13, 1974, following a four-year battle with cancer. She is buried beside her husband in Saint Joseph Catholic Cemetery in Evansville.

LIBBE K. HUGHES

For Further Reading

Nolan, Alan T. "Jeannette Covert Nolan: A Writing Life." *Traces of Indiana and Midwestern History* 12, no. 4 (Fall 2000): 3–13.

Nolan, Jeannette Covert. Private Papers. Lilly Library. Indiana University, Bloomington, IN.

Spritzer, Gertrude Fink. *A Guide to the Books of Jeannette Covert Nolan with a Biographical Essay*. Master's thesis, Kent State University, 1961.

O'Brien, Cornelius

February 12, 1883–July 16, 1953

Businessman, banker, U.S. Senate candidate, and pioneering historic preservationist.

In 1933 Cornelius O'Brien purchased, improved, and cherished Veraestau, a stately early-nineteenth-century estate overlooking the Ohio River near Aurora in Dearborn County, Indiana. A country retreat for his family and a place to entertain guests, preservation of the home culminated his accomplishments in Indiana business and politics, as well as his lifelong interest in state history. Rehabilitation of the Veraestau mansion, along with his leadership in the Whitewater Canal Association to restore the southern section of the historic canal, established O'Brien as one of Indiana's earliest historic preservationists.

The eldest of seven children, O'Brien grew up in Lawrenceburg, Indiana, where his father was president of a bank and co-owned the local newspaper. O'Brien attended Moores Hill College, now the University of Evansville, for two years and then Purdue University for a year, an experience that broadened his statewide political and business affiliations. In 1902 he returned to Dearborn County to work for his father at Citizen's National Bank, and then as assistant cashier of the larger institution over which his father presided, the consolidated Citizen's National and People's National Bank. In 1933 O'Brien became the bank's president. Meanwhile, he had married Anna Belle Cook in 1909 and become president and general manager of her family's company, A. D. Cook Pump Works, in 1921. Much was handed to O'Brien, but his peers recognized his financial and organizational acuity and he rose to direct the State Chamber of Commerce for nine years (1941–50), direct the Indiana Manufacturers' Association for six years, and join the Indiana Economic Council in 1943.

Saying that he was well connected in the southeastern region of the state bordering Ohio and, increasingly, across the state, might be an understatement. In addition to his own family's banking and political power, and his role in his father in-law's company, from at least his thirties he was a member of the Free and Accepted Masons, the Royal Arch Masons, the Knights Templar, the Knights of Pythias, and was a prominent alumnus of his college fraternity, Phi Kappa Psi, as well as a highly active member of the Methodist Church. At a young age O'Brien had been a director of the Dearborn County Building and Loan Association. During both world wars he was central to the county's fund-raising efforts.

O'Brien's father and grandfather, an immigrant from Ireland, were, like their heir, influential members of the business community and prominent Democratic officeholders in Indiana. Upon reaching voting age, O'Brien himself was elected precinct committeeman of the Democratic Party in Dearborn County and served as delegate to the Democratic State Convention, positions he held many times throughout his life. He also was elected precinct treasurer and chairman repeatedly. O'Brien's political network eventually covered the state and reached across the country, thanks to these strong, local party roots. In 1936 and 1940 he was the Ninth Congressional District delegate to the Democratic National Convention and then became the Democratic candidate for the U.S. Senate in 1944 to fill the seat left vacant by the death of Senator Frederick Van Nuys. Although he was not elected, his standing in the national party and lifelong cultural and historical interests resulted in his being invited in 1953 to serve on a commission to establish the Franklin D. Roosevelt Library.

Twenty years prior to his own death, O'Brien began to immerse himself in documenting and preserving Indiana's past. In 1933 he purchased Veraestau, the magnificent hilltop mansion of the Holman family in Aurora. O'Brien was interested in local history and knew the significance of the Holmans, early settlers of the region, who had lived there for more than a century and with whom his grandfather had worked. JESSE LYNCH HOLMAN had built Veraestau after moving to Indiana from Kentucky in 1810, and he was a delegate to the Indiana Constitutional Convention at Corydon, a judge of the Indiana Supreme Court, and a founder of the Indiana Historical Society in 1830. His son, William S. Holman, was a Democratic U.S. congressman elected to office sixteen times. O'Brien sponsored the publication of biographies of both Holmans, and preserved their house. He also operated Veraestau as a gentleman farmer, adding Hereford cattle, Percheron draft horses, and extensive fruit orchards. In 1937 he added three rooms to the house and a brick garage and clapboard stable outbuildings in the style of the 1913 portion of the house.

O'Brien enjoyed documenting the past on his own and with colleagues. He was intensely interested in the history of his corner of Indiana, writing short articles about sites in Dearborn County, checking the accuracy of and restoring historic maps and photographs of Lawrenceburg, and collaborating with others researching the region's past. In 1938 he served on Dearborn County's Northwest Territory Celebration Commission for planning the area's celebration of the territory's 150th anniversary. From 1939 to 1951, for example, O'Brien personally kept in touch with a man who had contacted the IHS about repositioning a large cylindrical stone boundary line marker placed in 1837 on the Ohio River to mark the Indiana-Ohio border, but which had become nearly lost beneath several feet of mud. His affinity for history included the mundane, writing the history of bridges in Dearborn County; to the noteworthy, authoring a history of Lawrenceburg; to the spectacular, helping to place markers along the 1863 invasion route of Confederate General John Hunt Morgan and his cavalry troops across Indiana and into Ohio. In 1945 O'Brien fondly recalled for Z. C. Sanderson, associate editor of *Outdoor Indiana*, that in 1927 he had "made the bronze markers which were placed on the boulders" along the trail of Morgan's raid.

Understanding and preserving state history was a defining passion for O'Brien in the final two decades of his life. He was a member of the Indiana State Library and Historical Board in 1940, an elected member of the Indiana Pioneers Society, and an elected member of the Sons of the American Revolution. From 1933 to 1953, he was a member of the IHS's Executive Committee and became its third vice president. While helping to guide the IHS, he was appointed as one of a four-man, bipartisan Conservation Department Commission by Governor Ralph Gates in March 1945. The department had been created in 1919, and in 1965 became the Indiana Department of Natural Resources, home to today's Division of Historic Preservation and Archaeology.

Other than Veraestau, O'Brien's greatest contribution to the state's early historic preservation movement was his work on behalf of the Whitewater Canal Association, which he founded in 1941 with John P. Goodwin of Brookeville. The effort to restore the southern end of the 1830s canal—between Brookeville and Lawrenceburg—demanded O'Brien's associational, financial, and political skills, especially to obtain title to parts of the route from a railroad and to raise the money for substantial reconstruction of the canal and locks. In 1946 the Indiana General Assembly agreed to take over fourteen miles of the canal as the Whitewater Canal State Historic Site. In fitting tribute to her father, Mary Cornelius Gibson established a historic preservation lectureship series in his name in 1972 with her mother, and it continues to this day, administered by the Indiana University Committee on Historic Preservation.

JOHN DICHTIL

For Further Reading

"The Life and Times of the O'Brien Family." Special presentation to the Hillforest Historical Foundation, November 16, 1972. Lawrenceburg Public Library Genealogy Room, Lawrenceburg, IN.

O'Brien, Cornelius. Papers, 1938–1944, Indiana Historical Society William Henry Smith Memorial Library, Indianapolis.

Shaw, Archibald, ed. *History of Dearborn County, Indiana: Her People, Industry and Institutions.* Indianapolis: B. F. Bowen and Company, 1915.

Oliver, James

August 28, 1823–March 2, 1908

Inventor and industrialist.

Why would nineteenth-century farmers want to use a "chilled plow"? Were they supposed to keep their plows in the icehouse with their butter? In fact, the "chilled" referred only to the process of manufacturing the plow patented and promoted by James Oliver of South Bend, Indiana.

Oliver, who was born in Scotland in 1823, moved with his family to Saint Joseph County

James Oliver

when he was thirteen. As a boy he worked as a farmhand, a riverboat crewman, and a cooper, but as a young man he discovered a liking for foundry work at the Saint Joseph Iron Works in Mishawaka. He learned the iron business in the heat of the blast furnace and the pounding of the forge, and he learned it well. In 1855 he invested his savings of $88.96 to purchase a one-quarter interest in the South Bend Foundry, a small firm located on the millrace on the western bank of the Saint Joseph River in downtown South Bend. The firm made a wide variety of iron products for builders and hardware dealers. The following year, Oliver and his friend, Harvey Little, who had also invested in the business, bought out the other owners of the foundry, which became known as Oliver and Little.

At the time Oliver and Little started their business, frontier plows were usually crude wooden devices with an iron plowshare at the cutting edge of the plow blade. Improved models offered an iron moldboard, a curved piece of metal that turned the earth in the furrow. Farmers frequently cursed their plows when they broke against a stone and cursed them even more often when the damp earth stuck to the moldboard and forced them to stop their teams and scrape away the mud with a wooden paddle.

Oliver experimented with building a better plow, and in 1857 he received a patent for "An Improvement in Chilling Plowshares." A chill is a metal mold or portion of a mold in which molten metal is cooled rapidly and the surface of the metal is hardened. By using an iron "chill" in a portion of the sand mold, Oliver produced a hard surface on the cast-iron plowshare, the cutting edge of the plow blade. The resulting plowshare retained its sharp cutting edge much better than traditional plows, and the cast iron was less brittle than usual because the interior portion of the iron cooled slowly.

During the recession year of 1857, Oliver and Little sold only about fifty of the improved plows. Most of the firm's business was still in general foundry work. Oliver entered several plows at the Saint Joseph County Fair and took two first prizes in competition with larger firms, leading to gradually increasing sales throughout northern Indiana. The "Indiana Plow" of 1858 was an improved model, and it triumphed over the competition at the Elkhart County Fair of 1859. The Model Number 40 reached the market in 1860 and remained Oliver's best-selling walking plow into the early years of the twentieth century. Also in 1860 machinist T. M. Bissell bought into the growing company, now known as Oliver, Little and Company.

A devastating fire on Christmas Eve that year destroyed the foundry, but the company began to rebuild within twenty-four hours. As the firm's only traveling salesman, Oliver traveled widely demonstrating his improved plows. Little left the partnership in 1863 and the company became known as Oliver and Bissell. Bissell increased production while Oliver concentrated his efforts on improving his plows in both design and composition. The first big year for the business was 1864, and the workforce increased to twenty-five men and boys; previously the company had employed no more than six. That same year, George Milburn, a Mishawaka wagon manufacturer, bought into the company and the name was changed to Oliver, Bissell and Company.

In 1868 Oliver received a patent for "Improvements in Mold-Boards for Ploughs." After eleven years of experimenting, he had perfected a much larger chilled mold that allowed him to cast the entire moldboard of the plow. His process used large iron chills that were cooled by hot water, reducing the temperature differential when the molten cast iron came into contact with the chill. His process also provided for the escape of hot gasses, which eliminated the tiny bubbles that usually marred the surface of castings. The resulting plow blades were polished to a very smooth finish, producing plows with smooth and durable cutting and turning surfaces made of a resilient cast iron that resisted cracking and breaking when the plow struck a stone in the fields. Oliver now had a plow that was clearly superior to others on the market.

In July 1868 Oliver, Bissell, and Milburn joined with CLEMENT STUDEBAKER, a South Bend wagon manufacturer, and John Brownfield, a South Bend merchant, to incorporate the South Bend Iron Works, makers of the Oliver Chilled Plow. The firm was initially capitalized at $100,000, and its sales increased rapidly. Oliver was the guiding genius of the company and eventually acquired full control. He advertised his "chilled plows" to farmers throughout the United States and developed an extensive export business as well. By 1874 South Bend Iron Works turned exclusively to the manufacture of plows and other farm implements, opening sales and distribution centers from New York City to San Francisco, although chiefly in the Middle West and the South.

By the turn of the century, Oliver employed more than a thousand men and boys at one of the nation's largest agricultural equipment factories. In prosperous years it could turn out as many as 300,000 plows, with specialized models for every purpose from breaking the thick prairie sod of Nebraska to cultivating the cotton fields of Alabama or the sugar plantations of Cuba. There was even a model for use in the steep hillside vineyards of the Rhineland, designed to throw the earth to the uphill side whichever direction the plow was moving. "Plowmakers for the World" was the company's proud advertising slogan, and Oliver jealously guarded his chilled plow trademark, warning farmers against imitations and filing suit against anyone who infringed his design patents. One style of plow Oliver resisted manufacturing for years, though, was the riding plow, insisting that farmers preferred to walk. He was even more stubborn in resisting the use of steel for plow blades despite the growing competition from John Deere, and he flatly refused to join the "plow trust" that became International Harvester.

The plows were always known as Oliver Chilled Plows, but the corporate name was not changed to Oliver Chilled Plow Works until 1901, becoming the Oliver Corporation when the family firm went public just before the Great Crash in 1929. The Oliver Chilled Plow was one of the most successful agricultural implements of the nineteenth century, and the firm remained an important manufacturer of farm equipment into the 1970s, when it disappeared into a succession of mergers and plant closings. Today the company is only a fading memory in South Bend.

"I was classed with the fools who pursue the fallacy of perpetual motion," Oliver once said of his quest to invent a completely chilled plow. "Although feeling keenly the cuts of former friends, I determined to succeed." As a result of Oliver's determination, farmers around the world plowed their fields with Oliver Chilled Plows.

PATRICK J. FURLONG

For Further Reading

Meikle, Douglas L. "James Oliver and the Oliver Chilled Plow Works." PhD diss., Indiana University, 1958.

Romine, Joan. *Copshaholm: The Oliver Story*. South Bend: Northern Indiana Historical Society, 1978.

Orr, Robert D.

November 17, 1917–March 10, 2004

Indiana state senator, lieutenant governor, governor, and U.S. ambassador to Singapore.

Described as "the consummate gentleman and Indiana's elder statesman," Robert D. Orr was a Republican politician and business leader who served two terms each as lieutenant governor and governor and went on to be named U.S. ambassador to Singapore. During his time at the helm of Indiana state government, he distinguished himself as a bold thinker and a reformer, especially in the areas of education policy and economic development. Indiana Supreme Court Chief Justice Randall Shepard, an Orr appointee and protégé, said "[Bob Orr] thought the state needed a great leap forward in education and pressed us to confront the challenges of a globalizing economy."

A sixth generation Hoosier, Robert Orr grew up in Evansville, Indiana, until he was sent to Hotchkiss Preparatory School in Connecticut in 1936. He graduated from Yale University in 1940 with a degree in history. He began attending the Harvard Graduate School of Business, but left to join the U.S. Army upon the outbreak of the World War II. He reached the rank of major and earned the Legion of Merit for his service in the Pacific theater. In 1944 Orr married Joanne (Josie) Wallace, a debutante from the East Coast who was a squadron commander and military pilot.

Upon returning to Evansville after the war, Orr quickly established himself as a business and civic leader. The end of the wartime mobilization had left Evansville with many shuttered factories, and he set about to find profitable uses for them. In 1953 he was named the Jaycees Young Man of the Year and received the organization's Distinguished Service Award. At that time, he was a director of twelve different companies and held leadership positions in thirteen service organizations.

Beginning in the 1950s, Orr held a series of positions in the Republican Party, making his way up from precinct committeeman to Vanderburgh County chairperson. In 1968 he was elected to the Indiana State Senate.

During his first term as a state legislator, Orr became the Republican nominee for lieutenant

Robert D. Orr

governor on a ticket led by OTIS R. BOWEN in 1972. The "Bowen Team" was elected that year with 56.8 percent of the vote. A change to the state constitution allowed Bowen to be the first governor since 1851 to seek a second consecutive term, and the Bowen-Orr ticket was reelected in 1976. Four years later, Orr secured the Republican nomination for governor with Bowen's blessing. Running on a slogan of "Let's Keep a Good Thing Going," Orr and his running mate, John Mutz, won by the largest margin in Indiana electoral history at that time, with 57.7 percent of the vote. The Republican landslide of 1980 also spelled the end of the political career of several prominent Hoosier Democrats, including U.S. Senator Birch Bayh and U.S. House Majority Whip John Brademas.

The lingering effects of the 1982 recession made Orr's re-election campaign in 1984 more challenging. The Orr-Mutz ticket beat back a stiff challenge that year, winning with just 52.8 percent in a strongly Republican year. Significantly, Orr's vote totals lagged behind the rest of the statewide ticket. When he left office in 1988 his transition was unusual in that one of the nation's oldest governors, age seventy-one, was replaced by one of the nation's youngest, Evan Bayh, age thirty-three.

Economic development was a special passion throughout Orr's long career in and out of public service. "I have no doubt that Bob Orr's economic development work as lieutenant governor and governor from 1973 to 1989 enabled Indiana to shuck off its 'Rust Belt' image," Bowen noted in his memoirs. Orr actively sought to promote the export of Indiana-made goods, and he worked at attracting foreign investment in the Hoosier State. A particular triumph was his successful effort to attract a $500 million Subaru-Isuzu plant to Lafayette in 1986.

His background as a successful businessman was valuable as he confronted severe economic challenges and laid the foundation for Indiana's strongest economic recovery in over forty years. In the 1980s Indiana saw dramatic declines in truck and automobile manufacturing, and the recession brought rates of unemployment as high as 20 percent in cities such as Muncie and Kokomo. The statewide unemployment rate exceeded 11 percent for four consecutive years. Orr furnished each state lawmaker with a copy of David Halberstam's book, *The Reckoning*, which examined the threat posed by Japan's economic resurgence.

As governor Orr also displayed a keen interest in education reform. He was responsible for two major legislative programs, Prime Time and A Plus. Orr helped push through a tax increase in 1987 to pay for his expansive plans for Indiana education. At one point, Indiana was second in the nation in the percentage of education spending by state and local governments. Orr showed particular skill in fashioning the A-Plus program in a way that overcame initial resistance from teachers unions on the one hand and business interests on the other. At one point, he went so far as paying a visit in person to the House Education Committee to promote his legislative goals, an unusual practice for a governor. His education policies created the Indiana Statewide Testing for Educational Progress-Plus testing program and reduced class sizes in the early grades, along with an incentive pay program for teachers.

Another significant reform put in place by Orr was the creation of a bipartisan commission to manage the Bureau of Motor Vehicles. For years, it had been under the control of the party in power in the statehouse, and license branches provided a source of revenue and patronage for local and state party organizations. Orr was a moderate who strongly supported Planned Parenthood and believed that government had a role in advancing societal aims. The Indiana Department of Environmental Management was created under his administration.

On occasion, Orr had to take the difficult step of raising taxes on Hoosiers. When serving under Bowen, Orr cast the tie-breaking vote in the state senate in 1973 to pass a bill that would double the state sales tax in order to pay for a series of property tax cuts. Almost a decade later, the dramatic recession of the early 1980s turned the state surplus into a projected $450 million deficit. After the November 1982 elections, Orr called a special session of the legislature to pass an emergency plan to increase the state sales tax and the state income tax.

Orr was chair of the Republican Governors Association and the Midwestern Governors Association and president of the Council of State Governments. He was awarded seven honorary doctorates and has a highway named after him in southern Indiana.

After leaving the governor's office, Orr was

selected by President George H. W. Bush to serve as U.S. ambassador to Singapore, a position he held from 1989 to 1992. In his later years, he lived in Indianapolis and ran a consulting firm, the Alliance for Global Commerce. After fifty-six years of marriage, he and Josie divorced in 2000. In 2001, at the age of eighty-three, he married Mary Kay Davis. Orr died of heart arrhythmia at eighty-six in Indianapolis, and his casket lay in state in the rotunda of the Indiana Statehouse. He was buried in Crown Hill Cemetery in Indianapolis.

ROBERT L. DION

For Further Reading

Mullaney, Marie Marmo. *Biographical Directory of the Governors of the United States, 1988–1994*. Westport, CT: Greenwood Press, 1994.

Gray, Ralph D. "Robert D. Orr." In Linda C. Gugin and James E. St. Clair, eds. *The Governors of Indiana*. Indianapolis: Indiana Historical Society Press, 2006.

Margaret, McKinney, "The Orrs," *Evansville Courier and Press*, September 19, 1982.

The Ostroms

Elinor, August 7, 1933–June 12, 2012; and Vincent, September 25, 1919–June 29, 2012

Globally influential political scientists and longtime Indiana University faculty members.

Elinor and Vincent Ostrom made Bloomington, Indiana, an internationally renowned destination for scholars seeking to better understand how people govern themselves and solve problems. They influenced the direction of social science research throughout the world. The Workshop in Political Theory and Policy Analysis they established and codirected—known now as the Vincent and Elinor Ostrom Workshop in Political Theory and Policy Analysis—became an intellectual center to which students and faculty were drawn and from which significant work of continuing vitality emerged. The awarding of the Nobel Prize in Economics to Elinor Ostrom in October 2009 shined a public spotlight on their work, but their impact on thought and policy was recognized worldwide well before then.

Elinor and Vincent Ostrom came from California to Indiana in 1964 and remained here until both passed away in 2012. During those decades, they worked daily to make Indiana University a destination for scholars and students from around the world, and a force for policy relevant social

Elinor Ostrom

science research and teaching. Many of the intellectual questions they pursued, however, they brought with them from earlier experiences in the West. Vincent had grown up in the state of Washington and Elinor in Los Angeles. Both had received their bachelor's, master's, and doctoral degrees from the University of California, Los Angeles, where they met in the early 1960s and married in 1963. A year later, Vincent was recruited by IU to become a professor of political science and the couple moved to Bloomington. Elinor received her PhD from UCLA in 1965 and joined the IU political science faculty shortly thereafter.

The Ostroms shared a fascination with natural resources, especially but not exclusively water. Vincent had studied and written about the formation of the massive Metropolitan Water District of Southern California and its construction and operation of an aqueduct carrying water hundreds of miles from the Colorado River to the Los Angeles Basin. He also served as a consultant to the Alaska Constitutional Convention and played a key role in the drafting of the article on natural resources for that new state's constitution. In the early 1960s Elinor conducted her dissertation research on the formation of associations, agencies, and rules for restoring and sustaining the groundwater supplies underlying several coastal cities in the Los Angeles metropolitan area.

Also while in California they witnessed an

approach to metropolitan government that called into question conventional wisdom about how governments should be organized and function. The "Lakewood Plan," named for one of the first cities to try it in the Los Angeles metropolitan area, involved residents of a community incorporating as a municipality but contracting with other municipalities and with county and/or state agencies and even private contractors to deliver most public services. The Lakewood Plan presented a challenge to notions about what it means to be or to have a government, and called into question the belief that decision making and service delivery had to be unified in a single government.

The study of local government in metropolitan areas became one of the most influential areas of the Ostroms' research. Vincent and other colleagues developed concepts of polycentricity (multiple governing jurisdictions), public choice, and local public economies to help explain how noncentralized systems could function and sometimes outperform large-scale governments. Elinor and teams of graduate students took to the streets in Indianapolis and elsewhere to research how services such as public safety and street maintenance actually functioned. Their findings undermined long-standing assumptions that larger-scale jurisdictions provide better services at lower costs. The study of polycentric governing systems altered the understanding of governmental organization, function, and performance worldwide over the following decades.

For Vincent, questions of governmental organization ran to more fundamental matters about how people can live together, cooperate with one another, address and resolve conflicts, and live in peace. Intensely influenced by the Federalist Papers and by Alexis de Tocqueville's *Democracy in America*, Vincent asked how people could develop and maintain their capabilities for democratic self-governance. His inquiries for the remainder of his life centered on how people learn and strengthen their capacities for cooperative self-government, what kinds of constitutional conditions promote that kind of human development, and what threats people face in maintaining those conditions and that development. He also directed his attention to how government and public administration were being taught and researched, a subject he explored in his most influential book, *The Intellectual Crisis in American Public Administration*. He became fascinated by language and how the ways in which people think about and talk about governing affect how we identify problems and envision remedies. Vincent's body of work was aptly characterized by some of his colleagues as "Vincent Ostrom's quest to understand human affairs."

Elinor's research took their shared interest in social organization and problem solving further into the study of human interactions with natural resources and with each other. Elinor had become deeply interested in how rules order relationships among people, how complex problems often involve multiple scales of causes and effects from very localized to widespread, and how institutions—rules and organizations—perform over time and under changing conditions. In this context Elinor began building her response to an influential 1968 article in the journal *Science*, "The Tragedy of the Commons" by Garrett Hardin. Hardin argued that common-pool resources such as grazing areas and water would be destroyed by the immutable logic of overuse, unless and until a central authority took over the resource and mandated sustainable use. Elinor's experience reaching back to her dissertation told her it was possible instead to show that people could work out solutions to problems of overuse and degradation of a shared natural resource. She began to look for more examples, and thus launched the work for which she is best known and has had the greatest impact.

With her graduate students and other colleagues, Elinor began developing a database of common-pool resources. She was willing to explore any cases where people had tried to sustain or recover shared resources, anywhere in the world and as far back as reliable recorded history would reach. There were failures—cases where shared resources had been destroyed. There were successes, where patterns of overuse and degradation had been overcome and shared resources had been sustained. Some of these successes had persisted for decades, even centuries. "The commons" was not always doomed to a tragic end, but there were no easy recipes for success either. It was important to identify what the successes had in common, and the failures.

This work culminated in Elinor's landmark 1990 book, *Governing the Commons: The Evolution of Institutions for Collective Action*. In that book and several other publications afterward, she made the case that no one organizational size, shape, or structure produces success or failure in managing a common-pool resource, but there are some basic characteristics, "design principles," among the successes—particularly the longer-lived ones. Beyond those common principles, however, a great diversity of institutional arrangements could and did flourish and no simple structure or policy was guaranteed to work everywhere.

Elinor's work on the commons crossed several academic disciplines. Good work on common-pool resources was being done by anthropologists, historians, geographers, sociologists, economists, political scientists, and others. The Workshop's reputation as a haven for interdisciplinary research rose and expanded. As the Internet came into wide usage in the 1990s, Bloomington became home to a "Digital Library of the Commons" where scholars could find and add to the storehouse of case studies and data on common-pool resources. An important interdisciplinary field of study emerged, with scholarly associations, research journals, and the like. Students and scholars flowed into and out of the Workshop, carried the study of the commons to other universities, and provided advice and consultation to governmental policy makers and nongovernmental organizations.

For her body of work on the commons, the Royal Swedish Academy of Sciences in October 2009 awarded Elinor Ostrom the Sveriges Riksbank Prize in Economic Sciences in Memory of Alfred Nobel—more popularly known as the Nobel Prize in Economics. She was the first female Nobel laureate in Economics. She also was not an economist. The award therefore stands also as recognition of the reach and impact of her work beyond her home discipline of political science. She was, like Vincent, an unusual sort of political scientist.

The time in Stockholm in December 2009 was joyous, but Elinor could not wait to get back home to Indiana, to Vincent, to the Workshop, and the work. She had expanded her interest in the commons to the general phenomenon of social-ecological systems, and was working with a new generation of colleagues on how to understand and characterize them. That work was her primary scholarly focus up to the time of her death from pancreatic cancer in June 2012. Vincent succumbed to complications of cancer just seventeen days later.

Indiana remains home of the Vincent and Elinor Ostrom Workshop in Political Theory and Policy Analysis, and the Workshop remains one of the world's foremost sites for research and teaching on how people can govern together to face challenges, resolve conflicts, and live together in prosperity and peace while protecting the natural environment on which we all depend. They deliberately named it the "workshop," to signify a place where people practice and refine their craft together, with a focus on practical matters, even when those matters are of vital and profound significance. They built it here in Indiana, but its effects have been felt around the world.

WILLIAM BLOMQUIST

For Further Reading

Aligica, Paul Dragos, and Peter J. Boettke. *Challenging Institutional Analysis and Development: The Bloomington School.* London: Routledge, 2009.

Ostrom, Elinor. *Governing the Commons: The Evolution of Institutions for Collective Action.* New York: Cambridge University Press, 1990.

Sproule-Jones, Mark, Barbara Allen, and Filippo Sabetti, eds. *The Struggle to Constitute and Sustain Productive Orders: Vincent Ostrom's Quest to Understand Human Affairs.* Lanham, MD: Lexington Books, 2008.

Overbeck Sisters

Margaret, July 3, 1863–August 13, 1911; Hannah Borger, March 14, 1870–August 28, 1931; Elizabeth Gray, October 21, 1875–December 1, 1936; and Mary Frances, January 28, 1878–March 20, 1955

Potters and artists of the arts and crafts movement who worked in Cambridge City, Indiana, from 1911 until 1955.

In the midst of the arts and crafts movement of the late nineteenth and early twentieth centuries, four sisters in east-central Indiana set up a ceramics workshop in their home with a goal of producing quality pottery without regard to quantity. None had any prior experience working with clay but all were schooled in the arts. Begun in 1911, Overbeck Pottery was the first undertaking in Indiana to produce entirely handmade art ceramics; during the sisters' lifetimes the pottery achieved recognition and awards far beyond the borders of the state.

The Overbeck family, consisting of six daughters and one son, lived in Cambridge City, Indiana. While their parents, John and Sarah, were farmers, they were also practicing artisans—the father an amateur cabinetmaker and the mother engaged in quilting, weaving rugs, and sewing lace. The family believed in living a cultured, unpretentious, and industrious life, stressing creativity and experimentation. All the children were educated, and their mother disapproved of marriage for her daughters, believing it would limit their ability to fulfill their creative potential. Only one daughter not engaged in the pottery enterprise married; the others chose to remain single.

Margaret, the second oldest daughter, attended the Cincinnati Art Academy in the 1890s and also studied under noted teacher Arthur Wesley Dow of Columbia University. She was an instructor in art at several schools, including DePauw University in Greencastle, Indiana, where she taught drawing, watercolor, and china painting from 1899 to 1910. Margaret is generally credited with proposing the idea that the sisters open a pottery studio in their home. She was focused on developing shapes of pottery that were well-suited for decoration. Unfortunately, she died in 1911, the year the studio was established, due to injuries suffered in an automobile accident in Chicago.

Three of Margaret's sisters carried on her dream with each taking on a specific specialty. Hannah, the next oldest, attended Indiana State Normal School (today Indiana State University) at Terre Haute and graduated in 1894. Her skills lay in sketching, watercolor, and design with a focus on plants and trees, so she became primarily responsible for the decorative designs on the pottery. Elizabeth, two years younger than Harriet, studied with Margaret and also under Charles F. Binns during 1909 and 1910 at the College for Clay Working and Ceramics at Alfred University in Alfred, New York. She was the only one of the sisters who mastered the use of the potter's wheel, turning out the clay forms on her wheel and formulating and preparing the glazes. Mary, the second youngest of the six sisters, also studied with Margaret and may have attended Indiana State Normal School. She studied with Dow at Columbia University and taught in Colorado and Indiana, and was well known for the bookplates she designed. Mary painted in both oil and watercolor, with her specialty being bird paintings. Along with Harriet, she designed and decorated the pottery forms.

The sisters' workshop was simple, consisting of an electric potter's mill, a portable kiln fueled with coal oil, and a clay-sifter. The sisters agreed that the idea for the shape of a pot must be carefully planned in advance. Any work that came out other than as planned was to be destroyed. Each piece of pottery was unique; no assembly-line production was tolerated. They guided their decorative design work by two principles—first, that all borrowed art, such as motifs and designs from Europe and Japan, was dead art; and second, that all good applied design was original. As a part of the arts and crafts movement, the Overbecks often based their design motifs on nature, especially plants, trees, birds, and animals indigenous to the Midwest. Their goal was to create an entirely American product free from foreign influences. Elizabeth explained the rationale for their process, stating that the American craftsman has "too little in the way of tradition or anything of natural or indigenous growth to build upon. If anything characteristic or original is to be accomplished, it is necessary to begin at the beginning and build up the foundation for oneself."

The Overbeck pottery studio generally made functional pieces such as teapots, pitchers, and tea sets, in simple shapes in the art nouveau and later the art deco styles. Only Elizabeth used the wheel; Hannah and Mary did all of their pieces by hand. They experimented with their own glazes, keeping their formulations secret. Since each piece was unique, their output was modest along with their income. To keep expenses low, the sisters performed almost all of their work themselves and used only basic tools. They opened a showroom in their home for sales to the public, taught pottery classes, and presented demonstrations to women's clubs around the state. Other than from their home studio, the pottery was sold almost exclusively at L. S. Ayres and Company in Indianapolis.

In a departure from their more serious pieces of pottery, the sisters developed a line of miniature figurines. Most were of people, including local notables and historical figures, but they also made pets and other animals, always coloring them true to nature and none more than a few inches tall. Begun as a way to test glazes, the sisters also sculpted what they called "grotesques," caricatures of people and wildlife and fantastical creatures. These humorous pieces made with exaggerated features and decorated in whimsical colors, became some of the sisters' most reliable sellers. Mary sculpted most of the grotesques, which Elizabeth called "humor of the kiln."

The Overbeck pottery received recognition far beyond the borders of Indiana. In the first twenty-five years of the studio's operation, the ceramics were exhibited in Paris, Chicago, Saint Louis, Baltimore, Detroit, Dayton, Indianapolis, at the Panama Pacific Exposition in San Francisco in 1915, as well as at Chicago's Century of Progress exhibit in 1933, often receiving prizes. A guestbook the sisters kept showed visitors to their studio from other potters and artists, journalists, educators, and interested parties from Europe and South America.

Hannah died in 1931 followed by Elizabeth in 1936. Mary continued making pottery on her own, focusing primarily on the figurines and whimsical animals rather than any larger pieces, until she died in 1955. Until the end, none of the sisters ever disclosed the formulas for the distinctive glazes for which the Overbeck pottery was known. They were women ahead of their time, having what was in the early part of the twentieth century, a radical goal of being economically and aesthetically independent. Their legacy of originality of shape, style of decoration, and notable colors in their glazes has earned them a deserved place in Indiana's history.

SUZANNE BELLAMY

For Further Reading

Denker, Ellen Paul. "Creating a Life: The Overbeck Sisters and their Cambridge City Pottery." *Traces of Indiana and Midwestern History* 17, no. 2 (Spring 2005): 20–29.

Newton, Judith Vale, and Carol Ann Weiss. *Skirting the Issue: Stories of Indiana's Historical Women Artists*. Indianapolis: Indiana Historical Society, 2004.

Postle, Kathleen R. *The Chronicle of the Overbeck Pottery*. Indianapolis: Indiana Historical Society, 1978.

Owen, Jane Blaffer

April 18, 1915–June 21, 2010

Known for dedicating her life to preserving and promoting the spirit of the utopian village of New Harmony, Indiana.

As a young bride in 1941, Houston, Texas, native Jane Blaffer Owen came to her husband's birthplace, New Harmony, for the first time. She found New Harmony, the site of two distinct attempts at building a perfect community, the first religious the second based on science and education, "covered in coal dust." An oil heiress by birth, Owen brought considerable intellectual and financial resources to her endeavor to revive the idealism of New Harmony. "My greatest education of all," Owen said, "was New Harmony, where I discovered America. . . . And it was an excitement for me to discover America in a small town . . . and what I found was good and wholesome in the people and the soil."

After establishing the Robert Lee Blaffer Trust in 1958 in honor of her father, Owen commissioned noted architect Philip Johnson to design a structure that demonstrated her belief that only the sky can contain the religions of the world—the Roofless Church. The catalyst for this commission was her purchase of a bronze casting, *Notre Dame de Liesse/Descent of the Holy Spirit* (1946–56) by artist Jacques Lipchitz. She orchestrated the establishment of Historic New Harmony Inc., which built New Harmony's education center, the Atheneum, an award-winning design by architect Richard Meier. Over nearly seven decades, Owen restored many original Harmonist structures and took a progressive approach to preservation by adapting them to contemporary use. Her first restoration and adaptation was a Harmonist single-family home that she called "No. V." This house became her New Harmony family home and remained her favorite project. For this effort she was given the Louise DuPont Crowninshield Award, the highest honor bestowed by the National Trust for Historic Preservation.

Always interested in the intersection of nature, spirituality, and art, Owen built gardens and sanctuaries throughout the town. In 1997 the Cathedral Labyrinth and Sacred Garden was dedicated. Inspired by the Harmonie Society that built a labyrinth in New Harmony, the Blaffer Trust commissioned this outdoor labyrinth made of granite to be a nearly exact replica of France's Chartres Cathedral. The memorial Carol's Garden and Paul Tillich Park invite contemplation. Other resources for reflection are Canon Herbert Waddams Chapel in the Entry House of the New Harmony Inn, the Chapel of the Little Portion north of the lake at New Harmony Inn, and the MacLeod Barn Abbey, named after George MacLeod, a pacifist Presbyterian minister who built the retreat center at Iona, off the coast of Scotland. The center-village green space, Church Park, commemorates the site of the original Harmonie Society church. The sculptural fountain in the center is dedicated to the memory of Owen's husband, Kenneth Dale Owen, who died in 2002. All of these public spaces were envisioned by Jane in collaboration with artists, architects, and religious leaders from around the world, many of them Hoosiers.

Owen facilitated connections between people, particularly in the areas of interfaith dialogue. Because of her vast experiences of travel and study—she went to the Ethel Walker School, a college preparatory school in Simsbury, Connecticut, and then studied at Bryn Mawr College in Pennsylvania, and Union Theological Seminary in New York City—she was afforded the acquaintance of luminaries in many fields. From the Archbishop of Canterbury to the magazine magnate Henry Luce, Owen invited legions of people from around the world to share her New Harmony. Through the sponsorship of the New Harmony Benedictine Retreat, spiritual leaders in all the world's faiths came to New Harmony, beginning in 1983. Illustrating her fearlessness in introducing the citizens of New Harmony to the wider world of religions, this retreat was picketed one year when she invited Buddhists to pray with the Benedictines.

Public sculpture is found throughout New Harmony. Placed by Owen over the decades, the works challenge and enrich the lives of townspeople and visitors alike. Owen's connoisseurship led her to choose well-known, international artists, as well as to support regional and local artists. The Blaffer Trust (now Foundation) has supported the arts throughout southern Indiana for more than fifty years. Grants continue the cultural traditions of the two founding utopian communities—the Harmonists and the Owenites—in music, theater, literary arts, fine arts, and fine crafts.

In 1978, in honor of her mother, the Sarah Campbell Blaffer Pottery Studio was opened. It supported a ceramics class run by the University of Evansville. Graduates from the university sought Owen's support when they created the New Harmony Project in 1987, with a goal to create, nurture, and promote new works for stage, television, and film that sensitively and truthfully explore the positive aspects of life.

Programs of the University of Southern Indiana, including the New Harmony Gallery of Contemporary Art (founded in 1975), the New Harmony Theatre, Ropewalk Writer's Retreat (now New Harmony Writers Workshop), and many other special events through Historic New Harmony endure because of Blaffer Foundation support.

A seminal experience for the village of New Harmony was the visit by the Perm Ballet from the Soviet Union in 1987. Acting through the Friendship Ambassadors Foundation, Owen hosted a visit by the famous young ballet troupe four years before the fall of communism. On three icy, snowy February nights in 1987, the troupe performed to sold-out crowds and changed the attitudes of the schoolchildren of New Harmony forever. "I know this is only a tiny drop in the bucket, but if it leads to something else then we're really accomplishing good here," she said. "I have tried for many years to get a group of young people there, because they are the future, the answer to these [world] problems."

In 2007, when Indiana Governor Mitchell E. Daniels Jr. bestowed the state's highest honor on her, the Sachem Award, he said, "You, like the Harmonist and Owenite founders, personify that insatiable striving for a better world for all humanity, a world that begins with the love of one individual and expands into the community, the state, the nation, and becomes the promised hope for peace on earth, goodwill toward men."

CONNIE WEINZAPFEL

For Further Reading

"Jane Blaffer Owen," Obituary, *New York Times*, July 4, 2010.

McCasling, Nancy Mangum, ed. *Jane Blaffer Owen, New Harmony, Indiana: Like a River, Not a Lake, a Memoir*. Bloomington: Indiana University Press, 2015.

Owen, Robert

May 14, 1771–November 17, 1858

Cotton manufacturer, social reformer, and founder of a utopian community in New Harmony, Indiana.

"It is of all truths the most important, that the character of man is formed FOR—not BY himself." On this terse assertion—this great truth revealed only to him—Robert Owen built an entire social movement to mold superior character from birth. In 1825 he purchased the former Harmonist town of New Harmony, Indiana, to become the preliminary model for his utopian communities. His "New System" enticed progressive educators, social and natural scientists, and socialistic communitarians to implement his plan. His "New Moral World" attracted common folk from the backcountry hoping to live in peace and plenty.

Owen was born into a large working-class family in Newtown, Wales, in 1771. With little schooling but a well-placed apprenticeship in London, this precocious lad was introduced to the textile business just as the spinning industry was bursting its seams with new mechanical inventions and power sources. First at Manchester, England, then at New Lanark, Scotland, the young Owen rose rapidly as a manager and part owner of cotton mills. The New Lanark Mills of David Dale had a company town already known for Dale's benevolent projects for hundreds of resident workers and their families. This became the venue for Owen to marry Dale's daughter, Anne Caroline, make a fortune as an innovative owner-manager, and expand Dale's initiatives into forming human character and ameliorating human suffering so exacerbated by the Industrial Revolution.

In 1813 Owen published *A New View of Society*. Influenced by Enlightenment rationalism and Scottish moral philosophy, it made him famous not only as an exceptionally humane and philanthropic capitalist but also as a socialistic utopian thinker and social reformer. In 1818 he established his Institute for the Formation of Character at New Lanark, providing free education from a pioneering infant school to adult classes. By then Owen had heard of the economic success of large Shaker and Harmonist communal settlements in the United States and became a convert to the communal method of reform. Whole communities are complicated to establish, but they promise rapid transformation on a small scale. So when GEORGE RAPP's religious Harmonists left New Harmony in 1824, Owen gladly paid $135,000 for their famous, ready-made town of 180 buildings and thousands of acres of land.

There, Owen expected his "preliminary society" to construct the first utopian Village of Unity and Mutual Cooperation south of town and predicted it would be replicated worldwide. In it, cutting-edge science and technology would provide physical comforts such as gas lighting, hot and cold running water, and laundries. Loving care and education would promote enlightenment in schools, libraries, museums, and botanical gardens. Universal goodwill would reign while private property, unhappy marriages, and organized religion would pass away. Although often branded an atheist, Owen was a deist in the mold of Benjamin Franklin, advocating a rational religion never in conflict with science and calling God "that Incomprehensible Power." Unfortunately Owen's ideal village, which was to be built as a huge quadrangle, never rose higher than 240,000 bricks piled upon the ground.

Owen was welcomed to the United States as a celebrated industrialist and philanthropic reformer. He socialized in elite circles, met with President James Monroe, and spoke twice to Congress. WILLIAM MACLURE, a rich Scottish merchant who had become the "father of American geology" and president of the Academy of Natural Sciences of Philadelphia, found Owen's plan so compelling he funded the transfer of some of the country's finest scientists and educators to New Harmony in 1826 on a keelboat that became known as the Boatload of Knowledge. Historian Arthur Bestor called this "one of the significant intellectual migrations of history." Owen made the crucial decision to put Maclure, by then his financial partner, in charge of New Harmony's educational program, the key to upgrading human character. Thus began America's first infant school followed by Pestalozzian classes that used a method of "learning by doing" that

Robert Owen

Maclure had introduced in Spain and Philadelphia. To this, Maclure added his School of Industry for teaching trades, perhaps the country's earliest, and lectures for adults by resident scientists. Boys who were taught printing made copper plates to publish the research of New Harmony's ichthyologists, conchologists, and geologists, as well as Maclure's widely circulated periodicals. Believing that practical knowledge could elevate the working classes, Maclure, in 1838, funded the Working Men's Institute in New Harmony, still Indiana's oldest continuously functioning library. In his will, like an early Andrew Carnegie, Maclure designated money used for 144 Working Men's Institutes in Indiana and sixteen in Illinois.

Noted natural scientists made New Harmony a center for research in a wilderness laboratory. Charles-Alexandre Lesueur, French naturalist and artist, made hundreds of invaluable sketches of his findings. Thomas Say produced his groundbreaking *American Entomology* (1824–28) and *American Conchology* (1830–36). Geology became the predominant scientific interest in New Harmony. Two of Owen's sons were lured into this promising new field by the mentoring presence of Maclure. Their explorations and teaching revealed the mineral resources that brought industrialization to the Midwest. David Dale Owen conducted the earliest state-commissioned survey of Indiana and became the first Indiana state geologist. Richard Owen became the second. Richard also became a professor of natural science at Indiana University and the first president of Purdue University. As a Civil War colonel, Richard's humanitarian upbringing came through so clearly in his kind treatment of Confederate prisoners at Camp Morton that they later donated a bronze bust of him, which is still in the Indiana State House.

Robert Owen's eldest son, Robert Dale Owen, championed the social and educational ideals of his father's New Harmony at the 1850 Indiana Constitutional Convention and as a state and national legislator. He fought for property and divorce laws to benefit women and designed Indiana's first public school system. He wrote the legislation that established the Smithsonian Institution as a free public national museum. In a now-famous letter, he urged President ABRAHAM LINCOLN to pursue peace through emancipation.

Owen's months-long absences contributed to the brevity of his two and a half year communal experiment in New Harmony. His twenty-three-year-old son, William, was left to deal with the overwhelming influx of settlers who regarded this place as the philanthropic project of a wealthy businessman. There were no membership requirements, so "free-lunchers" flooded into town. They and the eastern "thinkers" did not coexist well, which also helped bring Owen's community to an end. Yet, his bequest to Indiana rests upon his ability to attract talented people to his utopian vision. These teachers, scientists, and other intellectuals placed New Harmony and early Indiana in the vanguard of progressive education, cultural development, and discoveries in natural science for decades.

After his New Harmony initiative, Owen and his Owenite movement continued in a developmental process to exercise a profound effect on reforms that help define modern society—emancipation, women's and laborer's rights, tax-supported public schools, free public libraries and museums, producer-consumer cooperatives, and planned parenthood. Using organizations, lectures, and publications, Owenites gave effective voice to these causes. The utopian movements of New Harmony's dual founders, George Rapp and Robert Owen, left a legacy of the heart and mind still vitally alive in Indiana at its bicentennial.

DONALD E. PTIZER

For Further Reading

Bestor, Arthur. *Backwoods Utopias: The Sectarian Origins and the Owenite Phase of Communitarian Socialism in America, 1663–1829*. With an introduction by Donald Pitzer. Second Enlarged Edition. Eugene, OR: Wifp and Stock, 2012.

Owen, Robert. *The Book of the New Moral World*. New York: Augustus M. Kelley Publishers, 1970.

Pitzer, Donald E., and Darryl D. Jones. *New Harmony Then and Now*. Bloomington: Indiana University Press, 2011.

Peden, Rachel

December 17, 1901–August 16, 1975

Farm wife, newspaper columnist, and author.

In the 1940s a farmwife who lived west of Bloomington, Indiana, used letters to share with her sister living in Indianapolis the joys and sorrows of earning a living from the land. Nina Mason Pulliam showed the letters to her husband, newspaper publisher EUGENE C. PULLIAM, who, impressed by the writing ability of their author, Rachel Peden, offered her the opportunity to write a regular column. "I don't care what you write about, so long as it has a farm flavor," Pulliam said to Peden.

From February 1946 until her death in 1975, Peden imparted details of her life and the lives of her neighbors along Maple Grove Road to readers of her "The Hoosier Farm Wife Says" column in the *Indianapolis Star* and "The Almanac of Poor Richard's Wife" column in the *Muncie Evening Press*. "I'm just a farm wife with the good luck to have something to write about and a chance to write," she noted. Peden chronicled the difficulties faced by small American family farms in the twentieth century as they began to "erode away into large farms, like unprotected topsoil into the rivers." She also reported on the growing degradation of the land farmers depended upon for their livelihoods. "Man has an inescapable obligation to the land," Peden wrote. "It is his destiny to touch, observe, and learn from it, in his passionate effort to understand himself."

Born in Redkey in Jay County, Indiana, Rachel was third of seven children raised by Benjamin Franklin and Laura Mason. Rachel spent her formative years on her father's High Gap farm on land that eventually became part of the Morgan-Monroe State Forest. The family resided there for seventeen years before her father's injury in an automobile accident forced them to move. At an early age Rachel and the other children were

Rachel Peden

expected to help with the daily chores, including fetching and carrying firewood and water, washing dishes, sweeping floors, making beds, and looking after livestock. Often referring to her father as "the orchardist" in her columns, Rachel recalled that he knew the Latin names of plants and trees, and called them by those names. "My father planted orchards everyplace," she said. He became so adept at horticulture that his children considered him a magician of sorts when he successfully grafted an apple tree so it bore sweet apples on one side and sour apples on the other. Mason's real love, however, was peach trees, and he won fame by propagating a successful variety known as the Skipper's Late Red. "His trouble was that he had more talent than he could use," Rachel said of her father. While her mother, ten years younger than her husband, sought "small cozy security," Benjamin always wanted to "reach out for a grasp, however tentative, of some big, exciting thing."

Educated in a one-room schoolhouse that included eight grades, Rachel had early practice as a writer, as she and her siblings took to heart advice given to them by one of her father's hired hands, Bill Pofall, who told them if something "doesn't suit you, just write it down and burn it up." She noted that there were "so many things that didn't suit us that we had abundant practice in writing." As a young girl, her mother had wanted to become a writer and passed along a love of reading to her children. Rachel learned to type by sneaking into her father's office, supposedly off-limits to his children, and hurriedly pecking away at his old Monarch typewriter. "I never learned to type accurately," she recalled, "but I learned to type fast, because if the orchardist found one of us there it would be a painful encounter." (In addition to Rachel's later work as a columnist, her sister, Nina, published a book on her travels in Australia and won awards for her newspaper writing, and another sister, Miriam E. Mason Swain, wrote more than fifty children's books.)

After graduating from high school in Martinsville, Rachel attended Indiana University, majoring in sociology and psychology and graduating in 1923 with Phi Beta Kappa honors. She briefly worked as a reporter for the *Martinsville Reporter* before taking a job as women's editor at *Farm Life*, a national magazine based in Spencer, Indiana, with approximately a million subscribers. While at the magazine, where her sister, Nina, also worked, Rachel said she learned much about writing from its editor, George Weymouth, and treasured a letter from him complimenting her on a column she wrote. In 1929 she married Richard Peden, whose family had been farming in Owen County since Indiana became a state in 1816. The couple had two children; a son, Joe, born in 1939, and a daughter, Carol, born in 1942.

Farm Life went out of business during the Great Depression, and Rachel followed along as her husband decided to fulfill his dream of running a farm of his own. In 1941 the Pedens bought a farm on Maple Grove Road outside of Bloomington on which Richard raised feeder cattle, as well as corn, hay, and silage. By the 1960s the farm had grown from its original 130 acres to 239 acres. Before she started her newspaper column, Rachel wrote freelance articles for such magazines as *Country Gentleman*, the *Farm Journal*, and *Peoples Popular Monthly*, as well as several poetry periodicals.

For her newspaper columns, Peden wrote under the pen names "Mrs. R. F. D." and "the Hoosier Farmwife." (R. F. D. stood for Rural Free Delivery, the service first offered by the U.S. Post Office at the turn of the twentieth century.) She said she never went anywhere without carrying with her pencil and paper for her column's sake. "The farm always inspired something to bring back," Peden noted. She usually wrote in the morning, composing her columns on a typewriter set up on a small stand under a stairwell in her kitchen. "Sometimes I'm just certain there won't be anything important enough to write about," Peden said. "And then, I look out and the leaves are falling, or the sky is pink in the east, or there is hay baling to be done—so many wonderful things on the farm."

Peden's work proved popular with readers in central Indiana, with many telling her they saw themselves and their own experiences in her columns. A fan in Muncie helped bring her writing to a wider audience by convincing her son, Angus Cameron, an editor at the Alfred Knopf publishing firm in New York, to offer Peden a book contract. Peden eventually turned her columns into three books published by Knopf with illustrations by Sidonie Coryn—*Rural Free: A Farmwife's Almanac of Country Living* (1961); *The Land, The People* (1966), which received Indiana University's Author Award; and *Speak to the Earth: Pages from a Farmwife's Journal* (1974). As she did in her columns, Peden used her neighbors' actual names in her books and experienced a range of reaction when gaining permission to do so. When Peden asked one neighbor if she wanted to see what she had written about her, the neighbor declined, saying she would wait and see it when the book was published. "Still another said to just to make her really human, not too good," Peden recalled. "Neighbors are such a joy, and so close to my heart."

Peden died on August 16, 1975, and is buried at Payne Cemetery in Bloomington. Although her books went out of print for a time, she remained popular in her home community where, in 1976, she was a charter member of the Monroe County Hall of Fame. Starting in 2009, Quarry Books, an imprint of Indiana University Press, began reprinting Peden's books.

RAY E. BOOMHOWER

For Further Reading

Hiller, Nancy. "Rachel Peden Rediscovered." *Bloom Magazine*, August/September 2010.

Moore, Margaret. "Mrs. RFD Lets Cornstalks Stay." *Indianapolis News*, September 12, 1961.

Peden, Rachel. *Rural Free: A Farmwife's Almanac of Country Living*. 1961. Reprint, Bloomington, IN: Quarry Books, 2009.

———. *The Land, The People*. 1966. Reprint, Bloomington, IN: Quarry Books, 2010.

———. *Speak to the Earth: Pages from a Farmwife's Journal*. 1974. Reprint, Bloomington, IN: Quarry Books, 2011.

Stewart, Lotys Benning. "At Home with Mrs. R. F. D." *Indianapolis Star Magazine*, June 10, 1951.

Porter, Cole

June 9, 1891–October 15, 1964

Songwriter best known for his compositions for Broadway theater and Hollywood musicals.

A native Hoosier, Cole Porter is considered one of the greatest of American songwriters, and one of the leading composers of both stage and film during the golden age of the American musical. The author of nearly nine hundred songs, Porter's work includes numerous contributions to the Great American Songbook, which identified the popular songs deemed to be the most significant of the twentieth century. Noted for his sophisticated lyrics and deceptively simple melodies, his music is synonymous with the sound of the 1920s and 1930s and his best work remains both part of the nation's repertoire and an enduring contribution to world culture.

The only child of Samuel Fenwick Porter, a druggist and farmer from Vevay, Indiana, and his wife Kate Cole, Porter was born in Peru, Indiana, in 1891. Porter was educated at the Worcester Academy and Yale University, from which he graduated in 1913. While a student at Yale he wrote two of the most famous college fight songs in the United States: "Bingo Eli Yale" and the "Yale Bulldog Song." Although Porter had demonstrated a gift for music at an early age, his grandfather, who paid for his education, insisted that he pursue a law degree. Acquiescing to his grandfather's wishes, Porter entered the Harvard Law School in 1914. The following year, however, upon the advice of the dean, he transferred to the School of Music. With a fellow student, T. Lawson Riggs, supplying the book, Porter wrote the music and lyrics for his first Broadway show, *See America First*, in 1916. Following its failure, in 1917 he went to France, where he studied music and volunteered for the Duryea Relief Corps. Over the next two years he also contributed songs to several London shows, including *Very Good Eddie* (1918), *Telling the Tale* (1918), and *The Eclipse* (1919). In 1919 Porter married divorced socialite Linda Lee Thomas. A native of Louisville, Kentucky, Linda Porter was nine years older than her husband and fully aware of his homosexuality, but willing to turn a blind eye to his liaisons with other men. The couple remained devoted to one another until her death in 1953.

Between 1919 and 1929, Porter contributed songs to musical reviews produced in New York, London, and Paris. Like most theatrical songs of the era, Porter's compositions were stand-alone numbers that added nothing to either the show's plot or characterization. Frequently, however, numbers such as "I'm in Love Again" (*The Greenwich Follies of 1924*), "Let's Do It" (*Paris from 1928*), and "What Is This Thing Called Love" (from the London production *Wake Up and Dream* in 1929) were the most memorable aspect of the productions they appeared in. In 1929 Porter composed his first songs for a film, *The Battle of Paris*, starring Gertrude Lawrence.

The Broadway production of *The New Yorker* in 1930, featuring hits such as "Let's Fly Away" and "Love for Sale," which, to Porter's delight, was briefly banned from broadcast because of subject matter, launched what would be both the most productive and successful decade of Porter's career. In 1932 came *Gay Divorce* featuring what is generally considered Porter's most famous composition "Night and Day," sung by Fred Astaire in one of his final Broadway shows. Porter's next show, written for Lawrence, was *Nymph Errant* (1933). Although it was a major success in London, it was never produced in the United States. His next Broadway production *Anything Goes* (1934), however, proved to be one of the biggest successes of his career. Its sensational score, which included such standards as "All through the Night," "You're the Top," "Blow, Gabriel, Blow," "I Get a Kick Out of You," and the title song "Anything Goes," as well as a star-making performance by Ethel Merman, remains one of the few Porter shows that continues to be revived. The following year *Jubilee* produced another signature tune, "Begin the Beguine," although it was Artie Shaw's swing version of the tune that made the song an international hit. In December 1935 Porter accepted a lucrative offer from Metro-Goldwyn-Mayer to come to Hollywood and write an original score for a film *Born to Dance* (1936) that featured two well-known Porter songs, "Easy to Love" and "I've Got You under My Skin," which earned him his first Academy Award nomination.

Returning to New York, Porter's next musical was *Red, Hot and Blue* (1936), which produced two memorable songs for Merman, "Down in the Depths" and "It's De-Lovely," which was performed as a duet with Bob Hope. Returning to Hollywood in 1937, Porter wrote "In the Still of the Night" for the film version of *Rosalie*. Later that same year both of his legs were crushed in a riding accident. Although his wife and mother rejected the recommended amputation of both legs, Porter never fully regained use of his legs and remained in great pain for the rest of his life. In 1958, after thirty-four operations, his right leg was finally amputated.

In the decade that followed his accident, Porter alternated his time between New York and Hollywood. Although several of the shows that he composed during this period, which included *Leave It to Me* (1938), *DuBarry Was a Lady* (1942), *Panama Hattie* (1943), *Something for the Boys* (1942), *Seven Lively Arts* and *Mexican Hayride* (both 1944), were successful, their scores generally failed to live up to his earlier efforts. Aside from the song from *Leave It to Me*, "My Heart Belongs to Daddy" made famous by Mary Martin, the Bert Lahr/Ethel Merman duet "Friendship" from *DuBarry Was a Lady*, and "Ev'ry Time We Say Goodbye" from the *Seven Lively Arts*, very few of Porter's show tunes from this period have achieved lasting success.

Porter's work on film followed a similar pattern. In 1941 he received his second Academy Award nomination for what even his most ardent admirers consider to be a second-rate song, "Since I Kissed My Baby Goodbye" from *You'll Never Get Rich*. The 1942 film, *Something to Shout About*, produced "You'd Be So Nice to Come Home To," but it was the only real success out of an original score that initially included ten new songs. Ironically, perhaps the most successful film of Porter's career in this period was a film biography, *Night and Day* (1946), which starred Cary Grant, playing a highly fictionalized version of Porter. The film added to the increasing number of movies that featured songs from the Porter cannon, rather than new compositions, and only served to add to the growing sense that Porter's career was effectively over.

In 1948, however, that all changed when Porter wrote the score for what would be the greatest success of his Broadway career, *Kiss Me Kate*. Running for more than 1,000 performances, *Kiss Me Kate* was a clever reworking of Shakespeare's *The Taming of the Shrew*. It combined a witty "battle of the sexes" show-within-a-show plot, and some of the best tunes of Porter's career such as "Another Op'nin; Another Show," "Why Can't You Behave?" "Wunderbar," "So in Love," "Too Darn Hot," "Always True to You in My Fashion," and "Brush Up Your Shakespeare." It remains the most complete and well rounded of his theater work and that, combined with its strong book, has helped insure that *Kiss Me Kate* continues to be the best known of his musicals and, along with *Anything Goes*, one of the handful of Porter's book musicals still performed.

Porter never again achieved that same level of artistic, critical, and commercial success. In 1953, the same year that his wife died, came *Can-Can*, followed in 1955 by *Silk Stockings*, a musical version of the classic Ernst Lubitsch 1939 film *Ninotchka*. Although both productions were deemed hits neither came close to matching the lasting acclaim of *Kiss Me Kate*. In 1956 Porter wrote the score for the film *High Society*, a musical version of *The Philadelphia Story* (1940). It was for the song "True Love" from the film that Porter finally won the Academy Award for Best Song.

Porter's final two projects were composing a few unmemorable songs for the film *Les Girls*

(1957) and the score for a television musical, *Aladdin* (1958). Following the amputation of his leg in 1958, Porter retired. Becoming a semirecluse, he spent the last years of his life shuttling back and forth between his homes on both coasts, before dying in Santa Monica, California on October 15, 1964. He is buried in his hometown, Peru, Indiana.

JEFFERY A. DUVALL

For Further Reading

McBrien, William. *Cole Porter: A Biography*. New York: Norton, 1998.

Schwartz, Charles. *Cole Porter: A Biography*. New York: Da Capo Press, 1979.

Stempel, Larry. *Showtime: A History of the Broadway Musical Theater*. New York: Alfred A. Knopf, 2010.

The Pulliams

Eugene Collins, May 3, 1889–June 23, 1975, and Eugene Smith, September 7, 1914–January 20, 1999

Civic-minded newspapermen, editors, and publishers, with combined careers spanning more than a half of a century.

To a considerable degree, the father-son tandem of Eugene Collins Pulliam and Eugene Smith Pulliam exemplified old-fashioned newspaper publishing, leaving their mark on newspapers in Indiana and elsewhere for a combined five decades. Both father and son were roll-up-the-sleeves journalists, civic-minded, strong-willed, and passionate about their communities and their newspapers. Both were politically conservative, and the father, especially, was unapologetically outspoken in his beliefs; his news columns often reflecting that political favoritism.

As a student at DePauw University in Greencastle, Eugene C. founded the *DePauw Daily* and in 1909 helped establish Sigma Delta Chi, a professional journalism organization now known as the Society of Professional Journalists with headquarters in Indianapolis. Eugene C. began his reporting career in 1909 with the *Atchison Champion* before moving to the *Kansas City Star*. He took for his lifelong model William Rockhill Nelson, the *Star's* publisher. While Eugene C.'s politics were conservative and he naturally gravitated to the Republican Party, in a 1985 biography Russell Pulliam wrote that Nelson influenced his grandfather as "a firm individualist, independent in politics, not owing loyalty to any political or financial backers." Throughout his publishing career, Eugene C. kept Nelson's penchant for independence in mind.

Eugene C. purchased his first newspaper, the *Atchison Champion*, while still in his mid-twenties, partly with money from the family of his first wife. He eventually was owner and publisher of forty-six newspapers. His major holdings included the *Indianapolis Star, Indianapolis News, Muncie Star, Arizona Republic*, and *Phoenix Gazette*. He carried considerable clout in both Indianapolis and Phoenix, the flagship cities of the Central Newspapers Inc. chain that he assembled and oversaw. He was very much a working newsman as well as a publisher, and his editorials (which sometimes appeared on the front page) were reprinted extensively.

Between 1930 and 1960, Indianapolis gained a reputation for political conservatism, in part because publisher Eugene C. and another local power broker, Chamber of Commerce executive William Book Sr., became vocal spokesmen for free enterprise and patriotic causes. They also sought to influence the nomination of political candidates whose views mirrored their own. When prominent Republicans began in 1951 to recruit Dwight Eisenhower as a presidential candidate, Eugene C. noted to a confidant, Harry Darby, that "General Eisenhower is as completely fed up with socialism and bureaucracy as either you or I." Eugene C., however, did not limit his exposure to just national Republican figures. He interviewed three-time Democratic presidential nominee William Jennings Bryan, very much aware that his subject was wary of journalists. In order to gain his trust, Eugene C. showed him all the quotes he wrote down during their interviews so Bryan could check them.

True to his old-guard newspaperman image, Eugene C.'s public persona reflected an irascible side, demonstrated in his response to an item published in the trade publication, *Columbia Journalism Review*. The *Review*, citing *Time* magazine as the source, had Pulliam saying, "I've combed the whole goddam country. There are lots of good journalists around, but they're all cockeyed left-wingers." In his rebuttal, Eugene C. said, "Of course the statement attributed to me in *Time* was completely incorrect for two reasons: In the first place, I have never used the word goddam in an interview in my life. In the second place, we have about eight or ten of the finest editors in America

Eugene C. Pulliam

in our papers and not a single one of them are left-wingers. What I did say was that I looked all over the country for a good man—that there are a lot of good editors in America but too many of them, not all, are left-wingers. But, as usual, *Time* writes whatever it damn pleases."

Eugene C. was elected to the Associated Press board of directors in 1961 and served three successive three-year terms, the maximum permitted. He was given the John Peter Zenger Award in 1966 for journalistic merit from the William Allen White Foundation. In addition, he was selected a member of the Indiana Journalism Hall of Fame and honored multiple times by Sigma Delta Chi, the organization he founded.

Eugene C., who died in Phoenix at the age of eighty-six, was married three times: to Myrta Smith Pulliam in 1912 and who died in 1917; to Martha Ott Pulliam in 1919, a marriage that ended in divorce in 1941; and to Nina G. Mason Pulliam in 1941. Upon his death, his widow took over the presidency of Central Newspapers, a position she held until 1979. She also became publisher of the two Arizona newspapers.

Eugene S., meanwhile, became publisher of the *Indianapolis Star* and *Indianapolis News*. Under the younger Pulliam's leadership, the paper won a Pulitzer Prize in 1975 for an investigation of police corruption and another in 1991 for a series on medical malpractice.

Unlike his father, Eugene S., known as "Young Gene," was quiet and calm and did not allow his conservative views to leak into the news columns. But he also had a reputation as a penny-pincher and generally kept a close eye on the company's budget, except when the accountants suggested the newspapers start charging for obituaries. "People get mentioned in the paper only when they are born and when they die," Eugene S. once said, "so we're not going to charge them for dying."

Eugene S. was marinated in journalism from an early age. During summer vacations in the early 1930s he earned five cents an item writing news briefs for the *Lebanon Reporter*. After graduating from DePauw in 1935, he joined United Press (later United Press International) working in the news service's Chicago, Detroit, and Buffalo bureaus. Returning to Indianapolis in 1936, he became news director at radio station WIRE, then owned by his father, and became a familiar local broadcast voice.

During World War II, Eugene S. served four years in the U.S. Navy and later the Naval Reserve. He and his wife, Jane Bleecher, whom he married in 1943, had three children, all of whom continued the family tradition of journalism. After the war he served in several positions with the *Indianapolis Star*, among them aviation editor, assistant city editor, and city editor. In 1948 he became managing editor of the *Indianapolis News*, then was named assistant publisher of the *Star* and *News* in 1962, before becoming publisher upon his father's death.

Like his father, Eugene S. over his sixty-four-year news career was a staunch defender of press freedom and the First Amendment. In the early 1950s he assailed U.S. Senator Joseph McCarthy's smear tactics. Eugene S. served on an American Society of Newspaper Editors committee that investigated McCarthy's attack on *New York Post* editor James Wechsler. He concluded that McCarthy's attacks were "not only a threat to the freedom of the press, but also a peril to America." In addition, an award in his name is given annually to an individual, individuals, or organizations whose work protects and preserves the First Amendment.

Both father and son also established programs to help college students pursue journalism careers. The Eugene S. Pulliam Internship Program each year awards paid internships to ten college students to work on daily and nondaily newspapers in Indiana.

Eugene S. also believed the news media unfairly attacked his nephew, Dan Quayle, the oft-ridiculed 1988 Republican vice presidential nominee. After the election of George H. W. Bush and Quayle, Eugene S. defended his nephew in a signed editorial reminiscent of his father: "During a political campaign that abounded with attacks on his career, he kept his head high. He refused to be upset by unfair and inaccurate reporting." For his part, Quayle once described his uncle as "a man of independence and honor, and a leader who views life in terms of serving others and improving our city."

Eugene S. was ill for most of 1998 but continued to have a voice in the two newspapers' operations by telephone, then-executive editor Frank Caperton said. Eugene S. died at age eighty-four. About a year later the Central Newspaper holdings were acquired by Gannett Company Inc., bringing an end to the two-generation Pulliam newspaper dynasty.

ALAN K. WILD

For Further Reading

Connor, Lawrence S. "Bo." *Star in the Hoosier Sky: The Indianapolis Star in the Years the City Came Alive, 1950–1990*. Carmel, IN: Hawthorne Publishing, 2006.

"Publisher Gene Pulliam: Last of the Newspaper Titans." *National Review* 12, no. 2 (June 1985): 72.

Varnier, Josephine. "Pulliams keep alive family's century-long media legacy." *The EIJ News*, August 30, 2009. http://www.eijnews.org/2009/08/30.

Purdue, John

October 31, 1802–September 12, 1876

Businessman, merchant, supporter of civic causes, original benefactor of Purdue University, and lifetime Purdue trustee.

Legend has it that John Purdue and his friend, business partner, and fellow booster Martin L. Peirce, were riding past a Lafayette, Indiana, cemetery one day and commented on the dreadful amount of money spent on a particular grave marker. Peirce suggested that a more fitting and lasting monument to an individual as civic minded as Purdue would be a college named in his honor. No hard evidence supports this apocryphal story, but as Robert Topping, author of a history of Purdue University, noted "somewhere between legend and history, Purdue agreed to make his immortal gift."

Purdue was born in Huntingdon County, Pennsylvania, on October 31, 1802, the fifth child and only boy of Charles and Mary Purdue's nine children. Charles seems to have been a sharecropper and occasional employee at an iron smelter. Sometime around 1823, Charles and Mary moved their family west to Adelphi, Ohio, south of present-day Columbus. One of John's sisters died on the trek, and John's father died shortly after their arrival. Leaving John behind, likely apprenticed to a local merchant, Mary and her daughters moved to either Westerville or Worthington, north of Columbus.

The Purdue family was just one of countless others drawn westward in what historian Malcolm Rohrbough terms the "First Great Migration." The earlier pioneers had wrested the land from Europeans and Indians, established a degree of stability, and had begun breaking the land. Now the flood of new arrivals set about establishing farms and towns and commenced to make a living.

Purdue was also at the center of something even more profound than a great migration, what historians refer to as "The Market Revolution" that was transforming the nature and scale of American business. Working on a commission basis, Purdue began buying and selling almost anything available and in demand to the rapidly growing Ohio population. In the cash-poor environment of the Old Northwest, barter exchanges were common, meaning Purdue would have had to understand logistics beyond that required by modern-day cash transactions. Purdue excelled at anticipating what people needed, how much of it, and when, and he cultivated a reputation for fairness and effectiveness. A recent Purdue biography by a descendant, Irena McCammon Scott, described young Purdue as gregarious, with a good sense of humor, and a gifted conversationalist.

At the beginning of his career as a merchant, Purdue reportedly taught school in the winter months. The details for this are sketchy, but Purdue is supposed to have said that his teaching years were "the happiest of my life." This is undoubtedly when Purdue became committed to the importance of education, although he had little formal schooling himself. As his business dealings expanded, he abandoned teaching. Purdue biographer Robert Kriebel tells of one transaction in which Purdue drove four hundred hogs for neighbors to Cincinnati and collected a $300 commission, the equivalent of one year's teaching salary. Purdue also tried his hand at farming. Sometime between 1831 and 1832, he bought a 160-acre farm near his mother that he later sold for a profit. About the same time he went into business with one of his students, Moses Fowler, opening a general merchandise store in Adelphi.

In 1834 Purdue bought 240 acres in Lafayette, Indiana, from one of his customers for cash, store goods, and groceries. A few years later—the exact date is not clear—business took him to Lafayette, where he was impressed with the thriving town's business potential. Lafayette was located at the northernmost navigational point on the Wabash River, and close to the southern terminus of the soon to open Wabash and Erie Canal. Sometime in 1838 or 1839, Purdue and Fowler relocated their business to downtown Lafayette.

Over the next three decades Purdue's fortunes grew with Lafayette and Tippecanoe County. By 1847 Purdue's businesses were located in the Purdue Block, boasted as the largest business complex outside of New York City. Purdue served on the school board and city council, and he gave generously to local worthy causes, especially educational ones. Fowler left the business in 1844, but Purdue continued to mentor rising young entrepreneurs and helped provide startup money to many. Purdue never married, and lived in a suite in the Lahr House Hotel for the rest of his life. He did at times lament never marrying, and he did enjoy the company of children, especially his own nieces and nephews.

Purdue's business interests continued to diversify. In 1845 he and four other local merchants formed the Lafayette Bridge Company and built the first bridge spanning the Wabash River at Lafayette. He also was instrumental in three separate railroad projects. His expanding interests frequently took him to New York, where he marketed Indiana commodities and purchased eastern consumer goods. In 1866 Purdue purchased the *Lafayette Journal* newspaper, possibly in response to the rough treatment directed at him by the rival *Lafayette Courier* during Purdue's run for congress in 1864, or as a preemptive measure heading into his run in 1866. Neither bid was successful, his failure being blamed on his stubborn independent nature in an era of rabid political allegiance. He also purchased the Lafayette Agricultural Works, invested in the Lafayette Savings Bank, and a Colorado mining operation. But most significant was his purchase of Walnut Grove, a 1,695-acre farm in Warren County that he later mortgaged to the state.

The 1863 Indiana General Assembly set in motion the process of establishing a land-grant college after Congress passed the Morrill Act the previous year. Competing local interests stalled the decision until three of Purdue's associates from Tippecanoe County were elected to the legislature in 1866 and championed a proposal to locate the agricultural college in Tippecanoe County. Purdue had already floated a plan to locate the college in Battle Ground, near the site of the famous Battle of Tippecanoe, with cash and land inducements worth $100,000. Other localities including Bloomington and Marion County were preparing to raise their stakes when Purdue stepped in with a revised offer to donate $150,000 in ten equal installments and a donation of 100 acres, with the stipulation that the school would be named by an "irrepealable law" Purdue University, that he be installed as a member of the board of trustees, and that he had visiting privileges for the rest of his life. The bill creating Purdue University was signed into law on May 8, 1869.

The details establishing Purdue University were somewhat contentious. Purdue selected the location, arranged for land purchases, and was charged with oversight of construction. Trustees found him almost impossible to deal with, and often caved in to his desires out of exasperation. The university's first president, Richard Owen, resigned in frustration after only a few months. The trustees, in the absence of Purdue, appointed Abraham Shortridge, superintendent of Indianapolis public schools, as the next president, and gave him broad authority for overall operations of the university. Thirty-nine students were present on the first day of class in September 1874. Shortridge, too, would resign, to be replaced by Emerson Eldridge White, a man much more acceptable to Purdue. But Purdue, feeling slighted and citing poor health, became less involved in the university's affairs.

Purdue died from a stroke on September 12, 1876, after spending the afternoon touring the university's campus with his nephew. Shortly after a funeral fitting for a gentleman of Purdue's stature, attention turned to his estate. It came to light that Purdue had $700,000 in liabilities against $250,000 in assets, and he still owed the university $75,000 on his pledge. The final years of Purdue's life had been comprised of a series of ill-advised business decisions involving his partial ownership of the financially troubled LM&B Railroad, the Agricultural Works, and the Colorado mine. But there was a silver lining amidst the confusion. Purdue had mortgaged his Warren County farm to the state, the proceeds of the sale to be used to pay off the balance of his pledge to the university. His obituary in the *Journal* ended, "In short, he was a useful, public-spirited citizen."

DAVID CAMBRON

For Further Reading

Kriebel, Robert C. *The Midas of the Wabash: A Biography of John Purdue*. West Lafayette, IN: Purdue University Press, 2002.

Scott, Irena McCammon. *Uncle: My Journey with John Purdue*. West Lafayette, IN: Purdue University Press, 2008.

Topping Robert W. *Century and Beyond: The History of Purdue University*. West Lafayette, IN: Purdue University Press, 1988.

Pyle, Ernest "Ernie" Taylor

August 3, 1900–April 18, 1945

Widely read newspaper columnist best known for his reporting during World War II.

Ernie Pyle, perhaps America's most famous war correspondent, died in 1945 on the tiny island of Ie Shima, off the coast of Okinawa in the Pacific. Pyle's death came just six days after President Franklin D. Roosevelt died. In both cases, many Americans felt they had lost an old friend. Newspapers across the country editorialized about the man who gave readers a sense of what it was like being on the front lines.

No journalist since then has been able to establish a reputation equal to Pyle's, although many have dreamed of matching the accomplishments of this native of Dana, Indiana. Part of the reason was his talent. Part of the reason is that journalism has changed since Pyle's day.

Pyle attended Indiana University, but left one semester short of graduation. When the chair of the journalism department learned that the *La Porte Herald* was looking for a reporter, he nominated Pyle. Within a short time, though, he was on his way to join the staff of the *Washington Daily News*, a new tabloid founded by Scripps-Howard head Roy W. Howard. The journalists there worked hard and played hard. Pyle reveled in the environment. Just two years out of college he was writing about life in the nation's capital. He glowed as he wrote to a friend how he had covered a press conference given by President Calvin Coolidge.

At the age of thirty-one, Pyle was named managing editor at the *Daily News*, a position he held for three years. Copies of memos he wrote to the staff show someone who expected tough, persistent reporting and good writing. But he also recognized that how a paper played a story was important. It had to have stories to "smash" on page one.

To some degree, Pyle was a writer stuck in a journalist's skin. He was learning how to tell stories. He could write a story on deadline, but he preferred the chance to craft his work. Pyle honed his abilities to tell stories while writing about aviation, a field of heroes and heroines in the late

Ernie Pyle

1920s that naturally created stories. As Amelia Earhart put it, any aviator who did not know Pyle was "a nobody."

Pyle did not embellish. He did not have to because of his ability to see stories. He developed that skill as he crisscrossed the United States, Canada, and Latin America from 1935 to 1942, telling stories about interesting people and places. A trip to London at the end of 1940 to report on the Nazi bombing there catapulted Pyle to fame, launched by a brilliant word-picture of one of the biggest attacks of the war. "It was a night when London was ringed with fire," Pyle wrote. He demonstrated to his bosses at Scripps-Howard that he was more than just a provincial writer. For the first time, Americans could picture the war's impact in Europe. When Pyle returned to Great Britain in summer 1942, they knew who he was and what to expect from him.

Pyle's reporting from North Africa in late 1942 and early 1943 cemented his reputation as a war reporter. The secret of that success explains why no one has been able to take his place in the pantheon of war correspondents. Pyle did not have to file daily stories on the fighting and the strategic situation. Instead, he did as he had done before. He looked for stories and stored them up in his mind, then went away from the front lines and wrote them up. He did not have editors who choreographed his every move. He roamed about, following tellable stories. They were not all, however, about the men in the foxholes. Despite his reputation as the quiet, mild-mannered buddy of the GIs, Pyle was well connected. He treasured having Generals Omar Bradley and Dwight Eisenhower as friends. Eleanor Roosevelt, the president's wife, was an admirer, complimenting Pyle's work in her own newspaper column. At the very least, such friendships could open doors.

Several of Pyle's most famous columns were not the result of his planning, but of the chance of timing or of someone else's decision. "The Death of Captain Waskow," Pyle's most-famous column, appeared when the Allied forces were bogged down at the Anzio beachhead in Italy. In the column, which described how Waskow's men paid homage to him after the captain's body, one of many brought down from the mountainside, was laid alongside a stone wall. The column captured the tragedy of war, but also showed how the comradeship it built would win the war.

Pyle did not want to be on the beach at Normandy for D-Day. He hated invasions because he knew the chance of death was high. But General Bradley asked him to go. Without that request, readers would not have the picture of the beach one day after the invasion. The columns that he wrote from the beach are many layered. Those looking for inspiration will find it there. Those who abhor war will also find inspiration. In 1944 Pyle was awarded the Pulitzer Prize for his reporting, one of a bundle of prizes he won during the war.

Pyle's ability to tell stories explains in large part why he was so successful. Even censors were probably taken in by the stories. They found it difficult to remove even one word from the stories that Pyle had constructed. Readers at home or the soldiers and sailors who read his stories overseas remembered not the facts, but the stories. They could share the stories with others. The facts of other reporters were quickly forgotten as the front moved on. Pyle's stories survived.

The Allied drive across France to Paris took a severe toll on Pyle. Not only did he experience "friendly fire," but he also saw more dead people than he ever had before. Over time this unnerved him, just as it did so many soldiers during the war. He came home where he was overwhelmed and scared by the adulation that he received.

Early in 1945 Pyle headed to the Pacific. He resisted going, but at least publicly he said he owed it to the men and women there. Pyle never hit his stride in the Pacific. None of his columns there is among his famous ones. When he was on board ship the war seemed distant and impersonal. It only became real when he went ashore. He was scared about the landing on Okinawa, but he landed on a portion of the beach where practically no Japanese resistance was encountered.

A few days later, he came ashore on the small adjacent island of Ie Shima. It had been captured by the Allied Forces, but it had not yet been cleared of enemy opposition. On April 18, 1945, a Japanese soldier fired on the jeep in which Pyle was riding. Pyle and the others hit the dirt by the side of the road. When Pyle raised his head to check on the others, he was hit in the head and died instantly. Pyle was buried first on Ie Shima, and then in 1949 at the Punchbowl Cemetery in Honolulu.

In death, Pyle has remained on a pedestal. For those who lived during the war, his writing recaptures the quiet heroism of American troops. Like other journalists of the time, he supported the cause. He saw his role as one of helping the troops gain victory.

Pyle's stories remain eminently readable today. His powers of observation and description are still difficult to match. In 1944 Pyle was selected Hoosier of the Year by the Sons of Indiana in New York City. "To every Hoosier you are a modern Stephen Foster whose phrases, with simple perfection, contrive to bring into harmony the discordant overtones that try men's souls in wartime," read the award.

The generation he wrote about is rapidly passing from the scene. But the words of Ernie Pyle will endure to tell that generation's stories.

OWEN V. JOHNSON

For Further Reading

Boomhower, Ray E. *The Soldier's Friend: A Life of Ernie Pyle*. Indianapolis: Indiana Historical Society Press, 2006.

Nichols, David, ed. *The Best of Ernie Pyle's 1930 Travel Dispatches*. New York: Random House, 1989.

Tobin, James. *Ernie Pyle's War: America's Eyewitness to World War II*. New York: Free Press, 1997.

Pyle, Ernie. Online Wartime Columns Collection. Indiana University School of Journalism. http://journalism.indiana.edu/resources/erniepyle/wartime-columns/.

Ransom, Freeman Briley

July 13, 1882–August 6, 1947

General manager of the Madam C. J. Walker Manufacturing Company in Indianapolis and credited with leading the firm to dominance in business of hair care and beauty products for African Americans.

Freeman B. Ransom, who was born in Grenada, Mississippi, moved to Indianapolis in 1910 to become attorney for the MADAM C. J. WALKER Manufacturing Company, succeeding ROBERT L. BROKENBURR, whose other legal activities and political aspirations limited him to a part-time role as legal adviser. A year later, Ransom, who graduated in 1908 as valedictorian from the law department of Walden University in Nashville, Tennessee, with divinity and law degrees and did postgraduate work at Columbia University's law school, was named general manager, a position he held until his death.

Sales at the Walker Company began increasing almost immediately after Ransom's arrival and during his time as general manager the firm became preeminent in the field of hair care and beauty supplies for African Americans, both in the United States and abroad. The company's rapid growth made Walker wealthy, though she denied the often-repeated claim of being a millionaire.

Ransom's remarkable results at the Walker company came during a period when African American business successes were few. While his title was general manager, the breadth of his responsibility was the equivalent of chief operating officer and president, a position few black men had achieved prior to World War II. It is generally accepted that his steady stewardship at the controls of the company was responsible for both the survival of the firm during troubled times and its regeneration when business conditions improved.

Walker, unsure of her daughter A'Lelia's ability or willingness to supervise the enormous enterprise she had created, named Ransom manager of the business for life. Her trust in Ransom allowed her to travel a great deal to gain customers and to create a sales force of African American women that eventually led to branch offices in major cities throughout the eastern United States.

After Walker's death in 1919, Ransom assumed even greater responsibilities, adding marketing and management of the national sales force to his workload of supervising manufacturing as well as overseeing construction of the Walker Building west of downtown Indianapolis, completed in 1927 and home to not only the company's factory and offices, but also a theater, restaurant, drugstore, beauty salon and other establishments. Challenges to the firm soon followed, including, of course, the Great Depression, that sank a multitude of banks, insurance companies, and other businesses into bankruptcy.

Ransom's tenure also coincided with the rise of the Ku Klux Klan in Indiana and its campaign of violence and intimidation that targeted blacks, Jews, and Catholics, making life especially difficult and often dangerous for individuals and businesses in the minority. Beginning in the early 1920s, the Klan gained enough political and economic power to take control of the mayor's office in Indianapolis, a congressional seat, the city council, and the school board. While the double pressures of racial politics and economic instability were formidable challenges, the Walker company survived the turbulent times and was able to regain its footing after the Klan began losing its power by the mid-1920s and with the advent of the New Deal that powered an economic resurgence.

As the success of the Madam Walker Company grew, so did Ransom's influence and involvement in civic and political affairs, including service as a city councilman, alternate delegate to a Democratic national convention, trustee for the Indiana School for the Blind, and leading advocate when an antilynching bill was proposed by the Indiana legislature. Ransom also used his position in the Democratic Party to lobby for improving employment and educational opportunities for blacks and to fight for an end to the state's system of segregation. He was also vice president of the National Negro Bar Association; vice president of the National Negro Business League, a Booker T. Washington organization; a member of the Indianapolis mayor's relief committee; and an active supporter of the Senate Avenue Young Men's Christian Association, Phyllis Wheatley Young Women's Christian Association, and the Flanner House, a social-services agency for African Americans, which in 1946 named Ransom the city's "outstanding Negro citizen." Additionally, he was attorney for Doctor E. N. Perkins Cream Float Soap Company and the Frederick Douglass Life Insurance Company.

Through his position as a member of the board of directors of the National Association for the Advancement of Colored People, Ransom was often consulted by the organization's leadership on issues of race and segregation in the Midwest. For example, in 1924 Walter White, executive secretary of the organization's national office, sought Ransom's advice about the capabilities of three Indianapolis attorneys working for the NAACP to oppose the building of a segregated high school. When Ransom responded that the lawyers were not competent to handle the case properly, the NAACP withdrew from the case, which cleared the way for construction of segregated Crispus Attucks High School.

Although Ransom spoke in 1938 at a groundbreaking ceremony for a new addition to Crispus Attucks, he opposed segregated schools, believing they limited vocational and educational preparation for African American students. Yet, he realized such schools provided the only public education available at the time and declared that education "is the life blood of our democracy, and if democracy is to survive, our program of education must ever grow.

Years after his death, the name Freeman B. Ransom continued to be respected and admired in Indianapolis. In 1992 the area in which the Ransom family had resided was named the Ransom Place Historic District. The designation placed it in a position to receive special consideration from the city and from other organizations involved in neighborhood revitalization.

STANLEY WARREN

For Further Reading

Bundles, A'Lelia. *On Her Own Ground: The Life and Times of Madam C. J. Walker*. New York: Scribner, 2001.

Higbee, Mark David. "W. E. B. Du Bois, F. B. Ransom, the Madam Walker Company, and Black Business Leadership in the 1930s." *Indiana Magazine of History* 89 (June 1993): 101–24.

Taylor, Oliva, F. B. Ransom, and R. L. Bailey. *NAACP Branch Files*, Indianapolis, IN, 1912–1939. Frederick, MD: University Publications of America, 1991.

Ransom, Willard B.
May 17, 1916–November 7, 1995

Civic leader, attorney, business manager, civil rights leader, and advocate for social and economic justice.

When interviewed in 1982 for an *Indianapolis Magazine* article on black leadership, Willard "Mike" Ransom reminisced, "Causes have always been my avocation, but my wife says that causes are really my vocation." Indeed, throughout his long and active life Ransom was drawn to causes that reflected his commitment to broad-based social justice and devoted much of his adult life to fighting for progressive causes.

The son of the famous lawyer and MADAM C. J. WALKER Manufacturing Company general manager FREEMAN B. RANSOM, Willard was born and raised in the Indiana Avenue neighborhood that served as the hub of Indianapolis African American life at that time. The third of six children, Willard attended Crispus Attucks High School, where he was a star athlete and student. He then attended Talladega College, majoring in history and graduating with honors in 1936. Three years later, Ransom graduated from Harvard Law School—the only African American in a class of more than three-hundred students—and was admitted to the Indiana bar that same year. Following his return to Indianapolis, Ransom began to practice law with his father as well as serve as a deputy attorney general in the Indiana Attorney General's office.

The exigencies of World War II interrupted Ransom's bucolic career as a lawyer. Drafted into the army, Ransom was initially assigned to a chemical warfare unit, despite his repeated requests for an assignment that fit his legal training. Even within that unit, though, he frequently served as a defense counsel in courts-martial. Later transferred to the U.S. Army Air Corps, he was finally assigned to the judge advocate general section, becoming the first African American appointed to that legal unit, where he rose to the rank of captain.

Ransom spent much of his military service stationed in Tuskegee, Alabama. His wartime service, like that of so many African Americans of the greatest generation, was a transformative experience. He was outraged by the blatantly discriminatory and humiliating treatment visited upon African American military personnel by their own government. Ransom remembered his years in the army as a time of protests, rallies, and debates. "We were fighting discrimination," he said. "Black officers couldn't go into officers' clubs, enlisted men couldn't go into the noncommissioned officers' clubs."

Willard B. Ransom

After his honorable discharge from the army, Ransom returned to Indianapolis in 1946 to resume the practice of law with his father and with an intense determination to fight against racial discrimination. He threw himself into the local civil rights struggle. From 1947 to 1971 Ransom was a part-time attorney, dividing his time between the National Association for the Advancement of Colored People and his private law practice. He was elected state president of the NAACP five times from 1947 to 1951. In that capacity, he planned and participated in several direct action, nonviolent sit-ins and marches protesting racial discrimination in downtown Indianapolis restaurants, hotels, and other public accommodations to force them to comply with the state's existing, though rarely enforced, 1885 Civil Rights Law. Although his efforts eventually bore fruit, more than forty years later Ransom could still vividly remember the humiliation when he and a NAACP officer were served lunch at a downtown department store behind a screen "so the other customers couldn't see us." He also spent years helping develop legislation for equality in housing, education, and employment.

A tireless litigator, Ransom threatened to file a federal lawsuit in 1949 when the City of Indianapolis refused African Americans access to its public pools. In the early 1960s he pressured the Democratic Party to make open housing part of its platform. "We never intended to let up on housing. We never did," he declared in a 1990 interview. "We were always fighting the housing battle."

Riding a wave of reformist zeal at the local, state, and national levels, Ransom and other civil rights advocates lobbied vigorously to pass a state law to end segregation in Indiana's public schools. Obstructionists attempted to derail their efforts, not only employing procedural delaying tactics in the Indiana legislature, but also issuing verbal and written threats against the bill's supporters. Undeterred, Ransom and other civil rights leaders and groups engaged in a broad-based intraparty lobbying effort to ram the bill through the general assembly. Their efforts were eventually successful when the 1949 Hunter-Binder "Fair Schools" bill was passed by the legislature and signed into law by Governor Henry F. Schricker—five years before the U.S. Supreme Court's landmark *Brown v. Board of Education* decision.

None of Ransom's efforts on behalf of civil rights were achieved without a cost, though. He was reviled as an alleged Communist for his civil rights activities by foes of desegregation. White supremacists retaliated with constant harassment and threats against him. He was arrested and jailed several times, along with other civil rights protestors. Ransom's wife and sister-in-law lost their jobs as a consequence of his involvement with the civil rights movement in Indiana.

Ransom even became involved, briefly, in national politics. Deeply concerned about the Cold War policies of the Harry S Truman administration, as well as the anti-Communist hysteria of the late 1940s, he headed the Indiana delegation to the 1948 national convention of the Progressive Party and addressed the convention. He campaigned actively for the party's presidential candidate, Henry Wallace, and ran for Congress on its ticket. Although his announced candidacy earned him the distinction of being the first African American to run for Congress in Marion County, it was an action that horrified some of his fellow NAACP members at a time of rising anti-Communist hysteria and hostility to progressive politics.

After his father's death, Ransom and his brother took over management of the Walker Manufacturing Company, where he served as assistant manager from 1947 to 1954 and general manager from 1955 to 1971. He capped his lengthy association with the Walker company in 1990 as a director and trustee. In 1971 he joined the local law firm of Bamberger and Feibleman, making him the first African American attorney to work full time with a major white law firm in Indianapolis. He was also a director of the Indianapolis Chamber of Commerce and Merchants Bank, Madame Walker Urban Life Center board member, longtime trustee of the Young Men's Christian Association, member of the Marion County and National Bar Associations, and a cofounder of Indiana Black Expo.

Although Ransom believed things had gotten better in public accommodations, housing, and jobs by the early 1980s, serious problems of unemployment and economic underdevelopment persisted. He thought that African Americans needed to strengthen their economic base by creating more and expanding more businesses. "We have economic power," Ransom said, "if we could find a way of marshaling our strength."

Despite his many "firsts," as well as the important role he played in the civil rights movement in Indiana, Ransom was modest about his contributions to the advancement of social justice in the Hoosier State. When asked about the significance of his life he said, "Really the only thing I've tried to do is make a contribution to the black community in particular and the larger community in general." That he did—and more. His was a life well lived.

MONROE LITTLE

For Further Reading

Bryant-Willis, Wanda. "Spent Years in Equality Battle." *Indianapolis News*, July 26, 1982.

Lutholtz, William. "Who Speaks for the Black Community?" *Indianapolis Magazine*, July 1982.

Pierce, Richard B. *Polite Protest: The Political Economy of Race in Indianapolis, 1920–1970*. Bloomington, IN: Indiana University Press, 2005.

Thornbrough, Emma Lou. *Indiana Blacks in the Twentieth Century*. Edited by Lana Ruegamer. Bloomington: Indiana University Press, 2000.

———. "The Indianapolis Story: School Segregation and Desegregation in a Northern City." Unpublished Manuscript, Indiana Historical Society, 1993.

Rapp, George (Johan Georg)
November 1, 1757–August 8, 1847

Prophet of the Harmony Society and founder of New Harmony, Indiana.

"I am a prophet and am called to be one." George Rapp made this bold declaration in 1791 to officials investigating his separation from the state Lutheran Church in the German Duchy of Württemberg. With it, he defended the radical pietism, perfectionism, and postmillennialism that energized his celibate Harmonist movement. As a postmillennialist, Rapp preached an optimistic version of millennialism, which stressed dramatic improvements in modern times that were perfecting the world so Jesus Christ could return and establish his kingdom. Rapp's communal Harmony Society thrived on this premise for a decade in Indiana (1814 to 1824) and a century in American (1805 to 1905).

Rapp had been a humble religious seeker and weaver in and around Iptingen, Germany, his birthplace. But he and his wife, Christine Benzinger, became a threat to civil order when they rejected the cold and formal Lutheran Church of their day to return to Martin Luther's original emphasis on warm and emotional justification by faith and priesthood of believers. Rapp and his followers found inspiration in a personal relationship with God and salvation through a spiritual rebirth proclaimed by early German Pietists. When Rapp added to these beliefs the utopian hopes of alchemy and Christ's soon return, plus the personal magnetism of his own resounding voice and six-foot frame, he became the prophet of as many as 20,000 separatist disciples.

Rapp taught that his followers were God's only chosen people for the end times and that Christ could not return until they fulfilled their role as the church of Philadelphia and Sunwoman described in Revelation, chapters 3 and 12. Between 1803 and the mid-1820s, he induced some two thousand believers to flee to the protective wilderness and religious freedom of the United States—perhaps the largest group to immigrate to America following a single leader. When early arrivers began to scatter, he gathered 1,000 in Beaver County, Pennsylvania, where he directed the building of the first Harmonist town, Harmony. Rapp's use of the terms Harmonist, Harmony, and Harmony Society were calculated to inspire loyalty among his followers. He believed that God's ultimate objective was a cosmic harmony and that his people were playing an essential role in that preordained historical process. In 1805, to insure the security, solidarity, and survival of his movement, he adopted the communal method, organizing his disciples into the Harmony Society, which committed members to lifelong financial sharing. For biblical justification, he used the community of goods practiced by early Christians in Jerusalem according to Acts, chapters 2 and 4. Rapp summarized his views in *Thoughts on the Destiny of Man* (1824), which was the first book on religious philosophy printed in Indiana.

In 1814 Father Rapp—by then his title of endearment—moved 900 Harmonists to the Indiana Territory. Amid 30,000 acres on the navigable Wabash River in what became Posey County, they built a new town they called both Harmony and New Harmony. Here, Rapp and his Harmony Society helped lay economic and political underpinnings for the state of Indiana. With the astute direction of their multitalented—if patriarchal and authoritarian—prophet and with his competent adopted son, Frederick Reichert Rapp, as business manager, the unified and diversified labor force of skilled Harmonist tradesmen and craftsmen built New Harmony. A neighbor, Richard Flower, called it "that wonder of the West." Glowing reports of the community that eventually had 180 buildings—brick dwellings, two finely crafted churches, mills, and factories—began bringing Indiana to national and international attention. Many, including ROBERT OWEN, who bought the entire town in 1825 for his own secular utopian experiment, became curious how this community could become rapidly financially successful and virtually self-sufficient through a then-novel combination of agriculture, manufacturing, and commerce tied to communal living.

After only a decade on the Wabash River, Harmonist produce and products were traded with twenty-two states and nine foreign countries. Their commercial brewery, the first in Indiana, undoubtedly gave many Hoosiers their first taste of high-quality beer. The Harmony Society became so prosperous and wary of monetary instability that it initiated a sound banking tradition on the Indiana frontier. Its Farmers Bank of Harmony remained solvent as nearly all others failed. The Indiana treasurer requested a loan of $5,000 in 1823 to keep the fledgling state itself from bankruptcy. Frederick, the bank's president, had been the Harmony Society's representative at the 1816 constitutional convention when Indiana sought statehood. He made sure that this state the Harmonists helped create would stay afloat by loaning the money—at the usual 6 percent interest. Respect for Frederick permitted the Harmony Society to be influential in organizing the state's banking system. He became a director of the state bank at Vincennes. He and five other men were authorized to organize fourteen branch banks. Frederick also was put on the commission assigned to find a location for Indiana's capital city. His hand-drawn map of Indianapolis suggests he might have been involved in the planning and surveying as well.

As president of the flourishing Harmony Society in control of a large voting bloc, Rapp wielded political power at local, state, and national levels. After the ballots of the Harmonists were destroyed or stolen in one Posey County election, Rapp insisted his people abstain in the next. The winner that year apparently thought their united vote would have resulted in his defeat and wrote to thank them for not voting. One delegate to the Indiana Constitutional Convention warned the

Harmonist leader that if he used the overwhelming majority held by his male voters to determine every political decision in Posey County, his New Harmony community would reap the wrath of their neighbors and might jeopardize their safety and civil liberties. While the Harmonists supported the antislavery provision in the constitution, it was their desire to avoid military service that created controversy. One reason Rapp moved from Pennsylvania was his not being permitted to pay fines rather than have his purified, pacifistic men defile themselves by taking up arms. Frederick was able to insert a pay-rather-than-serve provision in the Indiana Constitution, which negated that dilemma, but not the animosity of many Hoosiers who charged this was a way for well-heeled Harmonists to escape their civic duty.

By 1824 the great influx of new German immigrants originally expected in New Harmony had not materialized, and Rapp moved his Harmonists back to the economic stability and greater acceptance of German culture in Pennsylvania. There, they built Economy (now Ambridge) on the Ohio River north of Pittsburgh. Rapp's sale of New Harmony to a single buyer, Owen, the wealthy cotton manufacturer and social reformer from New Lanark, Scotland, both helped preserve his town's remarkable heritage and brought new enduring benefits to Indiana through the progressive educators and natural scientists attracted to Owen's own secular utopian community.

Together, Rapp and Owen shaped a town that has become a living legacy enjoyed by citizens of Indiana and citizens of the world. Dotted with National Historic Landmarks, its gardens, labyrinths, musical performances, and sacred places still resonate with its Harmonist tradition. New Harmony has a profound universal spiritual appeal for many who visit, and Rapp's own utopian yearnings still linger in the aura of his Indiana town.

DONALD E. PITZER

For Further Reading

Arndt, Karl J. R., ed. *A Documentary History of the Indiana Decade of the Harmony Society, 1814–1825*. 2 vols. Indianapolis: Indiana Historical Society, 1975–78.

Arndt, Karl J. R. *George Rapp's Harmony Society, 1785–1847*. Rev. ed. Rutherford, NJ: Fairleigh Dickinson University Press, 1972.

Pitzer, Donald E., and Darryl D. Jones. *New Harmony Then and Now*. Bloomington: Indiana University Press, 2011.

Redenbacher, Orville Clarence
July 16, 1907–September 19, 1995

Agribusinessman, contributor to the creation of gourmet popcorn, and world traveler.

Mention the name Orville Redenbacher and one word immediately comes to mind—popcorn. Redenbacher's career, however, involved much more than just popcorn, though food and farming were at the heart of his varied endeavors in Indiana. He was a high school vocational agriculture teacher, county agriculture extension agent, adviser to 4-H clubs, manager of a large-scale farming operation, and co-owner of a company that sold an array of farm equipment and supplies in addition to growing and selling a product that eventually made him a household name.

Redenbacher's lifelong devotion to agriculture began at Brazil High School in Brazil, Indiana, where he studied the subject as well as participating in the school's farming and science clubs. After graduating from high school in 1924, he continued his focus on agriculture at Purdue University, making it his major and the center of his extracurricular activities. He was a member of Purdue's Agriculture Society and Press Club and was on the staff of the *Purdue Agriculturist*, a student-run magazine that covered the activities of the Agriculture School and Home Economics Department.

Upon his graduation from Purdue in 1928, Redenbacher taught agriculture and other subjects at Fontanet High School in Fontanet, Indiana. He combined traditional classroom instruction with field trips, taking students to apple orchards to trim trees and to farms to study dairy cows. Following his brief stint in teaching, Redenbacher moved to Terre Haute to join Purdue's agricultural extension service as a county agent for Vigo County, which mainly involved giving farmers practical instruction on how to make their operations more productive and profitable. As county agent, Redenbacher also worked with 4-H Clubs, the Terre Haute Fruit and Vegetable Association, and the Vigo County Beekeepers' Association. In 1930 he revived the county 4-H fair, which had not been held for twenty years.

Redenbacher also gave added meaning to the term extension agent by becoming the first one in the state to broadcast farm reports from the field through the use of the mobile unit of Terre Haute radio station WBOW, thereby expanding his outreach efforts to farm families who were increasingly adopting this relatively new form of communications. He also testified before the Federal Communications Commission in 1937 in support of increasing the station's transmitting power, which was granted.

One loyal listener to Redenbacher's radio reports was ANTON "TONY" HULMAN JR., a partner with Robert J. Smith in Princeton Farms, which was actually an amalgam of coal mining and agricultural operations in southwestern Indiana and southeastern Illinois. The farm broadcasts so impressed Hulman that he and Smith decided to hire Redenbacher to manage Princeton Farms, a position he held from early 1940 to the end of 1951. Redenbacher's years at Princeton Farms included his first involvement with the product that made him famous. During the Great Depression, Princeton Farms explored ways to diversify its corn acreage, which led Redenbacher to develop a hybrid dent seed corn and one of the first popcorn processing plants in the United States.

After leaving Princeton Farms, Redenbacher and Charles Bowman bought a seed company that they renamed Chester Hybrids. As president of Chester, renamed Chester Inc. in 1967, Redenbacher continued his work on popcorn, hiring plant breeder Carl Hartman in 1959 to conduct popcorn breeding experiments. Success was achieved in 1965 when this work ultimately resulted in a gourmet popcorn hybrid. Before this innovation, the raw popcorn industry was staid and parochial; unpopped popcorn was primarily a regional product sold in grocery stores in the Midwest and the South as a simple, inexpensive, and fun food. Quality and individual brand differences were rarely emphasized.

Everything changed in 1970 when Redenbacher and Bowman hired a Chicago marketing agency, which suggested putting Redenbacher's picture on the packaging and naming the product Orville Redenbacher's Gourmet Popping Corn. The following year Redenbacher convinced Marshall Field in Chicago to carry his product and later that year a subsidiary of Hunt-Wesson agreed to distribute the product in the southern United States with Redenbacher taking the starring role in promoting his popcorn. "I'm a people handler," Redenbacher said at the time. "It's pretty much my nature. We also had the big advantage that there are very few people who develop their own product and sell it."

The first sales of Redenbacher's popcorn in supermarkets also began in 1971, and it commanded the largest share of supermarket sales of popcorn by 1979, a position it continues holding today.

In 1976 Redenbacher and Bowman sold the popcorn business to Hunt-Wesson, which today is owned by agribusiness giant ConAgra. In a separate contract, Redenbacher agreed to be the face and chief promoter of his creation in a variety of ways, including appearing in those folksy television commercials wearing his trademark bow tie, which made him familiar to millions of American consumers. Redenbacher's fame was also stoked in 1979 when the city of Valparaiso, Indiana, created an annual Popcorn Festival, at which Redenbacher often appeared as grand marshal and by a nationwide publicity campaign in 1987 to celebrate his eightieth birthday.

While Redenbacher traveled the country and world promoting his popcorn, he was also a frequent traveler to other countries for People-to-People International, an organization dedicated to fostering peace and understanding among nations through personal connections—a goal that

Orville Redenbacher

perfectly aligned with his beliefs. In a letter to the author, his grandson, he wrote: "If we could get people to communicate we would not have nearly as many world problems."

Redenbacher's travels for the organization as part of its agriculture program took him to the Soviet Union in 1962, South America, and the organization's first trips to Mexico, Scandinavia, and Africa. His visit to Africa included a stop at a farm in the Republic of South Africa that handled the popcorn seed that his old firm Chester had sold to that nation.

In addition to People-to-People, Redenbacher was very active in the Kiwanis International. He first joined the Kiwanis in 1930 in Terre Haute, eventually serving as president in 1939 and as lieutenant governor in the Evansville Division in 1945. Redenbacher's efforts to promote popcorn were recognized when he was inducted into the first National Popcorn Hall of Fame in 1988. Also that year, he received an honorary doctorate in agriculture from Purdue, his alma mater.

Redenbacher died in 1995 at the age of eighty-eight in at his home in California, though his face is still identified today with the product he spent most of his life producing and promoting.

KEVIN R. FISH

For Further Reading

Fish, Kevin R. "More than Popcorn: The Life of Orville Redenbacher, *Traces of Indiana and Midwestern History* 20, no.1 (Winter 2008): 46–54.

Redenbacher, Orville. *Orville Redenbacher's Popcorn Book*. New York: Saint Martin's Press, 1984.

Sherman, Len. *Popcorn King: How Orville Redenbacher and his Popcorn Charmed America*. Arlington, TX: Summit Publishing Group, 1999.

Richardson, Henry, Jr.

June 21, 1902–December 5, 1983

Attorney, jurist, politician, civic leader, and civil rights pioneer.

It was an auspicious occasion when attorney Henry J. Richardson Jr. was awarded the Key to the City by Mayor Richard G. Lugar at the sixth annual Indianapolis Urban League's dinner meeting in May 1971. According to the *Indianapolis Recorder*, it marked "the first time a local citizen had been so honored." The Indianapolis Urban League recognized him as well by awarding Richardson a plaque for his outstanding contributions to the organization as one of its founders and for his continuous service to the organization and the entire community. Both awards were well-deserved honors, in recognition of Richardson's unflinching work on behalf of the civil rights movement and his tireless efforts to advance social justice in the Circle City.

Born in Huntsville, Alabama, Richardson arrived in Indianapolis during the second decade of the twentieth century. A member of what would become as known as the Great Migration, Richardson was sent to the city by his parents in search of greater educational opportunity, which was denied to African Americans in much of the South at that time. He attended Shortridge High School before the pall of racial segregation descended upon the Indianapolis public high schools. After graduating from Shortridge in 1921, he attended the University of Illinois for two years, serving as editor of the student newspaper, the *College Dreamer*. After a brief visit to Huntsville due to the death of his mother, he returned to Indianapolis in 1925 to attend the Indiana University Law School in Indianapolis and received his bachelor of laws degree in 1928.

After law school, Richardson was attracted to local and state politics. In 1930 he was appointed a temporary judge in the Marion County Superior Court—the first African American to serve in such a post. An active member of the state Democratic Party, Richardson was nominated for and elected to the Indiana House of Representatives on the Democratic ticket in 1932, making him one of the first two African American Democrats to be elected to that legislative body in the twentieth century. He served for three terms.

The 1930s was a decade of burgeoning civil rights activity at the national level as the National Association for the Advancement of Colored People, under the leadership of Charles H. Houston, embarked upon its lengthy legal challenge to *Plessy v. Ferguson*, the U.S. Supreme Court ruling that established the doctrine of separate but equal and permitted public schools to be segregated. In Indiana Richardson played a similar leadership role, serving as a tireless advocate for civil rights. During his first term in the Indiana House, Richardson lobbied to end racial segregation in dormitories at Indiana University at Bloomington, and joined with political allies to remove the state constitution's ban on African Americans in the Indiana National Guard.

Richardson also sponsored "a measure that required every contract made by a state or municipal corporation for construction or repair of a public building or public works contain an agreement that there be no racial discrimination in hiring." Emboldened by passage of this measure, he proposed a bill to strengthen Indiana's 1885 Civil Rights Law, but it died in committee. A second attempt by Richardson in the 1935 session of the general assembly to put teeth into the 1885 law not only went down to defeat, but also created the perception of him as something of a political maverick, leading the Democratic Party to withdraw support for his re-election in 1936.

Richardson's commitment to civil rights was also reflected in his activities outside the Indiana legislature. From 1932 to 1938 he served as director of the Civil Liberties Division of the National Bar Association. In 1938 he joined with Starling James of Indianapolis to promote the activities of the Federation of Associated Clubs—a coalition of African American social clubs whose members were committed to civil rights reform and spearheaded early efforts in Indianapolis to end racial segregation in local amusement and entertainment venues.

World War II's ideological challenge to and very real struggle against the evils of white supremacy reenergized the battle for civil rights in the United States as well as Indiana, and Richardson was in the midst of that struggle. Following the war, he chaired a committee that wrote the 1947 Indiana "Anti-Hate" Bill, which was designed to eliminate racial segregation in the state. In 1948 Richardson obtained an injunction in the Indiana court's to bar the white supremacist Dixiecrat Party from the ballot.

Richardson's signal contribution to the civil

Henry Richardson receives the key to the city from Indianapolis mayor Richard Lugar, May 1971.

rights struggle in Indiana was the pivotal role he played in passage of the 1949 Indiana school desegregation law or the Hunter-Binder "Fair Schools" bill as it was then called. The issue was both ideological and personal for him. His son was denied admission to his neighborhood public school. Following closely on the heels of Richardson's own personal communication with NAACP legal counsel Thurgood Marshall "for the purpose of soliciting your immediate interest aid and cooperation in the direction of abolishing our segregated school system here," and the proposal of the "Anti-Hate" Bill by state senators John Van Ness and ROBERT L BROKENBURR in January 1947, House Bill 406 called for the state "to provide equal educational opportunities and facilities for all," forbade school officials from maintaining or continuing "separate schools," discontinued enrollment "on the basis of race" in existing segregated schools, and prohibited any "tax-supported school, college or university" from discriminating "in any way against students on the basis of race, creed or color." The bill died in committee, but Richardson was undeterred.

The following year Richardson, representing the newly created Northside Parents' Association as well as legal representative for the state NAACP, threatened the Indianapolis Board of School Commissioners with legal action if it failed to eliminate racial segregation in the city's public schools In 1949 Richardson and a statewide phalanx of civil rights advocacy groups overcame opposition in the general assembly as well as Indianapolis white neighborhood associations to the Hunter-Binder Fair Schools Bill. It was signed into law by Governor Henry F. Schricker in March 1949, six years before the U.S. Supreme Court declared that segregated public schools violated the equal protection guarantee of the Fourteenth Amendment. The Indiana law mandated the complete integration of black and white students in Indiana's public schools by 1954. Beyond that year, state funds would be cut off for any school system that continued to practice racial segregation or that discriminated on the basis of color in the hiring, upgrading, or tenure of teachers.

Richardson actively continued his quest for equal rights throughout the 1950s and 1960s. In 1953, as state NAACP legal representative, he worked closely with Marshall and Constance Baker Motley to win a landmark housing discrimination lawsuit—*Jessie Woodbridge, et al. v. Housing Authority of Evansville, Indiana*—to desegregate public housing in that city. He also served on the board of the Indianapolis Church Federation, the Indiana Board of Public Welfare, the Indiana State Real Estate Commission, and the federal Civil Rights Commission. Five years later, he became the state's first life member of the NAACP. In 1965 he, along with Thomas Binford and other progressive local leaders, founded the Indianapolis Urban League and served on that organization's national board from 1966 to 1970. For many years, Richardson was also active with the United Negro College Fund, serving both as local chairman and a member of its national board. He remained an acerbic critic of racial prejudice and discrimination. In the early 1970s Richardson remarked that he had noticed "no great change in race and human relations" during his half century of work in Indianapolis and "felt that the black community still occupied a position of second class citizenship socially, economically and politically."

MONROE H. LITTLE

For Further Reading

Bodenhamer, David J., and Robert G. Barrows, eds. *Encyclopedia of Indianapolis*. Bloomington and Indianapolis: Indiana University Press, 1994.

Henry J. Richardson Jr. Papers. William Henry Smith Memorial Library, Indiana Historical Society Indianapolis, IN.

Thornbrough, Emma Lou., ed. *Indiana Blacks in the Twentieth Century*. Edited by Lana Ruegamer. Bloomington: Indiana University Press, 2000.

———. "The Indianapolis Story: School Segregation and Desegregation in a Northern City." Unpublished manuscript, Indiana Historical Society, 1993.

Richardville, Jean Baptiste (Peshewa or the Wildcat)

Unknown date approximately 1761–August 13, 1841

Mixed-lineage Miami tribal leader, fur trader, and merchant.

Born near modern-day Fort Wayne, Indiana, Jean Baptiste Richardville was the son of Joseph Drouet de Richardville, a French trader, and Taucumwah, a sister of the Miami chief, Pecan. In 1770 Joseph returned to Canada, where Jean Baptiste spent part of his childhood with his father and attended school at Three Rivers in Quebec. Well educated (he spoke French, English, and

Miami), Richardville returned in the late 1770s to Kekionga, the Miami village near Fort Wayne, and lived with his mother, who had remarried Charles Beaubien, another trader. As an adolescent, Richardville gained valuable experience working in his mother's trading house at Kekionga. Beaubien supported the Crown during the American Revolution, and following the war Richardville strengthened his ties with British merchants in Detroit and Ontario.

During the immediate postwar years Richardville remained part of his mother's tribal community, but he seems to have identified more as a creole Frenchman than a Miami, and at first was apparently reluctant to participate in tribal affairs. By all accounts Richardville dressed in French clothing and developed an interest in European music and literature. By the 1790s, however, he had emerged as a political ally of his uncle, Pecan, and of Little Turtle, another uncle who also lived near Kekionga. In 1800 Richardville married Natoequah, a Miami woman. The union produced four children: one son, Joseph; and three daughters, LaBlonde, Catherine, and Susan.

Richardville took little part in the border wars of the early 1790s. He may have been present at one of the battles resulting in Harmar's Defeat in 1790, but he did not participate in the Indian victory over Arthur St. Clair the following year. He favored a negotiated peace after the tribal defeat at the Battle of Fallen Timbers in 1794. In the aftermath, he signed the Treaty of Greenville the next year as a chief of the "Miamis and Eel Rivers." Closely associated with Little Turtle, by 1800 Richardville's political influence had increased. Richardville was aware that the United States had become the dominant political power in the region, and he attempted to protect Miami fortunes by cooperating with the government. Consequently, in 1802 and 1803 he signed treaties ceding Miami claims to lands in southern Indiana. Since few Miami resided in the region, most tribal members supported the cession.

In 1808 Richardville met with President Thomas Jefferson in Washington, D.C., and upon his return to Indiana he opposed the growing influence of TECUMSEH and the PROPHET. He initially resisted the cession of additional lands in Indiana, but eventually signed the Treaty of Fort Wayne in 1809 ceding territory along the Wabash River, but strengthening Miami claims to other regions in northern Indiana. When the War of 1812 erupted, Richardville fled to Canada, but Governor WILLIAM HENRY HARRISON still considered him to be friendly to the United States and instructed American troops not to destroy his property in the Fort Wayne region.

Richardville's economic success mirrored his growing political influence. An astute entrepreneur, he established trading posts at the forks of the Maumee and Wabash Rivers. His trading enterprises dominated the important portage between these two rivers and he charged travelers and other merchants a "carrying fee" to transport their goods overland between the two watersheds. In addition, as a "government chief" who exercised considerable influence over the dispersal of federal funds and annuity goods to the Miami tribe, he sometimes used his authority to penalize rivals and reward both political and business allies. According to local legend, he kept his profits in an iron-bound safe, and in 1816, when Indiana entered the Union, Richardville was reputed to be the wealthiest man in the state. Richardville maintained two residences, a brick home at Fort Wayne and another near his trading post on the Mississinewa River. The Fort Wayne residence was famous throughout the region for its size, architecture, and comfortable, sophisticated furnishings. Richardville was reputed to be a gracious host, entertaining guests at rather lavish dinners.

Yet in the quarter century following the War of 1812 Richardville identified less with the creole-French community and more with the Miami people; moreover during these decades he also emerged as the most prominent leader of the tribe. In 1818, although the Miami were forced to cede most of their remaining lands south of the Wabash River in the Treaty of Saint Marys, Richardville persuaded federal officials to exempt the Miami National Reserve, a tract of almost 875,000 acres located primarily in modern Cass, Clinton, Grant, Howard, Madison, Miami, and Tipton Counties.

In these treaty proceedings he also received, as his personal property, seven sections of land near Fort Wayne and two at the forks of the Wabash River. During the next two decades, in subsequent treaties, he also received another thirty-five sections and cash payments totaling more than $30,000. Some historians have criticized Richardville for his role in negotiating these land cessions, but he used his influence to obtain the highest prices possible for Miami lands. In addition, as the Miami land base shrank, Richardville welcomed many of the displaced Miami to new farms or village sites on his property.

Richardville initially opposed federal plans to remove the Miami from Indiana, but in 1838 and 1840 he signed two treaties that ceded most of the remaining Miami National Reserve and provided for the removal of the tribe to the West. The removal treaties also provided Richardville with additional personal lands and cash payments and exempted him and his heirs from being removed. Yet his remaining years in Indiana were brief. He died at his home near Fort Wayne on August 13, 1841.

Richardville exemplified many mixed-lineage tribal leaders who emerged in the Midwest in the decades following the War of 1812. Well educated, experienced frontier businessmen and traders, they negotiated with federal officials to protect tribal interests during a difficult time when tribal political and economic power was in decline while state and federal power was increasing. When removal became inevitable, they sought to obtain the highest possible price for the remaining tribal lands. During a period of rapid American expansion, Richardville could not stem the tide of white settlement, but he attempted to use his political experience and business acumen to protect the Miami people as best he could. Sometimes, however, like other entrepreneurs and political leaders of the Jacksonian Era, he also used his political power for personal advantage.

R. DAVID EDMUNDS

For Further Reading

Cayton, Andrew R. L. *Frontier Indiana*. Bloomington: Indiana University Press, 1996.

Chaput, Donald. "The Family of Drouet de Rocherville: Merchants, Soldiers, and Chiefs of Indiana." *Indiana Magazine of History* 74 (June 1978): 103–16.

Rafert, Stewart. *The Miami Indians of Indiana: A Persistent People, 1654–1994*. Indianapolis: Indiana Historical Society, 1995.

Riley, James Whitcomb

October 7, 1849–July 23, 1916

Writer, poet, and best-selling author.

The committee appointed to plan commemorations for the centennial of Indiana's statehood commissioned GEORGE ADE, the popular humorist and Kentland, Indiana, native, to produce a movie that would capture the essence of celebrations that took place across the state in 1916. The poet James Whitcomb Riley so exemplified what it meant to be a Hoosier that Ade had him appear as the narrator of the film. Unfortunately, no copies of this film have survived, but in the script Ade proclaimed that "Riley revealed the Hoosiers to themselves" and described him as "the triple extract of all that is worthwhile in the makeup of . . . a native son."

Riley's writing, which expressed the "local color" of the region, holds a particularly special place for Hoosiers. Because Ade and his contemporaries believed that life in Indiana was more typically American than in other parts of the United States, they also thought that Riley more broadly expressed the best in the American character. Best known for such poems as "When the Frost Is on the Punkin" and "Little Orphant Annie," Riley provided messages that endeared him to a wide range of Americans. He experienced fame and fortune as few writers do in their lifetimes. His unprecedented popularity as a poet led many critics and authors to believe that Riley would forever be recognized as a major figure in American literature.

Yet odds had been against Riley's success. Born in the small town of Greenfield, Indiana, on October 7, 1849, he had not done well in school. Riley explored several possibilities before settling on becoming a poet. He briefly studied law in the office of his father, Reuben, who had been a prominent Greenfield attorney, but the profession did not suit him. He worked as a shoe clerk, a house painter, a Bible salesman, a patent-medicine-show performer, and an itinerant sign painter. He also considered becoming an actor or musician.

In his twenties Riley enjoyed some success designing advertising signs that incorporated his own jingles. He identified himself as a "painter-poet" at this time. Yet he already took his poetry very seriously. Toward the end of 1876 Riley decided to send some of his poems to Henry Wadsworth Longfellow. The author of "Hiawatha" and "Paul Revere's Ride" was one of Riley's literary heroes. He did not have to wait long for a reply. Within a week, he had an answer. "I have read them with great pleasure," Longfellow wrote in response to Riley's poems, "and think they show the true poetic faculty and insight."

Longfellow's letter was pivotal to Riley's career. Although he continued to take sign-painting jobs, he looked for a position at a newspaper to transform himself into a professional writer. Newspapers were the first place that many aspiring writers first made names for themselves. Riley worked briefly as a local newspaper editor in Kokomo, and later was employed by the *Indianapolis Journal*, one of the most important newspapers in Indiana. Much of his writing first appeared in the columns of newspapers.

Riley also began performing on the lecture circuit during the early part of his career. His lecture appearances not only helped him financially but also gained him a wider audience. In 1887 in New York City, his performance at a lecture to benefit the International Copyright League brought him national fame. He appeared at Chickering Hall with the greatest American writers of the era, including Mark Twain and James Russell Lowell, yet the *New York Times* called Riley the "hit of the afternoon." Lowell's endorsement of Riley's poetry at this event transformed him into a publishing phenomenon. During the year that followed, the combination of his book sales and his lecture fees made Riley the wealthiest working poet in America. Only a few authors, such as Twain, earned more.

The Hoosier Poet

Riley's popularity never waned in the nineteenth century. His poems were read more than those written by any other nineteenth-century American poet, and his readings packed theaters from coast to coast. The management of his name and image anticipated the way celebrity would be handled in the twentieth century. Riley, his publishers, and his managers promoted him until his face and figure were known almost everywhere. His bespectacled face was caricatured in magazines and newspapers. Manufacturers used his image to promote their products.

Yet he also held a high status in the world of arts and letters. He became friends with some of the leading literary figures of his age, met internationally known artists and statesmen, and performed for presidents in the White House. In 1902 Yale University was the first prestigious university to award Riley an honorary degree. Wabash College followed in 1903, the University of Pennsylvania in 1904, and Indiana University in 1907. In 1908 the National Institute for Arts and Letters elected him to its membership, and in 1912 the National Academy of Arts and Letters conferred on him its medal for poetry.

Starting in 1911, children throughout Indiana celebrated Riley's birthday. U.S. Secretary of the Interior Franklin K. Lane called for its national observance in 1915. In Indiana, celebrating Riley's birthday became a tradition. Children continued to recognize it by reading his poems in the classroom until 1968.

Although his fame has faded, Riley's legacy remains important to children. In 1911 he made a gift of property at the northwest corner of Saint Clair and Pennsylvania Streets in Indianapolis for the construction of a new library because he wanted to make sure that all children in the city had free access to books. After his death in July 1916, a group of Riley's friends organized to establish a memorial in his name. With the contributions of more than 40,000 Hoosiers, the James Whitcomb Riley Memorial Association, now known as the Riley Children's Foundation, built the oldest hospital for children in the state. Part of Indiana University Health, the James Whitcomb Riley Hospital for Children opened on its namesake's birthday in 1924. The Riley Children's Foundation also established Camp Riley for Youth with Physical Disabilities at Bradford Woods, an IU camping and outdoor recreational facility located just south of Indianapolis.

Riley's contemporaries believed that he depicted his native state truthfully and accurately, but the Indiana countryside of his verse was essentially free from interaction with broader national patterns of societal change. It was not real. As the emotional range of his poetry is rather narrow and as he failed to address issues of any social gravity, Riley's literary star has fallen. Yet, some believe that Riley is underrated. "Good readers who emotionally respond to ink on paper can do me a favor . . . by reading at least one poem by James Whitcomb Riley," respected author and Indiana native KURT VONNEGUT said in January 2007. "If they do, they'll realize what a good poet he was. And I'll be so grateful." Riley wanted forever to be known as a good poet. He would be so grateful that someone of Vonnegut's literary stature still understood that his poetry had value in the twenty-first century.

ELIZABETH J. VAN ALLEN

For Further Reading

James Whitcomb Riley Papers. Lilly Library, Indiana University, Bloomington, IN.

Riley, James Whitcomb. *The Complete Poetical Works of James Whitcomb Riley.* Bloomington: Indiana University Press, 1993.

Van Allen, Elizabeth J. *James Whitcomb Riley: A Life.* Bloomington: Indiana University Press, 1999.

Rockne, Knute

March 4, 1888–March 31, 1931

All-America football player at the University of Notre Dame, renowned football coach and athletic director at Notre Dame, and football visionary and goodwill ambassador for the sport.

In the years before his death in a plane crash at age forty-three, Knute Rockne was as close to a rock star in the sports world as existed in that era. His name, his still-unparalleled winning percentage of .881 (105 wins, twelve losses, five ties) as head football coach at the University of Notre Dame, and his larger-than-life persona still constitute his legend. The Rockne name also evokes such iconic figures as George "Win One For the Gipper" Gipp and the Four Horsemen, the premier backfield of their day. Often, though, mythology obscures many of the more interesting and lasting facets of his life.

Behind the scenes and out of the spotlight, Rockne extended his coaching prowess by creating and running what are now known as coaching clinics. He tirelessly traveled coast to coast and all around Indiana, with Culver Military Academy near South Bend being one of his regular stops. In his travels, mostly by train, Rockne interacted with coaches and players on a personal level and shared his vision for not only the game of football but also the culture that should envelope it. If such a concept as clinics existed at other schools and with other coaches at the time, it did so on a smaller scale and without the barnstorming element Rockne brought to it.

"Wherever he went, they'd all adopt him as their coach from his week or two of having these summer clinics," according to Jim Lefebvre, speaker, sports historian and author of *Loyal Sons: The Story of the Four Horsemen* and *Coach for a Nation: The Life and Times of Knute Rockne*. "But it's the relationships he forms on a one-to-one basis, thousands of times over, with all these young coaches from all types of schools and colleges all across the nation that made him unique and made him so influential.

"That's why his story touches very part of the nation, because people go back to their local areas and espouse his values and his system in the way they coach. Just those relationships make him every bit a national coach as his feature articles for *Collier's* and other magazines, his newspaper columns and, of course, just Notre Dame's own fame and continuing to win game after game."

In his book, *Shake Down the Thunder: The Creation of Notre Dame Football*, Murray Sperber, a retired professor of English and America Studies at Indiana University and noted advocate of reforming college athletics, calls Rockne the "first great entrepreneurial coach" who pioneered a host of methods for college coaches to increase their outside income. For example, he noted that as his fame and drawing power increased, Rockne began transforming the summer clinics from a casual pastime into a highly organized and profitable business. He eventually entered into a partnership with University of Wisconsin basketball coach Walter E. "Doc" Meanwell to operate football and basketball coaching camps that by 1927 were generating the partners about $50,000.

Beyond just the Xs and Os, Rockne's message to his coaching brethren was also about the business of football and the promotion of it. According to Lefebvre, he understood what the public wanted and he helped craft a game of tremendous appeal far beyond college campuses. His attention to detail included designing uniforms and equipment at varying times—not for fashion sense, but to gain an advantage with a lighter and less wind-resistant package while increasing the protection qualities.

Rockne not only saw the big picture, but he also saw beyond it. And that helped lead to the university building Notre Dame Stadium, though Rockne faced much resistance to get fossilizing 27,000-seat Cartier Field replaced. "Notre Dame was increasingly falling behind other schools who were building the larger brick-and-mortar facilities to last a long time," Lefebvre said. "So he was trying to convince the administration that this was the route he needed to go." The new stadium, built in 1930 at a cost of $750,000, had a capacity of about 59,000. Rockne only got to coach five games there before his death, winning all five.

Rockne's visionary quality started when he was an ascending player for the Irish. The summer before the 1913 football season, Rockne (a senior end) and quarterback Gus Dorais went to great lengths to "systematize" the forward pass, a play that existed in college football but was hardly viewed as a legitimate offensive weapon.

The two friends got jobs as lifeguards at a hotel at Cedar Point, a resort and amusement park in northern Ohio on Lake Erie. Legend had it that the two spent countless hours on the beach, tossing the football back and forth while curious onlookers shook their heads in disbelief. The reality was that they often ran in the sand to build endurance in their legs, but worked mostly in seclusion on a grass field trying to figure out how the pass could become a legitimate weapon. The grass field allowed them to perfect timing, to develop pass patterns, and to try different angles and approaches.

It all came together in on a national stage on November 1, 1913, in a shocking 35–13 upset of powerful Army team at West Point, New York. To save money, Notre Dame coach Jesse Harper had only brought eighteen players with him on the 718-mile train trip. "Initially, I was just happy we were going to come out $83 ahead on the deal," a laughing Harper told the *South Bend Tribune*'s Joe Doyle three decades after the fact.

Rockne was on the receiving end of most of those Dorais strikes that day, including one for a touchdown. The teammates certainly did not invent the pass that day, but they came close to perfecting it and introduced it as a viable option for moving the football rather than the gimmick or desperation play the forward pass had been perceived as to that point in football history. In addition to showcasing the forward pass and heralding Notre Dame's emergence on the national stage, Lefebvre said the game clarified Rockne's vision that football can be "artistry on grass," can be wide open, and can allow someone of his size (five foot, eight and 165 pounds) to have a role. "It can be about scoring from anyplace on the field. It can be about speed, shiftiness and deception—those were the terms he used—as opposed to two groups of eleven behemoths smashing into each other," Lefebvre noted. And if Rockne were alive to see today's game, Lefebvre contends he would smile at the way the offenses have spread the field and created even more space for the little guy to make an impact.

"He'd be at the forefront of the whole concussion issue, because the game was challenged back then for its brutality," Lefebvre said. "I think he'd want to regulate it as much as it makes sense, and let's teach it the right way to minimize the brutality and to emphasize the artistry."

Knute Rockne

And if history is any guide, he would go to great lengths not to keep it to himself but to spread the word.

ERIC HANSEN

For Further Reading

Lefebvre, Jim. *Coach for a Nation: The Life and Times of Knute Rockne*. Minneapolis: Great Day Press, 2013.

———. *Loyal Sons: The Story of the Four Horsemen and Notre Dame Football's 1924 Champions*. Minneapolis: Great Day Press, 2008.

Sperber, Murray A. *Shake Down the Thunder*. Bloomington: Indiana University Press, 2002.

Rumely, Edward Aloysius

February 28, 1882–November 26, 1964

Trained physician, educator, industrialist, editor, economist, and political activist whose work greatly influenced American Constitutional law.

Edward Rumely was a complicated mix of privilege, self-reliance, idealism, pragmatism, tenderness, and thick skin. This unusual combination of traits brought him both prominence and disdain. He was bold and creative in business, innovative and caring as an educator, but his greatest strength was his ability to bring people and ideas together while defying the backlash he created.

At sixteen, Rumely entered the University of Notre Dame against his father's will, intent on becoming a priest. Once there, a professor recommended that he reconsider because his "obstinate nature and independent viewpoint" would make ecclesiastical discipline too difficult. After two years at Notre Dame, Rumely withdrew just hours before being expelled. He then studied abroad, initially at Ruskin Hall, a small cooperative institution in Oxford, England. After a year there, he attended the German universities of Heidelberg for one year and then Freiburg, from which he graduated magna cum laude with a degree in medicine and having met the requirements for a degree in economics. In Germany Rumely became a vegetarian and annoyed his fellow students by wearing unconventional clothing.

When Rumely returned to Indiana, he told his family he would not practice medicine; he would pursue his dream. In 1907, using techniques he had learned in Germany, Rumely opened the Interlaken School, combining physical work with classroom training to prepare boys for life in an industrial world. To finance his school, Rumely worked in the family business, gradually taking it over.

Under his leadership, the M. Rumely Company grew from a small manufacturer of farm equipment into an industry leader, but not without controversy. Rumely poached a key executive from a competitor along with, some claim, an unpatented tractor design. Then, he lured an engineer named John Secor from New York City to La Porte, Indiana, to develop an engine. Together, in 1907, they created what is believed to be the first reliable kerosene-burning tractor, the Kerosene Annie.

By early 1915, an economic downturn and overexpansion drove the M. Rumely Company into receivership. The business fell out of Rumely's hands, and he was fired. In June 1915 Rumely moved into a brownstone in Manhattan and acquired control of the *New York Evening Mail* through a complex matrix of financiers with ties to Germany. Then everything changed.

On April 6, 1917, America entered World War I. By early 1918 Rumely's German connections led A. Mitchell Palmer, alien property custodian and soon-to-be U.S. attorney general, to investigate ownership of the *Evening Mail*. In July 1918 Rumely and his attorneys were arrested for crimes involving failure to report German government ownership of the paper.

Rumely's friend, Henry Ford, publicly defended him. Former president Theodore Roosevelt, who used the *Evening Mail* to publish his writings, also lent support. Journalist H. L. Mencken claimed Rumely was "more the dreamer than the intriguer," but through the lens of war others saw it differently. Those colleagues deserted Rumely, some attacking him to distance themselves. Yet Rumely insisted the *Evening Mail* was his alone, and he was "absolutely and aggressively loyal to [his] country."

By September 1918 sensational press attention and anti-German fervor had closed the Interlaken School so abruptly that one biracial student found himself adrift in a nearby town. Free on bail in 1919, Rumely returned to Indiana to sell the school property. He also found the abandoned student, and became a "proxy father" to him. That student, Isamu Noguchi, went on to become a world famous artist and landscape architect.

Although a jury found Rumely and his attorneys guilty of only the least serious charges and recommended leniency, the judge sentenced them to one year and one day, thereby requiring that the sentences be served in federal prison. Although their convictions were upheld by the U.S. Supreme Court, somehow in 1920 Rumely helped launch a business marketing vitamins. The business survived until 1928 in spite of a trade journal recommendation against it based largely upon Rumely's German ties.

In 1925, with war hysteria fading, President Calvin Coolidge first reduced the sentences for Rumely and his attorneys. Then he pardoned them. When Rumely's attorneys applied for reinstatement to the New York bar, Chief Justice of New York and future U.S. Supreme Court Justice Benjamin Cardozo explained: "The President in granting this pardon acted . . . with the recommendation of his Attorney-General, now Mr. Justice Stone of the Supreme Court . . . who . . . expressed a belief that the petitioners were innocent." However, because Rumely was neither a lawyer nor a petitioner in that case, Cardozo's comments did not necessarily extend to him. Rumely had lost his reputation, his newspaper, and his school, and Cardozo's ambiguity haunted him for the rest of his life.

Yet Rumely persevered. In 1932 he assembled a nonpartisan committee known as the Committee for the Nation in an effort to rebuild the shattered farm economy. Rumely's committee, which included soon-to-be secretary of agriculture and future vice president Henry Wallace, persuaded President Franklin D. Roosevelt to abandon the gold standard and adopt the Agricultural Adjustment Act. But in 1937, when Roosevelt tried to enlarge the Supreme Court, the Committee for the Nation morphed into the National Committee to Uphold Constitutional Government to oppose him.

During the battle, Rumely refined the process of direct mailing, reaching out only to selected voters rather than to members of Congress or all voters. His effectiveness put him in the crosshairs of Congress for years thereafter. In 1938 U.S. Senator SHERMAN MINTON of Indiana ordered Rumely to surrender materials concerning the NCUCG's opposition to Roosevelt's court packing plan. Rumely refused, and Minton's committee considered but declined to prosecute him for contempt. In 1946 a House committee on lobbying charged Rumely with contempt when he refused to turn over the NCUCG's list of contributors, but a jury acquitted him.

In 1951 the House committee on lobbying again charged Rumely with contempt for refusing to disclose the names of bulk purchasers of books the NCUCG had distributed. This time a jury convicted him, but the U.S. Supreme Court upheld the reversal of his conviction, recognizing for the first time First Amendment implications in lobbying activity. Justices William O. Douglas and Hugo Black, Minton's predecessor on the Senate Lobby Investigation Committee, went further, asserting, "Once the government can demand of a publisher the names of the purchasers of his publications, the free press as we know it disappears." Given his history with Rumely, Minton, by then also a Supreme Court justice, took no part in the decision.

In 1959 Rumely returned to La Porte in failing health, musing in his autobiography: "Here I was born. . . . Here I returned after tasting university life abroad. Here I met and wed my bride. . . . No matter where I am . . . my roots are in this pleasant, homelike northern Indiana city close by the Lake Michigan dune country." He spent his last days distributing information about cancer, against smoking, and promoting the Papanicolaou (Pap) test. And to this day a few Kerosene Annies still visit county fairs and sometimes even plow a field.

WILLIAM J. BOKLUND

For Further Reading

Rumely, Edward A. Papers. University of Oregon Libraries Special Collections and University Archives, Eugene, OR.

Rumely, Edward. A. *The Gravest 366 Days: Editorials Reprinted from the* Evening Mail *of New York City*. New York: New York Evening Mail by the Throw Press, 1916.

"The Autobiography of Dr. Edward A. Rumely." Edited by Philip Morehouse McGarr. *Indiana Magazine of History* 66 (March, 1970): 1–39; (September, 1970): 197–237; 67 (March, 1971): 1–44.

Scheele, Leonard A.

July 25, 1907–January 8, 1993

Architect of mid-century America's foundations of biomedical research, education, and public health.

In mid-twentieth century America, the country faced the enormous challenge of providing science-based health care and preventive-health services to all its citizens. The responsibility for overseeing the response to national health needs, amid growing public expectations post-World

War II, fell to the Secretary of the Federal Security Agency (later the Department of Health and Human Services). In 1948 Secretary Oscar R. Ewing, from Greensburg, Indiana, recommended and President Harry S Truman accepted the appointment of Leonard A. Scheele for the position of U.S. Public Health Service Surgeon General, often called the "Nation's Doctor." This wise decision, with Scheele's adroit leadership, dramatically expanded the country's public and private sector capacity for quality biomedical research, health professions' education, health-care services, and public health.

Born on July 25, 1907, in Fort Wayne, Indiana, of parents with German and Swiss heritage, Scheele, an only child, was named after the famous physician Major General Leonard Wood, who commanded the Rough Riders during the Spanish-American War and played an important role in ending the dreaded yellow fever epidemics in Cuba. Scheele showed brilliance as a student at Central High School and was urged to become a doctor by his father, who worked at a pharmacy in Fort Wayne. Graduating from the University of Michigan and from the Detroit College of Medicine and Surgery, Scheele developed an interest in preventive medicine, and his historic career in public health began on July 2, 1934, when he received a commission as an assistant surgeon in the U.S. Public Health Service.

Scheele's research and leadership potential were soon recognized, and he was sent to New York City Memorial Hospital for Cancer and Allied Diseases, now Sloan-Kettering, to use the new field of epidemiology in research designed to find the cause of cancer. But his career was interrupted following the attack on Pearl Harbor, when New York mayor Fiorello H. LaGuardia assigned Scheele to the Office of Civilian Defense. From there Scheele was sent to the School of Military Government to learn how to reestablish governments in war-torn countries.

As General Dwight Eisenhower prepared for the invasion of Sicily and Italy, Scheele was sent on a top-secret mission to deliver plastic models of Sicily showing deployment of enemy soldiers and military targets. His public health skills were put to use in quelling a typhus outbreak in Naples, and, in 1944, Scheele was assigned to Eisenhower's Supreme Headquarters Allied Expeditionary Force, first in London and then in Versailles. Serving as chief medical officer of the Government Affairs and Public Health Section, Scheele was responsible for preserving health and preventing epidemics and civilian chaos at war's end. He debriefed Nazi physicians soon after Germany's surrender on May 7, 1945, and helped repatriate thousands of slave laborers. His final assignment was to attend the Potsdam Conference with General Lucius Clay. Eisenhower personally recognized Scheele's work in preventing typhus in the civilian populations of northwestern Europe, and he was awarded the U.S. Typhus Commission Medal for his innovations that saved thousands of lives.

On his return from Europe, Scheele was appointed director of the National Cancer Institute and associate director of the National Institutes of Health; on April 6, 1948, Truman appointed Scheele surgeon general, the youngest ever to hold the position. A tall man of pleasing and commanding appearance, Scheele had consummate administrative skills, and his quiet, thoughtful, and friendly demeanor, helped him develop excellent relationships with Congress and the public.

Scheele oversaw an unprecedented expansion of biomedical research and education. His public-health programs were varied and numerous. Following decades of research in the Midwest, including Indiana, Scheele approved on April 24, 1951, fluoridation of public drinking water. Other priorities included addressing the problems associated with aging, control of infectious diseases, research into smoking and lung cancer, and programs to control air and water pollution. He used the new medium of television to communicate with the American public.

Two accomplishments in particular shaped Scheele's legacy: the creation of new research institutes at the NIH and the introduction of Jonas Salk's polio vaccine. With the former, he demonstrated visionary leadership and with the latter, skills in managing a public health and political crisis.

From 1948 to 1956 Scheele oversaw the development of five new institutes at NIH, in collaboration with the visionary philanthropist, Mary Lasker. Following the creation of the National Heart Institute, National Institute of Dental Research, National Microbiological Institute, National Institute of Arthritis and Metabolic Diseases, and the National Institute of Neurological Diseases and Blindness, Scheele oversaw development of a landmark advance in clinical science: the 500-bed Clinical Center in Bethesda, Maryland, a world-renowned center for clinical research.

Scheele's skills in conflict management were put to the test with the controversy that erupted after the release of the Salk polio vaccine in 1955. There was intense public pressure to release the vaccine quickly, and a breakdown in testing procedures at one of the six pharmaceutical company production sites, created the "Cutter Incident." Some children who had received the Cutter Laboratory vaccine developed polio. Scheele immediately brought national leaders together and they quickly diagnosed and solved the problem, thus minimizing delay in vaccinating America's children. The effectiveness of Scheele's management of this politically explosive issue was recognized publically when Eisenhower reappointed Scheele as surgeon general.

By November 1955, children who had received Salk vaccine had 67 to 90 percent fewer paralytic polio attacks. In May 1956 Scheele and Salk addressed the American Medical Association and predicted that mass vaccination of children was the dream that, if realized, could lead to a "final conquest" of polio. The last cases of paralytic polio in the United States were reported in 1979.

Scheele retired from the Public Health Service in 1956 and another Indiana native, Leroy E. Burney, became surgeon general. Scheele became president of Warner-Lambert Research Institutes, but he was often called on to consult on national and international health issues. In 1962 Attorney General Robert Kennedy oversaw secret negotiations with Fidel Castro to release 1,180 prisoners held in Cuba following the April 17, 1961, U.S. invasion of Cuba at the Bay of Pigs. Kennedy met with Eugene Beesley of Eli Lilly, who represented the U.S. Pharmaceutical Manufacturer's Association, to gain its support for medical drugs- for- prisoners' exchange. A friend of both President John F. Kennedy and Robert F. Kennedy, Scheele was asked to meet with Castro to answer his questions about the drug inventory under review. Scheele joined the small negotiation team in Havana at a pivotal time, and their success was rewarded with the return of the prisoners; President Kennedy thanked Scheele for his "energetic and devoted participation in the rescue program."

When asked in 1989 by OTIS R. BOWEN, former Indiana governor and at time Secretary of the Department of Health and Human Services, to reflect upon his distinguished career, Scheele said three things gave him the greatest satisfaction: creation of the National Library of Medicine on NIH grounds, approval of the polio vaccine, and the building the Clinical Center at NIH.

At his death at eighty-five in 1993, scholars suggested that another legacy be added to this list: Scheele's raising the once obscure position of the U.S. Surgeon General to national and international prominence by speaking forcibly and clearly on the importance of science and public health in America. Scheele closely adhered to the adage: "Knowing is not enough; we must apply; Willing is not enough; we must do."

STEPHEN J. JAY

For Further Reading

Furman, Bess. "Surgeon General Leonard A. Scheele, 1948–1956." Bess Furman Papers, Modern Manuscripts Collection, History of Medicine Division, National Library of Medicine, Bethesda, MD.

Interview of Leonard Scheele by George Rosen, March 22, 1963. George Rosen Public Health Oral History Collection, National Library of Medicine.

Jay, Stephen J. "Leonard A. Scheele: Hoosier Sage of Science and Public Health." *Traces of Indiana and Midwestern History* 20, no. 4 (Fall 2008): 42–49.

Schweitzer, Ada Estelle

1872–June 2, 1951

Advocate for pre- and postnatal care of infants and head of Indiana's Division of Infant and Child Hygiene.

Ada Schweitzer, leading proponent of pre- and postnatal care of infants and positive eugenics, was born in Lagrange County, Indiana in 1872. After attending Michigan State Normal College, and subsequently teaching for several years, Schweitzer entered Indiana University's medical college. She graduated in 1902 and soon began the work that would be her legacy to the state.

Schweitzer had studied bacteriology while in medical school, with a special emphasis on diseases that affected pregnant women and their babies. Not only did her work lead to opportunities to speak and present at national conferences about the subject, but it also led to a job at the Indiana State Laboratory. Here, she studied the impact of diseases such as malaria, typhoid fever, and diphtheria in the state, but also expressed an interested in the spread and prevention of "social diseases." It was here as well that she caught the attention of the very influential Doctor JOHN HURTY, who, in 1906, gave her a platform from which to work for nearly a quarter of a century.

Hurty, secretary of the state board of health from 1896 to 1922, was a leading advocate of progressive reforms (both medicinal and political) as well as a eugenicist. Indeed, the reforms he advocated married well with the "science of the well born," including helping to craft the historic eugenic sterilization law in 1907. While it is likely that Schweitzer had encountered both strains of reformist thought before, it was under Hurty that they were encouraged to blossom and where "hygiene" was able to take on a reformist connotation to address societal ills in her work. Originally tasked with pediatric infectious diseases, by the 1910s Schweitzer became focused on children's health. She believed that better babies could be produced by better rearing as well as "superior breeding" by the wellborn. And she soon became the state's leading advocate for such a cause.

Early twentieth-century Indiana was home to a host of public-health initiatives keyed to eugenics. For Schweitzer, reading the reports and findings generated by Hurty and his allies, especially those from the Eugenics Records Office and the Indiana Committee on Mental Defectives, seemed to indicate that many poor, rural Hoosiers were living in squalor and rearing children unprepared both intellectually and physically for the demands of the modern world. While some might see in such reports the need for sterilization, Schweitzer saw a chance for education and to increase the health of the oft-maligned poor, while also showcasing the middle-class values she embodied. As head of Indiana's Division of Infant and Child Hygiene, created in part from state and federal grants, Schweitzer had the perfect platform from which to act.

Starting in 1920, the state board of health, under Schweitzer's direction, sponsored a Better Babies Contest at the Indiana State Fair. The goal was to help educate the public, especially parents, about raising healthier children. For twelve years the contests were a popular and well-publicized part of the fair. Babies were separated into groups based on age, sex, and place of residence. Doctors looked over the entrants—all adorned in matching togas—and ranked the babies. They were then rated by development, height, weight, mental aptitude, and checked over by a team of doctors and nurses, all with standardized forms to be filled out, which might be crossed-checked with forms that parents had to fill out as part of the enrolling process, generating a record used not only for judging, but also for the families of the contestants. Although scores were kept high, comments on the health of each child was medically accurate. Under Schweitzer's close scrutiny, the contests were run fairly and with a good deal of precision year in and year out.

There were benefits to the Better Babies idea, among them that infant mortality in Indiana dropped considerably. That being said, Schweitzer was also a firm believer in what later scholars labeled as negative eugenics, including advocating for limiting the procreation rights of some Hoosiers, as well as tightening marriage laws to prevent the breeding of "any person who is not well born." The very notion of breeding and judging babies, as if they were another category of species to be viewed at the State Fair, was not lost on either supporters or detractors of the contests. Likewise, the Better Babies contests tended to exclude both African American and immigrant babies. Indeed, the contests helped go a long way in normalizing the very concept of eugenics for many Hoosiers.

Schweitzer used her time at the state board to write extensively about the topic of children's health. Among her writings include "Infant Conservation" (1919), "Child Hygiene and the Doctor" (1920), "Vitamins and Health" (1928), and "A Doctor Looks at a Child's Teeth" (1932). These were in addition to various "notes from the field" as well as her own pamphlet writing for the Better Baby contests. She was considered among the leading experts in the field and did not confine herself merely to the State Fair, traveling the state speaking to civic groups and meetings across Indiana making the case for better pediatric care. Schweitzer also spearheaded "mothers' classes," reaching thousands of pregnant Hoosier moms-to-be with her message of the importance of prenatal and baby care.

Her career largely came to an end because of the Great Depression and the shift in both Indiana's politics and economy. A staunch Republican, Schweitzer found herself out of a job shortly after the Democratic administration of Paul V. McNutt came to power in 1933. She largely faded from public view, devoting more time to the Methodist

Church and less time to her signature reforms. The Better Baby Contests also did not survive the Depression. In many respects a pioneering woman in the field of public health, Schweitzer died in June 1951. Her legacy of promoting better health for infants and mothers, influenced as it was by eugenics, continued on.

JASON S. LANTZER

For Further Reading

Huerter, Mary Elise. "Prenatal Screening: Quality Control and the Genetics Gateway." Master's thesis, Indiana University, 2007.

Stern, Alexandra Minna. "'We Cannot Make a Silk Purse Out of a Sow's Ear': Eugenics in the Hoosier Heartland." *Indiana Magazine of History* 103 (March 2007): 3–38.

Scott, William Edouard

March 11, 1884–May 16, 1964

Noted African American artist, muralist, and portrait painter.

William Edouard Scott was once described "as a Rembrandt of race artists, a master wielder of brush and pen, whose love of beauty and high ideals are apparent in every one of his master pieces" He is best known for his portraits, murals and Haitian scenes. He sought to portray African Americans in a positive and uplifting way, in an effort "to perpetuate a type of painting and create racial pride."

Scott was born in Indianapolis in 1884, the son of Caroline Russell and Edouard Miles Scott, who worked in a wholesale grocery business. William studied art at Manual Training High School under OTTO STARK, one of the five famous impressionist painters known as the Hoosier Group. After graduating from Manual he returned to assist Stark in the art department. In 1904 Scott enrolled at the Art Institute of Chicago, where he began painting some of his famous murals.

Scott was awarded the Frederick Magnus Brand Prize for $50, which he used to support his first trip to France. He became closely associated with Henry O. Tanner, an acclaimed African American painter who left the United States to escape racial prejudice. Tanner encouraged Scott's interest in blacks as subject matter. Scott returned to Chicago, where he exhibited and sold some of his artwork but returned to France two other times.

He studied at the Académie Julian and the Colarossi Académie. In 1912 and 1913 he had paintings accepted at the Salon de la Societe des Artists Francais in Paris and at the Royal Academy in London. Scott's work in France focused on scenes that emphasized peasant life, a direct influence of Tanner. Two of his most famous French works were painted at Étaples, Tanner's summer home. One of those, *La Misèrie* (1913), was awarded the Tanqueray Prize of 125 francs. Another of the paintings, *Rainy Night, Étaples* (1912), was purchased by the John Herron Art Institute and is now at the Indianapolis Museum of Art.

With the outbreak of World War I, Scott returned to the United States. He painted numerous murals in Chicago and Indianapolis. In 1915 Booker T. Washington invited Scott to visit Tuskegee Institute. While there he painted several portraits of Washington. Years later he combined a portrait of Washington with George Washington Carver, famous for his work at Tuskegee with peanuts and sweet potatoes. One art historian observed "by placing these two prominent African Americans in the same portrait, Scott emphasized the importance of working together for the betterment of the black population." Scott painted more than thirty portraits of prominent black Americans including a posthumous portrait of Frederick Douglass, social reformer, orator and abolitionist leader. One of Scott's most famous murals features Douglass. Entitled *Douglass Appealing to Lincoln*, Scott painted it when he was chosen in 1943 as one of seven artists in a juried contest for the Recorder of Deeds building in Washington, D.C. Scott was the only black artist among the finalists. A noted art historian said that Scott's numerous murals "allowed black people, for the first time in the history of American culture, to see themselves through the eyes of their own artists."

Highlighting pride in the race was also evident in a series of murals illustrating seventy-five years of black history Scott completed for the 1940 American Negro Exposition in Chicago. Some of the titles of the murals were *Haiti; Negro Congressmen*, depicting the seven post-Civil War congressmen; and *One Way Out*, featuring Washington, Carver, and philanthropist Julius Rosenwald. Although he was not black, Rosenwald, former president of Sears Roebuck and Company, had donated millions of dollars to support the education of southern black children. Ernest L. Heitkamp, art editor and critic, said that Scott's canvases for the exposition "showed that the Negro, against crushing odds, had fought his way from poverty to an honored place."

In 1931 Scott began perhaps his most important artistic journey when he was awarded the Julius Rosenwald Fellowship to study subjects in Haiti. There he painted more than a hundred works, capturing the essence of the nation's people, culture, and landscape. In *Night Fishing in Haiti* (1931), which shows five Haitian men hoisting a turtle into a small fishing boat, the influence of Tanner is apparent in its use of color and light. *Haitian Market* (1950) reflects one of Tanner's favorite Haitian subjects—the colorful market.

Scott received warm praise by Haitians for his work. L. H. Dorrett, director general of the Bureau of Professional Instruction, wrote a letter to Scott saying that because of him hundreds of Haitian schoolchildren were given the "opportunity to see how every one of the few who draw in Haiti may find in our beautiful nature an inexhaustible sources of inspiration." Haitian painter Antoine Derencourt hoped that "following the example of this master of our own race, our local artists will leave off in the future copying views of Venice and of Fountaine-bleau, etc., and go and set up their easel right before Nature." Haitian President Stenio Vincent purchased several of Scott's paintings and awarded him the distinction of "Officer in the National Order Honneur of Merite," an honor equal to that of the French Legion of Honor.

Although known mainly for creating portraits, murals, and genre scenes, Scott also illustrated several covers for *The Crisis*, the magazine of the National Association for the Advancement of Colored People. W. E. B. DuBois, founder of the NAACP and editor of *The Crisis,* commissioned Scott to paint a cover for the Easter 1918 issue. *Indianapolis Star* art critic columnist Louise E. Morehouse described that painting, *Lead Kindly Light*, as "one of Scott's most poignant issues." It portrays two figures in a wagon driven by the man with his wife's head on his shoulders. The picture conveys black struggles in their "constant search for a better life."

Scott made one last trip outside the United States, to Mexico, in 1955. There he hoped to replicate his Haitian experience by painting rural scenes. However, failing health forced him to return home. He suffered from diabetes, had a leg amputated, and had impaired vision. He died in Chicago on May 15, 1964. He was survived by his wife, Esther, and his only daughter, Joan.

Scott's artistic legacy is enormous as testified by the numerous portraits, murals, and genre scenes that are displayed throughout the United States in schools, public buildings, art galleries, and museums. The most significant aspect of his work is the emphasis on the black condition and the achievements of African Americans, and for this he became known as "the Dean of Negro artists."

Several years after Scott's death, his daughter, Joan Scott Wallace, paid tribute to her father: "By painting African Americans like George Washington Carver and Booker T. Washington, he taught me about people who would have been in a course on African-American history if there had been one when I was growing up. It was part of his saying, 'These are all your people. Look at the barriers they had; see how they rose above them.' That was his philosophy—rise above the barriers."

KISHA TANDY

For Further Reading

Hardman, Della Brown. "William Edouard Scott Remembered: Lessons from a Remarkable Life." PhD diss., Kent State University, 1994.

William Edouard Scott Collection. Vivian G. Harsh Research Collection of Afro-American History and Literature. Woodson Regional Library, Chicago Public Library, Chicago, IL.

———. Schomburg Center for Research in Black Culture. NewYork Public Library, New York, NY.

Taylor, William E., Harriet G. Warkel, and John Geiser. *A Shared Heritage*. Indianapolis: Indianapolis Museum of Art, 1996.

Sewall, May Wright
May 27, 1844–July 22, 1920

Educator, women's rights pioneer, and peace activist.

While preparing for classes one day on the third floor at Indianapolis High School, later to become Shortridge, a teacher who had come to the city with her husband in the 1870s was interrupted by a distinguished visitor: ZERALDA WALLACE, widow of Governor David Wallace and president of the Woman's Christian Temperance Union's Indiana chapter. Wallace had come to the school to ask the teacher, May Wright Sewall, to sign a petition in favor of temperance that Wallace planned on presenting to the state legislature.

As Sewall prepared to add her name to the document, her eye caught some words indicating

May Wright Sewall

that those who signed did not intend to "clamor" for any additional civil or political rights. "But I do clamor," Sewall exclaimed to Wallace. Throwing the paper on the floor, Sewall stalked out of the room, "vexed in soul that I had been dragged down three flights of stairs to see one more proof of the degree to which honorable women love to humiliate themselves before men for sweet favor's sake." Sewall's anger at Wallace faded over time, and the two joined forces to found the Indianapolis Equal Suffrage Society. The Society came about in large part due to the "open contempt" showed to Wallace by Hoosier legislators when she attempted to present her temperance petition to the Indiana General Assembly.

To ensure that women's voices would indeed be heard by those in power, Sewall worked tirelessly on behalf of rights for women in the United States—and around the world—during the late nineteenth and early twentieth centuries. She served as an invaluable ally to such national suffrage leaders as Susan B. Anthony and Elizabeth Cady Stanton, and gave the woman's movement an international focus through her pioneering involvement with the International Council of Women and the American National Council of Women. By the turn of the twentieth century, *Harper's Bazaar* magazine claimed that Sewall had "an 'eternal feminine' following of 5,000,000 in eleven countries."

Her work on behalf of suffrage for women was just one of the many reform and cultural endeavors Sewall became involved in during her life. Described by one Indianapolis acquaintance as "a large woman of sturdy carriage," Sewall played a significant role in the cultural and social life of the capital city. At first with her second husband, the Harvard-educated Theodore Lovett Sewall, and later alone, she operated the influential Classical School for Girls, located on the southeast corner of Pennsylvania and Saint Joseph Streets. The private school provided hundreds of young women with the rigorous mental and physical training they needed in order to further their education in such respected institutions of higher learning as Vassar, Smith, Wellesley, and Mount Holyoke. Sewall championed reform not only for what women were taught, but also for what they wore, advocating a "simple school dress" that enabled her students to participate in physical fitness exercises, including daily gymnastics.

The Sewalls' residence served as a cultural showcase for the city, hosting a variety of nationally known literary and political figures. Every Wednesday in the home's drawing room approximately one hundred to two hundred people of all types gathered to discuss the issues of the day. "This salon is distinctively the social and literary centre of all Indiana, and, for that matter, many a distinguished sojourner from antipodal parts had enjoyed this rare hospitality," noted *Harper's Bazaar*. Another journalist who visited the house's library marveled over the fact that more "schemes for social progress have been conceived in this room . . . than in any other room on this continent." A bold statement, but not surprising considering Sewall enriched the city's intellectual life through her efforts to form such organizations as the Indianapolis Woman's Club, the Art Association of Indianapolis (the forerunner of the Indianapolis Museum of Art), the Indianapolis Propylaeum, the Contemporary Club, the Ramabai Circle (a group working to aid women in India), the Alliance Francaise, and the Indiana branch of the Western Association of Collegiate Alumnae. No less an authority on life in Indianapolis than BOOTH TARKINGTON boldly claimed that in company with BENJAMIN HARRISON and JAMES WHITCOMB RILEY, Sewall would have been selected as one of the city's three most prominent citizens.

Efforts by Sewall to improve life for people were not merely parochial in nature, but international as well. In addition to lecturing widely across the United States on behalf of women's rights, she also strove to win people's support for another cause: world peace, an effort she called her "absorbing ideal." Following the motto "My country is the world, my countrymen are all mankind," Sewall promoted the cause of peace through membership in the American Peace Society and through her work with both the National Council of Women and the International Council of Women, both of which adopted peace programs after intense lobbying by Sewall.

Sewall's work for the peace movement came to a climax in November 1915 when automobile tycoon Henry Ford asked Sewall to join him and others interested in securing an end to the war that had engulfed Europe. Sewall became one of sixty delegates to join Ford aboard the *Oscar II*, which sailed for Norway in hopes of getting the boys out of the trenches before Christmas. The Ford expedition failed, however, and World War I dragged on until American intervention helped to turn the tide for the Allies. But Sewall's other numerous local, national, and international achievements won her a well-deserved reputation for possessing the "organizing touch." In a sketch of her work for the *Indianapolis Sentinel*, a reporter noted that Sewall had "a faculty for getting people to work together and setting them at work in useful lines—a sort of social clockmaker who gets human machinery into shape, winds it up and sets it to running."

Fellow suffragists viewed their colleague as a common-sense woman. Unbeknownst to all but a handful of friends, however, Sewall led a secret life—one involving communicating with loved ones after their deaths. Left "stunned and desolate" by her husband's death from tuberculosis in 1895, Sewall attempted to forget her grief through work, especially her responsibilities at the Classical School for Girls and on behalf of world peace. Her journey into the spiritual world began two years after her husband's death while attending a Chautauqua meeting at a Spiritualist retreat located in Lily Dale, New York.

Until her death on July 22, 1920, Sewall claimed to be in almost constant contact with her dead husband, who told her to be very cautious in revealing her discovery to others as they would not believe her experiences of life after death. The few people to whom she related her fantastical adventures with the spiritual world were unanimous in their belief that their friend was suffering from a mental delusion. Sewall related her remarkable time with spiritualism in her book *Neither Dead nor Sleeping*, published by Bobbs-Merrill of Indianapolis in 1920 just a few months before her death.

RAY E. BOOMHOWER

For Further Reading

Letters and other documents about Sewall and her life can be found at the Indianapolis–Marion County Public Library and the Indiana Division at the Indiana State Library.

Boomhower, Ray E. *Fighting for Equality: A Life of May Wright Sewall*. Indianapolis: Indiana Historical Society Press, 2007.

Hale, Hester Anne. "May Wright Sewall: Avowed Feminist." Indiana Historical Society William Henry Smith Memorial Library, Indianapolis, IN.

Stephens, Barbara Jane. "May Wright Sewall (1844–1920)." PhD diss., Ball State University, 1977.

Sharp, Zerna

August 12, 1889–June 17, 1991

Educator, creator of *Dick and Jane*, and editor of popular reading series for grade-school children.

Zerna Addis Sharp had a long reach in time and space and in setting standards as an American author, writer, and teacher. As creator of the *Dick and Jane* beginning readers, her texts were mainstays throughout the United States and in many other English-speaking countries for nearly forty years. Though replaced as reading texts in most schools today by demands for standards-based literacy competencies and redefinitions of family and economic units, Sharp's *Dick and Jane* series remains in the minds of many as a definer of the American Dream middle-class family composed of a father, mother, three children, a dog and cat, and, of course, a teddy bear.

A lifetime Hoosier, Sharp was born in Hillsburg in Clinton County on August 12, 1889. Described by biographers as a highly intelligent and beautiful woman, she was also a person with convictions developed from her year of teacher training at Marion Normal School and several years in Indiana classrooms. Sharp recognized that textbooks for children were full of words and no pictures, and she firmly believed that children could learn to read more easily if they identified with other children through pictures and stories from their own experiences. With these ideas she incorporated her formula of repetitions into a pattern: Introduce a new word, "Run, Spot, run!" or "See, Jump, Oh," on one page and repeat it three times or more by the third page. Over and over the pattern was used to introduce new words and stories and to reinforce vocabulary growth.

Convinced of the correctness of her approach, Sharp arranged an interview with Doctor William S. Gray, a reading expert renowned for his scientific approach to learning to read and who served as director of the Curriculum Foundation Series for Scott, Foresman and Company. Sharp must have been very convincing because Gray hired her to develop a family of characters around which to mold her approach with his own ideas for the process of learning to read. Thus, was born the perception of the American family that lasted decades.

Although Sharp is often called the "Mother of *Dick and Jane*," she was not the author or illustrator of the series. She was, however, very much the designer of both format and content that she believed enabled youngsters to read. Rather than writing and illustrating any of the *Dick and Jane* stories as far as they are known today, Sharp chose stories from storylines submitted by others, named the characters, and supervised the layouts and illustrations—including clothing, toys, and settings—as the reading text took shape and the textbook series grew. The large watercolor pictures teamed with key words carried the storyline throughout the texts. The clothing styles and toys were actually copied from Sears and Roebuck and Montgomery Ward catalogs. Most important to the process, she was careful to check the authenticity of the language patterns and vocabulary by observing children at play.

The textbooks held a monopoly in the beginning readers market for many decades. The *Dick and Jane* series first appeared in schools in 1930 and, by the 1950s, 80 percent of first graders in the United States learned to read with the series. Although the texts held a monopoly in classrooms for many decades, critics emerged during the 1960s to point out stereotypes and errors. No longer was the family unit and economic status typical of the majority of U.S. homes, and critics began asking troublesome questions: "Were Mother and Jane subservient to Father and Dick?" Gradually the texts were replaced by other content and learning approaches that tended to feature literary-styled stories. Being very proud of her *Dick and Jane* family, Sharp was outraged with the criticisms.

Gradually, the *Dick and Jane* readers disappeared from schools as the adopted reading texts. Sharp retired to travel and remain active as an educator, but she still visited the Scott Foresman offices. She returned to her roots in Indiana to make her last home in Frankfort, where she died in a nursing home on June 17, 1981, at the age of ninety-one. She was buried in a local cemetery. As a Clinton County citizen, Sharp is recognized by the local historical society as "one who has made a significant impact on society." Although *Dick and Jane* readers are no longer used in today's classrooms, the pattern that Sharp designed for early readers remains today as a guide for more recent authors of children's early literature.

CLAUDIA C. CRUMP

For Further Reading

Clinton County Historical Society and Museum. http://srv1.geetel.net/~cchsm/zerna/htm.

Kismaric, Carole, and Marvin Heiferman, *Growing Up with Dick and Jane: Learning and Living the American Dream*. New York: Collins Publishers, 1996.

TagNwag Books and Bears. http://www.tagnwag.com/dick_jane/.

Treaster, Joseph B. "Zerna Sharp, 91, Dies in Indiana; Originated 'Dick and Jane' Texts." *New York Times*, June 19, 1981.

Shaw, Wilbur

October 31, 1902–October 30, 1954

Racecar driver, three-time winner of the Indianapolis 500, and president of the Indianapolis Motor Speedway.

Had it not been for Wilbur Shaw, the Indianapolis Motor Speedway most likely would not exist today. The three-time winner of the Indianapolis 500-Mile Race (1937, 1939, and 1940), and arguably the most successful American driver of the first half of the twentieth century, Shaw almost single-handedly saved the track from extinction following World War II.

Born Warren Wilbur Shaw in Shelbyville, Indiana, on October 31, 1902, he spent his formative years being shuttled back and forth between Shelbyville and Greensburg, Indiana, eventually settling in Indianapolis while still in his teens. Between 1927 and 1941 Shaw had thirteen starts in the Indianapolis 500, winning three times (including being the first to win in consecutive years), finishing second three times, and leading for a total of 508 laps, which more than seventy years after his last start still ranked him fifth all-time.

A number of Shaw's early races at the Speedway were almost worthy of hall of fame consideration before he ever won for the first time. He had a substantial lead in 1932 when a broken rear axle knocked him out with just over a hundred miles remaining. In 1933 he finished second, and he co-drove the car that finished third in 1934. In 1935 he was second again, driving a car that he had helped construct in Los Angeles with builder Myron Stevens. Shaw and Stevens built another car for 1936, and appeared well on the way to victory when its futuristic streamlined body became dislodged from its moorings, requiring two lengthy pit stops, and dropping them to seventh at the finish.

In 1937, driving the same car on a brutally hot day, Shaw managed to overcome late race fuel-pressure problems to nurse his car home to victory by a mere 2.16 seconds over Ralph Hepburn. With riding mechanics no longer required for 1938, Shaw drove the streamliner again as a single-seater and finished second. In 1939 and 1940 he became the first person to win in consecutive years driving a straight-eight dual-supercharged Italian Maserati grand prix car.

In 1941 Shaw appeared headed to a third consecutive victory (and fourth overall) when his right-rear wire wheel collapsed going into turn one on the 152nd lap, causing him to hit the wall tail-first and severely injuring his back. The start of the race had been postponed by approximately two hours due to a major fire in the garage area. Days before the race, Shaw had been balancing wheels, chalking the letters "OK" on each tire after completing his inspections. When one wheel presented some difficulty, Shaw chalked on the tire "OK—USE LAST." While never proven, Shaw always contended that water from hoses during the fire might have washed off the chalk lettering, permitting the offending wheel to be inadvertently placed on the right rear of his car.

In another memorable mishap, Shaw, as a relief driver in 1931 for owner Fred Duesenberg, was involved in a multicar tangle and hit the turn three outer wall with such force that the car leapt over the wall and landed on the grassy bank on the other side. Amazingly, Shaw and his riding mechanic were not injured and he returned to the race as a relief driver in an identically painted team car (except for the number). A friend of Shaw's who was a riding mechanic in another car, fearing for his friend's life after seeing him go over the wall, was astounded some time later when seeing him go roaring by in what appeared to be the same car.

With all of automobile racing curtailed during World War II, Shaw took a job in Akron, Ohio, as manager of Firestone Tire and Rubber Company's Aviation Division. The company, heavily involved at the time in developing a new synthetic rubber tire it planned to introduce soon to the public for highway driving, was granted special permission by the government to test this new product at the IMS. The initial phase of the test was very basic, consisting of several passenger cars being driven around the two-and-a-half-mile track at moderate speeds, but on November 29, 1944, a considerably more vigorous test was conducted, with Shaw driving a race car on a solo 500-mile run and averaging approximately 100 mph.

Shaw was appalled by the deplorable conditions at the facility. It was still under the stewardship of World War I flying ace Eddie Rickenbacker, who drove in pre-World War I Indianapolis 500 races before ever learning to fly. During World War I, the track's infield had served as an aviation repair depot for the military, but when Rickenbacker offered the facility to the government for similar purposes in early 1942, it was determined it could not accommodate the considerably more advanced aircraft of the time. Rickenbacker promptly shut everything down and when Shaw came to visit the Speedway resembled an abandoned army post. Weeds grew up through cracks in the track's surface and the infield had been overgrown into a virtual jungle to the point that locals believed the track would be razed after the war to make way for a housing development.

Shaw quickly headed for New York to meet with Rickenbacker, who was now, among other things, head of Eastern Airlines. Although Rickenbacker claimed he planned to reopen the

Wilbur Shaw drove this Maserati to victory at the 1939 Indianapolis 500.

track as soon as the hostilities ended, Shaw also determined that the facility might be for sale for about $700,000. He immediately began trying to raise the money, seeing himself as the principal investor along with twenty partners who would put up $25,000 apiece. Although his proposal attracted some interest, Shaw eventually decided another approach would be necessary.

One of his colleagues during his very early dirt-track racing days was Homer Cochran, who had long since retired from racing and had become a successful real-estate broker. Cochran told Shaw about ANTON "TONY" HULMAN JR. of Terre Haute, with whom he had been involved in several real-estate deals. Sometime in the fall of 1945, Shaw and Cochran drove to Terre Haute to meet with Hulman. Shaw was delighted to learn that Hulman was very familiar with both him and the 500-Mile Race, and expressed fond memories of having gone to the track many time as a boy with his father. Hulman was intrigued by the fact that the track was for sale, and that it could be Hoosier owned. In rapid order, negotiations took place at the Indianapolis Athletic Club on November 14, 1945, and the track officially changed hands, with Hulman becoming the owner, Shaw installed as president and general manager, and T. E. "Pop" Myers, the longtime beloved general manager, named vice president.

The Hulman and Shaw pairing was considered an ideal mix because while Hulman was exceedingly shy and retiring and not very well known in Indianapolis, the positively dynamic and charismatic five-foot, seven-inch Shaw was universally known and respected. For the next several years, the always-dapper Shaw tended to be the front man, while Hulman, who insisted on being called Tony, was happy to remain in the wings.

On the evening of October 30, 1954, Shaw was returning home from a trip to Detroit, where he had tested an automobile for an upcoming magazine article, when the small private aircraft in which he was flying encountered difficulties near Decatur, Indiana, and went down, killing all those aboard. Shaw had been quite intent on getting home because the following day would be his fifty-second birthday. He was survived by his wife, Catherine, and his ten-year-old son, Billy. Tributes and floral displays came in from all over the world. Shaw was buried in Vernon, Indiana, just yards from where his widow had been raised.

DONALD DAVIDSON

For Further Reading

Fox, Jack C. *The Illustrated History of the Indianapolis 500*. Madison, IN: C. Hungness Publishing, 1994.

Popely, Rick, and L. Spencer Riggs. *Indianapolis 500 Chronicle*. Lincolnwood, IL: Publications International, 1998.

Shaw, Wilbur. *Gentlemen, Start Your Engines*. New York: Coward-McCann, 1955.

Shepherd, Jean

July 26, 1921–October 16, 1999

Writer, broadcaster, storyteller, and humorist.

Like fellow Hoosier humorist GEORGE ADE, Jean Parker Shepherd was a master of limning the lives of everyday midwesterners in words. He was a consummate storyteller in print and on the air. His fictionalized tales of life growing up in Indiana often seemed more truthful than reality to many fans. Some of his characters, such as young Ralphie Parker, his family, and friends, have become almost iconic, especially during the Christmas season.

Shepherd was born in Chicago in 1921, but his family moved to the Hammond, Indiana, area when he was young. His father was an office worker for Borden Milk Company, but Hammond was a blue-collar mill town. It was from Hammond that Shepherd drew many of his later fictional characters. He worked a series of menial jobs around Hammond, including a brief stint as mail boy in a steel mill. He joined the U.S. Army in 1942 and was assigned to the Signal Corps (he was a licensed ham radio operator at sixteen), and the army also became a source for many of Shepherd's short stories and monologues.

After the war, when he may or may have not attended college, Shepherd began his radio career at WKRC in Cincinnati in 1948. Fired from that station for talking too much between records, he moved to rival station WSAI later in that year. He also did brief stints on television. He then became a radio nomad, moving to Philadelphia, where he worked from 1951 to 1953. He returned to Cincinnati, taking a job at radio powerhouse WLW. Shepherd found both his radio niche and home when he joined WOR in New York City in 1956.

It was at WOR that Shepherd connected with his core audience he called "the night people." To the iconoclastic Shepherd, the world was divided into the conformist "day people" and nonconformist "night people." His twenty-one years at WOR were the jumping off point for other areas in his career. It was there he honed his superb skills as a storyteller, regaling listeners with tales that had such a ring of truth that they thought he was recounting actual events in his life. He developed a cult following, where, as *Publishers Weekly* noted, "Railing against conformity, he forged a unique bond with his loyal listeners."

Shepherd's writing career partly grew out of a literary hoax. After fulminating against those who took polls and lists too seriously, in 1956 he and his listeners concocted a nonexistent book called *I, Libertine*, supposedly written by a British author who was an authority on eighteenth-century erotica. Shepherd's "night people" flooded bookstores with requests for the "book." The satiric effort was so successful that the "book" made it to the best-seller list (at that time requests for a book were added to actual sales to create the lists). Because of the demand, the "book" was actually published and sold more than 200,000 copies. Shepherd provided the outline of the book, but the majority was written by science fiction writer Theodore Sturgeon.

Shepherd began writing short stories and articles mainly based on his childhood and army stories. His work appeared in a wide range of publications, including *Mad Magazine, Field and Stream, Mademoiselle*, and *Playboy*. It was the later collections of these stories beginning in 1966, particularly *In God We Trust: All Others Pay Cash* and *Wanda Hickey's Night of Golden Memories*, that brought widespread fame to Shepherd and led to his most enduring work.

The stories from *In God We Trust* were the main source of the 1983 film *A Christmas Story*. Shepherd collaborated on the story and screenplay. But equally important to the film's success was Shepherd's narration of the film. His droll, knowing voice added great depth to the movie by hinting at the harsher elements of childhood embedded in the seemingly lighthearted yarn. Initially considered a sleeper movie when released, the film found its audience when it began appearing on television. It has since become as much a part of Christmas as Bing Crosby or *Rudolph the Red Nosed Reindeer*, with one network often staging twenty-four hour marathons of the movie. For many it is not Christmas until they see the story of Ralphie Parker's Christmas travails in northern Indiana.

The success of the film led to further work for Shepherd in television. He played the adult Ralph in a television movie, *Ollie Hoopnoodle's Haven of Bliss*, and appeared in productions on PBS and Showtime, among others. In 1985 he began a thirteen-part series on PBS called *Jean Shepherd's America*, featuring his quirky look at American life and culture.

A lifelong jazz devotee, Shepherd's stream of conscious storytelling may be likened to the improvisation inherent in that art form. Shepherd could be an enigmatic, often difficult person. As with many of his tales and characters, there seemed to be a wistfulness and sadness lurking just under his humor. He would hint at the truth of his life, but never quite confirm it. One longtime friend noted that "trying to make a point with Shep was useless: he entertained no ideas other than his own." He could be aloof, mysterious, and an extremely inward person. He played little role in the lives of his two children from his (perhaps) second marriage, Adrian and Randall. He had little to do with his children after his 1957 divorce. In fact, Randall was quoted in Shepherd's obituary as saying he was not even aware that his father had been married to actress Lois Nettleton, whom Shepherd had met when appearing on Broadway. Shepherd was married for the third or fourth time in 1977, this time to his agent-producer Leigh Brown. Their marriage lasted until her death in 1998

Shepherd died in Florida on October 16, 1999. He had inspired many with his storytelling and style of humor, including Garrison Keillor and Jerry Seinfeld. His legacy is a rich one and he is regarded as one of the finest storytellers of the twentieth century.

TIM CRUMRIN

For Further Reading

Bergman, Eugene. *Excelsior, You Fathead: The Art and Enigma of Jean Shepherd*. New York: Hal Leonard Corporation 2005.

Grant, Ed. "The Heyday and Dark Nights of Jean Shepherd." *Time*, June 11, 2001.

Ramrez, Anthony. "Jean Shepherd, a Raconteur of Radio, Dies in Florida." *New York Times*, October 17, 1999.

Paley Center for Media. "Remembering Master Storyteller, Jean Shepherd: With Jerry Seinfeld." Recorded January 23, 2012. http://www.paleycenter.org/2012-spring-remembering-master-storyteller-jean-shepherd-with-jerry-seinfeld-and-keith-olbermann

Shriner, Herb

May 29, 1918–April 23, 1970

Television and radio humorist, storyteller, and Broadway performer.

As a harmonica-playing, homespun entertainer often billed as "the Hoosier Humorist," Herb Shriner drew national attention to both himself and his adopted home state with a multimedia career that peaked during the 1950s. On network television variety and quiz shows, as well as during countless appearances across the country at state fairs, festivals, and civic events, Shriner told yarns about a small, mythical hometown designed to typify Everytown USA in an easy-going, low-key style considered reminiscent of Will Rogers.

"I was born in Ohio, but I came to Indiana as soon as I heard about it" was a favorite line of Shriner, a native of Toledo who moved to Fort Wayne as a young child with his mother. He became a fixture of early television as the host of programs such as *The Herb Shriner Show* and *Herb Shriner Time* as well as a popular quiz program, *Two for the Money* (1952–56), which served as a vehicle for Shriner's quips and yarns that often involved a "small town Indiana" theme. "Hoosiers are congenitally inquisitive," went one remark. "That means nosy, in a nice sort of way." A typical line about his mythical hometown: "Back home, we had a beauty contest once, and nobody won."

Although he grew up in Fort Wayne and his rise in radio also began in the state's second largest city, Shriner seldom referred to it by name; instead, much of his humor pivoted on the notion that his hometown was miniscule. Even so, he invariably identified himself as a Hoosier during his performances, typically depicting the state as being inhabited by folksy types such as himself. Indiana is so peaceful, he once remarked, "if you dropped an atom bomb on it, the bomb would just lay there and grow." During Shriner's rather fleeting heyday on network television in the 1950s, he hovered just a few rungs below fellow Hoosier entertainer RED SKELTON and was nominated for two Emmy Awards in consecutive years as Best Comedian. The decade of his greatest triumphs was bracketed by significant success on radio and Broadway in the late 1940s and, for the final decade of his life, steady bookings as an after-dinner speaker or comedian at civic events and concerts across the country. However, during the ten years before his tragic death at age fifty-one in a car crash in 1970, he almost vanished from network television, making only a handful of appearances on variety shows.

Throughout his career, which began during the 1930s on WOWO Radio in Fort Wayne, Shriner often was promoted as "Harmonica Herb." For two generations of children, he established harmonica clubs across the country, furnishing them with "how-to" kits; by some accounts, he helped teach a 100,000 boys and girls how to play the instrument.

As a child in Fort Wayne, Shriner began playing the harmonica in a band at his elementary school. On WOWO Radio and at barn dances, church socials, and other gatherings across northeastern Indiana, the lanky, sandy-haired entertainer landed enough steady gigs that he dropped out of Central High School as a junior at age seventeen. He crisscrossed the country as part of a harmonica quintet, then auditioned for—and was picked up in 1940 by—network radio in New York City as a monologist and harmonica player. His career leaped forward with regular appearances on *The Camel Caravan*, a CBS Radio variety show that featured singers and orchestras.

During World War II, Shriner performed in USO shows for troops stationed in Europe, alternating harmonica playing with his yarns, told in deadpan style. His humor rarely was confrontational or political, but Shriner enjoyed great success with a zinger told during his World War II service: "The mail service in our unit is very good. The mailman delivers packages to us as fast as he can smash them."

Following the war, he reaped increasing popularity as a regular on various network radio series and with a nightclub act. His big break came when he was cast in *Inside USA*, a lavish musical revue that opened on Broadway in 1948. The anecdotes he told between musical numbers brought down the house, were credited with the show's yearlong run, and resulted in offers to headline regular series in radio and early television. The *Herb Shriner Show* aired on CBS-TV five times per week beginning in 1949; each show lasted only five minutes, just long enough for the host to tell a couple of Hoosier tales and play a harmonica number. It meant that for much of 1948 and 1949 he was performing in eight shows on Broadway a week as well as in five radio or television shows, for which he wrote his own material.

Although the initial *Herb Shriner Show* on CBS was short-lived, it was followed by *Herb Shriner Time* on ABC-TV amid a major national publicity splash in 1951. He also appeared as a guest on most of the top television shows of the era, from variety programs such as *The Ed Sullivan Show* to panel shows such as *What's My Line?* as a mystery guest. He also served as a substitute host for *Arthur Godfrey's Talent Scouts*.

Shriner's popularity was such that in 1953 he was cast in *Main Street to Broadway*, a movie about backstage doings in which more than a dozen major Broadway stars appeared as themselves. The quiz show *Two for the Money* was built around Shriner's strengths as a folksy storyteller, much the way the popular series *You Bet Your Life* had been launched earlier as a showcase for the wisecracks of its host, Groucho Marx. Before the low-key competition between contestants on *Two for the Money*, each show featured a monologue by Shriner, who shared a "small-town Indiana" story or two.

In his adopted home state, some Hoosiers objected to Shriner's tales, feeling that they depicted the state's residents as provincial, with the *Fort Wayne Journal-Gazette* reporting complaints about his "Shrinerisms." He occasionally explained that his "small town" jokes were derived, not from Fort Wayne, but from his forays into nearby communities such as Montpelier, Leo, Monroeville, and Wabash. In any case, most Hoosiers apparently were more amused than offended; Shriner regularly returned to Indiana for successful appearances before business groups, trade associations, and local celebrations. During summer vacations from *Two for the Money*, he also performed in Las Vegas and cut an album for Columbia Records.

Shriner's final regular network television series, *The Herb Shriner Show*, a musical variety program on CBS-TV that featured top-name guests such as actor-director Orson Welles, was abruptly canceled in late 1956. The subsequent, rather swift, drop off of his television stardom was attributed to several factors, including changes in popular culture. By the early 1960s, the bow-tied, straight-laced "Hoosier Humorist" and his homespun style were not considered enticing to younger viewers. Some sources, however, indicate that Shriner, disillusioned by the cancellation, soured on California-based show business and deliberately refocused his career. In 1960 he moved his family to Fort Lauderdale, Florida, so he could indulge his lifelong fascination with the sea. (The Shriners spent their summers at a lakeside cottage near Angola, Indiana.) He continued to enjoy steady work across the country as an after-dinner speaker and as a storyteller at concerts and fairs.

Shriner and his wife, Pixie, were killed when his restored vintage car, an Indiana-made Studebaker, crashed into a palm tree in Florida as he was returning home from a business meeting. Amid much publicity in the early 1950s, the Shriners had given their children names that reflected his Hoosier heritage: They had a daughter named Indiana (known as "Indy") and a son, Kin, named in honor of Abe Martin creator FRANK MCKINNEY "KIN" HUBBARD. Kin Shriner became a soap opera actor; his twin brother, Wil (named for Will Rogers, but with one l), became a comedian, television director, and a talk show host with a laid-back style reminiscent of his father.

NELSON PRICE

For Further Reading

Blue, John S. *Hoosier Wit and Wisdom*. Rensselaer, IN: Published by author, 1985.

Brooks, Tim, and Earle Marsh. *The Complete Directory to Prime Time Network and Cable TV Shows, 1946–Present*. 8th rev. ed. New York: Ballantine Books, 1977.

Price, Nelson. "The Life of Indiana Funnyman Herb Shriner." *Traces of Indiana and Midwestern History* 16, no. 1 (Winter 2004): 16–27.

Shulz, Ada Walter

October 21, 1870–May 2, 1928

Artist, painter in Brown County Art Colony, and first wife of Adolph Robert Shulz.

When she first arrived in Nashville, Indiana, in 1908, artist Ada Walter Shulz saw something more than picturesque landscapes, for which the early Brown County Art Colony painters were known. She saw rural children playing outdoors in barnyards, shallow creeks, and sunlit meadows. And she felt inspired to paint them.

Ada Walter, a native of Terre Haute, Indiana, had been raised by her mother and grandmother after her father's untimely death when she was three years old. Her mother moved the family to Indianapolis in 1884, where Ada had the good fortune to attend Shortridge High School, then known as Indianapolis High School, and study with art teacher Roda Selleck. Ada's younger brother died the year she graduated, and she and her mother then moved to Chicago. For the next four years she studied at the Art Institute.

Ada's mother, her staunchest supporter, died in early 1892. The following summer, the young artist took an outdoor sketching class in Delavan, Wisconsin, taught by the Chicago Art Institute's John Vanderpoel and Charles Edward Boutwood, with help from Delavan artist, Adolph Robert Shulz. Adolph took a special interest in Ada, and when she returned to Chicago a discreet courtship developed. Their wedding in September 1894 surprised Adolph's colleagues.

Only a few days after their marriage, the Shulzes sailed to France. While Adolph enrolled in the Académie Julian and in the Académie Colarossi, Ada entered the new art school, Académie Vitti, which allowed women students. She studied under Luc Olivier Merson and Raphael Collin, receiving a bronze medal for the best figure drawing. In the spring of 1895, the Shulzes exchanged Paris for Munich, Germany, where they set up a studio and awaited the arrival of their first and only child, Walter, born on June 10, 1895. Three months later, Ada and her husband brought their son back to Delavan, Wisconsin.

Ada devoted herself to being a wife and mother during her first decade of parenthood. While Adolph supported the family by teaching art and occasionally selling his landscape paintings, Ada took care of the household. When Walter was almost ten, Ada began to paint again, sending her paintings to Chicago art galleries. She later wrote: "children and sunlight were the two words that were always ringing in my ears—would they not bring joy to the heart if painted right?" She was encouraged by the sales of two of her paintings to pursue her artwork more seriously.

Unhappy with the encroaching dairy farms in Delavan, Adolph took an exploratory trip to Brown County, Indiana, after reading a small newspaper article about it in 1900. Upon returning from a sketching trip in 1907, he praised his newly discovered painting grounds to Chicago artist friends, and brought his family to Nashville, Indiana, in the summer of 1908.

Encouraged by welcoming lodging accommodations and the newly built railroad through the northwest corner of the county, other curious artists made the trip from nearby cities, and eventually many of them chose to settle permanently in Nashville. From 1908 until 1917 the Shulzes wintered in Delavan while Walter attended school. He enrolled in the Art Institute of Chicago in the fall of 1913, and he and his parents displayed a family exhibition at the Milwaukee Art Society the following year.

Each summer the three returned to Nashville, where they stayed at the Pittman Inn, painting and socializing with the growing community of artists. Liberated from domestic chores, Ada found time to paint the people of Brown County. For her concentrated efforts she enjoyed significant recognition. She won a Chicago Art Institute award for *The Picture Book* in 1916 and the Chicago Art League purchase prize in 1917 for *Mother and Child*. With both Shulzes' growing success, they were able to buy land on the northeast side of Nashville in 1917.

The couple relocated to Brown County to oversee the construction of their new home on Hoop Pole Ridge, and Walter embarked on a late spring rafting trip down Salt Creek. But he then traveled back to Chicago, where he impulsively enlisted in the U.S. Army without notifying his parents. After surviving trench warfare in the Sixteenth Infantry of the First Division in France, he contracted diphtheria while on leave to sketch in the German countryside. He died on December 12, 1918.

Ada found solace in her faith and community involvement. She had helped organize Nashville's Christian Science Society, and worked to establish the Brown County Public Library in 1919. In 1926 both Ada and Adolph were founding members of the Brown County Art Gallery, where they showed artwork in the gallery's semiannual shows.

In addition to their success in marketing locally, the Shulzes always exhibited in the Hoosier Salon annual exhibitions, beginning in 1925. Ada's paintings, *Mother from the Hills* and *The Pet Duck*, won prizes in 1926 and 1928, respectively. The Shulzes were also both associate members of the Chicago chapter of the Society of Western Artists, a national organization that organized an annual yearlong traveling exhibition.

The only time Ada painted outside Brown County after their move from Delevan was during a trip she and Adolph took to Monticello, Florida, during the winter of 1920–21. True to her penchant for seeking out women and children, she painted canvases of black nannies with white children.

In 1921 a young woman named Alberta Rehm appeared in Brown County with a small infant and a professed desire to learn how to paint. Adolph agreed to be the young woman's art instructor, eventually allowing her and her child to move into the Shulzes' home. Three years later, Adolph and Alberta moved into a new cabin and studio on the east side of North State Road 135.

Living alone on Hoop Pole Ridge, Ada threw herself into her art with renewed vigor. She took it upon herself to create renditions of all the existing log cabins in Brown County, an unrealized goal, and painted more landscapes in 1924 than in any other year.

After her divorce from Adolph was finalized in September 1926, Ada concentrated on her newfound subject niche of children with barnyard pets. Her solo exhibition at the Milwaukee Journal Gallery of Wisconsin Art from March 5 to 31, 1928, proved to be Ada's last. By mid-April an undiagnosed illness prevented daily activity, and she died May 2, at age fifty-eight.

Ada Shulz's artwork is inherently autobiographical, portraying the people and places that populated her world. Without sentimentalizing her subjects, she painted rural people doing things they enjoyed in natural settings. True to her Christian Science philosophy of painting only uplifting images, she left a legacy of work reflecting the simple joys and freedoms of childhood.

RACHEL BERENSON PERRY

For Further Reading

Newton, Judith Vale, and Carol Ann Weiss. *Skirting the Issue: Stories of Indiana's Historical Women Artists*. Indianapolis: Indiana Historical Society, 2004.

Perry, Rachel Berenson. *Children from the Hills: The Life and Work of Ada Walter Shulz*. Nashville, IN: Artist Colony Press, 2001.

Shulz, Adolph Robert. "The Story of the Brown County Art Colony." *Indiana Magazine of History* 33 (December 4, 1935): 282–89.

Simon, Melvin

October 21, 1926–September 16, 2009

Founded Melvin Simon and Associates, which became Simon Property Group Inc., a worldwide leader in mall development, leasing, and management.

Today, millions of Americans do it every day without a second thought. They drive or walk or take public transportation to the mall. Once there they will encounter a kaleidoscope of shops, restaurants, and entertainment options under one roof. Many will return to the same malls their parents took them to when they were children.

It was not always this way, of course. Returning World War II servicemen and women came back to a commercial landscape filled with stores and markets located in downtowns. But soon, a transplanted New Yorker who had been stationed with the U.S. Army at Fort Benjamin Harrison on Indianapolis's east side would change shopping patterns and a way of life for an entire nation.

Melvin Simon was a pioneer, blazing a path with malls. By 2014 Simon Property Group, the public company that resulted from his vision, was a global leader in retail real estate with an interest in more than 325 retail real-estate properties in North America, Asia, and Europe.

Simon arrived in central Indiana shortly after receiving a bachelor's degree in accounting from the City College of New York. His ticket to the Hoosier State was his enlistment in the army, reporting to work in the finance office at Fort Benjamin Harrison. When his military obligation ended, Melvin stayed in Indianapolis and married. He worked for Albert J. Frankel, an Indianapolis real-estate developer, as a leasing agent for Frankel's Eastgate Shopping Mall.

In 1960 Simon founded Melvin Simon and Associates. Later that year, MSA completed its first fully owned shopping center, Southgate Plaza in Bloomington, Indiana. Four years later, MSA opened Mounds Mall in Anderson and College Mall in Bloomington, Indiana's first enclosed malls, each about 400,000 square feet of space.

By the end of 1967, the company owned and operated more than three million square feet of retail space and was opening new facilities at a rate of more than one million square feet annually. Towne East Square opened in Wichita, Kansas, in 1975, becoming the company's first enclosed mall of more than one million square feet.

By the early 1980s, Simon was opening as many as three or more enclosed malls each year. The company's development portfolio contained a healthy balance of regional malls and open-air community shopping centers.

Melvin and his brother, Herbert, provided the catalyst for the transformation of the state's capital city with the development of Circle Centre Mall, an 800,000-square foot retail and entertainment complex in the heart of downtown Indianapolis. This project demonstrated one of Melvin's hallmark qualities, perseverance, as he marshaled a group of private and public entities to execute his vision, which took nearly fifteen years to complete. In November 1992, more than a decade after initial planning for a downtown mall had begun, the city of Indianapolis began construction on parking garages that would be part of Circle Centre. From its opening day in September 1995, this urban mall has lived up to its promise of becoming a crown jewel of a city that had already established a reputation as a world-class destination. Circle Centre has been recognized throughout the country as a successful model of the marriage of public and private resources and the impact a successful downtown project can have on a city's vitality, continued economic development, and tourism appeal.

Melvin developed another signature property that remade the retail landscape when the landmark the Forum Shops at Caesars opened in Las Vegas in May 1992. This 670,000 square foot, anchorless center was erected between Caesars Palace and the Mirage hotels. Inside, visitors see a stunning re-creation of a Roman streetscape, complete with Roman village storefronts, magnificent statues, fountains, and piazzas.

Since its debut, the Forum Shops at Caesars has gone through numerous expansions, but it is still the hub of luxury fashion in Las Vegas, if not the entire country. On a sales-per-square-foot measure, the property is at the top of all U.S. shopping centers.

In December 1993, Melvin's son, David, led efforts that transformed the firm into a public company with a nearly $1 billion initial public offering, which at the time was the largest IPO in the country's history. The company, now known as Simon Property Group, began trading under the symbol "SPG." Less than ten years later, SPG was added to the S&P 500 Index and in 2012 became the first real estate company in the S&P 100.

In addition to his business successes, Melvin was a benefactor to a wide array of charitable, political, and civic organizations. He and Herb purchased the downtrodden National Basketball Association's Indiana Pacers in 1983, saving them from possible relocation to another city and built the team into a model franchise. In their first year at the downtown Indianapolis arena that has frequently been recognized as the top venue in the league for watching basketball, the Pacers reached the NBA finals, falling to the Los Angeles Lakers in six games.

Melvin and his family also donated generously to educational and health-related causes as well, often benefiting Indiana University. Simon Hall, a life sciences building, was dedicated on the Bloomington campus in 2007. A transformative gift of $50 million supported expansion of the IU Melvin and Bren Simon Cancer Center as well as funding cancer research. The Bess Meshulam Simon Music and Recital Center opened at the Jacobs School of Music in 1995. Other gifts include the Reading Room at the Indianapolis Public Library's Central Library in downtown Indianapolis and the Riley Hospital for Children Simon Family Tower at IU Health.

Simon also earned his fair share of distinctions, including Jewish Welfare Federation's "Man of the Year," The Horatio Alger Award, and induction into the Central Indiana Business Hall of Fame. In 2003 he was named a lifetime trustee of the Urban Land Institute and was a former trustee of the International Council of Shopping Centers. He was inducted into the Indiana Academy in 2007, a recognition bestowed by Indiana's private colleges and universities. Simon held honorary doctorates from IU's School of Business and Butler University, and was a member of the Real Estate Legends Hall of Fame housed at the School of Urban Planning and Development at the University of Southern California.

In an editorial after his death, the *Indianapolis Star* wrote: "To a society grown all too cynical about business, Mel Simon provided a living reminder that it's possible to do well with an idea and a handshake. To those who were privileged to shake his hand, he taught the obligation to do good. From the city's skyline to the news and sports pages to the good news that will be delivered to generations of cancer patients, his spirit will be ever-present."

LES MORRIS

For Further Reading

Carberry, Sonja. "Melvin Simon's Hustle Brought Bustle to Malls." *Investors.com*, June 23, 2011. http://news.investors.com/management-leaders-in-success/062311-576258-melvin-simons-hustle-brought-bustle-to-malls.htm?Ntt=it.

Martin, Douglas. "Melvin Simon, Pioneer of the Suburban Mall, Dies at 82." *New York Times*, September 18, 2009.

"Mel and Herb Simon—Mall Developers, Owners of the Indiana Pacers." *Indianapolis Star*, June 2004.

Sissle, Noble Lee
July 10, 1889–December 17, 1975

Musician, playwright, composer, arranger, bandleader, and vocalist.

Noble Sissle's career encompassed almost every aspect of the musical world—composer, songwriter, bandleader, playwright, and vaudeville performer. He is probably most famous for his collaboration with Eubie Blake, another African American musician, with whom he wrote several songs and musicals that achieved wide acclaim. Sissle's music was performed by leading singers of his day, including Lena Horne, Sophie Tucker, and Josephine Baker.

Born in Indianapolis, Sissle seemed to have music in his blood from birth. His mother, Martha Scott Sissle, not only worked both as a teacher and probation officer, but also spent a good deal of time nurturing her son's interest in the arts. She began his piano lessons by the time he was six years old. Sissle's love of music and singing blossomed from that time on. Noble's father, Reverend George Sissle, was pastor of Simpson Methodist Episcopal Chapel. Through elementary and high school, Noble gained quite a reputation for his singing, songwriting, and musical idealism. While attending Shortridge High School, Noble worked as an office boy for Doctor Sumner Furnace, a well-known black Indianapolis physician. In 1906 the family moved to Cleveland, Ohio, where Noble completed high school. The family returned to Indianapolis in 1913 after the death of Reverend Sissle.

The combination of family financial pressures and the desire to attend college caused Sissle to launch his professional career in his teenage years. One of his first "gigs" was with the Redpath Jubilee Quartet. He attended DePauw University for one semester in the fall of 1913, earning a total of three credits in German, math, and gym. He transferred to Butler College in Indianapolis for the 1914–15 school year. While at Butler he wrote at least two yells for the football team and was a song leader at athletic events.

Sissle's reputation as a singer, lyricist, and entertainer spread throughout the Midwest. The owner of the Severin Hotel in Indianapolis, in spite of the segregated nature of the city, hired him to form a dance band to perform at the hotel. The future looked very bright until the United

States' entry into World War I. Thousands of young Americans, including Sissle, volunteered for military service. Fortunately, he became a major part of the James Reece Military Band, which played for troops in the war zone. Reports of the bands actual involvement in fighting may be exaggerated. In a letter from Sissle to Ben Holliman, noted Indianapolis musician, he said:

> Boy, I guess you read about the bombardment on the 14th of July. Well, all I can say is that all the noise that fireworks ever made would be just the same as a cap pistol going off in comparison to the rumbling of cannons on that night. I am in the band, thank God, and we were not right up in the thick of it, but the big shells from the big Boche guns were bursting all around us. I went up on a hill where I could see the whole front for miles both directions.

Much of Sissle's success was based on partnerships and coproductions. He teamed with Blake, a brilliant pianist and composer. In 1921 this union led to the creation of the musical *Shuffle Along*. Written and produced by Sissle, Blake, Flournoy Miller, and Aubrey Lyle, the musical marked the revival of African American folk humor, jazz dance, and ragtime. The public had become enamored with dancing of all types, a fact that led to huge crowds at the performances of *Shuffle Along*. Many of the five hundred performances of the musical broke new ground by appearing on Broadway in New York City.

Shuffle Along served as a beacon to other talented blacks interested in the theater. It introduced such performers as Florence Mills and Baker. Soon, both became famous performers in the United States and abroad. Following the success of *Shuffle Along*, Sissle and Blake continued their success with 1924's *Chocolate Dandies*. The songs of Sissle and Blake were so infectious that they danced across the color line to find their way to the lips of Americans of every kind, especially the songs "Love Will Find a Way" and "You Were Meant for Me." White performers took note of the captivating songs being written by the two black entertainers. Tucker, who had a reputation for being a maverick, sang "It's All Your Fault," a Sissle and Blake song, in one of her shows. "You Were Meant for Me" became known from shore to shore because two stars of the theater, Gertrude Lawrence and Noel Coward, chose it as part of their repertoire. Sissle and Blake also wrote for two other well-known shows, *The Begère* and *The Brown–Skin Models*.

Sissle and Blake's vaudeville act helped to create a more dignified image of black performers. They were able to partially break down the segregated seating arrangements that prevailed in most theaters at the time by playing in theaters patronized by both races, instead of performing in theaters that catered mostly to blacks. They also refused to wear the blackface makeup that was common for both black and white minstrel performers of their day.

One of the most durable Sissle and Blake songs was "I'm Just Wild about Harry." Following the death in office of President Franklin D. Roosevelt in the spring of 1945, the unknown, unsung, Vice President Harry S Truman became President of the United States. The country was at war, plans for use of the atomic bomb were on the table, and Truman was thought to be too inexperienced to lead the country during this time of great adversity. The years until the 1948 presidential election were filled with more difficult decisions for Truman. In an attempt to

Noble Sissle

increase his name recognition during the election campaign, the Truman campaign decided that the song, "I'm Just Wild about Harry" was just what was needed to get voters to support their candidate. Truman's victory over Thomas E. Dewey, governor of New York, is considered one of the greatest political upsets in history.

Sissle continued writing and performing into the 1960s. He died in 1975 in Tampa, Florida, at the age of eighty-six. He is buried at the Long Island Veterans National Cemetery. The contributions of Noble Sissle and the Negro Actors Guild, of which Sissle was organizer and first president, have provided an immeasurable source of inspiration to musical theater in the United States and abroad.

STANLEY WARREN

For Further Reading

Ambrose, Stephen. *To America*. New York: Simon and Shuster, 2002.
Schiedt, Duncan. *The Jazz State of Indiana*. Pittsboro IN: Published by author, 1977.
Southern, Eileen. *The Music of Black Americans*. New York: W. W. Norton and Company, 1971.

Skelton, Richard "Red"

July 18, 1913–September 17, 1997

Popular comedian of stage, screen, radio, and television.

The most pivotal public statement this man-child ever made was, "That's my trouble. If you want a good story—talk to me. If you want the facts—talk to Edna [Skelton's first wife and writer/manager]." Skelton was the product of such a dysfunctional Vincennes, Indiana, family that his talent for and need to create "a good story" or cover applied equally to his private and professional life. Indeed, he took this protective trait to such an extreme I titled my second biography of him, *Red Skelton: The Mask behind the Mask* (2008).

Skelton carried the burden of being born to a prostitute named Lillian from his paternal grandmother Ella Cochran's brothel in Washington, Indiana, a small town near Vincennes. The prostitute doubled as the mistress of the comedian's father, Joseph, who fluctuated between using the surnames of Skelton and Ehart, the monikers of Ella's first two husbands. Joseph's wife, Ida Mae, who was credited on Red's birth certificate with being his biological mother, had also been pregnant at the time but her child was stillborn. After Lillian either died in childbirth or committed suicide (stories vary), Ida Mae received Skelton as a replacement child.

Red's father, a Vincennes grocer and frequently jailed roughneck, died less than two months before the comedian's birth, presumably from alcoholism. Widowed Ida Mae was frequently forced to work multiple jobs, which left little supervision for Red and his three older half-brothers, who often bullied him for being an outsider. His difficult childhood was only made bearable by a knack for making people laugh, such as clowning in the streets for pennies, but it was really attention and love he was after. Later on he would claim his father was an "internationally famous clown"; while there is *no* evidence, why not fill a blank spot with a unique father? Skelton's revisionist history helped make an embarrassing family tree go away.

Even the alleged catalyst for Red becoming a clown was puffed up. A vaudevillian passing through Vincennes treated the impoverished boy with a pass and the youngster was mesmerized by the show. Though that part is probably true, it was only years later Red said the entertainer was the

Red Skelton

legendary comedian Ed Wynn, who was then coincidently appearing on Skelton's television program. However, during the period in which young Red had his career epiphany, Wynn was nowhere near Vincennes. The most prominent visiting vaudevillian to fit Red's timeframe would have been the lesser known comic Raymond Hitchcock. Remember, though, the Rosetta Stone to understanding Skelton is to gild the facts—all in the spirit of telling a better story. To paraphrase Hoosier humorist FRANK MCKINNEY "KIN" HUBBARD, via his Abe Martin character, "It's pretty hard to be interesting without embellishing the truth a little."

Regardless, young Red did have surrogate father figures, with the most important being Clarence "Professor" Stout, who wore several entertainment hats, from being a pit musician at Vincennes's Pantheon Theatre to leading a summer Midwest touring company, Stout's Minstrel Follies. He also wrote songs, one of which, the dark comedy number "Death Where Is Thy Sting," was featured in Broadway's *Ziegfeld Follies of 1919*.

Though Skelton later claimed to have run off from home as a child to join the circus, Stout's Follies was Skelton's first taste of on-stage local fame, which occurred in 1929. Prior to this he had also periodically worked for "Doc" Lewis's summer medicine show, where he learned his *key* comedy lesson—pratfalls are *funny*. In an innocent attempt to merely bring "Doc" some "medicine" bottles, the boy's accidental fall produced such laughter that Lewis kept it in his con-artist routine; but since bottles had been broken, "Doc" had the "medicine" safely stored offstage *before* Red's slapstick!

After leaving Vincennes around 1930 to become an entertainer, Skelton met and married another teenager, Edna Stillwell, in 1931. Red was performing in grade-Z burlesque and Edna was a vaudeville usherette, with Skelton always hanging around, hoping to be a last-minute substitute. Initially, she did not find him funny, since he often depended upon old joke books; but after their marriage, her writing, more than anything else, made Red into a vaudeville star. Starting with a sketch on the many ways people dunk donuts, and culminating with the "Guzzler's Gin" routine (the basis for Lucille Ball's much later "Vitameatavegamin" sketch), Skelton was a headlining vaudeville star by the mid-1930s.

This eventually led to Skelton becoming a major Metro-Goldwyn-Mayer 1940s movie star, patterned after Paramount's Bob Hope persona. This new type of antihero fluctuated between cowardly incompetent and cool, egotistical wise guy. Skelton's breakout film, *Whistling in the Dark* (1941, with two sequels), was a parody horror film like Hope's career changing *The Cat and the Canary* (1939) and *The Ghost Breakers* (1940). The Hope-Skelton link was so successful that NBC put the popular Hoosier's new radio show, starting in 1941, on the air following the Hope program.

Unfortunately, MGM did not give its clowns the creative freedom of Hope's comic studio, Paramount, and Skelton was unhappy with the situation. Though he had at least one classic MGM picture, *The Southern Yankee* (1948, with the behind-the-screen help of Buster Keaton), Skelton was more interested in jumping to the new medium of vaudeville in a box—television. As with his radio show, Skelton would also control his television program; and for the next twenty years (1951 to 1971), with characters such as his tramp Freddie the Freeloader and his Hoosier hayseed Clem Kaddlehopper, he became a pioneering television star, as important as *I Love Lucy*'s Ball and *The Honeymooners*'s Jackie Gleason.

After having a hit television program on longer than anyone else during the medium's golden age of comedy, ranging from Milton "Mr. Television" Berle and Jack Benny, to the small screen innovator Ernie Kovacs, Skelton was an early victim of demographics. His top-ten ranked program was canceled because it appealed to an older, more rural, small-town audience, when corporate-driven networks were targeting a younger urban base. Skelton never got over his bitterness and refused to put his program into syndication. With this decision he destroyed his television legacy, because it translated into "out of sight, out of mind," with only the senior set now remembering his work.

Still, Skelton's career represented arguably the greatest cross-section of twentieth-century entertainment, including medicine shows, the circus, burlesque, depression-era walkathons and danceathons, vaudeville, radio, movies, television, and college concert dates—proving he could connect with younger audiences. His family was his fans, to whom he was so devoted, while his workaholic private life (including his success as a painter of clowns) was filled with travail (two more troubled marriages and the loss of a young son) and an ever-revised life story. Still, to paraphrase what he told me and many others, "I'm crazy but as long as I keep making money, they won't put me away." The man Groucho Marx felt was *the* comedian second only to the Hoosier's hero, Charlie Chaplin, was the stereotypical tragic clown.

WES GEHRING

For Further Reading

Gehring, Wes. *Red Skelton: The Mask behind the Mask.* Indianapolis: Indiana Historical Society Press, 2008.

———. *I, Red Skelton: Exit Laughing or a Man, His Movies and Sometimes His Monkeys.* Albany, GA: BearManor Press Fiction, 2011.

Hyatt, Wesley. *A Critical History of Television's* The Red Skelton Show, *1951–1971.* Jefferson, NC: McFarland and Company, 2004.

Smith, Walter Bedell

October 5, 1895–August 9, 1961

General, chief of staff for General Dwight D. Eisenhower, diplomat, and Central Intelligence Agency director.

As the lead car in the parade reached Monument Circle in Indianapolis late in the morning of June 20, 1945, a U.S. Army band swung into "Back Home Again in Indiana" and the crowd roared its welcome. More than fifty thousand people had turned out to view the victory parade, celebrating the end of World War II in Europe and honoring the man of the hour—native son and three-star general Walter Bedell Smith.

"Beetle" (or sometimes "Beedle") as he had been called since his teens, had distinguished himself for almost three years as chief of staff to General Dwight D. Eisenhower, during the Allies' campaigns through North Africa, Sicily, Italy, France, and Germany. He contributed much to the victory; Eisenhower called him "the general manager of the war."

Born in Indianapolis on October 5, 1895, to William Long Smith, a silk buyer for the Pettis Dry Goods Company, and Ida Frances Bedell, Walter grew up at 1713 Ashland (now Carrollton) Avenue. As a boy he was fascinated with things military, later recalling, "I always wanted to be an army officer; I never thought of anything else."

He achieved that goal, and more, but by a circuitous route. On his sixteenth birthday he joined the Indiana National Guard. Smith impressed his company officers and quickly earned promotions to corporal, sergeant, and to first sergeant at the age of eighteen. Graduating from Industrial Manual High School in 1913 with an undistinguished academic record, Smith applied to Butler University, but withdrew his application when he had to become the family's chief means of support after his father's health failed. Instead of going to college, he secured a job as a die maker at the Marion Railroad Company, continuing his National Guard drilling. Smith's principal biographer, D. K. R. Crosswell, described him as possessing "a first-rate intellect" and an "analytical and retentive mind," though apathetic about school.

In mid-1916, with World War I raging in Europe and the U.S. Army preparing to police the border with Mexico, the National Guard was federalized and expanded. Smith was assigned full time to the Indiana Guard's headquarters staff in Indianapolis. After the United States declared war on Germany in 1917, he received an army commission as a reserve officer. Also in 1917, Smith married Mary Eleanor "Nory" Cline of Indianapolis; they had no children.

In the spring of 1918, Smith's unit arrived in France and went into combat in mid-July. A second lieutenant in an infantry unit, he was wounded within thirty-six hours. Smith expected to return to his unit after convalescing. Instead, because of his staff experience at the Indiana Guard headquarters, he was assigned to the expanded General Staff of the War Department in Washington, D.C. In 1920 he received his regular army commission.

During the 1920s and 1930s Smith held staff positions at various posts, and at the U.S. Bureau of the Budget for four years. He also attended several army postgraduate schools. At Fort Benning's Infantry School, future generals Omar Bradley and George C. Marshall were much impressed with Captain Smith. Although he had not attended college, Smith demonstrated what Bradley recalled as an "absolutely brilliant and analytical mind."

In 1939, with Marshall now army chief of staff, Major Smith was appointed assistant secretary of the general staff and two years later its secretary. Shortly after Pearl Harbor, he began handling the same duties for the Anglo-American Combined Chiefs of Staff. It was from this position that Eisenhower selected him in September 1942. With the U.S. invasion of North Africa that November, Smith was a major general working for Eisenhower as chief of staff of the Anglo-American forces in North Africa and the Mediterranean.

In 1943, as Allied armies conquered Sicily then invaded Italy and advanced up the Italian boot, Smith remained at Eisenhower's side. He not only negotiated the difficult Italian surrender during a nine-hour marathon session in Lisbon, Portugal (a veteran British ambassador who was present considered Smith's performance "brilliant"), but he also signed the Italian armistice agreement for the Allies.

At the end of the year Eisenhower moved much of his staff to London to prepare for the invasion of France, with Smith in charge of planning. Following the successful Normandy landings in June 1944, they moved their headquarters to France to continue the drive eastward toward Germany. Eleven months later, on May 7, 1945, Lieutenant General Smith led the Allied team in Reims, France, accepting the German army's surrender. The *Indianapolis Star*'s lead editorial on the day of the parade six weeks later observed that although Smith held "the unique honor of a place in history" as the American representative at Germany's surrender, "far more notable was his staff work that speeded the victory of Allied arms."

Smith was well suited to serve as a senior staff officer. He was exceptionally bright and efficient, with a prodigious work ethic and a near-photographic memory. His written and oral presentations were models of clarity and succinctness. A few weeks after joining the army's general staff in 1939, it took Smith only three minutes to persuade Marshall and a roomful of skeptical generals to approve expenditure for a type of small truck to serve light transport needs. The army had already twice rejected the experimental vehicle; it would become well-known as the Jeep.

Smith was widely viewed by historians and contemporaries alike as "blunt, profane, and bad-tempered." One army officer called him "tougher than a 25-cent steak." He frequently suffered from ulcers. Smith's work as a staff officer also included a diplomatic touch. When working for Marshall in Washington, D.C., he served as the general's liaison officer to President Franklin D. Roosevelt's White House. As Eisenhower's top associate, Smith often found himself cultivating British officers (who generally held him in high regard) and mollifying French leader Charles de Gaulle. Prime Minister Winston Churchill referred to Smith, affectionately, as "the American bulldog."

Early in 1946 Smith was appointed American ambassador to the Soviet Union, where he served ably for three years but without much opportunity to impact significantly U.S.-Soviet relations. He took command of the U.S. First Army in New York in 1949, and the following year President Harry S Truman appointed him head of the fledgling Central Intelligence Agency. From 1950 to January 1953, Smith improved that agency's organization and helped ensure its permanent status through what later observers termed his "determination, personal prestige, and an understanding of the national security bureaucracy." While at the CIA Smith received his fourth star, becoming a full general in 1951.

In January 1953, frustrated that he had not become army chief of staff, Smith resigned from the army after thirty-six years as an officer. That same month he joined President Eisenhower's administration as Undersecretary of State, the number-two position in the department, and in 1954 headed the U.S. delegation to the international Geneva Conference on Indochina. There he helped bring the contesting parties toward

Walter Bedell Smith

a formal agreement that called for elections throughout all Vietnam in two years. But the United States was not a signatory to the settlement. Instead, the Eisenhower administration began to build up South Vietnam as an independent entity and declined to go along with the elections. Smith advised congressional leaders that communist leader Ho Chi Minh would have received 80 percent of the vote because of the Saigon government's perceived corruption and connection with French imperialism.

Also laden with far-reaching consequences was the administration's practice of overthrowing foreign governments. Smith successfully managed the coup that used the CIA to topple the elected president of Guatemala in June 1954. The year before he had played an important role in employing CIA operatives in Iran to oust the government of Mohammed Mossadegh, an event that continues to bedevil U.S.-Iranian relations today. The short-run success of both coups helped set the stage for another such attempt in 1960–61, the ill-fated Bay of Pigs operation in Cuba.

In October 1954, in ill health, Smith retired from government service. He died on August 9, 1961, at the age of sixty-five, and was buried in Arlington National Cemetery near the grave of his mentor and idol, Marshall.

RICHARD HUME WERKING

For Further Reading

Crosswell, D. K. R. *Beetle: The Life of General Walter Bedell Smith*. Lexington: University of Kentucky Press, 2010.

———. *The Chief of Staff: The Military Career of General Walter Bedell Smith*. Westport, CT: Praeger, 1991.

Montague, Ludwell L. *General Walter Bedell Smith as Director of Central Intelligence*. University Park: Penn State University Press, 1992.

Snyder, William P. "Walter Bedell Smith: Eisenhower's Chief of Staff," *Military Affairs* (April 1984): 6–14.

Sorin, Edward Frederick

February 6, 1814–October 31, 1893

Priest, missionary, educator, founder and first president of the University of Notre Dame.

Late in the morning of April 23, 1879, fire engulfed the Main Building of the University of Notre Dame, leaving the domed heart of the campus, as well as four nearby buildings, in smoking ruins. The inferno erased the labor of decades, and the blow to the young school might have been mortal—dormitories, library, infirmary, classrooms, all gone—with insurance sufficient to cover but a fraction of the $200,000 loss. Instead, the school's indomitable president and founder, Father Edward Sorin, transformed this moment of heartbreak into the catalyst for a new beginning. Rallying his devastated community to the nearby Sacred Heart church, the sixty-five-year-old Sorin committed himself to immediate rebuilding, thundering, "If it were ALL gone, I should not give up!" And, by the start of the same year's fall term, a new, larger and far more elaborate edifice replaced that lost in the fire.

Single-minded determination in the service of Catholic education was the characteristic quality of Sorin's career as priest and missionary. His family background undoubtedly shaped the devotion that marked his later life. Born in the hamlet of La Roche in the French province of Mayenne, he was the seventh of nine children in a devout Catholic household. The Sorin family, while not of the high aristocracy, was nonetheless distinguished in the vicinity, and had won some renown for courage in sheltering hunted priests at the height of the French Revolution's anticlerical persecutions.

Educated from the age of five by the parish priest, Sorin as a child already showed the combination of charisma and domineering will that marked his later undertakings in the New World. "Of the five of us, Edward Sorin was always first," one of his schoolmates later recalled. "And he knew how to profit by it to boss the others. He was born for that."

As a young man studying for the priesthood at Le Mans, Sorin heard Simon Brute, the bishop of Vincennes in Indiana, who visited Sorin's seminary in 1836, plead for missionaries to serve the Indians and whites. Ordained a priest in 1838, Sorin in the following year met the Abbé Basile Moreau, the founder of the Congregation of the Holy Cross, the religious community that established and still maintains the University of Notre Dame. Sorin began his career in Catholic work in Indiana as Moreau's protégé in the Congregation, later becoming his superior's dogged adversary in administrative quarrels, and, eventually, succeeding the old abbé at the head of the congregation.

In August of 1841 Sorin led six fellow brothers across the Atlantic Ocean, bound for Indiana at the request of Moreau and the new Bishop of

Vincennes, Celestine de la Halandiere. Sorin's group first established a school at the parish of Saint Peter's, a community of fifty poor Catholic families around Black Oak Ridge, located west of Washington, D.C. However, the strong-willed Sorin quickly clashed with Halandiere, who quarreled with many of his clerical subordinates, over control of school administration.

It was in this context that Sorin received an offer of land in northern Indiana that was purchased earlier from the Indians by Father Stephen Badin, who intended it for some religious purpose. Sorin was only too happy to accept, and in November 1842, accompanied by four brothers, he arrived at the south bend of the Saint Joseph River, determined to establish a school along the lines of a French lycee, or elite high school. He named the new institution the University of Notre Dame du Lac, or the University of Our Lady of the Lake. Within a few years of its founding, Sorin had guided the underdeveloped campus of a few small buildings, "attended by no more than a half-dozen students, and staffed by a faculty only a few of whom spoke English with any facility," onto the path that would make it one of the world's premier institutions of Catholic higher education. During the next four decades Sorin exhibited a blend of entrepreneurship, sales know-how, pragmatic administrative flexibility, ruthlessness, and faith that established Notre Dame as a university of national repute.

Adopting American citizenship in 1850, Sorin embraced the entrepreneurial ethos of his adopted nation with gusto. He founded the "Manual Labor School" for Catholic boys. He peddled fifty years of daily Masses for fifty dollars to raise money for Sacred Heart church, built in 1869. He built kilns, made and sold for three dollars per thousand yellow bricks from the lime-rich beds of the local lakes, giving the campus its characteristic and unusual shade. He ingratiated himself with wealthy local dignitaries such as the STUDEBAKERS, wining and dining them with "lavish dinner parties." And he was a skilled and tireless diplomat, crossing the Atlantic nearly sixty times to maintain his connections with the hierarchy of the Catholic Church in Europe.

No expedient was overlooked by Sorin and his Holy Cross Brothers to raise money and the profile of his new school. He founded the Saint Joseph's Company in 1850 to prospect during the rush to California, dispatching four brothers to the far West in a failed search for gold. Determined that Notre Dame should have its own postal station, he solicited the help of elder statesman Henry Clay to overcome objections that Notre Dame was too close to South Bend to deserve its own postal office. Sorin got the post office, and he got the job of postmaster to add to his other posts. When typhus struck the community in the summer of 1854, infecting many and killing eighteen faculty and students, Sorin had the dead buried secretly at night to quell panic, and carried on with business as usual under circumstances "almost surreal."

Such single-mindedness produced results, although the decisive turn in Notre Dame's fortunes may have come with the arrival of the railroad at South Bend in 1851. Thereafter, enrollment grew steadily, flourishing in the post-Civil War decades to around four hundred students by the 1880s, and drawing what Sorin described as students "of a higher and more comfortable class."

The bullheadedness that ultimately ensured Sorin's success came with a price, however, most clearly in a series of acrimonious battles waged with his erstwhile mentor Moreau, battles in which Sorin's unscrupulous tactics sometimes assumed aspects of the Machiavellian. He waved off debts his superior claimed were owed to the order, he browbeat the old abbé with threats to resign and requests for release from his vows, he refused orders to take up mission appointments in India, declined to heed a call to return to France to offer explanations, and more. Ultimately, however, Sorin's strengths were too much for Moreau to compete with, and he was elected to replace the abbé as superior general of the order in 1868.

The resounding success of Sorin's undertaking at South Bend is beyond question his most noteworthy achievement, and by far his greatest contribution to the history of the Hoosier State, but he was also instrumental in the success of other significant ventures, both within Indiana and beyond. He was a collaborator with Eliza Marie Gillespie, who as Mother Angela led the foundation of what became Saint Mary's College. With her, he also began publication of the successful periodical *Ave Maria* in 1865. And, despite his commitments at Notre Dame, he also found time and energy late in life, in 1878, to journey to Austin, Texas, to found another Holy Cross college, Saint Edward's University.

Sorin turned the presidency of the University of Notre Dame du Lac over to Father Patrick Dillon in the year 1865, spending the following decades trying to cultivate the expansion of the Holy Cross and helping to promote and consolidate the gains of Notre Dame. The Golden Jubilee of his priesthood in 1888 brought progressive American leaders from all around the country to South Bend to fete his life and achievements with an extravagant celebration. His final years were marked by declining health, and he died on the eve of All Saints' Day in 1893.

DAVID MURPHY

For Further Reading

Hope, Arthur J., C.S.C. *Notre Dame: One Hundred Years*. Notre Dame, IN: University of Notre Dame Press, 1943.

O'Connell, Marvin R., C.S.C. *Edward Sorin*. Notre Dame, IN: University of Notre Dame Press, 2001.

Spruance, Raymond A.

July 3, 1886–December 13, 1969

Admiral, hero of the Battle of Midway, and ambassador.

Raymond Ames Spruance, described by his biographers as "the quiet warrior" and "the thinking man's admiral," was born in Baltimore, Maryland. His parents, Alexander and Annie Ames Hiss Spruance, were residents of Indianapolis, where his mother was an editor at Bobbs-Merrill Publishing and his father was a businessman. Annie had returned to her family home in Baltimore to give birth to Raymond, the first of her three sons.

By the time Raymond graduated from Indianapolis's Shortridge High School in 1902, his father was bankrupt. His mother was the family's sole breadwinner, and little money was available for college tuition. She decided that Raymond should attend the Naval Academy in Annapolis, Maryland, some thirty miles from Baltimore. There he would receive a good education at no cost to the family and be launched on a respectable career. Through her position at Bobbs-Merrill she had made influential contacts. To obtain for Raymond a congressional appointment to Annapolis, she sought help from Hoosier author Booth Tarkington and Harry S. New, *Indianapolis Journal* publisher and member of the Republican National Committee. Her determination was rewarded, and the appointment was obtained in May 1903.

Meanwhile, Spruance was attending Stevens Institute of Technology in Hoboken, New Jersey, living with his mother's relatives. There he had secured the offer of an appointment to the Naval Academy from New Jersey due to his stellar performance on a competitive examination sponsored by the local congressman. He preferred to accept it, having earned it himself. But he reluctantly acceded to the argument made by his mother's relatives that he must accept the Indiana appointment that Annie had worked hard to obtain. On July 2, one day before his seventeenth birthday, he took the midshipman's oath. Spruance graduated from the Academy in September 1906. Because America's growing navy was facing a shortage of officers, the upper one-third of the class of 1907 graduated nine months early. Spruance ranked twenty-fifth out of 209 midshipmen.

In the years following his graduation from the Academy, Spruance rose through the officer ranks. During the 1920s and 1930s his many duty assignments included three tours at the Naval War College in Newport, Rhode, Island, one as a senior student and two as a faculty member. Throughout his career he consistently impressed superiors,

Raymond Spruance

peers, and subordinates with his calm, knowledgeable, and thoughtful approach to decision making.

In 1915 he married Margaret Dean, also of Indianapolis. The couple had two children: son Edwin, who would follow his father to Annapolis and a naval career, and a daughter, also named Margaret.

In September 1941 Rear Admiral Spruance took command of a division of four heavy cruisers at Pearl Harbor, part of Vice Admiral William "Bull" Halsey's aircraft carrier taskforce built around the carrier USS *Enterprise*. On December 7 they were hundreds of miles away, delivering planes to the marine garrison on Wake Island, when the Japanese bombed the American fleet at Pearl Harbor. The only other carrier then deployed in the Pacific, USS *Lexington*, was on a similar mission to Midway Island and hence also escaped damage.

During subsequent weeks and months, the Japanese military and naval advance continued throughout Southeast Asia. With much of America's naval fleet destroyed or severely damaged, it would be months before the United States would be able to mount a sustained offensive.

In late May 1942, Halsey became ill and was hospitalized. He recommended Spruance as his replacement to head the taskforce, although the latter was a surface warfare officer and had never served on a carrier. But Spruance possessed those special qualities of intellect and temperament that made both Halsey and Admiral Chester Nimitz, the Pacific commander, consider him the logical choice. Spruance took command of a taskforce that included the carriers *Enterprise* and USS *Hornet*, and a number of supporting vessels.

Meanwhile, a large Japanese force of four carriers, plus battleships and other vessels, was moving against Midway Island, 1,300 miles west of Honolulu. Aware of the threat, thanks to his code breakers, and intending to surprise the Japanese, Nimitz ordered Spruance's task force, along with another commanded by Rear Admiral Frank J. Fletcher built around the carrier USS *Yorktown*, to a position north of Midway. On June 4, dive-bombers from the American carriers sank all four enemy carriers. When the *Yorktown* was severely damaged that afternoon, Spruance assumed tactical command of both taskforces. Exercising well-founded prudence, he chose not to pursue the still-formidable Japanese surface fleet that night, which would have put his ships at great risk. Excellent night fighters, the Japanese would almost certainly have inflicted serious, perhaps fatal, damage on the Americans and their two still-functioning carriers, whose planes would not have been effective in the darkness.

The Battle of Midway is generally considered the turning point of the Pacific war, and it brought to an emphatic conclusion Japan's six-month offensive. Henceforward American forces held the strategic initiative. Noted historian Samuel Eliot Morison provided his assessment: "Spruance's performance was superb. Calm, collected, decisive, yet receptive to advice; keeping in his mind the picture of widely disparate forces, yet boldly seizing every opening, Raymond A. Spruance emerged from the battle one of the greatest admirals in American naval history."

Immediately after the battle Spruance became Nimitz's chief of staff and principal adviser. In the summer of 1943, he took command of the Navy's "Big Blue Fleet" for the drive across the Central Pacific. In this capacity, over the next two years he oversaw the successful amphibious operations that conquered the Gilbert, Marshall, and Mariana Island chains, as well as Iwo Jima and Okinawa, often using the USS *Indianapolis* as his flagship. Had the Pacific fighting not ended in August 1945, he would have commanded the invasion of Japan itself, planned for November.

When Nimitz was promoted to Chief of Naval Operations later that year, Spruance took his place as Commander in Chief, Pacific Ocean Area. The next year he assumed the presidency of the Naval War College, his fourth tour at the school and his last navy assignment—an especially fitting appointment for "the thinking man's admiral." Spruance Hall at the college is named in his honor.

On July 1, 1948, Spruance retired from the navy, completing forty-five years of service since taking his oath as a Naval Academy midshipman. He and Margaret moved to Pebble Beach, California, into the first house they had owned during their thirty-three years of marriage. Until then, their permanent mailing address through many duty stations had been the Spruance family home at 103 East Pratt Street (now Ninth Street) in Indianapolis.

In 1952 President Harry S Truman appointed Spruance U.S. ambassador to the Philippines, and he continued to serve in that post under President Dwight D. Eisenhower. The *Washington Post* greeted Spruance's nomination warmly, describing him as "one of his generation's most prominent members." Just as he had not been experienced in carrier or amphibious warfare before being assigned to oversee those operations, he was similarly inexperienced as an ambassador. Yet here too Spruance performed admirably, despite his reserved demeanor and aversion to public speaking.

In Manila Spruance continued to demonstrate his talents as an administrator. Displaying traits observed by historian Morison, he held frequent meetings, listened quietly to the various points of view expressed by his embassy staff during frequently spirited discussions, and then often concluded by saying: "Gentlemen, I thank you very much for your views and your comments. I've thought this over, and this is what I think we'll do." One participant recalled, "We all admired him so much, and his views were always so damned sound, that when he got through telling us what he wanted, the answer was 'yes sir.'" For her part, when asked to identify her principal job as the ambassador's wife, Margaret replied, "smiling."

In 1955 Spruance retired from public service. He died on December 13, 1969, and was buried next to two wartime comrades, Nimitz and Admiral Richmond K. Turner, in Golden Gate National Cemetery overlooking San Francisco Bay and the Pacific Ocean beyond.

RICHARD HUME WERKING

For Further Reading

Buell, Thomas B. *The Quiet Warrior: A Biography of Raymond A. Spruance*. Annapolis, MD: Naval Institute Press, 1987.

Forrestel, Emmet P. *Admiral Raymond A. Spruance: A Study in Command*. Washington, D.C.: U.S. Government Printing Office, 1966.

Lundstrom, John B. "Raymond A. Spruance: The Thinking Man's Admiral." *The Great Admirals: Command at Sea, 1587–1945*. Edited by Jack Sweetman. Annapolis, MD: Naval Institute Press, 1997.

Symonds, Craig L. *The Battle of Midway*. New York: Oxford University Press, 2011.

Stark, Otto

January 29, 1859–April 14, 1926

Hoosier Group artist; supervisor of art at Manual Training High School, Indianapolis; and teacher at John Herron Art Institute, Indianapolis.

To mangle an oft-cited saying of Winston Churchill, the Hoosier Group painter Otto Stark was an enigma wrapped in a contradiction. As supervisor of art at Manual Training High School and a teacher at the John Herron Art Institute in Indianapolis, he was beloved by students who were charmed by his gentle, kind manner that "got results out of [them]." As a parent, though, his four motherless children saw him as an exacting disciplinarian, one who was fair but not overly affectionate. Even as a painter, Stark was a paradox. Accomplished in the traditional academics of art, he wholeheartedly flirted with Impressionism. He was the only one of the five Hoosier Group artists to have studied in Paris and his work expresses a duality in approach not possessed by his four colleagues.

When the twenty-six-year-old Stark, born in Indianapolis, enrolled in the Académie Julian in Paris, the city was awhirl with the dancing light of Impressionism. Its official schools, however, were intent upon the preservation of art within very narrow aesthetic bounds. As such, his training at the Académie Julian and later in the atelier (workshop) of Fernand Cormon exposed him to the academic principles of perspective, anatomy, composition, and color harmony. By virtue of his technical mastery in this regard, Stark placed his work repeatedly in the grande dame of international art exhibitions: the Paris Salon.

But outside these formal strictures, the vitality of Paris beckoned to the young American. Using the city of winding cobblestoned streets, eccentric people, cabarets, half-wild gardens, windmills, and narrow footpaths as grist for his paintings, he, along with those avant-garde artists experimenting with the new Impressionism, sought out simple subject matter and everyday life incidents. Instead of the historical, literary, and exotic subjects preferred by the academicians of the Paris Salon, they focused on impressions of the visible world rather than its exact appearances. For them, light was to be perceived as color sensations, and they were concerned about the fluidity of changing light patterns. In their midst, Stark learned these lessons well.

Stark returned to New York City in 1888. There—with his French wife, Marie Nitschelm, whom he wed in 1886, and their one-year-old daughter, Gretchen—he took a job in commercial art. Shortly after the couple's arrival, a second daughter, Suzanne, was born. Money was scarce, and Stark supplemented his earnings with illustration work for such journals as *Scribner's Monthly* and *Harper's Weekly*. Within three years, his family had grown to six, with the addition of sons Paul Gustav and Edward Otto. Soon after the delivery of their last child, though, Marie's health seriously declined, and she died in November 1891.

Stunned by his loss and faced with the reality of earning money while raising four very young children alone, Stark turned to his family in Indianapolis for help. His father, then a widower, agreed to look after the three older children. One of his sisters volunteered to take care of his newborn baby. Within weeks of Marie's death, the grieving Stark left to begin a lonely vigil in Cincinnati, working as a designer with a lithography company there. In 1893 he returned to Indianapolis to set up housekeeping with his other two sisters, several nieces, and his four children.

Focused on little else but supporting his extended family, he opened a studio downtown to offer classes in oil and watercolor. Freed from day-to-day child care, he was able to teach as well as allot the time necessary to his development as an artist. Unable to generate a steady income, though, Stark took the position of supervisor of art at Manual Training High School in 1899. Six years later, he also became an instructor in composition and illustration at the city's John Herron Art Institute.

Between the demands of his two jobs and his children, Stark managed to place his paintings in local, regional, national, and international exhibitions. Consistent with the Impressionistic emphasis upon simple subject matter, the motifs in his work often were drawn from his everyday life experiences of sleeping babies and playing children. One art critic in Chicago so noted: "It gratifies me to find a man who can do a thing like that, turning to such pretty little subjects as the baby asleep yonder, the child with the long-suffering tabby cat, these sunflowers with the nasturtiums, they give a pleasant suggestion of the man's interests and sympathetics." Surrounded by four children, two nieces and all their playmates, it is little wonder that Stark painted the small moments in a child's life with such tenderness.

Always an innovative teacher, he had made his mark at both schools. Banishing the traditional drawing book method of teaching in which pupils were set to copying little lithographs, Stark encouraged them to work in various mediums and to develop their individual skills. Through the decades, he taught and his students responded. Artist Elmer Taflinger was in several of his classes at Manual during the early 1900s. "Most people don't realize what Otto Stark did for the art world of Indianapolis. He is the man who inspired us all to go to New York, to do something. He was a high school teacher, but he kept abreast of New York, Chicago, Paris," Taflinger said. "One thing a lot of people don't realize is that Otto Stark had an independent reputation on the East Coast. He won his spurs in Paris, New York, Philadelphia. Then, because his wife died, he decided to raise his four children in a healthier atmosphere. He was a human being above all else."

Not until 1919 did Stark feel that his family commitments were at an end. His grown children, with the exception of Gretchen, who stayed with him until his death, had married and settled elsewhere with families of their own. He finally felt free to resign from teaching at Manual and Herron and to devote all his energies to painting.

Rarely on display, restrained by long hours and rigid schedules, a whimsical sense of humor graced Stark's life. Even as a student in Paris, this comedic streak was there. After interrupting his charcoal drawing class at Julian with a spirited Native American war dance, Stark had been affectionately dubbed "Le Peau Rouge" (Red Skin) by his classmates. It was not until he retired, though, that he was able to give free rein to the jokester within.

As a yearly guest at the Michigan summer home of Hoosier Group artist J. OTTIS ADAMS, he not only painted but also felt free to be silly. Adams's niece remembered: "My older brothers and sisters had a circus one summer, and they wanted Mr. Stark, who was a little, thin, sort of bony man with a mustache, to be the ballet dancer. Uncle Jack [Adams], Mr. Stark and Aunt Winnie [artist Winifred Brady Adams], painted the scenes. . . . Another aunt made a ballet costume for Mr. Stark to wear, and he came tripping out to the music . . . and did a ballet around the ring. We all thought he was such a good sport about it."

In February 1925 the sixty-six-year-old painter was honored by his former students with a reception and exhibition at Manual. Although Stark had been gone from Manual for six years, the contributions of this modest, unassuming teacher had not been forgotten. Letters, tributes, and samples of work arrived from all over the world, sent by twenty-nine working artists who had studied with him. WILLIAM EDOUARD SCOTT, an African American artist who had won a scholarship to Paris under Stark's tutelage, spoke for decades of grateful students: "We cannot do too much for Mr. Stark. All I am I owe to him."

JUDITH VALE NEWTON

For Further Reading

Burnet, Mary Q. *Art and Artists of Indiana*. New York: Century Company, 1921.

Howard, Leland G. *Otto Stark: 1859–1926*. Indianapolis: Indianapolis Museum of Art, 1977.

Newton, Judith Vale. *The Hoosier Group: Five American Painters*. Indianapolis: Eckert Publications, 1985.

Steele, Theodore Clement

September 11, 1847–June 24, 1926

Artist in the Hoosier Group and Society of Western Artists and the first artist to settle in Brown County, Indiana.

Indiana's best-known historical artist, Theodore Clement (T. C.) Steele, led a uniquely American midwestern art movement while creating a market for Indiana landscapes. His decision to return to the Hoosier State after studying in Munich, Germany, helped bring esteem to Indiana in its cultural golden age at the turn of the twentieth century.

Born into a pioneer family with high ideals, T. C. Steele's Gosport birthplace in Owen County, Indiana, was soon replaced by a move to Waveland in Montgomery County, where his opportunity to study at the Waveland Academy was a primary focus. His penchant for drawing elevated him to a teaching role as early as age thirteen, and he painted portraits of fellow citizens soon after his studies were completed.

Steele met his future bride, Mary Elizabeth "Libbie" Lakin, at the academy and the two never wavered from their mutual adoration. They married on February 14, 1870. The young couple moved to Battle Creek, Michigan, where the artist painted commissioned portraits and taught a drawing class. The Steeles returned to Indianapolis less than three years later, already blessed with a son and daughter.

Theodore Clement Steele

With limited art instruction in the Midwest and the expectation for serious artists to study abroad, Steele formulated a method of support with friend and benefactor, Herman Lieber. For $100 each, donors would be guaranteed a portrait upon his return after two years of study at the Royal Academy of Art in Munich.

Already a father of three, Steele, with his wife and family, set sail for Antwerp, Belgium, on July 24, 1880. Two years became five as Steele studied drawing with Hungarian painter Gylua Benczur and graduated to painting classes with Ludwig von Löfftz, a German landscape painter. In summers he pursued his love of landscape painting with expatriate J. Frank Currier in the village of Schleissheim. Classes at the academy were rigorous, following the style of the Dutch Masters in the use of dark colors and accuracy of form. Steele's silver medal for his painting *The Boatman* at the 1884 student exhibition meant more to him, perhaps, than any later award.

In the summer of 1883 in Munich, Steele, along with fellow Hoosiers J. OTTIS ADAMS and WILLIAM FORSYTH, viewed the triennial Ausstellung International Exhibition. The three agreed that paintings by the Hollanders surpassed any others in the exhibit. The Dutch artists had applied their formal training to paintings of familiar home terrain. Inspired, the Indiana artists envisioned expressing their own national identity after finishing their studies.

But Steele's first order of business when he returned to Indianapolis in early June 1885 was to paint portraits owed to his patrons. Settling in the Tinker Mansion, which he rented at Sixteenth and Pennsylvania Streets, he doggedly worked for two years. As he repaid his commitments to influential community leaders, he became the premier portrait painter in Indiana.

Steele opened his Art School of Indiana in 1889. His interest in teaching waned and Forsyth took over all classes by the spring of 1895. Although commissioned portraits were Steele's livelihood, his passion was painting landscapes, and he built a horse-drawn studio/wagon just for that purpose. Traveling to southern Indiana, he reveled in the varied subject possibilities in Vernon and Metamora.

Steele and Forsyth, along with RICHARD GRUELLE and OTTO STARK, were invited by the Art Association of Indianapolis to exhibit their summer work in the fall of 1894. The Central Art Association of Chicago then urged the four artists, with the addition of Adams, to show their paintings in Chicago's Athenaeum Building.

The exhibition, called *Five Hoosier Painters*, caused a stir in the midwestern art world, and was touted by critics as the American western art movement. The much-quoted exhibit catalog, written by author Hamlin Garland, Lorado Taft, and artist Charles Francis Brown, stated that the artwork "exemplifies all the difficulties in the way of original western art and foreshadows its ultimate victory."

Steele's seasonal forays to southern Indiana eventually led him to Brookville. He was so enthused by the hilly village, quaint church steeples, and nearby Whitewater River that he purchased a home there with Adams in 1898. They rebuilt studio wings and named their sanctuary the Hermitage. A pivotal time in Steele's development, he produced significant landscapes, painting side by side with Adams along the sparkling river.

But his joyous summers at the Hermitage were marred by the illness of his beloved Libbie. Efforts to relieve her rheumatoid arthritis with treatment at a Spencer sanatorium and later a trip to Tennessee were to no avail, and she died of tuberculosis on November 14, 1899.

When the Tinker Place was sold to the Indianapolis Art Association to build the John Herron Art Institute in 1901, Steele rented a house on East Saint Clair Street, where he lived with his daughter, Daisy (Margaret) and eldest son, Brandt. Daisy accompanied her father by train to Oregon and California in 1902. The artist, inspired by changes in scenery and atmospheric light, painted lavender mountains and rocky beaches. His western expedition was repeated the following year.

In his efforts to establish a market for Indiana landscapes, Steele gave lectures, exhibited widely, and served on international art juries, including the 1904 Louisiana Purchase Exposition in Saint. Louis, Missouri and the 1914 Panama-Pacific Exposition in San Francisco, California. He was a founding member of the Society of Western Artists.

Steele sold his share of the Hermitage to Adams in 1906, and decided to explore the forested hills of Brown County. He purchased hilltop acreage south of Belmont and oversaw construction of the House of the Singing Winds. There he wrote to Selma Neubacher, an art teacher in Indianapolis, on June 21, 1907, "Some day artists will come to this county. So possibly you and I will be pioneers to blaze the way." Selma became his bride two months later.

With the advent of a nearby railroad stop and hospitable lodging, many Chicago artists, lead by Adolph Robert Shulz, eventually settled in Nashville. Steele never tired of his hilltop views and steep ravines where shaded creeks meandered. He followed his muse in all seasons. His 1913 election to associate membership in New York's National Academy of Design elevated his distinction.

Invited in 1922 by Indiana University president William Lowe Bryan, Steele established a library studio and fulfilled his position as "artist in residence" by painting outside on campus. He painted almost to the day of this death on July 24, 1926. His passing was mourned by all art-loving Hoosiers. Following a well-attended ceremony, his ashes were buried on his Brown County property and marked by a carved stone, which read, "Beauty Outlives Everything."

Steele's long list of portraits includes several Indiana governors as well as President BENJAMIN HARRISON, COLONEL ELI LILLY, and JAMES WHITCOMB RILEY, among others. His landscape paintings won significant awards, including Honorable Mention at the 1900 Paris Exposition, the Richmond Art Museum's Mary T. R. Foulke prize in 1906, and the 1909 Fine Arts Building Prize at the Society of Western Artists annual exhibition.

Steele's greatness was in helping people in his home state appreciate the beauty of their surroundings. His quiet paintings bear witness to his tireless inspiration and love of Indiana.

RACHEL BERENSON PERRY

For Further Reading

Krause, Martin. *The Passage*. Indianapolis: Indianapolis Museum of Art, 1990.

Newton, Judith Vale. *The Hoosier Group*. Indianapolis: Eckert Publications, 1985.

Perry, Rachel Berenson Perry. *T. C. Steele and The Society of Western Artists, 1896–1914*. Bloomington: Indiana University Press, 2009.

Stephenson, David Curtis

August 21, 1891–June 28, 1966

Grand Dragon of the Ku Klux Klan and powerful figure in Indiana politics during the 1920s.

On July 4, 1923, thousands of people jammed the roads leading into Malfalfa Park, three miles west of Kokomo. Families from all over Indiana and surrounding states arrived to participate in the largest Ku Klux Klan gathering in the state's history. It had been a hot and humid day, so many of the men removed their masks and walked openly among others in the county-fair atmosphere. Above the hooded throngs, a plane flew over with "K.K.K. No. 1" painted under the wings. Inside that aircraft sat David Curtis Stephenson, who was about to be anointed Grand Dragon of the KKK for Indiana and twenty-two other northern states. What must he have been thinking as he peered down through the treetops to see so many people waving and cheering for him? In just a short time, he had risen from obscurity to becoming one of the most powerful men in Indiana's history. He could not know it then, but just as fast as he soared, he would also tumble and take down some of the most important figures of his day.

Stephenson arrived in Evansville in early 1920 to take a job as a coal salesman. He had spent most of his previous life nomadically roaming from one small town to another in Oklahoma and Iowa writing for newspapers. In most of those places the young man had developed a reputation for being a drinker and ladies' man. He was married briefly in 1915 and fathered a daughter, but he spent most of his early adult life running from his responsibilities and into the arms of the next unsuspecting young woman. In Evansville he completely reinvented himself.

While there, Stephenson came into contact with a recruiter from the Ku Klux Klan's headquarters in Atlanta. The reinvented organization saw opportunity north of the Ohio River. Indiana, with its largely white, native-born, and Protestant population turned out to be fertile territory for expansion. Stephenson, a charismatic talker, signed on to help recruit members for the organization. He became so successful that the Klan asked him to move to Indianapolis to expand the membership in central and northern Indiana. Eventually, 250,000 Hoosiers joined the Klan, nearly 30 percent of the state's white male population.

An opportunist with grand political ambitions, Stephenson changed political views in every location he lived. In Oklahoma he worked for Socialists. In Evansville he had been a Democrat, and in Indianapolis he quickly surmised that he would now have to become a Republican. Stephenson convinced Hoosiers that the Klan was a patriotic organization that promoted "100 Percent Americanism." His subordinates recruited through the Protestant churches and encouraged ministers through financial incentives to promote the Klan. Stephenson became a millionaire within a very short time by selling memberships, Klan robes, and other paraphernalia. From those profits he bought a beautiful home in the leafy suburb of Irvington in eastern Indianapolis, where he added two-story Corinthian columns like those found on southern plantation homes. He also bought a yacht that he moored in Lake Erie and a fleet of sedans.

Klan crosses illuminated the night skies all across Indiana and the country causing great anxiety among Roman Catholic, Jewish, and African American populations. Klan rallies and parades dominated headlines in many Hoosier cities throughout the 1920s. Some local governments tried to pass antimask policies and some banned the burning of crosses within city limits. In South Bend a riot between University of Notre Dame students and Klan marchers on May 17, 1924, made national headlines. *The Fiery Cross*, a Klan newspaper, published the names of Catholic and Jewish-owned businesses so that members could boycott such establishments. In response, *Tolerance*, an anti-Klan newspaper, published the names of Klansman and Klan-dominated businesses. Burglars invaded some Klan offices, including the Indianapolis branch, to obtain the secret names for publication.

Stephenson loved the power that came with the title of Grand Dragon. He continued to recruit new members primarily in Indiana and Ohio. In August 1923 he hosted a party on his new yacht. Guests on the boat read like a who's who of Indiana and Ohio officeholders. Ed Jackson, the popular secretary of state and future Indiana governor, dined with U.S. Senator James Watson of Indiana and Ohio governor Victor Donahey. John Duvall, the Marion County treasurer and future mayor of Indianapolis, also joined the crew among other notables. Most people on that boat would later rue their association with a man who had already begun to boast to his friends that he was the "law in Indiana."

By the autumn of 1923 Stephenson found himself locked in a power struggle with Hiram Evans, the Imperial Wizard in Atlanta. In October Evans defrocked Stephenson as the Grand Dragon of the North. Not to be outmaneuvered, Stephenson and the Indiana Klan seceded from the national organization. In retaliation, Evans appointed Walter Bossert to lead the Indiana Klan; however, most local chapters remained loyal to Stephenson. Bossert, ever the faithful Klansman, managed to find Indiana legislators to introduce anti-Catholic measures, including the banning of Catholic teachers in the public schools. Most of his measures failed. Stephenson, on the other hand, went in a different direction and found success.

Relishing his role as the Indiana kingmaker, Stephenson supported the Republican candidate, Jackson, for governor in 1924. The popular Kokomo native benefited greatly from Klan support and he did not mind riding in the Lexington Touring Car driven by one of Stephenson's chauffeurs. Nor did he object to the thousands of dollars given to him by the Klan. In fact, the two men gave each

D. C. Stephenson

other generous Christmas presents. Jackson, along with numerous other Klan-sponsored politicians, easily defeated their opponents in 1924. Stephenson saw only dollar signs. Instead of supporting anti-Catholic measures, the "Old Man" as he liked to be called, touted bills that linked the Indiana Klan to government contracts. Utility executives paid Stephenson to lobby legislators to drop regulatory measures. The cash kept flowing into his coffers.

If 1924 had been a good year for Stephenson then 1925 had the potential to be his best, but his own problems with alcohol and his violent urges changed everything. Throughout most of the year he worked to ensure the election of Duvall for mayor of Indianapolis. In exchange for cash, Duvall signed a contract with Stephenson so that all city appointments would first have to be approved by Stephenson. The newly Klan-backed Indianapolis School Board immediately proposed an all-black high school to be called Crispus Attucks. Six members of the Indianapolis City Council owed their jobs to Stephenson. Local sheriffs, town officers, state legislators, judges, and small-town mayors took oaths of office because of Klan support.

The beginning of Stephenson's downfall came in March 1925 when he abducted a neighbor and statehouse employee, Madge Oberholtzer. He violently raped and assaulted the young woman on a train to Hammond. After the brutal attack, Oberholtzer managed to take several poisonous pills in an attempt to take her life. She died one month later in her parents' home from a staph infection from the wounds inflicted by Stephenson. His arrest and conviction in a sensational trial in Noblesville mesmerized the nation and damaged the reputation of the Klan. From his prison cell, Stephenson released names of politicians he had bribed, including Duvall and Jackson. Neither man recovered from the scandal. The *Indianapolis Times* received a Pulitzer Prize for its courageous coverage of the story. Stephenson languished in jail for thirty years and after his release died in obscurity in a small Tennessee town with his fourth wife.

WILLIAM GULDE

For Further Reading

Lutholtz, M. William. *Grand Dragon: D. C. Stephenson and the Ku Klux Klan in Indiana*. West Lafayette, IN: Purdue University Press, 1991.

Gray, Ralph, ed. *Indiana History: A Book of Readings*. Bloomington: Indiana University Press, 1994.

Stewart, George Pheldon

March 13, 1874–August 28, 1924

Cofounder with William H. Porter of the *Indianapolis Recorder* and business, civic, and community leader.

In 1895, shortly after moving to Indianapolis from Vincennes, Indiana, George Pheldon Stewart and William H. Porter started a single-sheet circular called *The Directory*, which contained advertising and church news. Two years later, their venture evolved into the *Indianapolis Recorder*, which is the longest continuously operating African American newspaper in Indiana and the third oldest of its kind in the nation.

Stewart became sole owner when Porter sold his share of the newspaper to him in 1899 for $300. He remained editor and publisher of the *Recorder* until his death in 1924. His widow, Fannie Caldwell, became owner and publisher; their son, Marcus C., became managing editor; and their daughter, Joyce Thompson, continued in her role as business manager—a position that her son, George, later held. The purchase of the *Indianapolis Recorder* in 1988 by Eunice M. Trotter, an *Indianapolis Star* journalist, marked the first time in the paper's history that the Stewart family did not own controlling interest. Chemical company entrepreneur William G. Mays assumed control of the newspaper in September 1990.

Like most African American papers, the *Recorder* promoted racial pride through stories about the achievements and accomplishments of blacks. However, unlike its early competitors, including the *Indianapolis Freeman* and the *Indianapolis Colored World*, the *Recorder* regularly published news and features that appealed to both Indianapolis and statewide black communities during a period of racial progress. Though the focus of the newspaper was local people and events, the early *Recorder* also reported national news. For such expanded news coverage, the paper relied on a network of sales agents, who in addition to selling subscriptions, served as local correspondents.

The early issues of the *Recorder* consisted of four pages, each six columns wide with the last column used as advertising space. Much of the content concerned ministers, churches, and general religious news. The front page carried a limited amount of local news along with national news, which often took the form of an appeal.

For example, one article in 1904 called for "Negro teachers all over the country" to organize. Many of the articles that promoted and examined black achievements ran in a column labeled "Race News." Church news was found on page two, and society activities were on page four. An outlet for information about local African American communities in other cities was published in a section on page three titled "From around Indiana."

At the turn of the century the paper published several articles with photographs about prominent black leaders visiting Indiana, including Booker T. Washington, who was in Indianapolis on numerous occasions. He spoke to the Flanner Guild, the first settlement house for African Americans in the city, on May 7, 1903, and he returned the following year to attend the annual meeting of the National Business League, of which he was president. He was also in the city at various times to help raise funds for the Senate Avenue Young Men's Christian Association and was keynote speaker for the dedication ceremony for the YMCA in July 1913. Washington's ideological rival, W. E. B. DuBois, also visited Indianapolis during the early 1900s, though his coverage in the *Recorder* was not as extensive as Washington's. The paper did give ample coverage to the feats of world champion bicyclist and Hoosier Marshall "Major" Taylor, from his defeat of thirty riders in a 1901 race in France to a collision he suffered during an international competition in Australia in 1904. The activities of Indianapolis entrepreneur MADAM C. J. WALKER were regularly featured in the *Recorder*.

By 1916, as the *Recorder* continued to develop as a community newspaper, there was a marked increase in advertising, especially from white businesses. The importance of education was a theme throughout several issues during this time, notably the education of women. Wedding announcements were confined to a "Woman's World" column located on the social page. Vital statistics and a classified advertising section were also prominent features. During the 1916 election year the paper carried numerous political advertisements and stories, including reports of the activities of the Colored Republican Committee, of which Stewart was chairman.

Throughout the Stewart era, the *Recorder* generally supported the Republican Party, though at times its editorials showed disillusionment with the party and the policies of President William McKinley during his first term in office. It did, however, endorse his re-election in 1900 and resisted suggestions that it abandon its allegiance to the national party as inconsistent and impractical.

To keep in touch with the African American community, Stewart was active in several religious, business, civic, political, and fraternal organizations. He joined Bethel African Methodist Episcopal Church soon after his arrival in Indianapolis. To promote the business and political progress of blacks, he joined, and more often than not, took a leadership role in the Colored Republican Committee, Indiana Association of Colored Men, Indiana chapter of the National Negro Business League, and the Indiana Negro Welfare League.

Although Stewart was associated with several fraternal organizations, he was most active with the black Knights of Pythias, an organization he and Porter joined soon after it was established in Indiana. The organization performed many acts of charity, offered an insurance plan for families of members, invested in real estate, constructed cemeteries, and operated the Union Amusement Theatre through a subsidiary corporation. Stewart also actively supported the Alpha Home for Aged Colored Women, the Indianapolis Community Chest, and the capital campaign for Second Baptist Church. He was also a member of the National Association for the Advancement of Colored People and the Negro Business League.

The *Recorder*, with its rich repository of articles and columns chronicling the activities and achievements of African Americans, is the single, most important publication that captures a panoramic view of twentieth-century black Indianapolis. It has supplied remarkable help to graduate students working on theses and dissertations, news reporters looking for black historical perspectives, and the general public seeking details about an event, not provided by the dailies. Stewart's activities testify to his role as an energetic participant during the era of Washington and the Age of Accommodation, a belief that economic self-help and education were better paths to equality than confrontation.

WILMA L. MOORE

For Further Reading

Barrows, Robert G., and David J. Bodenhamer, eds. *The Encyclopedia of Indianapolis*. Bloomington and Indianapolis: Indiana University Press, 1994.

Stewart, George P. Papers, 1894–1924. Manuscript and Visual Collections Department, William Henry Smith Memorial Library, Indiana Historical Society, Indianapolis.

"Indianapolis Recorder." Center for Digital Scholarship, Indiana University–Purdue University at Indianapolis. Ulib.iupui.edu/digitalscholarship/collections/Recorder.

Stout, Elihu

April 16, 1782–June 22, 1860

Publisher of Indiana's first newspaper.

During the early candlelit evening of October 8, 1855, Elihu Stout, who was seeking re-election as recorder of Knox County, appeared in Vincennes, Indiana, with other candidates to speak to voters. Stout, described by a contemporary as being "of medium height, of a wiry frame, possessing a massive head, who wore his hair long and combed back," was well known to his audience, having been the longtime owner and editor of the *Vincennes Western Sun* and *General Advertiser*. Not surprisingly, Stout handily won another term as recorder. His newspaper, originally named the *Indiana Gazette* when he started it in 1804, was the first to be published in the Indiana Territory and one of the first in the Northwest Territory, and it continues today as the *Vincennes Sun-Commercial*. A Stout descendant, Gayle Robbins, was named its editor in 2006.

Stout, who was born on April 16, 1782, in Newark, New Jersey, to Jediah and Polly Stout, moved to Lexington, Kentucky, after obtaining "a good common school education" in Newark. He eventually became employed as an apprentice compositor for the *Kentucke* (later changed to *Kentucky*) *Gazette*, an early Kentucky newspaper published by the Bradford family, and he also worked as an apprentice in their print shop.

In 1804, after being recruited by WILLIAM HENRY HARRISON, territorial governor, to print the laws of the territory, Stout left for Vincennes, but he was also "determined to start a paper of his own." Vincennes, where Stout and his wife, Lucy, whom he married in 1805, would raise their family, was then a remote village inhabited by such political notables as two future presidents, Harrison and Zachary Taylor, as well as Jefferson Davis. According to Henry S. Cauthorn, the grandson the couple raised, Stout "brought with him [to Vincennes] a handsome patrimony, afterwards doubled by in amount by the dowry of his wife."

The first issue of Stout's *Indiana Gazette* appeared in the summer of 1804. Stout used a laborious printing process, much like what Johannes Gutenberg developed in the fifteenth century, in which type was locked on an iron form and inked with buckskinned balls, after which paper was placed on the inked type form and a press was used to produce the individual printed page. Until a paper mill was established near Madison, Indiana, several years later, Stout obtained paper, type, and his press from Kentucky with money borrowed from his father. All of his equipment and supplies for the newspaper were shipped on a small, hand-propelled watercraft known as a pirogue and then brought the rest of the way to Vincennes on horseback. In declaring the principles that would guide his newspaper, Stout wrote that "essays of any political comple[x]ion, couched in decent language, shall find a ready insertion—but the Editor pledges himself that the columns of the *Gazette* shall never be tarnished with matter that can offend the eye of decency, or raise a blush upon the cheek of modesty and virtue."

Much of the news and many of the articles that Stout published originated in other journals and came in on horseback. As a consequence, he was sometimes unable, due to the varying accounts, to report precisely what had occurred. On one such occasion, the perplexed editor observed: "From all these various and contradictory accounts we can collect one fact only, that all in Spain is not right." Similarly, when the mail did not arrive Stout sometimes found himself without anything to publish. For example, on January 27, 1808, Stout reported "[w]e have had no mail for the last two weeks, for which we shall not pretend to assign a cause—we have consequently nothing new on the subject of peace or war."

The economic reality for Stout and other pioneer editors and printers was challenging at best. By 1808 the editor resorted to publishing the names of subscribers who were in arrears, some of whom had been so for years. Stout survived due to being named, as Harrison had promised, the official printer for the Territory of Indiana (until the capital was moved to Corydon in 1813), and because Stout accepted payment in goods (such as beef, pork, whiskey, tobacco, salt and tallow) and various services from his subscribers.

Stout had various business partners through the years, including JONATHAN JENNINGS, who became Indiana's first governor. More than one of his partnerships ended due to differences of opinion regarding important political issues such as slavery. Stout later partnered with his son, Henry. For most of his career, Stout did it all, serving as writer, editor, proofreader, compositor, pressman, and deliveryman, in addition to teaching printing to his assistants.

The significance of Stout's contributions cannot be overstated. As Indiana's first newspaper publisher, he was responsible for informing early residents of the important news of the day, thereby also providing future generations a valuable insight into this critical period of the state's history. Some of the most historically significant articles published included a description of the celebration of the Fourth of July of 1807, a description of the Battle of Tippecanoe in 1811, news accounts of the War of 1812, and a verbatim report of Harrison's nearly two-hour March 4, 1841, inaugural address as president and his death shortly thereafter. On April 16, 1836, Stout reported the news of the siege of the Alamo and its aftermath, and on June 6, 1844, he editorialized about the "disgraceful administration" of President Martin Van Buren.

Besides providing news and opinion in his newspaper, Stout served Vincennes in other ways as well, including holding a number of public officers, being active in civic and political organizations, and proposing ideas for community improvement. In addition to serving as recorder, Stout was a common pleas judge, a justice of the peace, and treasurer of the common fund of Vincennes. He was president of the Vincennes Theatrical Society and grand master of the Vincennes Masonic Lodge, the first lodge in Indiana. In the September 17, 1814, edition of the *Western Sun*, Stout proposed giving Vincennes residents an additional source of news and opinion through the establishment of what he called a "newsroom," which was to be something of a reading room. It would be open for use by "Subscribers, Strangers, and Friends of Subscribers, who do not reside in the town or neighborhood" and which would feature two of the "best constructed papers printed in each of the principal seaports throughout the U. States and two from the interior of each state and territory" as well as various noncirculating publications including medical, legal, literary, political and religious periodicals. Stout believed such a facility would allow users to "examine for themselves the ground on which they speak" and that by examining publications from different parts of the country users would be able to "throw light upon" interesting events occurring in the United States and elsewhere.

In August 1845 Stout was appointed by President James K. Polk as Vincennes's postmaster, which led him to sell the newspaper he had created and nurtured for so many years, ending his decades-long career as Indiana's pioneer journalist. Stout died on June 22, 1860, at the Vincennes home of his grandson, Cauthorn, who was then clerk of the Knox County Courts and who would go on the serve as a longtime state representative and an esteemed historian. Following a Masonic funeral, Stout was buried in Vincennes's public cemetery, his grave being marked by a simple stone. Cauthorn, in his *A Brief Sketch of the Past, Present, and Prospects of Vincennes*, wrote that Stout "le[ft] behind no evidence of any necessity of taking an inventory of his estate." A newspaper obituary expressed the hope that Stout would "rest in peace until called upon to occupy a higher and more blest estate."

DONALD B. KITE SR.

For Further Reading

Boomhower, Ray E. "Destination Indiana: Elihu Stout and the Vincennes State Historic Sites." *Traces of Indiana and Midwestern History* 12, no.4 (Fall 2000): 26–31.

Cauthorn, Henry S. *A Brief Sketch of the Past, Present, and Prospects of Vincennes*. Vincennes, IN: A. V. Crotts, 1884.

Denehie, Elizabeth M. "Indiana's First Newspaper." *Indiana Magazine of History* 31 (June 1935): 125–30.

William H. English Collection. University of Chicago Library, Special Collections Research Center, Chicago, IL.

Smith, Solomon, *The Theatrical Journey-Work and Anecdotal Recollections of Solomon Smith*. Philadelphia, PA: T. B. Peterson, 1854.

Stratton-Porter, Gene

August 17, 1863–December 6, 1924

Naturalist, novelist, essayist, photographer, and film producer.

For all her relevance to many of today's most potent issues, Gene Stratton-Porter remains little known—except in her home state, where not one but two state historic sites honor her memory and bring attention to her work. Today her books are sometimes mistakenly relegated to the children's literature section, in spite of dark themes in her

Gene Stratton-Porter

novels of abuse, prostitution, and abandonment. Present too, in *Her Father's Daughter*, are the anti-Asian sentiments, in cringe-worthy prose, prevalent in the early twentieth century. World War I and its aftermath horrified her, but she often expressed jingoistic attitudes common in 1920s America.

Yet Stratton-Porter was once one of the most popular writers in America and brought the themes of the growing conservation movement to ordinary people. She believed, with no idle boast, that her "Nature books and Nature novels have sent as many people afield in the past twenty years as the work of the combined scientists of the world in that period." She wrote for everyone, in mainstream as well as specialty publications. Apart from some of her nature study books, her proliferation of nonfiction—frequent essays, editorials, and monthly columns for numerous magazines—is virtually unknown today, yet her place in the pantheon of proto-environmentalists rivals that of John Muir. Still, she was a pragmatic conservationist even as she embraced Muir's concepts of nature's spiritual values. She found in nature solace and strength, but also practical value. She agreed with the principles of advocates such as Gifford Pinchot, first chief of the U.S. Forest Service, regarding stewardship and wise use, abhorring profligate waste and greed.

Some today are troubled by what they perceive as hypocrisy; her husband invested in gas and oil drilling during the boom of the 1890s, and indeed, income from many of these investments allowed for the construction of the first Limberlost cabin on the edge of Geneva, Indiana, close to the swamp she later made famous. Ultimately, however, the oil and gas exploitation and draining of the wetlands for truck farming also destroyed her outdoor workplace by the early 1910s. By then Stratton-Porter had become a successful novelist and popular nature writer, having struck a deal with Doubleday, her publisher, to alternate works of nonfiction nature lore, which sold well enough, with her novels, heavily laced with detailed descriptions of the swamps, woods, fields, as well as its denizens.

She illustrated her books with her own exquisite photographs. The stiffly posed taxidermy specimens that editors of the nature and outdoor magazines had suggested to accompany her first articles in the 1890s, when such publications began to proliferate, were not for her. Photography, cumbersome as it was, allowed her to show the birds, moths, and other creatures of which she wrote in their natural environment, engaged in their normal activities. These photographs remain today, more than a hundred years later, among the most amazing portraits of nature to be found anywhere.

Now that Stratton-Porter was wealthy enough to finance the building of a house that met all her needs as both a workshop—with library, darkroom, and conservatory—and a comfortable woodland retreat, she set about to find a suitable spot. Leaving the Limberlost area, she settled on Sylvan Lake, some eighty miles north, which itself was not pristine. It was an enlarged reservoir constructed for a proposed canal in the 1830s, a place she knew well from decades before when she attended the Island Park Chautauqua with her sisters. It was there that she had eventually made the acquaintance of Charles Dorwin Porter, whom she married in 1886. Theirs was an unusual union for its time; Charles supported Gene's career while avidly pursuing his own entrepreneurial interests, and after the house on Sylvan Lake was completed in 1913, they lived together only on weekends. Nonetheless, the bonds of affection remained strong until her death.

At first the couple lived in Decatur, Indiana, Porter's hometown, but after the birth of her daughter, Jeannette, Stratton-Porter persuaded Charles to move the family to the edge of Geneva, the location of one of his drugstores. Here she discovered the nearby Limberlost swamp, her inspiration and the start of her life's work. She felt that as long as she tended to all the needs of her family, any time that she could snatch could be devoted to her field observations and eventually, to her writing. After Stratton-Porter's work became successful, she was able to hire both household and secretarial help to keep things running smoothly.

The youngest of twelve children, Geneva Stratton had very little formal education, falling just short of completing high school; her university was the forest and fields of her Indiana homes, begun in her earliest childhood when she freely roamed as a "happy little wild thing" on her family's farm in Wabash County, Indiana. With unusual patience and concentration, the child observed the habits of her beloved birds and other wild creatures even to the point of feeding nestlings with the proper sort of food in the presence of the parents. Her true education was interrupted with the family's move to Wabash owing to her mother's increasingly poor health and the death of her brother, Leander "Laddie," who was the mainstay of the farm.

Her mother died soon after, and Geneva felt stifled in the town. She dropped out of school in her senior year in order to care for an older sister whose health was failing, but "unlike my schoolmates, I studied harder after leaving school than ever before and in a manner that did me real good. . . . The others of my family had been to college; I always have been too thankful for words that circumstances intervened which saved my brain from being run through a groove in company with dozens of others of widely different tastes and mentality. What small measure of success I have had has come through preserving my individual point of view [and] method of expression." She read voraciously and studied painting and music; she burned for a creative outlet that much later, after several years of marriage and motherhood, she came to realize was writing—and in particular, writing about that which she knew and loved best, nature.

Stratton-Porter wrote of the birds and the landscape and the people of the Limberlost area, and when she moved north to Sylvan Lake, she used that location to its utmost, continuing her fieldwork while also setting about to save all the native flowers and shrubs that she could as the areas around her were being developed. She loved the Cabin in Wildflower Woods, intending it to be her home for the rest of her days, but a bout with the influenza that racked the world at the end of World War I, as well as increasing legions of her fans invading her property, instigated a move to Southern California. Initially she planned to spend only the winters there, but the wealth of fresh air, sunshine, and new plant life drew her in, as did the community of artists, writers, and movie folk. Stratton-Porter became a pioneer in the latter industry as well, establishing her own production company in order to make proper movies of her books. She produced two and was at work on a third when she was killed in a streetcar accident in 1924.

GLORY-JUNE GREIFF

For Further Reading

Long, Judith Reick. *Gene Stratton-Porter: Novelist and Naturalist*. Indianapolis: Indiana Historical Society Press, 1990.

Meehan, Jeanette Porter. *Lady of the Limberlost: The Life and Letters of Gene Stratton-Porter*. Garden City, NY: Double Day, Doran and Company, 1928.

Morrow, Barbara Olenyik. *Nature's Storyteller: The Life of Gene Stratton-Porter*. Indianapolis: Indiana Historical Society Press, 2010.

Sexton, Eugene Francis, ed. *Gene Stratton-Porter: A Little Story of the Life and Work and Ideals of "The Bird Woman."* Garden City, NY: Double, Page and Company, 1926.

Strauss, Juliet V.

January 7, 1863–May 28, 1918

Writer and newspaper and magazine columnist.

Indiana's Turkey Run State Park, located in Marshall, Parke County, has within its 2,382 acres some of the Hoosier State's finest scenery. RICHARD LIEBER, noted environmentalist and the first director of the Indiana Department of Conservation, described the area as "a paradise of rocky gorges, glens, bathing beaches and waterfalls, a retreat for song birds, and a garden of wild flowers." Each year thousands of visitors hike through the park's thirteen miles of trails, marveling at such natural features as Rocky Hollow, Gypsy Gulch, Wedge Rock, Turkey Run Hollow, and Devil's Ice Box.

On May 18, 1916, however, most of the land that now makes up Turkey Run, also known as

Bloomingdale Glens, seemed under threat. For years the land, which had been originally settled in 1826 by Captain Salmon Lusk and passed on to his son John, had been open for Hoosiers to visit and enjoy. After John Lusk died in 1915, however, his heirs planned to auction off the land. A parks committee of the Indiana Historical Commission (created by the state legislature to commemorate the nineteenth state's centennial) made a valiant effort to buy the land and save it for future generations to enjoy, but the Hoosier Veneer Company of Indianapolis outbid the committee by the slim margin of $100, purchasing the property at auction for $30,200.

On assignment covering the auction for the *Indianapolis News* that day was its ace reporter William Herschell. To Herschell, who had been one of more than two thousand people who attended the auction, it seemed as though Turkey Run had "passed into the hands of those who, for the dollars of today, would wreck a State's happiness tomorrow." Walking along a path skirting Sugar Creek, which meanders its way through the area, and reflecting on the day's events, the reporter met by chance a member of the delegation brought by the parks committee to save the land from the woodsman's axe—a local woman who had often played in Turkey Run's woods as a child, whose own children had followed in her footsteps, and who had been among the first to call for the area to be conserved. "I am sick of soul," she told Herschell. "Who would have dreamed that a few men's dollars could step in and destroy all this, the most beautiful spot in all Indiana, one that all the money in the world could not restore once it is gone."

Herschell soon realized that the woman's tears were not those of resignation at a lost cause, but "fighting tears, the kind that the bravest warrior sheds when he is going into battle." The journalist's assessment proved to be true; the fight to save Turkey Run from destruction was far from over. Six months after the initial auction, the parks committee—bolstered by financial contributions from the public and the owners of the Indianapolis Motor Speedway—reached a settlement with the Indianapolis timber company, which accepted a $40,200 offer for the site.

The tears that had so moved Herschell had come from Juliet Virginia Strauss, well-known to the citizens of her hometown, Rockville, Indiana, and to readers nationwide under her nom de plum, "The Country Contributor." This homemaker who struggled so hard to save the forests of her youth wrote a steady stream of common-sense, down-to-earth observations on life for local readers of her weekly "Squibs and Sayings" column in the *Rockville Tribune*, for Indiana readers of her weekly "Country Contributor" column in the *Indianapolis News*, and for the approximately one million subscribers to *Ladies' Home Journal* who read her column "The Ideas of a Plain Country Woman." Edward Bok, longtime *Journal* editor, said that Strauss's contributions were "more widely read and . . . are more popular than the writings of any single contributor to the magazine."

During Strauss's childhood in Rockville, her family, who had roots in the South, was excommunicated from the Presbyterian Church for supposedly being Confederate sympathizers during the Civil War. Following the death of her carpenter father, who had nicknamed the young Juliet "Gypsy" (later shortened to Gyp) because of her constant wanderings in Parke County's lush forests, Strauss and her family had been looked down upon for their poverty by the upper ranks of Rockville society. Pretty, poor, talented, and

Juliet V. Strauss

fatherless girls, noted Strauss, always made a "fine target for village gossips and for the slings and arrows of outrageous fortune as dealt out by more fortunate girls who have fathers and big brothers and money and 'social position.'"

Although no scholar, Strauss did excel in one area—writing. Discovering her talent, fellow classmates, especially boys, often used her skills to improve upon their writing assignments. Her teacher, familiar with Strauss's style, soon discovered the ploy and marked entire paragraphs in blue pencil with the word "Gyp" in parenthesis beside them. Her writing talent caught the eye of John H. Beadle, a roving correspondent for the Associated Press and editor of the *Rockville Tribune*. Beadle convinced Strauss's mother to let her daughter write for the newspaper, starting the young woman on her newspaper career.

After a short stint teaching, she was married at a young age to a boy from the "wrong side of the tracks." Juliet and her husband, Isaac, who struggled to earn a living as operators of the small-town weekly newspaper they bought from Beadle, were excluded from the literary and other social clubs that sprang up in the community in the 1900s. Although she claimed that these experiences failed to embitter her, Strauss did emphasize in her writings the overwhelming importance of a woman finding her place at home, and the dignity and worth of such a life as opposed to the doings of fashionable and elegant society ladies. "Being a plain home woman," she argued, "is one of the greatest successes in life, if to plainness you add kindness, tolerance, and interest, real interest in simple things."

Strauss's writing found—in addition to frequent hardships and struggles—joy, beauty, and art in a homemaker's daily life. "I know what it is to be poor and to be held down seemingly to a level beneath my natural abilities," Strauss wrote. "I know what it means to be tired of the dishrag and sick of the coal-scuttle, but I have learned . . . that there is a way of accepting these things which lift them to the level of the brush and the pen and the strings of the harp or the violin." Her efforts to glorify homemaking struck a chord with her female readers across the country who grew, through long association, to consider the Rockville housewife "as friend and counselor," the *Indianapolis News* commented upon Strauss's death on May 22, 1918.

Her readers recognized Strauss as one of their own. Homemakers continually turned to her for the homespun advice and encouragement she offered and mourned her passing with poems and letters praising her work printed in newspapers throughout the state. In 1922 the Woman's Press Club of Indiana erected a more concrete tribute to Strauss, dedicating a statue titled *Subjugation* in her memory at Turkey Run. Sculpted by Myra R. Richards of Indianapolis, the monument, the Press Club claimed, captured the true spirit of Strauss's writing—the subjugation of the material to the spiritual. The work also honored the Rockville native's role in saving Turkey Run's lush forests from destruction.

RAY E. BOOMHOWER

For Further Reading

Boomhower, Ray E. *The Country Contributor: The Life and Times of Juliet V. Strauss*. Carmel: Guild Press of Indiana, 1998.

Hoy, Suellen M. "Governor Samuel M. Ralston and Indiana's Centennial Celebration." *Indiana Magazine of History* 71 (September 1975): 245–66.

Shumaker, Arthur W. *A History of Indiana Literature: With Emphasis on the Authors of Imaginative Works Who Commenced Writing Prior to World War II*. Indianapolis: Indiana Historical Bureau, 1962.

The Country Contributor [Juliet V. Strauss]. *The Ideas of a Plain Country Woman*. New York: Doubleday, Page and Company, 1908.

Studebaker, Clement

March 12, 1831–November 27, 1901

Founder, H. and C. Studebaker and Studebaker Brothers Manufacturing Company.

Most biographies of Clement Studebaker lead with mention of his and elder brother Henry's establishment of a South Bend blacksmith shop in 1852 and its subsequent growth and success. This focus is certainly warranted, as Studebaker was a global presence crossing two centuries and was the only wagon maker to successfully transition to automobiles. The Studebaker Brothers Manufacturing Company, later refinanced and incorporated as the Studebaker Corporation, built more than five million vehicles in its lifetime and remains an icon of Indiana's industrial heritage. However, to view Studebaker as merely a successful industrialist is an incomplete view of a man who was also teacher, blacksmith, politician, and philanthropist.

Studebaker was born just outside of Gettysburg, Pennsylvania, in 1831, and moved with his family to Ashland, Ohio, as a young boy. He learned blacksmithing and wagon making from his father, John Clement Studebaker. The elder Studebaker's talents did not extend to business, however, and Clement's childhood was quite austere.

At age nineteen, Clement and his brother, Henry, traveled to northern Indiana to join their sister and her husband at their home south of South Bend. Clement was employed as a schoolteacher for two terms before putting his blacksmithing to use at a local shop. In 1852 he and Henry pooled resources and opened the H. and C. Studebaker blacksmith shop in downtown South Bend.

The brothers' business endured early struggles and by the late 1850s the Studebaker shop was short on cash. Although sources differ as to the exact course of events, the arrival of younger brother John M. and, more importantly, his $8,000 in gold nuggets, righted the ship and allowed for expansion. J. M. also bought out elder brother Henry's share of the firm at this time. Brothers Peter and Jacob soon joined Clement and J. M., and by the end of the 1860s wagon production at the Studebaker Brothers Manufacturing Company, as it was then known, grew rapidly, spurred by sales to the military during the Civil War, to pioneers headed westward, to farmers, and to others for general transportation purposes.

In addition to his duties as company president, Clement, who held that position until his death in 1901, gave freely of his time and talents to numerous civic boards and institutions, serving as a trustee of Indiana's DePauw University as well as being a noted benefactor to the college. DePauw's administration building bears Clement's name in recognition of his family's many contributions.

Studebaker was a member of both the South Bend City Council and the Saint Joseph County Council. In addition to local politics, he was active on the state and national level as well, serving as a delegate to the Republican National Convention in 1880 and 1888 and was an oft-rumored Indiana gubernatorial candidate. He was also a U.S. commissioner to the Expositions in Paris and New Orleans and presided over Indiana's board of managers for the 1893 Columbian Exposition in Chicago.

In 1889 President BENJAMIN HARRISON appointed Studebaker to the country's ten-member delegation to the Pan-American Congress. As part of this delegation, Studebaker arranged for a visit by the Congress to South Bend for a tour of his company's facilities and a reception at his elegant new forty-room mansion, Tippecanoe Place. The plans were jeopardized when he received a telegram on October 9 reading, "The house is burning. The family were [sic] alarmed in time to make their escape. Come home at once." No one was seriously injured in the blaze, but much of the grand home's upper floors were destroyed. The dining room, however, was judged serviceable, and the Pan-American Congress visit took place as scheduled.

Tippecanoe Place today houses a restaurant of the same name and is but one of several South Bend landmarks made possible by Studebaker. South Bend's present-day Memorial Hospital began as Epworth Hospital, and was underwritten in large part by Clement and Anne Studebaker. The Studebakers also substantially financed the construction of South Bend's Saint Paul Methodist Church. During the church's construction, he arranged to have his image placed in the stained glass windows overlooking the sanctuary. Although Studebaker died prior to its completion, he literally looks down on every one of the church's congregants.

Studebaker, a devout Methodist, was a regular participant in church affairs and on three occasions represented the church at its national conferences. He was also a trustee of the Chautauqua Assembly and served as its president until his death. Additionally, Studebaker was a Knights Templar Mason and an Odd Fellow.

In spite of his great wealth and vast responsibilities, Studebaker never lost sight of his humble upbringing and early struggles. He is quoted as saying later in his life, "Those were about as pleasant days I ever knew—days when I was young and vigorous, able to do the blacksmithing for the farmers of the county. I like to recall the experiences of this kind and heartily appreciate the acquaintance and friendship of those who were my patrons in those days." In June 1891 he declared a half day of vacation for Studebaker employees so they could attend the circus: "I know how the average small boy would feel to be cheated out of [going to] a circus, for when I was the smallest of the small boys of my town I walked sixteen miles to see a show. I had 14 cents and gave 12 cents to get into the tent, and spent the other 2 cents for ginger bread, but I had more fun than I have ever had since in my life."

Studebaker Vehicle Works, South Bend, Indiana

An 1881 incident revealed another side of his personality that anyone with siblings will understand. Younger brother J. M. believed that his new horse was faster than his elder brother's mount. Clement, as one might expect, disagreed. The brothers took to the streets for an impromptu horse race. Clement prevailed, but the local marshal had the last say. The Studebaker brothers were cited and were each fined two dollars.

At the time of Studebaker's death on November 27, 1901, the blacksmith shop he founded some forty-nine years earlier was the world's largest wagon manufacturer with sales exceeding $3.5 million. Just three months later, the Studebaker Brothers Manufacturing Company introduced a new product—the automobile. Some of the world's most innovative and breathtaking cars left Studebaker's assembly lines over the next sixty-four years.

While much of Studebaker's work may be measured in production or sales figures, his other works give the full picture of the man. Regardless of the metrics used, Indiana is innumerably richer for his efforts.

ANDY BECKMAN

For Further Reading

Erskine, Albert. *History of the Studebaker Corporation*. Chicago: Poole Brothers, 1924.

Press Clipping Collection 1872–1896. Studebaker National Museum Archives, South Bend, IN.

"Obituary of Clement Studebaker." *South Bend Daily Times*, November 27, 1901.

"The Life and Times of Clement Studebaker." Unpublished manuscript, circa 1910. Saint Joseph County Library, Local History Department, South Bend, IN.

Sunday, William "Billy" Ashley

November 19, 1862–November 6, 1935

Professional baseball player who became the early twentieth century's most prominent evangelist.

In April 1917 as the United States entered World War I, William Ashley "Billy" Sunday launched his most spectacular campaign against the devil and his minions with a ten-week revival in New York City. As the controversial, flamboyant baseball player turned revivalist looked out over the thousands who had come to hear him preach, he could not resist observing that it had been a long way from a two-room log cabin on the Iowa prairie to a 20,000-seat tabernacle on

Sunday delivering a sermon at a tent meeting in Winona Lake, Indiana, circa 1910s.

Broadway. For Sunday that observation reflected the enormous satisfaction he took in his remarkable success. For many in his audience, however, the imagery of his journey from prairie log cabin to Broadway tabernacle appealed at least in part because it, as did other aspects of the evangelist's life and work, seemed a vindication of traditional values and of the national myth of social mobility and economic opportunity in an era of unprecedented and sometimes unsettling change.

The base path, not the pulpit, was Sunday's initial avenue out of an impoverished and troubled childhood in rural and small-town Iowa. In 1883 he began an eight-year career in Major League Baseball, first with the Chicago White Stockings and then with teams in Pittsburgh and Philadelphia. In the mid-1880s Sunday experienced a religious conversion through the street ministry of Chicago's Pacific Garden Mission and he met and married Helen Amelia Thompson, daughter of a middle-class Chicago family steeped in evangelical Protestant values. His conversion experience helped Sunday cope with what seems to have been a growing sense of sinfulness and disorientation, and his marriage to a devout and remarkably able woman provided a familial and religious anchor crucial to his future success.

While playing professional baseball Sunday began sharing his religious convictions with young men under the auspices of the Young Men's Christian Association in Chicago and other National League cities. After the 1890 season he retired from baseball and became a full-time Chicago YMCA worker. In 1893 he accepted an invitation to become an advance man for the well-known Indiana evangelist J. Wilbur Chapman, with whom he worked until late 1895, when Chapman announced his return to parish ministry. Sunday, who had learned the basics of professional evangelism from Chapman, then launched his own evangelistic career with a revival in Garner, Iowa, in January 1896. During the first decade of his ministry more than half of Sunday's one hundred revivals took place in the small towns of Iowa, while the remainder were in small venues in other midwestern states. After 1906 he began expanding his work into larger towns and cities, conducting his first revival in a city of a 100,000 with an evangelistic campaign in Spokane, Washington, in 1909.

Indiana was one of those states where Sunday had a large imprint. He conducted forty-eight revivals and speaking engagements throughout the state. In 1913, in South Bend, he led his largest revival in the state, a seven-week campaign that resulted in 6,098 converts. When it was over, it was hailed as "Indiana's Greatest Revival" by newspapers throughout the state.

By the 1910s Sunday had become a colorful and controversial national celebrity whose revivals were often regarded as the best show in town. His worship services were unquestionably entertaining and drew the curious as well as the devout, but showmanship was by no means the only reason for his success. The essence of his appeal lay in the fact that he conveyed a largely traditional social and religious message stressing the importance of family, community, individual responsibility, hard work, material success, and evangelical Christian piety in an often unorthodox style that resonated with many of the changes occurring in American life.

In an era in which sports were becoming an increasingly important part of the nation's popular culture, Sunday's sometimes exaggerated reputation as a professional ballplayer contributed to his rapport with audiences and provided familiar sports imagery and anecdotes that helped give his evangelism its unique character. He made the most of his reputation as a professional athlete, punctuating his sermons with astonishing feats of athleticism, including sparring with the devil, stealing bases, hitting imaginary home runs, and sliding home to eternity. His athletic prowess, coupled with his assertive, sometime pugnacious demeanor in the pulpit, appealed to those who longed for a more muscular, manly Christianity at a time when some were deeply concerned about the perilous state of American manhood in general and about the feminization of American Christianity in particular. His battle against demon rum made him the darling of many prohibitionists in an era rife with reform. Although Sunday believed that social reform began with the transformation of the human heart, he was convinced that his revivals had social, as well as personal, consequences. His credentials as a Progressive Era reformer, however, were modest at best. He never grasped and thus never challenged the complexities and inequities inherent in the industrial capitalism of his day.

The saving of souls turned out to be lucrative. Sunday biographer Lyle Dorset has estimated that between 1908 and 1920 the evangelist earned more than a million dollars in an era when the income of the average American worker totaled far less. While many Americans admired the businesslike character of Sunday's evangelism, there were many who found such personal gain from religious work unseemly. Sunday, who believed financial reward one measure of God's favor, never apologized for his wealth.

As Sunday's ministry expanded, he increasingly needed a respite from the accelerating pace of his work. Through his affiliation with Chapman, the evangelist and his family had begun to make summer visits from Chicago to Winona Lake, Indiana, site of the Winona Christian Assembly's Bible Conference Center. The resort-like surroundings afforded the relaxing environment for which he longed. After raising their four children in Chicago for twenty-three years, the Sundays built a Craftsman-style bungalow at Lake Winona in 1911 that became the couple's home and sometimes refuge for the rest of their lives.

Named Mount Hood, their home was an outstanding example of the American arts and crafts style, a movement that began in England in response to the Industrial Revolution and mass-produced goods. In the United States it became known as "blue architecture" because of its reliance on local labor and materials. Typical of the Arts and Crafts style, the Sundays' bungalow was simple in form and comfortable in design. They furnished it with decorative art pieces, naturalistic art prints, and furniture exemplary of the Arts and Crafts style. Nell Sunday, the last surviving member of the family, left Mount Hood and all of its contents to the Winona Christian Assembly as a place where visitors could come to hear the Billy Sunday story.

During the first two decades of the twentieth century, Sunday's life story, public persona, and dramatic revivalistic campaigns enabled him to package conventional norms in a way that made both him and his ministry appear relevant to millions in an era of unprecedented change. However, after 1920 the aging evangelist's popularity steadily declined. In the aftermath of the Great War, the nation made a decisive turn toward modernity. Accelerating urbanization and industrialization, with their corollary demographic and cultural changes, rendered the evangelist's message and methods less appealing and less necessary than in an earlier era. By the time of his death in November 1935

Sunday had preached to perhaps eighty million people, some of whom he had helped to negotiate the social and economic changes of the early twentieth century and others whom he had enabled to cope more effectively with the spiritual and emotional challenges of their lives. In the process Sunday, for good or for ill, had contributed much to the popular image of modern American evangelism and had helped to refine techniques upon which subsequent generations of evangelists built.

ROBERT F. MARTIN

For Further Reading

Firstenberer, W. A. "Indiana's Sacred Mount Hood: The Billy Sunday Home." *Traces of Indiana and Midwestern History* 18, no. 2 (Spring 2006): 26–35.

Martin, Robert F. *Hero of the Heartland: Billy Sunday and the Transformation of American Society, 1862–1935*. Bloomington: Indiana University Press, 2002.

Sunday, Billy. *The Sawdust Trail: Billy Sunday in His Own Words*. Iowa City: University of Iowa Press, 2005.

William Ashley Sunday and Helen Amelia Thompson Papers. Microfilm edition. The Billy Graham Center at Wheaton College, Wheaton, IL.

Taggart, Thomas

November 17, 1856–March 6, 1929

Mayor of Indianapolis, chairman of the Democratic National Committee, Democratic political boss of Indiana, U.S. senator, and owner of the French Lick Springs Hotel.

Thomas Taggart was a legendary figure in late-nineteenth-century and early-twentieth-century Hoosier politics and business. He was a classic example of the immigrant success story, achieving the American Dream after coming to America from Ireland as a young child. In politics, he was the powerful Democratic boss of Indiana who, unusual for a political boss, had a record in public office as mayor of Indianapolis and U.S. senator. Also unusual was that he was the boss of a statewide, not a city, organization, and that there was a progressive cast to many of his positions and achievements. He played a major role on the national political stage. In business, he was successful in a number of ventures, ranging from investments in Miami with CARL FISHER to a lucrative copper mining business in northern Mexico, but his signature business was the famous French Lick Springs Hotel.

Born in Amyvale, County Monaghan, Ireland, Taggart came to the United States in 1861 with his family, settling in Xenia, Ohio, where his father had secured a job as a railroad station agent. He went to work at age fifteen as a clerk for the N. and G. Ohmer Company in their railroad restaurant and hotel. Taggart never completed high school and was transferred to the depot restaurant in Garrett, Indiana, in 1875, where he met his future wife, Eva Dora Bryant, whom he married in 1878. In 1877 he was transferred to the company's restaurant at Union Station in Indianapolis. In 1887 Taggart became the sole proprietor of the depot restaurant in the new Union Station. He later acquired control of the Grand and Denison Hotels in downtown Indianapolis.

Taggart had a famously winning personality that led to success in both business and politics. After being courted to run for various offices, he was elected auditor of heavily Republican Marion County in 1886 and reelected in 1890. While auditor, Taggart served successively as city, county, and state Democratic chairman. As county chairman in 1888, he carried Marion County for Democratic presidential candidate Grover Cleveland over hometown favorite son BENJAMIN HARRISON. As state chairman in 1892, Taggart carried Indiana for Cleveland in Harrison's reelection bid. Knowing him to be a master political organizer, Indianapolis Democrats nominated Taggart for mayor in 1895. He won three successive contests, defeating Republicans Preston C. Trusler that year, William M. Harding in 1897, and Charles A. Bookwalter in 1899. Taggart's three city administrations were marked by public improvements and fiscal efficiency. His major achievement was the purchase of 953 acres along the White River to form the nucleus of an extensive public parks system, making Taggart a leader in the national movement to conserve urban green space for public use.

After leaving the mayor's office in 1901, Taggart embarked upon a business venture that shaped the rest of his life when he organized a syndicate that purchased the French Lick Springs Hotel in Orange County. He had a number of fellow investors in this enterprise, including the Monon Railroad, but he bought them out quickly because he wanted to invest profits in the further expansion of the hotel property, while his partners wanted to take out profits as dividends. And expand he did. He added an Annex to the front wing (1905–6) and constructed the Main Wing

(1910–11), Deluxe Wing (1914–15), Convention Wing (1924–25), and the Pluto Water Plant. The property increased from 350 to 2,800 acres. The nation's social and political elite began to frequent the hotel, especially in the spring and fall seasons, on their way to and back from winter sojourns in Florida. Kentucky Derby weekend, the first Saturday in May, was the height of the social season at French Lick Springs. An added attraction for many was the thriving illegal gambling at both the French Lick Springs and West Baden Springs hotels. The hotel soon acquired a reputation as one of the world's most elegant spas, propelled by Taggart's rising star on the national political stage.

With his final term as mayor of Indianapolis ending and the French Lick business venture just ahead, Taggart was named to the Democratic National Committee in 1900, a seat he held until 1916. Indiana, with its fifteen electoral votes, was an important swing state and presidential elections here were often decided by razor-thin margins in the last quarter of the nineteenth century and the first quarter of the twentieth. This fact gave Taggart an outsized importance in the national Democratic Party. He was elected chairman of the Democratic National Committee for the term 1904–8, leading the cause for Judge Alton B. Parker of New York against incumbent President Theodore Roosevelt in 1904 During these years when he was at the height of his power, Taggart helped secure vice presidential nominations for Hoosiers John W. Kern in 1908 on the ticket with William Jennings Bryan and THOMAS R. MARSHALL in 1912 and 1916 with Woodrow Wilson, as well as New York's Franklin D. Roosevelt in 1920 with James M. Cox. He is also credited with swinging the Democratic nomination to Wilson at the 1912 Baltimore convention.

In March 1916, upon the death of Democratic Senator Benjamin Franklin Shively, Governor Samuel M. Ralston, an old Taggart friend, appointed him to the vacant U.S. Senate seat. His short tenure was marked by attention to fiscal efficiency in the federal government. He lost the seat to Republican James E. Watson in the November 1916 election and again in 1920, when he ran to regain the seat. He was bitterly disappointed in 1924 when he had virtually nailed down the presidential nomination for now Senator Ralston, who withdrew at the last minute because of health considerations. By 1928 Taggart was too ill to play a major role at the national convention in Houston, but he did instruct the Indiana delegation to nominate banker and railroad attorney Evans Woollen as a favorite-son candidate on the first ballot. An interesting social and political footnote is that Taggart and his family summered in the village of Hyannis Port on Cape Cod from the early years of the twentieth century, where he built a compound of three summerhouses. Just before his death, Joe and Rose Kennedy purchased the house next door for their famous political family.

After battling health issues for several years, Taggart died on March 6, 1929. Happily, he and his wife had celebrated their fiftieth wedding anniversary in June 1928 with their children and grandchildren. Episcopal Bishop Joseph M. Francis read the funeral in the Taggart home at 1331 North Delaware Street just across the street from the late President Harrison's home. Taggart was buried in the Taggart family lot at Crown Hill Cemetery in Indianapolis. Two years after Taggart's death, friends and the city of Indianapolis erected a beautiful colonnade memorial along the

Thomas Taggart

White River in Riverside Park, at the center of his most enduring legacy as mayor of Indianapolis.

JAMES P. FADELY

For Further Reading

Fadely, James Philip, *Thomas Taggart: Public Servant, Political Boss: 1856–1929*. Indianapolis: Indiana Historical Society, 1997.

Taggart, Thomas. Papers. Indiana State Library, Indianapolis.

Fadely, James Philip. "Thomas Taggart." *Encyclopedia of Indianapolis*. Edited by David J. Bodenhamer and Robert G Barrows. Bloomington: Indiana University Press, 1994.

Tarkington, Newton Booth

July 29, 1869–May 19, 1946

Celebrated author from Indiana's golden age of literature.

In the summer of 1925, after a night of partying, a young and relatively unknown Ernest Hemingway and newly published *Great Gatsby* author F. Scott Fitzgerald, called upon Booth Tarkington at a café in Paris. The fifty-six-year-old Tarkington had spent most of the year traveling with his wife in North Africa and Europe. The celebrated Hoosier author had already won two Pulitzer Prizes and had been named the most significant living American writer by the readers of *Literary Digest* in 1921. It is no surprise that the budding writers would want to meet one of the most famous authors of the early twentieth century.

When Tarkington was not sojourning through Europe or summering in his Kennebunkport, Maine, mansion, the millionaire wintered in Indianapolis, his childhood home. Many of his short stories, novels, plays, and juvenile literature took place in Indiana locales. His childhood home in the 1100 block of North Pennsylvania Street featured prominently in some of those works. Born into a comfortable status, Tarkington grew up in a large Italianate brick home with his sister, Haute, and parents, John and Elizabeth Booth Tarkington.

Unhappy with their son's performance in the local public schools, in 1887 the Tarkingtons sent their young son off to Phillips Exeter Academy, a boarding school in New Hampshire. Later, he matriculated at both Purdue University, where he remained for one year in 1890, and then to Princeton University, where he stayed until 1893. While at Princeton, he immersed himself in reading great American and foreign writers. Tarkington particularly enjoyed Mark Twain, Henry James, Rudyard Kipling, and Leo Tolstoy. His greatest literary find while at Princeton was the realist William Dean Howells, whom he idolized through much of his literary career.

In 1893 Tarkington returned to Indianapolis without a college degree, but with the goal of writing a novel. He had already found some success selling a few short stories. He lived at home with his parents, but spent much of his time drinking with friends at clubs around the city. He garnered no measurable income during these lost years, but did receive an inheritance from his namesake and uncle, Newton Booth, who had been a California governor and U.S. senator. Tarkington was not unproductive during this time period. He wrote numerous poems and plays, and he completed a novel titled *Monsieur Beaucaire*, a romantic and sentimental tale set in Europe. He was also close to finishing another novel, *The Gentleman from Indiana*.

For five years Tarkington labored over the story of John Harkless, an easterner who assumed control of a newspaper in Plattville, Indiana. The young hero spends much of the novel defeating corrupt government officials, routing a gang of hooligans, and trying to win the heart of Helen Sherwood. Tarkington modeled his central character in *The Gentleman from Indiana* upon John Cleve Green, a Princeton friend who had died prematurely. With two unpublished novels now finished, his sister, Haute Tarkington Jameson, could stand it no more. She thought her brother to be an exceptional writer so she traveled to New York City to visit S. S. McClure, the publisher of *McClure's Magazine*. While McClure was not impressed with *Monsieur Beaucaire*, he was impressed with the idea of *The Gentleman from Indiana*, as regional fiction was very popular in the late nineteenth century. Hamlin Garland, a well-known author and serial writer for the magazine, read Tarkington's novel and wrote him a note. "You are a novelist." Tarkington treasured the note for the remainder of his life.

The Gentleman from Indiana became an instant best seller in 1900 and made Tarkington famous. He also began earning a handsome income. *Monsieur Beaucaire* came out in 1900 and also sold well. Tarkington continued to dabble in playwriting and spent much of the next decade trying to balance his time writing plays and novels. During this prolific time period, he wrote *The Van Revels*, a romance novel set in Terre Haute, Indiana, around the time of the Mexican-American War. While Tarkington later distanced himself from these early novels, they continued to be popular in early-twentieth-century America.

In 1902 he married Laurel Louisa Fletcher, the daughter of a wealthy Indianapolis banker. The marriage was troubled and eventually ended in divorce in 1911. The couple did have one child, Laurel, who died at the age of fourteen. Curiously, the author ran for and was elected to the Indiana House of Representatives in 1903. He served only one term, but the moment provided fodder for a series of short stories called *In the Arena* (1905). President Theodore Roosevelt enjoyed the stories so much that he invited Tarkington to the White House soon after the book's publication.

Tarkington's life took a new direction when he married Susannah Robinson in 1912. He swore off alcohol and produced work praised by critics and the public alike. His "Growth" trilogy placed him on the literary map. *Turmoil* (1915), *The Magnificent Ambersons*, (1918), and *The Midlander* (1924) traced the lives of three families living in a midwestern city. Each of the families had to deal with industrial, economic, and class issues of the day. The books somewhat mirrored Tarkington's own life. As the city of Indianapolis grew, his childhood playground started to vanish. The author loathed the soot that rained down upon his genteel neighborhood. Eventually, he moved from the family home to a beautiful Tudor Revival mansion in the 4200 block of North Meridian Street. The fictional Ambersons faced a similar dilemma in his Pulitzer Prize–winning novel of old-moneyed people who refused to move from their mansion near the city center. As the nouveau riche invested in automobile companies and relocated to country additions, the Ambersons clung to the past while their world changed around them. The Sheridans and Oliphants faced similar crises. Tarkington received further acclaim with the publication of *Alice Adams* (1921), which also won a Pulitzer.

Amazingly, during this same productive period, the prolific author managed to pen a series of popular juvenile works, including *Penrod* (1914) and *Seventeen* (1916). Sales from these books added to his already substantial income. Flush with cash, Tarkington began to collect expensive art pieces for his mansions in Maine and Indiana. During the height of the Great Depression, while many Americans suffered, Tarkington continued

Booth Tarkington

to write and collect art pieces by Titian, Velazquez, Goya, and others.

Much like the city that overtook his childhood home, the literary world also seemed to pass Tarkington by. By the 1930s critics found his work old fashioned and formulaic. The author himself once boasted that readers would never find profanity or sex in any of his novels. Despite health problems, he continued to churn out one novel after another. A staunch Republican, the author railed against the New Deal and became a supporter of another Hoosier, Wendell Willkie. With the start of World War II, Tarkington offered his talents as a writer to drum up support for the U.S. involvement in that conflict.

Tarkington died in 1946 at his Indianapolis home. He left his thirty-first novel unfinished. Upon his passing, Indiana lost yet another writer from the state's golden age of literature that included the likes of JAMES WHITCOMB RILEY, MEREDITH NICHOLSON, GEORGE ADE, and others. Tarkington's tales have been spun into Broadway plays, radio shows, and Hollywood films. He chronicled the lives of Hoosiers in a time of great change, and tapped into popular genres from his day.

WILLIAM GULDE

For Further Reading

Mayberry, Susanah. *My Amiable Uncle*. West Lafayette, IN: Purdue University Press, 1983.

Tarkington, Booth. *The Magnificent Ambersons*. Garden City, NY: Doubleday, Page and Company, 1918.

Woodress, James. *Booth Tarkington: A Gentleman from Indiana*. 1955. Reprint, New York: Greenwood Press, 1969.

Tecumseh and Tenskwatawa

Tecumseh (1768–October 5, 1813) and Tenskwatawa (March 1768–November 1836)

Shawnee Indian leaders who advocated uniting various tribes to halt westward expansion of white settlers.

In early 1808 two Shawnee Indian leaders, Tenskwatawa (the Prophet) and his brother, Tecumseh, trudged west into the Indiana Territory. A host of followers accompanied them on their journey through the woods bordering the Miami and Maumee Rivers. Here they would build the community of Prophetstown, which is located today outside of Lafayette. Three years earlier, in the spring of 1805, Tenskwatawa slipped into a deep trance in which the Great Spirit revealed a plan that would allow Indians to renew their culture. These visions became the basis for Tenskwatawa's community at Prophetstown. Tenskwatawa declared that Indians needed to unite politically and militarily in order to resist the destructive forces of Euro-American culture. Otherwise, solitary native communities would find themselves at the mercy of a white onslaught. The pan-Indian alliance that the Prophet and his brother hoped to create would require Indians to segregate themselves from Euro-Americans.

The Prophet hoped that such an alliance would stop the further westward encroachment of whites. Instead, his efforts ended up fueling violence and leading to the Indians' forced removal to the trans-Mississippi West. Prophetstown was a place where a variety of Indian communities—Kickapoo, Potawatomi, Ho-Chunk, Miami, Shawnee, and many others—visited, settled, and, in some cases, died. At the town's height, Indian residents cultivated between one hundred and two hundred acres of corn in order to feed indigenous visitors. Native peoples came and went to Prophetstown throughout the year; these migrations reinforced fears among many settlers that Tenskwatawa had created a native army bent on destroying whites.

In the years leading to the War of 1812, the Prophet, Tecumseh, and WILLIAM HENRY HARRISON, governor of the Indiana Territory, bickered over land cessions, treaty negotiations, and the Indians who had massed at Prophetstown. These debates culminated in the Treaty of Fort Wayne in 1809, a land cession that both Tecumseh and the Prophet adamantly opposed. The treaty ceded three million acres to the United States and represented a deep blow to the Prophet's efforts to unify Indians against white interference.

Scholars Gregory Dowd and R. David Edmunds identified this treaty as an important juncture—one where Tecumseh began to transform his brother's religious revival into a pan-Indian movement. After 1809 Tecumseh's efforts were transformed into an alliance with Euro-Americans, namely the British. Tecumseh accepted French traders and gunsmiths at Prophetstown because they provided tools necessary for uniting various Indian communities. Tecumseh boasted that a "considerable number of the Wyandots" and "some of the Six Nations" planned on joining the Shawnee brothers in the fall of 1811. Tecumseh's trip to the American southeast worried Harrison, which he viewed as an effort to win support for the Prophet's plans at Prophetstown. Believing that Prophetstown was the logical result of this growing polarization and represented an immediate threat to the region, the governor moved to destroy the nativist settlement.

Whites worried that the Prophet would help usher in a new era of British domination in the young American republic. These fears led Harrison and his supporters to construct a fort at present-day Terre Haute as a staging area for an expedition to Prophetstown. Many Americans believed that such a fort was necessary to prevent the Prophet from attacking Vincennes. The dense thickets, swamps, and small lakes of Indiana would prevent an attack by American cavalry and slow any infantry advance.

Despite the fact that nervous Indians had begun to leave Prophetstown in droves, Harrison was determined to confront Tenskwatawa. Making matters worse, Prophetstown lacked the unity Tenskwatawa desired and he believed that a small skirmish between Terre Haute and Prophetstown might convince hundreds of Indians to join him. French traders deliberately misled Harrison with false intelligence and convinced him to make a preemptive attack on Prophetstown.

Tecumseh

Bloodshed erupted between the two groups on November 7, 1811. Lieutenant Josiah Bacon watched it unfold, horrified as Indians with "their faces painted black" appeared in the darkness as the muskets flashed and lighted up the surrounding areas. The battle continued until sunrise. At the end, anywhere between thirty and fifty Indians were killed and almost 160 Americans had been killed or wounded. Tenskwatawa abandoned his town to avoid capture by the American forces. Harrison ordered the settlement burned, including all of the wigwams, the meetinghouse, and 5,000 pounds of stored food. But this desperate act did not stop Tenskwatawa. He kept his influence within the Wabash-Maumee Valley. In fact, Tenskwatawa remained a significant force in the region and rebuilt his town during the winter of 1811.

As the Prophet recovered from the violence at Tippecanoe, Tecumseh sought to unify the Indians through militarism. Rather than demand that the Indians operate under a singular ideology, Tecumseh hoped that they would fight against a single enemy, the Americans. Tecumseh used the Mississinewa Council of 1812 to defend Prophetstown particularly because he was busy trying to unite Indian groups throughout the northern and southern Ohio Valley. His plans included visiting Creek, Osage, and even Choctaw villages. The last thing Tecumseh wanted was for the Americans to destroy Prophetstown again and permanently drive away potential Indian allies. Tecumseh promised that the Indians would never initiate an attack, but that they would always defend their town to the last man. The Miami and Kickapoo demanded that the Potawatomi refrain from such attacks, and Tecumseh promised to control the Potawatomi who had caused the violence that spring. Although Tecumseh's efforts were geared toward protecting his growing pan-Indian confederacy, Harrison thought that Tecumseh's comments hinted toward his long-term goal to destroy the Americans.

Tecumseh succeeded in uniting various Indian communities throughout the region largely because of the growing diplomatic crisis between the United States and Britain. They had failed to reach a compromise over free trade and sailors' rights during the spring of 1812, which pushed President James Madison toward declaring war. Madison signed the declaration of war against Great Britain on June 18, 1812, which drastically altered the dynamics in the Wabash-Maumee Valley. Britain could distribute goods to its Indian allies throughout the Ohio valley, and many of the Indian communities gladly accepted them. War presented Indian groups with an opportunity to renew their old relationships with the British but also to acquire weapons they could use to defend themselves in a region flooded by American settlers.

Tecumseh's confederacy played an important role in the British war effort against the United States during the War of 1812, including the siege and capture of Fort Detroit. Ultimately, the Indian confederacy born at Prophetstown collapsed after the death of Tecumseh at the Battle of the Thames in 1813 and the subsequent end of hostilities between the United States and Great Britain. Tenskwatawa found himself exiled in Canada after the war, trapped between his former British allies and an American government that refused to allow him to return to Prophetstown.

During the summer of 1824, Lewis Cass, then governor of Michigan Territory, sent a letter to the Prophet. Cass hoped that the isolated, aging, and politically weakened Prophet might aid the federal government's plans to force Indians to leave their homes in the Ohio Valley and move west. The chance to take part in plans for Indian removal provided an excellent opportunity for

Tenskwatawa to undercut the influence of an old Shawnee adversary, Black Hoof. Cass hoped for the same thing; Black Hoof's Shawnee resisted efforts to push them from their homes. The Prophet had accepted the fact he would not return to Prophetstown, but he also recognized that helping the Americans would let him reassert his authority within the Shawnee community.

Isolated for nearly a decade from his community in Indiana, Tenskwatawa had little choice but to pacify Cass in order to survive. The Prophet deftly used Cass to work his way back into the United States by agreeing to lead a contingent of Shawnee to the Kansas River in the late 1820s. The Prophet would resurrect his town in Kansas. Tenskwatawa remained at the last iteration of Prophetstown near the Argentine district of present-day Kansas City, Kansas, until his death in 1836. He isolated himself from the majority of the Shawnee who had begun working with the missionaries and government agents. Few Indians sought his counsel largely because he did not support any sort of collaboration with the Americans. He spent his last few years in relative obscurity.

Despite their portrayal as "bad" Indians by American newspapers, political leaders, and amateur historians, Tenskwatawa and Tecumseh were in fact complicated figures who transformed the early history of Indiana. Not only did the development of frontier violence lead to the relocation of Indiana's capital from Vincennes to Corydon, but Tenskwatawa's and Tecumseh's actions also pulled the British west into Indiana during the War of 1812 and provided greater motivation for British traders and agents to get involved in Indian communities. As a result, calls for the removal of American Indians from Indiana grew more vocal in the postwar period, eventually leading to the forced removal of various Indian tribes from the area.

PATRICK BOTTIGER

For Further Reading

Bottiger, Patrick. "Prophetstown for their Own Purposes: The French, Miamis, and Cultural Identities in the Wabash-Maumee Valley." *Journal of the Early Republic* 33 (Spring 2013): 29–60.

Cave, Alfred. *Prophets of the Great Spirit*. Lincoln: University of Nebraska Press, 2006.

Edmunds, R. David. *The Shawnee Prophet*. Lincoln: University of Nebraska Press, 1983.

Jortner, Adam. *The Gods of Prophetstown*. Oxford: Oxford University Press, 2013.

Thomas, Mary Frame Myers
October 28, 1816–August 19, 1888

Physician and leader in the Indiana woman's suffrage movement.

Mary F. Thomas was a physician and prominent leader in the national movement for female suffrage and married women's property rights. She was the first woman to address the Indiana state legislature when she presented a petition to that body in 1859 arguing for married women's property rights and a female suffrage amendment to the Indiana Constitution.

Mary Frame Myers was born in North Carolina to Quaker abolitionist parents who instilled in their three daughters the value of education. According to one source, Mary's family lived for a time in Washington, D.C., where her father took her to hear congressional debates, which may have prompted her political connections later in life. In 1833 her family moved to Lisbon, Ohio, and six years later Mary married Owen Thomas.

In 1845 Mary heard suffragist Lucretia Mott speak at a Quaker meeting and became a proponent of women's rights. She also became a woman extraordinary in her time. After marrying Owen in Lisbon, Ohio, she studied medicine under his tutelage in Wabash County, Indiana. She attended Penn Medical University in Philadelphia from 1851 to 1852, took a course at Cleveland Medical College from 1852 to 1853, and then returned to Penn. She graduated in 1854 and is shown in the Penn catalog in 1860 among the school's "lady graduates," with her specialty listed as "ovarian dropsy."

Mary and her husband lived and practiced medicine in Fort Wayne, Indiana, for a time and then moved to Richmond. In 1857 the couple advertised their practice in the *Richmond City Directory*: "Dr. Thomas will attend to surgery and general practice. Dr. M. F. Thomas will give particular attention to Obstetrics and Diseases of Women and Children. Office and Residence on Fort Wayne Avenue (opposite Friends' Meeting House)."

Along with her medical practice, Mary also worked to better the situation of women. She was a member of the Indiana Woman's Rights Society and became president of the society in 1856. She became coeditor, along with Mary Birdsall, of the *Lily*, a national woman's magazine in 1857. The magazine focused on issues of temperance, dress reform, suffrage, and women's rights, including the repeal of unjust marriage and inheritance laws.

In 1859 Thomas, Birdsall, and another suffragist, Agnes Cook, took their concerns to the Indiana General Assembly. In a rare joint session of the legislature, the women requested a legal remedy to protect married women's property rights and to allow them the vote. Thomas read her petition first and thus became the first woman to address the Indiana legislature. In her eloquent argument for equal right to the vote, Thomas countered any argument that women were not capable of voting: "Mrs. Stowe can produce a sensation throughout the literary world by her "Uncle Tom;" Miss Hosmer chisels statues; Rosa Bonner and Lily Martain paint pictures; Lucy Stone, Frances D. Gage, and other women can lecture; Lucretia Mott, Antoinette L. Blackwell and Mrs. Jenkins can preach the gospel in American pulpits; women can edit newspapers with ability; while scores of ladies make fortunes as merchants, and last, though not least, your humble petitioner with hundreds of other lady physicians in our country, can follow the calling of the medical profession with the approval of the refined and intelligent among men and women."

Thomas went on to state that a woman should have same rights as a man to the vote and to her property. She concluded: "If she be granted human, with human faculties and human needs, then are the rights of humanity for the protection of these faculties, and the supply of these needs, assuredly hers—and no accident of sex, no prejudged inferiority, no plea of expediency, or fear of confidence, can at all militate against the soundness of the argument, modify the injustice of withholding or the rightfulness of granting such rights."

Unfortunately for Indiana, the legislators treated the reading of the petition as a joke, one of them calling it a "jollification." Perhaps Thomas expected no more, but she must have been disappointed. She continued, however, to pursue female suffrage in subsequent sessions of the general assembly, returning to lobby the legislature in 1877, 1879, and 1880. During these years, Thomas served as an officer in the Indiana Woman's Suffrage Association and of the American Association for Woman's Suffrage.

Never neglecting her medical practice, Thomas continued to work during these years as she lobbied for equal rights. During the Civil War, Governor OLIVER P. MORTON appointed her to hospital service. She served in Washington, D.C., and Nashville, Tennessee. She cared for soldiers wounded at the Battle of Vicksburg in one of her appointments.

After the war Thomas served on Richmond's Board of Public Health. Beginning in 1867, she was the physician for the Home for Friendless Women in Richmond, continuing her efforts to improve all women's lives. Although the Wayne County Medical Society twice rejected her application for membership due to her gender, she persisted and eventually became a member in 1875. A year later, she became the first woman member of the State Medical College.

Although Thomas was extraordinary for her time in her work and activism, she was also known as a good mother and homemaker. She was an apt seamstress and reputedly sewed the clothing for her three daughters, along with performing her other domestic duties.

Throughout her life Thomas continued to work to make other women's lives better, lobbying for a separate women's prison and separate reformatory for girls, and for female doctors in state mental hospitals. Even in death, she made a statement for women's equality.

Thomas died on August 19, 1888. She had requested that her six pallbearers be women. Four of them represented the organizations that Thomas belonged to and supported: the Good Templars, the Woman's Christian Temperance Union, the Woman's Suffrage Association, and the Home for Friendless Women. Two African American women represented "the Abolition cause and their race."

CONNIE ZEIGLER

For Further Reading

"Dr. Mary F. Thomas." Morrison-Reeves Library, Richmond, IN. http://www.mrlinfo.org/history/biography/thomasmf.htm.

King, Lucy M. "Pioneer Women's Physicians in Indiana." Ruth Lilly Medical Library, Indianapolis, IN. http://library.medicine.iu.edu/

Scholten, Pat Creech. "A Publlic 'Jollificaiton': The 1859 Women's Rights Petition before the Indiana Legislature." *Indiana Magazine of History* 72 (December 1976): 347–59.

Stanton, Elizabeth Cady, Susan Brownwell Anthony, Matilda Joslyn Gage, Ida Husted Harper, eds. *History of Woman Suffrage, 1876–1885*. Volume 3. Rochester, NY: Charles Mann Printing Company, 1886.

Thompson, "James" Maurice
September 9, 1844–February 15, 1901
Author, naturalist, and state geologist.

Scarcely known today except, at most, as the author of the once-popular novel *Alice of Old Vincennes*, Maurice Thompson lived during the fabled golden age of Indiana literature. *Alice*, a regional romance set during the American Revolution, at last brought Thompson the fame and financial reward he had long sought as a writer, but sadly, he died only months after its publication.

He was born in Fairfield, Indiana, a hamlet near Kokomo now known as Oakford. His father, a Baptist minister, moved the family to serve congregations in Missouri and Kentucky, but by 1854 he had left the ministry and settled on a plantation in Georgia. Thompson's early exposure to southern culture found its way into much of his writing. He and his younger brother, Will, enjoyed a good liberal arts education through tutors, along with instruction in outdoor skills from the locals. Maurice also studied mathematics, hoping to become a civil engineer.

Thompson fought for the South in the Civil War, chiefly as a scout, as did his brother. General William Tecumseh Sherman's March to the Sea left the family home in shambles, and afterward Thompson made his way to Calhoun, Georgia, where he studied civil engineering and later law. He wrote a few pieces for struggling southern literary magazines and also conducted a number of naturalist surveys of flora and fauna in the wilds of Georgia and Florida.

With few opportunities in the South after the war, Thompson and his brother decided to seek their fortunes in the North and in 1867 settled in Crawfordsville, Indiana, where both found work as civil engineers on a railroad under construction in the area. Within a year Maurice had married Alice Lee, the daughter of his employer, and later Will married her sister. The brothers opened a law office in the county seat town in 1871. But Maurice, who had wanted to write from an early age, also published in a variety of magazines numerous poems, essays, and articles on the outdoors and active pursuits in nature. While not anywhere near as prolific as his brother, Will, too, wrote a few articles and poetry.

The Thompson brothers were both skilled and avid archers, collaborating on a book of tips to prepare for competitions, *How to Train in Archery* (1879), which followed the publication the previous year of Maurice's *The Witchery of Archery*, his second book. *Witchery* was subtitled *A Complete Manual of Archery* and certainly the book, a compendium of practical instruction and essays on all aspects of the sport, appeared to cover the topic thoroughly. Indeed, Maurice is credited with stimulating a national interest in archery in the late nineteenth century. Long after his death, the National Archery Association in the 1930s named an annual award for Thompson to be given to the person "who has labored most earnestly and unselfishly for the advancement of archery."

With one foot in the South and the other in Indiana, Thompson put his various interests and experiences to good work in his short stories and novels. His first published book was a collection of nine stories and sketches called *Hoosier Mosaics* (1875). Among the chief supporting characters are a county seat lawyer and a civil engineer, and the locations are real towns in Montgomery County and adjacent counties with which Thompson was intimately familiar. In most there is an underlying theme of unrequited—indeed, unnoticed—love involving any of a number of Hoosier males of varying ages pining for a perceived paragon of womanhood of whom he suddenly becomes aware. In general, that comprises the sum of the plot; invariably, the object of the man's dreams moves away or is found to be involved with another, and thus the narrative ends. The stories are rich in descriptive detail, however, and reveal much of small-town and rural life in nineteenth century Indiana, as well as vivid pictures of the countryside.

More fiction followed; two novels in 1882 and 1883, respectively, aroused modest interest. In the latter year, Thompson also offered his first book of poetry, *Songs of Fair Weather*, most of which had previously been published in several different magazines. Thompson went at writing with a vengeance after that, ultimately giving up the practice of law entirely to devote full time to his calling. He published more novels alternating with collections of essays on nature and outdoor pursuits, such as *By-Ways and Bird Notes* (1885) and *Sylvan Secrets in Bird Songs and Books* (1887). The perspective in these essays was more toward that of the active outdoorsman than the contemplative naturalist, and these works also tended to be more popular than his novels. During this time, owing in part to his having served briefly in the state legislature—no mean feat for an ex-Confederate—and no doubt also for his prolific output of nature writings, Thompson served as Indiana's state geologist and head of the department of natural history.

Thompson even wrote a historical geography, *The Story of Louisiana* (1888), but for all his output, real financial success eluded him. In his short novel *A Fortnight of Folly* (1888), Thompson satirizes writers of all stripes—including himself—and has a character declaim:

> The really successful author in America is . . . never visible, except on the remote horizon. You hear much of him, but . . . [t]he fact is, he is a myth. On the other hand, however, the American cities are full of successful publishers who have become millionaires upon the profits of books which have starved their authors. Of course this appears to be a paradox, but I suppose that it can be explained by the rule of profit and loss. The author's loss is the publisher's profit.

One strongly suspects these are Thompson's true feelings, barely disguised. In the same novel he also pokes considerable fun at the contemporary craze for "dialect stories," a genre in which, of course, he indulged frequently.

Although he maintained his residence in Indiana, Thompson, in 1889, became literary editor for *The Independent*, a New York publication for which he wrote countless book reviews and unsigned editorials, along with more than two hundred articles and poems. Books of poetry, essays, criticism, and juvenile stories flowed from his pen in the 1890s with settings in both Indiana and the South.

Popular from the moment of its release in 1900, *Alice of Old Vincennes* was different from anything Thompson had written before and is cited by many as the model for a historical novel. Although Thompson represented the work as based on true characters and incidents during the time of the British occupation of Vincennes, no evidence has been found to support this assertion. Regardless, the book called attention to Indiana's prestatehood involvement in the American Revolution. Sadly, Thompson did not live long enough to enjoy the success of his book, which was later made into a play. He died of pneumonia in his Crawfordsville home before the winter was out.

Thompson lived in Crawfordsville nearly all his adult life, spending winters on the Gulf Coast. Indiana may claim Maurice Thompson as her own, but so does Georgia, his boyhood home and for whom he fought in the Civil War.

GLORY-JUNE GREIFF

For Further Reading

Banta, R. E. *Indiana Authors and Their Books, 1816–1916: Biographical Sketches of Authors Who Published during the First Century of Indiana Statehood with Lists of Their Books.* Crawfordsville, IN: Wabash College, 1949.

Russo, Dorothy Ritter, and Thelma Lois Sullivan. *Bibliographical Studies of Seven Authors of Crawfordsville, Indiana.* Indianapolis: Indiana Historical Society, 1952.

Maurice Thompson Papers. Emory University, Atlanta, GA.

Shumaker, Arthur W. *A History of Indiana Literature: With Emphasis on the Authors of Imaginative Works Who Commenced Writing Prior to World War II.* Indianapolis: Indiana Historical Bureau, 1962.

Thornbrough, Emma Lou
January 24, 1913–December 19, 1994

Black history pioneer, Indiana historian, and civil rights activist.

Emma Lou Thornbrough, a national pioneer in black history and a lifelong worker for civil rights in Indiana, wrote a seminal state-level study of African Americans in Indiana, *The Negro in Indiana before 1900*, and influential studies of national black leaders Booker T. Washington and T. Thomas Fortune. Her *Since Emancipation: A Short History of Indiana Negroes, 1863–1963* and her manuscript for *Indiana Blacks in the Twentieth Century* (published posthumously in 2000), which she continued to work on until her death in 1994, brought up to date her lifelong project of documenting and analyzing Indiana's experience of racial inequality.

Thornbrough's articles on racial barriers to public accommodations in Indiana, and "The Indianapolis School Busing Case" were harbingers of her accelerated research agenda after her retirement in 1983. At her death, she left behind two large works in manuscript, the above-cited *Indiana Blacks in the Twentieth Century* and her still unpublished "The Indianapolis Study: School Segregation and Desegregation in a Northern City."

Her scholarship was sound and her research exhaustive, while her essential commitment to equality and fairness were transparent. These convictions led her to combine social action as a concerned citizen with her scholarly research and teaching at Butler University from 1946 to

1983 and into retirement. Aside from a brief and unsuccessful venture into politics as a Democratic candidate for the state legislature in 1952, she worked for civil rights via local organizations throughout her adult life—she helped organize the Indianapolis Human Relations Council with Bishop Paul Moore and Rabbi Maurice Davis in the late 1950s and served as chair of its education committee, and she was on the executive boards of the Indiana Civil Liberties Union and the Indianapolis National Association for the Advancement of Colored People and received awards for her devoted service from these and other civil rights organizations. And her research obviously served her cause; she was proud that "my research on Indiana was used by the lawyers in the Indianapolis schools case, and Judge [S. Hugh] Dillon's first opinion in the Indianapolis case drew heavily upon my research."

To some, Thornbrough seemed incongruous as a pioneer in black history and as a civil rights worker: How does a white woman born into an Indiana Republican family in 1913 come to write black history? She was the first child of inventor Harry C. Thornbrough and his wife, Bess Tyler, of Indianapolis. Her younger sister, GAYLE, shared both her interests and their childhood home for nearly all their lives. Both took undergraduate degrees from Butler University (Emma Lou in 1934, Gayle in 1936), though Emma Lou also acquired a master's degree from Butler in 1936 and began teaching history at George Washington High School in Indianapolis after graduation, while Gayle went to work for the Indiana Historical Society. Both attended graduate school at the University of Michigan in the 1940s, Gayle for one year to get a master's, while Emma Lou completed her doctorate in 1946 and returned to Indianapolis to teach at Butler. Emma Lou lived in New York and Washington in 1955 and 1956 on a Ford Foundation fellowship to gather material on Thomas Fortune; Gayle left Indianapolis to work at the Library of Congress in 1967 and 1968; and Emma Lou was a Mather visiting professor of history at Case Western Research in the fall semester of 1977–78. They regularly traveled together to history conventions and to Europe, often with friends, and enjoyed theater, classical music, and a wide variety of literature. Theirs was a thoroughly upper-middle-class and Indianapolis-centered life; and they both worked against the city's endemic

Emma Lou Thornbrough

racism while living genteelly as elegant lady scholars with their parents until their parents' deaths in the early 1970s.

Certainly one key to the seeming incongruity of Emma Lou's life as a historian of black Americans and an activist for civil rights is her education in the early 1940s at the University of Michigan, where Dwight Lowell Dumond was a star in the history department and a powerful revisionist in the interpretation of the causes of the Civil War and the role of abolitionism. Dumond argued that the abolitionists were right in their condemnation of slavery and its conflict with the values embedded in the Constitution, at a time when most American historians accepted the view that they were unbalanced radicals with little impact on the war, which was seen as a conflict between economic interests. Thornbrough acknowledged in *The Negro in Indiana* that her interest in black history grew out of Dumond's graduate seminar at Michigan. Her dynamic teacher, himself the student of U. B. Phillips, the preeminent scholar of slavery, lit a torch that was passed to an apt pupil, who kept it burning in Indiana.

Emma Lou's third major contribution, in addition to scholarship and social action, was teaching. A powerful teacher, she won an outstanding professor award at Butler in 1965 and accolades from students over the years. She was a forceful and attractive person, with a husky voice and a valiant manner, with her head held high and her mind sharp, good-humored but ready for intellectual combat. Butler valued her highly; she was appointed to an endowed professorship and received the university's highest honor, the Butler Medal in 1981, and was awarded an honorary doctorate in 1988.

Her profession also honored her: she received the American Historical Association's Scholarly Distinction Award in 1993. Although working in a field dominated by men, she once said she had never felt discrimination. But she also noted during the relatively new Women's History Month in 1984 that "when I had become so steeped in the black experience, I could better understand the plight of women." Her first publication in 1956 was a study of kindergarten pioneer ELIZA A. BLAKER, who was able to attract considerable support from Indianapolis women in the late nineteenth century to establish a training school for kindergarten teachers, using the philosophy of Friedrich Fröebel, and whose school became a part of Butler University after her death. Thornbrough's career reflected a time of enormous social and political change, and she was one of its agents. She was interested in the new women's history that emerged in the 1970s and 1980s, but, aside from an essay she contributed on "The History of Black Women in Indiana" for a book published in 1981, she did not publish in this field.

Thornbrough was drawn more strongly to legal and constitutional history, one of the two subjects she most enjoyed teaching and which, along with black history, was the subject of her dissertation, *Negro Slavery in the North: Its Legal and Constitutional Aspects*. How the law was used to deal with gross inequality of condition, from slavery to segregation, was a continuing subject of her interest and analysis in monographs on the Fugitive Slave Law in Indiana, the civil rights movement of the mid-twentieth century, and the legal history of Indianapolis school desegregation. And in writing the history of the civil rights movement in Indiana, she had the advantage of knowing its leaders and working with them to end discrimination and expand opportunity.

Thornbrough considered herself a pioneer in her profession, both because of her sex and because of her field. There were relatively few women historians in academic appointments when she was establishing herself as a productive and influential researcher in post-World War II America, and few people of either sex were working in what was then called Negro history. It is remarkable that she was able to establish herself as both a leader in that field and as the complete historian that she was. In addition to major works in black history, she wrote the comprehensive *Indiana in the Civil War Era, 1850–1880*, volume three of the five-part history of Indiana commissioned by the Indiana Historical Society for the state sesquicentennial. In both her scholarly work and her life as a reformer, Thornbrough worked to shape Indiana history.

LANA RUEGAMER EISENBERG

For Further Reading

Thornbrough, Emma Lou. *The Negro in Indiana before 1900: A Study of a Minority*. Indianapolis: Indiana Historical Bureau, 1957. Reprint, Bloomington: Indiana University Press, 1993.

———. *T. Thomas Fortune, Militant Journalist*. Chicago: University Press of Chicago, 1972.

———. Papers. Irwin Library, Butler University, Indianapolis.

Thornbrough, Gayle
October 29, 1914–November 8, 1999

Indiana historical editor and transformative leader of the Indiana Historical Society.

Gayle Thornbrough's life was devoted to Indiana history, which she served in three stages of her career: as editor of historical documents and monographs for the Indiana Historical Society and the Indiana Historical Bureau, as director of the IHS's library and publications, and as the Society's leader in the wake of enormous resources inherited from ELI LILLY. A dedicated historian with scholarly habits, Thornbrough's responsibilities expanded exponentially in response to the confidence expressed in her abilities by Lilly, the Society's principal patron. While she was recognized nationally as an historical editor in the first stage of her career and throughout her life, her leadership of the country's wealthiest historical society after Lilly's death in 1977 was groundbreaking.

Thornbrough was the younger of two daughters born to Harry C. Thornbrough, an inventor (he patented an invention to improve variable speed transmissions in 1931), and Bess Tyler. Gayle's older sister, EMMA LOU, became a pioneer in the field of African American history, and she preceded Gayle to Shortridge High School and Butler University, as well as to the University of Michigan for graduate work in history. Lifelong companions, they shared a profound interest in history and culture as well as a home. Both brilliant students, they had very different temperaments; Emma Lou was bold and forceful, while Gayle was retiring and uncomfortable in the spotlight. Both forged important careers in history; Emma Lou as an academic historian at Butler University, Gayle as editor and administrator at the IHS.

Gayle was hired by the Society in 1937 to edit its new Prehistory Research Series, which grew out of Lilly's interest in the prehistoric Indian mounds in Indiana. She edited ten highly technical publications on Indian languages between 1937 and 1940. She spent most of 1941–42 earning a master's degree at the University of Michigan, where Emma Lou was pursuing a doctorate. After returning to the IHS as an editor, she moved into documentary editing and also coauthored a book, *The Buffalo Trace*, with George Wilson in 1946.

From 1947 to 1966 Thornbrough worked for both the Bureau and for the Society, replacing the Bureau's first editor Nellie Armstrong Robertson and beginning a partnership with editor Dorothy L. Riker that lasted for most of the rest of her life. Together in this twenty-year period they edited most of the papers that constitute the building blocks of Indiana's early political history: *Executive Proceedings of the State of Indiana*; the messages and papers of governors James Brown Ray, Noah Noble, Samuel Bigger, and David Wallace; *1805–1815 Journals of the General Assembly of Indiana Territory*; and *Indiana Election Returns*. During this period Thornbrough also edited R. C. Buley's two-volume *The Old Northwest*, the only book published by a historical society to win a Pulitzer Prize. She copyedited about twenty other publications for the IHS, not counting publications for the Bureau. She also provided heroic and indispensable service for Glenn Black's two-volume magnum opus, *Angel Site*, when he died before it was completed. After the coded dummy for the book, with hundreds of illustrations, was stolen from a car belonging to the printer, she painstakingly re-created the lost document and saved the publication.

Thornbrough also moved into editing and annotating personal documents, including correspondence between Josiah Harmar and John Francis Hamtramck, U.S. Army officers during the American Revolutionary War and Indian wars; between lifelong friends Treasury Secretary Albert Gallatin and John Badollet of the Vincennes Land Office; and records of Indian agents at Fort Wayne during the War of 1812.

Offered a position at the Library of Congress as a manuscripts specialist in 1967, Thornbrough moved to Washington, D.C., for twenty months, shocking her IHS coworkers, whom she only informed that she was leaving the day before she left. The move prompted Lilly to initiate a study of the Society that led to a major reorganization of the institution that created a major leadership role for Thornbrough. Lilly quietly gave the Society $2.5 million in Eli Lilly and Company stock to fund the new initiatives.

Thornbrough returned to the Society in 1968 in an entirely new role, director of publications and the library, the chief figure in the organization's research mission. When she left, she was one of a group of women who had been friends and lunch companions for twenty years. When she returned, she reinvented herself as an administrator, a lonelier and more responsible position. Some of her former colleagues admitted later that they had been initially skeptical about her ability to make the transition, but they expressed profound admiration for what she accomplished.

In her new position Thornbrough inaugurated a lecture series, worked through the library committee to make the crowded library more accessible to researchers by hiring cataloguers and storing some holdings, and undertook two major long-term documentary editing projects: the nine-volume *Diary of Calvin Fletcher* and the two-volume *Documentary History of the Indiana Decade of the Harmony Society*. She also had a large role in planning the new Library and Historical Building, largely funded by a gift from Lilly and dedicated in 1976. The present IHS building was constructed after she retired.

In 1976 the Society separated from the Bureau following the retirement of Hubert Hawkins, the last of the Society's executives to also head the Bureau. The IHS had shared an executive with the Bureau since the Progressive Era and depended upon the Bureau for leadership for many decades. The new independence of IHS was the result of Lilly's investment in the kind of history Thornbrough and her colleagues had created for forty years, and he entrusted to Thornbrough the

Gayle Thornbrough in her Indiana Historical Society office

leadership of the Society in its new independence, which was heightened considerably by Lilly's bequest in 1977 of 10 percent of his holdings in Eli Lilly Company stock. Lilly's philanthropy, as his biographer James H. Madison has noted, was linked to his personal interests and his personal friendships. It is difficult to imagine that the Society would have been given this legacy without Lilly's confidence in Thornbrough.

Thornbrough responded with a burst of projects: microfilming Indiana newspapers, creating a new version of the Works Progress Administration's *Indiana Guide*, editing the WILLIAM HENRY HARRISON Papers, inaugurating a dissertation fellowship competition to encourage work in Indiana history, funding a faculty position in history of medicine at Indiana University, expanding the Society's manuscripts collections, publishing historic recordings and a monograph on Indiana ragtime, and supporting a newsletter and collecting program in black history. She launched these, and more, while continuing editing the massive Fletcher diary and overseeing the regular production of smaller history publications distributed to IHS members.

In her last sixteen years at the Society, Thornbrough moved from the kind of career her predecessors Robertson and Riker had pursued to the creative leadership of the wealthiest historical society in the country. This was unprecedented. Few women had headed state historical societies and none led the most important ones. She accomplished this without ever having made a speech or writing a monograph and without a PhD, although her contributions to Indiana history were acknowledged by an honorary doctorate from Indiana University in 1982. Despite this unusual career path, no one in her generation made more important contributions to Indiana history and to the American historical society movement. The legacy of the Indiana Historical Society of Gayle Thornbrough and Eli Lilly is secure in the body of work that represents the preservation and dissemination of the materials of the state's early existence and in its prehistory.

LANA RUEGAMER EISENBERG

For Further Reading

Ruegamer, Lana. *A History of the Indiana Historical Society, 1830–1980*. Indianapolis: Indiana Historical Society, 1980.

———. "Gayle Thornbrough and the Indiana Historical Society." *Indiana Magazine of History* 80 (September 1984): 271–77.

Thornbrough, Gayle, and Dorothy Riker. *Readings in Indiana History*. Bloomington: Indiana University Department of History, 1956.

———. Papers. Indiana Historical Society William Henry Smith Memorial Library, Indianapolis.

Van Camp Family

Gilbert, December 25, 1817–April 4, 1900; Cortland, 1850–August 7, 1923; George, January 29, 1861–January 28, 1926; and Frank, 1864–November 11, 1937

Entrepreneurs, businessmen and innovators in the manufacturing, packaging, and retail businesses.

In the nineteenth and early twentieth centuries, the Van Camp family of Indianapolis was among Indiana's most prominent entrepreneurs and business professionals. The family patriarch, Gilbert, built a grocery and food packing business that dominated the canned baked bean market in the Midwest at the turn of the twentieth century. Van Camp's son, Frank, carried on with management of Van Camp Pork and Beans, while a second son, Courtland, broke away from the family business to establish one of the capital city's most successful wholesale and retail hardware businesses.

The descendant of Dutch immigrants, Gilbert C. Van Camp was born in Brookville, Indiana, on Christmas Day, 1817. Van Camp's father, Charles, had come to the Indiana Territory in 1804 and settled in Dearborn County near Harrison before moving north into the Whitewater Valley of Franklin County shortly before Gilbert was born. In the 1830s Gilbert apprenticed as a miller in Brookville and later established a partnership to sell tinware and stoves. Van Camp learned tinsmithing and practiced the trade in Brookville and Greensburg from 1845 to 1860, when he and his second wife, Hester, moved to Indianapolis.

Van Camp then joined grocer Martin Williams and banker CALVIN FLETCHER in the firm of Fletcher, Williams and Van Camp, which operated a cold-storage warehouse for fruits and vegetables. The firm reportedly supplied food to Union army encampments in Indiana during the Civil War, and Van Camp was soon calling upon his skills as a tinsmith to begin canning fruits and vegetables. He and his son, Frank, incorporated the company in 1875 as G. C. Van Camp and Son Packaging Company, which sold canned goods to wholesale grocers from a canning plant in the 300 block of Kentucky Avenue in Indianapolis.

The company's signature product was introduced in the early 1880s and was improved in the 1890s by another son, George, who spent his career with the company in the lab and on the factory floor. Van Camp's Pork and Beans was advertised as canned Boston Baked Beans, but in reality had no molasses or brown sugar in the syrup. According to company legend, Frank opened a can of competitors' beans one day for lunch, and finding them tasteless, mixed them with ketchup from the Van Camp plant. Company legend also stated that each can had one piece of pork, which was inserted by hand on a moving line; the absence of a piece of pork turned the beans gray, and two pieces of pork made the canned beans oily.

The Van Camps advertised the tomato sauce-based beans heavily, and by 1898 Van Camp and Son was shipping more than eight million cans of pork and beans from Indianapolis each year. Shortly after Gilbert died in 1900, Frank began bottling a brand of Worcestershire sauce and canning packed tomatoes in the company's Indianapolis plant. The firm also began experimenting with producing canned condensed milk.

Cortland, Frank's older brother, struck out in a different direction. After completing his college education in 1868, he worked for a few years in the family business, but then in 1876 he purchased Anderson, Bullock and Schofield, an Indianapolis wholesale hardware firm. In the 1880s the company merged with Hanson and Bergunthal, a local blacksmith supply firm. In 1884 the business was incorporated as the Hanson-Van Camp Company; two years later when Hanson left the business, it became Van Camp Hardware and Iron Company. In 1889 Bergundthal retired, and Cortland became sole owner.

In the 1890s and early 1900s the wholesale district surrounding Union Station south of Washington Street in Indianapolis supplied retail outlets in the cities and small towns of Indiana, Illinois, Ohio, Michigan, and Kentucky with everything from hardware to groceries to clothing and dry goods. From its eight-story office and warehouse at 401 West Maryland Street, sales personnel fanned out from Van Camp Hardware to service accounts in Indiana and surrounding states. The city's location at the hub of an expanding passenger, freight, and interurban rail network ensured timely delivery of goods across the region.

Courtland remained active in the business until his death in 1923, and his heirs ran the business until 1967. During the 1930s, 1940s, and 1950s, Van Camp Hardware was a household name in Indianapolis, and employed up to three hundred people at its peak. Changes in wholesale distribution doomed the company, and it dissolved in 1977 following the move of its headquarters to New York City.

While Van Camp Hardware was enjoying rapid growth in the first two decades of the twentieth century, Van Camp and Son entered the new century with plans for expansion despite facing increased competition from such canners as Franco-American and H. J. Heinz. In 1905 Van Camp sold more canned evaporated milk than Borden, the longtime leader in the field. Frank, who had taken over the company following the death of his father in 1900, was a strong believer in advertising in the mass circulation magazines of the day, and with the help of the Lord and Thomas Agency in Chicago, he made Van Camp products a staple in America's kitchen pantry.

Like many of his contemporaries in the cut-throat world of early-twentieth-century business, Frank was a gambler who lived large. His construction of a huge mansion on North Meridian just north of Fall Creek in 1906–7 was the talk of Indianapolis. But when Van Camp attempted to corner the Midwest tomato market in 1911 the move proved disastrous. When the carnage had settled in early 1912, Frank was in debt by more than $1 million to New York and Indianapolis bankers, Albert Lasker of the Lord and Thomas Agency, and his brother, Cortland. The company was effectively broke.

Creditors decided to convert their debt to ownership, and Frank's 100 percent share of the company was diluted to 20 percent. He sold his minority share in the company to Columbus banker W. G. Irwin, also known for providing the financial support that launched Cummins Engine Company in 1919. The investors who controlled Van Camp eventually sold out to Campbell Soup, which spun out the company in 1933 to the Stokely family, a Tennessee packer. Stokely merged the two companies into Stokely-Van Camp and made the flagship plant on South East Street in Indianapolis one of the nation's most productive tomato-packing plants.

Stokely-Van Camp became the nation's first marketer of sports drinks after it acquired the rights to make Gatorade in 1967. The company was sold to Quaker Oats in 1983, which then sold the Stokely brand to Seneca Foods in 1985 and the Van Camp brand to ConAgra in 1995. Today, Van Camp Pork and Beans remain the second most popular brand of canned beans in North America.

After leaving his hometown in disgrace, Frank moved to San Diego, California, and established a second iconic name in American canned foods. He and his son, Gilbert, bought the California Tuna Canning Company and changed the name to Van Camp Seafood Company. With two plants in San Diego and two in San Pedro, Van Camp Seafood quickly became a leader in the Pacific Coast tuna-canning business, becoming the first California canner to utilize Yellowfin tuna. Using tactics he had developed in the pork and beans business, Frank spent lavishly on advertising in the 1920s. He remained president of the company until his death in 1937, and Gilbert eventually sold the company to Ralston Purina in 1963. By then, the son, had used advertising and the little mermaid logo to popularize what had become known as the Chicken of the Sea brand of canned tuna.

BILL BECK

For Further Reading

Cruikshank, Jeffrey L., and Arthur W. Schultz. *The Man Who Sold America: The Amazing (But True) Story of Albert D. Lasker and the Creation of the Advertising Century*. Cambridge, MA: Harvard Business Review Press, 2010.

Grace, Roger M. "History of Van Camp's Beans Is Utterly Mangled." *Metropolitan News-Enterprise*, July 20, 2006

Smith, Andrew. *American Tuna: The Rise and Fall of an Improbable Food*. Berkeley: University of California Press, 2012.

Vonnegut, Kurt Jr.

November 11, 1922–April 11, 2007

Writer and novelist.

On May 29, 1945, twenty-one days after the Third Reich surrendered to the Allied armies, a father in Indianapolis received a letter from his son who had been listed as missing in action following the Battle of the Bulge. The young man, an advance scout with the 106th Infantry Division, had been captured by the Germans after wandering behind enemy lines for several days. "Bayonets," he wrote his father, "aren't much good against tanks."

Eventually, the Indianapolis native was shipped to a work camp in the open city of Dresden, where he helped produce vitamin supplements for pregnant women. Sheltered in an underground meat storage locker, he survived a combined American/British firebombing raid that devastated the city and killed an estimated 135,000 people. Freed from captivity by the Red army's final onslaught against Nazi Germany and returned to the United States, the soldier, Kurt Vonnegut Jr., used his experience in World War II to produce one of the landmark books of the 1960s, *Slaughterhouse-Five; or, The Children's Crusade, A Duty-Dance with Death*. The book made his literary reputation and led to a long career in writing that included a string of novels and essays criticizing what he saw as the increasing militarization of the United States.

The connection between the Vonneguts and Indianapolis dates to the 1850s when Clemens Vonnegut Sr., formerly of Westphalia, Germany, settled in the city and became a business partner with a fellow German named Vollmer. When Vollmer disappeared on a trip out West, Vonnegut took over a business that grew into the profitable Vonnegut Hardware Company.

Kurt's grandfather, Bernard Vonnegut, disliked working in the hardware store. Possessing an artistic nature, he studied architecture at the Massachusetts Institute of Technology and also received training in Hannover, Germany. After briefly working in New York, Bernard returned to Indianapolis in 1883 and joined with Arthur Bohn to form the architectural firm of Vonnegut and Bohn. The firm designed such impressive structures as the Das Deutsche Haus (The Athenaeum), the first Chamber of Commerce building, the John Herron Art Museum, Methodist Hospital, the original L. S. Ayres and Company department store, and the Fletcher Trust Building.

Kurt Vonnegut Sr. also became an architect, taking over the family firm in 1910. On November 22, 1913, he married Edith Lieber, the daughter of millionaire Indianapolis brewer Albert Lieber. The couple had three children, Bernard, born in 1914; Alice, in 1917; and, Kurt Jr. in 1922. As the offspring of a wealthy family, the two eldest Vonnegut children had been educated at private schools—Bernard at Park School and Alice at Tudor Hall School for Girls. The Great Depression, however, reduced the elder Vonnegut's commissions to a mere trickle. As a result, the Vonneguts pulled Kurt from a private school after the third grade and enrolled him at Indianapolis Public School Number 43, the James Whitcomb Riley School, located near the family's home at 4365 North Illinois Street.

Along with instilling Vonnegut with a strong sense of ideals and pacifism, his time in Indianapolis's public schools started him toward a writing career. Attending Shortridge High School from 1936 to 1940, Vonnegut during his junior and senior years edited the Tuesday edition of the school's daily newspaper, the *Daily Echo*. His duties with the newspaper, then one of the few daily high school newspapers in the country, offered Vonnegut a unique opportunity to write for a large audience, in this case, his fellow students. Because he was writing for his peers, and wanted them to understand what he was saying, Vonnegut developed a simple writing style, emphasizing clear, short sentences and paragraphs with strong verbs and using little or no adverbs and adjectives.

After graduating, Vonnegut enrolled at Cornell University. If he had gotten his way, he would have become a third-generation Indianapolis architect. His father, however, still bitter about having had no work during the Great Depression, persuaded him to study something useful, so he majored in chemistry and biology. In hindsight, Vonnegut believed it was lucky for him as a writer that the studied the physical sciences instead of English. Because he wrote for his own amusement, there were no English professors telling him how bad his writing might be or to tell him what to read.

To the young Vonnegut, Cornell itself was a "boozy dream," partly because of the alcohol he imbibed and also because he found himself enrolled in classes for which he had no talent. He did, however, find success working for the *Cornell Daily Sun*. In his freshman year, Vonnegut took over the "Innocents Abroad" column, which reprinted jokes from other publications. He later had his own column, called "Well All Right," in which he produced a series of pacifistic articles. Vonnegut's college days were interrupted by America's entry into World War II. In January 1943 he volunteered for military service. Rejected at first for health reasons (he had caught pneumonia while at Cornell), Vonnegut was later accepted and sent to study mechanical engineering at the Carnegie Institute of Technology in Pittsburgh and at the University of Tennessee. Although Vonnegut received instruction on the 240-millimeter howitzer, he eventually became an intelligence scout with the 106th Infantry Division, which was based at Camp Atterbury, just south of Indianapolis.

Three months after his mother's suicide on Mother's Day in 1944, Vonnegut was sent overseas just in time to become engulfed in the last German offensive of the war, the Battle of the Bulge. Captured by the Germans, Vonnegut and other American prisoners were shipped in boxcars to Dresden. On February 13, 1945, the air-raid siren went off in Dresden and Vonnegut, some other POWs and their German guards found refuge in a meat locker located three stories under the slaughterhouse. "It was cool there, with cadavers hanging all around," Vonnegut said. "When we came up the city was gone. They burnt the whole damn town down."

Freed from captivity by Russian troops, Vonnegut returned to the United States and married Jane Marie Cox on September 1, 1945 (they divorced in 1979 and Vonnegut married photographer Jill Krementz in 1979). The young couple moved to Chicago, where Vonnegut pursued a master's degree in anthropology at the University of Chicago. He also worked as a reporter for the Chicago City News Bureau. Failing to have his thesis, "Fluctuations between Good and Evil in Simple Tales," accepted, Vonnegut left school to become a publicist for General Electric's research laboratories in Schenectady, New York. He also began submitting stories to mass-market magazines. His first published piece, "Report on the Barnhouse Effect," appeared in *Collier's* February 11, 1950 issue.

Vonnegut quit GE in 1951 and moved to Cape Cod to write full time. His science background—the courses he took in high school and college and his work at GE—influenced his work. Although he sold a steady stream of stories to various magazines, he supplemented his income by teaching English at a school on Cape Cod, writing copy for an advertising agency, and opening one of the first Saab dealerships in the United States. With his short stories, and novels such as *Player Piano*, published in 1952, and *The Sirens of Titan*, released in 1959, Vonnegut was often typecast by critics as a science fiction writer.

Kurt Vonnegut at an L. S. Ayres book signing for Slaughterhouse-Five.

After briefly touching on his World War II experience in other work—the main character in *God Bless You, Mr. Rosewater* (1965), hallucinates that Indianapolis becomes engulfed in a firestorm—Vonnegut, in 1969, delivered his book dealing with the Dresden bombing, *Slaughterhouse-Five*. The book's fantastic success, and the release of a feature film based on it in 1972, gained Vonnegut a position as an American cultural icon. College students, in particular, responded well to Vonnegut's sense of the absurd and his Cassandra-like warnings about the bleak future the planet faced.

Although he never again found the best-selling success he had enjoyed with *Slaughterhouse-Five*, Vonnegut did produce a solid string of novels and essay collections, including *Breakfast of Champions* (1973), *Jailbird* (1979), *Palm Sunday* (1981), *Galápagos: A Novel* (1985), *Bluebeard* (1987), *Fates Worse Than Death: An Autobiographical Collage* (1991), *Timequake* (1997), and *A Man without a Country* (2005). In 2007 Vonnegut died of injuries suffered from a fall down a flight of stairs at his home in New York City at the age of eighty-four.

RAY E. BOOMHOWER

For Further Reading

Klinkowitz, Jerome. *The Vonnegut Effect*. Columbia: University of South Carolina Press, 2010.

Marvin, Thomas F. *Kurt Vonnegut: A Critical Companion*. Westport, CT: Greenwood Press, 2002.

Shields, Charles J. *And So It Goes: Kurt Vonnegut: A Life*. New York, NY: Henry Holt and Company, 2011.

The papers of Kurt Vonnegut Jr., including his correspondence and manuscripts, are located at Indiana University's Lilly Library, Bloomington, IN.

Walker, Madam C. J.

December 23, 1867–May 25, 1919

Entrepreneur, hair-care industry pioneer, philanthropist, arts patron, and social activist.

Madam C. J. Walker arrived in Indianapolis, Indiana, in February 1910, attracted by its thriving Indiana Avenue black business community, its access to the railroad, and respect for forward-thinking leaders such as the *Indianapolis Freeman* publisher George L. Knox and local physician Doctor Joseph H. Ward. That year the city's 21,816 black residents comprised 10 percent of the local population and were the nation's sixth largest urban black enclave.

Walker—who began life as Sarah Breedlove on the same Delta, Louisiana, plantation where her parents, Owen and Minerva Anderson Breedlove, had been enslaved—was then on her way to becoming one of the most successful black and female entrepreneurs of the early twentieth century. Orphaned at seven, she married Moses McWilliams, about whom little is known, at fourteen. Her only child, A'Lelia, was born in 1885. Soon after McWilliams's death, she and her daughter moved to Saint Louis to join her three older brothers, who were barbers. Having almost no formal education, she found work as a laundress, making as little as $1.50 a week. The middle-class women of nearby Saint Paul African Methodist Episcopal Church embraced and encouraged the struggling young widow. As a member of the choir and women's missionary society, she was exposed to educated, accomplished teachers and civic leaders, many of them members of the National Association of Colored Women.

Around 1900, after developing a severe scalp ailment that caused her to lose most of her hair, she experimented with curative ointments and ingredients, briefly selling the products of Annie Turnbo Malone, another Saint Louis resident, who became her fiercest competitor. In part to escape an abusive second marriage to a man named John Davis, she moved in 1905 to Denver, where a sister-in-law lived. Charles Joseph Walker, a newspaper advertising salesman she had known in Missouri, then joined her in Colorado. After their marriage in 1906, she began calling herself "Madam" C. J. Walker and began manufacturing her own hair-care line.

With such a limited market for her products among the small black population then living west of the Mississippi River, she and her husband spent the next year and a half traveling throughout the South and East selling their Wonderful Hair Grower, Vegetable Shampoo and Glossine, and training a network of Walker agents in beauty culture, hygiene, and direct sales. They settled briefly in Pittsburgh, but judged Indianapolis a more suitable location for their burgeoning mail-order operation because of its extensive railroad and highway network.

Quickly immersing herself in the civic and social activities of the city, Madam Walker joined Bethel AME Church. The following spring, she purchased a home and factory at 640 North West Street and enlisted the aid of two young attorneys, FREEMAN B. RANSOM, who served as her

Madam C. J. Walker

general manager for more than three decades, and ROBERT L. BROKENBURR, who went on to become Indiana's first black state senator.

As part of a national campaign to build Young Men's Christian Association facilities in black communities, Jesse Moorland—one of the organization's first black international secretaries—had persuaded Sears, Roebuck and Company president Julius Rosenwald to pledge $25,000 to any city where black and white residents would collaborate to raise $75,000 to construct a $100,000 building. At a rally in October 1911, Walker stunned the crowd when she added her own $1,000 contribution to those offered by the city's wealthy white businessmen.

The gift catapulted her onto the national scene as the *New York Age*, the *Baltimore Afro-American*, the National Association for the Advancement of Colored People's *Crisis*, and dozens of black newspapers chronicled her inspirational rags-to-riches rise. With the *Freeman*'s Knox among her strongest advocates, she appeared at Booker T. Washington's National Negro Business League convention in Chicago in August 1912. Rebuffed by Washington—then the most powerful black leader in America—throughout the first two days of the gathering, she pushed her way forward during the final plenary and dramatically seized the opportunity to speak. "Surely you are not going to shut the door in my face," she declared. "I am a woman who came from the cotton fields of the South. From there I was promoted to the washtub. From there, I was promoted to the cook kitchen. And from there, I promoted myself into the business of manufacturing hair goods and preparations. I have built my own factory on my own ground." The next year, Washington invited her back as a keynote speaker. She, in turn, hosted him in her home when he visited Indianapolis for the July 1913 dedication of the Senate Avenue YMCA.

Later that year, Walker traveled to Cuba, Haiti, Jamaica, Costa Rica, and the Panama Canal Zone to expand her international market. Increasingly involved in national civil rights matters, she moved in 1916 to Harlem, where her daughter had opened a Walker beauty school and salon just as that community was becoming a black cultural and political mecca. As Walker's annual sales passed the $100,000 mark, she confidently left the day-to-day operations to attorney Ransom and factory manager Alice Kelly in Indianapolis, where the cost of doing business was less expensive than in Manhattan. By the time she hosted her first national convention of Walker sales agents in Philadelphia in 1917, she claimed nearly 20,000 women trained in the Walker System of Beauty Culture.

With America's entry into World War I, Walker became a leader of the Circle For Negro War Relief and an outspoken advocate for a training camp for black army officers, whose ranks included her personal physician, Ward; her New York architect, Vertner Woodson Tandy; and James Reese Europe, a frequent guest in her home, who would lead the celebrated 369th Regiment's military band. As a member of the executive committee of the NAACP's massive Silent Protest Parade on New York's Fifth Avenue, she helped bring attention to the atrocities of the July 1917 East Saint Louis riot and joined a group of Harlem leaders who visited the White House to present a petition to President Woodrow Wilson urging him to support legislation to make lynching a federal crime.

In the spring of 1918 Walker moved into her newly constructed Irvington-on-Hudson, New York, mansion, just a few miles from John D. Rockefeller's Westchester County estate. Named Villa Lewaro by Italian opera tenor Enrico Caruso for her daughter by combining two letters from each three words of her full name, A'Lelia Walker Robinson, the home was the site of numerous social and cultural gatherings.

Just before she died of kidney failure and complications of chronic hypertension on May 25, 1919, Walker bequeathed $100,000 to dozens of black colleges, social welfare organizations, cultural institutions and political causes, including $5,000 to the NAACP's antilynching fund.

Today two National Historic Landmarks are associated with her legacy: Villa Lewaro in New York and the Madam Walker Theatre Center in Indianapolis. In 1998 Walker was honored with a U.S. Postal Service Black Heritage Series stamp.

A'LELIA BUNDLES

For Further Reading

Bundles, A'Lelia. *On Her Own Ground: The Life and Times of Madam C. J. Walker*. New York: Scribner, 2001.
———. *Madam Walker Theatre Center: An Indianapolis Treasure*. Charleston, SC: Arcadia, 2013.
Peiss, Kathy. *Hope in a Jar: The Making of America's Beauty Culture*. Philadelphia: University of Pennsylvania Press, 2011.
Madam C.J. Walker Papers. Indiana Historical Society William Henry Smith Memorial Library, Indianapolis, IN.

Wallace, Lew

April 10, 1827–February 15, 1905

Lawyer, politician, Civil War general, diplomat, author of best-selling novel *Ben-Hur: A Tale of the Christ*.

Born in Brookville, Indiana, Lew Wallace was the son of David Wallace, a soldier and politician who was the state's governor from 1837 to 1840, and Esther French Test Wallace, the daughter of a judge and congressman. She died when Lew was seven years old, and his father later married ZERELDA G. SANDERS, a leader in Indiana for such causes as prohibition and women's suffrage. Lew, frequently in trouble with his parents for constantly skipping school, was sent at age thirteen to Professor Samuel K. Hoshour's school in Centerville, which had a reputation for helping troubled youth. Hoshour inspired a love of learning in Wallace, who later said the experience was a turning point in his life.

Returning to Indianapolis, Wallace set his sights on a writing career. He joined a local literary society, wrote poems that were published in Indianapolis newspapers, and completed 250 pages of a romantic novel. During the 1848 presidential election, Wallace edited, with William B. Greer, the *Indianapolis Free Soil Banner*, a weekly campaign newspaper in support of Martin Van Buren's candidacy. When erstwhile supporters failed to pay the newspaper's expenses, it took Wallace six years to pay off the debt.

Wallace was also drawn to the military, perhaps influenced by his father, a graduate of West Point and leader of a local militia formed in Covington (where the family had moved) to defend against possible attacks by Native Americans. Wallace also followed in his father's footsteps by becoming a lawyer, but before earning a license to practice, he raised a volunteer company, part of the First Indiana Volunteer Infantry Regiment, in which he served as a lieutenant during the Mexican War.

Admitted to the bar in 1849, Wallace began practicing law in Indianapolis. As a Democrat during the 1850s, he adhered to his free-soil and

Lew Wallace writing under the shade of a beech tree on the grounds of his study in Crawfordsville, Indiana.

popular sovereignty ideology, opposing the extension of slavery into the territories and the admission of slave states into the Union. In Covington he served as prosecutor for the First Congressional District. He married Susan Elston in 1852 and moved to Crawfordsville, where, with interruptions during military duty and other public service, he lived for the rest of his life. During the belligerent antebellum period, he formed a volunteer militia company, served a term in the Indiana State Senate, and worked on a novel, *The Fair God*.

Wallace was pleading a case in Frankfort in April 1861 when the Civil War broke out and Governor OLIVER P. MORTON summoned him to Indianapolis. At Morton's request, he served as adjutant general (commander and recruiter of the Indiana volunteer forces) for a month, after which he assumed command of the Eleventh Indiana Volunteer Infantry Regiment, which Wallace turned into a Zouave unit, adopting the distinctive uniform and drill of the French Algerian infantry. The regiment saw its first action at Romney, Virginia (now West Virginia) in June, routing a Confederate force nearly double in size. Promoted to brigadier general, Wallace was then given the newly formed Third Division to command by Major General Ulysses S. Grant for campaigns against Confederate forts in north-central Tennessee. Wallace won praise for his actions that aided the Union victory at Fort Donelson and was subsequently promoted, becoming the youngest major general in the Union army. Attaining the rank from the state volunteer forces, coupled with his prickly personality, served to create resentment toward Wallace among West Point regulars.

Wallace's performance at Fort Donelson, however, was soon overshadowed by events at the Battle of Shiloh. Still in command of the Third Division and stationed at Crump's Landing, Tennessee, Wallace, anticipating attacks by Confederate forces, ordered improvements to the Shunpike Road, which provided access to the remainder of Grant's Army of the Tennessee. But neither Wallace nor Grant mastered the topography of the area or planned in advance the route by which Wallace and his troops should join the main army. On April 6, 1862, about 45,000 soldiers of the Confederate Army of Mississippi, under the command of General Albert Sidney Johnston, launched an attack at dawn on Union positions, surprising Grant, who ordered Wallace to move his men out to support Union forces. Wallace advanced according to his plan along the restored Shunpike, but when the Third Division took longer than expected to arrive, Grant then ordered Wallace to advance by a different route, which meant marching through unimproved swampland, adding to the delay in reaching the battlefield.

Despite the late arrival of Wallace's Third Division, Union soldiers drove Confederate forces from the field after a two-day battle. Grant's initial after-action report did not criticize Wallace. But the Battle of Shiloh incurred more casualties (23,746 on both sides, 3,482 killed) than all preceding North American wars combined. Because he had sustained so many casualties, Grant was an obvious target for blame, which prompted his aides to begin a whispering campaign faulting Wallace.

In June 1862 Wallace served as military governor of Memphis and then requested leave from the army. Thereafter he chose not to return to Grant's army, and General-in-Chief Henry W. Halleck—also protector-in-chief of West Pointers—blocked him from other major regular army commands. However, Wallace still had a role to play in the war effort. In the fall of 1862, Wallace went to Cincinnati, Ohio, and in a matter of days mobilized its citizens to defend against an expected attack. Apparently, the preparations so impressed Confederate spies that an assault never came. Later, President ABRAHAM LINCOLN selected Wallace to command the Eighth Army Corps and the Middle Department, an administrative military district based in Baltimore, Maryland. At the Battle of Monocacy (near Frederick, Maryland), Wallace and his troops delayed the Confederate advance on Washington, D.C., for a full day, effectively preventing seizure of the Union capital.

In the waning days of the war and beyond, Wallace was called upon to serve in a number of high-profile roles. In consultation with Lincoln, Wallace orchestrated a convention in Maryland, one of four Union slave states, for a state constitutional amendment that banned slavery, which preceded ratification of the federal Thirteenth Amendment that abolished slavery. He also presided over a panel that examined charges that Major General Don Carlos Buell had been derelict against Confederates in Kentucky and a military court that tried and convicted Captain Henry Wirz for war crimes committed at the Andersonville, Georgia, prisoner-of-war camp he commanded. In addition, Wallace was appointed a judge on a military court that tried those charged with conspiracy to kill Lincoln and other government officials.

After the war, Wallace practiced law in Crawfordsville, made an unsuccessful run for Congress as a Republican, and returned to writing. Twenty years in the making, *The Fair God*, a historical novel about the Spanish conquest of Mexico, was published in 1873. Wallace also served on an electoral commission that determined Rutherford B. Hayes the winner of the disputed presidential election of 1876. The decision included a compromise that resulted in the termination of Reconstruction in the South. The new president rewarded Wallace with appointment as territorial governor of New Mexico. There he dealt with the lawlessness and corruption known as the Lincoln County War and even negotiated with Billy the Kid. Wallace also found time to complete *Ben-Hur: A Tale of the Christ* (1880), which became the best-selling American novel of the nineteenth century. After reading *Ben-Hur*, President James A. Garfield was so impressed that he appointed Wallace as U.S. minister (ambassador) to Constantinople, where he served from 1881 to 1885.

Wallace, largely self-taught as a writer, was a prodigious researcher. He immersed himself in West Point textbooks during the 1850s; researched colonial Mexican history while writing *The Fair God*; carefully investigated Jewish, Christian, and Roman history while writing *Ben-Hur*; and studied the details of Byzantine history for background on *The Prince of India* (1893). Other works include a campaign biography of his friend, BENJAMIN HARRISON (1888, revised edition 1892), and his own *Autobiography* (1906), which Susan Wallace and Mary Hannah Krout, also a Crawfordsville writer, completed after Wallace's death in 1905 at age seventy-seven.

THOMAS A. MASON

For Further Reading

Boomhower, Ray E. *The Sword and the Pen: A Life of Lew Wallace*. Indianapolis: Indiana Historical Society Press, 2005.

Mason, Thomas A., project director. *The Papers of Lew and Susan Wallace*. Microfilm. Indianapolis: Indiana Historical Society Press, 2008.

Morsberger, Robert E., and Katherine M. Morsberger. *Lew Wallace: Militant Romantic*. New York: McGraw-Hill, 1980.

Stephens, Gail. *Shadow of Shiloh: Major General Lew Wallace and the Civil War*. Indianapolis: Indiana Historical Society Press, 2010.

Wallace, Zerelda G.
August 6, 1817–March 19, 1901

Temperance and women's suffrage leader and stepmother of author LEW WALLACE.

Although she did not set out to be a social reformer, she became an avid supporter and leader of two major reform movements of the late nineteenth century. Gentle in spirit and proper in demeanor, she was ardent in her beliefs. Coming from a devoutly religious family she was first attracted to the temperance movement and became a leader of that cause. Her participation in that crusade led inevitably to her involvement with the women's suffrage movement when she came to realize that women without the vote lacked the standing in society to achieve political goals.

Zerelda G. Sanders was born in Millersburg, Kentucky, August 6, 1817, the eldest of five girls born to Doctor John and Polly Gray Sanders. Zerelda's education consisted of grammar school and two additional years at a boarding school in Kentucky. However, at the encouragement of her parents, she read widely, especially the classics and the law.

Sanders moved the family to Indianapolis in 1830, where he established a medical practice and, once settled, he and Zerelda helped establish the Christian Church (Disciples of Christ). In 1836, at the age of nineteen, she married Indiana's lieutenant governor, David Wallace, almost twice her age and a widower with three boys, one of whom was LEW WALLACE, a future Union army general, governor of the New Mexico Territory, and author of *Ben-Hur*. Together Zerelda and David had six additional children, with three surviving to adulthood. A prominent Whig politician in the state, David served as governor from 1837 to 1840 and then served one term in Congress from 1841 to 1843. He died in 1859. Zerelda had a close relationship with her husband and advised him on issues as well as critiquing his speeches and writing.

Zerelda's public career commenced after she became involved with the temperance movement. Her conviction about the evils of alcohol were so strong that she announced to her church congregation that she would no longer take communion unless unfermented grape juice was substituted for wine. Her church became the first to switch, and the rest of the Disciples of Christ churches soon followed suit. Her involvement with the temperance movement led her to become active in the women's suffrage reform. This path of reform—from temperance to woman suffrage—paralleled the course of pre–Civil War reforms. Women usually started out in the temperance movement, but they ultimately embraced other reforms, most notably the abolition of slavery and women's rights.

After the Civil War, Wallace, like many other middle-class women, despaired of the damage alcohol abuse inflicted on the family, especially on women and children. Hence, she actively engaged in the temperance crusade that was rapidly gathering steam in the 1870s. Wallace served as one of the founding members of the Woman's Christian Temperance Union, organized in 1874. Not only did she hold the office of vice president of the national organization, she also was the first president of the Indiana chapter, which she helped to create. She served as president of the local WCTU from 1874 to 1877, and again from 1879 to 1883.

Immediately Wallace began speaking publicly about temperance reform, and in 1875 she addressed the Indiana legislature on the subject and presented the legislators with a memorial signed by 10,000 women, representing almost half of Indiana's counties. Some of the legislators treated her rudely and ridiculed or denounced the very idea of temperance reform. One senator told her that the petition "might as well have been signed by 10,000 mice." He added that legislators were not there to "represent their consciences but to represent their constituents." Wallace later said that "a light broke over her" because she realized she, too, was a constituent. The senator had succeeded in making Wallace a suffragist.

After this episode, Wallace realized that little could be done to advance the cause of temperance unless women had the right to vote. Before long she championed both temperance and woman suffrage. She and a few others, most notably fellow reformer May Wright Sewall, founded the Equal Suffrage Society of Indianapolis in 1878; Wallace served as the group's first president. Now she worked tirelessly for two reforms that were inextricably bound. In addition to her active role in the WCTU, both in Indiana and nationally, she eventually joined the National Woman Suffrage Association, founded by among others Elizabeth Cady Stanton—a dedicated advocate since 1840—and Susan B. Anthony. Devoting herself to both causes, Wallace traveled the country speaking and participating in a variety of conventions and gatherings. Another Hoosier suffragist, Grace Julian Clarke, said that Wallace's effectiveness as a speaker was due to the "richness and power of her voice," as well as "the magnetism of her presence."

By joining the NWSA, Wallace embraced an organization that advocated not only the right to vote but also a broad platform that included a host of reforms that affected women, ranging from better working conditions and pay to more liberal divorce laws. Prior to joining the NWSA, Wallace loosely connected with a rival, more conservative organization—the American Woman Suffrage Association, which campaigned only for women's suffrage. In addition, while the NWSA's strategy consisted of a federal constitutional amendment for guaranteeing the vote, the AWSA's focused on effecting change by campaigning in individual states. While Wallace was familiar with both organizations, it is telling that she identified with an organization that advocated broad reforms for women, even though its major focus was on suffrage.

Regardless of what her broader views may have been about a host of other issues, Wallace was widely known by the 1880s as one of the foremost crusaders for woman suffrage and temperance. In addition to urging state and national audiences to take up these two causes, Wallace also actively took part in the affairs of the NSWA, speaking at the national conventions and, at one time, serving as vice president. In that role she closely worked with Stanton and Anthony on national issues and strategies. She also testified before the Judiciary Committee of the U.S. Senate on behalf of women's right to vote. At the same time she continued to be active in the WCTU, urging some of its more skeptical members to embrace women's suffrage as an important component that would ultimately advance temperance.

In 1890 the NWSA and the AWSA joined forces to create the National American Woman Suffrage Association, which is what most Indiana suffragists had recommended for years. The NAWSA combined the strategies of the former organizations, concentrating on state action as well as continuing to pursue a federal constitutional amendment. This organization in turn eventually became the League of Women Voters. Wallace addressed the formal union of the two associations in a speech titled "A Whole Humanity." Speaking forcefully and eloquently she said: "as sure as you live, every argument you use against the enfranchisement of women deals a death blow against the fundamental principle which lies at the base of our government, and it is reason to bring an argument against it."

Wallace, for her part, continued to champion both temperance and voting rights for women, but by the 1890s she began slowing down, and on March 19, 1901, she died of a bronchial infection, nineteen years before her goal of women's suffrage was achieved with the passage of the Nineteenth Amendment to the U.S. Constitution. For her efforts the National League of Women Voters selected Wallace to represent Indiana on a bronze plaque in its Washington, D.C. headquarters.

Zerelda's step-son, Lew, paid tribute to her with these words: "The world has been unable to resist her as I was. In all the states of the Union, in every village and city, there are good people who know and speak of her as Mother Wallace, the sweet-tongued apostle of temperance and reform."

STEPHEN L. COX

For Further Reading

Boomhower, Ray E. *Fighting for Equality: A Life of May Wright Sewall*. Indianapolis: Indiana Historical Society Press, 2007.

Scott, Ann Firor, and Andrew MacKay Scott. *One Half the People: The Fight for Woman Suffrage*. Urbana: University of Illinois Press, 1982.

Sewall, May Wright. "Zerelda Wallace." *The Woman's Magazine* 10, no. 1 (September 1886).

Vogelgesang, Susan. "Zerelda Wallace: Indiana's Conservative Radical." *Traces of Indiana and Midwestern History* 4, no.3 (Summer 1992): 34–41.

Webster, Marie Daugherty

July 19, 1859–August 29, 1956

Textile artist and designer and author who changed the face of quilting.

Who would have thought that the slender, hazel-eyed girl from Wabash, Indiana, would become one of the most influential textile artists in the world of quilting? Even though Marie Webster was celebrated for the quilt designs she created during her lifetime, lasting acclaim came only after her death. It was then she was recognized for the fundamental role she had played in changing the look and the artistry of quilting.

According to a nationally known quilting expert, "Today it is a wonder how this woman born in (the) mid-nineteenth century . . . could be so completely a twentieth-century woman in her outlook, so modern in her creativity, to have had so much influence, even indirectly. . . . The spread of her patterns, even when no longer bearing the names she originally gave them or when she was no longer acknowledged as the original design source, has been phenomenal."

Webster married a banker in Marion, Indiana, on Valentine's Day of 1884 and gave birth to their only child by year's end. For the next several decades, she led a life devoted to her family and defined by social duties, volunteer activities and hours spent in sewing, reading, and amateur dramatics. Webster loved to travel, which she and her husband did until 1910 when he became crippled by rheumatoid arthritis and had to retire from the bank.

As his painful disease progressed, Webster needed to care for him, and her interests focused on hearth and home. At the age of fifty, with skills in needlework that she learned from her mother as a child, she took up quilting. Rather than work geometric pieces for her first quilt, however, she picked a traditional Rose of Sharon pattern for her inspiration. One of her granddaughters described how "she appliqued [sic] petals cut from soft shades of linen, adding a graceful curving trellis to unify the design [and then] quilting around each leaf and flower, she created a stunning three-dimensional effect." Her daughter-in-law said the quilt was "so much admired by her friends," that they urged her to send it to the *Ladies' Home Journal*, the leading woman's magazine of the time. Webster's submission could not have been better timed. The *Journal* was at the lead in promoting the arts and crafts ideals of the early twentieth century, and her quilt encompassed all the elements of this movement. Eloquent in its simplicity and craftsmanship, unique in its reliance upon nature as a design reference, Webster's quilt captured the attention of the magazine's editor who requested additional examples of her work.

Flattered and more than a little surprised, Webster went back to her garden for further inspiration. There she gathered flowers and leaves that she dried and pressed. Then she traced and cut their shapes on pastel linens that captured their subdued colors. As Webster would arrange and rearrange these pieces, patterns began to emerge. After settling on one, she would hand-appliqué the linen pieces onto quilt tops which were taken to women living in a nearby Home for the Elderly to be quilted. Four of Marie's quilts appeared, in full color, in the January 1911 issue of the *Journal* and, almost immediately, she was caught up in a whirlwind of converts.

Scores of the magazine's 1.5 million readers embraced Webster's designs, and an overwhelming number of them responded to the *Journal*'s offer for her to answer inquiries regarding her quilts if they provided a stamped, addressed envelope. Within weeks, she was inundated by requests for templates of her quilts.

Fortunately, her family came to the rescue. Her twenty-seven-year-old son, Lawrence, a mechanical engineer, made blueprints of her patterns and her sister, Emma, assembled full-size colored tissue-paper replicas of the quilt blocks and borders. The entire kit, which included directions, templates, and a picture of the finished quilt as well as fabric swatches glued to the back of the direction sheet, sold for fifty cents.

As Webster's quilts appeared in succeeding issues of the *Journal*, her home business thrived, and her reputation grew. In 1912 Doubleday, Page and Company asked her to write a book on the subject. Several years in the research and writing of the book, the budding author investigated needlework traditions of countries across Africa, Central Asia, Europe, and America from antiquity to her own time. She also delved into private and public quilt collections in order to compile an extensive listing of quilt designs. Published in the fall of 1915, her illustrated *Quilts: Their Story and How to Make Them* was the landmark study on quilting.

News of her accomplishment appeared in *New York Times*, the *Chicago Tribune*, the *Christian Science Monitor*, and the *Marion Daily Chronicle*. The latter reported that Webster's "book was enthusiastically praised by critics and it immediately placed Marie D. Webster in a position of honor as an authority on this subject." The newspaper declared that her approach to quilting put her work "in the realm of art." It noted her belief that quilts "should not be haphazardly thrown together with no art. She did not believe in countless long patches of color, but designed with an artist's eye for color scheme and design."

Letters by the thousands from admirers worldwide made their way to her home in Marion. Overwhelmed by the sheer volume of requests for kits, Webster asked two of her friends for help. Together, they founded the Practical Patchwork Company in 1921. The three women, with the continuing assistance of several Webster family members, decided to specialize in basted quilts and kits of stamped or precut fabric for bridge and luncheon sets as well as for bedspreads and quilts. Their motto was: "A Thing of Beauty Is a Joy Forever."

In addition to promoting their products through a series of catalogues and various periodicals, they also sold to an occasional retail shop. For under $100 a customer could order a finished quilt as well: one designed by Webster, appliquéd by her or another of the women, and quilted by one of the groups with whom she contracted for this service. For the next two decades, Webster operated a flourishing cottage industry out of an extra bedroom on the second floor of her home.

In 1938 Webster's husband became seriously ill and died. The seventy-nine-year-old widow and her sister remained in her home, while her son lived around the corner with his wife and two daughters. Blessed with good health, she reveled in playing with her granddaughters and was even able to do a bit of traveling. In 1942 her son and his family moved to Princeton, New Jersey. After being in business for some three decades, Webster and Emma decided to follow them, even though it meant leaving close friends behind in Marion. The needlewoman par excellence kept her vigor well into her nineties, when she suffered a stroke from which she never recovered. Shortly after her ninety-seventh birthday, she died on August 29, 1956.

Decades have come and gone since Marie Webster started quilting, and her patterns have stood the test of time. Grounded in her experiences as a female and shaped in large part by the social politics of the times in which she lived, she and her artistic quilting patterns offer testimony to the ingenuity of her creative spirit. Hampered by cultural expectations, fettered by familial constraints, she nevertheless followed her own muse. Because of her contributions to the art of Indiana, the state is far richer.

The Marie Webster House in Marion, Indiana, is now the home of The Quilter's Hall of Fame. Charged with documenting America's quilt-making heritage, it is open to the public. In 1992 the house was designated a National Historic Landmark and a Landmark of Women's History.

JUDITH VALE NEWTON

For Further Reading

Newton, Judith Vale, and Carol Ann Weiss. *Skirting the Issue: Stories of Indiana's Women Artists*. Indianapolis: Indiana Historical Society Press, 2004.

Perry, Rosalind Webster, and Marty Frolli, *A Joy Forever: Marie Webster's Quilt Patterns*. Santa Barbara, CA: Practical Patchwork, 1992.

Webster, Marie D. *Quilts: Their Story and How to Make Them*. Rev. ed. Santa Barbara, CA: Practical Patchwork, 1990.

Wells, Herman B

June 7, 1902–March 18, 2000

Indiana University faculty member, IU School of Business Administration dean, and IU president and chancellor.

In 1921 Herman B Wells enrolled at Indiana University, beginning a relationship that continued until his death nearly eighty years later. He relished the IU collegiate culture that included hijinks at the Book Nook, the campus hangout that classmate HOAGY CARMICHAEL made famous; observations and conversations with painter T. C. STEELE, the visiting professor of art; and glimpses of intellectual horizons and cosmopolitan perspectives in his academic coursework in the recently opened School of Commerce and Finance.

Wells, a fifth-generation Hoosier, was the only child of Joseph Granville and Anna Bernice Harting Wells. The "B" that was the whole of his middle name was due to his parents' inability to agree on a name. He spent his childhood and adolescence in Boone County, a rich agricultural area in central Indiana. His father, prone to depression, was a respected bank cashier and former elementary school principal; his mother, possessed of a strong will and stable temperament, provided a dependable source of love and security to her son. Wells grew up in the country village of Jamestown, attending the Methodist church regularly, playing in the boys' band, and visiting the occasional traveling Chautauqua. When his father was appointed deputy county treasurer, the family moved to Lebanon, the county seat, where Wells attended Lebanon High School and frequented the new Carnegie Public Library down the street. At fifteen he contracted a serious case of mumps with complications of orchitis. The sensitive and obedient boy, with his rounded shape and perpetual smile, became popular among his classmates, especially for his business and organizational skills, while maintaining high grades. Graduating in 1920, his high school peers voted him the "Best Boy" and "Funniest." Determined to pursue business in college, he spent his freshman year at the University of Illinois before transferring to IU.

In Bloomington he immediately joined Sigma Nu social fraternity and lived in the chapter house at the corner of Grant Street and Kirkwood Avenue, on the main street connecting the town and the university. Fraternity life offered him an elective family, united by shared interest and experience rather than blood ties. His social intelligence and interpersonal skills were honed by an extensive array of activities, both curricular and noncurricular, as he enthusiastically sampled collegiate life. Graduating with a bachelor of science degree in commerce in 1924, he later summed up his undergraduate career, "It was for me a time of response, growth, transformation, and inspiration"

In the next few years, Wells found himself betwixt banking and academic life, as he gained experience in the bank where his father worked before returning to Bloomington, where he earned a master of arts degree in economics in 1927 and then became a doctoral student at the University of Wisconsin. His student days came to an end in 1928, when he accepted the position of field secretary of the Indiana Bankers Association, a trade group representing nearly 1,100 banks in the state. Managing to keep his job with the banking group, in 1930 Wells landed an instructorship in the IU Department of Economics and Sociology.

His expertise in banking was in demand during this period of economic depression, which hit Indiana especially hard because of the agricultural recession starting a few years earlier. By 1931 Wells became the research director for the state-sponsored Study Commission for Indiana Financial Institutions, adding a third position to his full plate. He was the chief author of its 174-page report that called for thoroughgoing reform of state banking policies and regulations, published at the end of 1932. Those recommendations were pushed by Governor PAUL V. MCNUTT and quickly passed into law by the Indiana legislature in the spring of 1933, placing the state at the national forefront of banking reform. On leave from IU for two years, Wells worked for the Indiana Department of Financial Institutions as bank supervisor, as well as head of its research division.

In 1935 IU president William Lowe Bryan called Wells back to Bloomington to serve as dean of the School of Business Administration. In 1938 he was selected as president of IU after a few months of serving as the acting executive. Guided by a thoughtful university-wide self-study, he hired research-oriented faculty; brought the arts from margins to the center of campus life; and united faculty, students, alumni, staff, state legislators, and the public in a quest to advance IU. Possessed of a rare vision of academic quality and a sensitive appreciation of individuals, he drew strength from his huge social network and deep understanding of the Hoosier milieu.

Wells was determined to "bring culture to the crossroads," supporting the enhancement of fine and performing arts in the curriculum. Completed in 1941, the IU Auditorium was the first building of the Wells administration and provided the anchor for an ambitious plan to create a campus arts precinct. During World War II, Wells was involved in foreign economic analysis for the U.S. State Department in Washington, D.C., and he emerged as a national figure in educational policy circles. The war reinforced his interest in international education, leading to impressive efforts to enroll foreign students as well as expand IU area studies, foreign-language teaching, and international university assistance in the postwar period. In 1947 Wells served as cultural affairs adviser to the U.S. Military Government in West Germany for six months, responsible for reconstructing education, libraries, the press, and other cultural institutions in the war-ravaged country, and he played a vital role in the establishment of the Free University of Berlin.

In Bloomington veterans funded by the GI Bill were flooding the campus, causing great strain upon the physical plant. In order to provide classroom facilities and living accommodations for a doubling of the student body, from 5,000 to 10,000, the start of the 1946–47 academic year was delayed for three weeks. To accommodate unprecedented growth in personnel and facilities, the Wells administration purchased contiguous land from willing sellers, expanding the campus from less than two hundred to more than eighteen hundred acres in size, and oversaw a vigorous construction program. Mindful of the attractions of handsome limestone halls and green woodlands, he insisted on beauty in Indiana's architecture and landscape. Faculty quality remained Wells's highest priority, and he hired ambitious deans and directors to build strengths in music and the arts, graduate education, and the library system, as the university rose in stature. Vigorously protecting zoologist Alfred Kinsey's right to purse research on the subject of sex, Wells withstood much criticism upon the publication of Kinsey's landmark studies on male and female sexual behavior in 1948 and 1953, respectively.

Wells presided at his last IU commencement in 1962, where he was taken by a surprise ceremony to bestow upon him an honorary doctorate, summa cum laude, to join his other honorary degrees, which eventually numbered twenty-six. Only sixty years old, the IU trustees created a new post—university chancellor—to reflect his administrative stature as he became a senior counselor, extraordinary fund-raiser, and a radiant presence

A note from Herman B Wells that accompanied this image read: "The school bell denotes the school master. This bell was used by my father as a country school teacher for many years. The Tibetan Monk's begging bowl symbolizes that a University President must ask for financial support for his Institution. The globe denotes the worldwide concern of the University. All the world is our parish."

to the extended IU clan. That included the system of regional campuses that had matured during his tenure as president and chancellor from a handful of extension centers into a system of seven autonomous campuses. Wells faithfully attended regional campus commencement ceremonies year after year.

Wells continued to work in international education, serving as chairman of the board of the Education and World Affairs organization from 1962 to 1970. Acquiescing to entreaties to tell his life story, he wrote an autobiography, *Being Lucky: Reminiscences and Reflections* (1980). Gracefully aging in place, he maintained his work habits and social networks for decades, faithfully keeping his beloved alma mater and its welfare paramount. At the end of spring break in 2000, he died peacefully at his campus home. The funeral was held in Bloomington on March 22, exactly sixty-two years to the day after his selection as IU president.

Wells was the major architect for a prominent exemplar of one of our most distinctive modern institutions—the American research university—by building upon a premodern sensibility of place and altruistic devotion to others, using the tools he acquired from the political, bureaucratic, and technological developments of the twentieth century. He built an institution, and in the process, became one himself.

JAMES H. CAPSHEW

For Further Reading

Capshew, James H. *Herman B Wells: The Promise of the American University*. Bloomington: Indiana University Press, 2012.
———. "Making Herman B Wells: Moral Development and Emotional Trauma in a Boone County Boyhood." *Indiana Magazine of History* 107 (December 2011): 361–376.
Clark, Thomas D. *Indiana University, Midwestern Pioneer: Volume III: Years of Fulfillment*. Bloomington: Indiana University Press, 1977.
Wells, Herman B. *Being Lucky: Reminiscences and Reflections*. Bloomington: Indiana University Press, 1980.
———. Papers. Indiana University Archives, Bloomington, IN.

Welsh, Matthew Empson

September 15, 1912–May 28, 1995

Member of the Indiana House of Representatives, Indiana Senate, and governor of Indiana.

The administration of Governor Matthew E. Welsh was significant for the change it brought in fiscal responsibility, governmental efficiency, education, and social reform in Indiana. Elected

Matthew Welsh addressing a National Association for the Advancement of Colored People Freedom Rally, August 10, 1963.

in 1960, Welsh was arguably the most progressive governor since PAUL V. MCNUTT. His tenure in the statehouse was marked by a state budgetary crisis that required new sources of revenue, the streamlining of state government, a reorganization of the state's educational system from primary school through college, and responses to the fast-developing civil rights movement. At the center of these accelerating forces of change in Indiana was the scholarly, dignified, attorney from Vincennes, Indiana.

Welsh was born on September 15, 1912, to Matthew William and Inez Empson Welsh. He graduated from Lincoln High School in Vincennes in 1930 and went to the Wharton School at the University of Pennsylvania, graduating in 1934. He then enrolled at Indiana University School of Law in Bloomington, before transferring to the University of Chicago Law School, where he completed his degree. While in Bloomington, Welsh met Mary Virginia Homann of Washington, Indiana, whom he married in 1937, the year he received his law degree and passed the bar exam. The newlyweds moved to Vincennes, where Welsh decided to practice law, and became parents of twins, Kathryn and Janet, in 1942.

In 1940 Welsh was elected to the Indiana House of Representatives. Reelected in 1942, he resigned the following year to serve as an officer in the U.S. Navy during World War II, returning to civilian life in 1946. In 1950 President Harry S Truman appointed him U.S. attorney for the Southern District of Indiana, a post he held until resigning in 1952.

Welsh rejoined his private law practice, but politics, clearly, was in his blood. In 1954 he ran successfully for the Indiana Senate. Two years later, in 1956, Welsh narrowly lost the Democratic nomination for governor to Mayor Ralph Tucker of Terre Haute. The following year, and again in 1959, he was chosen as the Democratic floor leader in the state senate. Welsh's political star was rising and culminated in his election as governor in 1960 over Republican Crawford F. Parker.

Welsh faced a daunting budget crisis upon taking the reins of power in January 1961. Both the property tax, the mainstay of local government, and the gross income tax were not effectively administered and could not produce sufficient revenue to meet the demand for public services. Making matters more difficult, the 1960 election had given Welsh a Republican-controlled House and only a two-vote Democratic margin in the Senate. Despite the challenges of this split, the 1961 legislature passed three Welsh initiatives designed to improve the efficiency of the tax structure. The first of these was the Property Assessment Act of 1961, which was the first recodification of the state's property tax law since 1919. The other two measures were designed to improve the administration of the state's revenue system.

After the 1962 election both houses of the legislature were controlled by Republicans. When the regular session of the general assembly failed to act, Welsh called the legislature into special session on March 12, 1963, to resolve the tax issue. When the session ended the legislature had passed the compromise "2-2-2 Plan." It called for a 2 percent retail sales tax with a six dollar per capita credit against the state income tax; a 2 percent net income tax on individuals to replace the old gross income tax; and a 2 percent net corporate income tax as a minimum alternative to the gross income tax on corporations. The legislature also passed Welsh's increase in the cigarette tax, which made possible the construction of two toll bridges across the Ohio River at Mauckport and Cannelton, spurring economic development in southern Indiana.

The effort to revamp the state's tax structure was the best example of Welsh's considerable political skill, combining leadership and compromise. He was joined in this effort by his Republican lieutenant governor, Richard O. Ristine, who cast the tie-breaking vote in the state senate to pass the sales tax. Welsh, as well as Ristine, paid a heavy political price for the new tax plan. His opponents branded him "Sales Tax Matt" and car plates appeared across the state proclaiming "Indiana–Land of Taxes."

Welsh also sought to streamline state government. In 1961 the general assembly passed his proposal to create the Department of Administration to achieve more efficiency in state government operations through reorganized purchasing, personnel, and administrative procedures. The state highway department was also thoroughly reorganized. The Department of Mental Health was created, consolidating the administrative responsibility for all eight state mental hospitals under the department instead of separate boards of trustees. It was given oversight for two schools for the mentally challenged and a center for the treatment of alcoholics. The Department of Correction underwent considerable change, with an emphasis on the rehabilitation of offenders. Welsh issued an executive order in January 1964 creating Indiana's first arts commission, the Governor's Commission on the Arts.

Change was also the watchword of the state's educational system. Welsh aggressively pursued the implementation of the 1959 School Corporation Reorganization Act, which eliminated ineffective and uneconomic primary and secondary school units. The number of school units in the state was reduced from 966 to 466.

Concerned about the relative lack of access to postsecondary education in Indiana, Welsh encouraged the legislature to create the Post-High School Education Study Commission in 1961, chaired by Doctor John W. Hicks of Purdue University. The commission recommended that the state accelerate secondary school consolidation; expand and fund regional campuses of Indiana and Purdue universities; establish a state-funded scholarship program for all Indiana colleges; and create a new state school for vocational education. In response to this report, the general assembly established the Indiana Vocational Technical College in 1963.

Under Welsh's leadership Indiana became one of the most progressive midwestern states with regard to civil rights in the early 1960s. In 1961 he persuaded the legislature to pass a law that made the Fair Employment Practices Commission an independent agency under the merit system. The law also doubled the commission's budget, broadened the coverage of the public accommodations law, and increased penalties for violators. In addition, Welsh directed all state government agency heads to end all discrimination and to actively hire African Americans at upper management levels. He issued an executive order on December 12, 1961, that required a nondiscrimination clause in all state contracts.

In 1963 the general assembly passed a law giving the Indiana Civil Rights Commission power to issue enforceable cease-and-desist orders when it discovered discrimination. That same year Welsh directed all departments of state government to prevent discrimination in places of public accommodation through their various licensing powers, and asked all state departments to appoint an equal opportunities officer to work with the civil rights commission to end discrimination in state government and throughout Indiana. Significantly, these Indiana initiatives preceded the federal Civil Rights Act of 1964. Welsh sealed his reputation as an advocate for civil rights when he stood in for President Lyndon B. Johnson against Alabama governor George C. Wallace in Indiana's Democratic presidential primary in 1964. He scored a resounding victory over Wallace, defeating him by a vote of 376,023 to 172,646. Of all his accomplishments as governor, Welsh was most proud of the progress made in civil rights.

Constitutionally prohibited from seeking a second term, Welsh returned to the practice of law in Indianapolis, which he continued until his death. He served as Democratic national committeeman from Indiana from 1964 to 1968. In 1965 President Johnson appointed him as the part-time chairman of the U.S. Section of the International Joint Commission for the United States and Canada, which protected water levels along the U.S.-Canadian border. He served in this role from 1966 to 1970. Welsh won the Democratic nomination for governor in 1972, but lost to Republican OTIS R. BOWEN.

Welsh died in Indianapolis on May 28, 1995, at age eighty-two. His favorite saying, "It doesn't cost you anything to be a gentleman," summed up his life and career. He is buried at Memorial Park Cemetery in Vincennes.

JAMES PHILIP FADELY

For Further Reading

Madison, James H. *The Indiana Way: A State History*. Bloomington: Indiana University Press, 1986.

New, Jack. Interview with the author. February 28, 2004.

Peat, Wilbur D. *Portraits and Painters of the Governors of Indiana, 1800–1978*. Indianapolis: Indiana Historical Society and the Indianapolis Museum of Art, 1978.

Walsh, Justin. *Centennial History of the Indiana General Assembly, 1816–1978*. Indianapolis: Indiana Select Committee on the Centennial History of the Indiana General Assembly, 1987.

Welsh, Matthew E. Papers. Indiana State Archives and the Indiana State Library, Indianapolis.

———. *View from the State House: Recollections and Reflections, 1961–1965*. Indianapolis: Indiana Historical Bureau, 1981.

White, Esther Griffin

1869–September 28, 1954

Suffragette, electoral candidate, journalist, author, and art collector.

A small gravestone in Richmond, Indiana's Earlham Cemetery marks the final resting place of Esther Griffin White. Inscribed with her name and the year of her death, the plot is dwarfed by larger and more significant markers for many of Richmond's famous residents. However, the small size of the stone belies the significant of White's accomplishments, which spanned politics, journalism, art, and culture in the state of Indiana.

Born in 1869 to Oliver and Mary White, Esther was raised in a progressive Quaker family in Richmond that prized education and equality. Surrounded by her father—a merchant, newspaper publisher, and teacher—mother, and three siblings, White recalled early years full of "a brilliant flow of wit, epigram, and repartee." Her family encouraged her to attend Earlham College to supplement her public school education and in 1886, at the age of seventeen, she took classes there before entering professional life as a journalist.

With no formal training and with a writing style that was personal, inflated, and, at times, unprofessional, she was frequently at odds with the editorial staff of the major newspapers in the city. As a result, she worked only sporadically for the *Richmond Morning News*, *Richmond Sun-Telegram*, *Richmond Item*, *Richmond Palladium*, and the combined *Richmond Palladium-Item*, intermittently resigning or being fired. White was known as the journalist of record on all matters artistic and cultural in Richmond. Her understanding of the Quaker faith was a valuable asset and she frequently reported on the Yearly Meeting held in Richmond. She also covered the Chautauqua, a traveling assembly of authors, lecturers, artists, performers, and preachers that traveled to Richmond for years in the early twentieth century.

When not employed by local or national newspapers, she published her own, *The Little Paper*. Officially a political weekly, the *Little Paper* covered the artistic, cultural, and daily life of Richmond. Written, edited, designed, and published entirely by White, the *Little Paper* addressed her run-ins with other publishers, editors, shopkeepers, and workers in the city, as well as gossip on notable figures in the community.

White considered her greatest accomplishments, however, to be in the political arena. Her foray into politics began as early as 1912 with her participation in the women's suffrage movement. She served as an officer for the Women's Franchise League, the Indiana affiliate of the National American Woman Suffrage Association, and attended conferences, hosted speakers, and gave a series of short talks on the fight for the right to vote. Her interest in the movement took her to Indianapolis and then to Chicago in 1916, where she participated in a massive parade and show of strength at the Republican and Progressive Party meetings.

Guided by a deep belief in egalitarianism, she felt spurred into action. In 1920 she fought to have her name included on the ballot for the Republican state convention. After a lengthy battle that eventually involved the Indiana attorney general and the governor, she was selected to serve. White paved the way for future female politicians in Indiana, becoming not only the first woman to appear on a ballot for office in the state, but also the first to serve as a delegate for any party's convention. She renewed her position in 1922 and 1924.

White's political career did not end with her time as a Republican delegate. In 1921 she sought the Republican nomination for Richmond mayor, placing fourth out of eight in the Republican primary. In 1926 she challenged a Republican incumbent for a seat in the Indiana House of Representatives, becoming the first woman to attempt that feat in the state. Undoubtedly interested in politics, White also enjoyed the publicity her runs attracted and she appeared in newspaper articles in Chicago, Atlanta, New York, and Detroit. Coming in second in the Republican primary, she renewed her campaign in 1928, again without success. In 1938 she ran for mayor in Richmond as an independent with a campaign platform that focused superficially on park beautification and traffic laws. As noted in the *Little Paper*, however, "her "sole and only purpose in running for mayor [was] for the salary."

The political and professional met in White's career as a journalist and she used her journalistic endeavors to enact political change. Through her writings and a legal challenge, she was instrumental in blocking alterations to Richmond's portion of the National Road. A series of exposés on the unsanitary placement of privies near park springs ended in the offending structures being moved. Through the *Little Paper* she strenuously campaigned against changing to a city manager form of government, a reform supported by the major newspapers in town and the local Chamber of Commerce. Showing a strong grasp of the issue and substantial research on its potential effects, White's tenacity led to the proposal's defeat by a three-to-one margin. Wielding the power of the pen through the

Esther White

Little Paper, White was able to influence politics, a rarity for a woman of her generation.

A total of seventy-three issues of the *Little Paper* were published in her lifetime, sometimes with decades of hiatus as White's health faltered. The paper was never profitable, but was always popular, as readers knew that each edition would be as brash and entertaining as White herself. In 1992 White was inducted into the Indiana Journalism Hall of Fame in recognition of her nearly five decades of service to the profession. In the induction speech, the organization described her as a "woman ahead of her times" and her writings as "forceful, crusading, and sometimes eccentric."

White's writings were also profiled in two other mediums. She published at least four small collections of her own poems and short stories and a volume featuring bookplates created by and for famous Hoosiers. Her passion for art and music was well known. Unhappy with the cultural options available for Richmond residents, she frequently brought performers, lecturers, and artists to the area and maintained correspondence with poets and painters. She was personally responsible for eliminating Richmond's Blue Law, which prohibited artistic performances on Sundays. For years, her home doubled as a salon where Richmond's cultural elite met and discussed art and music. She was also a founding member of the Richmond Art Association.

In increasingly poor health and nearly blind in her later years, White was housebound and entirely removed from the civic and cultural life of Richmond. Upon her death and with no family remaining in the area, her personal collection of works from noted local artists, including George Baker and John Elwood Bundy, were donated to Earlham College and displayed at the Richmond Art Museum. Her papers, personal correspondence, and journal are now housed at the Earlham College Archives, much of which has been digitized and is available online.

CHERA A. LaFORGE

For Further Reading

Blakey, George. "Esther Griffin White: An Awakener of Hoosier Potential." *Indiana Magazine of History* 86 (September, 1990): 281–310.

Stout, Kristin. "A Passion for Politics: Esther Griffin White's Role in Indiana Politics, 1912–1938." Honors Thesis, Ball State University, May 2005.

Esther Griffin White Papers. Earlham College Archives, Richmond, IN.

White, Ryan
December 6, 1971–April 8, 1990

Teenage crusader for people with AIDS.

Hailed as a "kid pioneer," Ryan White of Kokomo, Indiana, became the focus of national attention during the 1980s with his crusade to attend school after he was diagnosed with acquired immune deficiency syndrome during an era when the disorder, then regarded as inevitably fatal, caused widespread panic. Only fourteen years old when the news broke that he would fight to be readmitted to Western Middle School in Russiaville, White eventually was credited with humanizing AIDS patients to millions of Americans because he came across on national television as a typical midwestern teenager, broadening the image of people struggling with the terrifying disorder.

In disarming testimony before a U.S. Congressional commission and during appearances on national television shows, White spoke in simple, powerful ways about the hostility his family endured with his crusade, as well as the acceptance he enjoyed during the final years of his life after his family moved to the Hamilton County town of Cicero, and he enrolled in Hamilton Heights High School. By the time he died at age eighteen in Riley Hospital for Children in Indianapolis, White had been befriended by international celebrities including pop singers Elton John and MICHAEL JACKSON; his life was dramatized in an ABC-TV movie, and his memorial service was attended by First Lady Barbara Bush, Indiana's top political leaders, and thousands of mourners ranging from high school students to health care workers.

Presidents from George H. W. Bush to Barack Obama have, in White's name, signed legislation to help thousands of Americans with AIDS. "We owe it to Ryan to open our hearts and our minds to those with AIDS," former President Ronald Reagan wrote in a tribute. "We owe it to Ryan to be compassionate, caring, and tolerant toward those with AIDS, their families, and friends. It's the disease that's frightening, not the people who have it."

Scrawny, sandy-haired White dealt with health challenges all of his life. Shortly after his birth at an Indianapolis hospital, medical specialists told his mother, Jeanne, that her son was afflicted with severe hemophilia, the blood clotting disorder. His diagnosis of AIDS—which White received shortly after his thirteenth birthday, during the holiday season of 1984—was attributed to contaminated vials of a blood clotting agent that had been used to treat his hemophilia during an era when thorough testing of such products was rare.

"I Know I'm Somebody 'Cuz God Don't Make No Junk" was a message on a bumper sticker that Ryan affixed to his bedroom wall in Kokomo after he launched his crusade to be readmitted to Western Middle School. A group of residents called the Concerned Citizens of Kokomo reacted with a lawsuit to block him; parents and some teachers sided with them as did others in Howard County, splitting the community amid heated, emotional debates. When the Concerned Citizens group exhausted their appeals after having obtained a restraining order at one point, and a court ruling cleared the way for White's return to the classroom, some parents pulled their children and set up a private school.

In his posthumously published autobiography, White wrote that he often felt isolated. "Other kids backed up against their lockers when they saw me coming, or they threw themselves against the hallway walls, shouting, 'Watch out! Watch out! There he is!'" In her own autobiography and in media interviews, Jeanne, a single parent who worked at a Kokomo factory, reported her family endured months of hostility that included trash dumps on their lawn and vicious phone calls and letters. However, other residents of Kokomo and Russiaville expressed support for the Whites, including classmates who circulated petitions urging school officials to welcome him.

The controversy, and White's steely resolve, made him a household name across the country, particularly once he began accepting invitations to appear on television programs for young people. Although he eventually spoke everywhere from a national teachers convention at the Superdome sports stadium in New Orleans to a Capitol Hill commission that included congressmen and the U.S. surgeon general, White always preferred making presentations to children and teenagers. "Kids listen," he explained in his typically direct style. Appearing before the congressional commission in March 1988, he wore jeans, a casual shirt, and high-topped sneakers with untied laces. White opened his testimony by saying, "I came face-to-face with death at thirteen years old." Emphasizing that he refused to capitulate to a diagnosis of a terminal disorder, White explained that he decided instead "to live a normal life, to go to school, be

Ryan White with his mother, Jeanne.

with my friends, and enjoy day-to-day activities."

In his choosing to do so as a young person with AIDS, he became a national celebrity, and so did his mother. Jeanne, who had been divorced from Ryan's father for several years before the boy's crusade to attend school, went from working at Delco Electronics in Kokomo to being a national advocate for families of AIDS patients. She testified before public officials, delivered keynote speeches at conferences, and put together presentations about AIDS awareness events across the country. Two years after her son's death, she married a neighbor in Cicero who had befriended her son and became known as Jeannie White-Ginder.

In the final years of his life, Ryan battled various health issues and was frequently absent from Hamilton Heights High School, where classmates and faculty were commended for their tolerance. For two weeks prior to White's enrollment in the fall of 1987, students at his new school received special AIDS education. In spite of his frail health, White made several appearances at events in New York and southern California—with athletes, television personalities, and pop singers—designed to increase AIDS awareness. He also found himself the focus of media attention at events such as the 1987 Pan American Games hosted by Indianapolis when the victorious diver, Greg Louganis, presented his gold medal to White and called the teenager a "hero."

A few months after White's death in April 1990, Congress passed, and President Bush signed, the Ryan White Care Act, which authorized $875 million in funding for programs to help people with HIV, the virus that causes AIDS. In 2009, with Jeanne White-Ginder at his side, President Obama signed the Ryan White HIV/AIDS Treatment Extension Act, the country's largest federally funded program for people living with HIV.

NELSON PRICE

For Further Reading

Price, Nelson. "A Quiet Hero: Ryan White Twenty Years Later," *Traces of Indiana and Midwestern History* 22, no. 1 (Winter 2010): 14–23.

———. *The Quiet Hero: A Life of Ryan White*. Indianapolis: Indiana Historical Society Press, 2015.

White, Jeanne, with Suzanne Dworkin. *Weeding Out the Tears*. New York: Avon Books, 1997.

White, Ryan, and Ann Marie Cunningham. *Ryan White: My Own Story*. New York: Dial Books, 1991.

Wiley, Harvey Washington

October 18, 1844–June 30, 1930

Chief chemist of the U.S. Department of Agriculture, a leading opponent of food adulteration; instrumental in developing the national Pure Food and Drug Law of 1906.

As a scientist of the early twentieth century, one might presume that the man dubbed "The Crusading Chemist" would have patented a drug or formulated the solution to a problem. Instead Doctor Harvey Wiley's contribution was a humbling one for science, for it revealed that scientists can be tempted to sacrifice data for government and corporate support. Sodium benzoate, formaldehyde, copper sulfate, sulphur dioxide, sweeteners derived from coal tar, misleading toxic medications, flour bleached of its nutrients, and contaminated meat from diseased animals were among the adulterations in the food and drug industries that Wiley became famous for exposing in his time, and some are still consumed by Americans today. Yet now his name is rarely recognized and the original purpose of his Pure Food and Drug Act of 1906 has long been undermined by the very bureaucracy charged with enforcing it.

Harvey Washington Wiley was born October 18, 1844, near Kent, Jefferson County, Indiana, the sixth of seven children on a working family

Harvey Wiley

farm. One influential project assigned to Wiley was the planting and harvesting of sorghum sugarcane, which gave him a sense of the American sugar industry's value. Wiley earned a bachelor of science degree from Hanover College in 1867 and an medical degree from Indiana Medical College in 1871. Two years later he received a bachelor of science in chemistry from Harvard University.

After graduating from Harvard, Wiley worked in Bismarck, Germany, at the Imperial Food Laboratory. He returned to Indiana for a post at Purdue University, where he conducted research on the adulteration of sugar with glucose. This background and experience helped to set him on his life's course as an advocate for safe food. He began his crusade against adulterated food in 1883 when he was appointed chief chemist of the U.S. Department of Agriculture, which eventually became the Bureau of Chemistry. Wiley observed that industrialization following the Civil War generated an increase in centralized city dwelling and dependence on manufactured food instead of food from one's homestead or local farmers. Furthermore, there was the burgeoning pharmaceutical industry that promised a cure for everything in a pill or spoonful. Wiley lamented that newspapers carried plenty of ridiculous and fraudulent "before and after" ads of people who used adulterated products or miracle drugs at the expense of articles about the problems that resulted from such use. States had worked to protect their citizens from food adulteration, but interstate industrialization of food production made this effort difficult. Wiley thus set his eye on Congress's constitutional authority to regulate interstate commerce.

In 1902 Wiley obtained permission from Congress to conduct experiments on a group of students from Georgetown Medical College, nicknamed "the Poison Squad," to scientifically test the effects of consuming foods that contain toxic preservatives and additives. For five years Wiley and his assistant, Doctor W. D. Bigelow, meticulously collected data in the Bureau of Chemistry kitchen, requiring study participants to eat every meal there, have vital signs monitored, and submit waste for examination. Wiley presented his findings in a congressional hearing. On June 30, 1906, with vast support from Congress, the president and the public, Wiley's brainchild, the Pure Food and Drug Act, was passed and signed into law, outlawing the sale of adulterated and misbranded food and drugs.

Wiley opposed food adulteration on grounds of honesty because adulterated products cheat the consumer into spending more than the degraded product is worth, and it compromised health since corrupting the natural makeup of a food substance can cause gradual damage to consumers' internal organs. When speaking to a group of businessmen who were skeptical of making food purity a matter of law, Wiley garnered applause by putting it in capitalist terms: "Is there a man in this audience who would put his hand in his neighbor's pocket, take a dollar from it and put it in his own pocket? . . . Is there a man in this audience who would so adulterate, so degrade and so misbrand a package of his goods as to cheat the consumer out of a dollar of his money when he bought that package?" No hands went up, and the point was taken. Purity of food would promote prosperity rather than hinder it.

One day a ketchup manufacturer from Terre Haute, Indiana, tearfully approached Wiley's office and entreated the good doctor to reconsider pure food standards, believing his business could not survive without the use of sodium benzoate. Instead, Wiley offered to fund a batch of nonadulterated ketchup as an experiment and see how it turned out. The ketchup manufacturer learned his customers preferred the flavor of the pure ketchup, and when Wiley asked if he still wanted sodium benzoate legalized, he replied, "Neither the law nor money could drive me back to its use again."

Some food industrialists remained opposed to the regulations, but they knew overturning such a popular law was out of the question. Manipulating the enforcers and regulations was their only option. Their propreservative agenda was gladly utilized by ambitious George McCabe, solicitor in the USDA, as he rose through ranks in the department. McCabe influenced Secretary of Agriculture James Wilson and President Theodore Roosevelt to trust him with more power, appoint probusiness bureaucrats to cancel out Wiley's decisions, and shorten food inspectors' deadlines, thereby thwarting conviction of Pure Food Law violators.

At times, Wiley's own scientific perfectionism and impulsiveness hindered his attempts at defeating cronyism. When Roosevelt assembled members of the Agriculture Department to settle complaints from the company Williams, Curtice, and Sherman Brothers about preservative use, Roosevelt resoundingly endorsed Wiley's ban on sodium benzoate. With a pound of his fist the president ordered, "This substance that you are using is injurious to health and you shall not use it any longer." When the topic arose of sweetening canned corn with saccharin, Wiley explained: "Everyone who ate that sweet corn was deceived. He thought he was eating sugar, when in point of fact he was eating a coal tar product totally devoid of food value and extremely injurious to health." He did not realize that Roosevelt's own doctor prescribed saccharin for him. Angrily, Roosevelt announced, "Anybody who says saccharin is injurious to health is an idiot."

Roosevelt promptly issued an executive order creating the Remsen Board of Consulting Scientific Experts, headed by Doctor Ira Remsen, himself the codiscoverer of saccharin. Remsen's men ran experiments that contradicted Wiley's Poison Squad experiments, but Wiley noticed flaws in their technique that corrupted the data. A subsequent committee investigation, headed by Congressman Ralph W. Moss, cleared Wiley of wrongdoing and concluded McCabe had been meddlesome. Even some of the antagonistic industrialists became convinced that Wiley was right. But the damage was done. Soon the standards of the Pure Food and Drug Law required manufacturers only to name the preservatives on their labels rather than abstain from adulterating their products. To this day, the Food and Drug Administration allows numerous preservatives on the market.

Frustrated with the success of special interests and government officials in watering down the provisions of the Pure Food Act, Wiley resigned in 1912. He continued, however, his mission to educate the public about the dangers of adulterated foods. In 1912 he accepted a position with *Good Housekeeping* as director of the Bureau of Foods Sanitation and Health, enabling him to continue his laboratory work. It was in this capacity he developed the famous "Good Housekeeping Seal of Approval" that most Americans today recognize. Wiley remained with *Good Housekeeping* for eighteen years.

In 1929, a year before his death, Wiley self-published *The History of a Crime against the Food Law*, an exposé on the politics and influence of the food and drug industry on food policy. It was his last act of public advocacy. He died on June 30, 1930, twenty-four years after the passage of the pure food law. He is buried in Arlington National Cemetery.

AMANDA CHRISTINE READ

For Further Reading

"Dr. Harvey W. Wiley," *New York Times*, July 2, 1930.

Wiley, Harvey W. *Harvey W. Wiley: An Autobiography*. Indianapolis: Bobbs-Merrill Company, 1930.

———. *The History of a Crime against the Pure Food Law: The Amazing Story of the National Food and Drugs Intended to Protect the Health of the People, Perverted to Protect Adulteration of Foods and Drugs*. Washington, DC: Harvey W. Wiley, 1929.

Willkie, Wendell

February 18, 1892–October 8, 1944

New Deal critic, Republican presidential candidate in 1940, and advocate for internationalism and for civil rights.

Remembered primarily as the dark-horse presidential candidate, Wendell Willkie's career reached importantly into business, international affairs, and civil liberties.

Born in Elwood, Indiana, in 1892, Willkie grew up in a German American family of lawyers, his father and, unusually, his mother. Although always a gregarious person, he was also an avid reader. After graduation from his hometown high school, he studied at Indiana University, where he toyed with socialism before becoming a Woodrow Wilson Democrat. Willkie, along with PAUL V. MCNUTT, were among the most well-known students on campus. After a brief stint teaching history, Willkie returned to Bloomington to earn a law degree and then practiced briefly in his hometown. He served in France during World War I and then set up a legal practice in Akron, Ohio.

Willkie's legal skills pulled him into corporate law, eventually with Commonwealth and Southern, a large public-utilities holding company, whose president he became in 1933. From his Manhattan base, he soon joined the attack on President Franklin D. Roosevelt. The New Deal's Tennessee Valley Authority was a direct threat to Willkie's utilities company. Quickly Willkie became a nationally known critic of government regulation of business.

One source of Willkie's growing popularity was his style. This sophisticated businessman lawyer came across as a friendly, down-to-earth midwesterner. His suit was always rumbled, his hair tousled, his conversation full of wit and warmth, and his Hoosier accent charming. Reporters loved his magnetism and candor. The *New Republic* tagged him as "a rumple-haired simple-hearted boy from Indiana." The *New York Times* wrote he had "an almost boyish exuberance of spirit and a natural straightforwardness which left untouched no one who knew him."

Adding to Willkie's appeal was his purchase of several farms near Rushville, Indiana, the hometown of his wife. He had no intention of farming himself, but the farms were great places for photographers. One wit claimed that hogs struck poses when Willkie showed up. As his national visibility increased, Willkie switched from the Democratic to the Republican Party. The GOP was in dire straits, weakened by the blows of the Great Depression and the popularity of Roosevelt's New Deal. The Republican Party's Old Guard leaders seemed aged and out of touch. With no political experience, Willkie burst onto the scene fresh and eager.

The 1940 Republican nominating convention in Philadelphia was one of the most exciting in American history. The combination of weak Republican leadership and Willkie's business success and personal charisma pulled him to the spotlight. As gallery chants of "We Want Willkie" reached deafening levels, the dark-horse candidate began to gather votes. On the sixth ballot he won, prompting U.S. Senator James E. Watson of Indiana to comment that it was okay for the town prostitute to join the church, but she should not lead the choir the first Sunday.

A triumphant Willkie traveled to Elwood to make his acceptance speech. As the temperatures reached 100 degrees Fahrenheit that August day and as 150,000 people overwhelmed the town and facilities, the candidate spoke. Usually a superb orator, his speech that day was a bit dull.

A rocky start to the campaign grew rockier. Willkie's unfocused and unprofessional campaign could not counter Roosevelt's masterly political skills and wide popularity, even as the president sought an unprecedented third term. And with war growing fiercer in Europe and Asia, many voters preferred an experienced leader in the White House. Roosevelt handily beat the Republican dark horse by nearly 10 percent—54.7 to 44.8 percent. The president carried thirty-eight states and Willkie carried ten. He did win his native state, but not by much. In Indiana Willkie won 50.5 percent of the vote to 49 percent for Roosevelt.

Rather than slumping into a corner after his defeat, Willkie emerged as a bright light of progressive Republicanism and internationalism. Some of his strength came from Irita Van Doren, the sophisticated book review editor of the *New York Herald Tribune*. Van Doren became Willkie's tutor and his lover. She was, he wrote, the woman "I admire inordinately and love excessively." Edith Willkie likely knew. So did many journalists. But not the general public.

Willkie moved far from the isolationism of his fellow midwestern Republicans. In early 1942 he accepted Roosevelt's invitation to visit war-ravaged Britain, carrying a letter from the president to Winston Churchill. Willkie spoke widely in favor of the necessity of standing up to Adolf Hitler and lend-lease aid. Under the lend-lease program, the United States transferred arms and other war materials, without compensation, to Britain, China, the Soviet Union, and other countries whose defense was deemed vital to the nation's security. The plan marked the end of the United States' noninterventionist policy and the pretense of neutrality.

Willkie's greatest international contribution came in late 1942 when, at Roosevelt's invitation,

Wendell Willkie

he boarded a military plane to travel around the world, covering 31,000 miles in forty-nine days, long before such travel was common or comfortable. He met with leaders in the Middle East, Africa, the Soviet Union, and China. His radio address on his return home captured an audience of thirty-six million listeners. Soon he was at work on a book, encouraged and helped by Van Doren.

One World appeared in spring 1943. Describing his travels and the people he met in clear and engaging prose, Willkie asserted that, "our thinking must be world-wide." Visiting with farmers in Russia, he found people there and elsewhere similar to those back home in Indiana. He sharpened his criticism of Western colonialism and his case for a "United Nations" organization. *One World* sold more than a million copies in two months, many more in the months after. BOOTH TARKINGTON, a fellow Indiana Republican and Pulitzer-prize winning author, lauded the book as "written with a breathless honesty" by a leader who "has personally experienced the small roundness of the twentieth century world."

Willkie also became in the early 1940s one of the nation's most visible advocates of civil liberties and racial equality. The great irony of World War II was that Americans fought for the four freedoms with a segregated military. Segregation and discrimination were rampant at home as well as overseas, as Willkie said again and again. He worked closely with the National Association for the Advancement of Colored People. As chairman of the board of Twentieth-Century Fox, he pushed against the racial stereotyping so commonplace in Hollywood films. Willkie wrote and spoke widely on civil rights with a passion unmatched by few, if any, prominent white Americans. He even suggested the possibility of federal government action if progress was denied. And he returned often to one of the lessons learned from his global trip—America's own race problems connected to struggles against racism and colonialism overseas.

Willkie's global vision and advocacy of racial equality were too advanced for many Americans. He considered a presidential run in 1944, but many Republicans had always thought of him as an outsider. The Republican convention of 1944 had no room for even a speech by the party's 1940 nominee.

Willkie's death at age fifty-two removed a progressive voice from the postwar era. In the next years, as Cold War animosities and McCarthyism took hold, many forgot this advocate of internationalism and civil rights. They remembered instead the dark-horse candidate who appeared briefly on the national stage in 1940. Such memories missed the point. Like a few other great Americans, Willkie became greater as the decades passed and as the full meaning of his life became clearer.

JAMES H. MADISON

For Further Reading

Dunn, Susan. *1940: FDR, Willkie, Lindbergh, Hitler—The Election and the Storm*. New Haven, CT: Yale University Press, 2013.

Madison, James H., ed. *Wendell Willkie: Hoosier Internationalist*. Bloomington: Indiana University Press, 1992.

Neal, Steve. *Dark Horse: A Biography of Wendell Willkie*. Garden City, NY: Doubleday, 1984.

Woodburn, James Albert

November 30, 1856–December 12, 1943

Indiana University historian, teacher, and writer whose ties to his family and campus shaped the historical understandings of Indiana residents for generations.

James Albert Woodburn lived almost his entire life in Bloomington, Indiana, where he spent most of his career as a professor of American history and politics at Indiana University. A member of the first generation to professionalize the historical discipline, Woodburn obtained his PhD in history from Johns Hopkins University in 1890, just six years after the founding of the American Historical Association. Woodburn came from a long line of educators, making his career choice a somewhat obvious one. Born to parents who were both teachers, Woodburn represented the beginning of his family's fourth generation in the United States. An understanding of his family and hometown remain vital to any full appreciation of his later writing, teaching, and career.

Woodburn routinely demonstrated a keen appreciation for the ways his family, hometown, and national histories intertwined. His family's deep roots afforded him many practical and intellectual advantages as a student and teacher. Woodburn used his family's rich records, today archived at IU's Lilly Library, to frame and give shape to many of his writings and teachings. Papers in Woodburn's personal possession date to the arrival of his ancestors to the United States in 1767, when his great-grandfather, the original James

Woodburn, first immigrated. One of the few records documenting him, tellingly, is an inventory of the books he collected dated November 24, 1799. From the beginning, the Woodburns were a family that valued education.

In addition to this passion for learning, the family's antislavery views also left a lasting impression upon Woodburn. The Woodburns migrated from South Carolina to Indiana as South Carolinians with antislavery sentiments felt increasingly unwelcome. When his grandfather, Dorrance Beatty Woodburn, endured repeated threats in the form of public broadsides posted by his neighbors outside local tavern doors beginning in 1823, the Woodburns were forced to leave. In 1830 they settled in and around Bloomington.

Woodburn developed a deep contempt for slavery from these and other stories. With his disdain came a simultaneous respect for those institutions, such as public schools, that helped sustain debate and the free flow of ideas—precisely the kinds of things he saw slaveholders trying to suppress. Woodburn seemed to especially admire and emulate the experiences of his father, James Woodburn II, who continued the family's antislavery and educational traditions. He was one of the first state residents to study at IU, where he was enrolled from 1838 to 1842 before becoming a public school teacher.

Woodburn saw that IU opened opportunities for his father that had not been available to his grandfather and great-grandfather in South Carolina. His father, for example, became active in the Athenian Society, one of the school's literary and debate clubs. For much of the nineteenth century, the Athenian and its rival organization, the Philomethean Society, shaped the lives and social activities of students. The education and experiences Woodburn's father gained in college helped him launch his teaching career, a trajectory and career path his son clearly admired and emulated. But when James II died an untimely death in 1865, young Woodburn faced the prospect of adulthood without a father and mentor.

Woodburn's life work made it clear that this loss had left a lasting impression. He began by enrolling at IU in 1872, also becoming active with the Athenians. Early on, he borrowed heavily from his father's writings and teachings. In 1873, for example, he used several of his father's words in his speech, "Mr. President." As he matured, Woodburn started developing his own ideas. "Hero Worship" (1874) critiqued the cult of soldier worship becoming commonplace during Reconstruction. "The Irrepressible Conflict" (1876) offered a pointed appraisal of the direction of the nation's partisan politics. Two decidedly polemical speeches, "Decoration Day" (1875) and "A Political Harangue" (1876) were written but never delivered, perhaps as Woodburn worried they would be perceived as overly partisan. Outside the Athenian's halls, however, his partisan identity deepened. His first ballot from 1878 had the words "My First Vote" scribbled across its top and listed several Republican Party candidates he favored.

After graduation, Woodburn saw a need for greater training. With new standards now governing entrance into the profession, Woodburn used his high marks and glowing recommendations from teachers to begin doctorate work at Johns Hopkins in 1886. After completing his PhD in 1890, Woodburn returned to Bloomington and renewed his work at IU.

In the early 1890s, Woodburn became an increasingly regular feature of the local lecture and visiting professor circuit, frequently invited by area communities to talk about his research. At one such lecture in Indianapolis, Woodburn met a young woman named Caroline Louise Gelston, whom he later married on November 20, 1893. The couple's first son, fittingly named James, was born in 1894, followed by a daughter, Janet McMillan, in 1900. A third child, Edward Albert, born in 1903, died in infancy. As the family took shape, Woodburn also took a number of visiting professorships at a number of other universities.

For the most part, however, Woodburn lived and worked in Bloomington. Edward Albert's death aside, the years the family spent in Bloomington seemed like happy ones. Woodburn emerged as a prolific writer and scholar, establishing a reputation in his field. He corresponded with a number of early and influential historians, including Herbert Baxter Adams, Frederick Jackson Turner, and Reuben Gold Thwaites. Still active in partisan politics, he also corresponded with William Jennings Bryan, EUGENE VICTOR DEBS, Theodore Roosevelt, and Woodrow Wilson. Woodburn also established contact with influential African American leaders such as Booker T. Washington, at one point orchestrating Washington's visit to the campus for a lecture. In 1903 Woodburn won the prestigious John Marshall Prize, given by Johns Hopkins University for the year's best book in political science.

As his career progressed, Woodburn authored several works. He continued using his own family's papers and letters as primary sources, offering as they did a frontline view of nearly a century of American history. An essay in the 1936 *Indiana Magazine of History*, for example, detailed the life of his father. But he also wrote widely on a variety of subjects of broader focus. Some of his favorite themes included the emergence of national politics and political parties, the American West, and the sectional crisis. He published in a variety of scholarly journals and wrote several books. Perhaps his most controversial work was his biography of the antislavery leader and Radical Republican Thaddeus Stevens. Radical Republicans of the Civil War era were not highly regarded at the time, and his detractors did not muzzle their critiques.

Woodburn seemed unwilling to forget or deny the trials his family had faced in the 1820s and 1830s, however, and refused to portray slavery or the South in the softer tones used by historian William A. Dunning and others. Undaunted, Woodburn remained active and much beloved on campus. He served on the editorial board of the *Indiana Magazine of History*. He also became active in the Indiana Historical Society, the Indianapolis Literary Club, the Kiwanis Club, and professional organizations such as the American Historical Association and American Political Science Association. He served as the first chair of the IU History Department in 1914 when it split from political science to become its own, autonomous unit. In 1924 Woodburn retired.

He continued to publish until his final years. One of his last works, *History of Indiana University*, published in 1940, might well be considered his most personal labor of love, given that it allowed him to finally thread together so many elements of his family's (and especially his father's) story, his personal upbringing, and the place where he had lived and worked for so long. Woodburn died during a bout of pneumonia in Madison, Wisconsin, on December 12, 1943. When his body returned home, his family, friends, and mourners gathered at Bloomington's Rose Hill Cemetery to celebrate him. On October 24, 1971, the building directly next to Lilly Library on the present-day IU campus was renamed in his honor. The plaque posted inside the door remembered a campus teacher, scholar, and friend.

JESSE J. GANT

For Further Reading

Barnhart, John D. "James Albert Woodburn, 1856–1943." *Indiana Magazine of History* 39 (December 1943): 362.

Gant, Jesse J. "'Younger and More Irreconcilable': James Albert Woodburn's Undergraduate Orations at Indiana University, 1875–1876." *Indiana Magazine of History* 108 (June 2012): 146–85.

Morris, Martha Tucker. "Indiana Genealogy: The Woodburn Family." *Indiana Magazine of History* 33 (September 1937): 363–65.

Wooden, John

October 14, 1910–June 4, 2010

Renowned men's basketball coach at the University of California, Los Angeles, whose teams won a record ten National Collegiate Athletic Association titles. A three-time All-American basketball player at Purdue University. Legendary speaker and mentor in leadership.

Hall of Fame broadcaster Dick Enberg, who has midwestern roots himself, in describing John Wooden, said, "He's a sports Abraham Lincoln, a Winston Churchill; one of the greatest athletes the game of basketball has every produced as a three-time All-American at Purdue. He was a scholar. Plus, he was a nice man."

Enberg's words accurately described the essence of Wooden and his legacy to not only basketball around the world, but also especially to those who follow the sport so passionately in Indiana, which Hoosiers say is where the sport enjoys its greatest popularity. The state can also take pride as the place where one of the legends in sports history blossomed. Wooden was named in 2009 by *The Sporting News* as the greatest coach of all time in any sport after winning ten National Collegiate Athletic Association men's basketball championships at UCLA over a twelve-year span, a record not likely to be approached, let alone broken.

Yet, Wooden's life and impact go beyond basketball. His story is rooted in the experiences of growing up in Indiana and living in the state for nearly four decades of his ninety-nine years. In time, Wooden's legend grew to almost mystical proportion, expanding even more later in his life. Although flawed as any other human, he appeared to live a life so rich and full of character that it seems natural that his story would inspire others.

His unprecedented success at UCLA provided him fame and had he chosen, fortune. Yet, he chose to live a life entrenched in principles that he learned from his parents growing up in Morgan Country and shared those lessons with as many people as possible. He was born in Martinsville, not Hall, as many previous stories on Wooden have stated. His life skills were taught to him mostly from his father, Hugh. Though simplistic in nature, they helped Wooden develop his guiding principles to be used in all arenas of life, not just in basketball.

One of the simple gifts he received from his father came after he graduated from a small country grade school in Centerton. On a three-by-five-inch note card, his father wrote in pencil "7 Suggestions To Follow," including be true to yourself, help others, and make friendship a fine art. His dad also offered Wooden, and his two brothers, the Two Sets of Threes. The first set was a simple message of never lie, never cheat, never steal, followed with don't whine, don't complain, don't make excuses.

Wooden kept the note card until it wore out. Then he rewrote Hugh's message again on a fresh card. After he retired from coaching in 1975, following a twenty-seven-year career at UCLA, he reproduced laminated versions of the card that he handed out to anyone who would take one. It was his way of carrying on his father's legacy and values, rooted in his upbringing, which meant so much to him.

Wooden loved sports in grade school, especially baseball and basketball. But Martinsville High School did not have a baseball team, so he turned to basketball. He later played in three consecutive state basketball championships, winning the crown for the Martinsville Artesians in his junior year of 1927. In his senior year he experienced the disappointment of missing a critical free throw in the closing seconds that would have given his team its second state title.

Wooden knew full well about disappointment. He said later in his life that the greatest lesson he learned while growing up was watching his father deal with losing the family farm a couple years earlier. "Seeing my father abide by them [his principles] as he lost the farm had a most powerful effect on me," Wooden said. "That's where I came to see that what you do is more important than what you say you will do."

In the fall of 1928 Wooden headed to Purdue hoping to be a civil engineer. He ended up with a degree in English, with his love for poetry and thirst to be a teacher expanding at West Lafayette as did his prowess in basketball. His spectacular

Coach John Wooden instructs his Indiana State University basketball team.

athleticism allowed him to bounce all around the court, and into the bleachers if necessary to retrieve the basketball. Wooden is credited as being one of the game's fastest, and most skilled, dribblers.

In his sophomore and senior seasons Wooden led Purdue to Big Ten titles, the latter team, in 1932, considered by experts as the best team in the land nearly a decade before the first NCAA Tournament was played. He left Purdue as the conference's all-time leading scorer, but Wooden believed his most important accomplishment was winning the Big Ten Medal of Honor for academic achievement. He placed the medal prominently in the entrance of his condominium for the thousands of visitors who stopped by until his dying day seventy-eight years later.

Wooden's love for teaching and coaching burgeoned thanks to the mentoring of his college coach, WARD "PIGGY" LAMBERT. It was also Lambert's love for fast break, up-tempo basketball that shaped how Wooden coached his teams during his forty-three-year career as a coach.

Upon graduating from Purdue, he married his hometown high school sweetheart, Nell, and the newlyweds moved to Dayton, Kentucky, where Wooden got his start in coaching. There he fine-tuned his Pyramid of Success, a step-by-step depiction of how success is defined that later became his calling card for leading others. After two years, Wooden was back in Indiana after taking a job at South Bend Central High School. But Wooden's playing days were not over. Long before the days of the National Basketball Association, Wooden supplemented his income, and his desire to remain competitive, by playing professionally for the barnstorming Indianapolis Kautskys.

Wooden never won a state title at South Bend Central, but relished his role as a teacher as much as a coach. After service in World War II, he decided it was time to try college coaching and began at Indiana State Teachers College (now Indiana State University) in 1946. In two seasons, his Sycamore teams twice made the national tournament.

Yet, the biggest impact in Terre Haute might have been his association with the Sycamores' lone African American player, Clarence Walker. Wooden had witnessed racism growing up in Martinsville. His experience with Walker, though not without difficulty that was consistent with the times, furthered Wooden's reputation for having empathy toward all people. "Coach Wooden saw the Ku Klux Klan at its worse in the 1930s so he understood what the fight was all about," said Kareem Abdul-Jabbar, his star center at UCLA in the late 1960s.

Wooden passed on a couple of opportunities to return to Purdue as its head coach in the late 1940s and early 1950s. Yet, when he was honored in 1969 in his hometown of Martinsville, Wooden was still a Hoosier at heart. As one national sportswriter put it, "He goes better with sycamores than palm trees."

Wooden remained involved in Indiana basketball well into his nineties, lending his name to the John R. Wooden Tradition event held annually in Indianapolis from 2000 to 2009, and attending the event for as long as he could. In a life that lasted nearly a century, Indiana was never far from his heart or conscience.

ALAN KARPICK

For Further Reading

Davis, Seth. *A Coach's Life*. New York: Times Book, Henry Holt and Company, 2014.

Karpick, Alan. *Boilermaker Basketball: Great Purdue Teams and Players*. Chicago: Bonus Books, 1989.

May, Chris. "John Wooden 1910–2010: Saying Goodbye to a Legend." *Indiana Basketball History Magazine* (Fall 2010).

Morrow, Barbara Olenyik. *Hardwood Glory: A Life of John Wooden*. Indianapolis: Indiana Historical Society Press, 2014.

Wylie, Andrew

April 12, 1789–November 11, 1851

First president of Indiana University.

Indiana University is recognized today as one of the most successful public universities in America. Few know, however, about its early history or the highly charged battles that public education advocates had to win to ensure that all Indiana citizens had the opportunity to pursue college degrees in an institution funded by the state and in an environment open to all, regardless of their religious beliefs.

Two hundred years ago, there were few colleges in the nation, and most were controlled by religious denominations. Formal education of any kind was virtually nonexistent in Indiana. Nevertheless, the farsighted founders of Indiana wanted a public college established. No individual played a more significant role in ensuring the success of that goal than did Andrew Wylie, the first president of Indiana University and a committed supporter of public education.

Wylie was born in Washington County, Pennsylvania, on April 12, 1789. He graduated with honors from Jefferson College, and became president of Washington College in 1817 while still a young man. In May 1828 Wylie was elected president of the newly established Indiana College, which had previously been Indiana Seminary and would become IU in 1838. Wylie was thirty-nine at the time of his unanimous election by the board of trustees. Evidence suggests that Wylie did not even know he was a candidate. Although well-regarded and already a successful educator, one aspect of Wylie's resume would haunt him throughout his long tenure at IU and would contribute significantly to the animosity directed toward the institution, marring its newly forming reputation in the state legislature and with the citizens of Indiana: Wylie was an ordained Presbyterian minister. For many in Indiana, his affiliation with the Presbyterian Church implied that the new college was controlled by that denomination.

Not only was Wylie an ordained Presbyterian minister, but his two faculty members, hired before he arrived, were also Presbyterian, which further aggravated the situation. Many asked why the state should fund Indiana College for the Presbyterians and not also fund a college for each of the other denominations. Wylie spent many years reassuring the legislature and Indiana citizens that IU was not controlled by the Presbyterian Church and was, in fact, an institution where no specific religious tenets were taught. Still, the battle for state funding raged on for most of Wylie's tenure. The most formable opponent in that battle was the state's largest religious denomination, the Methodists.

The issues were further complicated by Wylie's own views on education. Although he was committed to ensuring that no church would control the new college, he also believed that education should be based on a religious foundation. The difference for Wylie was that he believed that religious instruction should not be sectarian—that is, influenced by the specific beliefs of the various religious denominations or "sects." It was left to Wylie, therefore, to develop a plan for providing collegiate education with a religious yet nonsectarian base. Adding to the competition and complexity of the issues was the fact that state colleges were a relatively new phenomenon on the scene. Indiana College was only the eleventh such institution founded in the nation and the first, for many years, in Indiana. Few citizens, therefore, understood how a college could possibly exist that was funded by the state and yet not controlled by a religious sect. In his writings on IU's history, David Banta suggests that to most in the early days of Indiana, "it was inconceivable how a college that was not under some sort of church supervision could exist and not be infidel."

In his first address before the state legislature, Wylie introduced his plan for providing nonsectarian education. He hoped to foster a type of generic Protestantism, a model reminiscent of Benjamin's Franklin's "public religion," which would find a home eventually in the Common School movement. Wylie referred to his plan as a "middle course," or a way to provide collegiate instruction respectful of religion without inculcating specific sectarian tenets. His plan would avoid the "dark and thorny wilderness of mystical Theology." He claimed that "the evils of sectarianism could be prevented" if religion and morality were taught in a "system of liberal public instruction." Wylie implored the legislators to "let our youth be taught to fear God and keep his commandments, but let their teachers be enlightened, liberal-minded men."

Wylie championed this position throughout the next twenty-one years of his presidency, but many continued to doubt the sincerity of his claims, especially the Methodists. Wylie tried to appease the Methodists and the other denominations. Non-Presbyterians were appointed to the faculty and to the board of trustees, and Wylie accepted a cut in his salary when enrollment dropped, a fact partially attributed to the competition for students from the newly forming religious colleges. In 1841 Wylie published his book, *Sectarianism is Heresy*, in which he outlined his frustration over the ongoing battles and recounted a story of his reaction to a Methodist board member who wanted him to create a Wesleyan professorship. Wylie objected because Wesleyan was a sectarian title and added: "By accepting the place which I held in the Institution I have virtually pledged myself to the public to keep it clear of sectarianism . . . to call any professorship by the name of Wesley" would be "inconsistent" with that pledge.

In a report to an investigating committee of the legislature in 1841, Wylie outlined the type of students who were most likely to attend IU. He stated that those from smaller sects that could not afford to establish their own colleges, those indifferent to sects, and those who are "the more liberal and enlightened of all sects" may be expected to send their sons to IU, which could be "managed as not to offend the prejudices of any liberal-minded good man."

In his May 1841 baccalaureate address, Wylie insisted that although he recognized the right of religious sects to educate their sons in their own institutions, he wanted them to also acknowledge the state's right to provide public education in an institution not controlled by a particular sect. Wylie admitted that such an institution, free from the control of religious denominations and subject to state supervision, was still vulnerable to "the restless jealousy of party spirit" and to the "private ambition of unprincipled demagogues." Nevertheless, "as long as the State Legislatures shall be governed by the spirit of that liberal policy in regard to religious matters . . . no very great danger is to be apprehended."

Nearly two centuries later, it is difficult to appreciate how critical Wylie's commitment was to the establishment of IU as the only state-funded, nonsectarian college. By Wylie's death in 1851, the battles to ensure IU's unique position in the state were virtually over. Unfortunately, Wylie's contribution to that status would be largely forgotten. Nevertheless, Wylie's own words, spoken early in his administration, best foretold the future of IU when he stated that it: "shall become, before long, the pride and glory of the State, the loved and revered spot to which her sons shall resort, to enjoy advantages, equal, at least, to those of any other seat of learning west of the Alleghenies."

GAYLE A. WILLIAMS

For Further Reading

Woodburn, James Albert. *History of Indiana University, 1820–1902*. Bloomington: Indiana University Press, 1940.

Williams, Gayle. "Andrew Wylie and Religion at Indiana University, 1824–1851: Nonsectarianism and Democracy." *Indiana Magazine of History* 99 (March 2003): 3–24.

Wylie, Andrew. Papers. Indiana University Archives, Bloomington, IN.

Zimmer, Justin O.

August 31, 1884–March 19, 1951

Entrepreneur and founder of orthopedic giant Zimmer Manufacturing.

Justin Zimmer was twenty years into a sales career when his Hoosier and American success story began, hatched from a rejected proposition that he parlayed with risk, conviction, and innovation into a global giant in the orthopedics industry. With some seed money from two investors and help from a former cabinetmaker, Zimmer turned a basement operation making artificial splints in Warsaw, Indiana, into a company that grew to employ more than 8,000 people in corporate and manufacturing faculties around the world and sell its extensive line of orthopedic equipment in more than a hundred countries.

Zimmer Manufacturing Company, now Zimmer Holdings Inc. was instrumental in transforming Warsaw—a northern Indiana community of still fewer than 14,000 people—into the orthopedics capital of the world. Hundreds of researchers and engineers call it home and thousands of surgeons, salespeople, and technical experts visit every year, sharing ideas and fueling medical advancements. It is home to DePuy—the orthopedic company Zimmer broke away from in 1927—and Zimmer and Biomet, a company formed by two former Zimmer executives in 1977. There are offshoots and suppliers supporting these enterprises, all forming a cluster industry that feeds on competition and proximity with products and processes that reach worldwide.

This "cross-pollinated" brotherhood, as one news account called it, began in June 1905 when Revra DePuy hired Zimmer to help his company make wooden splints. Zimmer, a twenty-year-old Western Union telegraph trainee at the time, soon began selling the splints on his way to becoming DePuy's national sales manager. Zimmer knew the market and, recognizing the growing use of aluminum, became convinced that splints made from aluminum—which do not interfere with X-ray imaging—would be preferred by doctors and be a market success. He took his idea and a request to buy an interest in DePuy to the founder's widow and was told, "You know, Justin, you are small potatoes."

Zimmer, who was born on a family farm south of Warsaw in 1884, told his wife, Janet, and daughter, Betty, in 1926 that he wanted to form his own company. "Nobody but my father thought the business could succeed," his daughter recalled. "My mother was opposed, as were my grandparents." In February 1927 Zimmer called fellow salesman Joe

Ettinger into his office at DePuy and told him his plans, saying, "I'm going to start my own business and I want you to be my factory superintendent." Ettinger, recalling the moment, said, "All right. I'll go with you. I've tried to talk you out of this before, but this time I'll go with you." Two others put up some cash, Zimmer hired Donna Belle Harmon Cox as a secretary and bookkeeper, and they started making and selling their own orthopedic products, primarily arm and leg splints.

The designing and manufacturing started in the basement of Zimmer's Warsaw house and, with help from Doctor C. F. Lytle, they arranged a display of products that within three months was presented to doctors in Washington, D.C. "We ran a one-horse show at first: from a few persons and nothing," Ettinger said. "But from the beginning sales were good because Zimmer had sales managing ability and a good line of products." The company soon moved to a building in Warsaw and within seven months, sales reached $160,000—topping DePuy. As one trade magazine put it, "Mr. Zimmer and his crew delighted in proving wrong all those who'd predicted that demand for splints could not support one or both companies, and one or both would fail."

The early strength of Zimmer's company was evident during the Great Depression. Sales dipped from 1930 to 1932, but not badly. There were only two weeks—in 1933—when employees worked fewer than forty hours a week, and they often worked overtime. They did so even during the Bank Holiday of 1933 in order to make and ship a large number of splints for hospitals in New York City. There were no layoffs during the decade and the company played a key role in assisting patients during the polio epidemic of the late 1930s, developing custom braces that could be fit to each person's specific measurements.

Zimmer died in 1951 while on vacation in Florida, but the company continued to grow and pioneer medical advancements. It marketed the first hip prosthesis, which was developed by Doctor Palmer Eicher, and developed a spinal instrument used to treat scoliosis in 1958. Zimmer became a subsidiary of Bristol-Myers Squibb in 1972 and continued to develop new devices, including a fully integrated modular system to replace artificial knees created in the 1980s.

Taking a page from the company's own start under Zimmer fifty years earlier, two Zimmer executives formed Biomet in 1977. Now those companies, and a host of others that serve them, employ thousands and, as the *New York Times* noted in 1994, "helped Warsaw sail smoothly through the recessions that socked most of the Midwest during the 1980s." The competition is fierce but can also be friendly, the latter evident in a golf tournament between teams of competing employers known as the Lesser Trochanter Open. It is a reference to a bony protrusion on the hip where leg muscles are attached. "I'm always amused at how many people from this small town I run into places like Seoul or San Francisco at international medical meetings," Ron Davis, who was president of Zimmer in 1994, told the *Times*.

In 2001 Zimmer Holdings Inc. spun off from Bristol-Myers and began trading on the New York Stock Exchange as an independent company once again. Zimmer and its competitors continue to advance products and procedures in the industry, drawing top engineers and researchers to Warsaw, as well as growing their own. Indiana's Ivy Tech Community College has an advanced orthopedics manufacturing program—designed with input from industry representatives—that trains machinists for the industry, and other Indiana colleges and universities provide support. The medical device makers in northern Indiana also receive training grants and tax incentives from state and local governments.

As the *Times* wrote twenty years ago, Warsaw is to bone surgery what Detroit is to cars and Hollywood is to movies. A trade publication said in 2006, "Tracing the industry's history reveals how homegrown entrepreneurship and specialized local skills have led to a series of small-town players to seize a spot in the global economy."

MICHAEL SMITH

For Further Reading

"In the Land of the Orthopedic Implant." *New York Times*, September 18, 1994.

DuLong, Jessica. "Welcome to Warsaw: Indiana's Orthopedics Capital of the World." *Today's Machining World* 2, no. 5 (May 2006). http://todaysmachiningworld.com/magazine/welcome-to-warsaw-indianas-orthopedics-capital-of-the-world/.

"In the Land of the Orthopedic Implant." *New York Times*, September 18, 1994.

Vrabel, Jo Ann. "Joe Ettinger: Dovetailed into Cabinet Crafting." http://yesteryear.clunette.com/ettinger.html.

Zollner, Frederick

January, 22, 1901–June 21, 1982

Industrialist, owner of Zollner Corporation, founder of Fort Wayne Pistons pro basketball team (later the Detroit Pistons), and helped found the National Basketball Association.

By almost any measure, Fred Zollner was a phenomenal man. Although small in stature, Zollner towered over most of his competitors in engineering, community building, marketing, sports, and patience. Some people called him an engineering genius; others praised him for bringing fast-pitch softball and pro basketball to the forefront of American society. His employees, though, found him to be a kind, accessible individual who often worked side by side with them on the factory floor as well as in the business office.

Fred, as he was known, was the son of Theodore Zollner, founder of the Zollner Manufacturing Company in Duluth, Minnesota. The firm rebuilt automobile engines, pistons, and precision parts for mining tools. In 1914, at age thirteen, Fred went to work for his father as an apprentice. His routine involved going to school in the morning and working at the shop in the afternoon. When schools closed for a holiday or summer vacation, he worked in the factory. By 1918 he had become a full-fledged machinist with the company, but his drive for a better education continued. From 1919 to 1927 Fred attended evening classes at the University of Minnesota and earned a degree in mechanical engineering.

By that time, business was booming for the company. Demand was unprecedented. The business, though, needed a better location to improve production and facilitate shipping. In 1931 Fort Wayne was selected as the new home of what was then called Zollner Machine Works.

Business continued accelerating for Zollner Manufacturing after America's entry into World War II. By the summer of 1942 the plant was operating seven days a week and Fred had succeeded his father as head of the company, which by then was playing a vital part in the war effort by producing 70 percent of the world's heavy-duty aluminum alloy pistons for combustion engines.

The new chief executive was not one who lorded over his employees. In fact, he preferred that they call him Fred rather than Mr. Zollner. He oversaw the creation of a monthly magazine to keep workers abreast of stories about such developments as production achievements, workers drafted into the military, men killed or missing in combat, and women taking on new responsibilities.

In its heyday, Zollner Manufacturing had more than 12,000 employees, but with the changing nature of the domestic automotive industry in the late twentieth and early twenty-first centuries, which included shifting manufacturing jobs overseas, company fortunes steadily declined. By the time the former Zollner piston plant closed in 2009, then under a different owner, employment had dropped to fewer than fifty production workers.

In addition to his notable business achievements, Zollner also made his mark in the sports world. More than just an avid fan, he started softball and basketball teams that played in industrial leagues and competed against other company-sponsored teams, including the Akron Firestone Non-Skids, Akron Goodyear Wingfoots, and Toledo Jeeps. His semiprofessional and professional teams, known as the Fort Wayne Zollner Pistons, were widely respected and drew large crowds whether they were playing slow- or fast-pitch softball or basketball. Throughout much of the late 1940s, the Pistons were recognized as one of the best amateur softball teams in the country. The fastball titles were claimed by the team in 1949 and 1951 through 1953. In 1941 the basketball team went professional, joining the National Basketball League and soon became a dominant force, winning championships in 1944 and 1945. The success of the softball and basketball teams and the resulting publicity had the added benefit of increasing the visibility of Zollner products in particular and Fort Wayne in general.

By 1949, however, the NBL began losing talent to the new Basketball Association of America, and in a move led by Zollner, the two leagues merged into the National Basketball Association. Once in the NBA, Zollner was dropped from the team's nickname, becoming the Fort Wayne Pistons and then the Detroit Pistons when Zollner moved the team in 1957 to remain competitive with teams drawing bigger crowds in metropolitan cities. In addition, the team's moniker was an obvious fit for the Motor City.

Zollner helped keep the league afloat during its early years by lending it large sums of money when other teams failed to pay their dues. He was, according to one writer, the "old Pop who always comes through when you write home for money." In another example of his generosity, Zollner purchased a DC-3 in 1952, becoming the first NBA owner to fly players to away games.

The Piston franchise also had a major impact in the early days of pro basketball after the team's defeat of the defending champion Minneapolis Lakers in a November 1950 game by the anemic score of 19–18. To insure more scoring and prevent the stalling tactics used in this contest, the league adopted the rule, still in effect, that required players to attempt a shot within twenty-four seconds.

Zollner's involvement in and support of athletics extended beyond softball and basketball. He also developed a program for young people interested in sports known as the Zollner Knot Hole Gang that eventually involved thousands of children. Zollner built a professional-class football stadium in Fort Wayne used by local high schools and a world-class, eighteen-hole golf course north of Angola. The Fred Zollner Memorial Stadium and Athletic Complex is home to teams of Concordia Lutheran High School. In addition, his company built and entered a race car in the 1941 Indianapolis 500.

Understandably, given his many contributions to the sports world, Zollner, who died in 1982 at age eighty-one, received a host of awards and honors. He was posthumously enshrined into the Naismith Memorial Basketball Hall of Fame in 1999 and named "Mr. Pro Basketball" at the silver anniversary NBA all-star game in 1975. While many words of praise also were bestowed upon him, the most appropriate came not from sports figures, but from those who worked side-by-side with him: Fred Zollner was "a great boss and friend."

SCOTT M. BUSHNELL

For Further Reading

Beatty, John D., and Phyllis Robb. *The History of Fort Wayne and Allen County, Indiana*. Vol. 1. Evansville, IN: M. T. Publishing Company, 2006.

Cope, Myron. "The Big Z and His Misfiring Pistons." *Sports Illustrated*, December 18, 1967.

Nelson, Rodger, and Ryan Taylor. *The Zollner Piston Story*. Fort Wayne, IN: Allen County Public Library Foundation, 1995.

CONTRIBUTOR BIOGRAPHIES

James S. Aber, Roe R. Cross Distinguished Professor, Emporia State University, Kansas. PhD in geology from University of Kansas. His primary teaching and research interests include glaciation, remote sensing and aerial photography, tectonics, wetlands, wind energy, global climate change, and history of geology. Coauthor of William Maclure essay.

Susan W. Aber, Emporia State University, Kansas. PhD in library and information from Emporia State University. She teaches courses via distance learning on science and technology resources and information services in Library and Information Science graduate programs for North Carolina Central University, Durham, North Carolina, and San Jose University, San Jose, California. She is the director of the Science and Math Education Center, Library, and Planetarium at Emporia State. Coauthor of William Maclure essay.

Marc Allan is the news manager at Butler University, where he has worked since 2004. Prior to that he spent twenty-four years in the newspaper business, the last two-thirds of those at the *Indianapolis Star*. His work has also appeared in the *Washington Post*, *Los Angeles Times*, *Writer's Digest*, *Indianapolis Monthly*, *Nuvo*, and many others. Author of Tony Hinkle essay.

Judith A. Allen is professor of history at Indiana University, Bloomington, and senior research fellow of The Kinsey Institute for Research in Sex, Gender and Reproduction. Her research interests are comparative histories of feminist theory and politics, the history of sex research, histories of interpersonal crimes, and changing historical childbearing patterns. She is the author of: *Sex and Secrets: Crimes involving Australian Women since 1880* (1990), *Rose Scott: Vision and Revision of Feminism, 1880–1925* (1994), and *The Feminism of Charlotte Perkins Gilman: Histories/Sexualities/Progressivism* (2009). Author of Alfred Kinsey essay.

John G. Baker, judge, Indiana Court of Appeals since 1989; chief judge, Indiana Court of Appeals (2007 to 2010). He is the author of "Now or Never: Reforming Indiana's Court System," *Indiana Law Review* (2008); "Indiana Judge: A Portrait of Judicial Evolution" in *The History of Indiana Law* (2008); "The History of the Indiana Trial Court System and Attempts at Renovation," *Indiana Law Review* (1997); and "Jesse L. Holman," in *Justices of the Indiana Supreme Court* (2010). Author of Jesse Holman essay.

Daryl Baldwin, director of the Myaamia Center at Miami University, is a citizen of the Miami Tribe of Oklahoma. His forefathers were active in the affairs of the Miami Nation dating back to the eighteenth century, and he continues this dedication through his work in language and cultural revitalization. He graduated in 1999 from the University of Montana with a master's degree with emphasis in Native American linguistics. Since 1995 he has worked with the Myaamia people developing culture and language based educational materials and programs for the tribal community. The Myaamia Center is a joint venture between the Miami Tribe of Oklahoma and Miami University. Coauthor of Mihšihkinaahkwa (Chief Little Turtle) essay.

Margaret Banks, professor of music, senior curator of musical instruments at the University of South Dakota. Author of "Conn," in *The Grove Dictionary of American Music* (2013). Author of Charles Conn essay.

Robert G. Barrows is professor of history at Indiana University–Purdue University, Indianapolis. In addition to his biography of Albion Fellows Bacon, he coedited the *Encyclopedia of Indianapolis* (1994) and he has published several articles and book chapters dealing with aspects of Indiana history and American urban history. Author of Albion Fellows Bacon essay.

William E. Bartelt is a retired high school and university educator. He served as president of the Vanderburgh County Historical Society and as a member of the board of trustees of the Indiana Historical Society from 2011 to 2014. He is a director of the Abraham Lincoln Association and a member of the board of directors of the Friends of Lincoln Collection of Indiana. He is the author of *"There I Grew Up": Remembering Abraham Lincoln's Youth* (2008) and received the IHS's Hoosier Historian Award in 2005. Author of Abraham Lincoln essay.

Timothy Bauman is the curator of archaeology at the University of Tennessee's McClung Museum of Natural History and Culture. He obtained a bachelor's in anthropology from the University of Missouri, a master's in anthropology from the University of Wisconsin-Milwaukee, and a PhD in anthropology from the University of Tennessee. His research interests focus on late prehistoric and historic periods. He is best known for community-based research on African American heritage in Missouri from enslavement to civil rights, for which he was honored in 2006 with the John L. Cotter Award by the Society for Historical Archaeology. Coauthor of Glenn Black essay.

Bill Beck is a writer and historian who has covered the iron and steel industry since the 1970s. He has done extensive writing about business history. He wrote his first history for Minnesota Power in 1986, and has published more than seventy-five books. Beck is a 1971 graduate of Marian College (now Univeristy), Indianapolis, and did graduate work in American history at the University of North Dakota. Beck started Lakeside Writers' Group twenty-one years ago following ten years as a business reporter for newspapers in Minnesota and North Carolina and seven years as the senior writer in the public affairs department at Minnesota Power and Light Company in Duluth, Minnesota. Author of Van Camp Family essay.

Andrew Beckman is archivist for the Studebaker National Museum. He has been with the museum since 1999, and previously worked at the Sheboygan County Historical Society in Sheboygan, Wisconsin, and Wade House State Historic Site in Greenbush, Wisconsin. He has a degree in history from the University of Wisconsin-Green Bay. In 2009 he received a mid-level certificate in collections preservation from the Campbell Center for Historic Preservation Studies in Mount Carroll, Illinois. He is the author of two books: *The Studebaker National Museum: Over a Century on Wheels* and *Studebaker's Last Dance: The Avanti*. In addition to his duties at the Studebaker National Museum, he serves as vice president of the Society of Automotive Historians. Author of Clement Studebaker essay.

Ray Begovich is a journalism professor at Franklin College. He made national and international news in 2013 with his discovery of an eight-second video clip of President Franklin D. Roosevelt being pushed in his wheelchair abroad the cruiser USS *Baltimore* in July 1944. The discovery was made while he was doing research at the U.S. National Archives for a biography of Elmer Davis. Author of Elmer Davis essay.

Suzanne S. Bellamy, JD, is a researcher and writer. She is the author of *Hoosier Justice at Nuremberg* (2010), a former editorial assistant of the IHS's *Papers of Lew and Susan Wallace*, and served as assistant general counsel, Anacomp Inc. Author of Overbeck Sisters and Virginia Jenckes essays.

Jon M. Bill is the director of education and archives at the Auburn Cord Duesenberg Automobile Museum in Auburn, Indiana. A graduate of Purdue University, he taught industrial technology for thirty-four years before joining the museum staff in 2001. Bill is the author of several books on Auburns, Cords, and Duesenbergs. Author of Duesenbergs essay.

William Blomquist is dean of the IU School of Liberal Arts and professor of political science and adjunct professor of public and environmental affairs at IUPUI. He received his bachelor's and master's degrees from Ohio University and his PhD in political science from IU, Bloomington. His research interests concern governmental organization and public policies, with a specialization in the field of water institutions and water management. Author of Ostroms essay.

William Boklund has served as judge of LaPorte Superior Court 4 in Michigan City, Indiana, for more than twenty-one years. He is currently working on documentaries on the evolution of free speech from the beginning of the twentieth century to the present and on the court-packing plan of President Franklin D. Roosevelt. Author of Edward A. Rumley essay.

Ray E. Boomhower is senior director, IHS Press, and editor of *Traces of Indiana and Midwestern History*. He is the author of a number of books about Indiana history, including *Gus Grissom: the Lost Astronaut* (2004); *Robert F. Kennedy and the 1968 Indiana Primary* (2008); *The People's Choice: Congressman Jim Jontz of Indiana* (2013); and *John Bartlow Martin: A Voice for the Underdog* (2015). His articles have appeared in *Traces* and the *Indiana Magazine of History*. In 2010 he received the Eugene and Marilyn Glick Indiana Authors Award in the regional category. Author of May Wright Sewall, Eliza Blaker, Julia Carson, Carl Fisher, William Powers Hapgood, Kin Hubbard, Juliet Strauss, Virgil "Gus" Grissom, John Bushemi, Goethe Link, Kurt Vonnegut, George Ade, John Brown Dillon, Jacob P. Dunn Jr., John Bartlow Martin, Rachel Peden, and Albert Beveridge essays.

Patrick Gary Bottiger, PhD, is a history professor at Kenyon College. He has also taught at Florida Gulf Coast University and Mount Allison University in New Brunswick, Canada. His teaching interests include the American history survey, American Indian history, colonial and Revolutionary America, and comparative frontiers. His work has appeared in the *Journal of the Early Republic* and other scholarly periodicals. He has held a fellowship at the Filson Society and participated in a National Endowment for the Humanities Summer Seminar. His current book-length project, "Prophetstown, Vincennes, and the Invasion of the Miami Frontier," examines ethnic factionalism in the Ohio River Valley at the turn of the nineteenth century. Author of Tecumseh and Tenskwatawa essay.

James E. Brunson III, an art historian, retired as assistant vice president for diversity and equity, Northern Illinois University. He is the author of *The Early Image of Black Baseball: Race and Representation in the Popular Press* (2009). His essays have appeared in *Base Ball: A Journal of the Early Game* and *NINE: A Journal of Baseball History and Culture*. He received his master's of fine arts degree from Northern Illinois University and his PhD in art history from the University of Chicago. Author of George Knox essay.

Contributor Biographies

Keith Buckley is assistant director for public services (library) and lecturer in law at the IU Maurer School of Law. He is coauthor of *Indiana Stonecarver: The Story of Thomas R. Reding* and he continues to research the lives of Reding and the other Hindustan Whetsstone carvers of southern Indiana. His other major area of research is the treatment of women and families under the Civil War pension statutes. Author of Leander Monks essay.

A'Lelia Bundles is the author of *On Her Own Ground: The Life and Times of Madam C. J. Walker* (2001), the award-winning, *New York Times* bestselling biography of her great-great-grandmother. During a thirty-year network television news career, she was a producer with NBC News and later a producer, Washington, D.C. deputy bureau chief and director of talent development with ABC News. She is chair of the board of the National Archives Foundation and a trustee of Columbia University. She serves on the advisory boards of the IHS's Publications Committee and the Radcliffe Institute's Schlesinger Library at Harvard. Her young adult biography, *Madam C. J. Walker: Entrepreneur* (1991), received a 1992 American Book Award from the Before Columbus Foundation. *Madam Walker Theatre Center: An Indianapolis Treasure* was published in 2013. She is at work on her fourth book, *The Joy Goddess of Harlem: A'Lelia Walker and the Harlem Renaissance*, the first comprehensive biography of this 1920s icon. Author of Madam C. J. Walker essay.

Scott M. Bushnell has written five books about Indiana history as well as contributing to *Justices of the Indiana Supreme Court* published by the IHS Press in cooperation with the Indiana Supreme Court in 2010. Author of Fred Zollner essay.

J. Kent Calder was formerly an editor with the IHS and executive director of the Texas State Historical Association. He is now acquisitions editor at the University of Oklahoma Press in Norman, Oklahoma. Author of Floyd Hopper and David Laurance Chambers essays.

Charles W. Calhoun is Thomas Harriot College Distinguished Professor of History at East Carolina University. He is the author of *Benjamin Harrison* (2005); *Conceiving a New Republic: The Republican Party and the Southern Question, 1869–1900* (2006); *Minority Victory: Gilded Age Politics and the Front Porch Campaign of 1888* (2008); and *From Bloody Shirt to Full Dinner Pail: The Transformation of Politics and Governance in the Gilded Age* (2010). He is the founder and past president of the Society for Historians of the Gilded Age and Progressive Era. Author of Benjamin Harrison and Oliver Morton essays.

David Cambron is currently completing a PhD in history at Purdue University following a thirty-year career as an architectural-graphic designer. He lives north of Lafayette, Indiana, on property overlooking the Wabash River, Prophetstown State Park, and bisected by the Wabash and Erie Canal. All of the places are significant for the subject of the essay he wrote for this volume. Author of John Purdue essay.

James H. Capshew is a historian of science and learning at IU, Bloomington, where he is a faculty member in the Department of History and Philosophy of Science and Medicine. He teaches courses on the scientific dimensions of society, the history and culture of the modern university, and the environmental humanities, among other topics. He is author of *Psychologists on the March: Science, Practice, and Professional Identity in America, 1929–1969* (1999); *Herman B Wells: The Promise of the American University* (2012); and several journal articles and book chapters. He also served as editor of *History of Psychology* (2006-09). Author of Herman B Wells essay.

Sally Childs-Helton holds her MLS, master's, and PhD in ethnomusicology from IU. As a graduate student, she worked as a sound archivist at the Archives of Traditional Music and became interested in the broader world of archives. She worked at the IHS's William Henry Smith Memorial Library as a manuscripts processor and cataloger for fifteen years before coming to Butler University in 2000, where she is the head of special collections, rare books, and university archives at Irwin Library. She also teaches world music and ethnomusicology courses at Butler. Author of Ovid Butler essay.

Linda Cochran is secretary of the Lawrence D. Bell Aircraft Museum board of directors and has been a museum director since 1982. She has worked in an elementary school library and enjoys sharing Larry Bell's historical accomplishments. Author of Lawrence Bell essay.

Rachel Graham Cody is coauthor, with her father, Tom Graham, of *Getting Open: The Unknown Story of Bill Garrett and the Integration of College Basketball* (2006; 2008), which won the Indiana Center for the Book's "Best in Indiana" award for nonfiction in 2007. She has won investigative reporting awards for her coverage of education issues in Portland, Oregon. Coauthor of Bill Garrett essay.

James J. Connolly is professor of history and director of the Center for Middletown Studies at Ball State University. He writes about American urban, ethnic, and political history and his publications include *An Elusive Unity: Urban Democracy and Machine Politics in Industrializing America* (2010) and *What Middletown Read: Print Culture in an American Small City* (forthcoming). Author of Robert and Helen Lynd essay.

Stephen L. Cox is the retired IHS Press vice president and former historian and vice president of programs for the Conner Prairie Pioneer Settlement in Fishers, Indiana. He is the author of "Back to the 1820s: the Re-reconstruction of the William Conner House," *Traces of Indiana and Midwestern History* and "New Life: Eli Lilly and the First Restoration of the William Conner House," also in *Traces*; and also coauthor of *Building a Home, Preserving a Heritage: The Story of the Conner House* (1993). Author of Zerelda Wallace essay.

Claudia D. Crump is professor emeritus of elementary education, IU Southeast, and current founding director of the IUS Center for Cultural Resources, which among other things houses information about more than three hundred Hoosier women. She was educated in one-room schools in rural Kentucky, Western Kentucky University, and IU. She earned her doctorate in elementary social studies and language arts education in conjunction with a Ford Foundation Field Experience Program and taught methods courses at IU Southeast for twenty-five years. She has been an officer of and received many teaching and service awards from world, national, state, and local professional organizations. She is also the author of fourth-grade-social studies texts. Author of Zerna Sharp essay.

Tim Crumrin retired after twenty-five years a historian at Conner Prairie and is president of the Historiker Consulting Group. From 1992 to 1996 he was adjunct professor of history at Saint Mary-of-the-Woods College. He holds a bachelor's (summa cum laude) in European history and a master's in American history from Indiana State University. He has written or edited more than thirty-five scholarly publications and made numerous presentations at conferences sponsored by the Organization of American Historians and the IHS, among others. In addition to his duties as historian, he was the creator and designer of the Conner Prairie website during its first five years and project coordinator during the implementation and initial programming phase of the museum's distance-learning program. He received the IHS's Eli Lilly Lifetime Achievement in History Award in 2014. Author of William Conner, Powel Crosley Jr., and Jean Shepherd essays.

Leigh Darbee was formerly head of reference and curator of printed collections at the IHS's William Henry Smith Memorial Library. She is the author of several articles published in *Traces of Indiana and Midwestern History* and *The Hoosier Genealogist*. Author of Ida H. Harper, Eugene Debs, and Powers Hapgood essays.

Donald Davidson, Indianapolis Motor Speedway historian, is believed to be the only full-time salaried historian at any racetrack in the world. Heard annually on the worldwide Indianapolis Motor Speedway radio broadcast ever since being hired by the late Sid Collins in 1965, the British-born-and-raised raconteur has written hundreds of magazine articles and newspaper columns, and made hundreds of television and radio appearances in addition to having presented a four-week course on 500 history for IUPUI's Continuing Studies program every spring since 1986. He was inducted into the Auto Racing Hall of Fame in 2010 and is the only living member who was never a participant. In 2013 he was inducted into the Indiana Broadcast Pioneers Hall of Fame. Author of Tony Hulman and Wilbur Shaw essays.

John Dichtl is the president and CEO of the American Association for State and Local History. He earned his master's and PhD in U.S. history at IU in 2000 and later served as deputy executive director for the Organization of American Historians, and exectutive director of the National Council on Public History. He is the author of *Frontiers of Faith: Bringing Catholicism to the West in the Early Republic* (2008) and is part of the IndyHistorical smartphone app project that provides historical tours for Indianapolis and New Albany. Author of Cornelius O'Brien essay.

Robert L. Dion is chairperson of the Department of Law, Politics, and Society at the University of Evansville, where he specializes in teaching American politics. Author of Robert Orr essay.

Rachael L. Drenovsky is the Learning Center Coordinator for the Michigan Supreme Court. She holds a master's degree in history with a concentration in pubic history from IUPUI. Author of William Fletcher essay.

Jeffery A. Duvall is a research associate for the Institute for American Thought at IUPUI, and assistant editor of the Frederick Douglass Papers. He holds a PhD in history from Purdue University. Author of Cole Porter, Efromyson Family, and James F. D. Lanier essays.

David Edmunds is the Anne Stark Watson and Chester Watson History Professor at the University of Texas at Dallas. An historian of Native American people and the American West, he has written extensively about Native American-white relations in the eighteenth and nineteenth centuries. He is an expert on the Potawatomi, Shawnee, Mesquakie, Miami, Seneca-Cayuga, Otoe-Missouri, Omaha, and other Native American tribes. His current research focuses on the history of Native American identity, Native Americans on the Great Plains, and Native American biography. Edmunds was a content and historical adviser to PBS's *American Experience* program for the five-part series "We Shall Remain." Edmunds has also been recognized with awards or fellowships from the NEH, Guggenheim Foundation, the Ford Foundation, and the Newberry Library, in addition to winning five teaching awards from four universities. Author of Jean Baptiste Richardville essay.

Lana Ruegamer Eisenberg was editor of the IHS from 1975 to 1984, taught at IU, Bloomington, from 1986 to 1998, and was associate editor of the *Indiana Magazine of History* from 1998 to 2003. She is the author of *A History of the Indiana Historical Society* (1980) and editor and coauthor (final chapter) of *Indiana Blacks in the Twentieth Century* (2000). Her article, "Dorothy Lois Riker, 1904-1994: Reflections on Indiana History, Historical Editing, and Women in the Historical Profession" won the 1995 Thornbrough Prize for best article published in the *IMH*. Born in Lafayette, Indiana, and educated in its public schools, she received her bachelor's from Harvard University and PhD from IU. Author of Emma Lou Thornbrough and Gayle Thornbrough essays.

James Philip Fadely, a sixth-generation Hoosier, is director of college counseling at University High School of Indiana in Carmel. He has a bachelor's in history from Hanover College and a master's and PhD from IU. He is the author of *Thomas Taggart: Public Servant, Political Boss, 1856–1929* (1997). Fadely's interest and involvement in Hoosier politics include being a nominee for the U.S. House of Representatives. He has been a lecturer in history at IUPUI, Butler University, and the University of Indianapolis. He has also taught U.S. history at four independent college preparatory schools. Author of Thomas Taggart and Matthew Welsh essays.

E. Rae Ferguson is associate professor of history, University of Rhode Island. Her publications include *Stepping Forward: Black Women in Africa and the Americas* (2002) and several articles and book chapters about the black women's club movement in Indianapolis. Author of Lillian Thomas Fox essay.

Kevin R. Fish is a freelance writer living in San Jose, California. The eldest grandchild of Orville Redenbacher, Fish received his associate's degree in history from DeAnza Community College in Cupertino, California, in 1974; his bachelor's degree in history from Southern Oregon State College (now Southern Oregon University) in Ashland, Oregon, in 1976; his master's degree in social science (mainly history) from San Jose State University in 1984; and his paralegal degree from DeAnza College in 2013. Author of Orville Redenbacher essay.

A. James Fuller, professor of history, University of Indianapolis, has published six books, including *The Election of 1860 Reconsidered* (2013) and is completing *The Great War Governor: Oliver P. Morton and the Politics of the Civil War and Reconstruction*, a biography of Indiana's Civil War governor. Author of Ray Crowe essay.

Patrick J. Furlong is professor emeritus of history at IU, South Bend. He is author of *Indiana: An Illustrated History* (2001) and a forthcoming history of Saint Joseph County. Author of James Oliver essay.

Jesse Gant is a PhD candidate in the Department of History at the University of Wisconsin–Madison. He is currently working as a Public Humanities Fellow with the Wisconsin Center for the Humanities in partnership with the Wisconsin Humanities Council. The project for the 2014–2015 academic year is to help develop the Council's Working Lives project. Author of James A. Woodburn essay.

Wes D. Gehring is a professor of film at Ball State University and associate media editor for *USA TODAY Magazine*, for which he also writes the column, "Reel World." He has written nearly three dozen film-related books, including award-winning biographies of Red Skelton and James Dean. He is a frequent contributor to *Traces* magazine and has been selected for *Who's Who in America* for 2012, 2013, and 2014. Author of James Dean and Red Skelton essays.

George Geib is professor emeritus of history at Butler University. His books include *Indianapolis: Hoosiers' Circle City* (1981); *Lives Touched By Faith: Second Presbyterian Church, 150 Years* (1987); *Indianapolis First: The Centennial History of the Indianapolis Chamber of Commerce* (1990; Miriam K. Geib, coauthor); and *Federal Justice in Indiana: The History of the United States District Court for the Southern District of Indiana* (2007; Donald B. Kite, coauthor). He was awarded the Doctor John Morton Finney Award for Excellence in Legal Education by the Indianapolis Bar Association in 2007. Author of Calvin Fletcher essay.

Tom Graham is coauthor with his daughter, Rachel Graham Cody, of *Getting Open: The Unknown Story of Bill Garrett and the Integration of College Basketball* (2006; 2008), which won the Indiana Center for the Book's 2007 "Best in Indiana" award for nonfiction. He grew up in Bill Garrett's hometown. Graham, an international lawyer, currently serves as an international judge on the Appellate Body of the World Trade Organization, the appeals court for deciding international trade disputes between governments. He has headed the international trade practice of a large multinational law firm, served as a trade negotiator for the U.S. government and a legal officer of the United Nations, and taught law at Georgetown University and the University of North Carolina. A graduate of IU and Harvard Law School, Graham divides his time between Geneva, Switzerland, and Portland, Oregon. Coauthor of Bill Garrett essay.

Ralph D. Gray, professor emeritus of history at IUPUI, is an Indiana native and a graduate of Hanover College. After studying abroad as a Fulbright Scholar and teaching in Delaware, Illinois, and Ohio, he returned to Indiana in 1964 to teach history at IU, Kokomo, where he began his study on the life and work of Elwood Haynes. He moved to Indianapolis in 1968, where he taught at

IUPUI until 1997. Holding advanced degrees in history from the University of Delaware and the University of Illinois, he has specialized in recent years in Indiana and midwestern history and is the author and editor of numerous books and articles in American economic, political, and cultural history, including *Gentlemen from Indiana: National Political Candidates, 1836–1940* (1977); *A History of the Haynes Stellite Company, 1912–1972* (1974); *Alloys and Automobiles: The Life of Elwood Haynes* (1979); *Public Ports for Indiana: A History of the Indiana Port Commission* (1994); *IUPUI: The Making of an Urban University* (2003); *Meredith Nicholson: A Writing Life* (2007); and *A Meredith Nicholson Reader* (2007). Author of Elwood Haynes, Thomas Hendricks, and Meredith Nicholson essays.

Glory-June Greiff is a public historian, preservation activist, professional narrator, and performer. She regularly presents poetry programs around the state. A native of Hudson Lake in northern Indiana, Greiff earned a bachelor's in Radio-Television/English from Butler University and a master's degree in public history from IU. She is the author of *Remembrance, Faith and Fancy: Outdoor Public Sculpture in Indiana* (2005) and *People, Parks, and Perceptions: A History and Appreciation of Indiana State Parks* (2009). Author of Gene Stratton-Porter, Sarah Bolton, and J. Maurice Thompson essays.

David L. Gugin is an associate professor of English at the University of Guam. He has taught English in the United States, Japan, Tonga, Myanmar, and the United Arab Emirates. He has most recently published in *Micronesian Educator: The Handbook of Research on Assessment Technologies, Language and Literature* and *Literature and Stylistics for Language Learners*. Author of Theodore Dreiser essay.

Linda C. Gugin, PhD, is professor emeritus of political science at IU Southeast. She is coauthor of *Sherman Minton: New Deal Senator, Cold War Justice* (1997) and *Chief Justice Fred M. Vinson: A Political Biography* (2002); coeditor of *The Governors of Indiana* (2006) and *Justices of the Indiana Supreme Court* (2010); coeditor of *Indiana's 200: The People Who Shaped the Hoosier State* (2015); and author of "Sherman Minton; Restraint Against a Tide of Activism," *Vanderbilt Law Review* (2009). Author of Grace Julian Clarke and Koch Family essays and coauthor of Sherman Minton essay.

William F. Gulde is a history teacher at North Central High School in Indianapolis and author of *Irvington in 1910: A Year in the Life of an Indianapolis Neighborhood* (2010) and of *Hopes, Dreams, and Books: The Story of North Central High School 1956–2004* (2004). Author of Booth Tarkington and D. C. Stephenson essays.

Judith P. Hallett is professor of classics and distinguished-scholar teacher at the University of Maryland, College Park. She received a bachelor's in Latin from Wellesley College, where she was elected to Phi Beta Kappa, and a master's and PhD in classical philology from Harvard University. She has published widely in the areas of Latin language and literature; women, the family, and sexuality in Greek and Roman society; and the study and interpretation of classical antiquity in twentieth-century America. A collection of nineteen essays in her honor, *Roman Literature, Gender and Reception: Domina Illustris*, was published by Routledge in 2013. Author of Edith Hamilton essay.

Bob Hammel was sports editor of the *Bloomington Herald-Times* from 1966 to 1996. Prior to covering the IU Hoosiers, he was with newspapers in Huntington, Fort Wayne, Peru, Kokomo and Indianapolis. In 1995 he received the highest honor given to a basketball writer, the Curt Gowdy Award from the Naismith Hall of Fame in Springfield, Massachusetts. He has been selected the top sportswriter in Indiana seventeen times by the National Sportswriters and Sportscasters Association. Has written seven books about Hoosier basketball and was editor of the *Bob Hammel Indiana Basketball Magazine*. He is the author of *The Bill Cook Story: Ready, Fire, Aim!* His second Bill Cook book, *The Re-Visionary*, covering the last four years of Cook's life after the publication of *Ready, Fire, Aim!* is due out from IU Press in February 2015. Author of Bill Cook and Doc Counsilman essays.

Eric Hansen has won more than fifteen national awards from the Football Writers Association of America and numerous state awards while covering college football since 1983. He currently serves as the University of Notre Dame football beat writer for the *South Bend Tribune* and as assistant sports editor. He has authored two books, *Stadium Stories: Notre Dame Fighting Irish* (2004) and *Notre Dame: Where Have You Gone?* (2011). He also serves as cohost for WSBT's Weekday SportsBeat radio show. Author of Knute Rockne essay.

Jennifer Yantis Harrison is an independent scholar and communications generalist. Her interest in conservation and natural history arose from many happy hours of hiking, paddling, and exploring the outdoors in Indiana and elsewhere. She has been a contributor to numerous publications, including *Traces* magazine. She now resides near Denver, Colorado. Author of Charles Deam essay.

Carolyn Harstad is the author of *Go Native! Gardening with Native Plants and Wildflowers in the Lower Midwest* (1999); *Got Shade? A Take It Easy Approach for Today's Gardener* (2003); and *Got Sun? 200 Best Native Plants for Your Garden* (2013). A graduate of the University of Minnesota, Minneapolis, and Bethany Lutheran College, Mankato, Minneapolis, she is a regular contributor to several gardening magazines including *The Hosta Journal* and *Minnesota Gardener*. Author of Richard Lieber essay.

Peter T. Harstad earned his PhD from the University of Wisconsin and taught at several universities. He served as CEO of the State Historical Society of Iowa from 1972 to 1981 and as CEO of the Indiana Historical Society from 1984 to 2001. He has published essays about Thomas Marshall in journals and books including Facts on File's *The Vice Presidents: A Biographical Dictionary* (1998). Author of Thomas Marshall essay.

Gregg Hertzlieb is the director/curator of the Brauer Museum of Art at Valparaiso University in Valparaiso, Indiana. He is an exhibiting artist working primarily in watercolor and pen and ink. His edited works include *The Calumet Region: An American Place* (2009); *Heeding the Voice of Heaven: Sadao Watanabe Biblical Stencil Prints* (2010); and *Domestic Vision: Twenty-Five Years of the Art of Joel Sheesley* (2008). He is also a contributor to the books *The Art of George Ames Aldrich* (2013); *The Indiana Dunes Revealed: The Art of Frank V. Dudley* (2006); and *American Railroad China: Image and Experience* (2008). Author of Frank Dudley essay.

Libbe K. Hughes is a local history researcher, writer, and lecturer residing in Hendricks County, Indiana. She also wrote the profile of John V. Hadley in *Justices of the Indiana Supreme Court* (2010). Author of Jeanette Nolan essay.

Melanie E. Hughes is an associate librarian at IU Southeast. She holds an MLS degree from IU, Bloomington, and an MBA from IU Southeast. Like the subject of her essay in this volume, and Amelia Earhart, she too lived in Windsor Halls at Purdue. Author of Lillian Gilbreth essay.

George Ironstrack, assistant director of the Myaamia Center at Miami University, has participated in Myaamia language renewal projects as both a student and a teacher since the mid-1990s. He is a citizen of the Miami Tribe of Oklahoma and has assisted in the organization and administration of the tribe's Eewansaapita Summer Educational Experience since its inception in 2005. He received his master's degree in history from Miami University. His graduate work centered on the Miami Indian village of Pickawillany, which was located in western Ohio near the city of Piqua. He continues to regularly research and write about Myaamia history. Examples of his work can be found on the Myaamia Community History and Ecology Blog: Aacimotaatiiyankwi. Coauthor of Mihšihkinaahkwa (Chief Little Turtle) essay.

Peter P. Jacobi is emeritus professor in the School of Journalism at IU, Bloomington, and former professor and associate dean of the Medill School of Journalism at Northwestern University. His professional credentials range from magazines to broadcasting and newspapers as staffer and freelancer. Since 1986 he has served as music columnist and critic for the *Bloomington Herald-Times*. Author of Hoagy Carmichael and Josef Gingold essays.

Stephen J. Jay, MD, is a practicing physician and professor emeritus at the IU School of Medicine and Richard M. Fairbanks School of Public Health. His interests are in the history of medicine and public health policy. Author of Alice Hamilton and Leonard A. Scheele essays.

Owen V. Johnson taught for thirty-four years in the IU School of Journalism, served as director of the university's Russian and East European Institute, as acting director of the Polish Studies Center (twice), and as director of graduate studies in the journalism school. Author of Ernie Pyle essay.

Alan Karpick is a Purdue sports historian who has interviewed John Wooden several times. He has served as president and publisher of *Gold and Black Illustrated*, an independent publication and website focusing on Purdue University sports. Author of John Wooden essay.

Jon Kay is executive director of Traditional Arts Indiana, a statewide folk-arts program based at IU, and serves as a professor of practice in the IU Department of Folklore and Ethnomusicology. Kay conducts fieldwork, supports public programs, and produces exhibitions and documentary videos about Indiana's traditional artists and art forms. He also teaches public folklore and provides professional development training for artists, community scholars, and heritage professionals. Prior to working at IU, Kay directed the Florida Folk Festival. He also hosts the podcast Artisan Ancestors, which explores ways to research and understand the creative lives of people from the past. Author of Frank Hohenberger essay.

Dina Kellams is an associate archivist, IU Office of University Archives and Records Management. Author of Joseph Muhler essay.

Rick Kennedy is the author of *Jelly Roll, Bix & Hoagy: Gennett Records and the Rise of America's Musical Grassroots* (2000), and coauthor (with Randy McNutt) of *Little Labels–Big Sound: Small Records Companies and the Rise of American Music* (1999). He lives in Cincinnati, Ohio. Author of Gennett Family essay.

Donald B. Kite Sr., JD, is Of Counsel with the Wuertz Law Office, LLC., Indianapolis. He is author of several biographical sketches that were included in *Justices of the Indiana Supreme Court* (2010), coauthor of *Federal Justice in Indiana: The History of the United*

States District Court for the Southern District of Indiana* (2007), recipient of the Defense Trial Counsel of Indiana's Defense Lawyer of the Year Award (2005), and corecipient of the Indianapolis Bar Association's Doctor John Morton Finney Jr. Award for Excellence in Legal Education (2007). Author of Edmund Hovey, David Maxwell, Caleb Mills, and Elihu Stout essays.

Alfred L. Knable Jr., MD, is a practicing physician in New Albany, Indiana, and Louisville, Kentucky, and an associate professor of dermatology at the University of Louisville. He attended Purdue for his undergraduate work and remembers a brief but inspiring pep talk that the subject of his essay gave to students before their organic chemistry final exam in 1985. Author of Herbert C. Brown essay.

Dean J. Kotlowski is professor of history at Salisbury University in Maryland. He received his PhD in U.S. history from IU, Bloomington. He is the author of *Paul V. McNutt and the Age of FDR* (2015); *Nixon's Civil Rights: Politics, Principle, and Policy* (2001); and numerous refereed journal articles on U.S. politics and public policy. He also has edited *The European Union: From Jean Monnet to the Euro* (2000). In 2005–06 he was Paul V. McNutt Visiting Professor of History at IU and in the fall of 2008 he was a Fulbright Professor at De La Salle University in Manila. Author of Paul McNutt essay.

Carl E. Kramer is adjunct assistant professor of history and retired director of the Institute for Local and Oral History at IU Southeast. He also coowns Kramer Associates, Inc., a public history consulting firm. He is the author of twelve books, including *This Place We Call Home: A History of Clark County, Indiana* (2007). He earned his PhD in American history from the University of Toledo. Author of Jonathan Jennings and George Rogers Clark essays.

Martin Krause is curator of prints, drawings, and photographs at the Indianapolis Museum of Art. He is the author of numerous books on European and American artists including *The Passage: Return of Indiana Artists from Germany, 1880–1905* (1990); *Turner in Indianapolis* (1992); and *The Essential Robert Indiana* (2013). Author of J. Ottis Adams essay.

Carolyn R. Lafever, Wayne County historian, is the author of *The Biggest Little Wild West Show on Earth: The Story of Buckskin Ben Stalker's Family Wild West Show* (1997); *The Pictorial History of Wayne County, Indiana* (1998); and *Wayne County, Indiana: The Battles for the Courthouse* (2010). Author of George Julian essay.

Chera A. LaForge is an assistant professor of political science at IU East. She teaches courses in American politics and quantitative analysis. Her research interests include Congress and legislative politics. Author of Esther White essay.

James Lane is professor emeritus of history at IU Northwest, codirector of the Calumet Regional Archives, and editor of *Steel Shavings* magazine. Author of Vivian Carter essay.

Jason S. Lantzer is a historian interested in the intersection of religion, politics, and law in American society and culture. A native Hoosier, he holds three degrees from IU. He is the author of three books and numerous articles and book chapters. He serves as an instructor and University Honors Program Coordinator at Butler University. Author of Oscar McCulloch and Ada Schweitzer essays.

Monroe H. Little is associate professor of Africana Studies and History at IUPUI. He is the recipient of numerous honors and awards, including a Lilly Foundation Faculty Grant, IUPUI Joseph Taylor Diversity Award, and the Director's Award from the Center for Leadership Development. He is the author of several publications about African Americans in Indiana. His most recent is, "The Battle for Educational Freedom: The 1949 Indiana 'Fair Schools' Bill," to be published in *Ohio Valley History*. Author of Willard Ransom and Henry Richardson essays.

Doria M. Lynch is the administrative specialist and historian at the U.S. District Court for the Southern District of Indiana. She is a 2003 graduate of Kalamazoo College and received her master's degree in public history from IU in 2007. She was a contributing author to *Justices of the Indiana Supreme Court* (2010) and an editorial assistant on *Finding Indiana Ancestors* (2007). Author of Clowes Family and Marilyn and Eugene Glick essays.

James H. Madison is the Thomas and Kathryn Miller professor emeritus of history at IU, Bloomington. He is the author of *Indiana through Tradition and Change* (1982); *The Indiana Way: A State History* (1986); *Eli Lilly: A Life, 1885–1977* (1989); *Wendell Willkie: Hoosier Internationalist* (1992); *A Lynching in the Heartland: Race and Memory in America* (2001); and *Hoosiers: A New History of Indiana* (2014). He has won numerous awards for distinguished teaching. Author of Flossie Bailey, Wendell Willkie, and Eli Lilly essays.

Robert F. Martin holds a PhD from the University of North Carolina, Chapel Hill, and is professor and head of the Department of History at the University of Northern Iowa. He is a specialist in the history of the American South and the Gilded Age/Progressive Era in the United States. He is the author of *Howard Kester and the Struggle for Social Justice in the South, 1904–1977* (1992) and *Hero of the Heartland: Billy Sunday and the Transformation of American Society, 1862–1935* (2002). Author of Billy Sunday essay.

Thomas A. Mason is adjunct lecturer in history at IUPUI and coauthor with J. Kent Calder of *Writing Local*

History Today: A Guide to Researching, Publishing, and Marketing Your Book (2013); project director, *The Papers of Lew and Susan Wallace*, (microfilm, 2008); edited, with Robert A. Rutland, et al., *The Papers of James Madison*, vol. 14, *1791–93* (1983), vol. 15, 1793–95 (1985), vol. 16, *1795–97* (1989); and *Serving God and Mammon: William Juxon, 1582–1663, Bishop of London, Lord High Treasurer of England, and Archbishop of Canterbury* (1985). Author of Lew Wallace essay.

Harry McCawley retired in 2014 as the associate editor of the *Columbus Republic* after a fifty-year career with Home News Enterprises, the paper's parent company. He became known as the mirror and storyteller of the community and its people through his columns. McCawley started his career with the *Daily Franklin*, a sister paper. Author of Clessie Cummins and J. Irwin Miller essays.

G. William Monaghan is a senior scientist at the Indiana Geological Survey, IU, and specializes in Quaternary geology and geoarchaeology. He served as associate and interim director of the Glenn A. Black Laboratory of Archaeology (2005–14) and associate director of the Mathers Museum (2011–13). Monaghan has authored more than a hundred publications about archaeology, geology, and geomorphology, including several about his work at Angel Mounds. Some of his most recent monographs include *Modeling Archaeological Site Burial in Southern Michigan: A Geoarchaeological Synthesis* (2005); *Minnesota Deep Test Protocol Project* (2006); and *Geoarchaeology and Taphonomy of Lake Michigan Coastal Dunes: Activation, Stabilization, Cycling and Archaeological Site Formation Processes* (2012). Coauthor of Glenn Black essay.

Wilma L. Moore is senior archivist, African American history, at the Indiana Historical Society William Henry Smith Memorial Library. She edits the "Black History News and Notes" department in *Traces* magazine. As a member of the Manuscripts Department within the IHS library, she serves as a specialist for black history and assists with general and manuscript reference work. Author of George P. Stewart essay.

Les Morris is director of public relations for Simon Property Group, Indianapolis. Author of Melvin Simon essay.

Ronald Vaughan Morris, PhD, is a professor and Presidential Immersive Learning Fellow in the Department of History at Ball State University. He is the author of several works related to teaching history and social studies and has produced DVDs for elementary and social studies classroom use, for which he won an Emmy. He is presently restoring Civil War Governor Oliver P. Morton's home. Author of Levi and Catharine Coffin essay.

David Thomas Murphy is professor of history at Anderson University. He earned his PhD at the University of Illinois in 1992, with a specialization in modern German history. He is the author of many articles, as well as three books, most recently *Murder in Their Hearts: The Fall Creek Massacre* (2010). Author of Edward Sorin essay.

Judith Vale Newton is the author of *The Hoosier Group: Five American Painters* (1985). She is also coauthor with Carol Ann Weiss of *A Grand Tradition: The Art and Artists of the Hoosier Salon, 1925–1990* (1993); *Beyond Realism: The Life and Art of Frederik Grue* (1995); and *Skirting the Issue: Stories of Indiana's Women Artists* (2004). Former editor in chief of *Arts Indiana* magazine and a columnist for the *Saturday Evening Post*, she has contributed features and reviews to such publications as *ARTnews*, *Antique Review*, and *Traces*. In 2005 she and Weiss received the IHS's Dorothy Riker Hoosier Historian Award. Author of Otto Stark and Marie Webster essays.

John Norberg is a writer, author, and humorist. Before retiring in 2013 he was first a reporter and then a columnist for the *Lafayette Journal and Courier*. He also served as a presidential speech writer and director of development communication at Purdue. He is the author of seven books, including *Spacewalker: My Journey through Space and Faith as NASA's Most Frequent Flyer* (2013), with Jerry L. Ross, and *Hail Purdue* (1987). Author of Paul Emrick essay.

Elizabeth R. Osborn is the coordinator for court history and civic education and is responsible for the educational outreach programs of the Indiana Supreme Court, including the Indiana Supreme Court Legal History Series and Courts in the Classroom. She is the author of numerous publications about the history and operation of Indiana's courts and contributor to the *History of Indiana Law* (2008). Author of Helen Gougar essay and coauthor of Antionette Leach essay.

Rachel Berenson Perry is the former fine arts curator of the Indiana State Museum, where she organized and curated all of the art exhibitions at the ISM from 2003 through 2011. Her books include *William J. Forsyth: The Life and Work of an Indiana Artist* (2014); *Painting Indiana III: Heritage of Place* (2013); *Barry Gealt: Embracing Nature* (2012); *Paint and Canvas: A Life of T. C. Steele* (2012); *T. C. Steele and the Society of Western Artists, 1896–1914* (2009); and *Children from the Hills: The Life and Work of Ada Walter Shulz* (2001). Author of William Forsyth and Ada Shulz essays.

William B. Pickett, emeritus professor of history at Rose-Hulman Institute of Technology, is author of *Homer E. Capehart: A Senator's Life, 1897–1979* (1990); *Dwight David Eisenhower and Americana Power* (1995); *Eisenhower Decides to Run: Presidential Politics and Cold*

War Strategy (2000); and *To Be the Best: Rose-Hulman Institute of Technology, 1974–1999* (1999). Author of Homer Capehart essay.

Jennifer Burek Pierce is associate professor in the School of Library and Information Science at the University of Iowa, where she also has an appointment with the University of Iowa Center for the Book and serves on the board of the Iowa Initiative for Sustainable Communities. She is the author of *What Adolescents Ought to Know: Sexual Health Texts in Twentieth Century America* (2011). Her writing has also appeared in American Libraries and *The Chronicle of Higher Education*. Author of John Hurty essay.

Donald E. Pitzer is professor emeritus of history and director emeritus of the Center for Communal Studies at the University of Southern Indiana in Evansville. He earned his PhD in history at Ohio State University and was a scholar-in-residence at Harvard University. He is a founder and first president of the Communal Studies Association and International Communal Studies Association. He edited and contributed to the anthology *America's Communal Utopias* (1997) and, with photographer Darryl Jones, published *New Harmony Then and Now* (2011). In 2011 he received the Indiana Historical Society's Dorothy Riker Hoosier Historian Award. Author of Robert Owen and George Rapp essays.

Evelyn Pockrass earned a bachelor's degree from Hunter College and a master's degree in social work from New York University. She has been a member of Indianapolis Hebrew Congregation since 1979, was president of the Temple Sisterhood, and has been librarian at IHC since 1990. She is a member of the Association of Jewish Libraries, served three terms as president of the Church and Synagogue Library Association, and for more than twenty years has written book reviews for CSLA's journal, *Congregational Libraries Today*. Author of Howard Feuerlicht essay.

Nelson Price is an Indianapolis-based author, journalist, historian, and radio personality. An award-winning, former feature writer/columnist for the *Indianapolis Star*, he specializes in writing books about famous Hoosiers and Indianapolis city history. He is the author of *Indianapolis: Leading the Way* (2000); *Legendary Hoosiers* (2001); *Indiana Legends: Famous Hoosiers from Johnny Appleseed to David Letterman* (2005); and *Indianapolis Then and Now* (2004). He hosts *Hoosier History Live!*, a weekly call-in talk show on WICR-FM (88.7) in Indianapolis. He has been named a Sagamore of the Wabash by two Indiana governors. Author of Ryan White and Herb Shriner essays.

Russell Pulliam is the associate editor of the *Indianapolis Star* and director of the Pulliam Fellowship Program, which provides internships at the *Star* and *Arizona Republic*. He has been a reporter for the *New York Times*, *Washington Post*, *Springfield Union*, *Indianapolis News*, the *Star*, and the Associated Press. He is the author of *Publisher: Gene Pulliam, Last of the Newspaper Titans* (1984). Pulliam has earned numerous journalistic awards and has his bachelor's degree from Williams College. Author of Washington DePauw, Francis Jenkins, and Otis Bowen essays.

Barbara Quigley is senior archivist, visual collections, for the Indiana Historical Society William Henry Smith Memorial Library. She previously was assistant archivist at Bellarmine University in Louisville and also was an intern at the John F. Kennedy Presidential Library. She has a master's degree in library science from Simmons College in Boston. Author of Ball Brothers essay.

Amanda Read is a former columnist of the *Communities* at the *Washington Times* and is a screenwriter based in Alabama. Her first screenplay was a historical drama about the life of Doctor Harvey Wiley, which is yet to be produced. She graduated from Troy University in 2013 with a bachelor's degree in history. Author of Harvey Wiley essay.

Ruth D. Reichard is a doctoral candidate in U.S. history at IU. She graduated with honors from Ball State University in 1982 and earned her JD from the IU Robert H. McKinney School of Law in 1985. A former deputy prosecutor and criminal court judge, she works as a staff attorney at the Indiana Supreme Court Division of State Court Administration. Author of Logan Esarey essay.

C. Martin Rosen is director of library services at IU Southeast. He is a frequent contributor of feature stories and performance reviews to the *Louisville Courier-Journal* and the *Louisville Eccentric Observer*. Author of Elieen M. Ahern and Paul Dresser essays.

James E. St. Clair is professor emeritus of journalism at IU Southeast. He is coauthor of *Sherman Minton: New Deal Senator, Cold War Justice* (1997) and *Chief Justice Fred M. Vinson: A Political Biography* (2002); coeditor of *The Governors of Indiana* (2006) and *Justices of the Indiana Supreme Court* (2010); and coeditor of *Indiana's 200: The People Who Shaped the Hoosier State* (2015). Author of Clarence F. Cornish essay and coauthor of Sherman Minton essay.

Eric Sandweiss is Carmony Chair and professor of history at IU, Bloomington, and editor of the *Indiana Magazine of History*. He received the James P. Holland Award for Exemplary Teaching and Service to Students and Fulbright Distinguished Scholar Award. Author of *The Day in Its Color: Charles Cushman's Photographic Journey through a Vanishing America* (2012). Author of Charles Cushman essay.

Lee Ann Sandweiss has been working on publications about the Midwest for three decades. As an acquisitions editor for Wayne State University Press in the 1980s, she helped develop that press's successful Great Lakes Books series. She served as director of publications for the Missouri Historical Society from 1993 to 2002 and authored two books during that period, *Seeking St. Louis: A Guide to the River City, 1670–2000* (2000) and *St. Louis Architecture for Kids* (2001). She has taught classes on midwestern literature for IU Lifelong Learning and is coauthor with James H. Madison of *Hoosiers and the American Story* (2014). Author of William Henry Harrison essay.

Carrie Schwier holds a bachelor's degree in art history from Hanover College and an master's degree in art history and master's of library science with a specialization in archives and records management from IU. She is the assistant archivist at the IU Archives, where she participates in reference, instruction, digitization, and outreach efforts and supervises the arrangement and description of the papers of notable IU faculty, staff, and students, in addition to university records. Author of Robert Borkenstein essay.

Peter J. Sehlinger is professor emeritus, IUPUI. He taught Latin American history there for thirty years and is the coauthor, with Holman Hamilton, of *Spokesman for Democracy: Claude G. Bowers, 1878–1958* (2000). Author of Claude Bowers essay.

Randall T. Shepard served as Chief Justice of the Indiana Supreme Court for twenty-five years, longer than anyone else in the state's history. He is the former president of the Conference of Chief Justices and teaches periodically at IU, Yale Law School, and Notre Dame. He is the author of "Jesse W. Weik: The Young Indiana Lawyer who made Herndon's Lincoln Possible," *Indiana Magazine of History* (2009) and coauthor (with David J. Bodenhamer) of *The History of Indiana Law* (2006). Author of Conrad Baker and Issac Blackford essays and coauthor of Antionette Leach essay.

Michael Skaggs is a doctoral candidate in the Department of History at the Notre Dame. His dissertation is a study of midwestern Catholicism and the Second Vatican Council. Author of Andrew Grutka and Theodore Hesburgh essays.

Paul William (Bill) Smart, graduated from Southport High School and served in the U.S. Navy during World War II. He holds a bachelor's degree from the University of Cincinnati and a master's of fine arts from Yale University. He worked with New York advertising agencies and for international publishers, including McGraw-Hill, Franklin Book Programs, and Presbyterian Publishing House of Brazil. He was director of the University of Cincinnati Foundation and later operated Smart-Williams Associates advertising agency in Cincinnati. Smart is the nephew of Justin Gruelle. Author of the Gruelle Family essay.

Michael Smith is currently a freelance reporter and writer after a rewarding career with the Associated Press, working mostly during twenty years as chief statehouse reporter in Indianapolis. Author of Justin O. Zimmer and Donald Carmony essays.

Cary Stemle is managing editor of *Business First Louisville*, a newspaper of business and finance. He was formerly editor of *Louisville Eccentric Observer* and staff writer for the *Corydon Democrat*. He wrote the profile of Frank O'Bannon for *The Governors of Indiana* (2006). Author of Bill Monroe and Wes Montgomery essays.

Andrew E. Stoner is an assistant professor at California State University at Sacramento. He holds a PhD in public communication and technology from Colorado State University. A native of Indiana, he has previously taught as an adjunct professor or graduate teaching assistant at Colorado State University, IUPUI, Ivy Tech Community College of Indiana, Franklin College, and the University of Wisconsin-Stevens Point. He is the author of books covering Indiana history and true crime. Author of John Dillinger essay.

Geri Strecker is an assistant professor of English at Ball State University and is writing a book-length biography of Oscar Charleston, plus a history of pre-World War I baseball in the Philippines. In 2011 she directed a Virginia Ball Center for Creative Inquiry project that produced the Emmy Award-winning documentary *Black Baseball in Indiana*. Author of Oscar Charleston essay.

Ellen D. Swain is archivist for Student Life and Culture at the University of Illinois at Urbana-Champaign, where she administers the University Archives' Student Life and Culture Archival Program. She has a bachelor's degree from Earlham College, a master's in American history from IU, and a master's in information science from the University of Illinois at Urbana-Champaign. She is a past president of the Midwest Archives Conference (2011–13) and a Distinguished Fellow of the Society of American Archivists (2013). Author of Rhoda Coffin essay.

Kisha Tandy is an assistant curator at the Indiana State Museum. In this position, she researches, collects, and presents content and exhibitions related to Indiana's cultural heritage, in particular African American history. She holds a bachelor's degree in American history and master's of library science. Author of John W. Hardrick and Edouard Scott essays.

Ken Thompson is a sports writer and columnist for the *Lafayette Journal and Courier* and has been with the newspaper since 1984. Author of Ward Lambert essay.

Stephen E. Towne is associate university archivist at IUPUI. He has written and edited books and articles on the American Civil War, including *Surveillance and Spies in the Civil War: Exposing Confederate Conspiracies in America's Heartland* (2014). Author of Lambdin Milligan essay.

Elizabeth Van Allen is assistant director, Civil War Governors, Digital Documentary Edition, for the Kentucky Historical Society. She is the author of *James Whitcomb Riley: A Life* (1999). Author of James Whitcomb Riley essay.

Stephen Vaughn has been a historian and professor in the School of Journalism and Mass Communication at the University of Wisconsin, Madison, since 1981. His books include *Holding Fast the Inner Lines* (1980), *The Vital Past* (1985), *Ronald Reagan in Hollywood* (1994), and *Freedom and Entertainment* (2006). He is also the editor of *The Encyclopedia of American Journalism* (2008), *New Communication Technologies* (2010), and coeditor (with Gregory Downey and Rima Apple) of *Science in Print* (2012). Author of Will Hays essay.

Stanley Warren is emeritus professor, DePauw University. He earned a bachelor's degree from Indiana Central College, and a master's degree in teaching and an EdD degree from IU. His publications include: *Crispus Attucks High School: Hail to the Green, Hail to the Gold* (1998) and *The Senate Avenue YMCA for African American Men and Boys* (2005). Author of Noble Sissle, Robert Brokenburr, and Freeman B. Ransom essays.

Connie A. Weinzapfel is director, Historic New Harmony, a unified program of the University of Southern Indiana and the Indiana State Museum and Historic Sites. A native and resident of Posey County, she had the pleasure of collaborating with the subject of her essay in this book, for nearly twenty-five years in their beloved New Harmony. Author of Jane Blaffer Owen essay.

Carol Ann Weiss is the former visual arts editor, columnist, and feature writer for *Arts Indiana* magazine. She is the coauthor with Judith Vale Newton of *A Grand Tradition: The Art and Artists of the Hoosier Salon, 1925–1990* (1993); *Beyond Realism: The Life and Art of Frederik Grue* (1995); and *Skirting the Issue: Stories of Indiana's Historical Women Artists* (2004). In 2005 she and Newton received the IHS's Dorothy Riker Hoosier Historian Award. Author of Marie Goth essay.

Richard Hume Werking, professor of history and library director, emeritus, at the U.S. Naval Academy in Annapolis, Maryland, grew up in Evansville, Indiana. Following service in the U.S. Army and Indiana National Guard, he graduated from Evansville College, now the University of Evansville, and received his PhD from the University of Wisconsin. He is the author of *The Master Architects: Building the United States Foreign Service, 1890–1913* (2014) and has taught history at several colleges and universities, specializing in U.S. foreign relations, military, and naval history. Author of Walter Bedell "Beetle" Smith and Raymond A. Spurance essays.

Wendy Read Wertz, a native of England, began her career with the London publishing company of Hodder and Stoughton and later held positions as executive secretary to corporate management in Madrid, Spain, and Saudi Arabia. She completed a bachelor's degree with highest distinction at IU, Bloomington, where she met the subject of her essay and assisted him with his last book *The Latter Days* (unpublished). She has since written several articles about Caldwell and is the author of *Lynton Keith Caldwell: An Environmental Visionary and the National Environmental Policy Act* (2014). Author of Lynton Keith Caldwell essay.

Frederick Whitford has worked for the Purdue University Cooperative Extension Service for twenty-two years. He has authored three books on the history of Purdue and Indiana agriculture: *The Grand Old Man of Purdue University and Indiana Agriculture: A Biography of William Carroll Latta* (2005); *The Queen of American Agriculture: A Biography of Virginia Claypool Meredith* (2008); and *For the Good of the Farmer: A Biography of John Harrison Skinner, Dean of Purdue Agriculture* (2013). Author of Virginia Meredith essay.

Alan Wild is a freelance editor/writer who lives in New Albany, Indiana. He is a former copy editor at the *Louisville Courier-Journal* and also has worked for several small newspapers in southern Ohio. He has been an adjunct lecturer in journalism at IU Southeast since 1996. He has bachelor's and master's degrees in journalism from Ohio University. Author of Eugene C. and Eugne S. Pulliam essay.

Gayle A. Williams retired in 2011 from IUPUI, where she served as assistant dean of academic affairs in University College. She has an EdD in higher education and student affairs and a master's degree in religious studies from IU. One of her primary research interests is religious history and its role in American higher education. She is the author of "Biography of David Starr Jordan," in *The Dictionary of Unitarian and Universalist Biography* (2005) and "Andrew Wylie and Religion at Indiana University, 1824–1851: Nonsectarianism and Democracy," *Indiana Magazine of History* (March, 2003). Author of Andrew Wylie essay.

Wanda Lou Willis is a folklore historian and well-known Indiana personality and speaker giving programs throughout the state and appearing on radio and television. She is an award-winning author of the *Haunted Hoosier Trails* series of books, and soon to be released *Ghosthunting: Indiana, America's Haunted Road Trip* series. She also coauthored *Bedlam at the Brickyard* (2010), contributed to *Racing Can Be Murder* (2007), and is a columnist for *Country Roads: Southeastern Indiana's Lifestyle* magazine. She has been a consultant for movie and television productions and also appeared in paranormal movies produced by Dan T. Hall. Author of James Allison essay.

Julie Young is a freelance writer and author in the Indianapolis area who has written six books on local history, including *A Belief in Providence: A Life of Saint Theodora Guérin* (2007); *Historic Irvington* (2008); *Eastside Indianapolis: A Brief History* (2009); *A Brief History of Shelby County, Indiana* (2010); and *The CYO in Indianapolis and Central Indiana* (2011). Author of Saint Theodora Guerin, and Michael Jackson essays.

Connie Zeigler is a writer and historian and owner of C. Resources, a preservation consulting firm. She writes a monthly history column for an Indianapolis newspaper, has published numerous magazine articles and exhibitions, and has contributed to or coauthored six books, including *Advancing the Cause of Education: A History of the Indiana State Teachers Association, 1854–2004.* (2004) and *Indiana's State House* (2000). Author of Howard Cadle and Mary Thomas essays.

INDEX

Page numbers for illustrations are in italics

"7 Suggestions to Follow," 383
1805–1815 Journals of the General Assembly of Indiana Territory, 354

A. D. Pump Works, 257
A Plus program, 262
Abbott, Alice Reid, 151
"ABC" (song), 186
ABCs (baseball team), 57, 58
Abdul-Jabbar, Kareem, 384
Abner, Ewart, 54
Académie Julian (Paris), 324
Academy of Natural Sciences (Philadelphia), 219, 269
acquired immune deficiency syndrome, 374, 376
Actors Studio, 91
Actual Detective magazine, 224
Adams, Alban Housely, 1
Adams, Edward Wolfe, 2, 3
Adams, Elisha, 1
Adams, George Matthew, 182
Adams, Herbert Baxter, 381
Adams, J. Ottis, *1*, 1–3, 123, 124, 177, 325, 327
Adams, John, 161
Adams, John Alban, 2, 3
Adams, John Quincy, 176
Adams, Robert Brady, 2, 3
Adams, Wayman, 177
Adams, Winifred Brady, 2, 3, 325
Addams, Jane, 148, 149
Adderly, Cannonball, 247, 249
Addressograph Corporation, 85
Ade, Adaline Bush, 3
Ade, George, 3–5, *4*, 56, 254, 292, 308, 345
Ade, John, 3
Ade, William, 5
Adler, Mortimer, 166
Administrative Theories of Hamilton and Jefferson, The (book), 44
Adventure magazine, 86
Aereco. *See* Auto Electric Radio Equipment Company
Aeronautics Commission of Indiana, 75, 76
Aero-Notes (newsletter), 76
Aesop's Fables, 144
Afro-American National Business League, 199
Agabashian, Fred, 84
Agamemnon (play), 151
Agricultural Adjustment Act, 242, 297
Ahern, Mary Eileen, 5–7

Akira Suzuki, 37
Aladdin (television musical), 274
Aladdin and the Lamp, 144
Alice Adams (novel), 345
Alice of Old Vincennes (novel) 350
"All through the Night" (song), 274
Allen Whitehill Clowes Charitable Foundation Inc., 65
Allison, James A., 7–8, 118
Allison, Lucy Musset, 8
Allison, Myra Jane, 7
Allison, Noah Samuel, 7
Allison, Sarah Cornelius, 8
Allison Engineering Company, 8
Alpha Home for Aged Colored Women, 126
"Always True to You in My Fashion" (song), 274
American Association for Woman's Suffrage, 349
American Automobile Accessory Company, 79
American Bureau of Industrial Research, 152
American Colonization Society, 23
American Dental Association, 253
American Entomology, 270
American Home Missionary Society, 178
American Journal of Insanity, 122
American Jurist and Law Magazine, 22
American Legion, 229, 231, 242
American Library Association, 5, 6
American Peace Society, 304
American Philosophical Society, 219
American Railway Union, 93
American Woman Suffrage Association, 365
An American Tragedy (novel), 100, 101
"Another Op'nin; Another Show" (song), 274
Angel Mounds, 20, 21, 22, 212
Angel Site, 354
Anthony, Susan B., 138, 157, 158, 207, 208, 303, 365
Anything Goes (musical), 274
"Anything Goes" (song), 274
Apollo program, 140, 142
Appeal to Reason (journal), 93
Apperson, Edgar, 164
Apperson, Elmer, 164
Arizona Republic, 275
Armat, Thomas, 190
Armstrong, Louis, 48, 102, 130, 236, 249
Armstrong, Neil, 113
Art and Artists of Indiana, 143
Art Association of Indiana, 64
Art Association of Indianapolis, 124, 303, 327

Arthur Godfrey's Talent Scouts (television program), 310
Ashe, Arthur, 77
Astaire, Fred, 274
Atlanta Journal, 232
Atlantic Monthly magazine, 149
Auburn Automobile Company, 107
Auto Electric Radio Equipment Company (Fort Wayne, IN), 75
Autry, Gene, 130
Ave Maria magazine, 321
Avery, Fred, 118
Avery, Percy, 7
Ayala, Eusebio, 255

"Back Home Again in Indiana" (song), 102
Bacon, Albion Fellows, 8–10; *9*
Bacon, Hilary, 9
Bacon, Josiah, 347
Bad (album), 187
Badin, Stephen, 321
Badollet, John, 354
Bailey, Katherine "Flossie," 10–12
Bailey, Walter, 10, 12
Bailey, Walter Charles, 10
Bain, Wilfred, 134
Baker, Conrad, 12–14, 68, 168, 169
Baker, George (artist), 374
Baker, George (cartoonist), 38
Baker, Josephine, 314, 315
Baker, Matilda Escon Sommers, 12
Baker, Thaddeus, 12
Baker, William, 12
Balch, Emily, 148
Baldwin, Elihu, 180
Baler, Charlotte Francis Chute, 12
Ball, Edmund B., 14, 15, 16
Ball, Edmund F., 15
Ball, Frank C., 3, 14, 15
Ball, George Alexander, 14, 15
Ball, Lucille, 317
Ball, Lucius L., 14, *14*
Ball, William C., 14, 15
Ball Brothers Foundation, 14, 16
Ball Brothers Glass Manufacturing Company (Muncie). *See* Ball Corporation
Ball Brothers, 14–16
Ball Corporation (Muncie), 14, 15, *15*
Ball Family, 218
Ball Memorial Hospital (Muncie), 14, 16
Ball State University (Muncie), 14, 16
Ball Teachers' College. *See* Ball State University
Baltimore Afro-American, 361
Bamberger and Feibleman (law firm), 284
Bannister, Roger, 77
Banta, David, 385

Banting, Frederick, 64
Barbee, Clarissa. *See* Jennings, Clarissa, Barbee
Barnhart, John, 50
Barrett (Barritt), Sarah Tittle. *See* Bolton Sarah T.
Barrows v. Jackson, 243
Barry Barton's Mystery, 256
Barton, Bruce, 57
Barton, Laura Bartlow, 224
Basketball Association of America, 388, 389
Battle of Fallen Timbers, 291
Battle of Monocacy, 363
Battle of Paris, The (film), 273
Battle of Shiloh, 363
Battle of the Thames, 162, 347
Battle of Tippecanoe, 162, 347
Baumann, Gustave, 173
Bay of Pigs, 47, 320
Bayh, Birch, 31, 47, 262
Bayh, Evan, 230, 262
Baylen, Sarah. *See* Brown, Sarah Baylen
Baylor, Elgin, 128
Bays, John S., 297
Beadle, John H., 337
Bean Blossom (IN), 246, 247
"Beat It" (song), 187
Beatles (music group), 54, 186
Beaubien, Charles, 291
Beauty for Ashes, 10
Bedell, Ida Frances. *See* Smith, Ida Frances Bedell
Beesley, Eugene, 211, 299
"Begin the Beguine" (song), 274
Beiderbecke, Bix, 48, 49, 130
Being Lucky: Reminiscences and Reflections, 370
Bell, Cool Papa, 58
Bell, Grover, 16
Bell, Jousha, 134
Bell, Lawrence D., 16–17
Bell Aircraft Corporation, 16
Belmont, Alva, 208
"Ben" (song), 186
Bench and Bar, The, 40
Benczur, Gyula, 2, 123, 327
Benedict XVI, pope, 147
Beneficence (statue), 16
Ben-Hur: A Tale of the Christ (novel), 364
Benner, Bill, 172
Benny, Jack, 317
Benson, George, 249
Bentley, Eric, 223
Benton, Thomas Hart, 177
Bergère, The (musical), 315
Bergundthal, D. C., 356
Berle, Milton, 317
Berline, Bylon, 247
Bernoulli's principle, 77
Best Years of Our Lives, The (film), 49
Better Babies Contest, 300, 301

Beveridge, Albert J., 17–19, *18*, 31
Beveridge, Catherine Eddy, 19
Beveridge, Frances Eleanor, 18
Beveridge, Kate Maude Langsdale, 19
Beveridge, Thomas, 18
Biddle, Horace, 99
Big Ten, 127, 128, 204
Bigelow, W. D., 377
Bigger, Samuel, 354
Biggers, Earl Derr, 57
Bill Monroe Music Park and Campground (Bean Blossom, IN)
Billboard magazine, 54, 102, 187
Billy the Kid. *See* Bonney, William
Binford, Thomas, 290
"Bingo Eli Yale" (song), 273
Binns, Charles F. 266
Biomet (company), 386, 387
Bird Songs and Books (essay collection), 350
Birdsall, Mary, 348
Bissell, T. M., 260
Black Hoof, 348
Black, Glenn, 19–20, *21*, 354
"Black or White" (song), 187
Blackford, Caroline MacDonald, 23
Blackford, Isaac, 22–24
Blackwell, Antoinette L., 349
Blackwell, Scrapper, 130
Blaffer Foundation, 267, 268
Blaffer, Sarah Campbell, 268
Blake, Eubie, 314. 215
Blaker, Eliza, 24–26, *24*, 353
Blaker, Louis J., 24
Bleecher, Jane. *See* Pulliam, Jane Bleecher
Blood on the Dance Floor (album), 187
Bloom, Sal, *32*
Bloomington (IN), 226, 227
Bloomington Indiana Gazette, 226
Bloomington Indiana Tribune, 227
Bloomington Post, 227
"Blow Gabriel, Blow" (song), 274
Blue Grass Boys (music group), 245, 246
"Blue Moon of Kentucky" (song), 247
Bluebeard (novel), 359
Blum, David, 133
Board of State Charities, 228
Boatman, The (painting), 327
Bobbs, Ruth Pratt, 124
Bobbs, William C., 56
Bobbs-Merrill (publisher), 55, 56
Bogart, Humphrey, 92
Bohn, Arthur, 358
Bok, Edward, 336
Bolton, Nathaniel, 26, 99
Bolton, Sarah T., 26–27, *27*
Bonner, Rosa, 349
Bonney, William, 364
Book, William, Sr., 275
Bookwalter, Charles A., 342
Boone, Pat, 54

Booth, Newton, 344
Borkenstein, Robert Frank, 27–29, *28*
Born to Build: The Story of the Gene B. Glick Company, 136
Born to Dance (film), 274
Bossert, Walter, 329
Boutwood, Charles Edward, 311
Bowen, Carol Mikesell, 31
Bowen, Elizabeth Anna Agnes "Beth" Steinmann, 30, 31
Bowen, Otis R., 29–31, 45, 262, 299, 372
Bowen, Robert, 31
Bowen, Rose Hochstetter, 31
Bowen, Stewart and Company. *See* Bobbs-Merrill
Bowen, Vernie, 30
Bowen Center for Public Affairs, 31
Bowen-Merrill Company. *See* Bobbs-Merrill
Bowers, Claude G., 31–33, *32*
Bowers, Pat, 32
Bowers, Sybil McCaslin, 32
Bowman, Charles, 287
Bowman, Joseph, 60
Boxwell, Mahala. *See* Dudley, Mahala Boxwell
Bracken, Jimmy, 54
Brackett, Rogers, 91
Brademas, John, 262
Bradley, Bill, 77
Bradley, Omar, 280, 318
Bradwell, Myra, 207
Brady, Diamond Jim, 74
Brady, Winifred. *See* Adams, Winifred Brady
Brando, Marlon, 92
Branigin, Roger, 225
Brauer, Richard H. W., 105
Brauer Museum of Art (Valparaiso, IN), 104, 105
Breakfast of Champions (novel), 359
Brearley, Harry, 163
Breathalyzer, 27, *28*
Breedlove, Minerva, 360
Breedlove, Owen, 360
Breedlove, Sarah. *See* Walker, Madam C. J.
Breen, Joseph, 166
Breman (IN), 30, 31
Brief Sketch of the Past, Present, and Prospects of Vincennes, A, 333
Briggs, John C., 207
Brighton, Lydia Dakin, 207
Brighton, Nettie. *See* Leach Antoinette Dakin
Bristol-Myers Squibb, 387
British Medical Journal, 122
Brokenburr, Robert L., 33–35 *35*, 281, 290, 361
Brook (IN), 3, 5
Brooklyn Brown Dodgers (baseball team), 59

Brooklyn Dodgers (baseball team), 59
Brookville (IN), 2, 327
Broonzy, Bill, 130
Brophy, John, 152
Brotherhood of Locomotive Firemen, 92, 157
Brovarnik, Herbert Charles. *See* Brown, Herbert Charles
Brown, Charles Francis, 124, 327
Brown, Herbert Charles, 35–37
Brown, James, 186
Brown, Leigh. *See* Shepherd, Leigh Brown
Brown, Sarah Baylen, 36, 37
Brown County (IN), 136, 137, 138, 173, 174, 181, 182, 311, 312, 327, 328
Brown County Art Gallery, 312
Brown County Art Guild, 137, 138
Brown County in Autumn (classical work), 49
Brown v. Board of Education, 243, 283
Browne, Thomas M., 169
Brownfield, John, 260
Brown-Skinned Models (musical), 315
"Brush Up Your Shakespeare" (song), 274
Brute, Simon, 320
Bryan, William Jennings, 3, 130, 138, 140, 182, 275, 343, 381
Bryan, William Lowe, 85, 328, 369
Bryant, Eva Dora. *See* Taggart, Eva Dora Bryant
Bryn Mawr, 150, 151
Buchanan, Sister Marie Antoinette, 147
Buckner, Rachel, 155, 156
Buechlein, Daniel M., 146
Buell, Juan Carlos, 363
Buffalo Trace, The, 354
Buley, R. C., 354
Bullock, William Avery, 40
Bundy, John Elwood, 374
Burbank, Lucinda. *See* Morton, Lucinda Burbank
Burnet, Mary Q., 143
Burney, Leroy E., 299
Burrell, Kenny, 249
Burritt, Ruth, 24
Bush, Barbara, 374
Bush, George H. W., 77, 263, 277, 374
Bush, Owen "Donie," 58
Bushemi, John A., 37–40, *39*
Bushemi, Pietro, 38
Bustin, Dillon, 174
But We Were Born Free (book), 57, 88
Butler, Chauncy (father of Ovid), 40
Butler, Chauncy (son of Ovid), 40
Butler, Cordelioa Cole, 40
Butler, Demia, 40, 41
Butler, Elizabeth Anne Elgin, 40
Butler, Jerry, 54
Butler, Ovid, 40–42, *41*, 120, 121
Butler, Scot, 40, 42

Butler Collegian, 171
Butler University (Indianapolis), 25, 26, 40, 41, 42, 171, 172
By-Ways and Bird Notes (essay collection), 350
Byrd, Cecil, 174
Byrd, Harry, 47

C. G. Conn Company, 71
Cadle, Buford, 43
Cadle, E. Howard, 42–43
Cadle, Helen, 43
Cadle, Ola M., 43
Cadle, Virginia Ann, 43
Cadle Tabernacle (Indianapolis), *42*, 43, 117
Caldwell, Fannie. *See* Stewart, Fannie Caldwell
Caldwell, Helen Walcher, 44, 45
Caldwell, Howard, 172
Caldwell, Lynton Keith, 43–45, *45*
Calhoun, John, 237, 238
Call It North Country (book), 224
Camel Caravan (radio show), 310
Cameron, Angus, 272
Camp Morton (Indianapolis), 239
Campanella, Roy, 59
Can-Can (musical), 274
Canton (IL), 74. 75
Canyon Passage (film), 49
Capehart, Alvin T., 46
Capehart, Homer E., 45–47
Capehart Corporation, 46
Caperton, Frank, 277
Capitol Records, 54
Capone, Al, 74
Capra, Frank, 38
Captian EO (film), 187
Cardozo, Benjamin, 297
Cariani, V. (Varaldo) J. (Giuseppe), 136, 137, 138
Carmichael, Hoagland "Hoagy" Howard, 47–49, *48*, 85, 130, 368
Carmichael, Hoagland, Jr., 49
Carmichael, Joanne, 48
Carmichael, Randy, 49
Carmichael, Ruth Meinardi, 49
Carmichael, Wanda McKay, 49
Carmony Golda, 50
Carmony, Bert, 50
Carmony, Diane, 50
Carmony, Donald, 49–51
Carmony, Duane, 51
Carmony, Edith, 51
Carmony, Lowell, 51
Carmony, Mary Hiatt, 51
Canal, Morning, The (painting), 143
Carnegie, Andrew, 95, 270
Carnegie, Tom, *82*
Carpenter, Malcolm Scott, 141
Carr, John, 193
Carson, Andre, 53

Carson, Julia, 51–53, *52*
Carter, Calvin, 54
Carter, Mary. *See* Hovey, Mary Carter
Carter, Vivian, 53–55, *55*
Caruso, Enrico, 361
Carver, George Washington, 301, 302
Cass, Lewis, 234, 347–48
Castro, Fidel, 299
Cat and the Canary, The (film), 317
Catt, Carrie Chapman, 158
Cauthorn, Henry S., 332, 333
Cavalier of Tennessee, The (novel), 255
Cavanaugh, John J., 170
Center for Studies of Law in Action, 29
Central Indiana Community Foundation, 110, 111
Central Newspapers Inc., 275, 276, 277
Century (publisher), 56
Chaffe, Roger, 140, 142
Chamberlain, Wilt, 128
Chambers, David (grandfather of David Lawrence), 55
Chambers, David Abbot, 55
Chambers, David Laurance, 55–57, *56*, 182
Chambers, YJean, 53, 55
Chandler, Gene, 54
Chapin, Francis, 177
Chaplin, Charlie, 318
Chapman, Elizabeth. *See* Conner, Elizabeth Chapman
Chapman, J. Wilbur, 340, 341
Charelston, Jane Blalock Howard, 58
Charity Organization Society, 24
Charles Scribner's Sons (publisher), 56
Charles W. Cushman Photograph Collection, 86
Charles W. Dahlgreen (painting), 138
Charleston, Oscar, 57–59; *59*
Chase, Salmon, 67
Chase, William Merritt, 1, 2
Chasseboeuf, Constantin-François de, Count of Volney, 219
Chatard, Silas, 147
Cheaper by the Dozen (book), 131
Cheronis, Nicholas, 36
Chester Hybrids, 287
Chicago, 84–85, 86
Chicago American Giants (baseball team), 58
Chicago Daily Globe, 100
Chicago Daily News, 39
Chicago Giants (baseball team), 58
Chicago Morning News, 4
Chicago Tribune, 39, 232
Chicken of the Sea, 357
Chief Anderson, 72
Chihuly, Dale, 237
Children's Aid Society, 25, 116
Chile, 31, 33
Chinese Nightingale, The, 144
Chocolate Dandies (musical), 315

Choice, Wally, 129
Christian, Charlie, 248, 249
Christian, Grant, 124
Churchill, Winston, 319, 324, 379
Chute, Charlotte Francis. *See* Baker, Charlotte Frances Chute
Ciardi, John, 223
Cicero (IN), 374
Cincinnati (OH), 79, 80, 363
Cincinnati Reds (baseball team), 80
Cincinnati Tribune, 181
Circle Centre Mall (Indianapolis), 313
Citizens' National Bank, 257
Citizen's Relief Committee, 117
Civil Rights Act (US, 1964), 372
Civil Right Law (IN, 1885), 283, 289, 372
Clabber Girl Baking Powder, 183
Clark, Ann Rogers, 60
Clark, Delectus "Dee," 54
Clark, George Rogers, 60–62, *61*
Clark, John, 60
Clark, Teresa, 102
Clark, Thomas D., 57
Clark, William, 61
Clark State Forest (Clark County, IN), 89
Clarke, Charles B., 62
Clarke, Grace Julian, 62–64, 365
Clarksville (IN), 60
Classical School for Girls, 303, 304
Clay, Henry, 19, 213, 321
Clay, Lucius, 298
Clements, Vassar, 247
Cleveland, Grover, 109, 160, 169, 181, 195, 342
Cleveland Press, 143
Cline, Mary Eleanor "Nory." *See* Smith, Mary Eleanor "Nory" Cline
Cloutier, Joseph R., 183
Clowes, Allen, 64, 65
Clowes, Edith Whitehill Hinkel, 64, 65
Clowes, George H. A., Jr., 64, 65
Clowes, George Henry Alexander, 64, 65, 211
Clowes Family, 64–65
Clowes Fund, 64, 65
Clowes Memorial Hall, 65
Coach for a Nation: The Life and Times of Knute Rockne, 294
Coats, Randolf, 124
Coburn, John, 42
Cochran, Ella, 316
Cochran, Homer, 183, 307
Coffin, Catharine, 65–67
Coffin, Charles, 68, 69
Coffin, Elijah, 68
Coffin, Levi, 65–67
Coffin, Rhoda M., 68–69
Cole, Cordelia. *See* Butler, Cordelia Cole
Cole, Kate. *See* Porter, Kate Cole
Cole, Nat King, 249
Coleman, Christopher B., 20, 115
College Widow, The (play), 5

Collier's magazine, 87, 253, 294, 359
Collin, Raphael, 311
Collins, Bob, 183
Coltrane, John, 249
Columbia Conserve Company, 151, 152, 153, 154, 155
Columbia Journalism Review, 275
Columbus (IN), 83, 84, 235, 236, 237
Columbus, Christopher, 109
Commercial Club, 210
Committee for the Nation. *See* National Committee to Uphold Constitutional Government
Commonwealth and Southern, 378
Comprehensive School Law (1852), 241
Compromise of 1820, p. 250
ConAgra, 287, 357
Congregation of Holy Cross, 170, 171, 320, 321, 322
Congress of Industrial Organizations, 152, 155
Conn, Charles (father of Charles Gerard), 70
Conn, Charles Gerard, 69–71
Conn-Selmer Inc., 71
Conn Conservatory of Music, 71
Conner, Elizabeth Chapman, 72
Conner, John, 72
Conner, Richard, 72
Conner, William 71–73, 212
Conner Prairie Interactive History Park, 212
Consolidated Aircraft Company, 16
Cook, Agnes, 349
Cook, Anna Belle. *See* O'Brien Anna Belle Cook
Cook, Gayle, 73
Cook, William Alfred "Bill," 73–75
Cook Inc., 73
Cooke, Sam, 54
Coolidge, Calvin, 33, 297
Cooper, Gordon, 141
Cooper, Ira, 79
Cooper, Jacob, 25
Cooper, Mary Jane Core, 24
Coppes, John, 30
Corbett, James "Gentleman Jim," 4
Cord, Errett Lobban, 107
Cormon, Fernand, 324
Cornelius, Sarah. *See* Allison, Sarah Cornelius
Cornell Daily Sun, 358
Corning Glass Works, 215
Cornish, Clarence F., 75–76
Corpuz, Paula, 120
Corydon (IN), 332
Coryn, Sidonie, 272
Costigan, Francis, 205
Cottman, George S., 99, 114
Coulter, John, 88
Coulter, Stanley, 88, 90
Counsilman, James E. "Doc," 76–78

Counsilman, Joe, 77
Count de Volney. *See* Chasseboeuf, Constantin-François de
Country Chairman, The (play), 4
Country Gentleman magazine, 272
Courts and Lawyers of Indiana, 245
Covert, Charles G., 256
Covert, Grace Tucker, 256
Coward, Noel, 315
Cox, Donna Belle Harmon, 387
Cox, James M., 343
Cox, Jane Marie. *See* Vonnegut, Jane Marie Cox
Cox, Lenora, 63
Crawford, Mary Hiatt. *See* Carmony, Mary Hiatt
Crawfordsville Record, 179
Crawfordsville Star, 180
Crest toothpaste, 253
Crisis magazine, 302, 361
Crispus Attucks High School, 35, 81, 82, 128, 330
Croghan Lucy, 61
Croghan, William, 61
Crosley, Charlotte, 79
Crosley, Lewis, 79
Crosley, Powel (father of Powel Jr.), 79
Crosley, Powel, Jr., 78–80, *79*
Crosley Aircraft, 80
Crosley Radio Company, 79
Crosswell, D. K. R., 318
Crowe, Ray P., 81–83, *82*
Cuffey, James, 215
Culberson, Dick, 127
Cummins Engine Company. *See* Cummins Inc.
Cummins Foundation, 237
Cummins Inc. (Columbus, IN), 83, 84, 235, 236, 237, 357
Cummins Machine Works. *See* Cummins Inc.
Cummins, Almira Josephine Eddleman
Cummins, Clessie Lyle, 83–84, 235
Cummins, Francis Marion, 83
Currier, J. Frank, 327
Curry, John Steuart, 177
Cushman, Charles Weever, 84–86
Cushman, Jean, 85, 86

Dabbert, James, 104
Dahlgreen, Charles, 138
Daily Echo, 358
Dale, Anne Caroline. *See* Owen, Anne Caroline Dale
Dale, David, 269
Dangerous (album), 187
Daniels, Edward, 14
Daniels, Mitchell E., Jr. (Mitch), 51, 268
Darby, Harry, 275
Darrow, Clarence, 117
Daugherty, Emma, 367
Davis, Elmer, 57, 86–88, *87*

Index

Davis, Jefferson, 195, 332
Davis, John, 360
Davis, Mary Kay. *See* Orr, Mary Kay Davis
Davis, Maurice, 352
Davis, Miles, 249
Dawes, Charles, 5
Day the Earth Stood Still, The (film), 86
Day, Harry, 253
Dayton (OH), 96
de Gaulle, Charles, 319
Deam, Charles "Charlie" C., 88–90; *90*
Deam, Stella Mullin, 88, 89
Dean, James, 90–92
Dean, Margaret. *See* Spruance, Margaret Dean
Dean, Mildred Wilson, 91
Dean, Winton, 91
"Death Where Is Thy Sting?" (song), 317
Debs, Eugene Victor, 92–94, *93*, 153, 157
Debs, Katherine Metzel, 92, 93
Deere, John, 260
DeFrantz, Faburn, 127–28
Delaware (tribe), 72
Dells (music group), 54
Democracy in America, 264
Denver Republican, 108
Denver Rocky Mountain News, 108
Denver Tribune, 108
DePauw, Catherine Newland, 95
DePauw, Charles (Washington C.'s grandfather), 94
DePauw, Charles (Washington C.'s son), 95
DePauw, Frances "Fannie" Leyden, 95, 96
DePauw, John, 94
DePauw, Newland, 95
DePauw, Sarah Malott, 95
DePauw, Washington C., 94–96
DePauw American Plate Glass Works (New Albany), 94–95
DePauw Daily, 275
DePauw University (Greencastle), 95
Dependent Pension Act, 160
DePuy, Revra, 386
Depuy (orthopedic company), 386, 387
Derencourt, Antoine, 302
Destiny (album), 186
Detroit, 60, 61
Detroit Pistons (basketball team), 388, 389
Dewey, Thomas, 44, 316
Diary of Calvin Fletcher, 354
Dick and Jane (reading series), 304, 305
Dillinger, John H., Jr. 96–98, *97*
Dillman, Dwight, 246
Dillon, John Brown, 98–99
Dillon, Patrick, 322
Dimmick, Mary Lord. *See* Harrison, Mary Lord Dimmick
Directory, The, 330, 331
Disciples of Christ, 40
Dixie Highway, 118, 119

"Doctor, The" (poem), 123
Documentary History of the Indiana Decade of the Harmony Society, 354
Documents Relating to the French Settlements on the Wabash (book), 109
Dodds, Johnny, 130
Dolan, Jon, 187
Dominican Republic, 225
Donahey, Victor, 329
Donovan, Mary. *See* Hapgood, Mary Donovan
"Don't Stop 'til you Get Enough" (song), 186
"Doomed Anarchists, The" (poem), 27
Dorrett, L. H., 302
Dorset, Lyle, 341
Dorsey Brothers, 49
Doughty, Drusilla. *See* Lanier Drusilla Doughty
Douglas, Stephen A., 19, 168
Douglass, Frederick, 126, 155, 301
Douglass Appealing to Lincoln (mural), 301
Dow, Arthur Wesley, 266
Dowd, Gregory, 346
Dowell, John, 247
Down Beat magazine, 249
"Down in the Depths" (song), 274
Doyle, Joe, 295
Dreiser Theodore. 100–101, *100*, 102
Dresden (Germany), 358, 359
Dresser, Paul, 100, 101–4
DuBarry Was a Lady (musical), 274
DuBois, W. E. B., 302, 331
Dudley, Frank V., 104–5
Dudley, Mahala Boxwell, 104
Dudley, Maida Lewis, 104
Duesenberg (automobile), *106*, 107
Duesenberg, August (Auggie), 105–7
Duesenberg, Friedrich (Fred), 105–7, 306
Duesenberg Automobile and Motors Company, 105, 106, 107
Duffy, Thomas, 170
Dumond, Dwight Lowell, 352
DuMond, Frank Vincent, 137
Duneland (painting), 104
Dunn, Caroline, 108, 109
Dunn, Charlotte Elliot Jones, 108
Dunn, Eleanor, 108
Dunn, Harriet Louisa Tate, 108
Dunn, Isaac, 108, 175
Dunn, Jacob P., Jr., 108–10, *109*, 222
Dunn, Jacob (father of Jacob P. Jr.), 108
Dunn, Mary E. *See* Maxwell Mary E. Dunn
Dunn, Williamson, 225
Dunning, Paris C., 214
Dunning, William A., 382
Dupont, Eugene, 70
Duryea, Frank, 164
Duryea (automobile), 164
Duvall, John, 329, 330
DuValle, Reginald, 48

Dye, John T., 254
Eaglesfield, Bessie, 207
Earhart, Amelia, 132, 280
Early Birds, The (mural), 144
East of Eden (film), 90, 91
Eastern Colored League, 58
Eastman Kodak, 85
"Easy to Love" (song), 274
Eckert, Mack, 202
Eclipse, The (musical), 273
Ed Sullivan Show (television program), 310
Eddy, Catherine. *See* Beveridge, Catherine Eddy
Edible Wild Plants of Eastern North America, 196
Edison, Thomas A., 190, 191
Edith Hamilton: An Intimate Portrait, 150
Edmondson, Frank K., 216
Edmunds, R. David, 346
Eepiihkaanita. *See* Wells, William
Efroymson Clarence W. 110
Efroymson, Daniel R., 111
Efroymson, Gustave A., 110, 111
Efroymson, Jacob, 110
Efroymson, Mamie W. Wallenstein, 110
Efroymson, Robert, 110, 111
Efroymson Family, 110–11
Ehart, Joseph. *See* Skelton, Joseph, 216
Eicher, Palmer, 387
Ei-ichi Negishi, 37
Eisenhower Dwight D., 33, 35, 47, 224, 275, 280, 298, 318, 319, 320, 323
El Dorados (music group), 54
Elgin, Elizabeth Anne. *See* Butler Elizabeth Anne Elgin
Eli Lilly and Company, 20, 64, 185, 210, 299, 354, 355
Eliza A. Blaker Club, 24, 25
Elkhart (IN), 70–71
Elkhart Lighting Company, 70
Elkhart Truth, 70
Elliott, Edward C., 132
Elmer Davis and the News (radio show), 87
Elston, Susan. *See* Wallace, Susan Elston
Emancipation Proclamation, 213, 238, 251
EMI (record company), 54
Emrick, Paul "Spotts." 111–13, *113*
Enabling Act, 19293
Enberg, Dick, 382
Engel, J. Ronald, 105
Engel, Joan Gibb, 105
England and the 1880s: Toward a Social Basis for Freedom, 218
Environmental Protection Agency, 74
Equal Suffrage Society, 303, 365
Erskine, John, 57
Esarey, Laura, 114
Esarey, Logan, 114–15, 245
Esarey, Solomon, 245
Esquire magazine, 224, 235

Estill, Robert G., 97
Ettinger, Joe, 386
Eugene and Marilyn Glick Family Foundation, 136
Eugene S. Pulliam Internship Program, 277
eugenics, 300
Europe, James Reese, 361
Evans, Dave, 84
Evans, Hiram, 329
Evansville (IN), 9, 10, 328
Evansville Courier, 256
Everett, Betty, 54
Everett, F. B., 139
"Evicted" (poem), 27
"Ev'ry Time We Say Goodbye" (song), 274
Ewing, Oscar, R., 298
Ex Parte Milligan, 237, 239
Executive Proceedings of the State of Indiana, 354
Explorer 1 (satellite), 141
Eyed, Abe, 138

Fables in Slang (book), 4
Fair Employment Practices Commission, 372
Fair God, The (novel), 363, 364
Fairbank, Caroline, 63
Fairbanks, Charles, 182
Farm Journal, 272
Farm Life magazine, 272
Farm Security Administration, 86
Farnsworth, Philo, 191
Farnsworth Television and Radio Corporation, 191
Farrakhan, Louis, 53
Fates Worse Than Death: An Autobiographical Collage (novel), 359
Federal Airport Act (1946), 76
Federal Radio Commission, 191
Federal Security Agency, 230
Federation of Associated Clubs, 289
Fellows, Albion, 9
Fellows, Annie, 9
Fellows, Mary Erskine, 9
Fendrich, Mary. *See* Hulman, Mary Fendrich
Ferber, Edna, 92
Ferguson, Allie, 174
Fesler v. Brayton, 245
Feuerlicht, Mildred M. Mayerstein, 117
Feuerlicht, Morris Marcus, 115–17
Field System (book),131
Fifteenth Amendment, 169, 251
Fishback, William P., 254
Fisher, Carl, 7, 8, 79, 117–19, *119*, 342
Fisher, Jane Watt, 117–18
Fitzgerald, F. Scott, 344
Five Hoosier Painters (exhibition), 124, 327
Flanner Guild, 126
Flatt, Lester, 246, 247

Flatt and Scruggs (music group), 247
Fletcher Sarah Hill, 120, 121
Fletcher, Agnes O'Brien, 122
Fletcher, Calvin, 40, 99, 119–21, *120*, 356
Fletcher, Frank J., 323
Fletcher, Laurel Louisa. *See* Tarkington, Laurel Louisa Fletcher
Fletcher, William B., 121–23
Fletcher, Williams and Van Camp, 356
Flora of Indiana, 89
Flower, Richard, 285, 286
fluoridation, 298
fluoride, 253
The Flying Preacher: One Night Revival Sermons, 43
Forbes magazine, 73
Ford, Gabriel, 23
Ford, Gerald, 77, 171
Ford, Henry, 296, 304
Ford, John, 94
Ford, Worthington S., 19
Forest and Trees of Indiana, 89
Forest Reserve Act, 160
Forest Tax Classification Act (1921), 89
Forsyth, William Jefferson, 1, 2, 3, 123–25, *125*, 155, 177, 327
Fort Sackville, 60, 61
Fort Wayne (IN), 75
Fort Wayne Journal-Gazette, 32, 310
Fort Wayne News-Sentinel, 75
Fort Wayne Zollner Pistons (basketball team), 388
Fortnight of Folly, A (novel), 351
Fortune, T. Thomas, 351, 352
Forum Shops at Caesars (Las Vegas), 313
Foster, Stephen, 103, 211, 281
Fountainhead, The (novel), 57
Four Seasons (music group), 54
Fourteenth Amendment, 24, 169
Fowler, Moses, 278
Fox, Lillian Thomas, 125–27
Foyt, A. J., 183
Francis, Joseph M., 343
Franco, Francisco, 33
Frank M. Hohenberger's Indiana Photographs, 174
Frank M. Hohenberger Photograph Collection, 174
Frankel, Albert J., 313
Frankfurter, Felix, 149
Franklin, Benjamin, 219, 385
Franklin College (Franklin), 176
Fred Zollner Memorial Stadium and Athletic Complex (Fort Wayne), 389
"Free Wheeling" (song), 48
Freedman's Bureau, 67
Freedom 7, p. 141
Freeman, John, 121
Freeman, Martha. *See* Hovey, Martha Freeman
French, Jesse, 129

French Lick Springs Hotel, 74, 342, 343
Freud, Sigmund, 78
Fried, Miriam, 134
Friends of Mr. Sweeney (novel and film), 87
Friends of Our Native Landscape, 104
"Friendship" (song), 274
Fröebel, Fredrich, 24, 353
Fugitive Slave Law (1850), 195

G. C. Van Camp and Son Packaging. *See* Stokely-Van Camp
Gage, Frances D., 349
Galápagos: A Novel, 359
Gallatin, Albert, 354
Gallmeyer, E. J., 251
Galt, Edith. *See* Wilson, Edith Galt
Gamble, George, 1
Gannett Company Inc. 277
Gardiner, Elizabeth. *See* Lanier, Elizabeth Gardiner
Garfield, James, 364
Garland, Hamlin, 124, 327, 344
Garrett, Betty Guess, 128
Garrett, Bill (son of William), 128, 129
Garrett, Judith, 128
Garrett, Laurie, 128
Garrett, Tina, 128
Garrett, William, 127–29; *127*
Garrett, William L., II (grandson of William), 129
Gary (IN), 38, 144, 145, 146
Gary Post-Tribune, 37
Gaskin, George, 102
Gates, Ralph, 259
Gather Ye Rosebuds (novel), 257
Gatorade, 357
Gavisk, Francis H., 117
Gay Divorce (musical), 273–74
Gelston, Caroline Louise. *See* Woodburn, Caroline Louise Gelston
Gemini project, 141–42
Gene B. Glick Company, 135, 136
Gennett, Clarence, 129
Gennett, Fred, 129, 130
Gennett, Harry, 129
Gennett, Henry, 129, 130
Gennett Family, 129–30
Gennett Records, 48, 129, 130
Gentleman from Indiana, The (novel), 344
Gentry, Allen, 213
George Koch and Sons, 201
George Rogers Clark National Historical Park (Vincennes), 61
George Rogers Clark, Soldier and Hero, 257
George, Kristi Koch, 201, 202
George, Walter, 47
"Georgia on My Mind" (song), 48
Gerdts, William H., 105
Ghost Breakers, The (film), 317
Giant (film and novel), 90, 92
Giant Killer (novel), 87

Gibbs, Reuben, 199
Gibson, Josh, 58, 59
Gibson, Mary Cornelius, 259
Giddings, Jousha, 62
Giddings, Laura. *See* Julian, Laura Giddings
Gilbreth, Frank, 131–32
Gilbreth, Frank (son of Lillian and Frank), 132
Gilbreth, Lillian Moller, 131–33
Gillespie, Eliza Marie, 321
Gingold, Gladys, 133
Gingold, Josef, 13–35, *134*
Gipp, George, 294
Gleason, Jackie, 317
Glenn A. Black Laboratory of Archaeology, 21
Glenn, John, 141
Glenn L. Martin Company, 16
Glick, Eugene C., 135–36
Glick, Marilyn Ruth Koffman, 137–36
God Bless You, Mr. Rosewater (novel), 359
Godfrey, Donald, 190
Goebbels, Joseph, 88
Goethe and Helen Link Foundation for Scientific Research, 215
"Going Out of My Head" (song), 247, 249
Goldblatt, Maurice, 116
Gomez, Juan Vicente, 255
Good Housekeeping magazine, 378
Goodman, Benny, 48, 248
Goodrich, James P., 63, 165, 210, 244, 245
Goodwin, John P., 259
Gookins, James F., 123
Goral Airways (Fort Wayne, IN), 75
Gordy, Berry, 55, 186, 187
"Got to Be There" (song), 186)
Goth, Charles, 137
Goth, Genevieve. *See* Graf, Genevieve Goth
Goth, Jesse (mother of Marie), 136
Goth, (Jesse) Marie, 136–38
Gougar, Helen Mar Jackson, 138–40, 207
Gougar, John, 138, 140
Gougar v. Timberlake, 139
Governing the Commons: The Evolution of Institutions for Collective Action, 264
Graetz, Heinrich, 116
Graf, Genevieve Goth, 137, 138
Graham, Gordon, 202, 204
Grand Ole Opry (radio program), 246, 247
Grant, Cary, 274
Grant, Ulysses S., 195, 251, 363
Grapes of Wrath, The (novel), 85
Grasses of Indiana, 89
Grateful Dead (music group), 247
Gray, Isaac, P., 70
Gray, William S., 305
Gray's Manual of Botany, 88
Great American Songbook, 49, 273
Great Gatsby (novel), 344
Great Migration, 288

Greater Indianapolis (book), 109
Greater Indianapolis Progress Committee, 111
Greek Way, The, 149, 150
Green, Dwight, 224
Green, Joe, 58
Green, John Cleve, 344
Greenfield (IN), 199
Greenhouse, Wendy, 105
Greenleaf, Carl Dimond, 71
Greenwich Follies of 1924, The (musical), 273
Greer, William B., 362
Griffith, Dick, 174
Grissom, Betty, 140
Grissom, Scott, 140
Grissom, Virgil I. "Gus," 140–42, *141*
Gru, Prudence. *See* Gruelle, Prudence
Gruelle, Alice, 142, 143
Gruelle, John Barton "Johnny," 142, 143
Gruelle, Justin, 142, 144
Gruelle, Marcella, 143
Gruelle, Prudence, 142, 144
Gruelle, Richard B., 2, 123, 124, 142–43, 327
Gruelle Family, 142–44
Grutka, Andrew Gregory, 144–46
Guérin, Anne-Thérèse. *See* Guérin, Saint Theodora
Guérin, Saint Theodora, 146–47, *147*
Guess, Betty. *See* Garrett, Betty Guess
Guinness Book of World Records, 76
Gurney, Joseph John, 68
Gutenberg, Johannes, 332

H. P. Wasson Company, 110
Hackney, Leonard J., 207
Hadley, Paul, 177
Haffner, Gerald, 95
Haiti, 302
Haiti (mural), 301
Haitian Market (painting), 302
Halandiere, Celestin de la, 321
Halberstam, David, 262
Hale, William Harlan, 223
Hall, Katie, 51
Halleck, Charles A., 197
Halleck, Henry W., 363
Halliburton, Richard, 57
Halsey, William "Bull," 323
Hamilton, Agnes, 149
Hamilton, Alexander, 19, 31, 33
Hamilton, Alice, 148–50, *149*
Hamilton, Allen, 148
Hamilton, Arthur, 149
Hamilton, Edith, 149, 150–51
Hamilton, Emerline, 148
Hamilton, Gertrude, 148, 150
Hamilton, Henry, 60, 61
Hamilton, Joseph R., 85
Hamilton, Margaret, 149, 150
Hamilton, Montgomery, 148

Hamilton, Nora, 149, 150
Hampton, Lionel, 248
Hamtramck, John Francis, 354
Handbook of the Mammoth Cave of Kentucky, 180
Hanley, James, 102
Hanly, J. Frank, 19
Hanson, J. A., 356
Hanson and Bergundthal, 356
Hanson-Van Camp Company. *See* Van Camp Hardware and Iron Company
Hapgood, Charles H., 153
Hapgood, Eleanor Page, 151, 153
Hapgood, Fanny Louise Powers, 153
Hapgood, Hutchins., 153
Hapgood, Mary Donovan, 152
Hapgood, Norman, 153, 154
Hapgood, Powers, 151–53, 154, 155
Hapgood, William Powers, 151, 152, 153–55, *154*
Hardin, Garrett, 264
Harding Warren G., 32, 93, 165, 222
Harding, William M., 342
Hardrick, Georgia Howard, 155
Hardrick, John Wesley, 155–56
Hargar, Rolla, 28
Hargrove, Marion, 38
Harmar, Josiah, 233, 291
Harmon, Tom, 38
Harmonie Society, 267, 268, 269
Harmonist movement, 284, 285, 286
Harmony Society, 284, 285
Harper, Frances, 126
Harper, Ida Husted, 63, 156–58, *157*
Harper, Jesse, 295
Harper, Thomas Winans, 157
Harper, Winnifred, 158
Harper's magazine, 87, 223, 224, 325
Harper's Bazaar magazine, 232, 303
Harris, William, 130
Harrisburg (PA) Telegraph, 58
Harrisburg Giants (baseball team), 58
Harrison, Anna Symmes, 161, 162
Harrison, Benjamin (father of William Henry), 161
Harrison, Benjamin (president), 51, 98, 109, 143, 158–60, *159*, 165, 199, 235, 304, 328, 338, 342, 364
Harrison, Caroline Scott, 159
Harrison, Christopher, 193
Harrison, Mary Lord Dimmick, 160
Harrison, William Henry, 72, 158, 160–62, *161*, 175, 191, 192, 291, 332, 333, 346, 347
Harroun, Ray, 118
Hartman, Carl, 287
Harvard Monthly, 153
Harvey, Aurilla. *See* Knox, Aurilla Harvey
Harvey, Flossie. *See* Bailey Katherine "Flossie"
Hatcher, Richard, 145
Havana, 299

"Hawk" (poem), 223
Hawkins, Hubert, 354
Hay, Ann Gilmore. *See* Jennings, Ann Gilmore Hay
Haydn, Hiram, 57
Hayes, Rutherford B., 169, 251, 364
Haynes, Bertha Lanterman, 164
Haynes, Elwood, 163–65, *163*
Haynes, Hilinda Haines, 163
Haynes, Jacob M., 163
Hays, Helen Louise Thomas, 167
Hays, Jessie Herron Stutesman, 167
Hays, John Tennyson, 165
Hays, Mary Cain, 165
Hays, William (Will) Harrison, Sr., 165–67, *167*
Hayworth, Rita, 103
Hearst, William Randolph, 32
"Heart and Soul" (song), 49
Heb Shriner Show (television program), 309, 310
Heitkamp, Ernest L., 301
Helfant, Art, 4
Hemingway, Ernest, 344
Hemmer, C. W., 112
Henderson, Clayton, 102
Henderson, Nellie, 156
Hendricks, Eliza C. Morgan, 168
Hendricks, John, 168
Hendricks, Thomas Andrews, 14, 176–69, *168*
Hendricks, William, 168
Henry, Patrick, 60
Hepburn, Ralph, 306
Her Father's Daughter (novel), 334
Herb Shriner Time (television program), 309, 310
Herbert C. Brown Center for Borane Research, 37
Herschell, William, 336
Hersey, John, 223
Hesburgh, Anne Murphy, 170
Hesburgh, Theodore Bernard, 170
Hesburgh, Theodore Martin, 169–71, *170*
"Hiawatha" (poem), 292
Hibben, Thomas, E., Jr., 123, 124
Hickcox, Charlie, 77
Hicks, John W., 371
High Society (film), 274
Hill, Fred, 50
Hill, Sarah. *See* Fletcher, Sarah Hill
Hines, Earl "Fatha," 130
Hinkel, Edith Whitehill. *See* Clowes, Edith Whitehill Hinkel
Hinkle, Paul D. "Tony," 171–73
Hispaniola, 109
Historic New Harmony Inc., 267
Historical Notes on the Discovery and Settlement of the Territory Northwest of the Ohio, 99
History: Past, Present and Future Vol. I (CD set), 187

History of a Crime against the Food Law, The, 378
History of Indiana, 98, 99
History of Indiana from 1850 to the Present, A, 115
History of Indiana from Its Exploration to 1859, A, 115
History of Indiana University, 382
History of the Jews, 117
History of the New York Times, 1852–1921, p. 87
History of Woman Suffrage, 158
Hitchcock, Raymond, 317
Hitler, Adolf, 33, 379
Ho Chi Minh, 320
Hochstetler, Rose. *See* Bowen, Rose Hochstetter
Hohenberger, Frank M., 173–74, *173*
Hohenberger, Grace, 174
Holiday World and Splashin' Safari (Santa Claus, IN), 200, 201–2
Holiday World. *See* Holiday World and Splashin' Safari
Holley, Lillian M., 97
Holliday, John H., 181
Holliman, Ben, 315
Holman William S., 258
Holman, Jesse L., 148, 175–76, 258
Holmes, Oliver Wendell, 212
Homann, Mary Virginia. *See* Welsh, Mary Virginia Homann
Home Mission Association, 68
Home Missionary, 240
Homestead Act (1862), 195
Homestead Grays (baseball team), 58
Honeymooners, The (television program), 317
Honor Bright (play), 255
Hooker, John Lee, 54
Hoosier City: The Story of Indianapolis, 257
Hoosier Group, 2, 3, 123, 125, 137, 142, 155, 177, 301, 302, 324, 325
Hoosier Holiday, A (travel book), 101
Hoosier Mosaics (story collection), 350
Hoosier Salon, 104, 138, 312
Hoosier Veneer Company, 209, 336
Hoosiers, The (book), 254, 255
Hoover, Herbert, 33, 149, 188
Hope, Bob, 274, 317
Hopper, Floyd, 124, 176–78
Hopper, Hazel, 177, 178
Hord, Oscar B., 14, 168
Horne, Lena, 314
Hoshour, Samuel K., 362
House of a Thousand Candles (novel), 255
House without a Key, The (book), 57
Hovey, Edmund Otis, 178–80, *179*, 240
Hovey, Horace C., 179, 180
Hovey, Martha Freeman, 178
Hovey, Mary Carter, 178
Hovey, Mary Freeman, 180
Hovey, Roger, 178

How the Other Half Lives, 9
How to Train in Archery, 350
Howard, Georgia. *See* Hardick, Georgia Howard
Howard, Jane Blalock. *See* Charleston, Jane Blalock Howard
Howard, Roy W., 279
Howells, William Dean, 4, 34
Howley, Haviland Company (publisher), 103
Hubbard, Frank McKinney "Kin," 174, 180–82, *181*, 311, 317
Hubbard, Thomas, 181
Hudson, James "Pookie," 54, 55
Hudson, Rock, 92
Hughes, Fred, 54
Hull House (Chicago), 148, 149
Hulman, Anton, Jr. "Tony," 182–84, *183*, 287, 307
Hulman, Anton, Sr., 183
Hulman, Herman, 184
Hulman, Mary (Mari) Antonia, 183
Hulman, Mary Fendrich, 183
Hulman and Company, 183
Hulman and Cox (Terre Haute, IN), 92
Humphrey, Hubert, 224, 225
Hunter-Binder "Fair Schools" Bill (1949), 283, 290
Huntington (IN), 238
Hunt-Wesson, 287
Hurty, John Newell, 184–86, 300
Huston, Charles H., 288
Hutsell, Kay, 78

"I Get a Kick Out of You" (song), 274
"I Get Along without You Very Well" (song), 49
I Love Lucy (television program), 317
"I Want You Back" (song), 186
Ie Shima, 280
If You Don't Outdie Me (book), 174
"I'll Be There" (song), 186
I'll Show You the Town (novel and film), 87
Illinois Survey, 148
"I'm in Love Again" (song), 273
"I'm Just Wild about Harry" (song), 315, 316
"In the Closet" (song), 187
"In the Cool, Cool, Cool of the Evening" (song), 49
"In the Still of the Night" (song), 48, 274
Immoralist, The (play), 91
Impressions (music group), 54
In God We Trust: All Others Pay Cash (story collection), 308
In re Clark, 175
In re Leach, 139
In re Petition of Leach, 207
In the Afternoon (painting), 124
In the Arena (short story collection), 345
Independent, The magazine, 351
"Indiana" (poem), 26

Index

Indiana: A Redemption from Slavery (book), 109
Indiana: An Interpretation (book), 224
Indiana: From Frontier to Industrial Commonwealth, 50
Indiana Aircraft Trades Association, 75
Indiana and Indianans (book), 109
Indiana "Anti-Hate" Bill, 289, 290
Indiana Asbury College (Greencastle, IN). *See* DePauw University
Indiana Astronomical Society, 214, 216
Indiana Blacks in the Twentieth Century, 351
Indiana Boys' School, 13
Indiana College. *See* Indiana University
Indiana Daily Student, 85
Indiana Democrat, 98
Indiana Dunes, 104, 105
The Indiana Dunes Revealed: The Art of Frank Dudley (book), 105
Indiana 1816–1850: The Pioneer Era, 50
Indiana Election Returns, 354
Indiana Federation of Clubs, 10, 62, 232
Indiana Federation of Colored Women's Clubs, 126
Indiana Federation of Women's Clubs. *See* Indiana Federation of Clubs
Indiana Gazette, 332
Indiana General Assembly, 9, 10, 13, 18, 30, 50, 68, 69, 75, 102, 193, 209, 213, 214, 226, 240, 241, 259, 278, 303, 348, 349, 365, 368, 372, 385
Indiana Guide, 355
Indiana High School Athletic Association, 34
Indiana Historical Bureau, 115, 353, 354, 355
Indiana Historical Commission, 115, 209, 336
Indiana Historical Society, 20, 108, 115, 144, 212, 258, 259, 353, 354, 355
Indiana Home, 115
Indiana Home Economics Association, 232
Indiana Hospital for the Insane, 69, 121, 122
Indiana in the Civil War Era, 1850–1880, p. 353
Indiana Jewish Chronicle, 117
Indiana Journal, 209
Indiana Landmarks, 73, 212
Indiana Local History: A Guide to Study, with Some Biographical Notes, 115
Indiana Magazine of History, 49, 50, 99, 109, 114–15, 245, 382
Indiana Manual Labor Institute. *See* Franklin College
Indiana Medical Journal, 185
Indiana National Guard, 70, 318
Indiana Pacers, 313
Indiana Reformatory Institute for Women and Girls, 68, 69
Indiana Seminary. *See* Indiana University

Indiana State Bar Association, 206, 207, 208, 245
Indiana State College. *See* Indiana University
Indiana State Board of Charities, 116, 117
Indiana State Library, 108, 115
Indiana State Library and Historical Board, 258
Indiana State Penitentiary (Michigan City, IN), 96
Indiana State Teachers' Association, 241
Indiana State University (Terre Haute), 13
Indiana Statesman, 240
Indiana Supreme Court, 244, 245
Indiana Union of Literary Clubs, 232
Indiana University (Bloomington) 20, 101, 114, 115, 215, 216, 128, 133, 134, 176, 225, 226, 263, 313, 368, 369, 370, 380, 381, 382, 384, 385, 386
Indiana Vocational Technical College, 372
Indiana Woman's Rights Society, 348
Indiana Woman's Suffrage Association, 39
Indiana Woolen Manufacturing Company (Mishawaka, IN), 148
Indianapolis, 10, 24, 25, 34, 35, 159, 193, 328, 329
Indianapolis and Bellefontaine Railroad, 120
Indianapolis Benevolent Society, 24, 228
Indianapolis Charity Organization Society, 228
Indianapolis Clowns (baseball team), 59
Indianapolis Colored World, 330
Indianapolis 500 Mile Race, 8, 84, 102, 107, 118–19, 183, 305, 306, 307
Indianapolis Foundation. *See* Central Indiana Community Foundation
Indianapolis Free Kindergarten and Children's Aid Society, 24
Indianapolis Free Soil Banner, 362
Indianapolis Freeman, 125, 199, 200, 330, 360
Indianapolis Gazette, 26
Indianapolis Hebrew Congregation, 116, 117
Indianapolis Human Relations Council, 352
Indianapolis Journal, 23, 92, 293, 322
Indianapolis Magazine, 282
Indianapolis Motor Speedway, 7–8, 80, 106, 113, 118, 183, 305, 306
Indianapolis News, 34, 108, 109, 126, 158, 180, 181,182, 200, 209, 254, 275, 276, 336, 337
Indianapolis Recorder, 11, 127, 128, 156, 288, 330–31
Indianapolis Sentinel, 32, 108, 206, 254, 304
Indianapolis Star, 50, 51, 108, 109, 110, 143, 155, 156, 173, 174, 177, 183, 212, 256, 257, 271, 276, 302, 314, 319
Indianapolis Symphony Orchestra, 64, 65

Indianapolis Times, 108, 330
Indianapolis Urban League, 290
Indianapolis Woman's Club 62, 64, 303
Industrial Toxicology, 149
Ingersoll, Robert G., 153
Institute of Saints Cyril and Methodius, 145
Institute for Sex Research. *See* Kinsey Institute in Sex, Gender and Reproduction
Institute for Social and Religious Research, 216, 218
insulin, 64, 211
Intellectual Crisis in American Public Administration, The, 264
Interlaken School, 296
Internal Improvements in Early Indiana, 114
International Astronomical Union, 215
International Business Machine Corporation, 132
International Council of Women, 158, 303, 304
International Harvester Company, 74, 260
International Violin Competition, 135
Invincible (album), 187
The Irish Orators: A History of Ireland's Fight for Freedom, 32
Irving, Washington, 22
Irwin, Joseph Ireland, 235
Irwin, W. G., 83,84, 235, 357
Irwin Management Company, 236
Irwin Sweeney Miller Foundation, 237
Isn't It Romantic? (film), 257
It Seems Like Only Yesterday: Memoirs of Writing, Presidential Politics and the Diplomatic Life, 225
"It's All Your Fault" (song), 315
"It's De-Lovely" (song), 274
Ittner, Robert T., 252, 253
"I've Got You under My Skin" (song), 274
Ivy Tech Community College, 387

Jackson, Andrew, 31, 175, 176, 205, 238, 255
Jackson, Ed, 329, 330
Jackson, Helen. *See* Gougar, Helen Mar Jackson
Jackson, Henry M., 45
Jackson, Janet, 187
Jackson, Michael, 186–87, 374
Jackson 5, p. 186
Jacobs, Andrew, Jr., 51
Jacobs Manufacturing Company, 84
Jailbird (novel), 359
Jake Brake, 84
"Jam" (song), 187
James, Henry, 344
James, Starling, 289
James Allison Manufacturing Company, 7
James Whitcomb Riley Hospital for Children (Indianapolis), 293
James Whitcomb Riley Memorial Associa-

tion. *See* Riley Children's Foundation
Jameson, Haute Tarkington, 344
Jazz Review magazine, 249
Jean Shepherd's America (PBS series), 309
Jefferson, Blind Lemon, 130
Jefferson, Thomas, 19, 31, 161, 291
Jefferson and Hamilton: The Struggle for Democracy in America (book), 33
Jeffersonian Democrat (periodical), 32
Jeffersonville Evening News, 95
Jenckes, Ray, 188
Jenckes, Virginia Ellis, 187–89, *188*
Jenkins, Ab, 107
Jenkins, Charles Francis 189–91
Jenkins, Grace Love, 190
Jenkins Automobile Company, 190
Jenkins Laboratories, 190
Jenkins Television Corporation, 191
Jennings, Ann Gilmore Hay, 192
Jennings, Clarissa Barbee, 192, 193
Jennings, Jacob, 191
Jennings, Jonathan, 23, 175, 191–93, *192*, 332
Jennings, Mary Kennedy, 191
Jensen, Jens, 104
Jessie Woodbridge, et al. v. Housing Authority of Evansville, Indiana, 290
Jewish Federation of Indianapolis, 110
Jewish Welfare Board, 116
John Herron Art Institute, 64, 124, 324, 325
John Sexton and Company, 155
John, Elton, 374
Johnny Appleseed (classical work), 49
Johnson, Andrew, 12, 169, 239, 251
Johnson, Jane Janette. *See* Thomas, Jane Janette Johnson
Johnson, Judy, 58
Johnson, Lonnie, 130
Johnson, Lyndon, 47, 142, 224, 372
Johnson, Rhoda. *See* Coffin, Rhoda M.
Johnston, Albert Sidney, 363
Johnston, Sarah Bush. *See* Lincoln, Sarah Bush Johnston
Jolson, Al, 102
Jones, Alexander, 173
Jones, Bobby, 77, 190
Jones, Charlotte Elliott. *See* Dunn, Charlotte Elliot Jones
Jones, Isham, 48
Jones, Quincy, 186, 187
Jones, William, 213
Jordan, David Starr, 101
Journal of Dental Research, 253
Joy, Henry B., 119
Jubilee (musical), 274
Julian, George Washington, 62, 193–95, *194*
Julian, Isaac, 194
Julian, Jacob, 194
Julian, Laura Giddings, 62

Julian, Rebecca, 194
Jungle, The (novel), 19

Kaltenborn, H. V., 87
Kansas-Nebraska Act, 195, 250
Kansas City Star, 230, 275
Kathie (painting), 124
Katz, Martin, 145
Kaufman, Nate, 128
Kazan, Elia, 91, 92
Keady, Gene, 204
Keaton, Buster, 317
Keepnew, Orrin, 247, 249
Keillor, Garrison, 309
Kelly, Alice, 361
Kennedy, Joe, 74, 343
Kennedy, John F., 47, 170, 201, 214, 224, 225
Kennedy, Robery F., 149, 151, 224, 225, 299
Kennedy, Rose, 74, 343
Kent, Chancellor, 22
Kentuckians (music group), 246
Keppard, Freddie, 130
Kern, John W., 31, 32, 343
Khrushchev, Nikita, 47
Kickapoo (tribe), 347
Kimball, Sumner, 190
Kimsey, Lois I. *See* Marshall, Lois I. Kimsey
Kindergarten Normal Training School, 24, 25
King Oliver, 130
King, Martin Luther, Jr., 145, 149, 151
Kinsey (film), 197
Kinsey, Alfred Charles 195–98, *196*, 369
Kinsey, Clara Bracken McMillen, 196
Kinsey Institute for Research in Sex, Gender and Reproduction, 196, 197
Kipling, Rudyard, 344
Kirby, Amanda, 138
Kiss Me Kate (musical), 274
Kizer, Margaret Monks, 244, 245
Knight, Bob, 204
Knopf, Alfred, 272
Knowledge for What?, 218
Knox, Aurilla Harvey, 199, 200
Knox, Elwood, 200
Knox, George Levy, 198–200, 360, 361
Knox, Nellie, 200
Knox, William, 200
Koch, Dan, 201, 202
Koch, Kristi. *See* George, Kristi Koch
Koch, Lori, 202
Koch, Louis J., 200–201, 202
Koch, Natalie, 201
Koch, Pat Yellig, 201
Koch, Philip, 201
Koch, William, Jr. (Will), 200, 201, 202
Koch, William A., Sr., 200, 201
Koch Development Corporation, 201
Koch Family, 200–202

Koffman, Marilyn Ruth. *See* Glick, Marilyn Ruth Koffman
Kokomo (IN), 164, 328, 329, 375
Koop, Everett, 31
Kountze, Eugenie. *See* Nicholson, Eugenie Kountze
Kovacs, Ernie, 317
Krementz, Jill. *See* Vonnegut, Jill Krementz
Kriebel, Robert, 278
Krout, Mary Hannah, 364
Ku Klux Klan, 50, 11, 110, 117, 130, 224, 256, 281, 328, 329, 384

L. S. Ayres and Company, 266
La Blame, Augustin de, 233
La Misèrie (painting), 301
La Porte Herald, 279
Ladies Home Journal magazine, 209, 336, 366, 367
Lafayette (IN), 277, 278
Lafayette Bridge Company, 270
Lafayette Call, 3
Lafayette Courier, 117, 139, 278
Lafayette Journal, 278, 279
Lafayette Journal and Courier, 112, 202
Lafayette Morning News, 3
Lafayette, Marquis de, 94
LaGuardia, Fiorello, 298
Lahr, Bert, 274
Lakewood Plan, 264
Lakin, Mary Elizabeth "Libbie." *See* Steele, Mary Elizabeth "Libbie" Lakin
Lamb, John E., 32
Lambert, Ward Lewis "Piggy," 202–5, *203*, 384
Lampland, Carol O., 215
Land O' Lakes Statement, 170
The Land, The People, 272
Land of Sky and Song (painting), 104
Landsberg, Clara, 150
Lane, Franklin K., 293
Lane, Henry S., 168, 250
Laney, Lucy, 126
Langsdale, Kate Maude. *See* Beverdige, Kate Maude Langsdale
Lanier, Alexander Chambers, 205
Lanier, Drusilla Doughty, 205
Lanier, Elizabeth Gardiner, 205
Lanier, James Franklin Doughty, 205–6
Lanier, Mary McClure, 205
Lanier, Sidney, 206
Lannon, Dorothy Wolfe. *See* Nicholson, Dorothy Wolfe Lannon
Lanterman, Bertha. *See* Haynes, Bertha Lanterman
Laramie (television series), 49
Laredo, Jaime, 134
LaSalle Business Bulletin, 85
Lasker, Albert, 357
Lasker, Mary, 298
Last Gleam, The (Painting), 124

Late Afternoon (painting), 124
Lawrence, Gertrude, 273, 274, 315
Laws, William, 236
"Lazy Bones" (song), 49
"Lazy River" (song), 48
Leach, Antoinette Dakin, 206–8
Leach, George, Jr., 201
Leach, George W., 207
Leach, Hortense Eugenia, 207
Lead Kindly Light (painting), 302
Leadville (CO) Chronicle, 108
League of Nations, 222
League of Women Voters, 64, 365, 366
Leave It to Me (musical), 274
Lebanon Reporter, 276
Lee, Alice. *See* Thompson, Alice Lee
Lee, Robert E., 195
Leedy, U. G., 113
Leedy Drum Company, 113
Lefebvre, Jim, 294, 295
Leopold, Aldo, 44
Les Girls (film), 274
Lesueur, Charles Alexandre, 270
"Let's Do It" (song), 273
"Let's Fly Away" (song), 273
"Letter That Never Came, The" (song), 103
Lewis, Jerry, 91
Lewis, John L., 152
Lewis, Maida. *See* Dudley, Maida Lewis
Lewis, Meriwether, 61
Lewis, Sinclair, 87
Lewis, William Draper, 22
Liberty Bell 7, p. 140, 141
Lie Down in Darkness (novel), 57
Lieber, Edith. *See* Vonnegut Edith Lieber.
Lieber, Emma Rappaport, 209
Leiber, Herman, 155, 327
Lieber, Richard N., 89, 90, 208–10, *208*, 335
Life and Poems of Sarah T. Bolton, 27
Life and Work of Susan B. Anthony, The, 158
Life as I Remember It: As a Slave and a Freeman, 200
Life magazine, 43, 224
Life of John Worth Kern, The (book), 32
Life with Health: A Textbook on Physiology, Hygiene, and Sanitation, 186
Lilly, Eli (Colonel), 20, 210, 211, 212, 328
Lilly, Eli (Mr. Eli), 73, 120, 210, 211, 212, 353, 354, 355
Lilly, Josiah K., Jr. (J. K. Jr., Joe), 210, 211, 212
Lilly, Josiah K., Sr., 210, 211
Lilly, Lilly Ridgely (Mrs. J. K. Sr.), 210
Lilly, Ruth, 212
Lilly Endowment, 212
Lilly Family, 210–12
Lilly Library (Indiana University), 211
Lilly magazine, 348
Lima (OH), 96
Lincoln, Abraham, 13, 19, 40, 51, 155, 168, 195, 212–14, 225, 250, 270, 363, 364

Lincoln, Nancy Hanks, 212, 214
Lincoln, Sarah, 213
Lincoln, Sarah Bush Johnston, 212
Lincoln, Thomas, 212, 213
Lincoln Boyhood National Memorial, 201, 214
Lincoln Highway, 118, 119
Lincoln Highway Commission, 119
Link, Goethe, 214–16
Link, Helen, 215, 216
Lipchitz, Jaques, 267
Literary Digest, 344
Little Anthony and the Imperials (music group), 248
Little Brown Girl, A (painting), 155, 156
"Little Orphant Annie" (poem), 143, 292
Little, Harvey, 259, 260
Little Turtle. *See* Mihšihkinaahkwa
Little Paper, The, 373, 374
Locomotive Fireman's Magazine, 92, 157
Loesser, Fank, 49
Löfftz, Ludwig von, 327
Logansport Canal Telegraph. See *Logansport Telegraph*
Logansport Telegraph, 99
Longfellow, Henry Wadsworth, 292
Look magazine, 224
Louisville Courier, 95
Love, Grace. *See* Jenkins, Grace Love
Love, John, 123
"Love for Sale" (song), 273
"Love Will Find a Way: (song), 315
"Love You Save, The " (song), 186
Lowe-Victor Company (Chicago), 106
Lowell, Abbott Lawrence, 149
Lowell, James Russell, 293
Lowell Observatory (AZ), 215
Loyal Sons: The Story of the Four Horsemen, 294
Lubitsch, Ernst, 274
Luce, Henry, 268
Lugar, Richard G. 53, 288, *289*
Lumsden, John, 129
Lusk, John, 209
Lusk, Salmon, 336
Luther, Martin, 284
Lyle, Aubey, 315
lynching, 11
Lynd, Andrea, 218
Lynd, Helen Merrell, 216–18
Lynd, Robert Staughton, 216–18, **216**
Lynd, Staughton, 218
M. Rumely Company, 296

MacBeth (play), 91
MacDonald, Ballard, 102
MacDonald, Caroline. *See* Blackford, Caroline MacDonald
MacDonald, George, 23
MacLean, Arthur, 20
MacLeod, George, 267
Maclure, William, 218–20, *219*, 269–70

Macmillan Company (publisher), 56
Macon, Uncle Dave, 130
Mad Magazine, 308
Madam C. J. Walker Manufacturing Company, 34, 281, 282, 284
Mademoiselle magazine, 308
Madison, James, 23, 162, 193, 347
Madison, James H., 49, 50, 51, 355
Madison and Indianapolis Railroad, 205
Magnificent Ambersons, The (novel), 345
Maier, Victor, 215
Main Chance, The (novel), 255
Malone, Annie Turnbo, 360
Malott, Sarah. *See* DePauw, Sarah Malott
Man Nobody Knows, The (book), 57
Man without a Country, A (essay collection), 359
Mandler, Henry, 139
Manhattan Melodrama (film), 98
Mann, Billy, 5
Mansfield (OH) News, 182
Mao Zedong, 235
Marion (IN), 11, 12
Marion County Superior Court, 288
Marion Daily Chronicle, 367
Marshall, Daniel, 220
Marshall, George C., 318, 319, 320
Marshall, John, 19, 22
Marshall, Lois I. Kimsey, 220, 222
Marshall, Martha, 220
Marshall, Sarah. *See* Mills, Sarah Marshall
Marshall, Thomas R., 88, 109, 220–23, *221*, 343
Marshall, Thurgood, 290
Martain, Lily, 349
Martin, Billy, 224
Martin, Clyde, *196*
Martin, Dean, 91
Martin, Dickie, 224
Martin, Frances Smethurst, 224
Martin, Glenn, 16
Martin, John Bartlow, 223–25, *223*
Martin, John Frederick, 224, 225
Martin, John W., 224
Martin, Mary, 274
Martinelli Stradivarius (violin), 133, 135
Martino, 249
Martinsville Reporter, 272
Marvin, John Gage, 22
Marx, Groucho, 310, 318
Mason (automobile), 105
Mason, Benjamin Franklin, 271, 272
Mason, Edward, 105
Mason, Laura, 271
Mason Motor Car Company, 105
Massacres of the Mountains: History of the Indiana Wars of the Far West (book), 108
Massey, Raymond, 91
Mastersounds (music group), 249
Matthews, Mary, 232
Matthews, Meredith, 232

Matthews, Victoria Earle, 126
Mattison, Donald Magnus, 124, 177
Mature, Victor, 103
Mauck, Mary Frances Ball, 16
Maxwell, Bazaleel, 225
Maxwell, David Hervey, 225–27
Maxwell, J. D., 227
Maxwell, Margaret Anderson, 225
Maxwell, Mary E. Dunn, 225
Mayerstein, Mildred M. *See* Feuerlicht, Mildred Mayerstein
Mayfield, Curtis, 54
Mays, William G., 330
Maysville (CO) Democrat, 108
McCabe, George, 377, 378
McCabe, James, 140
McCarthy, Eugene, 225
McCarthy, Joseph, 47, 88, 276
McCaslin, Sybil. *See* Bowers, Sybil McCaslin
McClean, John, 176
McClellan, George B., 195
McClellan, John, 47
McClure, Mary. *See* Lanier, Mary McClure
McCormick's Creek State Park (Owen County), 209
McCoury, Del, 247
McCracken, Branch, 128
McCray, Warren, 232
McCulloch, Alice, 227
McCulloch, Carleton, 227
McCulloch, Harriet, 227
McCulloch, Oscar Carleton, 24, 25, 227–28
McCullough, Fanny, 213
McCutcheon, John T., 3, 4, 138
McDonald, Butler and Mason (law firm), 19
McDonald and Butler (law firm), 108
McDowell, Ephraim, 225
McGovern, George, 224
McHale, Frank M., 229
McKay, Wanda. *See* Carmichael, Wanda McKay
McKinley, William, 160, 165, 331
McKinley Tariff Act, 160
McMillen, Clara Bracken. *See* Kinsey, Clara Bracken McMillen
McMurray, Fred, 102
McNagny, William F., 220
McNutt, John Crittenden, 228
McNutt, Kathleen Timolat, 229
McNutt, Louise, 229
McNutt, Paul V., 97, 138, 197, 210, 228–31, *229*, 241, 242, 300, 368, 370, 378
McNutt, Ruth Neely, 228
McTaggert, James, 108
McWilliams, Moses, 360
Meade, Kevin, 74
Meadow Folks Story Hour, The (children's textbook), 144

Meanwell, Walter E. "Doc," 204, 294
Meat Inspection Act, 19, 160
Meck, Mary Powers, 137
Meek, Alexander A., 205
Meier, Richard, 267
Meinardi, Ruth. *See* Carmichael, Ruth Meinardi
Mekinges (wife of William Conner), 72
Melvin Simon and Associates. *See* Simon Property Group
Mellencamp, John, 247
Mencken, H. L., 101, 296
Mentone (IN), 16, 17
Mercer, Johnny, 48, 49
Meredith, Emily. *See* Nicholson, Emily Meredith
Meredith, Henry, 231
Meredith, Solomon, 231
Meredith, Virginia Claypool, 231–33
Merman, Ethel, 274
Merrell, Helen, *See* Lynd Helen Merrell
Merrill, Catharine, 40
Merrill, Samuel, 40, 56
Merrill, Samuel, Jr., 56
Merson, Luc Olivier, 311
Messing, Mayer, 116
Metal Polishers, Buffers, Platers, Brass Moulders, Brasss and Silver Workers International Union, 71
Metheny, Pat, 249
Metro-Goldwyn-Mayer, 274
Merv Oasis, The (book), 148
Metzel, Katherine. *See* Debs, Katherine Metzel
Metzner, August, 1
Mexican Hayride (musical), 274
Miami (FL), 347
Miami (tribe), 233–35, 291, 292
Miami Beach (FL), 119
Miami National Reserve, 291, 292
Middletown (book), 216, 218
Middletown in Transition (book), 218
Midlander, The (novel), 345
Midway Island, 323
Mihšihkinaahkwa (Little Turtle), 233–35, *233*, 291
Mikesell, Carol. *See* Bowen, Carol Mikesell
Milburn, George, 260
Miller, Flournoy, 315
Miller, Hugh, 235
Miller, J. Irwin, 84, 235–37, *236*
Miller, Martin Boots, 244
Miller, Merle, 37, 38, 39, 40
Miller, Nettie Sweeney, 235, 237
Miller, Xenia, 237
Milligan, H. J., 240
Milligan, Lambdin Purdy, 237–39
Mills, Caleb, 23, 178, 179, 180, 239–41, *239*
Mills, Florence, 315
Mills, Sarah Marshall, 240
Mills Brothers (singing group), 102

Milton, John, 254
Minh, Ho Chi, 320. *See also* Ho Chi Minh
Minnetrista Cultural Center (Muncie), 14, 16
Minton, Sherman, 241–43, *242*
Mission on the Ouabache, The (book), 109
Mississippi Valley Historical Review (journal), 115
Missouri Compromise (1820), 195
Moberly, Stephen, 51
Modern Art (journal), 143
Moller, Annie, 131
Moller, Lillie Evelyn, *See* Gilbreth, Lillian Moller
Moller, William, 131
Molly Brown, 142
Mongomery-Johnson Quintet, 249
Monks, Agnes, 244
Monks, Alice, 244
Monks, Elizabeth White Teal, 244
Monks, George Washington, 244
Monks, Leander J., 244–45
Monks, Margaret, 244
Monks, Mary Irwin, 244
Monks, Mary. *See* Kizer, Margaret Monks
Monks Robbins Starr and Goodrich (law firm), 245
Monroe, Birch, 246
Monroe, Charles, 246
Monroe, James, 269
Monroe, William "Bill" Smith, 245–47
Monroe Brothers (music group)
Monsieur Beaucaire (novel), 344
Montgomery, Buddy, 249
Montgomery, Jim, 77
Montgomery, John Leslie "Wes," 247–49, *248*
Montgomery, Monk, 248, 249
Montgomery, Serene, 248
Moonrise and Twilight (painting), 124
Moore, Betty. *See* Grissom, Betty
Moore, Paul, 352
Moorehead, W. K., 20
Moores, Charles W., 56
Moorland, Jesse, 361
Morals for Moderns (short stories), 87
Moravians, 72
Moreau, Basile, 320, 321
Morehouse, Louise E., 302
Morehouse, Lucille E., 156
Morgan, Eliza C. *See* Hendricks, Eliza C. Morgan
Morgan, John Hunt, 259
Moriah Fund, 111
Morison, Samuel Eliot, 323, 324
Morland, Dorothy, 124
Morse, Elijah, 139
Morton, Jelly Roll, 130
Morton, Lucinda Burbank, 250
Morton Oliver P., 12, 13, 68, 159, 167, 168, 194, 195, 213, 250–51, *251*, 349, 363

Moss, Ralph W., 378
Mossadegh, Mohammed, 320
Mother Angela. *See* Gillespie, Eliza Marie
Mother and Child (painting), 312
Mother from the Hills (painting), 312
Mother Theodore Guérin. *See* Guérin, Saint Theodora
Motion Picture Association of America, 165, 166, 167
Motion Picture Producers and Distributors of America. *See* Motion Picture Association of America
Motley, Constance Baker, 290
Motown, 55, 186
Mott, Lucretia, 348, 349
Mount Palomar Observatory (CA), 215
Mug, Sister Theodosia, 147
Muhler, Joseph Charles, 252–54
Muir, John, 334
Mullen, Stella. *See* Deam, Stella Mullin
Muncie (IN), 2, 14, 15, 16, 216, 217
Muncie Art School, 124
Muncie Evening Press, 271
Muncie Star, 275
Munich (Germany), 1–2, 123–24, 326, 327
Murphy, Charles, "Stretch," 204
Murphy, Jimmy, 106
Murrow, Edward R., 87, 88
Musset, Lucy. *See* Allison, Lucy Musset
Mussolini, Benito, 33
My Gal Sal (film), 103
"My Heart Belongs to Daddy" 274
"My Resistance Is Low" (song), 49
Myaamiaki. *See* Miami
Myers, Mary Frame. *See* Thomas, Mary Frame Myers
Myers, T. E. "Pop," 307
Mythology, 150

Nabors, Jim, 102
Nall, Adeline, 91
National Aeronautics and Space Administration, 140, 141
National American Woman Suffrage Association, 63, 64, 365, 373
National Archery Association, 350
National Association for the Advancement of Colored People, 10, 11, 12, 282, 283, 284, 288, 290, 380
National Association of State Aviation Officials, 76
National Bar Association, 289
National Barn Dance (radio program), 246
National Basketball Association, 388
National Basketball League, 388
National Collegiate Athletic Association, 172, 202, 204, 382, 383
National Committee to Uphold Constitutional Government, 297
National Conference of Jewish Charities, 117
National Conference of Charities and Corrections, 228
National Conference on State Parks, 210
National Council of Churches, 235, 236
National Environmental Protection Act, 44, 45
National Institute of Occupational Safety and Health, 149
National Institutes of Health, 298, 299
National Invitational Tournament, 172
National Labor Relations Board, 145
National Safety Council, 29
National Woman Suffrage Association, 158, 208
Natoequah (wife of Jean Baptiste Richardville), 291
"Ne Dormiat Deus" (poem), 27
Nebergal, William, 253
Neely, Ruth. *See* McNutt, Ruth Neely
Negro American League, 59
Negro Baseball League, 200
Negro Congressmen (mural), 301
Negro in Indiana before 1900, The, 351, 352
Negro National League, 58
Negro Slavery in the North: Its Legal and Constitutional Aspects, 353
Neighbor (painting), 138
Neither Dead nor Sleeping (book), 304
Nelson, William Rockhill, 275
Nelson, Willie, 247
Nettleton, Lois, 309
Neubacher, Selma. *See* Steele, Selma Neubacher
Neumann, Georg Karl, 21
New Albany (IN), 94–95
New Albany and Salem Railroad, 94
New Harmony (IN), 218, 220, 267–68, 269, 270
New Harmony Project, 268
"New Muleskinner Blues" (song), 246
New Republic, 378
New View of Society, A, 269
New York Age, 200, 361
New York Evening Journal, 32
New York Evening Mail, 296
New York Herald, 143
New York Herald Tribune, 379
New York Lincoln Giants (baseball team), 58
New York Times, 23, 43, 86, 87, 171, 256, 293, 379, 387
New York World, 32
New Yorker, The (musical), 273
New, Harry, 322
Newby, Arthur, 7, 8, 118
Newcomb, Horatio, 40, 120
Newland, Catherine. *See* DePauw, Catherine Newland
Nicaragua, 255
Nicholson, Dorothy Wolfe Lannon, 255
Nicholson, Edward Willis, 254
Nicholson, Emily Meredith, 254
Nicholson, Eugenia Kountze, 254, 255, 256
Nicholson, Meredith, 3, 56, 254–56, 255, 345
Night and Day (film), 274
"Night and Day" (song). 274
Night Fishing in Haiti (painting), 302
Nimitz, Chester, 323, 324
Nineteenth Amendment, 63, 158, 366
Ninotchka (film), 274
Nitschelm, Marie. *See* Stark, Marie Nitschelm
Nixon, Richard, 149, 171, 235
Nobel, Alfred, 265
Nobel Prize, 36, 37, 265
Noble, Noah, 227, 354
Noblesville, 72, 73
Noguchi, Isamu, 296
Nolan, Alan, 256
Nolan, Jeannette Covert, 256–57
Nolan, Kathleen, 256
Nolan, Val, Jr., 256
Nolan, Val, Sr., 256, 257
Noll, John F., 170, 171
North Western Christian University. *See* Butler University
Notes: Critical and Biographical, Collection of W. T. Walters, 143
Notre Dame de Liesse/Descent of the Holy Spirit (sculpture), 267
Novick, Peter, 114
Nowlin Mound, 20
Nymph Errant (musical), 274

Obama, Barack, 374, 376
O'Bannon, Frank, 51
Oberholtzer, Madge, 330
O'Brien, Agnes. *See* Fletcher, Agnes O'Brien
O'Brien, Anna Belle Cook, 257
O'Brien, Cornelius, 257–59
O'Brien, Michael, 92
Observations on the Geology of the United States, 219
Occidental Literary Club (Terre Haute, IN), 92
Ochiltree, Sam, 224
O'Donovan, Edmond, 148
Off the Wall (album), 186
Office of Defense Health and Welfare Services, 230
Office of War Information, 87–88
Official Detective magazine, 224
O'Hara, Eliot, 177
Old Familiar Faces (essay collection), 255
Old Northwest, The, 354
Oldway and the New, The (film), 222
Oliver, James, 259–62, *259*
Oliver and Bissell, 260
Oliver and Little, 259, 260
Oliver Bissell and Company, 260

Oliver Chilled Plow, 260
Oliver Corporation, 261
Oliver Steel Plow Works. *See* Oliver Corporation
Ollie Hoopnoodle's Haven of Bliss (television film), 309
O'Malley, William Patrick, 97
On Being a Negro in America (book), 57
On Shame and the Search for Identity, 218
"On the Banks of the Wabash, Far Away" (song), 101, 102, 103
On the Banks of the Wabash: The Life and Music of Paul Dresser (book), 102
One Hundred Years of American Psychiatry, 1844–1944, 122
One Way Out (mural), 301
One World (book), 380
Oral Health Research Institute, 253
Orchard School, 64, 65
Order of American Knights, 238
organic chemistry, 36, 37
Orr, Joanne (Josie) Wallace, 261, 263
Orr, Mary Kay Davis, 263
Orr, Robert, 31, 261–63, *261*
Orville Redenbacher's Gourmet Popping Corn, 287
Ostrom, Elinor, 263–65; *263*
Ostrom, Vincent, 263–65
Our Alley (painting), 177
Our Temperance Herald, 139
Outdoor Indiana magazine, 258
Overbeck, Elizabeth, 266
Overbeck, Hannah, 266, 267
Overbeck, John, 265
Overbeck, Margaret, 266
Overbeck, Mary, 266, 267
Overbeck, Sarah, 265
Overbeck Pottery, 265–67
Overbeck Sisters, 265–67
Overtaken by Events: The Dominican Crisis from Fall of Trujillo to the Civil War (book), 225
Owen, Anne Caroline Dale 269
Owen David Dale, 270, 220,
Owen Richard, 270
Owen, Jane Blaffer, 267–68
Owen, Keith Dale, 268
Owen, Richard, 220, 278
Owen, Robert, 220, 268–70, *269*, 285, 286
Owen, Robert Dale, 26
Owen, William, 270

Pacific Jazz Records, 249
"Paddle Your Own Canoe" (poem), 26
Paddle Your Own Canoe and Other Poems, 27
Page, Eleanor. *See* Hapgood, Eleanor Page
Paige, Satchel, 58, 59
Palm Sunday (essay and short story collection), 359
Palmer, A. Mitchell, 296

Panama Hattie (musical), 274
Paraguay, 255
Paris, 324
Paris from 1928 (musical), 273
Parke, Benjamin, 175
Parker, Alton B., 343
Parker, Byrd, 125
Parker, Charlie, 249
Parker, Crawford F., 371
Parker, Dan, 53
Parker, John, 1
Parks, Rosa, 52
Parlin and Orendorff Plow Works (Canton, IL). *See* International Harvester Company
Party Battles of the Jackson Period, The (book), 32
Patton, Charley, 130
Paul, king of Greece, 151
Paul Baer Municipal Airport, 75
"Paul Revere's Ride" (poem), 292
Paulson, John, 71
Pecan (Miami chief), 290, 291
Peden, Rachel, 271–73, *271*
Peden, Richard, 272
Peggy from Paris (musical comedy), 4
Pei, I. M., 237
Peirce, Martin, 277
Pelli, Cesar, 237
penicillin, 211
Penrod (novel), 345
Penrose, Valentine, 174
Peoples Bank, 135
People's National Bank, 257
Peoples Popular Monthly magazine, 272
People-to-People International. 287, 288
Perkins, Paul, 249
Perkins, Samuel, 23
Pestalozzi, Johann Heinrich, 219, 220
Pet Duck, The (painting), 312
phantoscope, 190
Philadelphia Stars (baseball team), 59
Philadelphia Story (film and play), 274
Philanthropist (ship), 220
Philippines, 230, 323, 324
Phillips, U. B., 352
Phoenix Gazette, 275
Phyllis Wheatley Young Women's Christian Association, 126, 282
Picture Book, The (painting), 312
Pierce, Franklin, 23, 26, 168, 250
Pierce, Richard B., 81
Pike, Hezzie B., 155
Pinchot, Gifford, 334
Pioneer (automobile), 164
Pittsburgh Crawfords (baseball team), 58
Playboy magazine, 308
Player Piano (novel), 359
Plessy v. Ferguson, 288
Plump, Bobby, 171
Plymouth Congregation Church (Indianapolis), 227

Poe, Edgar Allen, 27
Poems, 26
Pofall, Bill, 272
polio vaccine, 298, 299
Polk, James K., 213, 333
Polk, Josiah, 72
Pomeroy, Wardell, 196
Popcorn Festival (Valparaiso, IN), 287
Porter, William H., 330
Porter, Albert G., 22, 69
Porter, Beulah Wright, 126
Porter, Charles Dorwin, 334, 335
Porter, Cole, 49, 273–75
Porter, Jeannette, 335
Porter, Kate Cole, 273, 274
Porter, Linda Lee Thomas, 273, 274
Porter, Russell W., 215
Porter, Samuel Fenwick, 273
Porter, Velma, 51, 53
Posey, Thomas, 23, 175, 189
Potawatomi (tribe), 347
Powers, Fremont, 34
Practical Patchwork Company, 367
Prairie Club, 104
Prang, Louis, 143
Presley, Elvis, 186, 247
Pressler, Menahem, 134
Prest-O-Lite Storage Battery Company, 7, 118, 119
Preucil, William, 133
Prime Time program, 262
Prince of India, The (novel), 364
Princeton Farms. 287
Private Life of Helen of Troy, The (book), 57
Proceedings of the Indiana Academy of Sciences, 89
Procter and Gamble, 253
Project Mercury, 140, 141
Prophet, The. *See* Tenskawatawa
Prophetstown, 346–47, 348
Prunk, Hattie, 125
Psychology of Management, The, 132
Public Administration Review (periodical), 44
Public Service Commission, 242
Public Welfare Loan Association, 110
Public Works of Art Project, 124
Publishers Weekly magazine, 308
Pugh, James A., 105
Puis X, pope, 145
Pulitzer, Ralph, 32
Pulitzer Prize, 345, 354
Pulliam, Eugene Collins, 270, 275–77, *276*
Pulliam, Eugene Smith, 275–77
Pulliam, Jane Bleecher, 276
Pulliam, Martha Ott, 276
Pulliam, Myrta Smith, 276
Pulliam, Nina Mason, 270, 272, 276
Pulliam, Russell, 275
Pullman Palace Car Company, 93
Purdue, Charles, 277

Purdue, John, 13, 277–79
Purdue, Mary, 277
Purdue Agriculturist magazine, 286
Purdue University (West Lafayette), 13, 36, 37, 132, 204, 231, 232, 277, 278, 286, 288; band, 112–13
Pure Food and Drug Act (1906), 376, 377, 378
Pure Food and Drug Act (IN), 185
Pyle, Ernest "Ernie" Taylor, 85, 279–81, *279*
Pyramid of Success, 384

Quakers. *See* Society of Friends
Quayle, Dan, 31, 277
Quezon, Manuel L., 230
Quilts: Their Story and How to Make Them, 367

Radio Corporation of America, 191
Raggedy Andy (doll), 143, 144
Raggedy Ann (doll), 143, 144
Raggedy Ann Stories, 143
"Raggedy Man, The" (poem), 143
Rainy Night, Étaples (painting), 301
Ralston, Samuel M., 18, 108, 109, 110, 117, 119, *192*, 209, 210, 343
Ralston Purina, 357
Rambler (automobile), 105
Rand, Ayn, 57
Rannels, William W., 112
Ransom, Freeman Briley, 281–82, 360, 361
Ransom, Willard B., 282–84, *283*
Rapp, Frederick Reichert, 285, 286
Rapp, George (Johan Georg), 269, 270, 220, 284–86
Rappaport, Emma. *See* Lieber, Emma Rappaport
Rawls, Lou, 54
Ray, James Brown, 115, 175, 354
Ray, Nicholas, 92
Readings in Indiana History, 115
Ready, Fire, Aim (book), 73
Reagan, Ronald, 30, 31
Real Silk Hosiery Mills, 110
Real Silk Investments Inc., 110, 111
Rebel without a Cause (novel and film), 90, 91, 92
Reckoning, The, 262
Red Bandana (painting), 177
Red Book magazine, 87
Red City, The (painting), 124
Red, Hot and Blue (musical), 274
Redding, Saunders, 57
Redenbacher, Orville Clarence, 113, 286–88, *287*
Redpath Jubilee Quartet, 314
Reed, Jimmy, 54
Reese, Addison, 26
"Regardin' Terry Hut" (poem), 92
Rehm, Alberta, 312

Reid, Dorian Fielding, 150, 151
Reid, Doris Fielding, 150
Reid, Edith Gittings, 150
Reid, Harry Fielding, 150
Reinhardt, Django, 249
Remember the Night (film), 102
"Remember the Time" (song), 187
Reminiscences (book), 66, 67
Remsberg, Rich, 86
Remsen, Ira, 378
Revised Laws of Indiana, The, 213
Rhyne, Melvin, 249
Rice, Alexander, 139
Richard, Samuel, 1
Richards, Myra R., 337
Richardson, Henry, Jr., 288–90, *289*
Richardville, Catherine, 291
Richardville, Jean Baptiste (Peshewa or the Wildcat), 290–92
Richardville, Joseph, 291
Richardville, Joseph Drouet de, 290
Richardville, LaBlonde, 291
Richardville, Susan, 291
Richie, Lionel, 187
Richmond Art Association, 374
Richmond Item, 372
Richmond Morning News, 372
Richmond Palladium, 372
Richmond Palladium-Item, 373
Richmond Sun-Telegram, 372
Rickenbacker, Eddie, 105, 183, 306
Rickey, Branch, 59
Ridgely, Lilly. *See* Lilly, Lilly Ridgely
Riggs, T. Lawson, 273
Riis, Jacob, 9
Riker, Dorothy L., 120, 354, 355
Riley Children's Foundation, 293
Riley, James Whitcomb, 3, 51, 56, 92, 123, 138, 143, 225, 254, *255*, 292–94, *293*, 304, 328, 345
Riley, Reuben, 292
Riley, Teddy, 187
Ris, Wally, 78
Ristine, Richard O., 371
"Riverboat Shuffle" (song), 48
Riverside (record label), 247, 249
Robbins, Gayle, 332
Roberson, Oscar, 128
Robert Lee Blaffer Trust. *See* Blaffer Foundation
Robert W. Long Hospital (Indianapolis), 11
Roberts, Fiddlin' Doc, 130
Roberts, Hadley, 24
Robertson, Nellie Armstrong, 354
Robertson, Oscar, 82
Robeson, Paul, 77
Robinson, A'lelia Walker, 281, 360, 361
Robinson, Jackie, 58, 59, 127, 128
Robinson, Susannah. *See* Tarkington, Susannah Robinson
"Rock with You" (song), 186

Rockefeller, John D., 95, 216, 361
Rockefeller Foundation, 197, 198
"Rockin' Chair" (song), 48
"Rockin' Robin" (song), 186
Rockne, Knute, 294–96; *295*
Rockville Tribune, 336, 337
Rogers, Edith, *32*
Rogers, Will, 86, 118, 309, 311
Rohrbough, Malcolm, 277
Rolling Stone magazine, 187
Rolling Stones (music group), 54
Roman Way, The, 150, 151
Roofless Church (New Harmony), 267
Roosevelt, Eleanor, 280
Roosevelt, Franklin D., 31, 33, 188, 189, 230, 241, 242, 243, 254, 255, 279, 315, 319, 343, 378, 379
Roosevelt, Theodore, 3, 5, 18, 88, 160, 165, 209, 222, 296, 343, 345, 377, 378, 381
Roppolo, Leon, 130
Rosalie (film), 274
Rosenwald, Julius, 117, 301, 361
Ross, David E., 5
Ross, Diana, 186
Ross-Ade Stadium (Purdue University), 5
Rother, Mark, 74
Rowan, Peter, 247
Royal Academy of Painting (Munich, Germany), 1–2, 123
Royal Road to Romance, The (book), 57
Rumely, Edward Aloysius, 296–97
Rural Free: A Farmwife's Almanac of Country Living, 272
Russell, Bill, 128
Russell, Caroline. *See* Scott, Caroline Russell
Russell, Richard, 47
Ryan White Care Act, 376
Ryan White HIV/AIDS Treatment Extension Act, 376
Ryman Auditorium (Nashville, TN), 247

Saarinen, Eero, 237
saccharin, 378
Sacco, Nicola, 152
Sailor Beware (film), 91
Saint Joseph Iron Works (South Bend), 259
Saint Louis Giants (baseball team), 58
Saint Mary-of-the-Woods, 146, 147
Salk, Jonas, 298, 299
Sam, Howard W., 56
Sanders, John, 364
Sanders, Polly Gray, 364
Sanders, Zerelda G. *See* Wallace, Zerelda G. Sanders
Sanderson, Z. C., 258
Sandland's Even Song (painting), 104
Santa Claus (IN), 200, 202, *202*
Santa Claus Land. *See* Holiday World and Splashin' Safari

Sarnoff, David, 191
Saturday Evening Post, 224
Sawyer, Lawrence E., 189
Say, Thomas, 270
Scheele, Leonard, 297–99
Schindler, Oscar, 231
Schirra, Walter, 141
Schleissheim (Germany), 2
Scholastic Magazine, 189
School Corporation Reorganization Act (1959), 371
Schoonover, Francis, 177
Schricker, Henry F., 47, 76, 136, 138, 283., 290
Schuller, Gunter, 249
Schulz, Arthur, 246
Schweitzer, Ada Estelle, 299–301
Science (journal), 264
Science of Swimming (book), 78
Scolar, Irwin, 22
Scott, Caroline Russell, 301
Scott, Caroline. *See* Harrison, Caroline Scott
Scott, Edouard Miles, 301
Scott, Esther, 302
Scott, Irena McCammon, 277
Scott, James, 175
Scott, Joan. *See* Wallace, Joan Scott
Scott, Walter, 148
Scott, William Edouard, 301–2, 326
Scribner's Monthly magazine, 325
Scruggs, Earl, 246, 247
Second State Bank of Indiana, 66, 67
Second Vatican Council, 145
Secor, John, 296
Sectarianism as Hersey, 385
Sedition Act (1918), 93
See America First (musical), 273
See Here, Private Hargrove (book), 38
See the Jaguar (play), 91
segregation, 81, 82
Seib, Phil, 87
Seinfeld, Jerry, 309
Selby, Robert, 124
Selleck, Roda, 311
Senate Avenue Young Men's Christian Association, 128, 282, 361
Seven Lively Arts (musical), 274
Seventeen (novel), 345
Seventeenth Amendment, 221
Sevitzky, Fabien, 138
Sewall, May Wright, 138, 158, 302–4, 303, 365
Sewall, Theodore Lovett, 303, 304
Shaffer, John C., 19
Shake Down the Thunder: The Creation of Notre Dame Football, 294
Shakespeare, William, 274
Shank, Samuel, 117
Sharp, Zerna, 304–5
Sharpe, Julia Graydon, 124
Shaw, Artie, 274

Shaw, Billy, 307
Shaw, Catherine, 307
Shaw, Wilbur, 183, 305–8, *307*
Shawnee (tribe), 348
Shelvador (Richmond), 80
Shepard, Alan, 141
Shepard, Randall, 261,
Shepherd, Adrian, 309
Shepherd, Jean Parker, 308–9
Shepherd, Leigh Brown, 309
Shepherd, Randall, 309
Sheppard-Towner Act (1921), 185
Sherman, John, 55
Sherman, William Tecumseh, 350
Sherman Anti-trust Act, 160
Sherman Silver-Purchase Act, 160
Shetron, H. C., 20
Shipp, Tom, 11
Shirer, William L., 87
Shively, Franklin, 343
Shockley, Ernest V., 245
Short Flights (poetry), 254
Shortridge, Abraham, 278
Show Window (essay collection). 87
Shriner, Herb, 309–11
Shriner, Indiana, 311
Shriner, Kin, 311
Shriner, Pixie, 311
Shriner, Wil, 311
Shrubs of Indiana, 89
Shuffle Along (musical), 315
Shulz, Ada Walter, 138, 311–12
Shulz, Adolph Robert, 138, 311, 312, 328
Shulz, Walter, 311, 312
Silk Stockings (musical), 274
Simon, David, 313
Simon, Melvin, 312–13
Simon, Herbert, 313
Simon Property Group, 313
Simonson, John, 191
Sinatra, Frank, 186
Since Emancipation: A Short History of Indiana Negroes, 1831–1963, p. 351
"Since I Kissed My Baby Goodbye" (song), 274
Sinclair, Upton, 19
Singapore, 261, 263
Sirens of Titan, The (novel), 359
Sissle, George, 314
Sissle, Martha Scott, 314
Sissle, Noble Lee, 314–16, *315*
Sister Carrie (novel), 100, 101
Sisters of Providence, 146, 147
Skelton, Edna Stillwell, 316, 317
Skelton, Ida Mae, 316
Skelton, Joseph, 316
Skelton, Richard "Red," 309, 316–18, *316*
"Skylark" (song), 49
Slaughterhouse-Five; or, The Children's Crusade, A Duty-Dance with Death, 358, 359

Slayton, Donald "Deke," 141
Slipher, Earl C., 215
Slipher, Vesto M., 215
"Small Fry" (song), 49
Smethurst, Frances. *See* Martin, Frances Smethurst
Smith, Abe, 11
Smith, Alfred E., 31, 33
Smith, Gipsy, 43
Smith, Ida Frances Bedell, 318
Smith, Mary Eleanor "Nory" Cline, 318
Smith, Robert, 287
Smith, Walter Bedell, 318–20, *319*
Smith, William Long, 318
Social History of Indiana, The, 177
Society for American Architecture, 20
Society of Friends, 68
Society of Motion Picture Engineers and Television Engineers, 191
Society of Western Artists, 2, 124, 312, 327
sodium benzoate, 376, 377, 378
Soldiers' and Sailors' Children's Home (Knightstown), 13
Soldiers' and Seaman's Home (Knightstown), *See* Soldiers' and Sailors' Children's Home
Solomon, Izler, 138
Somes, Virginia Ellis. *See* Jenckes Virginia Ellis
Something for the Boys (musical), 274
Something to Shout About (film), 274
Sommers, Matilda Escon. *See* Baker, Matilda Escon Sommers
Songs of a Lifetime, 27
Songs of Fair Weather (poetry), 350
Sons of Liberty, 238, 239
Sorin, Edward Frederick, 320–22
South Bend (IN), 321, 329, 338, 340
South Bend Foundry, 259
South Bend Iron Works, 260
South Bend Tribune, 295
Southern Yankee, The (film), 317
Spain, 31, 33
Spaniels (music group), 54
Speak to the Earth: Pages from a Farmwife's Journal, 272
Speedway (IN), 7, 8
Sperber, Murray, 294
Spink, Mary A., 123
Spink, Urbana, 123
Spitz, Mark, 77
Sporting News, The magazine, 382
Sports Illustrated magazine, 77
Spruance, Alexander, 322
Spruance, Annie Ames Hiss, 322
Spruance, Margaret Dean, 323, 324
Spruance, Margaret, 323
Spruance, Raymond A., 322–24, *322*
Sputnik (satellite), 141
Spy for the Confederacy: Rose O'Neal Greenhow, 257

St. Clair, Arthur, 233, 291
Stager, Joel, 78
Stagg, Amos Alonzo, 172
Standard and Poor's, 85
Standard Statistics Company. *See* Standard and Poor's
Stanton, Edwin, 67
Stanton, Elizabeth Cady, 303, 365
Stanwyck, Barbara, 102
Staple Singers, 54
Star Glass Works (New Albany). *See* DePauw American Plate Glass Works
"Stardust" (song), 48
Stardust Road, The (book), 47, 49
Stark, Edward Otto, 325
Stark, Gretchen, 324, 325
Stark, Gustav, 325
Stark, Marie Nitschelm, 324, 325
Stark, Otto, 2, 123, 124, 137, 155, 177, 301, 302, 324–26, 327
Stark, Paul, 325
Stark, Suzanne, 324
Starker, Janos, 133, 134
Starr Piano Company (Richmond), 129, 130
State Bank of Indiana, 12, 94, 193, 204
State Banking in Indiana, 1814–1873, p. 114
State Bar Association of Indian. *See* Indiana State Bar Association
State v. Lassalle, 175
Steele, Brandt, 327
Steele, Daisy (Margaret), 327
Steele, George W., 19
Steele, Mary Elizabeth "Libbie" Lakin, 326, 327
Steele, Selma Neubacher, 327–28
Steele, Theodore Clement (T. C.), 1, 2, 123, 124, 326–28, *326*, 368
Steinbeck, John, 85, 91
Steinmann, Elizabeth Anna Agnes "Beth." *See* Bowen, Elizabeth Anna Agnes "Beth" Steinmann
Steinway Musical Instruments Inc., 71
Stellite, 163, 165
Stephenson, David Curtis (D. C.), 224, 328–30, *329*
Steven, Myron, 306
Stevens, George, 92
Stevens, Thaddeus, 12, 382
Stevenson, Adlai, 224, 225
Stewart, Fannie Caldwell, 330
Stewart, George Pheldon, 330–32
Stewart, Marcus C., 330
Stillwell, Edna Skelton. *See* Skelton, Edna Stillwell
Stimson, Stella, 63
Stockton, Sarah, 69, 122
Stokely-Van Camp, 356, 357
Stone Quarry (painting), 177
Stone, Lucy, 349
Story, Joseph, 22

Story of Clara Barton of the Red Cross, The, 257
Story of Louisiana, The, 351
Stout, Clarence "Professor," 317
Stout, Elihu, 332–33
Stout, Henry, 332
Stout, Jediah, 332
Stout, Lucy, 332
Stout, Polly, 332
Stowe, Harriet, Beecher, 349
Strange Women (novel), 87
Strasberg, L., 91
Stratton, Geneva. *See* Stratton-Porter, Gene
Stratton, Leander "Laddie," 335
Stratton-Porter, Gene, 333–35, *334*
Strauss, Isaac, 337
Strauss, Juliet V., 209, 335–37, *336*
Stubbs, Gorge W., 116
Studebaker, Anne, 338
Studebaker, Clement, 260, 337–39
Studebaker, Henry, 337, 338
Studebaker, Jacob, 338
Studebaker, John (J. M.), 338, 339
Studebaker, John Clement, 338
Studebaker, Peter, 338
Studebaker Brothers Manufacturing Company. *See* Studebaker Corporation
Studebaker Corporation, 337, 338, *339*
Studebaker family, 321
Stutesman, Jessie Herron. *See* Hays, Jessie Heron Stutesman
Styron, William, 57
Sullivan, Ed, 54
Sullivan, John J., 4
Sultan of Sulu, The (play), 4
Summer Rain, A (painting), 177
Sunday, Helen Amelia Thompson, 340
Sunday, William "Billy" Ashley, 339–42, *340*
Sunny Corner (painting), 124
Swain, Miriam E. Mason, 272
Sweeney, Elsie Irwin, 237
Sweeney, Nettie. *See* Miller, Nettie Sweeney
Sweeney, Zachary Taylor, 235
Swing Raymond Graham, 87
Sylvan Secrets (essay collection), 350
Symmes, Anna. *See* Harrison, Anna Symmes
Symmes, John, 161
Szell, George, 134

Tacitus, 109
Taflinger, Elmer, 325
Taft, Lorado, 124, 327
Taft, Robert A., 47
Taft, William Howard, 3, 5
Taggart, Eva Dora Bryant, 342
Taggart, Thomas, 221, 222, 342–44 *343*
Taming of the Shrew, 274
Tandy, Vertner Woodson, 361
Tangeman, Clementine, 237
Tanner, Henry O., 301

Tarkington, Elizabeth Booth, 34
Tarkington, John, 344
Tarkington, Laurel Louisa Fletcher, 345
Tarkington, Laurel, 345
Tarkington, Newton Booth, 3, 254, 255, 304, 322, 344–46, *345*, 380
Tarkington, Susannah Robinson, 345
Taucumwah, 290
Taylor, Ben, 58
Taylor, C. I., 57, 58
Taylor, Creed, 247, 249
Taylor, Elizabeth, 92
Taylor, Fredrick Wilson, 131
Taylor, J. R., 248
Taylor, Marshall "Major," 331
Taylor, Olivia, 58
Taylor, Robert S., 19
Taylor, William, 156
Taylor, Zachary, 332
Teal, Elizabeth White. *See* Monks, Elizabeth White Teal
Tecumseh, 161, 162, 346–48, *347*
Telling the Tale (musical), 273
temperance, 365
Tennessee Valley Authority, 378
Tenskwatawa (The Prophet), 162, 291, 346–48
Terre Haute Daily News, 157
Terre Haute Saturday Evening Mail, 156
Theatre Arts Monthly, 150
"They Don't Care about Us" (song), 187
Thirteenth Amendment, 169, 213
Thirteenth and Roosevelt (painting), 177
Thomas, Helen Louise. *See* Hays, Helen Louise Thomas
Thomas, Jane Janette Johnson, 125
Thomas, Linda Lee. *See* Porter, Linda Lee Thomas
Thomas, Mary Frame Myers, 348–49
Thomas, Owen, 348
Thomas, Robert E., 125
Thompson, Alice Lee, 350
Thompson, George, 330
Thompson, Helen Amelia. *See* Sunday, Helen Amelia Thompson,
Thompson, Joyce, 330
Thompson, Maurice, 350–51
Thompson, Will, 350
Thompson, William A., 244
Thomson, James, 179
Thornbrough, Bess Tyler, 352, 353
Thornbrough, Emma Lou, 98, 351–53, 354; *352*
Thornbrough, Gayle, 120, 352, 33–56, *355*
Thornbrough, Harry C., 352, 353
Thought on the Destiny of Man, 285
Thriller (album), 186, 187
"Thriller" (song), 187
Thwaites, Reuben Gold, 381
Tilden, Samuel J., 169, 251
Time (magazine), 43, 98, 170, 197, 275–76
Time-and-motion research, 131. 132

Timequake (novel), 359
Times Have Changed (novel), 87
Timolat, Kathleen. *See* McNutt, Kathleen Timolat
Tinguely, Jean, 237
Tipton, John, 99
To Have and Have Not (film), 49
Tocqueville, Alexis de, 264
Tolstoy, Leo, 344
Tony Hinkle: Coach for All Seasons, 172
Topper (film), 49
Topping Robert, 277
Toscanini, Arturo, 133–34
Townsend, Clifford, 76
Tragic Era, The (book), 31
The Tragic Era: The Revolution after Lincoln, 33
Trans World Airlines, 75
Transactions of the American Philosophical Society, 219
Treaty of Fort Finney (1786), 61
Treaty of Fort McIntosh (1785), 61
Treaty of Fort Wayne, 291, 346
Treaty of Greenville, 291
Treaty of Paris, 61
Treaty of Saint Marys, 193, 291
Tribe of Ishmael, The, 228
Triumph (album), 186
Trotter, Eunice M., 330
Troy (IN), 213
"True Love" (song), 274
Trujillo, Raphael, 59
Truman, Harry S, 230, 241, 243, 284, 298, 315, 319, 323, 371
Trusler, Preston C., 342
Tucker, Glenn, 56
Tucker, Irene, 178
Tucker, Ralph, 371
Tucker, Sophie, 314, 315
Tumulty, Joseph P., 222
Turkey Run State Park (Parke County), 209, 335, 336, 337
Turmoil (novel), 345
Turner, Carl D., 215
Turner, Frederick Jackson, 381
Turner, Richmond K., 324
Tuttle, Joseph, 240, 241
Twain, Mark, 4, 144, 293, 344
Two for the Money (quiz show), 309, 310
Two Minutes till Midnight (book), 88
Two Percent Club, 230, 242
"Two Scenes" (poem), 27
"Two Sleepy People" (song), 49
Tyler, Bess *See* Thornbrough, Bess Tyler
Tyler, John, 162

"Uncle Pen" (song), 246
Underground Railroad, 66, 67
Union Carbide and Carbon Corporation, 7, 118
Union of American Hebrew Congregations, 110

Union Starch and Refining Company, 236
United Auto Workers, 51
United Mine Workers of America, 152
United Service Organizations, 230
University of California, Los Angeles, 382, 383
University of Minnesota, 232
University of Notre Dame (South Bend), 169, 170, 171, 294, 295, 320, 321, 322, 329
Unsinkable Molly Brown (musical), 142
Updyke, Wynn, 78
USS *Enterprise*, 323
USS *Hornet*, 323
USS *Indianapolis*, 323
USS *Lexington*, 323
USS *Randolph*, 141
USS *Yorktown*, 323

Van Buren, Martin, 162, 238, 333, 362
Van Camp, Charles, 356
Van Camp, Courtland, 356, 357
Van Camp, Frank, 356, 357
Van Camp, Gilbert (father of Frank and Courtland), 356
Van Camp, Gilbert (son of Frank), 357
Van Camp, Hester, 356
Van Camp Family, 356–57
Van Camp Hardware and Iron Company, 356, 357
Van Camp Pork and Beans, 356, 357
Van Camp Seafood Company. *See* Chicken of the Sea
Van Doren, Irita, 379, 380
Van Dyke, Henry, 55
Van Huysen, Grant, 253
Van Nuys, Frederick, 258
Van Revels, The (novel), 344
Vanderpoel, John, 311
Vandiver, Pen, 246
Vanzetti, Bartolomeo, 152
Vargas, Brian, 52
Variety, 200
Vee-Jay Record Company 53, 55
Veiller, Lawrence, 9, 10
Venturi, Robert, 237
Veraestau, 175, 176, 257, 258, 259
Verve Records, 247, 249
Very Good Eddie (musical), 273
Victor Records, 130
Vietnam, 320
Vincennes (IN), 23, 60, 61, 146, 191, 332, 333
Vincennes General Advertiser, 332
Vincennes Sun-Commercial, 332
Vincennes Western Sun, 332, 333
Vincent, Stenio, 302
Vincent and Elinor Ostrom Workshop in Political Theory and Policy Analysis, 263, 265
Vitascope, 190
Voegelin, Charles F., *21*

Von Löfftz, 123
Vonnegut, Bernard, 358
Vonnegut, Clemens, Sr., 358
Vonnegut, Edith Lieber, 358, 359
Vonnegut, Jane Marie Cox, 359
Vonnegut, Jill Krementz, 359
Vonnegut, Kurt, Jr., 294, 357–60, *359*
Vonnegut, Kurt, Sr., 358
Vonnegut and Bohn, 358
Vonnegut Hardware Company, 358
Vornbrock, Ernie, 77

Wabash College (Crawfordsville), 239, 240, 241
Wabash Manual Labor College and Teachers' Seminary. *See* Wabash College
Wagner, Harold, 97
Wagner, Robert F., 31, 33
Wainwright, Rufus, 102
Wake Up and Dream (musical), 273
Walam Olum, 21
Walcher, Helen. *See* Caldwell, Helen Walcher
Walk with Music (musical), 49
Walker, A'Lelia. *See* Robinson, A'lelia Walker
Walker, Charles Joseph, 360
Walker, Clarence, 384
Walker, Madam C. J., 11, 34, 35, 281, 331, 360–61, *360*
Wallace, David, 302, 354, 362, 364
Wallace, Esther, French Test, 362
Wallace, George C., 372
Wallace, Henry A., 230, 223, 284, 297
Wallace, Joan Scott, 302
Wallace, Joanne (Josie). *See* Orr, Joanne (Josie), Wallace
Wallace, Lew, 199, 254, 362–64, *362*, 364, 366
Wallace, Susan Elston, 363, 364
Wallace, William, 254
Wallace, William J., *21*
Wallace, Zerelda G. Sanders, 302, 362, 364–66
Wallenstein, Mamie W. *See* Efroymson, Mamie W. Wallenstein
Waller, Bret, 156
Walter, Ada. *See* Shulz, Ada Walter
Walters, William T., 143
Walton, Luke, 184
Wanda Hickey's Night of Golden Memories (story collection), 308
Ward, Joseph, 360, 361
Warner-Lambert Research Institutes, 299
Warsaw (IN), 386, 387
"Washboard Blues" (song). 48
Washington, Margaret (Mrs. Booker T.), 126
Washington, Booker T., 200, 282, 301, 302, 331, 351, 361, 381

Washington, Bushrod, 23
Washington (DC) Times, 70
Washington Daily News, 279
Wathall, Alfred, 4
Watson, Enos L., 244
Watson, James E., 221, 343., 379, 329
Watt, Jane. *See* Fisher, Jane Watt
Wayne, Anthony, 161, 234
Wayne, Florence, 126
"We Are the World" (song), 187
Weatherwax, Paul, 89
Webster, Daniel, 22
Webster, Lawrence, 367
Webster, Marie Daugherty, 366–68
Wechsler, James, 276
Weer, Paul, 20
Weizmann, Chaim, 117
Welles, Orson, 310
Wells, Anna Bernice Harting, 368
Wells, Herman B, 128, 215, 252, 368–70, *369*
Wells, Joseph Granville, 368
Wells, William, 234
Wells-Barnett, Ida, 126
Welsh, Inez Empson, 370
Welsh, Janet, 370
Welsh, Kathryn, 370
Welsh, Mary Virginia Homann, 370
Welsh, Matthew Empson, 30, 34, 370–72, *370*
Welsh, Matthew William, 370
West Baden Springs Hotel, 74, 343
Western Free Produce Association, 67
Western Freedman's Aid Commission, 67
Weymouth, George, 272
"What Is This Thing Called Love" (song), 273
What's My Line (quiz show), 310
Wheeler, Clifton, 177
Wheeler, Frank, 7, 8, 118
Wheeler, William A., 169
Wheeler, William Morton, 196
"When the Frost Is on the Punkin" (poem), 292
Whistling in the Dark (film), 317
Whitcomb, James, 240
White, Byron "Whizzer," 77
White, Charles, 180
White, Ed, 140, 142
White, Emerson Eldridge, 278
White, Esther Griffin, 372–74, *373*
White, Jeanne. *See* White-Ginder, Jeanne
White, Leonard D., 44
White, Mary, 372
White, Oliver, 372
White, Ryan, 374–76, *375*
White, Walter, 11, 12, 282
White, William Allen, 4
White-Ginder, Jeanne, 374, *375*, 376
Whiteman, Paul, 46
Whitewater Canal Association, 257, 259
Whitewater Canal Historic Site, 259

Whitman, Walt, 101
Whitmore, James, 91
Whittier, John Greenleaf, 27
"Why Can't You Behave?" (song), 274
Wickard, Claude, 47
Wiggins, Fred, 129
Wilcox, Howard "Howdy," 8
Wildermuth, Ora L., 128
Wiley, Harvey Washington, 185, 376–78, *377*
Willard, Ashbel P., 250
William A. Koch Sr. Memorial Highway, 201
William E. English Foundation, 110, 111
Williams, Fannie Barrier, 126
Williams, James "Blue Jeans," 159
Williams, K. P., 214
Williams, Martin, 356
Williamson, Bruce, 88, 89
Willkie, Wendell, 243, 345, 378–80, *379*
Wilson, Edith Galt, 222
Wilson, George, 354
Wilson, James, 377
Wilson, Mildred. *See* Dean, Mildred Wilson
Wilson, Woodrow, 19, 32, 220, 222, 245, 343, 361, 378, 381
Winslow, Marcus, 91
Winslow, Ortense, 91
Winslow, Richard H., 205, 206
Winslow, Lanier Company, 205–6
Wirt, William, 53
Wirz, Henry, 363
Wishard, William, 185
Wisler, Niley, 253
Witchery of Archery, 350
Wittig, Georg, 37
Wiz, The (film), 186
Wolf, George D., 185
Wolf, Louis W., 110
Wolfe, Thomas, 74
Wolff, Carrie, 1
Woman's Christian Temperance Union, 365
Woman's Improvement Club, 126
Women's Franchise League, 62, 64, 373
Women's School Commission. *See* Women's Franchise League
Wong Kai Kah, 116
Wood, Grant, 177
Wood, Leonard, 298
Woodberry, George, 254
Woodburn, Dorrance Beatty, 381
Woodburn James, II (father of James A.), 381, 382
Woodburn, Caroline Louise Gelston, 381
Woodburn, Edward Albert, 381
Woodburn, James (son of James A.), 381
Woodburn, James (great-great-grandfather of James A.), 380
Woodburn, James Albert, 380–82
Woodburn, Janet McMillan, 381

Woodbury, Levi, 205
Wooden, Hugh, 383
Wooden, John, 202, 204, 382–84, *383*
Wooden, Nell, 384
Woodland Brook, A (painting), 124
Woods Hole (MA), 64, 65
Woollen, Evans, 343
Words and Faces (book), 57
Workers, The (mural), 156
Working Men's Institute and Library (New Harmony), 219, 220, 270
Works Progress Administration, 22, , 85, 86, 144, 156
Worth, John, 51
Wright, Joseph, 241
Wright Brothers, 144
Wurlitzer Corporation, 46
Wylie, Andrew, 226, 384–86
Wynn, Ed, 317
Winona Christian Assembly's Bible Conference Center, 341

"Yale Bulldog Song," 273
Yandes, Simon 40, 120
Yank magazine, 37, 38
"Ye Sons of Toil" (poem), 27
Yeager, Chuck, 17
Yellig, Pat. *See* Koch, Pat Yellig
Yerkes, Charles T., 164
"You Are Not Alone" (song), 187
You Bet Your Life (quiz show), 310
"You Were Meant for Me" (song), 315
"You'd Be So Nice to Come Home To" (song), 274
You'll Never Get Rich (film), 274
Young, Arthur M., 17
Young, John W., 141, 142
Young, Jewel, 204
Young, Neil, 247
Young Man with a Horn (film), 49
Young Men's Christian Association, 15, 77, 117, 139, 340, 361
Young Women's Christian Association, 15
Your Money (magazine), 85
"You're the Top" (song), 274

Ziegfeld Follies of 1919 (musical), 317
Zimmer (company), 386, 387
Zimmer, Janet, 386
Zimmer, Justin O., 386–87
Zimmer Holdings Inc., 386
Zimmer Manufacturing Company. *See* Zimmer Holdings Inc.
Zale, Tony, 38
Zollner, Frederick, 388–89
Zollner, Theodore, 388
Zollner Machine Works, 388
Zollner Manufacturing Company, 388